W9-BGL-522

WITHDRAWN

BLACKS IN THE NEW WORLD
August Meier, Series Editor

Race Relations in the Urban South, 1865–1890

RACE RELATIONS IN THE URBAN SOUTH 1865-1890

HOWARD N. RABINOWITZ

UNIVERSITY OF ILLINOIS PRESS
Urbana   Chicago   London

Illini Books edition, 1980

By arrangement with Oxford University Press
Copyright © by Oxford University Press, Inc. 1978
Foreword © 1980 by C. Vann Woodward

Manufactured in the United States of America

LIBRARY OF CONGRESS CATALOGING IN PUBLICATION DATA

Rabinowitz, Howard N   1942–
  Race relations in the urban South, 1865–1890.

  Bibliography: p.
  Includes index.
  1. Afro-Americans—Southern States. 2. Afro-
Americans—Southern States—Segregation. 3. City
and town life—Southern States. 4. Southern States—
Race relations. 5. Afro-Americans—History—1863–
1877. I. Title. II. Series.
E185.2.R23 1980   305.8'96073   79-28674
ISBN 0-252-00811-1 pbk.

For Anita with Love

It is only natural that race relations in Southern cities during the generation after the Civil War should have been relatively neglected by historians. In that period the great majority of Southern people, black and white, lived in the country, and the attention of scholars has been mainly focused on rural life. Even by 1890 only some 15 percent of Southern blacks could be called urban dwellers. But urban life was to be the way of the future for both races, for blacks even more than for whites. The first generation of freedmen and their white contemporaries, Northern and Southern, set the pattern for race relations of the future and the present. This book by Howard Rabinowitz repairs the neglect and brings new understanding, fresh interpretation, and needed revision of older conceptions of the way race relations developed in the urban South during and after Reconstruction.

With patient, exacting, and thorough research, Rabinowitz has mined and explored the records of the five small cities he has selected as representative of the region and period. His findings are highly worth pondering for any student of the several subjects upon which he touches—racial, Southern, black, and urban history. Among these subjects are the black community and its relations to the courts, the economic structure, its residential patterns, public services, public accommodations, churches, schools, and politics. One of the large subjects that requires reassessment be-

cause of this study is the character of Reconstruction and especially its racial policies.

Perhaps the most revisionary part of the book is that dealing
with the origins and development of segregation. The revisions
stem in part from a new point of view. The issue from this point
of view is not "merely when segregation first appeared, but what
it replaced," and what it replaced was "exclusion." From that
starting point segregation appears as an "improvement." The radical white Republicans "initiated it" in *de facto* practice, the blacks
"supported and at times requested it," and the Redeemers continued it on an informal basis until the wave of legal, universal,
and rigid segregation and disfranchisement toward the end of the
century. Rabinowitz concedes that in public accommodations
race relations were "relatively fluid," and in spite of much *de facto*
separation, "there was a degree of integration throughout the
period not matched in other aspects of Southern life."

For students of race relations in the mid-1950s and later, when
segregation was still rigid, legal, and universal and was defended
on the ground that "things had always been that way" and law
could not change them, that "degree of integration" and relative
fluidity took on special significance and received corresponding
emphasis. A quarter of a century later, when legal segregation
is ended and there is less *de facto* segregation in Southern than
in Northern schools, that emphasis on the exceptional degree
of integration seems misplaced. Howard Rabinowitz began his
study in 1967, when the integrationist emphasis was still felt,
but he was able to break away and look at the subject from a
different point of view. The time has come to bring to bear a new
perspective, and in doing so this admirable study serves us well.

                                                    C. Vann Woodward

New Haven, Conn.

This is a book about race relations in the urban South during the years from 1865 to 1890. In the questions it asks and the answers it seeks it will straddle the fields of urban, black, Reconstruction, and Southern history.

Its purpose is threefold. First, it seeks to re-create the lives of urban Negroes during the painful transition from slavery to freedom. This means not only unearthing the actual conditions among blacks, but also examining white attitudes, especially with respect to what whites perceived as the proper role of Negroes in their communities. At the end of the period, which coincides with the beginning of significant Negro migration to the North, 90 percent of the country's blacks were still concentrated in the South. Roughly 15 percent of Southern blacks lived in cities in 1890, comprising almost a third of the region's urban population and almost 70 percent of the nation's Negro urban dwellers.[1] Better educated and more prosperous than their rural brothers, they played a major role in national Negro political, economic, and social affairs. Nevertheless, their imprint on urban society and the impact that city life had on them remain largely undocumented.

Urban historians have long slighted the South, preferring to concentrate on a few Eastern and Midwestern cities. Historians of the Reconstruction period have likewise been preoccupied with national policy-making and statewide trends, noting the urban scene only in passing. Students of black history also have tended to ignore the character of life of these new migrants to Southern towns, viewing emancipation, as well as slavery, primarily within a rural context. For detailed descriptions of black urban life in the postbellum years, students must turn, with a few recent exceptions, to the growing number of monographs about black communities in the urban North. As a result of these studies, it is commonly agreed that it was in the North during the twentieth century that the modern Negro ghetto first appeared.

In answering the questions of what it was like to be black in the Southern cities and what it was like for the urban South to absorb large numbers of blacks, I found it necessary to deal with the origins and development of segregation. This, the second major concern, in part accounts for the termination date of 1890, the time commonly accepted as the beginning of a rigid system of segregation. Disagreement persists as to the reasons for its appearance and for its evolution and extensiveness before this date.[2]

In order to get at the roots of segregation, it was essential to understand the meaning of Reconstruction. Thus the third aim of this study is to use the city as a microcosm in which to examine the larger issues of Reconstruction. Only one state study of Southern Negroes has taken into account the entire period of Presidential Reconstruction, Congressional Reconstruction, and Redemption.[3] By doing so for the urban South, I hope to present a more detailed account of the effects of so-called Radical Reconstruction, not only in an urban setting, but in the South as a whole. What difference did it make to the freedmen whether the men in power were Radicals or Redeemers? What did Reconstruction mean to them in their social, economic, and political relations with whites and among themselves?

To talk of "the urban South," of course, is as misleading as referring to "the South." Just as there were several Souths, so too were there differences among Southern cities. Considerations of time and energy made it impossible to study every Southern city; I therefore selected a sample of five cities for concentrated study, although information concerning other cities has been utilized as well. The sample includes Atlanta, Georgia; Montgomery, Alabama; Nashville, Tennessee; Raleigh, North Carolina; and Richmond, Virginia.

In conception this book has a kinship with a number of other works which employ a comparative framework to examine a given period of urban growth. Unlike those studies, mine is less interested in the cities themselves than in how they dealt with a common problem.[4] My work is also different in that my five cities do not possess a natural unity. Missing are such major Southern cities as New Orleans, Charleston, Birmingham, Savannah, Baltimore, Louisville, and Washington, D.C. The last three were eliminated when I decided to focus on the states of the former Confederacy. When I began this study, Savannah and New Orleans were already the subject of close investigation, and in the case of New Orleans I felt that its pattern of race relations was likely to be atypical. The Crescent City also was simply too large to treat systematically along with four other cities. Charleston blacks had been adequately if unsystematically treated in the numerous excellent studies of South Carolina during the period, and Birmingham was still less than twenty years old in 1890 with a population of only 3,000 in 1880.[5]

But why these particular five cities? With the exception of a seaport, together they represent a cross section of the Southern urban experience. They vary according to size, age, rate of growth, economic function, region, and in two ways especially important for this study, the length of Republican control in the state and city and the percentage of Negro residents. They are atypical, however, in that they are all capitals. This choice was the result of my belief that, as such, they provided maximum advantages to blacks during the period of Republican control. As headquarters for federal troops and the seat of government, for example, it was here that the Radicals were best able to put their ideas into practice. I was also interested in the possible effects that conditions in these cities might have had on white state legislators. Their experiences while living in the capitals might have had as much to do with their attitudes toward racial legislation as did circumstances in their home districts. I found little to support this view in the papers of the legislators which I examined, but this idea merits further investigation.

If these cities are truly representative, then we need to revise much of our thinking about the period. First, at no time, even at the height of Radical Reconstruction, were blacks accorded the same rights and privileges as whites. Second, in seeking to discipline blacks, whites very early resorted to various means of piecemeal disfranchisement in the political sphere and to *de facto* and *de jure* segregation in the social. Third, although Reconstruction witnessed the commonly acknowledged enfranchisement of blacks, it was not characterized by integration. Instead, Republicans championed the replacement of an earlier policy of exclusion with one of separate but equal treatment. Though backed

by most blacks, the long-term result was separate but unequal treatment and the emergence in the South by 1890 of the first black
ghettoes.

At times the interests of the whites and blacks coincided; more often,
however, they were in conflict. Out of this interaction between blacks
and whites there had evolved by 1890 a new pattern of race relations.
Its legacy remains today.

Acknowledgments

I am indebted to librarians and archivists throughout the South for their help and consideration. I want to thank especially Mr. Franklin M. Garrett of the Atlanta Historical Society; Mrs. Betty Gibson of Richmond's Valentine Museum; Mr. Milo B. Howard, Jr., and Mrs. Frances Clark of the Alabama Department of Archives and History; Mrs. Cleo A. Hughes and Mrs. Harriet C. Owsley of the Tennessee State Library and Archives; and Dr. H. G. Jones, then of the North Carolina Department of Archives and History, but now Curator of the North Carolina Collection, University of North Carolina, Chapel Hill. Many other Southerners too numerous to mention extended Southern hospitality to me during my lengthy stays in the South.

I would also like to thank the interlibrary loan office staffs at the University of Chicago and the University of New Mexico libraries for meeting what must have seemed to them as my almost insatiable desire to use their services. The University of Chicago's Department of History and Center for Urban Studies generously provided financial aid throughout my stay at the university. Mrs. Penelope Katson typed the final version of the manuscript with speed, accuracy, and a critical eye, and became a family friend in the process. Oxford's Sheldon Meyer was a continual source of encouragement and Susan Rabiner, Parke Puterbaugh, and Laura Seitel helped bring the book through the final stages of publication.

My thanks go to the editors of the *Journal of American History*, the *Journal of Southern History*, the *Journal of Urban History*, the *Social Service Review*, and the *Historian* for their permission to use material which appeared originally in those periodicals, although in different form.

As an undergraduate, I benefited greatly from my teachers at Swarthmore College. The history faculty was superb, and I want to thank especially James A. Field, Jr., and Robert C. Bannister, Jr., for their interest and understanding.

Several scholars noticeably improved earlier drafts of this book. Peter Kolchin and Walter B. Weare who read an almost final version made excellent suggestions which did not necessitate the broader revisions they may have preferred. Richard C. Wade, who introduced me to urban history and to the joys of financial aid, helped develop this topic as a dissertation and later offered his considerable editorial skill as my manuscript neared completion. August Meier offered his typically detailed and perceptive comments that resulted in major organizational revisions. This book originated in a memorable seminar that John Hope Franklin took "on the road" to North Carolina in 1967. Professor Franklin subsequently supervised my dissertation with his usual thoroughness and took time from his own work to read the revised manuscript. I have been fortunate to have had him as a teacher and a friend. My greatest intellectual debt is to Arthur Mann who has most influenced my approach to the study of history and whose ability to cut to the heart of an issue made me aware of the deeper implications of my findings. As an uncle and role model, he led me into academia; as a demanding critic, he made my book better than it would have otherwise been.

In the end, however, this book is a testament to the support of three people. My parents emphasized the importance of ideas and knowledge, encouraged my interest in an academic career, and provided timely moral and financial support. And without my wife, Anita, this book and the dissertation upon which it is based would never have been completed. She typed, edited, xeroxed, proofread the work's numerous drafts, compiled the index, and picked up my flagging spirits. Best of all, she provided a wonderful home for me and our two precocious daughters. For these and other reasons, I dedicate this book to her.

Howard N. Rabinowitz

Albuquerque, N.M.

Contents

Maps

Tables

I
THE MILIEU

The Civil War produced profound changes in Southern urban life. It led to the disruption of traditional trade routes, destruction of railroads, burning of factories and homes, ravaging of agrarian hinterlands, and neglect of urban services. Most of all, the emancipation of the slaves and widespread dislocation in the countryside left thousands of refugees to be assimilated.

Like the rest of American cities in the latter part of the nineteenth century, Southern cities grew in population largely as a result of in-migration. Elsewhere in the country the migrants were either foreigners or rural whites; in the South there were large numbers of rural whites, but the most significant group consisted of rural blacks. Like the East Europeans in the North, the Chinese in the Far West, and the former farmers in the Midwest, these new urban dwellers in the South were a source of instability and social disruption. But blacks presented Southern white urbanites with an even more serious problem than that faced by their counterparts in other sections. These newcomers were not only poor, unaccustomed to the conditions and responsibilities of urban life, and of a different ethnic or racial background than a majority of the resident population, they were tainted by slavery. The blacks, unlike other migrants, had long been assigned a role in the life of the region in which they settled. Their position had been one of subservience, as slaves controlled by the white race. A free Negro was an anomaly, someone whom Southerners had sought to banish from their midst. Now all blacks were free.

The influx of blacks and the resultant problem of social control greatly troubled whites. In their view the Negroes "infested" the cities, "clogged" the streets, and threatened the attainment of peace and prosperity. While whites sought to reestablish the control weakened by the defeat of the Confederacy and the emancipation of the slaves, blacks sought to use the urban environment to fulfill the dreams of freedom.

Once the reality of emancipation had been grasped by both whites and blacks, adjustments had to be made in the nature of urban life. Most pressing were the questions of how the blacks would support themselves and where they would live. The decisions concerning jobs and housing would affect not only these vital areas but all aspects of urban life as well. And in an effort to keep blacks "in their place," whites turned against them the full force of the legal system.

3

1

The Urban South

Urbanization in the eleven states that comprised the Confederate States of America lagged behind the rest of the country. In 1860, 7.1 percent of the population was urban compared to 19.8 percent in the nation as a whole; by 1890 the respective figures were 12.8 percent and 35.1 percent.[1] Nevertheless, Southern cities had long played a more important role in the region than their proportion of the population would indicate.

Prior to the Civil War the important cities were located on the perimeter of the South. Seaports such as Norfolk, Charleston, Savannah, Mobile, New Orleans, and Galveston and river ports like Richmond, Nashville, and Memphis were commercial centers which exported cotton, rice, tobacco, lumber, and other raw materials and imported manufactured goods from the North and overseas. Commercial elites, often with cotton factors the most prominent members, ran the cities, which exhibited the same kind of urban spirit found elsewhere in the nation.

While some cities suffered and others benefited from the Civil War, the war did not impede and perhaps even stimulated Southern urbanization. But in the postbellum period it was the railroad rather than a choice water location that determined urban success. Though New Orleans remained the largest Southern city, it and the other coastal ports except Norfolk suffered a relative decline in population, wealth, and commerce. Thanks to penetration of the railroads, interior towns like Atlanta, Dallas, San Antonio, and the totally new town of Birmingham rose to urban prominence. Meanwhile, Nashville, Memphis, Norfolk,

4

and Richmond were able to retain their commanding positions because of their expanding railroad networks. Whereas in 1860 the three largest cities after New Orleans were Charleston, Richmond, and Mobile, by 1890 they were Richmond, Nashville, and Atlanta. Though much of the postbellum urban growth was due to manufacturing, most Southern cities continued to serve primarily as commercial and administrative centers.

While continuing to lag behind their Northern counterparts, within the twenty-five years after the war Southern cities actively participated in the growing urbanization of the nation. The South initiated services and functions long before inaugurated by Northern cities. Systems of public education, uniformed and paid fire and police departments, paved streets, mass transit, and public welfare services either appeared for the first time or made significant advances. But Southern cities did more than merely reach the stage of antebellum Northern cities. As additional urban innovations appeared elsewhere, they were immediately adopted. These included improvements in street lighting, the electrification of streetcars, and the introduction of telephone service. In some cases, as in the conversion to electric streetcars, the South actually led the way.

The South did more than share in the benefits of urban life; it was also faced with some of the problems. Air and water pollution, epidemics, traffic congestion, and a lack of sufficient funds, for example, plagued Southern cities of all sizes. More importantly, though spared the influx of foreign immigrants which nearly overwhelmed the structure of Northern urban life, Southern cities faced a similar problem in the form of the newly emancipated former slaves.[2]

The five cities selected for closer examination reveal the variety, richness, and importance of Southern urban life.

Atlanta was the child of the railroad. In 1837 the eastern terminus of the Western and Atlantic Railroad was established seven miles east of the Chattahoochee River on a plateau formed by the eastern slope of the Allegheny Mountains. At the site grew a small settlement known as Terminus. The completion of the railroad encouraged growth, and in 1844 the settlers received a charter incorporating the village under the name of Marthasville. Within two years the prospects of the town had been improved by the completion of both the Macon and Western Railroad and the Georgia Railroad which linked it to Macon and Augusta. Buoyed by Marthasville's potential as a railroad center, a group of citizens obtained a city charter in 1847. By 1854 the population of Atlanta, as it was now known, increased twentyfold from 300 to 6,000 and the bustling town had sixty stores and several churches. By the eve of the Civil War, Atlanta's more than 9,000 residents made it the fourth largest city in Georgia. Located within comparatively easy reach of both the Gulf of Mexico and the southeast coast, the center of an impressive railway network, and surrounded by a hinterland with abundant resources, the city was already an important commercial center.[3]

As a major Confederate military base and supply depot, it increased in population and business activity until the Battle of Atlanta in July 1864. General William Sherman ordered the evacuation of all civilians, and before he left on his famous "March to the Sea" much of the central business area had been gutted by fire. Yet the extent of the destruction has been exaggerated. On arriving in the city in November 1865, Sidney Andrews, surprised to find the damage less than he had expected, wrote: "the City Hall and the Medical College and all the churches, and many of the handsomer and more stylish private dwellings and nearly all the houses of the middling and poorer classes, were spared."[4]

Nonetheless, there was much rebuilding to do and the residents impressed visitors with their determination to remake the city. "From all this ruin and devastation a new city is springing up with marvellous rapidity," reported Andrews.[5] "Atlanta is certainly a fast place in every sense of the word, and our friends in Atlanta are a fast people," observed the Milledgeville *Federal Union*. "They live fast and they die fast. They make money fast and they spend it fast. They build houses fast and they burn them down fast. . . . They have the largest public buildings, and the most of them. . . . To a stranger the whole city seems to be running on wheels, and all of the inhabitants continually blowing off steam." Visitors could get a hold on the city only by explaining it in terms of Northern rather than Southern cities. "Chicago in her busiest days could scarcely show such a sight," noted Sidney Andrews. "The four railroads entering here groan with the freight and passenger traffic and yet are unable to meet the demand of the nervous and palpitating city. . . . Rents are so high that they would seem fabulous on Lake Street and yet there is the most urgent cry for store-room and office-room." In 1874 Edward King described Atlanta as "a new, vigorous awkwardly alert city, very similar in character to the mammoth groupings of brick and stone in the Northwest. There is but little that is distinctly Southern in Atlanta."[6]

What seemed to provide the drive was a passion for material goods. According to Sidney Andrews, "The one sole idea first in every man's mind is to make money." No matter that the prosperity rested on a shaky foundation which might soon collapse. "Meantime Atlanta is doing more than Macon and Augusta combined." This striving for money was fueled by the influx of outsiders, especially from the North, who sought to make a quick profit: Andrews noted that "few of the present merchants were here before the war." More than a decade later an Atlantan sadly concluded that "our people are too utilitarian, too much absorbed in the cares and pursuits of the present, too money-loving." Because of this concentration on the present, Atlantans were quintessential Americans, though atypical Southerners. They lacked an interest in tradition or appreciation of history. ". . . Except by a few persons of leisure, the history of even last week is but slightly esteemed, only so far as it affects the present day." Or in the words of a French visitor, "The city is the creation of the day before yesterday."[7]

Atlanta had the raw character of a frontier town. "The middle of the city is a great open space of irregular shape, a wilderness of mud, with a confused jumble of railway sheds and traversed by numberless rails, rusted and splashed where strings of dirty cars are standing, and engines constantly puff and whistle," wrote John Dennett in December 1865. He found bones and skulls of animals collected for some factory lying in the street, unfinished houses everywhere, and added that "the city is hardly less pleasing to the eye than the people. A great many rough-looking fellows hang about the numerous shops and the shanties among the ruins where liquor is sold, and a knot of them cluster at each street corner." Yet despite its "cheap and squalid look . . . it evinces much energy and life." A local resident was less generous. Not only had the population increased rapidly, complained schoolteacher Elizabeth Sterchi, "but also the corruption, for it has a lottery, gambling houses, theatres and every bad thing invented in the world to corrupt humanity; added to this are headquarters and garrison." As the years passed, Atlanta accumulated the indicators of a prosperous city: new hotels, pleasant residential areas, several streetcar lines, and substantial shops. But the rawness of the immediate postwar years remained. Arriving in 1878, George Campbell was "disappointed to find

that it is not at all a pretty or nice town; very inferior in amenities to
all the other Southern towns I have seen. It is, in fact, a new brick
town built with no trees in the streets, but abundant mud, for there is
a good deal of rain." Nor was dampness restricted to the streets,
Campbell added. "I have here realized for the first time what American
spitting is. It really requires some nerve to walk across the hall [of the
Kimball House Hotel]."[8]

Above all, Atlanta struck the observer with her transitory, incomplete nature. Like the nation itself, Atlanta was in the act of becoming.
Right after the war, Robert Somers noted that "a general depot is being built, but like everything else in Atlanta, it is unfinished." A little
later Edward King concluded that "Atlanta has an unfinished air; its
business and residence streets are scattered along a range of pretty
hills; but it is eminently modern and unromantic." As late as 1889,
in the midst of still another building boom that had seen much downtown construction, the laying out of new residential neighborhoods,
and the electrification of the streetcars, the *Atlanta Constitution*
quoted a pedestrian as saying, "I wish they would finish Atlanta," as
he tried to pick his way among the scaffolding on Whitehall Street.[9]

By 1890 Atlanta had become the archetype of the New South. It
had grown from a prewar population of 9,554 to 21,789 by 1870 and
to 65,000 in 1890.[10] Georgia's largest city, it was designated the state
capital in 1868. Henry W. Grady, Joseph Brown, and Hoke Smith
were state and national leaders. The *Atlanta Constitution* was the
most influential Southern newspaper. A leading market for upper
Georgia and the major distribution point for Western products, Atlanta was also a financial, commercial, administrative, and light-manu-
facturing center.

Atlanta already had a reputation for racial moderation. Because the
Radicals never had a majority of the City Council or elected one of their
number mayor, the impact of Congressional Reconstruction was even
less in the city than it was on the state level. As a result, the Redeemers did not have to resort to violence and fraud.[11]

Few cities could have differed more from Atlanta than Raleigh. Rather
than a sprawling, irregular, and unplanned community, Raleigh was
the nation's first planned state capital. The state purchased land for
the site and in 1792 a plan for the city was completed. Modeled after
Philadelphia, it contained the same grid pattern interspersed with a large
public square in the center and four smaller ones in each quadrant of

the city. Although its original boundaries were extended during the nineteenth century, the city retained its compact character and even at the turn of the century still could be crossed easily by foot. From the beginning it served primarily as an administrative center. There was little manufacturing and, possessed of neither a choice river location nor exceptional rail facilities, it became only a minor distribution center to a limited hinterland. On the eve of the war it contained fewer than 5,000 people. Its major claim to fame was as the birthplace of Andrew Johnson.[12]

Raleigh was spared the suffering encountered by other cities during the war. The surrender of the city on April 12, 1865, to General Sherman prevented its burning and sacking. In the fall of that year John Dennett found little change from its antebellum character. "Raleigh is a less considerable city than I had supposed, and the business part of it is neither large nor handsome; but its broad avenues, abundant trees, gentle declivities and rather elegant private residences, make it the prettiest Southern town, and with the most external evidences of taste and refinement, that I have yet seen."[13]

The city did not lose its quiet charm during the ensuing years. George Campbell found it "a pretty country place, with plenty of flowers and good vegetation." Like Atlanta and other Southern cities, it added streetcars and imposing railroad depots, began paving its streets, and advocated civic pride and the need to bring in new industry. But lacking was the determination and drive to bring about rapid and far-ranging change. "How about that cotton factory?" chided the Raleigh *Daily Constitution* in urging local businessmen to "awake from your lethargy" in 1875. "Wilmington has one, Charlotte is thinking about establishing one and Raleigh should not be behind the times." Thirteen years later civic leaders were still trying to bring a factory to the city. "What is to become of Raleigh unless we do something to increase its business?" bemoaned the *State Chronicle*. Finally in 1891 a mill began operation. Two other mills followed soon after, but boosters were less successful in their attempts to start a cigarette factory. Although an outsider offered to give the city the machinery if it could raise $6,000, local businessmen failed to come up with this small sum. Equally unsuccessful were efforts to get a boiler and iron works. *State Chronicle* editor Josephus Daniels, Raleigh's counterpart of Henry Grady, sadly concluded that the city needed "a little more unity, a little more energy, and a little more snap."[14]

Attempts at public improvements also reflected the absence of the dynamic vitality that distinguished Atlanta. Although aldermen began discussing the need for a waterworks system in 1870, piped water was still not available to homes twenty years later. Horse cars did not appear until 1886 and street paving for even the main streets was not begun until 1885. Residents seemed happy with the slow pace of the town and, despite the proddings of Daniels and other New South advocates, change continued to come slowly.[15]

From fewer than 5,000 in 1860 the number of inhabitants rose to 8,000 in 1870 and only 12,600 two decades later.[16] By the end of the period there was more industry. In addition to cotton, local firms produced wagons, paper, ice, shoes, and granite. But Raleigh's main function remained that of an administrative center and minor market town for tobacco and cotton.

What makes Raleigh noteworthy is the length and strength of Radical rule. From 1868 to 1875 Republicans held the mayor's office and the majority of the council seats. It is thus representative of the handful of Southern cities in which the Radicals maintained power during more than three consecutive elections.[17]

Montgomery was the second largest city in a state commonly assigned a position with Mississippi as the most anti-Negro in the South. Its site was originally occupied by two rival towns. Northerners founded New Philadelphia in 1817 and a year later Georgians laid out East Alabama nearby. A third community named Alabama was also plotted but quickly disappeared. In 1819 the three villages were united by the state legislature and incorporated as the town of Montgomery, named in honor of General Richard Montgomery, the martyred hero of the battle of Quebec. Set on a bluff overlooking the Alabama River twenty miles below the confluence of the Coosa and Tallapoosa, the new town was surrounded by a fertile hinterland for which it was a natural commercial center. The river was navigable the year round and emptied into Mobile Bay 331 miles away. With the addition of several railroad lines, the city increased its economic dominance over the interior of the state. It received a city charter in 1837, became the state capital in 1846, and briefly served as the first capital of the Confederacy during 1861.[18]

A charming Southern town of less than 9,000 at the outbreak of the war, Montgomery impressed visitors with its beauty and substantial prosperity. "The position of Montgomery is commanding and picturesque in the extreme," wrote an observer in 1862. "It is an important town . . . a great depot for cotton, corn, tobacco and rice. . . . The view from the dome of the State House, on a fine day is very grand and very extensive; and looking . . . on a vast panorama of swelling hills and plains, mostly covered with ripe corn, wheat and cotton." Noting that the streets were wide, unmacadamized, ankle-deep in sand, and usually lined with trees, he concluded that "altogether the place had the air of a comfortable quiet country town."[19]

Confederates shattered the peace of the city shortly before the end of the war when they set afire 80,000 bales of cotton in order to prevent their capture by Union troops. A greater conflagration ensued, destroying many buildings. General Sherman added to the town's loss by razing the arsenal, railroad depots, and other buildings of public utility. Rebuilding began quickly, however, and the town retained its charming appearance. John Dennett arrived in the city in January 1866, near the end of his journey throughout the South. "The city of Montgomery is the most beautiful that I have seen yet," he reported, moving Raleigh into second place. He was especially impressed by the undulating country surrounding the city and the pleasant vista of the Alabama River. The many trees and broad streets were characteristics shared with other Southern towns, but "here the streets are clean and hard, and the elegance of the private residences is equalled by the handsome and substantial appearance of the business quarter." Two years later an English visitor cited the same factors and concluded that "Montgomery, Alabama, is one of the prettiest towns I have seen."[20]

Yet commercial activity was brisk. "Very heavy stocks of goods—far too heavy, one would think, for the impoverished country—had been sent down on credit by New York merchants, cotton filled the warehouses, and drays loaded with it, crowded the streets and the river bank, where it was shipped to Mobile," wrote Whitelaw Reid in 1865. It could not have been much different given the city's choice Black Belt location and ample transportation network. Five years later Robert Somers noted that the low price of cotton at Liverpool had done little to discourage the businessmen of the city. "Out from the central dial, along the business streets, an active country trade goes on all day long. The steamboats come to a high but sloping bluff near the warehouses and cotton yards, where the cotton bales are rolled down easily to the wateredge, and taken on board. The railway depots are in the same vicinity and carry off large quantities of cotton to Savannah and other seaports." By then local merchants had successfully challenged the seaport cotton factors for control of the area's crop.[21]

Montgomery was also an iron and coal distribution center, although the emergence of Birmingham was soon to reduce this trade. The capital did a large wholesale trade in groceries, dry goods, boots and shoes, hardware, crockery, drugs, and notions. By 1885 it was a horse and mule market extending as far as New Orleans and Jacksonville. Cotton, of course, was the staple product, but trade in lumber, farm produce, and hay was also extensive. Manufacturing centered upon cotton production. There was a cotton mill, a firm producing cottonseed oil, a manufacturer of cotton presses and other machinery, and a cotton press company. Other manufactured products included fertilizer, bricks, sash, doors, blinds, candy, and iron. Such economic growth spurred population growth. Montgomery was small compared to the major Southern cities, but its 1890 population of slightly less than 22,000 was twice that of twenty years before.[22]

Montgomery remained a provincial town, hostile to change and outside influences. Even by 1890 the downtown streets were unpaved and municipal services in general were inferior to those in other Southern cities. The absence of the United States flag from the capitol's flagpole when the state House of Representatives met at the end of 1865 symbolized this resistance to change. The passions of the war did not easily subside, and, as in Mobile and Selma, many Northerners who settled in Montgomery in the summer of 1865 were boycotted by local residents and often forced to sell their businesses at a loss.[23] Helping to keep alive old memories was the relative success of the Radicals. The state was not redeemed until 1874, while Republicans controlled city hall from 1868 to 1875 and the City Council for all but two of those years.[24]

Alone among the five cities, Richmond's roots went back to the colonial era. In addition to being the oldest of the five, it was the only one to be ranked among the major cities of the antebellum South. Founded in 1609 as an Indian outpost but not incorporated as a town until 1742, Richmond was situated at the head of navigation on the James River, only 150 miles by boat to the coast. The surrounding country was rich in tobacco, iron, copper, and manganese. Laid out in a gridiron pattern with little consideration given to the site's uneven topography, the city was built on two undulating plateaus, its length far greater than its depth, and cut into two unequal parts by the valley of Shockoe Creek and subdivided by smaller valleys and ravines.

In 1779 it became the state capital. Growth was slow but was stimulated in 1835 by completion to Lynchburg of the James River and Kanawha Canal which bypassed the falls of the river near Richmond. The construction of new railroads and the partial utilization of the river's water power helped the population to reach almost 38,000 by 1860. The city was a large processor of tobacco and flour and the home of the Tredegar Iron Works, destined to be the chief supplier of iron for the Confederacy. Richmond's prominence, elegant social life, and its central location led Jefferson Davis to designate it the permanent capital of the Confederate States.[25]

Throughout the war Richmond was under constant pressure from the Union forces. Food was scarce, public services declined, and prosperity vanished. Evacuating Southern troops in April 1865 set fire to supplies, arsenals, and bridges, producing a calamitous blaze in which more than $8,000,000 worth of property was destroyed.[26] Much of the spirit went out of the city. "The burnt district of Richmond was hardly more thoroughly destroyed than the central part of Atlanta," observed Whitelaw Reid in 1865, "yet with all the advantages of proximity to the North, abundant capital, and an influx of business and money from above the Potomac, Richmond was not half so far rebuilt as Atlanta." In ambition and drive Richmond seemed closer to Raleigh and Montgomery than to Atlanta. It lacked the rawness of the Georgia capital and its interest in tradition and history was more in line with what is ordinarily considered "Southern behavior." Visitors noted not only Richmond's beauty but its ordered appearance, which at times made it seem as much a country town as Montgomery or Raleigh. According to one English traveler, "Richmond is a most beautiful city, its streets are wide, many of its buildings elegant, and there is a picturesqueness in its general aspect which gives it a peculiar charm." It was a wealthy city with an impressive array of institutions and an elite which set the tone of life. "From a distance the city presents an imposing appearance," noted a former Union soldier. "It is situated on several hills, and its grand buildings, its spires, its monuments, its schools, speak to the greatness and splendid taste of the people. . . . Everything looks so monarchial, exclusive and lordly."[27]

In the postwar years the city strengthened its economic position. Clearly the tobacco capital of the nation, with more than fifty factories in operation by 1880, its rich hinterland also provided the resources for its flour mills and iron and steel foundries. Steamboats ran regularly between the city and Norfolk, New York, Baltimore, and Philadelphia. It was the terminus of six railroads, nearly all parts of trunk lines that connected Richmond with principal cities throughout the country. In short, it was the richest and most prosperous of the cities under discussion.[28]

Richmond was also among the best run. The gas and waterworks were municipally owned, paving was more extensive than in other cities, and there were numerous parks. Innovation was also encouraged, as demonstrated by the appearance on its streets of the first electrified streetcar in a major city. Yet the community lacked the booster spirit of its younger rivals. The pace of life was slow and perhaps its leaders too often looked to the past. Although the area of the city more than doubled through annexation of two and a half square miles of territory in 1867, the population rose from 51,000 in 1870 to little more than 81,000 two decades later. This rate of growth was even slower than Raleigh's.[29]

The Radicals enjoyed only a brief hegemony in the city. The administration appointed by the military authorities in April 1868 served until the Redeemers replaced it in March 1870. Republicans maintained minority representation in the City Council throughout the period, but never came close to gaining a majority or winning the mayoralty. The city was the personification of Bourbon Democracy.[30]

Nashville, likewise a significant community by the time of the Civil War, far outstripped Richmond in its postwar development, although it still had 5,000 fewer people in 1890. The city began as a small trading settlement in 1779 in what was then part of North Carolina's western frontier. It soon became headquarters for a number of stations in the area and prospered despite fierce resistance from Indians. A local government was formed, the town laid out, lots sold, and a court house, prison, and stocks erected. In 1790 North Carolina ceded the area along with the rest of its disputed western lands to the United States government. The early settlers had chosen a good location for their town. Built on a bluff overlooking the Cumberland River, the city was surrounded by a series of conical hills and was divided into four sections by valleys formed by three meandering streams. The adjacent countryside was rich in a variety of crops, especially tobacco and cotton.

By 1810 trade with the Indians had declined in importance as keel boats and barges took furs to Pittsburgh, Natchez, and New Orleans and brought back such products as dry goods, sugar, and coffee. When the steamboats replaced barges, Nashville citizens became full or part owners of vessels that worked the Cumberland, the Ohio, and the Mississippi. Nashville quickly recognized the importance of railroads and the Louisville and Nashville Railroad soon linked the city to Louisville, New Orleans, St. Louis, and Memphis.[31]

A thriving community of almost 17,000 in 1860, Nashville was one of several Southern cities favorably affected by the war. Confederate troops left the city in February 1862 and the leading citizens surrendered it to Union forces. Andrew Johnson served as Military Governor until he left to assume the vice presidency.[32] Nashville was spared the destruction of other cities and its function as headquarters for Union troops kept money in the pockets of local merchants. Like Atlanta, the town attracted emigrants from throughout the South and North and took on the character of a frontier community. "Every branch of business has been pecuniarily prosperous beyond all precedent," wrote one resident shortly after the war ended. "Everything is now in a transition state and no one is clear sighted enough to say what will be the consequences in Nashville—it may remain a large thriving city or it may go back and be a village again. . . . Lawyers, doctors, newspaper men, merchants, etc. are today making fortunes, tomorrow they may be packing up for some other region—all at least, but the lawyers."[33] Boom-town conditions persisted, however, despite a financially difficult five-year period following the Panic of 1873.

At its core was ambitious boosterism, though not quite as pervasive as in Atlanta. In 1881 Nashville hosted one of the earliest city expositions. Urging support of the endeavor, the *Nashville Banner* reminded its readers that "all progressive cities must have expositions. They advertise the city. They exhibit our industries and induce people to settle among us. A city which has no expositions, has no vitality, no vim. . . . A failure would reflect on the city." Visitors found tangible evidence of this spirit. "Of the old cities of the South," remarked Alexander McClure, "Nashville ranks next to Atlanta in rapid and substantial growth since the war. It has many signs of Northern energy and thrift, and it is advancing with healthy strides." To another visitor who had last seen the city in 1861, the contrast by 1881 was remarkable.

> Old Nashville lies in a dark mass of roofs, chimneys, spires and tree-tops, wreathed in a mist of smoke, on the slopes of the capitaline hill. Up and down the river, north and south stretches the new town until the houses become scattered and the country begins but the most impressive feature is the line of public institutions encircling the city like a line of fortifications.

While the site was impressive, the city itself had never been beautiful and it was now even less so. "There is too much a mixture of hovels and palaces; too much yellow clay and bare rock in sight."[34]

The public institutions were among the most visible signs of post-war progress. They included Fisk University, Vanderbilt University, Nashville Institute, University of Nashville, Central Tennessee College, State Capitol, City Hall, and various state asylums. In 1900 they were joined by a magnificent new Union Railroad Depot. The city was expanding horizontally as well as vertically. Two large annexations during the period added the adjacent territory on Nashville's side of the Cumberland and the neighboring town of Edgefield on the opposite bank of the river. From ten wards in 1865, Nashville grew to twenty by 1890; its population increased from fewer than 26,000 in 1870 to more than 76,000 twenty years later. By the middle of the 1870s it had surpassed Memphis as the state's largest city.[35]

By 1880 Nashville was the chief commercial center and wholesale market south of the Ohio. In addition to superb rail and water connections, twelve macadamized turnpikes entered the city, establishing better ties with its immediate hinterland. On its outskirts were imposing factories that produced cotton, lumber, oil, and iron. Here, too, processing turned grain from the surrounding territory into flour and good Tennessee whiskey.[36]

With all its advances, Nashville was still not a finished city. The *Republican Banner* complained in 1873 that "our city looks like a pig pen, and is profitable to the owners of city scum, but it speaks badly for our notions of health and cleanliness." As late as the eighties, swine roamed the streets as the chief sanitary force; alleys and streets were glutted with filth. Citizens and newspapers bemoaned the unpleasant smells noticeable even in the heart of the city. Slaughterhouses and tanneries were poorly regulated and, as was true of private individuals, dumped their waste directly into the streams which emptied into the river that furnished their water. Even in 1890 the drinking water was described as "warm and thick" and visitors unaccustomed to it were advised to flee to the suburbs for a purer version.[37] Like other Southern cities, Nashville paid dearly for its neglect of sanitary measures in the recurrent epidemics of smallpox, yellow fever, and cholera.

Nashville was in a unique position politically: Tennessee was the sole former Confederate state readmitted to the Union before the inauguration of Congressional Reconstruction. Nevertheless, the city experienced two stormy years of Radical domination under A. E. Alden. The Radicals were removed in 1869 and thereafter, despite the long reign of a Republican mayor, the Democrats enjoyed continuous control of the City Council. Nonetheless, the position of the Republicans was stronger than in any of the other four cities throughout the period, and Nashville thus represents those few Southern cities not safely in the hands of the Democrats after the overthrow of the Radical governments.[38]

These then are the cities. But what of the blacks? Where did they fit? Part of the problem, of course, was that they did not. Indeed, it will be argued that they were a persistent source of instability. As the next chapter will begin to explain, the increased black urban population after the war confronted Southern white urban dwellers with their most serious challenge.

2

Black Migrants and White Cities

In the antebellum South blacks had been assigned a place in the countryside, filling a role supposedly ordained by God. Though the great
majority remained where they were, the end of the Civil War brought
increasing numbers of blacks into the cities. Their presence continued
to trouble urban whites throughout the postbellum period.

Although both free and enslaved blacks had been part of antebellum
Southern urban life, whites had become increasingly upset with the
relative freedom enjoyed by blacks in the urban environment. Many
arranged for their own jobs, lived without white supervision, and had
considerable leisure time. Whites in Richmond, Nashville, and Raleigh
took some solace, however, in the decline in the relative number of
their Negro residents during the 1850s. This was part of a regional
trend; in 1820, 37 percent of all Southern town dwellers were black;
by 1860, this was true of less than 17 percent.[1] The postwar influx destroyed any illusions that the urban black population would continue
to decline. With the exception of Montgomery, the five cities which
constitute the core of this study witnessed a sharp rise in the percentage of their black populations in the first years after the war. Even
Montgomery showed a large increase in the absolute size of its Negro
population in the ten years after 1860, although percentage-wise the
Negroes failed to keep pace with the addition of whites. The growth
in the number of blacks continued throughout the period, often with
a corresponding increment in their percentage of the population. (See
Table 1.)

18

Table 1
POPULATION STATISTICS 1850–1890

	1850	1860	1870	1880	1890
Nashville					
White	7,626	13,043	16,147	27,005	46,773
Black	2,539	3,945	9,709	16,337	29,395
% Black	25	23	38	38	39
Atlanta					
White	2,060	7,615	11,860	21,079	39,416
Black	512	1,939	9,929	16,330	28,098
% Black	20	20	46	44	43
Richmond					
White	15,274	23,635	27,928	35,765	49,034
Black	12,296	14,275	23,110	27,835	32,330
% Black	44	38	45	44	40
Montgomery					
White	6,511	4,341	5,402	6,782	8,892
Black	2,217	4,502	5,183	9,931	12,987
% Black	25	53	49	59	59
Raleigh					
White	2,253	2,693	3,696	4,911	6,327
Black	2,263	2,087	4,094	4,354	6,348
% Black	50.1	44	53	47	50.1

SOURCE: Bureau of the Census, *Ninth Census: Population* (Washington, D.C., 1872), I, 81, 102, 225, 262, 280; Bureau of the Census, *Tenth Census: Population* (Washington, D.C., 1883), I, 416–17, 422, 424–25; Bureau of the Census, *Eleventh Census: Population* (Washington, D.C., 1893), I, 524, 527, 546, 555, 557.

Nor did the U.S. census figures given in Table 1 truly reflect the changes in population. The federal censuses for 1870 and 1890 under-enumerated blacks, especially those in Southern cities.[2] Then too because of their decennial nature they missed the ebb and flow of people within the decade. This problem is especially serious when trying to re-create the situation in Southern cities during 1865 and 1866. According to the *Nashville Dispatch*, there were 10,744 freedmen in Nashville in 1865 as compared to the prewar figure of fewer than 4,000; the 1870 census, however, counted only 9,709 blacks. Was this decline due to statistical inaccuracies or to an actual thinning out of the Negro population? Local censuses conducted in Atlanta in 1867 and 1869 found 9,288 and 13,184 blacks in the city for those years, but the 1870 census returned only 9,929.[3] Since the figure for the white population was approximately 4,000 below the 1869 tally, perhaps the local censuses were a product of a booster spirit which exaggerated the fledgling town's population. Considering the primitive state of statistics at the time, a definitive answer to such questions remains unlikely.

One possibility is that a return of freedmen to the countryside after 1866 did take place; in some towns it may have begun earlier. "Has the surplus negro population left the city?" asked the *Montgomery Daily Ledger* in the fall of 1865. "We make the inquiry for we hear a general complaint of their scarcity." A partial answer to the question was given by a Montgomery resident in the beginning of 1866 who reported that "there are scarcely any country people in town now. They are making contracts and going to work rapidly." The failure to find work in the cities was a prime reason for a return to the countryside, but there were others as well, including the unhealthy living conditions. Myrta Avary, whose former slaves had deserted her plantation near Atlanta for the attractions of the nearby town, noted that by 1866 "our negroes were all back, some ill from exposure." In the winter of 1866 the *Richmond Dispatch* also noted that many of Richmond's recent black migrants "have gone back to the cornfield, many have wandered to their old homes, many have died or disappeared mysteriously."[4]

The Freedmen's Bureau and the Army tried to keep the blacks in the countryside, and when this effort failed they sought to disperse the urban Negro population. "In the city of Richmond," complained a delegation of blacks in 1865, "the military and police authorities will not allow us to walk the streets day or night, in the regular pursuit of our business or on our way to church without a pass and passes do not in all cases protect us from arrest, abuse, violence and imprisonment." The protest came five days after the Richmond *Times* reported that "the stern decrees of the military" had encouraged the departure of thousands of blacks.[5] Circular Number 1 issued in September 1865 by General Wager Swayne, Assistant Commissioner of the Freedmen's Bureau in Montgomery, stated clearly that "as to both Freedmen and Refugees . . . all humane and rightful means should be employed to prevent their crowding into cities and towns, where they will suffer from high rents, scarcity of fuel and infectious diseases." Judicial agents of the Bureau were to send to specially designated farms "all Freedmen found sleeping in streets, or in excessively crowded rooms, or who are otherwise committed as Vagrants."[6]

Nashville, because of its early occupation by Union troops, was the first of the cities to experience the problem of mass influx. In June 1863 the Board of Aldermen, troubled by the presence of "a large unprecedented collection of runaway slaves, contrabands and free negroes without profitable occupation or place of residence and without means of subsistence," asked that the Army put them to work or else allow the municipal authorities to do so. Yet the following year a Union soldier using blunter language reported, "the negars is as thick as hell here."[7] The efforts of the Freedmen's Bureau's General Clinton B. Fisk to remove sizable numbers of blacks thus drew praise from the local press, and in the fall of 1865 Fisk was able to report that the Nashville camps, houses, and hospitals for freedmen, along with most of the other facilities in his district, had been closed, the majority of the former occupants "established in good homes in the country."[8] During the first winter after emancipation, the Bureau in Nashville contracted with fifty Negroes per day to work in the countryside.[9] As elsewhere, local authorities were further stimulated by General O. O. Howard's order to his Assistant Commissioners in February 1866 to "continue to use every possible effort . . . to reduce . . . any accumulations of people in the different cities and villages."[10]

Despite the departure of a portion of the Negro population, both visitors and residents were struck by the numbers of new Negroes in the cities. Whatever the actual count, it seemed to observers that the cities were teeming with blacks. Although whites actually comprised a larger percentage of Richmond's population throughout the period, the English traveler C. B. Berry observed in 1866 that "the black population seem to predominate over the white"; two years later another Englishman, George Rose, noted that the result of emancipation was "to fill the streets of Richmond and other Southern cities with crowds of great, hulking, idle black men, with their tattered and filthy women, and more than half naked, neglected children."[11] White Southerners experienced a sense of siege as they spoke of "swarms" of Negroes who were "engulfing" them and disrupting the previous pattern of urban life. Writing in the fall of 1867, the editor of the Raleigh *Weekly Progress* complained:

> For nearly three years Raleigh has been to the great mass of unbleached Americans in the western and contiguous counties of this state what Mecca is to the followers of Mohamet . . . caravan after caravan swarmed into the state capital—the immigrants being prin-

cipally the idle and the desolate thus overcrowding our beautiful city
with a population capable of at times being made a dangerous instru-
ment in the hands of vicious men.[12]

There were many reasons for this flow of freedmen to the cities;
and despite unsatisfactory living conditions the migration continued
and even intensified. Many former slaves were simply influenced by
the headiness of freedom which removed their bonds to the land and
permitted them to flee the control of their old masters. Often they
fled the countryside from fear of reprisals by whites who refused to
accept their new status. The cities served as sanctuaries housing the
federal troops and later the headquarters of the Reconstruction governments; there too was safety in numbers. "They leave the country
in many instances because they are outraged, because their lives are
threatened; they run to the cities as an asylum," testified the black
leader Henry M. Turner at the Congressional hearings investigating
the Ku Klux Klan in 1871. At the same hearings Negroes from Atlanta
and Montgomery confirmed that they had fled to those cities in order
to escape white violence in the rural areas.[13] Not only violence drove
them from the land. According to Henry Turner, another reason for
the migration was that many freedmen were tired of working all year
without getting the wages they had been promised.[14]

Most whites emphasized the attractions of the cities as the reason
for Negro migration. This approach undermined charges of outrages
in the countryside and at the same time demonstrated the alleged irre-
sponsibility of the blacks and the culpability of their Northern allies.
Charles Wallace Howard, editor of The Plantation and an Atlanta resident, thought that the exodus was the result of "the inherent love of
the negro for a crowd, for shows, for amusements, and for opportunities of making a precarious living by occasional jobs when they may be
idle at other times." Asked if it was the result "to some extent" of the
treatment they received in the countryside, he replied, "No, I think
not." A Republican who lived outside Atlanta agreed. "They are fond
of crowds and shows, and all such things as are going on in cities; and
they pick up a livelihood in cities without any persistent labor, with
more facility than they can in the country."[15]

Unsympathetic whites also attributed the urban migration to the
influence of the Northern intruders. Summing up events of the previous few years, the Nashville Union and American claimed in 1870
that many blacks were "lured to the cities by the wily Radicals who

. . . held out to the views of the darkies the glittering boon of the franchise, with hopes of office and position in the future." As an added incentive to migration, claimed the newspaper, "soup houses were established for them at public expense; fuel in many instances was furnished in the same manner. . . . The days when negroes had to work in Nashville, were, to appearances, at an end." Not only did Negroes come to the cities after the Northerners had been there a while, often they came into town with them. To Sarah Follansbee, witnessing line after line of occupation forces march past her home in Montgomery, "it seemed that thousands upon thousands of negroes had joined them." There were Negro soldiers as well. The 12th and the 15th U.S. Colored Infantry units were only two of several Negro companies mustered out in Nashville during 1865–1866. Many of these former defenders of the Union remained in the city and added to its growing black population.[16]

City services clearly attracted many blacks. One of General Fisk's methods of reducing the black urban population in the early postwar years had been to curtail the number of freedmen's schools. After the urban public schools started, they remained far superior to their rural counterparts and wherever such schools were founded, Negroes sought to take advantage of them. Shortly after Athens, Georgia, established free schools in 1886, the *Athens Banner Watchman* unhappily reported that because of the schools "negroes continue to pour into Athens in perfect swarms, and they are packing like sardines into the huts they rent."[17] The schools, together with welfare services such as hospitals and public relief inaugurated by the Freedmen's Bureau and Northern missionaries, remained strong magnets for freedmen throughout the period.

Most blacks drawn to the city for its services remained to swell the population. Others only temporarily contributed to the seemingly endless influx. Saturday nights, in particular, attracted blacks and whites to the city, but Negroes were more noticeable and newspapers lost no opportunity to list the frequent brawls that marked their visits.[18] Then too there were the special trips for celebrations or to contract for farm jobs during the year. "The negroes as usual at this season [Christmas] are coming to town in droves," wrote a Montgomery resident to his son. "The streets are blocked by them. . . . [They] come to trade and meet their friends and kindred, and make arrangements for the next year." He compared this gathering to "the saturnalia of Ancient Rome, when the slaves had greater privileges and license than at other times."[19]

There were also many Negro tourists. For example, in the summer of 1878 it seemed to the *Atlanta Constitution* that at least 10,000 Negro excursionists had jammed the city for the Fourth of July.[20] Another source of transitory blacks was the numerous emigrants heading west to new lands. The *Daily Atlanta Intelligencer* claimed that in one week of February 1867 one thousand Negroes had been seen in the city *"in transita"* heading for southwest Georgia or Mississippi.[21] Occasionally, however, Atlanta proved the unexpected terminus for some of them, as in 1883 when several carloads of Negroes emigrating from South Carolina to Texas found their funds exhausted upon reaching the city.[22]

Thus, the influx of blacks had many causes. As in all migrations, there were both push and pull factors at work. In the early postwar years the dislocation in the countryside along with white hostility was a major cause. But then, as later, the attractions of the city were of equal importance; together they caused a shift, if often only temporary, of many blacks from the farms to the cities. The influx persisted and though whites might disagree as to the reasons it was a reality they had to face.

White opinion was virtually unanimous that the city was no place for blacks. In freedom as in slavery their place was believed to be on the farms. "Our advice to them is to go into the country and cultivate the soil, the employment God designed them for and which they must do or starve," declared the *Montgomery Daily Ledger* in 1865. Added its editor, the city was "intended for white people." Few others would entirely exclude Negroes from urban areas, but most whites would have agreed with the *Atlanta Constitution* that "no better laborer for cotton than the colored man can be found" and shared its disappointment that "he is unwilling to leave the city to go into the country on a farm." In 1873 immigration agents in Nashville estimated that there were about two or three hundred able-bodied Negroes in the city without regular employment. The *Republican Banner* argued that their services were severely needed in the countryside, but

> they will not leave the city under any consideration, and when asked if they would like to work in the rural districts, scornfully reply that they have been living in the city for so many years, and if the agents wanted anybody to go, they had better go themselves.

Two years later the paper concluded that eight thousand of the city's ten thousand Negroes would be better off on farms.[23]

Given the prewar history of Southern race relations, it is not surprising that the majority of whites held such views. Negroes were seen as clearly better off on the land for the sake both of themselves and of the whites. Farming, to the basically agrarian Southern society in the words even of the *Atlanta Constitution,* an apostle of the New South creed, was "good honest work . . . the basis of all happiness and prosperity." The work was good for whites as well as blacks, but it was the latter group which was seen as especially suited for agriculture by temperament, experience, physical makeup, and level of intelligence. Above all, it was easier to control and take better care of the freedmen in the countryside. There, ran the argument, they could benefit from the careful supervision of their former masters and other whites who knew them. To become uprooted was to be placed at the mercy of the impersonal city. "Nothing can be more deleterious to the black race as their [*sic*] strong proclivity to congregate in the towns," argued the Raleigh *Daily Sentinel.* "The temptation to idleness, viciousness, and crime are ten fold what they are in the country."[24]

White paternalism in its various forms played an important role in developing this view. Although most whites accepted the end of slavery, the *Atlanta Constitution* still argued in 1881 that

> in its humane aspect and in the results that have followed, the system of slavery as it existed in the south never had and can never have its parallel in the history of the world. So far as the negro is concerned, it was the only field in which the seed of civilization could be sown. It was as necessary to his moral, mental and physical dissenthralment [*sic*] as the primary school is to the child.

This comparison of the Negro to a child was frequently made during the period and influenced white perception of the freedman. Like the child, he was imitative, in need of discipline, and someone to be "kept in his place." Often the two groups were lumped together. "The juvenile and colored population of East Side have been in ecstacies during the past week over the Italian, his organ and monkey," reported the *Nashville Banner.* In the same city during a crackdown on the violators of the Sunday baseball law, a Criminal Court judge told the grand jury that "if you should determine to indict spectators, then by all means begin with the intelligent class of the community, . . . leaving (if anybody) the more ignorant colored people and the small boys to

escape." As late as 1871, a Richmond city ordinance gave as one of the
duties of fire commanders "to prevent minors and colored persons from
running with the engine, taking hold of any part of the apparatus, or
meddling with the same in any way." And in an editorial defending
Southern treatment of Negroes, the *Richmond Dispatch* stated that
"the white men of Virginia have no more prejudice against the negroes
than they have against children."[25]

Some whites were genuinely concerned about the welfare of the former slaves and believed they would be better off away from the
cities, but the majority was more concerned with the impact of the
freedmen on the community. In private letters, city reports, speeches,
and columns of the newspapers, "the negro" appeared most prominently as a person who had to be controlled and disciplined. Whether
he was the invader from the countryside, the resultant vagrant, the
petty thief, the bolder criminal, the disorderly or drunken reveler and
fighter, the hackman who drove too fast and overwhelmed passengers
at the depot, the bootblack who crowded the depots and the streets,
or the Republican voter, "the negro" was to be kept in his place and
managed for the sake of the peace and stability of the white community. Of most concern to whites, especially during the first Christmas
after emancipation, was the threat of "negro insurrection." The fact
that such insurrections never took place tells much about the blacks
and even more about the frightened whites. Since whites insisted for
the most part in seeing an undifferentiated mass of blacks to whom
they ascribed the worst of motives and behavior, social control out-
weighed any desire to ease the transition of the blacks from slavery
to freedom in the urban South.[26]

The transition from the old world of slavery and subordination to
the new one of freedom and "insubordination" presented white residents with a severe shock. They felt threatened and betrayed by the
passage of the old order and therefore sought to hold on to as much
of their previous authority as possible. In the midst of such efforts they
proclaimed their disappointment with the behavior of their former
slaves. Out of these feelings was forged a mixture of anger, puzzle-
ment, and, predictably, nostalgia.

Few whites called for the reestablishment of slavery, but in their
comparisons of the past with the present Southerners left little doubt
as to their preference. "In times gone by, it was a rare thing to hear
negro swearing upon the streets or elsewhere," remarked the *Mont-*

gomery Daily Ledger in 1865. "But now, it is the most common occurrence in all public squares." After pointing out the alleged insolence of blacks on streetcars and on the streets throughout the South, Myrta Avary remembered that

> Southerners had taken great pains and pride in teaching their negroes good manners; they wanted them to be courtly and polished, and it must be said for the negroes, they took polish well. It was with keen regret that their old preceptors saw them throw all their fine schooling in etiquette to the winds.

In accounting for the appearance of a Negro named Cornelia before the Mayor's Court in 1866, the *Daily Atlanta Intelligencer* concluded that she "evidently entertained large ideas of her freedom, and believed it gave her license to apply all sorts of epithets to white ladies." Nor was she unique: "Cornelia is simply a specimen of that large class of worthless and abandoned creatures in this community. . . . They are respectful to no one. . . . They are no longer the contented useful house-girls of former years." The much-praised loyalty which the slaves exhibited during the war seemed to evaporate. A Montgomery editor summed up the feelings of many whites. "Ingratitude is one of the characteristics of the negro," he said. "However much you may do for him, and especially when sick, he is ungrateful; gratitude, that even a dog never fails to exhibit, seems to be a stranger to his breast."[27]

The world had been turned upside down. The "inherent vices" of the blacks which included "indolence, theft and sensuality," according to one Atlantan, had been "greatly increased since the abolition of slavery" because "restraints have been withdrawn." Worse still, these vices were accompanied by growing black influence. "Sir, you come to a Godforsaken country," a young Richmond man told an English visitor in 1868. "Those who lately had riches are now in want; and the whites are now ruled by blacks." The visitor during his stay in the city found this sentiment echoed many times by other citizens who believed that "their slaves had been made their masters." In 1889 the appointment of a black to the Atlanta post office led to the resignation of a white employee. "My father used to own 200 negroes," he explained, "and I used to have two negroes wait upon me when I was a school boy and of course, I can't work in the same office with a negro."[28]

It is not surprising that the whites wherever possible sought to retain their former authority or regain it when it had been lost. Yet keeping the Negroes in their place proved an elusive goal, especially as a new generation of young blacks born in freedom emerged in the cities. Whether part of the new educated middle class or of the lower-class vagrant variety, these young blacks confronted the white community with a long-term problem of social control. "These [lower-class] rascals are a great pest and nuisance. They are irrepressible. They are destined to annoy and perplex statesmen for years to come," stated the *Nashville Banner*.

> This class is composed exclusively of the young. As they grow older they are more dangerous, as they often resort to arson and murder. . . . They are the worst elements in Southern society, and if something is not done soon to put a check to their depreciations [*sic*], life in towns and cities will grow unbearable. Reform schools, whipping posts, stocks, each and all have been canvassed, but as yet nothing is done.

The newspaper claimed in another issue that while older black agricultural workers were dependable, their children preferred to spend "most of their time in town."[29] The more these young Negroes caused trouble and the more the cities were disrupted, the more often Southerners longed for the old plantation Negroes.

Nostalgia for the days of the "happy obedient darkey" expressed itself in many ways. Not wasting any time in recalling the superiority of the past, the *Montgomery Daily Ledger* in September 1865 devoted two columns to tell of a freedwoman, once a well-cared-for slave. She came into the office of the editor and offered to sell herself back into slavery in order to pay nearly $100 rent "and in order, too, to secure a permanent home, free from the anxieties and troubles she had experienced since she became free; she was tired of freedom." According to the editor, her case was not an isolated one for others also regretted "having no master to provide for [them] in sickness and health and relieve [their] mind[s] of the thousand perplexities that harass" them. The *Richmond Dispatch* printed a letter allegedly written by "an aged and polite colored man" who, although he had looked forward to freedom, now also wanted to return to his former master. "If I was back at Marsy's, I would give my zestance—let the balance do as they may." Whites often boasted of the superior health and well-being of the slaves, especially in light of the growing belief that the Negro population had been declining since emancipation. Another approach was to show that no matter how far the Negroes seemed to have departed from their earlier subservience, they were still the same old faithful souls at heart. The *Nashville Banner* told its readers in 1889 that James H. Jones, who had been body servant to Jefferson Davis at the time of his capture, was still strongly devoted to Davis despite the Negro's position as a leading Raleigh Republican politician.[30]

"Many Southerners look back wistfully to the faithful, simple, ignorant, obedient, cheerful, old plantation Negro and deplore his disappearance. They want the New South, but the old Negro. That Negro is disappearing forever along with the old feudalism and the old-time exclusively agricultural life." Although this statement of Ray Stannard Baker's was contained in a chapter on Atlanta written in 1908, it had long applied to the capital of the New South. Indeed, Atlanta, especially in the pages of the *Constitution*, was the most preoccupied with keeping alive the memory of the "old darkey." The newspaper was fond of comparing the "good negro" of slavery times with the "bad negro" of present. In one issue, for example, the increase of yellow fever among blacks since emancipation was attributed not to the greater malignancy of the disease, but rather to the decreased resistance of Negroes. "Cleanliness, temperance, due labor and regular proper habits" were seen as the four cardinal principles of health which had been assured by the white supervisor under slavery but had subsequently broken down in the absence of white control.[31]

Even more revealing were the frequent obituaries of "good negroes." When an "old before the war" black named Charles Farrall died suddenly in Atlanta, the *Constitution* carried a one and one-half column story, concluding that "old man Farrall was a polite negro. He never forgot his early training, and whenever he met an acquaintance it was his custom to raise his hat and bow. He was honest and had a great many friends among the white people." Most of the good Negroes had servant or menial occupations, like Aaron Harper, the porter at the Kimball House, who, under the heading of "Death of a Good Negro," was described as a "faithful, good negro, who won the esteem and confidence of all who knew him by his unfailing devotion to duty. He was punctual as a clock, always reliable and trusty."[32]

There was also proof that loyalty could still be found among the living blacks. Recounting the tale of John Wesley, a Negro who was once owned by one of the town's leading citizens, the *Constitution* told how the former slave returned from Virginia to be near his master's dying son. The man entered his son's room to find the former

slave rubbing the head of his young massa, leading the paper to conclude that "it was a touching picture, eloquent of that fidelity which
now and then is found in the old plantation negro as pure and beautiful as it ever gleamed in romance or poetry. John Wesley is still here
and we want more negroes like him."[33] Nor did the paper miss an
opportunity in 1890 to print an interview in which Peg Leg Williams,
one of the South's leading labor agents, compared urban and rural
blacks.

> A country nigger is the best laborer on earth, and is good for any
> work you put him at. He is a good farmer, a good merchant, a good
> railroad or boat hand, a good cook—a good anything. A town nigger
> is good for nothing, as a usual thing, and planters as much as they
> need labor, have no use for him.[34]

Perhaps it was such a view of the relative merits of the new town Negro and the "old plantation darkey" that led the newspaper's Joel
Chandler Harris to move his "old type darkey" Uncle Remus from
the streets of Atlanta to the country porches from which he told his
tales of Brer Rabbit. It certainly accounted for the popularity of such
groups as the Fisk Jubilee Singers whose initial successes performing
old slave songs came in Southern cities.[35]

The influx of blacks and the resultant problem of social control confronted urban whites with their greatest challenge. No matter how
much they wished that the freedmen would return to the countryside,
they were forced to find new ways to discipline blacks to replace the
old combination of slavery and free Negro statutes.

3

Justice

White Southerners sought in many ways to perpetuate their control over the newly freed black population. One way was the manipulation of the system of justice. Such action was required to keep blacks in an economic, social, and political position most beneficial to the white majority. Rather than functioning as a protector of Negroes, laws existed throughout most of the period to discipline them. Blacks suffered from explicitly or implicitly discriminatory laws, unequal administration of justice, and elimination from participation at all levels of the legal process.

During the antebellum period, the legal rights of blacks were sharply restricted. Slaves, in fact, had none, while free Negroes enjoyed only a quasi-free status in which they could sue and be sued, make contracts, inherit property, buy and sell goods, and marry. Yet they could not testify against a white man, could not serve as jurors or law officers, were barred from certain business pursuits, were denied full freedom of association and assembly, and, of course, were prohibited from marrying whites.[1]

The former Confederates who exercised power during the period of Presidential Reconstruction sought to minimize the changes between the old and new status of blacks. In July 1865 the Nashville City Council repealed all its laws pertaining to slaves, but provided that "hereafter they [the former slaves] shall be subject to the same pains and penalties for a violation of any municipal ordinance, as free persons of color have been subject to heretofore." Richmond and Atlanta, on

31

the other hand, simply repealed those ordinances which made Negroes guilty of different crimes than whites.[2] The ex-Confederates maintained that blacks could expect fair treatment from their former masters. In January 1866 Mayor J. E. Williams reminded the Atlanta City Council of the need to suppress crime "and especially such as may be attributed to the changed situation of the negro," but called for "even handed and impartial justice . . . [for] evildoers whether they be white or black."[3] In none of the cities, however, were any practical steps taken to provide blacks with equal judicial rights; there was no place for them on the juries and their access to the witness box was limited to cases in which whites were not parties.

Representatives of the victorious North were not convinced that Negroes would receive equal justice without federal intervention. Testifying before the Joint Congressional Committee on Reconstruction, the Freedmen's Bureau's Assistant Commissioner in Raleigh concluded that if neither U.S. troops nor the Freedmen's Bureau were present, Southern whites "would enact laws which would make them [the freedmen] virtual slaves."[4] His Richmond counterpart was equally certain that oppression would follow in his city and observed that "I have the assurance of one of the first lawyers in the city of Richmond that the negroes could not obtain justice before a Virginia jury."[5]

For this reason and especially because of the refusal of the regular courts to recognize black testimony against whites, cases involving freedmen were heard in Provost Marshal and Freedmen's Bureau courts for almost a year. Negroes often received harsh treatment in the military tribunals which at times seemed as interested as local whites in disciplining them. Penalties at the Raleigh Provost Marshal's Court, for example, were designed less to punish the offender in a manner to fit the crime than to deter similar behavior by others. Each day local newspapers reported punishments such as the following:

> Abram (colored) who was convicted of stealing a lot of bacon from the Southern Express Company exhibited himself, as many have done before him, near Turners corner, suspended by the thumbs to a lamp post. A card affixed to his back, marked "Abram stole meat," informed all passersby of the reason for his punishment.

Larcenous whites were subjected to the same fate, though in far fewer numbers and for shorter duration.[6]

Union troops also disciplined freedmen outside of the courts. The

military, in what Raleigh's *Daily Standard* described as "a move in the
right direction," rounded up loitering freedmen and set them to work
on the city streets; similar action was taken in Montgomery.[7] In Atlanta
and Montgomery U.S. troops enforced special curfews for blacks and
checked them for passes.[8] In Richmond an officer told a group of former slaves that they would be sent to prison unless they stopped asking
for wages owed them by their former master. Another officer decided
that a child of a former slave had to stay with the ex-owner. A Northern teacher sadly noted that "daily and hourly, instances of this sort
are coming to our notice."[9]

As upsetting were the frequent attacks upon innocent Negroes
by white soldiers. In one of the most blatant cases, John Dennett
reported walking along an Atlanta street with a soldier who proclaimed "I'm going to punch every d--d nigger I see." Whereupon
meeting two blacks the soldier proceeded to carry out his boast. Later
in the day an affray between white soldiers and Negroes left two of
the freedmen with gunshot wounds.[10]

The Freedmen's Bureau provided better protection for the rights of
blacks. Its courts tried both civil and criminal cases: contract disputes
between blacks and whites, marriage support disagreements, property
claims, misdemeanors, and felonies. In August 1865 the *Nashville
Daily Press and Times* observed that many of the cases involved "little
sums of money due to colored people for washing, etc." Most were
successfully settled out of court as whites preferred to pay rather than
confront the blacks as equals in the courtroom. In succeeding months
the Nashville Bureau found in favor of more than twenty Negroes who
sought back wages for a woodcutting job, sided with another group
which sued for wages at the Crystal Palace Saloon, and awarded $5 to
a hack driver who had not been paid for the hire of his cab. In December 1865 charges of discrimination against Negroes in the Recorder's Court led General Clinton B. Fisk to transfer all its cases
against blacks to the Freedmen's Court.[11] As elsewhere, however, there
remains the question as to how successful the Bureau was in enforcing
its decisions.

The continued intervention of the Bureau in the legal process was
one of the main reasons for the eventual acceptance of black testimony
by the postwar governments. This was a muted concession, since it
was initially admitted only in cases in which a black was a party.[12] The
distrust of Negro testimony was further evident in a special North

Carolina law which provided that "whenever a person of color is examined as a witness, the court shall warn the witness to declare the
truth." As late as 1871, Nedom Angier, one of Georgia's leading white
Republicans, was still against the use of testimony from blacks: "The
[blacks] are ignorant; they have seldom been before the courts and
they know nothing of the obligation of an oath."[13] Despite such feelings even among Unionists, the Freedmen's Bureau abolished its
courts as soon as the revised state laws went into effect, although federal officials kept a watchful eye to see if equal justice was meted
out.

The laws permitting Negro testimony were part of what has become
known as the Black Codes. Passed by the first popularly elected (by
white suffrage) state legislatures in 1865 and 1866, they consisted of
statutes regulating all aspects of black behavior, although few specifically mentioned race. As in the case of the restrictions on Negro testimony, the former Confederates were unwilling to do more than erase
the distinction between slave and free Negroes—the differences between Negroes and whites remained. With few exceptions all the
codes stated that criminal laws were to apply equally to both races.
In fact, however, important distinctions were made, especially in the
area of sexual contact. Under a law passed in January 1866 the North
Carolina legislature decreed that attempted rape of a white female by
a Negro was punishable by death; regardless of the victim's race, rape
by a white man was punishable by fine and the lash.[14] Although the
law was soon amended to apply without regard to race, appended to
the pronouncement of equal punishment was a new phrase, "due regard being had to the nature and circumstance of the offense."[15]

A related matter of social control was achieved by the prohibition
of racial intermarriage. In North Carolina a person knowingly performing such a ceremony was subject to a $500 fine.[16] In 1866 the
Georgia legislature passed a statute providing both a fine and a jail
sentence for anyone issuing a marriage license or performing the ceremony between a black and a white.[17]

The Black Codes circumscribed Negro behavior in other ways. As a
rule they prohibited blacks from selling liquor or owning firearms.[18]
The Alabama statute on apprenticing provided that when the child of
a freedman was apprenticed, preference should be given to the former
owner, "if he was a suitable person."[19] More subtle were the number
of laws which, while not specifically mentioning blacks, were clearly

meant to discipline them. Typically they included a vagrancy law, a law preventing the enticement of servants, and a variety of laws aimed at combating petty thefts. The same concerns were reflected in a series of new city ordinances that gave wide latitude to police officers. In Raleigh persons convicted of disorderly conduct, intoxication, cursing, and other forms of disagreeable behavior were to be fined as much as $25. If unable to pay, they could be put to work on the streets or bound out to private individuals. In the case of a freedman (who would have had great difficulty paying even a $5 fine), the former master was to have first claim in hiring him.[20]

Although they did not mention race, the vagrancy acts became the chief statutes for disciplining the freedmen. "If severe penal legislation shall become necessary to prevent the free negro from becoming a vagabond and thief," stated the Richmond *Times* in June 1865, "the Legislature will provide the remedy." And indeed the legislature did, despite the illusion of nondiscrimination it sought to foster. It empowered state officers to apprehend all idlers or those following no "labor, trade, occupation or business and [who] have no visible means of subsistence, and can give no reasonable account of themselves or their business." Such persons would be hired out for three months for the "best wages that can be procured." Runaways were to serve an extra month and be confined with a ball and chain. Additional legislation limited to two months contracts between whites and Negroes unless signed by a public official or finalized in the presence of two or more witnesses who explained the terms to the Negroes involved. If a laborer broke a contract, other employers could not hire him and he was therefore subject to arrest under the terms of the vagrancy act. General Alfred H. Terry declared the act inoperative upon Negroes nine days after its passage just as federal generals elsewhere countermanded the most objectional provisions of the Black Codes.[21]

The most blatant abuse of the vagrancy statutes, however, occurred in Nashville in 1866. Although atypical in its magnitude and gross irregularity, it accurately reflected the use of the judicial system as a means of keeping blacks in their place. In October the police cracked down on Negro vagrants. On one day they arrested twenty-seven. Fifteen were tried, convicted, and fined $5 and costs. Unable to pay, all were sent to the workhouse where, a few days later, twelve more Negroes arrested for vagrancy joined them. Convinced that it was unprofitable for the city to employ so many people, the Board of Aldermen permitted two local whites to take approximately fifty Negro vagrants, including a few women and several boys, to northern Mississippi to work on their cotton plantations. The two men signed contracts and paid the fines and costs in each case. Under heavy guard the group was spirited out of the workhouse at night and placed on a train. No one notified the parents of the children or relatives of the other prisoners. The episode received national attention, and the Northern press used it as an example of Southern determination to reinstitute slavery. A month later the head of the Freedmen's Bureau in Tennessee secured the release of the minors from the plantations. All the adults except one elderly woman had allegedly violated their contracts and deserted their employers.[22]

Laws might make no distinction as to race, but as the Nashville incident demonstrates, such was not necessarily true of the officials responsible for carrying them out. This became especially important after the new Republican governments eliminated the blatantly discriminatory sections of the early acts. To the dismay of Southern whites, for example, Radical constitutions did not ban intermarriage. In some instances, the mention of race in the laws would reappear with the defeat of the Republicans, but for the most part the Redeemers relied on more subtle means to challenge the gains of Radical Reconstruction. The key components of the legal system throughout most of the period were therefore the police, magistrates, and juries. And, in most of the urban South, black representation in these groups mirrored the changing fortunes of the Republicans. When Republicans were in power, Negroes were more likely to be found in the jury box, on the bench, or walking a beat. In most cases, however, such instances ceased with the return of the former Confederates to power.

In two areas the discrimination practiced by the first postwar governments was permanently overcome and was not altered by political changes. With the election of the Republicans the last restrictions on Negro testimony were removed. In Raleigh's Mayor's Court in October 1875, for example, one white man was convicted of robbing another through the testimony of a Negro. Ten years later the testimony of a Negro drayman in Atlanta offset opposing accounts of five whites in a suit by the city against the Western and Atlanta Railroad.[23]

Redeemer governments also recognized the foothold Negro lawyers obtained in the courts. Here, however, blacks made only limited gains, many of which did not come until after the period of Radical rule. Negro attorneys evidently appeared first in Nashville, where in 1870 a Negro Radical contested a case against a white Radical opponent. By the following year blacks were admitted before the Criminal Court, but it was not until the end of the decade that they were allowed to practice in the Chancery Court. As late as 1888, a white lawyer faced with a Negro opponent remarked that "it always irritated him to appear as counsel with a negro lawyer, and it was beneath his dignity to argue a point with one." When the Negro answered in kind, the white man hit him with a walking cane and both were fined $5 for contempt.[24] The progress of blacks in the legal profession was especially slow in Atlanta. Not until 1877 did Atlanta's Styles L. Hutchins, a graduate of the University of South Carolina Law School, become the first Negro attorney to plead a case before a judge in Georgia; it took eleven more years for C. H. J. Taylor to become the first to plead in the City Court.[25] The relative absence of black lawyers from courtrooms was due both to white opposition and to their small number.[26] As a result, throughout the period the defense as well as the prosecution of Negro lawbreakers was mainly in white hands.

Not only the lawyers but the judges and the juries were usually white. The two busiest courts were those presided over by the mayor and the recorder. No blacks held these offices in the five cities, an especially significant fact since these were juryless courts. There also were no black justices in the county criminal or circuit courts. The only judicial positions Negroes held were as justices of the peace, posts with very limited jurisdiction. Even here, it was a restricted tenure. There were no black justices of the peace in Atlanta and blacks served only briefly in Montgomery during the Radical administration. A few Raleigh Negroes such as the undertaker Handy Lockhart filled the position after the Radicals made it an elective office. When the Democrats gained complete control of the state government in 1877, however, they transferred the right of electing justices for counties, cities, and towns from the people to the legislature.[27] No Negro justices were ever chosen under the new procedure.

Richmond and Nashville blacks were more fortunate. As one of General Edmund Canby's last acts as military governor in 1870, he appointed the first Negro justice of the peace in Henrico County.[28] After the creation of Jackson Ward, which was largely Negro, in 1871, at least two and sometimes all of the three justices elected from the ward were black. None of the other five wards ever returned a Negro.[29] A few black magistrates were elected each year in Nashville and the surrounding county districts beginning in 1869. Prior to 1876 two justices were elected from each ward to the Davidson County Court, which, despite its name, was also an executive and legislative body. In that year there was a shift to the at-large selection of all judges, a tactic in part aimed at eliminating Negro justices. By 1888 the change proved successful. All of the black candidates from the city lost that year, the first time this had occurred since 1869. The new all-white County Court which met in 1889 made clear its determination to limit further black participation in the legal process as it failed for the first time in more than twenty years to name any Negro notaries public.[30]

The black justices rarely heard cases involving whites. In fact, if newspaper coverage was a true indication, black magistrates were far less busy than their white counterparts. For example, during 1869 and 1870 the *Nashville Union and American* mentioned only three cases heard before J. L. Lapsley, the city's only Negro justice; in all three the principals were black. The main function of the justices of the peace, especially black ones, was the performance of marriage ceremonies. And here, of course, the racial line was firmly drawn. According to Nashville's *Daily American*, a Negro magistrate reported in 1877 that since the abolition of the tax on marriage licenses, he had been kept busy "making the colored people happy."[31]

Magistrates and lawyers were important, but for whites and blacks the most controversial issue involved black jurors. The jury issue was considered significant enough to be covered in the Fourteenth Amendment and the various civil rights laws, including the Civil Rights Act of 1875, and was invariably discussed at Negro conventions held throughout the period. During Presidential Reconstruction, Negroes were totally absent from Southern juries. Black Codes made no mention of jury duty and it was understood that the prewar policy of exclusion would continue. In 1866 Tennessee became the first state to mention the matter in a law. A statute which gave Negroes the right to testify specifically withheld the right to sit on juries.[32]

The ban against black jurors began to crumble under Military Reconstruction and was further undermined by the Radical regimes. The United States Circuit Court which convened at Richmond on May 6, 1867, had six Negro grand jurors, a fact duly noted by the Republican judge. It was before twenty members of the court's petit jury, half of them black, that Jefferson Davis was scheduled to be tried.[33] In succeeding months Negroes in the other cities came to exercise similar duties.[34] By 1869 North Carolina and Georgia Radicals had established elaborate procedures to assure, at least in theory, that there would be no discrimination in the selection of juries. According to Raleigh's *Daily Standard,*

> There seems now to be no objection against the colored juror—he tries cases, and sits as a grand inquest, to decide on the merits of bills of indictments. At one time it seemed to be hard for some lawyers to address the jury as "gentlemen of the jury," if a colored man was in the box—this prejudice has ceased to exist and they are treated as a body of men entitled to the respect of judges as well as counsel. . . . Within the brief space of two years prejudice to their serving as jurors as well as legislators has well nigh faded out.[35]

Despite legal guarantees and the euphoria of the *Daily Standard,* few Southern whites were ready to accept black jurors. An independent Conservative who was seeking Negro support for election to the Virginia legislature candidly told a black leader: "As soon as your people are sufficiently educated to be able to intelligently discharge the duties of jurors they should go into the jury box, but not before."[36] This remark was made seven months after the passage of the Civil Rights Act of 1875, which barred discrimination in the choosing of juries "on account of race, color, or previous condition of servitude." It was this section which the *Nashville Union and American* described as "the most serious and dangerous provision of the entire bill." In 1878 a white Nashville resident urged the defeat of Republican magistrates who were planning to appoint Negroes to juries "where they will hold in their hands, *life, liberty and property.*"[37]

In the face of such opposition blacks had difficulty becoming jurors. A few blacks continued to serve on Republican-controlled federal juries,[38] but after the end of Radical rule they were largely excluded from state and local panels. Alabama Redeemers achieved this exclusion in 1876 by a change in the jury law which affected only the six counties (including Montgomery County) with Republican majorities. Under the old system juries had been chosen by probate judges, sheriffs, and clerks of the circuit or city courts, all of whom tended to be Republican. Now the selection was placed in the hands of five commissioners appointed by Democratic governors. Despite the fact that its own editorial acknowledged that the law applied only to the Black Belt and would eliminate "ignorant blacks" from the juries, the *Montgomery Daily Advertiser* asserted: "There is nothing in this bill that discriminates against race or color."[39] The County Commission in Wake County (Raleigh) supervised jury selection and by making positions on it appointive rather than elective the Democratic legislature, in 1877, accomplished the same result as had its Alabama counterpart.[40]

Further evidence of the exclusion of Negroes from juries comes from the blacks themselves in the form of numerous protests addressed to local, state, and federal authorities. The efforts of Nashville Negroes to gain access to juries best demonstrate both the tenacity of Negro interest and the strength of white resistance. A meeting of leading blacks held in 1872 cited the prejudice of all-white juries toward black defendants and asked that Negroes on trial be given the right to decide if they wanted blacks on the jury. Three years later a similar group met to protest two lynchings. In addition to decrying the lynchings and the unequal administration of justice, they resolved that "the color line is so closely drawn as to not only prevent us from sitting on juries when whites are interested, but also from sitting on those cases where only we are interested." The State Colored Convention held in Nashville in 1884 continued the attack.

> The colored citizens of Tennessee most emphatically condemn the continued, persistent and unlawful manner in which they are tried, condemned, hanged, and enslaved, by individuals who have been taught from cradle to the jury box, that the negro is naturally inferior to them, by men of reason and prejudiced views of them and their race.

And among the complaints expressed in a resolution passed at a meeting of blacks in 1886 was that "intelligent, honest and honorable citizens, and freeholders are not allowed a just representation in the jury box, the common right of Americans, because they are negroes."[41]

Negro participation in state and local courts was temporarily encouraged during the early 1880s thanks to Judge Alexander Rives of the Federal Court for the Western District of Virginia. He instructed a grand jury to indict justices in several Virginia counties for not allowing blacks on juries. Richmond was most directly affected. In March and April 1880 the first Negro jurors in history were chosen to serve in the Henrico County Court and the municipal Hustings Court. In 1885 a Negro was among one of the nine grand jurors chosen for the January term of the Hustings Court as were three of the twenty-four chosen for the February term. The number who actually served on juries is not known. Furthermore, Negroes were not even considered for the important trials. After one thousand white men were summoned in May 1885 as potential jurors in the T. J. Cluverius murder trial, the most sensational of the period, only twelve of the needed sixteen were accepted for duty. The *Richmond Dispatch* reported that this exhausted the field of potential jurors in the city and that fifty men from Alexandria would have to be summoned.[42]

After the United States Supreme Court upheld the Rives decision, the names of twenty blacks were added to the revised jury lists in Atlanta. "To escape all cavil and question it is deemed by the wisest to be best that intelligent and upright colored men should be put on the lists," noted the *Atlanta Constitution*. Lest its phrasing be misunderstood, it added that the names could then be accepted or rejected by the parties involved. Although there were as many as fifty blacks on the jury list in 1884, only one black actually served on a state court jury during the decade.[43] The Rives decision had greater impact in Montgomery, Nashville, and Raleigh, but even in these cities the evidence supports Gilbert Thomas Stephenson's contention that throughout the South the use of blacks on juries declined after 1885.[44]

Negro policemen were an even less familiar sight in Southern cities. To the whites in the postbellum South the policeman stood as the first line of defense against the freedmen. It was his responsibility to break up the black gambling and vice dens, clear the streets of vagrants, catch Negro lawbreakers, and on occasion keep black voters in check. In the minds of most whites, blacks could not be trusted to fulfill these vital functions. More importantly, black police might end up having authority over white citizens. For these reasons the first postwar governments hired only white policemen. Atlanta Negroes unsuccessfully petitioned the City Council in September 1867 to appoint one Negro from each ward to the police department since "justice demands that our color should be represented." White opposition remained strong and subsequent efforts to place blacks in the department also failed.[45]

The lack of Negro police in Atlanta, a city that avoided Radical domination, bears witness to the close relationship between Republican control of municipal governments and the hiring of black policemen. The coincidence of Republican rule and black police was naturally greatest during Reconstruction. In 1868, after a heated battle,

Montgomery blacks won almost half the positions in the police department under a Radical administration, but once the Conservatives regained power in 1875 black appointments ceased.[46]

The addition of Negro police was the most striking innovation during the period of Republican rule in Raleigh. In July 1868, under the headline "The Mongrel Regime!! Negro Police!!," the Conservative *Daily Sentinel* announced the appointment of four Negroes and concluded that "this is the beginning of the end." The Republican *Daily Standard* defended the action by appealing to practical politics, improved law enforcement, and principles of justice.

> If it is true . . . as obliged in certain quarters that a large portion of the thefts and burglaries are committed by the colored, the colored policemen will have means of information and consequently of bringing the perpetrator to justice, which never would have been extended to the former police. All classes will learn that the laws must be respected and the colored people will not feel that it is an oppression on them or their race when tried and punished by a Republican mayor.

Bryan Lunn, a Negro saloonkeeper, was appointed as one of the city's two assistants to the police chief. Although a black never became head of the force, there were always several patrolmen and one assistant chief. Despite the early opposition to Negro policemen, the Democrats on returning to power retained one black whom the *Daily Sentinel* described as "a very efficient officer."[47] After 1877, however, he too was gone.

But not even Republican victory assured the hiring of black policemen. Soon after the Radical triumph in September 1867, Nashville Negroes petitioned the new City Council to appoint blacks to the force. A resolution was prepared but not offered instructing the police department to make half of the appointments from the Negro population. When the force was chosen, it contained no blacks. Additional efforts during later years also failed. In 1884, for example, the Democratic mayor vetoed a council resolution supporting the principle of nondiscriminatory appointments because he thought it would fan, rather than allay, racial prejudice. The resolution's black sponsor, J. C. Napier, and the other black councilman were the only ones voting to override the veto.[48]

Even the Negroes' Radical allies often opposed giving the black police jurisdiction over whites. In Montgomery, blacks won the right to arrest whites only after a dramatic confrontation between the leading Negro politician and one of the city's most prominent white Republicans.[49] In most other cities it seems that blacks were supposed to arrest only blacks. This was true of the black special detectives appointed by Nashville's Republican Mayor Thomas A. Kercheval, as well as of the regular police in Mobile and in New Bern and Greenville, North Carolina.[50]

The basically white composition of the police, magistrates, and juries had serious implications for the kind of justice dispensed to Negroes. Although the great majority of urban blacks came from the lower class and thus were subject to the kinds of discrimination faced by poor people in general, they also suffered because of racial bias. A higher percentage were arrested and convicted of crimes and their sentences were more severe than those of whites charged with comparable offenses. At no time during the interval from arrest to punishment was it forgotten that the individual was black.

With few exceptions there were more Negroes than whites arrested each year. This was true in all five cities, although only in Montgomery and Raleigh did the blacks at any time constitute a majority of the population. The first postwar report on arrests in Richmond covering the period from December 1865 to April 1866 listed 429 whites and 581 blacks. In the succeeding twenty-five years white arrests never outnumbered black, and for 1890 the figures stood at 2,905 versus 3,665. In the latter year the figures for Raleigh were 461 and 549 and for Montgomery, 785 and 1,327.[51]

Whites viewed grievances between Negroes as a primary cause for the large number of black arrests. In doing so, they reflected a belief in the unimportance of Negro wrongdoing if it was confined to the black community and failed to appreciate what having resort to the legal system meant to former slaves.[52] But black leaders also criticized the apparent excessive adjudication. "Colored men cease being jealous of one another," the *Richmond Planet* told its readers. "Stop these intestine quarrels. Strive to live in peace with one another. Stay out of the Police Court with your petty quarrels." An irate Negro wrote to the Savannah *Colored Tribune* after a black woman had issued a warrant against her husband, who subsequently drowned while fleeing from the police.

> The habit of these dirty colored women, of arresting their husbands
> every time they have a family quarrel is becoming intolerable and
> should be either stopped or colored men should stop marrying. White
> families quarrel and disagree as much as colored do but you never
> hear of white women however low they may be running to the magis-
> trate to have their husbands jailed.[53]

Nonetheless, the white community and its law enforcement officials
were responsible for the great mass of Negro arrests. For them the
basic necessity was control, for most whites were convinced that Negroes comprised a criminal class which jeopardized the peace and
security of the city. "The truth is that the enfranchisement of the black
has worked the enfranchisement of his vices and the liberation of his
proclivities to crime," wrote the *Atlanta Constitution* in 1873. Placing
the blame on the Republicans, the newspaper concluded that "carpet-
bag Radicalism but encourages negro crime." The *Constitution* blamed
the Negro criminal for keeping the courts in business. Noting that during the last two weeks of the May 1877 session of the County Superior
Court only one white person was arraigned for trial, the editor concluded that without the black offenders "our courts now would have
but little to do."[54]

Although increasing numbers of blacks were arrested for serious
crimes, the great majority of Negro arrests were for vagrancy, disorderly conduct, petit larceny, and other misdemeanors. During a typical
two-day period in Nashville City Court, for example, ten blacks were
convicted of various forms of disorderly conduct, four of vagrancy, and
eight of assault and battery. Atlanta's City Court usually witnessed
the conviction of three or four Negroes per day for "larceny from the
house." At one point the *Montgomery Daily Ledger* ceased publishing
reports of the Mayor's Court since all the cases were allegedly the
same: "freedman stealing."[55] The most famous kinds of pilferage involved food, especially chickens. The stereotype of the Negro as
chicken thief received its classic representation in an 1890 cartoon in
the *Nashville Banner* which pictured a black preacher who, after
preaching against chicken-stealing to his congregation, commits the
same offense.[56]

Crimes of blacks against property tended to be committed against
whites, although many were directed at goods belonging to members
of their own race. This pattern was reversed in crimes against persons.
James H. Clanton of Montgomery told a Congressional committee in

1871 that Negroes "kill one another frequently." Although Clanton exaggerated, the great proportion of violent crimes by Negroes were indeed committed against other Negroes, including repeated cases of gambling altercations, barroom brawls, and domestic fights.[57]

Nowhere was the desire to control blacks (and in this case whites as well) more evident than in the passage and enforcement of anti-miscegenation laws. Even during Reconstruction, the Conservative-controlled Georgia Supreme Court held that intermarriage was forbidden since the new Radical constitution had not specifically repealed the section of the code proscribing such alliances. Once they returned to power, Democrats in other states moved quickly to restore the legal barriers to intermarriage.[58] Attempts to challenge such laws were successfully beaten back in the Redeemer-dominated courts. In 1878, for example, the Supreme Court of Alabama reversed a decision by a lower court that the Civil Rights Act invalidated the state's antimiscegenation statute. Three years later it upheld the assessment of heavier punishments for interracial fornication and adultery.[59]

Local governments diligently enforced these laws. In Nashville during the 1880s the annual number of arrests for interracial cohabitation never dropped below thirteen couples. One year it reached a total of fifty-seven individuals, some charged with more than one offense.[60] One of the cases in 1877 involved a white man who came to the city from North Carolina with his Negro wife. In keeping with the city's 1871 ordinance which prescribed stiffer penalties for the white partner in such situations, the man was fined $50 and the woman only $15.[61] Couples brought to trial ranged from those who were married or in love to those who had a single sexual liaison.[62] And in Atlanta, a young white girl was arrested in 1888 for dancing with Negroes at a Negro ball.[63]

In a related effort to "protect" whites from blacks who refused to follow the mores of the white community, city officials undertook periodic crusades against alleged Negro streetwalkers. These individuals were arrested, tried, and, if they could pay the fine, sent back to the streets again; if not, they would be sentenced to thirty days in jail. In either event they would eventually be re-arrested to repeat the cycle. Meanwhile, considerably less attention was paid to their white counterparts. Indeed the greater number of Negro women than white women arrested accounted for the excess of black over white arrests in the five cities. For a typical one-year period in Nashville ending

October 1881, there were 1,771 white males and 1,472 black males arrested, but the statistics for the females were 136 and 791 respectively. Nine years later only 269 of the 2,996 whites were women, while this was true of 1,086 of the 3,014 Negroes. Atlanta in 1890 listed 380 females among its 5,601 arrested whites as compared to 1,715 of the 7,236 blacks.[64]

White anger also focused on centers of urban Negro low life. Police raided brothels, gambling dens, saloons, and "negro balls."[65] Yet many centers of low life enjoyed impunity. In Nashville, Republican Mayor Kercheval evidently went easy on them for political reasons and in Atlanta, "lewd houses" confined to a certain locality were left alone if they caused no trouble to the surrounding community.[66] Then, too, many places where Negroes "drink and fight and gamble all day" were located outside the city beyond the reach of municipal authorities.[67]

The prostitutes and frequenters of the dives and dens were seen as part of a larger problem—the high number of Negro vagrants. To most whites a Negro without a regular job was a threat to the entire community. As had been the case in the years from 1865 to 1867, the Redeemers sought to meet this problem with the passage of strict vagrancy statutes and frequent roundups of vagrants.[68] Authorities took pains to disguise their motivation, claiming that both whites and blacks were targets, but their actions and often their words gave them away. In 1875, for example, the Nashville *Republican Banner* rejoiced at the passage of Tennessee's new vagrancy statute. Among those groups specifically singled out as vagrants by the newspaper were loiterers around the saloons, street corners, gaming houses, and brothels without evident means of support. Although race supposedly was not a factor, local authorities and the press frequently drew attention to the large number of Negroes who were engaged in such activities and rarely complained about similarly occupied whites. And lest the meaning of the act be lost upon its readers and the black community, the *Republican Banner* added that "there is labor for all, and *in labor there is liberty. Freedom is not vice, immorality and idleness.*"[69] Who else but the freedmen needed such advice?

Nashville was the scene of the single most concentrated attack against Negro vagrants and prostitutes. In September 1886 white citizens of South Nashville formed the South Nashville Law and Order League to combat the lawlessness in Black Bottom. They charged city officials with pampering vagrants and other criminals, a view shared by some police officers. At the meetings of the league and its North Nashville counterpart, the members always singled out Negroes as the primary lawbreakers. As a result of pressure from the leagues, officials increased fines against vagrants and prostitutes, installed electric streetlights, and directed police to round up vagrants and streetwalkers. Soon after the changes began, the *Nashville Banner,* a staunch supporter of the movement, observed that "people who pass through Black Bottom say that the improvement is already very apparent."[70]

The paucity of Negro policemen during most of the period exacerbated relations between Negroes and the police. The only contact that most white policemen had with blacks was with criminals. Such conditions fostered feelings of mutual distrust and hostility. As the *Atlanta Constitution* observed, "A negro with a bundle on his shoulders at the dead hour of the night is always an object of suspicion to a policeman."[71] An Atlanta black was arrested on "suspicion" after he sold a mule for what seemed to an officer to be too small an amount; another man was arrested on a similar charge for having a turnkey and a pair of shoes for which he could not establish ownership; a third had a handsome gold watch in his possession. A Richmond Negro charged with being "a suspicious character" was sent to jail for thirty days.[72] Richmond police often arrested large groups of Negroes on general warrants. Not only was this a method of Negro control, but since sergeants and captains of the force received fees as county constables, it was a way of earning extra money. Although the mayor said in 1874 that he had put a stop to this "most vicious and unlawful practice," it continued after that date.[73]

Selectivity in arrests was only one way in which the law was used to discipline Negroes. After the arrest, many whites received reprimands or paid their fines without being brought to trial. During his defense of three Nashville blacks accused of stealing lumber, a white lawyer maintained that had his clients been white, they would not have been indicted for such a small offense, a charge loudly endorsed by a Negro woman in the gallery.[74] When whites did come to trial, fragmentary evidence suggests that with the exception of miscegenation, they received lighter sentences than blacks for the same crimes.[75]

During the 1872 session of the Fulton County Superior Court, the judge sentenced two whites convicted of simple larceny to work on the county roads for six months, the same penalty assessed a white man convicted of fornication. Yet a Negro found guilty of fornication and another of simple larceny each received twelve month sentences on the public roads. In Montgomery a black was convicted on circumstantial evidence of killing a policeman and sentenced to life in the penitentiary. Soon after, "an aristocratic white man" attempted to kill the chief of police, but mistakenly murdered another policeman. He was tried, convicted of manslaughter in the first degree, and sentenced to the penitentiary for two and a half years. In comparing the two cases the *Herald,* a local Negro newspaper, asked, "Will God prosper a people that make such a mockery of justice?"[76]

Judges also meted out excessively high fines to blacks. The *Atlanta Constitution* welcomed the trial of an "idle and worthless" Negro in City Court "as a . . . tester to see what the temper of the court might be towards this type of offender." After the black was convicted, fined $50, a sum he "naturally" could not pay, and sent off for twelve months' work on the public roads, the *Constitution* saw the verdict as "a center shot at the offense of vagrancy [which] will have a salutary effect in driving scores of these idle loafers away from the city." Nashville's chief of police defended the high fine levied against nine young Negro bootblacks for "obstructing the sidewalk, using profane language, etc.," on the ground that "the city is more interested in the prevention of disorderly conduct and crime than [in] inflicting small fines."[77]

Richmond authorities used a variation of the high fine tactic to imprison Negroes for minor offenses. Rather than assess excessive fines, magistrates ordered defendants to post bonds for good behavior. John Pollard, charged with disorderly conduct, had to put up $100 "to keep the peace." When he could not raise the money, he received sixty days on the chain gang. Rarely used against whites, peace bonds frequently led to the confinement of Negroes found not guilty. After a black woman had been acquitted of assault and battery against a white woman, she was required "to give security for good behavior." When she failed to raise the money, she was sent to jail. The same fate met John T. Williams, "a suspicious character" acquitted of breaking into a white man's house, and Minor Poindexter acquitted of stealing iron from the Chesapeake and Ohio Railroad. Even if the individual could raise the bond money, his troubles were not over. Apparently the courts interpreted any arrest as sufficient evidence of default of the bond. In 1866 a Negro's bond was declared forfeited merely because she had been charged with a crime.[78] This practice no doubt led many blacks to leave the city to avoid future court appearances. Thus the city stood to benefit either by confining an unwanted Negro in jail, by receiving additional revenue if the bond were forfeited, or by driving alleged criminals from the city.

Whether the cities used high fines or surety bonds, the chain gang provided the primary means of punishment for minor offenses. Although used for a few whites, this institution—with its dual function of disciplining offenders and providing cheap labor for the city or county—was employed mainly for blacks. The device originated after the war as a means of effectively utilizing idle Negroes while keeping them out of trouble. "The chain gang in this city," noted the *Montgomery Daily Ledger* in December 1865

> is an "institution" introduced since the negroes became free; and a good substitute for imprisonment in the guard house. It cuts the pride of the freedmen who unfortunately get into trouble by their misdeeds, many of whom would probably prefer the old fashioned thirty-nine lashes well laid on.

Over 90 percent of the cases before the Montgomery Mayor's Court involved blacks and high fines were set for petty offenses in order to get recruits for the gang. While visiting Atlanta in 1878, George Campbell was told by a resident that "the blacks are sent to the chain-gang very readily; when men are wanted for a chain-gang they are always got."[79]

When the Richmond chain gang first appeared in December 1866, 12 of its 14 members were black. During 1871, 230 Negroes and only 34 whites worked on the gang; the figures for the following year were 305 and 40. These statistics reflect the higher incidence of black convictions and the inability of Negroes to pay their fines. This situation was especially clear for Montgomery which kept records of the number of days labored for the city by parties unable to pay fines. For the twelve-month period ending April 30, 1887, white males had worked 3,002 days compared to a total of 13,790 by black males, a much larger gap than would be expected from the arrest figures of 773 white and 1,104 black males. The totals for the females are even more revealing. Although there were approximately eight times as many black as white women arrested, blacks served 2,182 days on the chain gang and whites only 92. The presence of white women on city chain gangs was indeed a rare occurrence. In Atlanta a white female commonly hired a Negro man to work in her place while she remained in the chain gang stockade; black women, such as the one who gave birth while serving a short term, still worked on the roads.[80]

Negroes also were the primary if not the sole victims of a variety of other steps taken to use the judicial system both as an agent of social control and a source of labor. Blacks convicted in local courts for minor offenses often worked off their sentences under private employers. This form of peonage was most common during the first two years after the war. Berton Snellings, a Raleigh Negro convicted of larceny and unable to pay his fine, was bound out by the Wake County Superior Court for ten months. In Montgomery City Court a black orphan girl "who had been roosting on the sidewalk" was turned over to any one "that [sic] would make her work." The Daily Advertiser reported in 1866 that the chain gang had "lost five of its members yesterday, who were taken out of limbo by a gentleman who hired them to work upon his farm."[81]

Because of its "serious abuses," in 1867 General Wager Swayne, Assistant Commissioner of the Freedmen's Bureau, had outlawed the use of the chain gang throughout Alabama except in connection with the penitentiary; however, the gang reappeared with the return of civilian rule. In addition, the state act of 1866 which established the system of "Hard Labor for the County" remained on the books. The law provided a substitute for imprisonment in jail in cases where the defendants were unable to pay their fines and court costs. Although modified in 1876 so that sentences of more than two years were to be served in the penitentiary, judges often circumvented this restriction by imposing several consecutive sentences of two years each. As of 1886 the sixty-six prisoners at hard labor in Montgomery County were employed by Farris and McCurdy doing farm work; all of them were Negro. Although two years was supposed to be the maximum term, one prisoner was sentenced to four years, several others to three to thirteen years. Most were serving time for failure to pay the costs of their trials.[82]

Atlanta authorities made use of a Georgia statute which permitted those convicted of misdemeanors to hire themselves out to private parties. The court formally approved the contracts which had to be mutually agreeable to the convict and employer. Predictably, the system was subject to much abuse. In March 1883 a Negro named

Richard Turner was convicted of larceny in City Court and sentenced to pay a fine of $10 or spend six months on the public works gang. Instead, Turner made a contract to work for a local farmer for twelve months in return for board, clothing, and the payment of the fine and costs. When Turner failed to work as well as his employer wanted, the farmer sold Turner's contract to the lessee of state convicts. Though guilty of only a misdemeanor, Turner had to work in a brickyard where he was treated as a felon.[83]

The policy of whipping offenders lingered in Southern cities after the war. Although an occasional white might feel the lash, Negroes were more likely to be whipped and to be assigned a higher number of stripes. The practice reached its peak in most places before the Republicans came to power. A Montgomery youth indicted for stealing a hog in December 1865, for example, agreed to receive thirty-nine lashes, the traditional punishment of slaves, rather than be imprisoned.[84]

In Richmond, however, whipping continued to be used, especially for blacks, well into the 1880s. According to one report, this means of punishment was due to the overcrowding in the local jails.[85] The *Virginia Star* disagreed. "The whipping law was made especially for colored people and with respect to them, male or female, a true Southerner does not condescend to entertain any sentiments of decency and justice." Although not offered as a corroborating statement, a Richmond resident noted, "I don't go along with cruelty to the nigger at all. But you can take an oath of this—that there's no way but floggin' to punish them; it's the only way to make them feel. They don't mind anythin' else." One day at the Hustings Court in 1866 nine Richmond Negroes including two women received from ten to twenty lashes after being found guilty of petit larceny. The next day nine more received from ten to twenty lashes. In the same period five whites were assessed between five and twenty lashes. Fourteen years later a twelve-year-old Negro was sentenced to thirty-nine lashes for stealing a pocketbook, the same number assigned to an adult the month before. The few whites who were whipped never received more than twenty stripes and rarely that many. And unlike the situation among blacks, only an occasional white woman was whipped. One Virginia officer stated that he had never whipped a white woman, though he had whipped about as many Negro women as men. "We make them strip down to the waist," he said, "and I lay the stripes on pretty hard. An Ethiopian's back is tough and can stand it." But then in a moment of compassion, he added, "It's a mean business, though, this thing of whipping."[86]

Chain gangs, hiring out, and whippings were meant to deter Negroes from committing minor offenses. Different means were used to discourage more serious crime. The most brutal, though the least used, was the lynch mob. Even during the chaotic early postwar years, blacks in the five cities were spared organized attacks because of the concentration of federal forces in their midst. A white Republican who had fled to Atlanta from Warren County told a Congressional committee that bands of men were whipping and killing Negroes throughout the state, but "things are quiet about Atlanta. We have as much law and order in Atlanta as you have here [Washington, D.C.]."[87] Such conditions persisted in most of the urban South despite the rise in lynchings in the rural districts during the 1870s and 1880s. There were major disturbances in the five cities, but during the period there were evidently only four lynchings, all of which occurred or were said to have occurred in Nashville.

The first lynching took place in 1872. Davy Jones, a Negro charged with the murder of a prominent white citizen during a burglary attempt, was shot twice in his cell by a mob of white men who had wrenched the keys to the cell block from the Negro jailer. While still alive, Jones was taken from his cell, dragged through the streets, and hung from a lamp post. At this point the county sheriff, a white Radical, made an attempt to rescue him but was felled by a blow on the head. The city police dispersed the crowd and took the barely alive prisoner back to his cell. Still protesting his innocence, Jones died the following morning. The *Republican Banner* condemned the lynching in an editorial entitled "Let Us Preserve Our Civilization." An inquest, however, concluded that death had come at the hands of persons unknown; no one asked the jailer or his two aides if they had recognized any of the mob.[88]

A lynching surrounded by bizarre circumstances occurred three years later. Jo Reed, a Negro who had killed a policeman while resisting arrest, was spirited from the jail by a large mob and dragged through the streets by a rope tied to his neck. Before reaching the suspension bridge, he was shot in the head and then shot a second time after he was placed on the railing. He was then swung by his neck from the bridge until the rope broke, causing him to fall into the Cumberland River. Both Nashville newspapers condemned the lynching and blamed the police for offering feeble resistance. "Respect for law is civilization. Disregard of it is barbarism," argued the *Republican Banner*.[89] Yet neither paper called for the apprehension of the culprits. The incident so troubled the *Republican Banner* that it suddenly announced that Reed had miraculously escaped, basing its discovery upon "reliable authority." The newspaper continued to publicize this improbable view and featured an interview with the doctor who supposedly treated Reed. Thanks to these reports, when several whites were arrested for being involved in the lynching, they were charged with "rescuing and aiding in the escape of a prisoner." They were immediately released on bond and were evidently never brought to trial even on the absurd charge.[90]

Even more bizarre was a third lynching thought to have taken place in 1877. After a ten-day stretch of burglaries dubbed "almost a reign of terror" by the Nashville *Daily American*, a mob of thirty or forty whites reportedly took a Negro thief from arresting officers and, after killing him, threw his body into the river. The mayor argued that no lynching had taken place and that a hoax had been perpetrated to discourage further robberies by blacks. During a special investigation, the City Council endorsed the mayor's view of the incident. The *Daily American*, however, was unconvinced. Witnesses were certain that a man had been taken from the police and, more important, no one from the mob identified himself as part of the "hoax." As the editor asserted, "while public opinion might admit, for the sake of the city's fair name, that no man was lynched, it is none the less amused at the absurd failure of the so-called investigations."[91]

Nashville's growing concern for its image perhaps accounts for the failure of the city's newspapers to mention another alleged lynching of a Negro who supposedly had attacked a white man. The incident, however, was reported in the *Atlanta Constitution* on August 18, 1890. If the lynching did indeed occur, then perhaps others took place in the various cities without being acknowledged by local residents.

Even if the number of lynchings was small, whites used the threat of this form of retribution to control blacks. Newspapers commonly reported lynchings elsewhere with all their gory details. They decried the acts in general terms, but justified them in the end as dictated by circumstances. "A single day rarely passes that a case of lynching is not flashed over the wires and the cause is almost the same in each instance, the rape of a white woman or child by a big, burly negro," re-

ported the *Nashville Banner* in 1881. "It is rape and hang. As often as
it is done, that often will a devil swing off into eternity." The next year
the newspaper issued an almost identical warning, saying that Negroes
could expect hanging "swift and sure" for raping or attempting to rape
white women. In similar fashion the *Atlanta Constitution* gave much
attention to alleged attacks by blacks against white women, practically
all of which were followed by lynchings. After noting the attempt of
a "yellow scoundrel" to outrage a lady near Atlanta, the editor observed that "this sort of crime is becoming entirely too prevalent and
the best cure for it is lynch law."[92]

Hearing reports of violence elsewhere and observing the attitude of
the press and city officials, local Negroes, even when not the victims
of such brutality, expressed growing concern about the new tendency
toward vigilante justice. The editor of Montgomery's *Colored Citizen*
observed in 1884 that "mob law is getting to be as common in our
country as if we were all savages. We can say that lynch and mob law
is not now known in the city nor in Montgomery county, but we don't
know how soon, the indications are very favorable at times." Two years
later the editor of another Montgomery Negro newspaper commented
that "each day we see that some colored man is lynched or murdered
to the disgrace of American justice." According to the *Richmond
Planet,* "killing Negroes in the South is getting to be as contagious as
killing chickens when preachers are around."[93]

More frequent than lynchings were attacks on Negroes by individual
whites, often resulting in the deaths of the victims. The most celebrated cases involved police officers. Throughout the period black citizens met with occasional success in suits brought against white officers
for using excessive force. In 1866 two Nashville policemen were
charged with beating a Negro laborer without cause. The city's Democratic mayor, supported by the captain of police, dismissed the men
from the force after a brief hearing. In the same city in 1889 a longtime
member of the force was dismissed after he accidentally shot and
wounded a young Negro. The police commissioners ruled that he had
violated the regulation prohibiting the use of a weapon except in self-
defense. A similar regulation resulted in the suspension of an Atlanta
policeman, described as "one of the best officers of the force," for firing
at a black thief. Another Atlanta officer was suspended for thirty days
"due to a lick which he gave a negro." In a third Atlanta incident a

policeman was sentenced to three years in the penitentiary for killing a Negro who was allegedly resisting arrest.[94]

Despite these few cases, most of the officers charged with the use of undue force against blacks went unpunished. Richmond policeman Richard O'Dwyer, charged with kicking a Negro down the station house steps, was let off by the mayor in 1866 with the admonition that he be less aggressive in the future. The following year the mayor presided over a case in which a city policeman allegedly struck a young Negro without provocation. After reminding those policemen present that they were given clubs to defend themselves from attack and not to use as offensive weapons, the mayor postponed the trial until a later date. The trial never resumed, indicating either that charges were dropped or that a cash settlement was made out of court. The individual, however, remained on the force. In 1885 an Atlanta policeman was acquitted in the seemingly unnecessary and cold-blooded killing of a "bad negro."[95] Another city officer was tried and found not guilty for the killing of a black who allegedly resisted arrest for the theft of a pair of shoes. In 1891 an all-white jury took forty minutes to find a Raleigh policeman not guilty of the shooting of an unarmed Negro.[96]

More significant is that most cases of irresponsible police behavior did not even result in the bringing of charges by the victim. The *Atlanta Constitution*, for example, mentioned two cases in 1890 of apparent police brutality. In one a Negro was dragged through the street by three policemen "as though he had been a brute." In another, a drunken Negro who had resisted arrest was brought by two officers from the Kimball House with his face and head "covered with blood." No charges were filed against any of the policemen.[97]

On occasion blacks received a relatively fair hearing in cases that grew out of incidents between private citizens. Most of these instances, especially if they involved attacks on blacks by whites, occurred when the Republicans were in control of the city government. In 1870 a white man, fined $25 and costs for shooting at a Negro man who he said had "wantonly insulted and thrown a brick at me," petitioned the Montgomery City Council to remove or reduce the fine. The white man's employer endorsed the petition on the ground that the wounded Negro was "very ill tempered and frequently very insulting to white men in his manner." The Council defeated a motion that the fine be reduced to $15 by a vote of 7 to 5, with the Republican mayor voting with the majority. During the period of Radical control in Nashville, a black had a white conductor arrested and fined $10 for ejecting him from a streetcar and in another instance a white soldier was fined $3 and sent to the workhouse for thirty days for assaulting a Negro.[98]

More often local courts found the defendants not guilty or meted out light sentences. An issue of the *Richmond Dispatch* in 1875 reported the case of a black thief stabbed to death by a neighbor of the woman whose chicken he was stealing. At the inquest the homicide was deemed justifiable and the jury added that the neighbor deserved "the thanks of the community for his action under the circumstances." Two white brothers who allegedly attacked a Negro were acquitted by an Atlanta jury in 1883; three years later the attack of a white man upon a Negro girl resulted in the girl's having to post $100 for assault and battery. Montgomery blacks found it almost impossible to use the courts to deter unprovoked attacks. After a white man was found not guilty of killing a Negro, the *Colored Citizen* endorsed the view of a white newspaper which had termed the affair a simple case of cold-blooded murder and concluded that "this kind of business is common in this place." The previous week it had charged that "when a white man shoots a negro in this section he always has 'justifiable cause' for doing so—at least so our courts decide."[99]

Nashville Negroes also frequently expressed their dismay at the impunity enjoyed by white attackers. One such protest followed the acquittal in 1872 of a white grocer for the "accidental shooting" of a Negro whom he had hired to work for him. The incident resulted from a dispute over wages; the grocer got off with a reprimand for the careless use of firearms. Two whites who had killed two blameless blacks in separate incidents in May 1890 had still not been brought to trial by December although both were immediately captured. In one of the killings, described by the *Daily American* as "one of the most cold blooded that ever blackened Nashville's record of crime," the accused man claimed that while in a condition of "insane inebriety" he had simply awakened to the sight of a Negro boy leaning against a pole and had plunged a knife into his heart. After reporting the second murder and an unprovoked attack on still a third black, the newspaper warned, "Human life—*even though it be that of a negro*—is not of so little value that our whole people be shocked and astounded at seeing it snuffed out as if it were the insignificant candlefly which meets its doom in the blaze of the gas jet." A Negro protest meeting led by J. C.

Napier, however, charged that the murder was not the result of liquor as authorities maintained but rather of racial prejudice which infected the entire system of justice.[100]

Punishments actually assessed indicate the belief that a black's life or his person was worth less than a white man's. In one of the most celebrated cases of this kind, the white manager of Richmond's St. Charles Hotel, W. H. Godsey, was brought to trial for the murder of a Negro waiter named David Glass. Glass had been shot three times, once in the back. After the rejection of numerous Negroes, an all-white jury was chosen to hear the case. Despite the clear weight of evidence that Godsey was guilty of first-degree murder, ten of the jurors were for acquittal and two for imprisonment in the penitentiary. In a compromise verdict they found Godsey guilty of involuntary manslaughter and fixed punishment at four months in the city jail and a fine of 1¢. The judge increased the fine to $5, the smallest sum the law permitted.[101]

Equal justice was also denied in the great majority of rape cases. One of the few involving the rape of a white woman by a black man occurred in Raleigh in 1870; an all-black jury found him guilty and sentenced him to death.[102] More common were assaults of black men upon black women. The white community tended to look less seriously upon such violations than if white women were involved. An Atlanta jury found a Negro guilty of the rape of an elderly black woman but recommended mercy, enabling him to receive five years in the penitentiary rather than the death penalty. Another Negro was charged with the rape of a twelve-year-old black girl. After "a slight investigation," the magistrate concluded that the case was without foundation and the accused was required to give a small bond for fornication.[103]

Although a Negro who was arrested was more likely to be brought to trial and once tried more likely to be found guilty than his white counterpart, not every black accused of a crime was certain to be convicted. Even accused vagrants were found innocent, as were blacks brought in for gambling.[104] In Richmond's Mayor's Court a Negro charged with insulting and resisting a policeman "was discharged upon the hearing of the evidence." A Nashville black accused of assaulting a streetcar conductor was acquitted when the judge believed the Negro's version of the incident which was supported by several black witnesses. When a fifty-year-old Atlanta white woman charged a Negro, Abe Rucker, with assault and attempted rape, Rucker's alibi was supported by a black barkeeper. The case was dismissed and the *Constitution* termed it a clear example of mistaken identity.[105]

Two other cases, both of which took place in Atlanta, suggest that the Georgia capital was perhaps the fairest of the five cities in dealing with Negro defendants, but even they illustrate the difficulty in reaching a just decision when blacks were involved. In 1882 a Negro named Romulas Shields was tried for the murder of a white man named Joyner. Several black residents of the alley in which Joyner was found testified, as did Shields, that the defendant had been assaulted without provocation by three white men and, after unsuccessfully trying to ward off the blows, had stabbed the victim in self-defense. Doctors corroborated that Shields had been badly beaten and cut. Two white friends of Joyner, however, asserted that Shields had wantonly committed the murder, although Negro witnesses testified that these particular men were not even at the scene. Despite the existence of reasonable doubt, the jury found Shields guilty but recommended mercy; the judge sentenced him to life in prison. A few days later the *Atlanta Republican*, a weekly published by whites, charged with seeming justification that

> evidence preponderated for the defense and if the same law for white and black had existed, or if existing had been applied honestly to the case, the solicitor general should have been ordered by the court to have reduced the charge from murder to manslaughter and the evidence proved that involuntary.

Had the matter ended there it would have been a typical example of blacks not receiving fair hearings in court, especially if the other party were white; however, for unknown reasons, except perhaps the recognition of a miscarriage of justice, Shields was granted a retrial after serving a year in jail. Despite the opinion of the *Atlanta Constitution* that Shields' new case was weaker than before and that he should again be found guilty, this time without any recommendation of mercy, the jury found him innocent. Negroes in the segregated galleries of the courtroom cheered while whites on the main floor sat in shocked disbelief.[106]

In the second case, A. G. Rhodes, an installment furniture dealer, brought libel proceedings against Alonzo W. Burnett, one of the publishers of the *Weekly Defiance*. Burnett was especially vulnerable since the newspaper was frequently critical of white leaders and had been using strong language to condemn Atlanta's system of justice after the killing of two Negroes by white policemen. Required to post a $600 bond, Burnett faced a maximum penalty of a $1,000 fine, imprisonment for up to twelve months, and work on the public roads for six months. At the trial Burnett produced several witnesses who testified to the crookedness of Rhodes and documented specific examples of shady deals. Despite the obvious disrepute of the newspaper among whites, the all-white jury took only three minutes to find Burnett innocent.[107]

Nevertheless, it is not surprising that Negroes had little respect for the system of justice under which they lived. Citing the absence of Negro jurors as the main reason, a white Democratic candidate for sheriff in 1880 noted that "nine negroes out of ten in the county of Davidson believe that there's not one in every twenty of their color that are justly and fairly convicted [in the Criminal Court]." Three days later a black charged that he had been unfairly arrested and convicted for raising a disturbance. He would have been found innocent, he said, if all the witnesses had testified under oath and "if an honest colored man's word went as far before the court as a white man's." Another Nashville Negro succinctly voiced a typical complaint of blacks against the system of justice in the urban South.

> We cannot see why we should be watched more vigilantly by the police, apprehended for smaller offenses, and condemned with less hesitation than are the whites; why we are excluded almost invariably from serving on juries; why we are subjected to the awful lynch law, a visitation so seldom happening to a white man.[108]

Throughout the period whites sought to convince themselves and the blacks that the freedmen could expect equal justice. The *Atlanta Constitution* delighted in reporting cases which allegedly proved the respect accorded Negroes in local courts. A black was tried for the murder of his wife before a jury composed of "respectable and intelligent white citizens of the county." The paper saw the verdict of not guilty as "a notable example of the certain and evenhanded justice with which the humblest colored man in Georgia is treated." Yet even some whites realized that evenhanded justice remained a goal rather than a fact. In 1883 the mayor of Nashville urged that the new Police Court judge be a man "who will mete out equal justice to both white and black." Nonetheless, following the murder of two Negroes seven years later, the *Nashville Banner* felt it necessary to advise that the officers of the law should be as active in ferreting out criminals and bringing them to justice when a negro has been made the victim of a murderous assault as when a white man is slain. The humblest laborer, no matter how black his skin may be, is as much entitled to the protection of the law as the most influential citizen.[109]

Negroes clearly did not feel that they enjoyed such protection. Frequent protests about the treatment of accused black lawbreakers led the *Atlanta Constitution* to charge that

there is nothing more disheartening to the true friends of the negroes than the utter disregard of law manifested in this lawless loyalty to color. The meaning of the whole business is that negro thieves, negro murderers, negro lawbreakers of all kinds, are to be protected at all hazards.[110]

The blacks were closer to the truth in charging that it was the whites who suffered from an excessive loyalty to color.

4

The New Economic Structure

As slaves, the mass of antebellum blacks had been confined to the agricultural sector of the Southern economy. They lived in the countryside and worked as field hands, house servants, or artisans. Smaller numbers worked in factories and on railroads located in rural areas. The remainder, about 5 percent of the slave population, lived in cities where they were laborers, craftsmen, or servants, working directly for their masters or hiring their own time. They were joined by 35 percent of the region's free Negroes, some of whom were successful draymen and small shopkeepers or engaged in service occupations. But whether free or slave, Negroes in antebellum cities encountered growing hostility from the white community, which frowned upon competition between whites and blacks, especially when blacks seemed to be winning. Consequently, by the beginning of the war Southerners were seeking to control and limit the economic opportunities of blacks.[1]

The defeat of the South complicated efforts to discipline the Negro wage earners. After the war, the influx of former rural slaves flooded the urban labor market. Most of them, either as a result of white prejudice or of their own deficiencies, remained at the bottom of the economic ladder. Some, however, through hard work, connections with important whites, or the foresight to seek positions thought too demeaning for whites, succeeded in providing themselves with a decent standard of living. By the end of the period each city contained growing numbers of this rising black middle class. Still, the great mass of urban blacks were mired in low-paying, irregular, and low-status positions that came to be known as "negro jobs." Whites applauded the successes and condemned the failures, but perceived both within the same framework of questions. Were the blacks best serving the interests of the entire city or, more particularly, the white residents? Were they limiting themselves to the proper fields and posing no threat to white workers? And, most importantly, was the city really the best place for Negroes to earn their bread?

The largest number of blacks in antebellum cities were unskilled laborers. Whether free or slave, the men were concentrated on the street-work gangs, wharves, and docks and the women worked as domestics or laundresses. Occasionally they were employed in factories, as in Richmond where blacks comprised a large part of the workers in the tobacco and iron industries. A much smaller number earned a better living as artisans and skilled laborers or in service occupations frowned upon by whites. In every city successful blacks were among the leading barbers, draymen, and livery-stable operators.

Some of these men managed to accumulate property. A few, such as Hardy Perry of Nashville who had a line of hacks and transfer teams, were slaves who hired their own time. Most, however, were free. In Richmond the percentage of property holders among the free population steadily increased. Negroes had owned property in the city since the 1790s and by 1830 there were fifty owners of town lots valued at $18,435. Thirty years later the number had risen to 211 and the property was worth $184,971. In 1830 one free Negro family in fifteen owned property; by 1860 the ratio was one in four. Fifteen individuals were worth between $4,000 and $5,000. Reuben West, one of the two most successful barbers in the state, was the leading black property owner, with real estate valued at $7,000 and an additional $7,000 in cash and bonds. Not far behind was John Adams, a contractor and plasterer, who owned thirteen houses and lots, the largest number of separate pieces of property held by a free Negro in Virginia. Some women were successful as well: in 1860 there were at least six Negro seamstresses who had accumulated more than $1,000 in personal property, as had Patsy Brooks who worked in a tobacco factory.[2]

Though less numerous, free Negroes in other cities had become property owners by the eve of the war. John Ivy and Josephine Hassell of Montgomery were worth more than $5,300; David Farley, an illiterate butcher, was worth nearly $4,000.[3] In Nashville W. C. Napier,

Frank Akin, and William A. Sumner all owned homes, had hacks, and "made a comfortable living." Napier was the proprietor of a livery stable; Akin was a porter who, together with a number of free barbers including Nelson Walker, Frank Parrish, and Aaron Foster, was among the early leaders of the postbellum Negro community.[4] Living just outside the city were Alice Bosley and Manse Bryant, two free Negroes who owned several slaves and large amounts of land.[5]

After the war whites continued to see blacks as best suited for the kinds of jobs immigrants held in Northern cities. Rural blacks swelled the ranks of the unskilled and even those blacks who had been artisans before the war were often denied the opportunity to use their skills because of white prejudice or the more specialized demands of the urban labor market. As Tables 2–5 make clear, by 1890 the typical black was an unskilled laborer or engaged in personal or domestic service. And because of the resulting economic insecurity, black women formed a much larger part of their race's work force than their white counterparts.[6] Yet these characteristics had long been evident. In 1870 Atlanta Negroes held over 76 percent of the city's unskilled jobs. Six years later about 57 percent of Raleigh's Negro labor force was engaged in domestic and personal services. And in 1878 George Campbell learned that Atlanta whites considered blacks better than whites for manual labor, but they felt "he [the Negro] is not fit to rise higher; he has no 'judgment,' and does not make a skilled mechanic."[7]

Blacks were frequently employed in the region's growing manufacturing concerns. They comprised a large part of the work force at the Alabama Compress and Storage Company in Montgomery, Nashville Tannery, Nashville Cotton Seed Oil Company, Dixie Oil Company of Nashville, and in rolling mills throughout the South. Richmond, the most industrialized of the five cities, made the most extensive use of large-scale black industrial labor. An 1882 Chamber of Commerce publication, noting that "in temper he is tractable and can be easily taught," reported that the "negro in the heavier work of the rolling mills, and as stevedore, etc. is a most valuable hand." Although whites also sought Negro labor for the flour mills, black laborers were especially plentiful in the tobacco factories, where they monopolized the production of chewing tobacco but were largely excluded from the more desirable manufacture of cigars and cigarettes. Many of them had been employed as slaves and continued to work after emancipation. The owner of Cameron's tobacco factory which employed only

Table 2

MALE OCCUPATIONAL STRUCTURE OF ATLANTA, RICHMOND, AND NASHVILLE, 1890[a]

	Professional No.	%	Proprietary No.	%	Clerical No.	%	Skilled No.	%	Semiskilled No.	%	Unskilled No.	%	Domestic & Personal Service No.	%
Atlanta														
All workers	883	5.1	2242	12.9	3393	19.6	4995	28.8	812	4.7	3799	21.9	1354	7.8
Native whites	738	7.8	1768	18.6	3108	32.6	3057	32.1	594	6.2	345	3.6	53	0.6
Foreign whites	28	3.2	282	32.1	171	19.5	288	32.8	49	5.6	22	2.5	32	3.6
Colored[b]	117	1.7	192	2.8	114	1.6	1650	23.8	169	2.4	3432	49.4	1269	18.3
Richmond														
All workers	613	3.0	2633	12.8	3112	15.1	5772	28.1	2460	12.0	4648	22.6	1308	6.4
Native whites	490	4.2	1986	17.0	2987	25.6	3931	33.7	1033	8.9	1162	10.0	74	0.6
Foreign whites	48	3.7	401	31.2	47	3.7	513	40.0	139	10.8	128	10.0	8	0.6
Colored	75	1.0	246	3.2	78	1.0	1328	17.5	1288	16.9	3358	44.2	1226	16.1
Nashville														
All workers	768	3.9	2737	13.9	3017	15.3	5716	29.0	1348	6.8	4895	24.8	1237	6.3
Native whites	563	5.2	1988	18.3	2793	25.7	3543	32.6	935	8.6	952	8.8	98	1.0
Foreign whites	36	2.3	530	34.6	164	10.7	583	38.0	62	4.0	132	8.6	27	1.8
Colored	169	2.3	219	3.0	60	0.8	1590	21.7	351	4.8	3811	52.1	1112	15.2

SOURCE: Bureau of the Census, *Eleventh Census: Population* (Washington, D.C., 1893), I, Part II, 634, 696, 718.
[a] Occupations either unspecified by the Bureau of the Census or unclassifiable have been omitted. Their percentage of the male occupations was 14.3 in Atlanta, 12.4 in Richmond, and 14.1 in Nashville.
[b] "Colored" includes a very few Chinese, Japanese, and Indians.

Table 3

FEMALE OCCUPATIONAL STRUCTURE OF ATLANTA, RICHMOND, AND NASHVILLE, 1890[a]

	Professional		Proprietary		Clerical		Skilled		Semiskilled		Unskilled		Domestic & Personal Service	
	No.	%	No.	%	No.	%	No.	%	No.	%	No.	%	No.	%
Atlanta														
All workers	345	3.8	311	3.4	322	3.5	62	0.7	1529	16.7	61	0.7	6522	71.4
Native whites	221	10.1	214	9.7	294	13.4	53	2.4	1169	53.4	36	1.6	196	9.0
Foreign whites	15	13.6	16	14.5	11	10.0	5	4.5	35	31.8	0	0	30	27.3
Colored[b]	109	1.6	81	1.2	17	0.2	4	0.06	325	4.8	25	0.4	6296	92.0
Richmond														
All workers	481	4.2	282	2.4	493	4.3	156	1.4	3127	27.1	136	1.2	6870	59.5
Native whites	337	10.8	154	4.9	468	15.0	122	3.9	1778	57.0	24	0.8	233	7.5
Foreign whites	8	3.2	74	30.0	9	3.6	7	2.8	92	37.2	6	2.4	51	20.6
Colored	136	1.7	54	0.7	16	0.2	27	0.3	1257	15.4	106	1.3	6586	80.5
Nashville														
All workers	461	4.9	184	2.0	293	3.1	132	1.4	1907	20.3	70	0.7	6333	67.5
Native whites	344	13.0	101	3.8	267	10.0	123	4.6	1414	53.4	16	0.6	381	14.4
Foreign whites	18	6.9	50	19.1	18	6.9	7	2.7	65	24.9	1	0.4	103	39.3
Colored	99	1.5	33	0.5	8	0.1	2	0.03	428	6.6	53	0.8	5849	90.4

SOURCE: Bureau of the Census, *Eleventh Census: Population* (Washington, D.C., 1893), I, Part II, 634, 696, 718.

[a] Occupations either unspecified by the Bureau of the Census or unclassifiable have been omitted. Their percentage of the female occupations was 1.1 in Atlanta, 1.8 in Richmond, and 1.1 in Nashville.

[b] "Colored" includes a very few Chinese, Japanese, and Indians.

Table 4

"COLORED" PERCENTAGE OF SELECTED OCCUPATIONS IN
ATLANTA, RICHMOND, AND NASHVILLE, 1890[a]

	Profes-sional	Propri-etary	Clerical	Skilled	Semi-skilled	Un-skilled	Domestic & Personal Service
Atlanta							
Male	13.3	8.6	3.4	33.0	20.8	90.3	93.7
Female	31.6	26.0	5.3	6.5	21.3	41.0[b]	96.5
Richmond							
Male	12.2	9.3	2.5	23.0	52.4	72.2	93.7
Female	28.3	19.1	3.2	17.3	40.2	77.9	95.9
Nashville							
Male	22.0	8.0	2.0	27.8	26.0	77.9	89.9
Female	21.5	17.9	2.7	1.5	22.4	75.7	92.4

SOURCE: Bureau of the Census, *Eleventh Census: Population* (Washington, D.C., 1893), I, Part II, 634, 696, 718.
a "Colored" includes a very few Chinese, Japanese, and Indians. Occupations either unspecified by the Bureau of the Census or unclassifiable have been omitted.
b This figure is deceptive since 24 of the 29 laborers were black, while 31 of the 32 messengers, packers, and porters were white.

blacks preferred the system of free labor because "most of them [blacks] work better. They have the stimulus of remuneration." In addition, he thought that the labor was cheaper and more easily managed. If a worker did not do his job, he fired him, and if there was a slow season, he could dismiss all the men and close down.[8]

Throughout the South, however, cotton mills were reserved for whites. Often, as in the case of one Atlanta owner, the antebellum practice of employing Negroes in the mills was abandoned immediately after emancipation. In his trip to Nashville in 1881, Noble Prentis found that all three hundred hands at the large cotton factory were white with the exception of three or four black roustabouts.[9]

Outside the factories blacks took jobs whites did not want. They were in great demand as day laborers for such hazardous occupations as well-digging or sewer-building; they worked on the streets, in the railroad yards, and on the docks. The work was irregular and the pay low. What General Clinton B. Fisk said of Nashville in 1865 remained true of the urban South throughout the period. "In this city it is the

Table 5
DISTRIBUTION OF WORK FORCE BY SEX AND ETHNICITY IN
ATLANTA, RICHMOND, AND NASHVILLE, 1890

	Atlanta	Richmond	Nashville
% of Total Male Work Force			
Native Whites	55.8	56.9	56.8
Foreign Whites	5.1	6.4	7.9
Colored[a]	39.1	36.6	35.3
% of Total Female Work Force			
Native Whites	24.5	27.7	28.6
Foreign Whites	1.3	2.3	2.8
Colored	74.2	70.0	68.6
% of Work Force Female			
All Groups	31.3	33.4	29.3
Native Whites	16.7	19.6	17.2
Foreign Whites	10.2	15.1	12.8
Colored	46.4	48.9	44.6

SOURCE: Bureau of the Census, *Eleventh Census: Population* (Washington, D.C., 1893), I, Part II, 634, 696, 718.
[a] "Colored" includes a very few Chinese, Japanese, and Indians.

negroes who do the hard work. They handle goods on the levee and at the railroad; drive drays and hacks; lay gas pipes; and work on new buildings." Or as the Englishman Robert Somers put it, the black was "a natural-born Cockney."[10]

The white press was constantly on guard against the threat of black laborers replacing whites. In 1865 the *Nashville Daily Press* advocated the colonization of the former slaves because "their seeming interest is to burrow in large cities, where if they are so disposed, they . . . would at once come into rivalry with white labor." Especially unsettling was the threat to skilled laborers. "White mechanics in our midst are complaining that preference is given to negro mechanics by some of our citizens who have work to be done even at the same price," the *Montgomery Daily Ledger* reported in August 1865. Almost twenty-five years later "Sarge," one of the regular columnists in the *Atlanta Constitution*, urged his white readers to employ white brickmasons and carpenters. "Darn this idea of getting indignant at shaking hands with the nigger when you're slipping the quarters and halves and dollars into that same paw."[11]

By 1890 jobs which had once belonged to blacks were being turned over to whites. In that year, for example, Negro firemen on the Georgia Pacific left their jobs in opposition to the railroad's alleged systematic substitution of whites for black firemen. White replacements were easily found and the *Atlanta Constitution* concluded that "it is very probable that even if the strike don't [sic] take off all the negroes, their going in short order now is a reasonable certainty." In Richmond the City Council Committee on Grounds and Buildings rejected a request in 1887 by the chairman of the Colored Mechanics Committee to allow Negro mechanics to work on the construction of the new City Hall.[12]

Whites gave special attention to the replacement of black domestic help. Immediately following the war those who thought Negro help unreliable and insolent sought to hire white and especially immigrant workers. Such efforts continued to the end of the century. The daily newspapers were filled with letters and editorials condemning the poor quality of black help and urging the hiring of whites. Advertisements announced: "Wanted: a white girl to do general housework for a family of two persons. Irish or German preferred," "Wanted, a good white woman as a housekeeper," and "Wanted: A white girl for cook [sic] and housework. German preferred."[13] Nevertheless, the dependence upon blacks continued. (See Table 4.)

Negro skilled laborers were also still a factor in 1890. Robert Shields Crump of Richmond remembered that his father, a leading contractor, had employed a Negro named Holmes reputed to be the best bricklayer in the city. And despite the efforts of "Sarge" the black share of Atlanta's skilled male workers declined only slightly between 1870 and 1890 to 33 percent.[14]

Yet the situation of black skilled workers was actually worse than is suggested by Tables 2 and 4. The categories of steam railroad and streetcar workers were omitted from the tabulation and there were no census figures for waiters. Had they been included they would have increased the proportion of white clerical and skilled workers and black servants and lowered the share of black skilled laborers. Furthermore, the broad category of skilled workers blurs the fact that blacks had a large percentage of a few occupations such as barbering, plastering, and brickmaking, while being grossly underrepresented in the higher-paying and more prestigious fields of carpentry, plumbing, printing, and machine operation. Meanwhile, except in Richmond where the tobacco, flour, and iron industries provided opportunities, blacks even lagged seriously behind in the semiskilled category.

Both skilled and unskilled blacks often worked together with whites on the job, though not without some opposition. An irate Atlantan, for example, objected to the employment of white and black carpenters on the same building since "such miscegenation of labor will inevitably produce a hybrid architecture not pleasing to the chaste taste of Georgians." Despite such criticism, a visitor to Montgomery found that in 1885 "blacks and whites are indiscriminately intermingled on the street, at the cotton stores, and in all channels of business, and the shops and other mechanical pursuits exhibit the white and black man side by side in earning their bread." In 1889 Henry W. Grady pointed to this aspect of racial integration within the larger context of Atlanta and indeed of all Southern urban life:

> White and black carpenters and masons work together on the same buildings, white and black shoemakers and mechanics in the same shops. White and black hackmen drive on the same streets. . . . [But the] white and black carpenters, working together on the same building, go to separate homes at night, to separate churches on Sunday. White and black mechanics in the same shop send their children to separate schools.

Grady was exaggerating the extent of this mixture as well as the opportunity for the blacks to get the employment for which their skills had prepared them, but it is clear that as Ray Stannard Baker said twenty years later, "in the South while the social prejudice is strong, Negroes and whites work together side by side in many kinds of employment."[15]

Working side by side did not usually mean two equals working together. Although George Campbell, during his Raleigh trip of 1879, noticed some construction at Shaw Institute on which the master mason was black and two of his subordinates were white, he concluded that "this is an exceptional case and could not ordinarily occur." As Lady Duffus Hardy noted during her visit to Charleston in 1883, "the master mechanics, builders, carpenters, blacksmiths, etc. are generally white, while the journeymen and laborers are coloured, it is the same with the shopkeepers and small traders, their employees being of the opposite race."[16]

Race also played a central role in the formation of workers' associations and unions, often serving to isolate Negroes from whites in simi-

lar occupations. In 1866, for example, Negroes incorporated the Nashville Colored Mechanics Association "for the general promotion of all
trades among mechanics and for the improvement of its members in
virtue and knowledge." More often the formation of Negro organizations came as a response to exclusion by comparable all-white
bodies, as in the separate Negro unions among Richmond tobacco
workers and longshoremen. Most unions excluded blacks either because of racial prejudice or fear of black competition. Furthermore,
the unions, seen as antithetical to the American and especially the
Southern way of life, could not afford the additional stigma of being
labeled miscegenationist. The policy of exclusion sometimes led to the
weakening of their bargaining position when employers sought nonunion Negro labor in response to economic demands. Nonetheless, it
seemed preferable considering the repercussions that would follow
Negro admittance. Besides, the unions could resort to intimidation in
order to defeat efforts at employing nonunion labor. White Nashville
bricklayers who struck for higher wages in 1879, for example, succeeded in frightening away the five nonunion Negroes hired to do their
work.[17]

Union exclusion contributed greatly to the plight of potential as well
as existing black skilled laborers. In 1886 one of the loudest complaints
at a protest meeting of Nashville blacks was that racial prejudice prevented black youths from becoming apprentices in trades.[18] No figures
are available for Nashville, but the 1890 census revealed that Atlanta
had 135 white apprentices and 27 blacks while Richmond had 212 and
24 respectively. Twelve years later a Raleigh resident reported that
"the black artisan is losing here"; a key reason was that there were no
Negroes in the local unions and "it is doubtful they could get in."[19]

Some unions preferred to make separate provisions for blacks. One
example was the Brotherhood of Painters and Decorators (Colored)
of Nashville, founded by the white parent union. The two branches
met in separate union halls on different nights, but the Negro group
was clearly under white jurisdiction. The Knights of Labor in Richmond actively pursued the same policy. By 1885 Negroes had organized seven assemblies in the city. Three years later there were
twenty-three white assemblies and thirty black, six of the latter group
for females. Each race had district and local assemblies with their own
executive boards. When the two groups met together as they did in the
1888 national convention held in Richmond, members were seated by

race.[20] Even this careful segregation was not enough to soften the impact of white and Negro membership in what was a social as well as an economic organization. In the end the intermixture contributed to the movement's failure and its replacement by the racist American Federation of Labor.

Although comparative information concerning wages is fragmentary, the instances of equal pay for the races seem to have been rare and were evidently limited to the period of Radical control. One example was the payment of $1.25 per day in 1869 to each of the three whites and three Negroes hired to assist in the surveying of Wake County. More typical was the situation in Richmond in 1870 where blacks earned less than comparable white help, though the more skilled the job, the smaller the difference. John O. Kelly, a successful black businessman, found that in Raleigh during the 1880s "white folks won't give the same wages to colored brickmasons or carpenters." Judging from the complaints in the *Constitution* column by "Sarge," skilled Atlanta blacks could be paid less and were therefore often preferred to whites. A leading Atlanta businessman, Samuel P. Richards, frequently employed Negro contractors, brickmasons, and carpenters. It is doubtful that he could have paid a white painter the meager $9.35 which he gave to "an honest and capable [Negro] painter" for three days' worth of labor and material. Employers also took advantage of black unskilled workers. In 1870 the 320 white hands employed at the Atlanta Rolling Mills earned about $3 per day, the Negro employees, $1 per day. On the Raleigh and Gaston Railroad and the Raleigh and Augusta Air Line in 1887 white laborers made an average of 89¢ per day; Negroes, 80¢. The following year an Atlanta City Council resolution that would have ensured all city employees "the same amount of salary for the same work done, without regard to color or sex" was buried in the Street Committee.[21]

The wages the majority of blacks received were insufficient to provide for the necessities of life. Limited incomes meant poor housing and inadequate diet. Dr. R. F. Boyd, a leader of the Nashville black community, reminded delegates to the 1895 Tennessee State Convention of Colored Teachers that

> our people . . . go to the markets Saturday nights and buy the spoiled meats and vegetables on which the flies and smaller insects have preyed all day. In these vegetables are the seeds of indigestion disorders and death. The vegetables and meats which are left over

and not sold in the market and grocery houses are put in wagons and driven to the colored settlements where they are sold cheap for cash.

An 1896 survey of a typical working-class Negro section of Nashville by a Fisk professor helped to explain why so many blacks limited themselves to such poor food. The study included 145 families containing 649 people and representing fifty-one different occupations. Each family earned an average of $9.11 per week, but of the 133 families personally visited, 33 earned less than $6 per week and only 10 made more than $20. Nor was the work always regular. During the year 61 adults who were usually employed underwent a period of forced idleness totaling 749 weeks or an average of three months each.[22]

Throughout the period few blacks earned as much as $30 per month. In 1877 the *Atlanta Constitution* implied that Negroes could get along well on half that amount, observing that "smart colored washerwomen make $15 a month in this city." Compared to at least one female Negro in Nashville, the Atlanta washerwomen were prosperous. Brought into court for stealing from her employer, she listed her duties as "general housework, cooking, washing and ironing." In return for her services she was paid $1 per week with which she had to support five children. The judge dismissed the case because, in the words of the *Daily American*, he "knows where to draw the starvation line and he drew it."[23]

Lacking ready cash, blacks were easy prey for installment sellers. An Atlanta grocer who had been selling furniture as a side line decided to devote his efforts full-time to furniture. "I have a thousand dead beats," he said, "and if any of them want furniture on the installment plan they can get it." When asked by a naive reporter how he would get even with them, the man pointed to a cheap bureau which "looked like it might have been turned out by a boy with a jackknife." The reporter estimated the bureau's price to be a maximum of $6, but the grocer said it cost $15, $2 to $3 in cash and the balance in weekly installments of 50¢. He would, however, sell it for $8 in cash. As for the matter of finding buyers, there were "plenty of them . . . negroes and poor whites." Not only was the installment price almost twice the regular price, but according to this enterprising businessman, "I have a cast iron printed contract, which the buyer signs, agreeing that the furniture is only rented and not sold and forfeiting both furniture and the amount paid on it when a week's rent goes by default." Similarly, in Nashville when Queeny Johnson missed one 50¢ installment on a clock she had purchased, the agent repossessed it.[24]

Some blacks turned to the strike as a means of increasing their wages. In December 1866 the *Nashville Daily Press and Times* reported that "the laboring colored men of Nashville will hold a meeting tonight at Washington Hall for the purpose of taking preliminary steps towards organizing a strike for higher wages."[25] Evidently the meeting never took place and the proposed strike was not undertaken. Because of the nature of their occupations, which usually required scant skills and for which replacements, white or black, could easily be found, few of the strikers could bargain from a position of strength. Nor could they maintain unity within their own ranks.

Strikes that did occur among manual laborers were also handicapped by the hostility of local governments and, as a result, rarely succeeded. In February 1871 the Nashville *Republican Banner* reported that the Negro laborers who unloaded boats on the wharves would not work for less than 20¢ per hour. The strike continued for more than a month, but the steamboat owners easily undermined it by employing state convicts for the old rate of 15¢ per hour. Equally unsuccessful was a strike ten years later by one hundred laborers, mostly Negroes, employed in constructing new switches for the Nashville, Chattanooga, and St. Louis Railroad Company. The men had demanded an increase from $1 per day to $1.25 and had "announced publicly that they will steal rather than work for a dollar a day."[26] Although there was a well-developed strike mentality among both whites and blacks in Richmond, employers easily defeated several strikes involving Negro stevedores, coopers, truckmen, and common laborers.[27]

Negroes employed in service or domestic occupations had only occasional success striking for higher salaries. The waiters at Atlanta's National Hotel once declined to enter the dining room just before dinner time until their wages were increased to $14 per month. They got their raise, but two years later in 1883 the Hotel Waiters Union backed down from a confrontation with employers over the dismissal of several alleged agitators among the Markham House waiters. Often the employers could count on support from civic authorities in their efforts to dictate wages and working conditions. When the waiters at Richmond's St. James Hotel struck, they were immediately replaced "and the interests of the hotel suffered no detriment." The ringleader of the strikers was arrested and fined $10 for creating a disturbance and threatening to assault two nonstriking workers.[28]

The difficulties facing blacks can be seen in the washerwomen strike in Atlanta in 1881. The strike and the methods used to end it demonstrate the poor bargaining position of unskilled blacks in the face of a hostile white community. White Atlantans had been troubled by the unreliability of Negro domestic help since emancipation. In 1872 when Emma Jones, a washerwoman, was found guilty of failing to return clothes entrusted to her and sentenced to the penitentiary for two years, the newspaper noted that "we learn that this is a common practice and the punishment inflicted on Emma, we think, will exert a salutary influence in deterring others from continuing the practice."[29] The severe penalty and the praise from the *Constitution* suggest that the white community felt it was necessary to assume a further degree of discipline over black servants.

By 1881, however, that discipline and control seemed more absent than ever as the Negro washerwomen struck for higher wages. According to a police captain, an association of washerwomen had been organized the previous year in one of the black churches, but had failed to attract more than twenty or thirty members. Now, thanks to an anonymous white man, the movement had been revived and a strike begun for the payment of $1 per dozen pounds of wash. At its peak the strike involved an estimated three thousand Negroes. Churches hosted nightly meetings announced by preachers at Sunday services. The strike committee visited other women and either through the use of reason or intimidation enlisted their support. Some families had gone more than two weeks without any washing being done when the *Atlanta Constitution* reported that the strike is "causing quite an inconvenience among our citizens." Worse than the mere annoyance, it continued, "Not only washerwomen, but the cooks, house servants and nurses are asking an increase. The combinations are being managed by the laundry ladies."[30]

The discomfort of the whites was destined to be temporary for they had too much power over the lives of blacks. The economic sanction was paramount. The *Constitution* noted that winter was approaching and the strikers would be "calling for aid." But many whites threatened that "they will refuse to give anything towards those who now decline to work for a fair remuneration." When one man was told by his washerwoman, who was also his tenant, that she would not work for less than $1 per dozen pounds of wash, he told her that he would raise her rent to $25 per month. Reporting that the woman agreed to work for the usual price, the *Constitution* emphasized that if the strikers "persist in their exorbitant demands, they will find house rents going up so rapidly they will have to vacate."[31] In the face of such retribution and the absence of any other money coming in, the strike fund of $300 provided little reserve strength.

The public sector also undertook economic reprisals. The *Constitution* told its readers that at the next meeting of the City Council an ordinance would be offered requiring all washerwomen belonging to any "association" or "society" to pay a business tax or buy a license. At the same time the Council was planning to exempt a new steam laundry from city taxation for ten years. A law was indeed proposed requiring each member of the Washerwomen's Association of Atlanta to pay $25 for a license and 50¢ for the clerk's fee, the same amount levied against town merchants who owned their own businesses. After its introduction, many of the strikers decided to withdraw from the organization. The majority, however, "laughed at the resolution" and in a letter to the mayor announced that they

> are willing to pay $25 or $50 . . . so we can control the washing for the city. We can afford to pay these licenses and will do it before we will be defeated and then we will have full control of the city's washing at our own prices, as the city has control over our husbands' work at their prices. Don't forget this. . . . We mean business this week or no washing.[32]

Despite the bluster, the lack of resources in the black community meant that few if any washerwomen would be able to pay for the license. In any case, the strike was already being undermined through the active use of police power. Strike leaders were arrested and tried for "disorderly conduct and quarreling" when they sought to attract new recruits to the movement. During one day in Recorder's Court, five washerwomen were fined $5 and a sixth, $20. The following day "two more of the belligerent washerwomen" were fined $20 each. Judge Glenn, the recorder, warned that future offenders would be sent to the chain gang. One of the police captains promised to provide "additional subjects for his [Glenn's] consideration" for "then they will stop." During the next two weeks there was no mention of the strike, but evidently the combined efforts of private employers and the city government wore down the fragile solidarity of the workers. At the August 15 meeting of the Council the proposed $25 license law was returned from committee with an adverse report.[33] Together with the other measures, the threat of such action had been sufficient to defeat the strike.

As long as the great majority of black men were confined to the ranks of the unskilled and black women were laundresses or illiterate domestics, there was little prospect of economic improvement. To most black leaders industrial education provided the best means for economic mobility. Industrial education is often seen as either a white plot to perpetuate Negro inferiority or as a program blacks reluctantly adopted at the very end of the century in response to the prodding of Booker T. Washington. In fact, whites often advocated industrial education for members of their own race. Editorials in the Southern press during the 1880s supported this type of schooling for both races, but often emphasized its value for whites. Even when the blacks were singled out, it was understood that whites were included in the plan.[34]

The idea had come South with the Northern missionaries who conducted industrial arts classes in their primary schools and added industrial departments to their colleges. As early as 1867, the leaders of Nashville's black community joined ranks behind Peter Lowery's recently incorporated Tennessee Manual Labor University. Offering both academic and vocational courses, it was needed since "large numbers of our brethren . . . are thrown upon the community in an ignorant state, deprived of the means of acquiring an education."[35]

Interest in the movement remained at a relatively low level until the 1880s when the paucity of black mechanics became evident. By 1883 biracial interest in industrial education for Negroes emerged in Richmond and the privately-operated Moore Street Industrial School for Colored Youth became part of the public school system. In the same year R. H. Carter, the Negro principal of Atlanta's Gate City School, addressed the Georgia State Educational Convention of Colored Men and strongly urged teaching boys trades as one of the surest means of elevating the race.[36] Another Atlanta educator, Professor W. H. Crogman of Clark University, also praised the advantages of industrial education. During a speech in 1883 on "The Beneficent Effects of Christian Education," he pointed with pride to the industrial department at Clark with its lectures in architecture, school of carpentry, blacksmith shop, model home, and school of domestic economy, "the crown and capstone of all the rest," where girls were taught to sew, knit, cook, and how to "become worthy wives of worthy men." An 1885 editorial in the militant *Richmond Planet* summarized the attitudes of large numbers of blacks ten years before Booker T. Washington's Atlanta Compromise speech:

> We want educated mechanics. Let your boy finish school and if he has a disposition for some trade, instead of packing him off to some college let him follow his industrial inclinations and many a boy will prove the glory of his father and the honor of his race. By this we do not mean to disparage college learning, far from it. If he desires college training or some profession, let him have it and beneficial results will accrue; but do not force a carpenter into the profession of law nor a shoemaker into the profession of medicine, for they may both prove bunglers whereas in their proper sphere they would have been a brilliant example.[37]

Although the majority of blacks remained in manual labor or personal and domestic service, growing numbers turned to a variety of business activities. Some were peddlers, ranging from ragmen to women who sold flowers on the streets. Others sold produce from the countryside like those Charles Wallace fondly remembered on the Richmond streets when he was a boy.

> I got um green rind an' red meat an' full o' juice an' so sweet.
> All dat got money, come up an' buy, dose dat got none, stan' back an' cry, 'kose I'se got watermillions.
> I got um fresh, I got um fine, just come from de livin' vine—watermillions.
> Ladies, I am a goin' by! Aw it is a pity dat you will let me go! Aw it is a pity-pity-pity, a pity-pity-pity-pity-pittee-ee-ee, dat you don't by [*sic*] none o' dese hard head cabbage.

Most whites, however, were less sentimental about the presence of these hawkers who supposedly disrupted the community. "One cannot turn a corner without being invited by some enterprising representative of the African persuasion to partake of refreshments . . . it is 'lemonade, sir' about every four steps," the *Daily Atlanta Intelligencer* charged in July 1866. The large group of freedmen on the Thompson Hotel lot was a special target. "So long as that living mass of laziness can eke out a scanty subsistence by selling pea-nuts, green apples, musty pies, ginger cakes and stale bread and meats, they will never be useful to themselves or anyone else."[38]

Blacks drew praise from the local press when engaged in more substantial businesses. Despite inhibiting state legislation, the Raleigh *Weekly Progress* found in February 1867 that many blacks were "embarking in business." Thirteen years later the *Atlanta Constitution* cited the growing number of Atlanta Negro boot and shoemakers, undertakers, retail grocers, restaurant owners, boardinghouse keepers, and livery-stable operators. By 1886 the *Richmond Planet* could boast that "there are more business places conducted by colored men in this city than ever before, and they are steadily on the increase."[39]

City directories and census schedules documented these observations. Although the directories and, to a lesser extent, the censuses undercounted the number of self-employed blacks, sizable numbers of them began to appear.[40] Yet the range of black business was limited. A survey of Negro businessmen in the South made by W. E. B. Du Bois in 1899 disclosed that better than 40 percent were either grocers, general merchandise dealers, or barbers with $500 or more invested. The next two highest groups were printers and undertakers. An Atlanta survey revealed that groceries comprised more than one-third of the 61 Negro businesses in the city of sufficient size to be noticed. Even in those areas where they were most often found, with the exception of barbering, the blacks were underrepresented in relation to the white businessmen. Although 21 of the 31 barbers listed in the 1891 Atlanta directory were black, only 75 of the more than 450 retail grocers and none of the 27 wholesale grocers were Negro. The Montgomery directory of the same year identified 16 of the 17 barbers as black, but this was true for only 2 of the 118 retail and none of the 21 wholesale grocers and only 1 of the 18 retail dry goods operators.[41]

In other categories there were few if any Negro businessmen. None of the 63 Montgomery saloonkeepers, 4 hardware store owners, or 9 tailors were black; only 4 of the 22 fruit sellers and confectioners were Negro. In the Richmond directory of 1891 no Negroes were listed as commission merchants, hardware store proprietors, insurance or land agents, or wine and liquor dealers.[42]

One factor limiting the development of a large black merchant class was the difficulty encountered in obtaining stalls in the local markets. Either because of the lack of sufficient cash or discrimination in the awarding of the yearly market spaces, few Negroes ever got these valuable places. Nashville's market in 1878, for example, contained 115 stalls with yearly rentals ranging from $75 to $150. Issac Smith, who rented a vegetable stall for $75, was the sole Negro.[43] The number of black butchers in the Montgomery meat market fell from six in 1881 to only one ten years later.[44]

The most serious obstacle to the development of a strong black business class was the competition from white merchants. One response of Negro leaders, therefore, was an appeal to Negroes to "buy black." An 1865 issue of the *Colored Tennessean* contained several such entreaties to the Nashville black community. Edward Monahan notified readers that he had opened a carriage shop after many years of experience in the trade. The editor added that "he calls loudly on his colored friends to sustain him, as it is the duty of the race to patronize our own people." Among other advertisements making similar appeals were those of Pharro Benson's boot and saddlemaking shop, J. H. Sumner's saloon and grocery, Henry Young's carriage shop, and the O.K. Hair Dressing and Shaving Saloon. The following year the newspaper urged blacks to patronize the new drugstore opened by "go ahead colored men." Montgomery's Negro newspaper, the *Herald*, encouraged blacks in 1886 to frequent a local photography gallery where a Negro was in charge of the retouching and printing room. And when the State Colored Men's Convention was held in Richmond in 1890, the Richmond delegates helped pass a resolution which also called upon Negroes to patronize merchants and professionals of their own race.[45]

Because supporting black businesses would be impossible unless enough blacks were entrepreneurs, racial spokesmen also encouraged blacks to think of the opportunities a business career offered. "Many seem to think that the Negro should be and can only be educated to teach and preach," observed the *Fisk Herald* in 1887. But, the paper argued, some college graduates should enter the business world for "never will the Negro gain due recognition unless wealth keeps pace with his other development." According to Richmond's *Virginia Star*, more was needed than the opening of small-scale businesses. "We would like to see more started on a large scale. If single individuals are not able to conduct such, let several unite their means and do so." There should be Negro-owned banks, ships, cotton mills, sawmills, and tobacco factories. "Must we sit and pray and hope for better times when the white man will see our need and give us better wages? Certainly not. Let us put our shoulders to the wheel; imitate our white brother instead of abjectly depending upon him; establish and carry on every species of industrial enterprise for ourselves, employing and paying fair wages to our people." In fact, such enterprises were being started. The paper's news columns announced and the editor applauded the opening of a book and stationery business by two Richmond Negroes.[46]

The *Virginia Star's* view of the need to pool resources was shared by Negroes in the five cities who combined their meager funds in joint promotional efforts. Urban blacks played a disproportionate role in the statewide agricultural and mechanical associations formed after the war and were leaders in the organization of local, state, and national exhibitions aimed at demonstrating and further encouraging the industrial progress of the race. Nashville Negroes filled every office of the Davidson County Colored Agricultural and Mechanical Association founded in 1870. Fourteen years later the city's most famous black resident, J. C. Napier, served as State Commissioner of Colored Exhibits for the 1884 New Orleans Exposition. In the interim yearly fairs were held in Nashville to display the products of black labor. In 1879 twenty-two Raleigh Negroes organized the Colored Industrial Association of North Carolina with capital stock of $20,000. Two years later Montgomery Negroes served as officers of the Industrial State Fair Association for the upcoming Alabama Colored Fair. Other blacks led by W. A. Pledger obtained for Atlanta the National Colored Exposition held in 1888. When the Georgia Colored State Agricultural Society was founded that same year, the secretary and treasurer were Atlanta blacks.[47]

Urban blacks also sought to organize profitmaking enterprises. Usually these businesses were presented as endeavors to benefit the entire black community. Three former slaves replaced by whites in Richmond tobacco factories requested help from the Freedmen's Bureau in 1865 to start a tobacco business run by other displaced black workers.[48] Later efforts relied solely on black capital, but the pattern of seeking business opportunities to help other Negroes remained in effect. It is doubtful, of course, if any other policy could have been pursued since there were few whites eager to work for black employers.

In 1882 a group of Nashville business and political leaders headed by J. C. Napier and S. W. Crosthwaite tried to start the Colored Citizens Cotton and Manufacturing Company. Its charter stated that while white laborers might be temporarily employed to teach the necessary skills, the principal object of the corporation was to give employment to Negro operatives. There is no evidence that this factory or a similar one proposed in Augusta, Georgia, four years earlier was ever built.

More successful were the Negro publishing ventures such as Nash-ville's Sunday School Union Publishing House of the A.M.E. Church.[49]

As in the white business community, most of the large-scale efforts at joint business operations involved land development, insurance, and banking. One of the earliest was the Virginia Home Building Fund and Loan Association, chartered in 1868 by several Richmond Negroes and headed by Peter Woolfolk. Dissolved in 1879, its work was carried on by the Virginia Building and Savings Company, an offshoot of the orig-inal association. An advertisement in the *Virginia Star* aimed at "offi-cers of Churches, Institutions and Societies," clearly expressed the ra-cial nature of the enterprise.

> We confidently appeal to you to *deposit your money* with us, believ-ing that you are willing by this method to aid us in promoting indus-try among our people. By combining our means, great good can be accomplished: for *"in union there is strength!"* We desire to en-courage and support *our mechanics,* and to supply *capital and busi-ness* for *our merchants.*

A number of these same incorporators chartered the Mount Alto Mining and Land Company of Virginia in 1880. Nashville Negroes chartered similar companies such as the Southwestern Real Estate Company of Nashville in 1872, the Bilbo Avenue Building and Real Estate Loan As-sociation in 1888, and a local branch of the American Building and Loan Association in 1889. The most successful organization of this type was the Georgia Real Estate, Loan and Trust Company founded in 1890 by Atlanta Negroes. By 1894 it controlled more than $25,000 worth of Atlanta property.[50]

Negro businessmen turned to these local and state associations after the failure of the National Freedman's Savings and Trust Company. But before its collapse in 1874 the Freedmen's Bank had received some of its strongest support in the branches established in the five cities. The Richmond and Nashville offices, established in October 1865, were two of the first three opened. Raleigh followed in 1869 and by July 1870 operation had begun in Montgomery and Atlanta. Many blacks served as officers and members of the advisory committees, but white Republican politicians like North Carolina Governor William Holden also played influential roles.[51]

Blacks were encouraged to view the bank as a symbol of their free-dom. According to the members of the Nashville Advisory Committee, one of the most important means "well calculated to advance the interests of the colored race, and assist in elevating them above that low and degraded condition, to which slavery once reduced them is that of the 'National Freedmen's [*sic*] Savings and Trust Company.'" To those "many persons of color" who might be suspicious of such endeavors the committee ironically replied that "no fears need be indulged in respecting the safety and soundness of this institution." Deposits and accrued interest would provide funds for "our declining days" and cushion the effects of an accident or an illness. Also important was the effect that such activity would have on whites. For "by becoming economical and saving in our habits" blacks would gain the respect of their opponents and "do away with that oft repeated remark made use of by them that 'the negroes are thriftless, and nothing can be made of them.'"[52]

The local white press generally reacted favorably. On the occasion of the opening of the Atlanta branch, the *Atlanta Constitution* suggested that businessmen examine the claims of the institution "and if satisfied as to its character and safety" recommend it to their employees. Despite the low incomes of the black masses, the urging of Negro leaders and the encouragement of whites helped to get the branches started. In March 1872 the Richmond branch had assets of almost $131,000, the Nashville branch had $101,000, and the other three had between $19,500 and $27,400. By the end of the year the amount of deposits in the Richmond bank had increased to $162,000.[53]

The great majority of passbook holders had small accounts. The $162,000 in Richmond, for example, was divided among almost 3,400 depositors. In Atlanta most of the individual accounts were between $3 and $50, very few reaching $100 and perhaps none as high as $500. Between October 1865 and October 1871, 16,444 depositors put a total of $555,000 into the Nashville bank. As of January 1870, there was almost $60,000 on account, which averaged $90 for each depositor, the fifth highest figure among the twenty-six branches then operating. A fourteen-year-old Negro lad who sold sulfur water had saved almost $200 by 1871 through regular deposits of 50¢ to $1. A female servant who had begun making deposits in 1865 had accumulated about $300 in the bank six years later. No less diligent, though more successful, was Henry Harding, a member of the Executive Committee, who had been the bank's second depositor and by 1871 had $3,500 in his account.[54]

The local banks varied in the quality of their management, but all were undermined by mismanagement in the national office and had closed by the end of 1874.[55] The failure of the bank served to repel many blacks from such enterprises; for years the only banks they would trust were those owned by local whites. Even when in seemingly successful operation, the bank had often sapped rather than increased the strength of the local black communities. After the closing of the bank in the summer of 1874, a Nashville Negro correctly charged that since its establishment the deposits had been sent weekly to Washington instead of being invested locally. Noting that a bill had been introduced in the Senate to wind up the affairs of the "mismanaged institution," the *Virginia Star* editorialized in 1878: "Let this be the last bite at the cherry and give us no more 'piousness' for our hard earned money."[56]

Not until the end of the 1880s did Negroes again place their faith in a savings bank associated with racial aims. This time the enterprise was entirely black owned and operated. In January 1881 the Grand Fountain of the United Order of True Reformers was founded as a fraternal beneficiary institution. Two years later it received a charter as a joint-stock company from the Circuit Court of Richmond. The founder and Grand Worthy Master, the Reverend William W. Browne, established the headquarters in Richmond. Most of the officers were other Richmond blacks who, like Browne, were former slaves. The corporation's success and its unhappiness with placing its funds with whites resulted in the organization of the Savings Bank of the Grand Fountain United Order of True Reformers. In 1888 the organization obtained from the Virginia legislature the first charter issued to a Negro bank in America. When it opened in Richmond the following year, local Negroes expressed their support by depositing $1,200 on the first day. During the first five months there were deposits of almost $10,000; by 1907 the bank had amassed over $500,000.

Before the institution failed in 1910 because of mismanagement of the order, it had played a key role in overcoming Negro prejudice against black banks. In addition, it improved the lives of blacks, especially in Richmond, where in 1893 it lent the city $10,000 to help pay school expenses. Although it supported operations in cities throughout the South, the order, like the bank, had its greatest impact on the Richmond black community. It ran the Hotel Reformer for Negroes, chartered the Mercantile and Industrial Association and operated its most important store, published *The Reformer*, and managed an old-age home six miles from the city. Most importantly, the organization served as a model for the various large-scale Negro real estate, banking, and insurance companies which proliferated in the 1890s and the first decade of the twentieth century. These included the Mechanics Savings Bank, St. Luke's Penny Savings Bank, Nickel Savings Bank, and American Beneficial Insurance Company, all in Richmond, and the Atlanta Mutual Insurance Association.[57]

A growing number of black businessmen achieved a degree of economic security. As a result, they were able to expand the limited opportunities for white-collar employment within the black community. A survey of those individuals mentioned in newspaper stories and compilations of racial leaders suggests that they had much in common. All but a few had been born slaves and were still in their thirties and forties by the end of the period. Their roots were generally in the countryside, but they had been part of the urban migration in the immediate postwar years. They had little formal education. With a few notable exceptions, they served a black clientele and were concentrated in occupations such as liveryman, barber, undertaker, grocer, and caterer.

Estimates of their wealth must be viewed with caution. Tax records for the period are rarely extant and when found, often give only the tax assessed and not the value of the holdings. The biographies of racial leaders appearing in the increasing number of paeans to the race's progress clearly overestimate wealth. The 1870 census depended upon an individual's unsubstantiated assessment of his real and personal property. Nevertheless, two points are clear. Compared to the wealthiest whites in the city, black fortunes were quite modest. Viewed in light of the distance blacks had traveled in the twenty-five-year period since emancipation, their achievements were impressive.

There was already much evidence to support Ray Stannard Baker's later contention that "some of the most prosperous Negroes in every Southern city are undertakers, doing work exclusively . . . for colored people." According to his half-page advertisement in the 1891 Atlanta directory, David T. Howard was "the first colored undertaker who graduated from the Clark School of Embalming in Georgia." He assured potential customers that "Funerals and Everything pertaining thereto [would be] conducted in a strictly First Class manner" and guaranteed "Perfect Preservation of all bodies." Born a slave in 1850, Howard worked as a railroad porter after the war. In 1882 he opened a mortuary with $175 inherited from a white benefactor. Sixty years later he told an interviewer that he had chosen his occupation since "there wasn't anything like that here . . . for my people. . . . My folks were being buried in drays and hacks. And I knew I could beat that." By 1890 he had succeeded in his twin aims of helping the race and making a good living for himself: he had taxable property of $9,600. By the turn of the century he owned a lovely country home eight miles from Atlanta—replete with groves of fruit trees, several well-stocked lakes, game birds, and valuable Jersey cattle. Despite the trappings of a country gentleman, Howard did not forget the rest of his race. He lost money endorsing notes and going bond for less fortunate blacks and took particular pride in the number of students he had sent through college in order that "they could help our race forward to better things."[58]

Many undertakers were able to expand into other businesses. H. A. Loveless of Montgomery, a former slave who had walked sixty-five miles to the city in 1870, used his early success as a butcher to open an undertaking establishment. By 1895 he also operated a hack and dray line, a coal and wood yard, and sold real estate. He employed twenty-five persons in his various enterprises and was worth approximately $15,000. Seven years later his employees had grown to thirty-five with a weekly payroll of $400. A churchgoer who favored industrial education and good business training as a partial solution to the race problem, he advised laborers to "pay your own debts if it takes every cent you have."[59] Richmond's A. D. Price had also left the countryside after the war. By 1909 his undertaking operation had led him into a successful livery business. Together they provided enough capital for him to engage in real estate speculation and among his estimated $70,000 in holdings were three modern buildings in Richmond for Negro tenants. Price's economic success was further reflected in his positions as president of the Southern Aid Society of Virginia and director of the Mechanics Savings Bank, the Capital Shoe and Supply Company, and the American Beneficiary Insurance Company.[60]

Until the end of the century Negroes had a near monopoly in barbering in most Southern cities. They could easily enter the trade as journeymen, accumulate a small amount of money, and then branch out on their own. In 1866 the number of Richmond barbershops had grown to fifty-six, more than twice the prewar total of twenty-three.[61] The *Atlanta Constitution* perhaps had Moses H. Bentley in mind when it reported in 1877 that "there are colored barbers in Atlanta who wear diamonds that weigh two ounces." By 1890 Bentley employed eighteen men in his barbershop, the largest and oldest in the city, which was "patronized by the best class of citizens" in Negro society. He took an active part in community affairs serving as senior captain of the State Colored Military Company, president of the Social Etiquette Club of Colored People, and chairman of the Republican County Executive Committee. In addition to his barbershop he owned a confectionery and restaurant.[62] Nashville's Nelson Walker and Sampson W. Keeble, Montgomery's C. Patterson, and Richmond's William Lyons were among the wealthiest blacks in their cities.[63]

One barber who had not yet had his full impact on his hometown of Atlanta or the national Negro community was nevertheless already among the small number of successful blacks. Alonzo Herndon, born a slave in Social Circle, Georgia, came to Atlanta in 1882 at the age of twenty-four and found employment as a journeyman barber. Four years later he opened his own shop. His white clientele helped him become manager of the Markham House Barber Shop. When the hotel was destroyed by fire in 1896, he opened an elegant shop on Peachtree Street that featured crystal chandeliers and brass spittoons. He soon had three shops employing seventy-five men. He then launched what eventually became the Atlanta Life Insurance Company, the largest Negro stock company in the world.[64]

Like black barbers, blacks in the livery business benefited from white disdain of their occupation. "There are two or three negroes who have made a fortune on drays," remarked the *Constitution* in 1878. "One of them now runs a dozen teams and lives in a neat cottage of his own." At his death Bob Hooper of Nashville who had engaged in the business for several years was the owner and successful operator of four hacks.[65] W. C. Napier, also of Nashville and the father of the city's most prominent black, J. C. Napier, had amassed $5,000 in real estate and $1,200 in personal property by 1870 in a livery business which dated from the antebellum period. John O. Kelly of Raleigh listed among his employees two white omnibus drivers.[66]

Such success among Negroes led the *Atlanta Constitution* to decry the disinclination of white men "of humble station and limited means" to accept such positions. "They seem to think that such a place is utterly unfit for a white man, though well enough for a negro." Whites showed no such feelings toward accepting jobs as streetcar drivers from which blacks were excluded, and indeed by 1890 the development of horse-drawn and then electrified streetcars seriously threatened the economic security of the black hackmen. Yet as the *Nashville Banner* noted there were still over fifty good hacks in the Tennessee capital with a number of others in more or less dilapidated condition. Most were owned by white undertakers and the transfer company, but "the remainder . . . with very few exceptions, are owned by colored men."[67]

Several of the wealthiest blacks were contractors. The most successful was Alexander Hamilton, a veteran of the Union Army, Alabama state legislator, and city councilman in Eufaula, Alabama, who came to Atlanta in 1877. He served as superintendent of the W. L. Trainer Company, was contractor of Morris Brown College, supervised the erection of the Good Samaritan Building, and built many of the most beautiful houses in the city on Peachtree and Washington streets. In 1890 his son entered the business and during subsequent years they did as much as $70,000 worth of business annually. As a result of his financial success, he had an imposing residence and extensive real estate holdings. The older Hamilton became one of the largest Negro contractors in the country; he was employed by members of both races and in turn hired both white and Negro workmen for his jobs.[68]

In 1902 W. E. B. Du Bois singled out eight leading Nashville Negro contractors, all of whom owned "good homes," had other good rental property, and were "men of force and standing."[69] In 1882 Atlanta's Frank Jackson, described as the "largest colored rental agent in the city," erected six tenement houses on Mather Street.[70] Montgomery's James Hale, another former slave who became a contractor, was one of Alabama's richest blacks. In 1870 he had already accumulated $2,500 worth of real estate and $400 of personal property. Fifteen years later he was manufacturing his own doors, sash, and scrollwork needed for his business.[71]

A number of black merchants, especially grocers, amassed considerable wealth by serving the needs of the Negro community. James Tate, who had taxable property of $7,000 in 1890, came to Atlanta after gaining his freedom in 1865. He began selling goods with $16 in capital and, with the aid of credit supplied by whites, established James Tate and Son Dry Goods Store. By 1894 his stock was worth $6,000 and was housed in a two-story brick building. Willis Murphy came to Atlanta with $130. After accumulating additional funds as a carpenter, he opened his grocery store in 1881. By 1890 he paid taxes on more than

$6,700 worth of property. Grocer Floyd H. Crumbley, also of Atlanta, owned more than $7,000 of taxable property in 1890. In that year he was one of the five incorporators of the Georgia Real Estate, Loan and Trust Company. Two years later he became one of the directors of the Penny Savings Bank in Chattanooga. He was secretary of the Grand Lodge of Freemasons of Georgia from 1886 to 1894, secretary of the Board of Directors of the Carrie Steele Orphan Home for black children, and a founder of the Negro Historical Society of Atlanta.[72]

Nashville had the period's two most successful black merchants. Lewis Winter was born in Lebanon, Tennessee, in 1839 of slave parents. He worked on a farm until he left to seek his fortune in Nashville in 1865. With $40 he began business as a wholesale merchant and by 1889 he was described by a local newspaper as the richest Negro in the state with real estate valued at $70,000, "to say nothing of his bank account." By the turn of the century Winter was the largest egg and poultry dealer south of the Ohio River, employing more than a dozen persons at his four-story brick business house. In addition to his position as senior partner of L. Winter and Son, he was a leader of St. Paul's A.M.E., one of the founders and president of the Home Banking and Loan Association, owner of Little Bethel Church of Nashville, and a trustee of Wilberforce University.[73] Winter's friend Henry Harding was even more successful. At his death in 1888 he was one of the two largest Negro taxpayers in the county and had accumulated a fortune of $80,000. While still a slave of a leading Nashville family, he saved $3,500 through the sale of combs and trinkets to his fellow slaves. After emancipation, he opened a hotel on Cedar Street, but, though worth over $35,000 in 1870, he lost most of his considerable profits in the collapse of the Freedmen's Bank. He also was forced to pay the entire purchase price of $15,000 for the Colored Fairgrounds when the twelve other subscribers failed to meet their obligations. Undeterred, he built a profitable secondhand furniture business. He sold it a year and a half before his death and opened a real estate and brokerage house. At his death some of the city's leading blacks owed him more than $1,000 in rents and loans.[74]

There were other prominent businessmen as well. Jacob McKinley, an Atlanta coal and wood dealer, left an estate of $40,000.[75] Moses Calhoun, an Atlanta hotel owner and former grocer, survived several business failures to become by 1886 the "wealthiest colored man in Atlanta." He owned a handsome house on Wheat Street and his youngest child attended school in Boston.[76] G. W. Bragg of Richmond owned the Richmond Steam Laundry, by the turn of the century said to be the largest and best equipped black-owned business of its kind in the country.[77] But perhaps the best known was Richmond's leading caterer, John Dabney. According to one authority, "from the post–Civil War period until . . . 1900 there was rarely an entertainment of importance given in Richmond, whether a private dinner party or a large function, without [his] supervision."[78] The son of house slaves whose owner taught him to cook and hired him out as a bartender, Dabney gained instant fame when the Prince of Wales praised his mint juleps during a trip to Richmond in 1860. He purchased freedom for his wife and himself with money saved from his job and before the end of the war had opened his restaurant and catering business. Though he could neither read nor write in 1870, he was already worth $9,600. Thanks to his patrons among the city's leading white families, he was the caterer for two state dinners given President Grover Cleveland and was placed in charge of refreshments for the 1880 state fair. He owned several impressive residences and engaged in real estate speculation. All his children attended school and one, who went to Oberlin College, organized the Dabney Publishing Company and was editor of *The Union*. Dabney died in 1900 while preparing a banquet for the Seaboard Airline Railway and his funeral rivaled that of the Reverend John Jasper in the number of white persons who attended.[79]

Despite individual successes, the typical black businessman either failed or barely made a living, thus helping to account for the small number of black clerical workers. (See Tables 2–4.) Du Bois's study of Negro businesses in 1899 singled out seven Richmond enterprises for special mention because of the capital invested. Only two of the seven had as much as $10,000 and most had less than $3,000. Of the twenty Montgomery merchants considered noteworthy, only one had more than $5,000 invested. The sixty-one Negro businesses in Atlanta "of sufficient size to be noticed" had a combined total of $11,925 invested, more than one-fifth of this sum supplied by two undertaking establishments. Even the meager achievements of these few businesses were impressive when compared to the mass of Negro shops. Almost ten years after the Du Bois study, Ray Stannard Baker found that "Atlanta has many small Negro tailor and clothes cleaning shops." A number of groceries were scattered throughout the city, some of them prosperous, but "for the most part they are very small, many are exceedingly dirty and ill kept; usually much poorer than corresponding places kept by foreigners."[80]

There were several reasons for the stunted growth of black endeavors. The overwhelming majority depended almost entirely on Negro trade. This meant that their clientele was limited to the poorest minority of the population. Because of this situation, blacks were forced to rely more heavily on credit customers than whites and were also less able to compel payment. Then, too, the Negroes had to compete against more experienced and better-financed white merchants. A British Board of Trade committee found in 1910 that on Atlanta's Decatur Street, "practically all the shops, though doing a trade exclusively among the coloured people, are nevertheless kept by whites," especially immigrants.[81]

Many of the most prominent Negroes came from the small group of professionals found in each city. (See Tables 2 and 4.) The majority of these men combined their professional activities with business pursuits. This was true of the clergy, who were often among the richest blacks because of their investments in real estate and other ventures. It was also true of the doctors, dentists, lawyers, and even the wealthier schoolteachers and principals. Such intermixture was due to the limited resources within the black community and to the ease with which businessmen and even blue-collar workers could move into such professions as the law and, to a lesser extent, medicine. Nevertheless, the number in the professions, other than teaching and preaching, was pitifully small. The 1890 census-takers recorded two Negro lawyers in Atlanta, six in Richmond, and nine in Nashville. While the great majority of white lawyers were the children of native-born parents, even the total of foreign-born and the children of foreign-born parents exceeded by 26 the number of blacks. Of the 562 physicians and surgeons counted in the three cities, only 36 were black, 24 of them in Nashville. In 1876 professionals comprised only 1.6 percent of Raleigh's employed Negroes; by 1888 the percentage had reached a mere 3.8. None was a doctor or dentist; the overwhelming number were teachers and clergymen.[82]

Opportunities for black lawyers were greatest in Nashville. By the turn of the century there were sixteen worthy of special mention in a compendium of racial leaders. Several former slaves such as Taylor Ewing, Alfred Menefee, Samuel Lowery, and Nelson Walker had successful practices despite little formal education. All had first become interested in politics and their participation in Republican Party activities paved the way for their legal careers. During March 1872, Walker, who like Ewing was also a barber, was both admitted to practice as an attorney in the State Supreme Court and elected president of the Tennessee State Barber Association.[83] Others had the benefit of a more thorough education. Samuel McElwee, also a former slave, attended primary schools, taught after the war, and spent one year at Oberlin College. After teaching in Mississippi and Alabama, he returned to Nashville and graduated from Fisk University and Central Tennessee College Law School. While still an undergraduate, he served the first of three terms as a state legislator and subsequently remained active in national and Tennessee Republican politics. Another former slave, George T. Robinson, came to Nashville from rural Mississippi after the war and like McElwee graduated from Fisk and Central Tennessee. In addition to having an active law practice, he became Professor of Law at Central Tennessee College, a leading Republican politician, and the founder and editor of the *Tennessee Star* which later merged with the *Indianapolis Freeman.*[84]

J. C. Napier was the most successful lawyer. Born near Nashville in 1843 of free Negro parents, he was sent to Wilberforce University and Oberlin College. In his junior year he took a position in the War Department in Washington, D.C. He graduated from the law department of Howard University and was admitted to the Washington bar in 1873. After several years in government service, he established a law practice in Nashville. A leading Republican politician, he was a delegate to four national conventions, a member of the Tennessee Republican Executive Committee for sixteen consecutive years, and a city councilman for four terms. His career benefited from his marriage in 1878 to the daughter of John Mercer Langston, later the Negro Congressman from Virginia, and from his close association with Booker T. Washington. Like most wealthy blacks, he invested in real estate and owned much property including "Napier Court," a building divided into offices for Negro professionals.[85]

The only attorney elsewhere to match the Nashville leaders was C. H. J. Taylor, who came to Atlanta in 1888. He had been Minister to Liberia, was licensed to practice before the U.S. Supreme Court, and according to the *Atlanta Constitution* was "one of the foremost colored men of the country." He was "a man of extensive information, good character, and fine conversational powers."[86] The fact that he was also one of the few Negro Democrats probably influenced the newspaper's assessment. Other successful lawyers included Montgomery's A. A. Garner and Richmond's T. C. Johnson.[87]

Nashville, because of the presence of the Meharry Medical School, was also the leader in the medical profession. In 1880 the State Colored Medical Association was organized there and chose Dr. J. M. Jamison of the city as its first president.[88] One of its most outstanding members was Dr. R. F. Boyd, born a slave in Giles County, Tennessee, in 1858. His interest in medicine dated from 1866 when his mother took him to Nashville to live with Dr. Paul Eve, one of the greatest surgeons of the day. He attended night school at Fisk and for the next twelve years alternated teaching in rural areas, working in Nashville, and attending school. In 1880 he entered Meharry, from which he graduated with first honors. After a brief period of practicing medicine and teaching in Mississippi, he returned to Meharry as Adjunct Professor of Chemistry. At the same time he entered the college department of Central Tennessee College, graduating with honors in 1886. From 1884 to 1888 he was Professor of Physiology at Meharry and then Professor of Anatomy and Physiology for a year. In those five years he also graduated from the dental department. During the summer of 1890 he attended the Post Graduate School of Medicine at the University of Chicago and two summers later took the special course on diseases of women and children. He began his medical practice in 1887, working primarily with the lower class. By the turn of the century he was treating all classes, although he retained his interest in the care of the indigent. Continuing his education, he received a Master of Arts from Central Tennessee College in 1891. In 1893 he became Professor of Diseases of Women and Clinical Medicine and the head of the Meharry College hospital. A leader in the black community, he was a candidate for the General Assembly in 1891 and for mayor the following year. In the early 1890s he purchased a three-story brick house on Cedar Street for $14,000, the largest transfer of real estate to a Negro in Tennessee up to that time. Renamed the Boyd Building and rented to black business and professional men, it was valued at $20,000 in 1902. Boyd's other rental property included several houses leased to blacks. By 1900 he was president of the American Medical Association of Colored Physicians and Surgeons and was among the leading candidates for the position of Surgeon-in-Chief at the Freedmen's Hospital in Washington, D.C.[89]

The influence of Meharry was also evident in Atlanta where at least three of the most prominent black physicians were alumni. Two of them, Dr. Thomas Heathe Slater and Dr. H. R. Butler, opened the first Negro-owned and -operated drugstore in Georgia. By the 1890s it had become the largest black-owned retail drug business in the country.[90] In addition to several other doctors, Atlanta's medical community also included a dentist, Dr. Roderick D. Badger. Badger was born in 1834 in DeKalb County, Georgia, the son of a white dentist. He and his brother were taught dentistry by their father and Roderick began practicing in Atlanta in 1856. Freed soon afterwards, he spent the war years in Chicago. After the war he went to Nashville where he and his brother briefly practiced before returning to Atlanta. By 1870 when he was only thirty-five, Badger owned $2,900 in real and personal property. In 1882 the *Atlanta Constitution* reported that he was doing a good business and that "many of his patients are among the leading families of the city." In 1884 according to one of the city tax assessors, he was the city's richest Negro, being worth about $15,000. Six years later he was paying taxes on $9,600 of real estate.[91]

Montgomery also had a successful Negro dentist in Dr. T. A. Curtis. Born of slave parents in Marion, Alabama, in 1862, he later graduated from the State Normal School for Colored Children and taught in Alabama and Texas. As with many other black professionals, he abandoned his teaching career and entered Meharry Dental College from which he graduated with honors in 1889. After being chosen as the best practical dentist in his class, he became Alabama's first Negro dentist. During his first year he earned more than $2,000 and in each succeeding year his income increased.[92]

Less is known of the background of Montgomery's leading Negro physician, C. N. Dorsette, who arrived in the city in 1883. According to an article in the *Colored Citizen*, Dorsette was from Lyons, New York, where he had been a resident physician in charge of the county insane asylum. In his new home he organized the Dorsette and Company Pharmacy, was president of and physician at the James Hale Infirmary for Negroes, and was head of the Colored Orphan, Infirm and Aged Association. He also erected, probably with the aid of his father-in-law, James Hale, an impressive three-story building which housed his pharmacy, office, and meeting rooms for Negro lodges.[93]

Two other physicians deserve special mention. The first is Dr. Sarah G. Jones, the daughter of George W. Boyd, the wealthiest black contractor and builder in Richmond. Born in Albemarle County, North Carolina, she was educated in Richmond and later taught in the city's public schools for five years. After her marriage to M. B. Jones, who later became the G. W. A. Secretary of the True Reformers, she entered Howard Medical College and graduated in 1895 with an M.D. She then became the first woman licensed to practice medicine in Virginia.[94] Dr. I. W. Hayes, the other noteworthy doctor, demonstrates the supportive roles played by the various Southern cities. A mulatto born in Georgia in 1865, he was largely self-educated until he entered Cookman Institute in Jacksonville, Florida. After graduating at the head of his class in 1883, he attended Clark University in Atlanta briefly before finally graduating from Benedict College in Columbia, South Carolina. He taught in rural Georgia and then entered Raleigh's Leonard Medical College. After completing his medical courses, he spent two years in Georgia until the Nashville hospitals accepted Negro students. He entered the Clinical Sanitarium of Nashville and was awarded a second M.D. in 1892. Hayes then returned to practice in Atlanta. In less than thirty years he had used the institutions for blacks in Atlanta, Jacksonville, Nashville, Raleigh, and Columbia to catapult himself from humble origins to a successful career in medicine.[95]

By the end of the period urban black communities had made remarkable economic strides which were reflected in the tax rolls. During February 1869, Atlanta Negroes had an estimated $37,000 worth of taxable property. By 1874 the amount for Fulton County Negroes (owned almost entirely by Atlanta residents) had risen to $253,852; thirteen years later the city property alone had grown to $490,565; for 1890 the figure was $855,561 with an additional $94,985 worth of land outside the city.[96] In 1875 there were forty-two Atlanta and Fulton County blacks who had property worth more than $1,000; five years later there were over six hundred with holdings valued between $100 and $1,000, a fact which the *Atlanta Constitution* took "as an evidence of the general thrift and prosperity of the race." Most of these Negroes owned only their homes, although some had additional properties.[97] Richmond Negroes made advances comparable to those in Atlanta. In

1891 they owned real estate valued at $968,736. Four years later there were six blacks in Jackson Ward who owned more than $10,000 worth of property.[98] Even in Montgomery local blacks had amassed over $150,000 in real estate and personal property by 1878.[99]

Nashville Negroes had made the most gains. As early as 1868, there were twenty Negroes whose aggregate wealth was $227,000. By 1886 the combined wealth of the black population was approximately $1,000,000, with seventeen individuals worth more than $10,000.[100] In an effort to demonstrate how well the Negroes were prospering in the South and especially in Nashville, the *Nashville Banner* noted in 1890 that "there are many colored people worth from $5,000 to $10,000 each in this city. They have made this within the past twenty-five years." Among the sizable number worth even more was Lucinda Bedford, the richest black woman in the city, whose former master left her an estimated $100,000 in possessions.[101]

Yet at the time that Atlanta Negroes had $37,000 worth of property, local whites had approximately $10,000,000; by 1890 white-owned city property was worth almost $26,000,000. The *Constitution* article in 1875 that listed forty-two blacks owning more than $1,000 in property devoted two columns to whites owning $10,000 or more. The value of personal property in Richmond's Jackson Ward in 1890 when 13,530 of its 17,210 residents were black was $158,325; the next lowest sum was in Marshall Ward where $571,144 was divided among 5,900 fewer persons. All the other wards had at least $2,300,000. The $968,736 worth of real estate blacks owned throughout the city in 1891 was barely one-third of the total value of real estate in Jackson Ward alone. And in Nashville more than half of the $1,000,000 in the hands of the local blacks in 1886 was owned by only forty-four families.[102]

By 1890 a small number of black business and professional men had experienced considerable economic advancement. Most were former slaves who had succeeded in accumulating property and wealth and were able to provide their children with the advantages of higher education and a secure economic base. Below them was a modest-sized group of regularly employed hardworking petty tradesmen, artisans, and laborers who perhaps owned their homes and enjoyed some of the comforts of life. For the majority of urban Negroes, however, the first twenty-five years after the war were years of frustration and disap-

pointment. The year 1890 found them at the lowest levels of the economic ladder with little prospect of improvement. As Richard Hopkins
has suggested for Atlanta, the economic mobility of urban blacks was
even less than that of foreign immigrants with whom they often com-
peted for jobs.[103] The lack of economic power served to undermine the
strength of blacks in warding off the discrimination generated by the
white community.

5

Negro Housing and Neighborhoods

In the antebellum years the majority of urban blacks, as slaves, lived with their masters in enclosed compounds. Subjected to close supervision, they were nevertheless provided with adequate food and shelter. At the same time many fugitive and hired-out slaves joined free Negroes in colonies located on the periphery of the cities.[1] The emerging pattern of segregation was strengthened at the end of the war as numerous blacks vacated the old slave quarters. By 1890 separate black and white neighborhoods dominated the urban landscape.

As in other areas of Negro urban life, the existence of segregation paradoxically marked both the success of social control and a further threat to it. For if keeping Negroes out of white neighborhoods prevented racial mixture and the lowering of property values, it also brought together large numbers of Negroes in areas that whites could not easily control. As whites discovered, if one part of the city was unhealthy, the rest of the city might suffer. If crime flourished in one neighborhood, it might easily spread to others; fires begun in one locality might inflame the rest of the city. Throughout the period this dilemma baffled whites. How could blacks be kept out of the white neighborhoods without causing even more serious repercussions by compressing blacks into a united mass?

Even by the end of the period whites and blacks could still be found living next to one another in certain sections of the city. The extent of such intermingling is distorted if judged solely by ward population figures,[2] but even house-by-house examination reveals a certain amount

97

of racial intermixture within city blocks. Nevertheless, such occurrences were limited to special circumstances. Negroes either worked
for their white neighbors or lived among whites unable to move elsewhere. In the latter case, the pattern was clearly temporary, to be
ended either by the death of the whites or their financial improvement.
There were usually one or more main concentrations of Negroes and
numerous other smaller clusters. Some of the housing segregation was
voluntary: Negroes sought proximity to their jobs, welcomed the freedom from white surveillance, and enjoyed the company of other blacks.
Much of it, however, was due to black poverty, which limited housing
options, and to white pressures to keep blacks out of their neighborhoods. Some Negro neighborhoods had begun in antebellum times as a
result of the concentration of free Negroes and fugitive and hired-out
slaves. Others evolved after the occupation by federal forces. Whatever the origin, these areas were in the worst sections of the city: in
unkempt alleyways, on low-lying ground near contaminated streams,
or near slaughterhouses, flour mills, or other industrial sites. In short,
the Negroes occupied land considered unfit for white habitation.

Richmond's Jackson Ward contained the most famous concentration
of blacks. By the time it was organized in 1871 as the city's sixth political subdivision, the area had already become the center of Richmond's
Negro population. Its formation from territory taken out of three other
wards was a blatant case of gerrymandering in response to the reality
of Negro settlement. The ward was bounded on the west and north by
Bacon Quarter Branch which formed the northern limits of the city,
on the east by Shockoe Creek, and on the south by Leigh Street. By
1890 the ward contained 3,680 whites and 13,530 of the city's 32,330
blacks.[3]

Antebellum free Negroes had organized their first communities in
the midst of German and Irish immigrants. They built a number of
small frame houses on Leigh in the vicinity of Brook. Around this nu-
cleus the Third African Baptist Church was organized in 1858, two
years after construction of the nearby Second African Baptist. There
were similar antebellum concentrations of homeowning free Negroes
on Duval near Judah, on the 500 block of West Baker, and on the
northern parts of St. James, St. Peter, and St. Paul streets. In 1814
free Negroes in the vicinity had successfully petitioned the City Council for the right to operate a burial ground at the end of Third Street
near the poorhouse. Smaller concentrations of blacks were found else-

where: a settlement of free Negroes, for example, supported a clandestine church in Penitentiary Bottom in the southern part of the city near the docks and Tredegar Iron Works where many blacks worked.[4]

Thus, before the outbreak of the Civil War, Negro communities with the beginnings of an institutional framework had already begun to appear. Although most common in Richmond because of the size and wealth of the free Negro population, such communities were also found to a lesser extent in the other cities. The majority of the blacks, however, remained slaves living near their masters; only emancipation and the end of the war could produce the embryonic ghettoes that began to emerge.

In Richmond the areas of Negro settlement expanded from the antebellum nuclei. Blacks gradually occupied small houses in the western end of Leigh as they moved in the direction of Marshall and Clay streets. Evidently the larger houses to the east of First Street did not lend themselves well to this natural push south. Negroes began to move into the small frame houses on the seventh block of nearby Catherine Street as early as 1879, although the lower three blocks of the street remained predominantly white until the 1890s. Around 1866 the Negroes who had been on Duval began moving east and by the 1870s the street was primarily black, a transition affirmed by the sale of the white Presbyterian Duval Street Chapel to the Negro Sixth Mount Zion Baptist Church in 1870. Similar expansion on Baker, St. James, St. Peter, and St. Paul also began at this time. Meanwhile, Third Street from Shockoe Cemetery to Jackson Street, the corresponding stretch of Second Street, as well as Jackson itself, had become overwhelmingly black by the end of the decade.[5]

Changes in church ownership again reflected this shift in population. In 1880 members of the Fifth Street Baptist Church moved into the building "lately occupied" by the German Lutheran Church at the corner of Fifth and Jackson.[6] In the words of a longtime Richmond resident, "no section of our city . . . so completely changed its complexion and population."[7] By 1890 the whites in the ward were concentrated on several north-south streets east of St. James and Leigh streets between St. James and the creek with the exception of the undesirable marshy blocks from Tenth to the Shockoe.[8]

Negroes gravitated to other areas in and around postbellum Richmond. According to one resident, shortly after emancipation blacks "formed a circular belt around the city on both sides of the river."[9]

This arrangement was a continuation of the prewar settlement of slaves and free Negroes on the fringes of the city. The United States Army and the Freedmen's Bureau strengthened the pattern by organizing camps to house, care for, and facilitate the return of the former slaves to the countryside. On Chimborazo Heights in the eastern limits of Richmond, the freedmen were kept in low wooden buildings originally used as a Confederate hospital. Camps elsewhere were even more makeshift and unsatisfactory.[10]

Because of the great number of freedmen, the lack of resources at the disposal of the Freedmen's Bureau, and the desire to get the freedmen back to the countryside, these camps were closed as quickly as possible.[11] Rather than return to the rural areas, many of the freedmen stayed where they were or moved closer to the city limits. As a result, all of the cities came to have a ring of Negroes on their outskirts, forming anything but the affluent white band that the word "suburb" commonly brings to mind. In Raleigh during the early postwar years many of the freedmen occupied an area one mile northwest of the city where the town of Oberlin was soon incorporated. By 1881 almost all of the 750 inhabitants were Negro. An Atlanta guidebook of the same year suggested that its readers observe "the Negro villages located at several points near the city limit. . . . They are thickly populated and have their churches." As for the suburbs of Atlanta, they are "remarkably orderly," observed the *Atlanta Constitution*, "including the negro settlements, which are very numerous."[12]

In Nashville the settlements were also numerous, but far from orderly. "Nashville, a beautiful and attractive city, is possessed of filthy and repulsive suburbs," read a government report on the 1873 cholera epidemic. "The small streets and lanes that surround the base of Capitol Hill are occupied exclusively by the lower classes. The houses are dirty and filthy in the extreme; the streets and gutters are filled with filth. Gutters and sewers upon either side enter into the branches, which afford the only efficient drainage of the city." The *Republican Banner* traced the origin of these largely Negro areas to the early postwar period. Noting that the freedmen camps were broken up in 1866, the newspaper reminded its readers that

> it was about this time . . . that the classic localities of "Black Center" and "Hell's Half Acre" became known to fame. They were appropriately named from the numberless shanties which were

erected in the most confused and helter skelter style upon a small piece of ground south of Broad street and from the crimes constantly committed west of the Nashville and Chattanooga Road.[13]

Such concentrations of Negro population, especially outside the corporation limits, posed a clear problem of unsanitary conditions and lawlessness. There was, for example, New Bethel, a Negro settlement in the southern suburbs near a former freedmen camp. A reporter for the *Republican Banner* found in 1873 that white citizens living nearby complained about "the filthiness of some of the shanties and desire their removal." More than half a dozen petitions with this request had been presented to the county government and many of the houses had already been "disinfected, if not removed," but whites demanded further action.[14]

Because of the threat to the health and property of the nearby city, such neighborhoods were subject to periodic annexation attempts in order to extend the area of white control. Before the end of the century New Bethel, along with many other similar settlements in the districts of Davidson County adjacent to Nashville, were taken over by the city, largely during the mass annexations of 1879 and 1889. County districts filled with freedmen around Richmond, Atlanta, and Montgomery had already been subjected to the same treatment within five years after the war. Raleigh's Negro suburb of Oberlin met a similar fate later in the century. What this meant, of course, was that these new areas of the city would be brought in essentially as segregated communities. Like giant amoebas the spreading cities absorbed these foreign entities; unlike the amoebas' prey the entities were not broken down and consumed but rather remained as units within the larger body.

Many of these areas brought with them their own community institutions, such as public schools, churches, and meeting halls. If they did not, then the concentration of Negroes assured that the institutions would soon follow. Once this occurred, they in turn attracted still more Negro residents, reinforcing the developing 'pattern of segregated neighborhoods.

Churches and schools formed the core of Negro communities. In Atlanta, Summer Hill, a real estate subdivision on Martin, Richardson, and adjoining streets once used as the city dump, was "a respectable colored community centered around the Summer Hill Public School."[15] On the other side of town on Green's Ferry Street there was Willowtree

Church "surrounded by negro houses and young negroes."[16] Settlement followed so rapidly around Montgomery's Congregational Church and Swayne School that the area was dubbed "New Montgomery." In 1873 the church's pastor reported that the school, the church, "and the delightful . . . location, have drawn the better class of our colored citizens from all parts of the city to find permanent homes."[17]

The numerous Negro colleges that were organized in the Southern cities further contributed to the formation of Negro areas. One such community developed near Fisk University in Nashville.[18] This colony increased as the school prospered and in 1879 when the area was annexed by the city, another segregated unit of society replete with its own public schools, college, and churches was added to the larger segregated society. Because Negro colleges had religious connections, at least one church of the same denomination was usually founded in conjunction with a school. Not only was this true of Howard Chapel near Fisk, but of the churches associated with Central Tennessee College, Atlanta University, and Raleigh's St. Augustine's College.

The philanthropic societies which founded most of these colleges and churches also made provision for nearby black housing. Montgomery's Congregational Church occupied only one part of a three and one-half acre tract; the rest had been subdivided by the American Missionary Association and sold to black families. In 1881 the *Atlanta Constitution* praised the progress of Clark University run by the Freedmen's Aid Society of the Methodist Episcopal Church and noted that the trustees owned four hundred acres of land around the main hall which "will become a village in a few years where our colored citizens can find comfortable suburban homes." Raleigh's Josephus Daniels, then editor of the *News and Observer*, noted that Shaw Institute in the southern part of his city was "in the heart of the negro district." Established on South Street in 1866 because the neighborhood was already predominantly black, the school's presence helped to make the area even more segregated. When the American Missionary Association decided to open a primary school and a church on South and McDowell Streets, it was responding to the same conditions. By selling adjoining property only to Negroes, it further increased the racial imbalance.[19]

Businessmen also encouraged blacks to live among their own race. Advertisements in the *Colored Tennessean* announced in 1866 "land to rent to respectable colored people who have steady employment." Twenty-two years later J. H. Keeble, a leading Nashville Negro politician and businessman, ran a series of advertisements in a white newspaper urging blacks to see him about choice housing lots.

> Every colored man in Nashville ought to own a house. There is no use in saying you can't for no man is too poor to buy one or two lots at sale next Tuesday. . . . Beautiful lots, high and dry, at $80, $110, and $125 each, $20 down and balance in payments of $3 per month.

The land was adjoining Ashcraft Seminary, "one of the best schools in the country" for Negroes. A few months later Keeble reported that he had "desirable property for sale . . . near Fisk University."[20]

White real estate agents also saw the profit involved in selling to blacks. In 1887 two Atlanta Republican politicians, Campbell Wallace, Jr., and Colonel A. E. Buck, subdivided a fifty-acre property they owned near Clark University into 250 building lots and organized the South Atlanta Land and Improvement Company. A Clark professor was the general manager. Purchasers were assured "reasonable prices" and "exceedingly easy terms." They had two to four years to pay for the land and the corporation would erect the houses if the buyers desired. Several lots had already been sold to "well-to-do respectable colored people" and the company pledged to sell the remainder only to "a decent class of negroes."[21]

An added stimulus to segregated housing was the organization at the end of the 1880s of several black building and loan associations. Nashville's Negroes chartered the Bilbo Avenue Building and Real Estate Loan Association in 1888 and in the following year established both a branch of the American Building and Loan Association and an indigenous organization known simply as The Building and Loan Association. The latter organization was composed of the city's Negro business and political elite, who subscribed $3,000 at the first meeting.[22] Although there is no evidence that these efforts bore fruit, by 1889 a similar black society in Richmond was already selling the twenty-three houses it had built for black families.[23]

These burgeoning Negro communities did not develop solely in response to the needs of their residents nor did they represent merely voluntary action upon the part of the freedmen. At the heart of segregation lay the opposition of surrounding white areas to residential intermixture. Although laws proscribing integrated blocks or entire sections of the community were a product of the early twentieth century,[24] Southern whites sought to accomplish the same goals through the more subtle use of public and private power.

To whites who failed to distinguish among the various classes of blacks, Negroes in the neighborhood automatically meant poor housing. In 1865 Nashville's Board of Aldermen voted to repeal the municipal ordinance permitting the construction of frame buildings without the consent of the bicameral City Council. During the subsequent debate over the bill in the Common Council, a member argued that opposition to the ordinance arose less from the dread of fire than from the fact that most of these shanties were built for Negroes. An opponent answered that people were indeed tired of these shacks occupied by white and black prostitutes, thieves, and other disreputable people. The councilmen finally defeated the proposed change by a vote of 6 to 5. A similar situation arose in 1889 when white residents of one neighborhood protested to the city building commissioners against the planned erection of a one-story tenement. They charged that many Negroes would crowd into it and it would be an undesirable addition to the community. The commissioners, however, said that they were powerless to act since the building construction complied with the law. The final outcome is not known, but it is clear from these two illustrations that white residents, if not yet municipal officials, were mobilized against incursions by unwanted blacks.[25]

When Negroes succeeded in moving into a white neighborhood, it was often in the face of concerted opposition. Complaints to the Post-Adjutant of Montgomery in 1865 led to General Order Number 6 which stated that "negroes will not be permitted to occupy dwelling houses or tenements of any description in this city, without authority from the lawful owners." Blacks disobeying this regulation were ordered to vacate the buildings immediately. Those who were in rightful possession were required to show certificates as proof. In the eyes of the *Montgomery Daily Ledger* there was an even greater problem involving white owners who were renting to blacks for more money than whites could afford.

> We do not gainsay their right to obtain the most rent but we would suggest that they are giving not the best neighbor to many very worthy poor white families and may run the risk of the destruction of the property by fire or in the pulling down and burning of their fences. In not a few instances, houses are rented from the owner and then made a den for numerous other negroes who agree to pay rent

for a portion of the premises or of a room, thus settling in a particular locality parties who calculate to live by depredations upon hard working, honest white persons.

Two weeks later another attack appeared on "negro assignation houses" which have "the purpose of amalgamation, where the soul and body are debauched and the public morals are fearfully stabbed." Worse still, claimed the editorial, "they exist in every part of the city and are constantly on the increase."[26]

Black settlement was opposed on other grounds as well. Richmond officials sought to confine Negro voters to Jackson Ward in an effort to restrict their political power. Raleigh's blacks faced an even more blatant campaign in 1875 when they attempted to move in greater numbers into the Fifth Ward, the only ward which had not been racially gerrymandered by the Democratic administration. Allegedly the Republican leaders advised the Negroes to "rotate" to the Fifth Ward, but "the rotaters will find it difficult to get houses," said the *Daily Sentinel*, "when it is known they move only to carry the election and keep control of a much plundered city."[27] In fact, most of those who were able to get homes in the ward, notably near the railroad yards where many of them worked, remained as permanent residents. Nevertheless, whites in subsequent years succeeded (partly through the tactic of closing the ward's only Negro school) in keeping the main body of blacks confined to the Second and Fourth wards to the south, thus preventing Negro majorities in the Fifth Ward and assuring Democratic control of the city.

It is an arduous and time-consuming process to trace the shift from the prewar pattern of housing to that of the segregated postwar pattern. The nature of the sources makes it an almost insurmountable task for the immediate postbellum period. The 1870 federal manuscript census schedules list one household after another without indicating the street address; the same is often true for the 1880 census. Many city directories did not begin to list blacks until the late 1870s and then contained only a few names. Nevertheless, the 1870 and 1880 manuscript census schedules for Atlanta, Richmond, and Montgomery contain ample evidence of substantial early segregation which seemed to increase from decade to decade. A more systematic study of residential patterns in several Southern cities by John Martin supports these tentative conclusions about the extent of segregation. In Richmond, for example, 67 percent of the linear blocks were totally segregated in 1870, as were 74 percent of them in 1880; the respective figures for Atlanta were 73 percent and 76 percent.[28]

Fragmentary impressionistic evidence also suggests that segregated neighborhoods quickly came to predominate after the war. In 1881 an *Atlanta Constitution* reporter observed that "by far the largest proportion of Negroes are never really known to us. They are not employed in private homes nor in the business houses, but drift off to themselves, and are almost as far from the white people, so far as all practicable benefits of associations are concerned, as if the two races never met." He then took his readers on a tour of black Atlanta: Shermantown, Mechanicsville, Hell's Half Acre, Bone Alley, and Pigtail Alley. Had he continued, he well could have mentioned Darktown, a densely populated black district from Butler to Piedmont and Houston to Baker; Peasville, centered upon Fraser and Martin in the rear of the State Capitol; and Jenningstown near Atlanta University in the western part of the city where "the population consists chiefly of niggers, bobtailed dogs and babies."[29] By 1881 whites in other cities could also easily identify the Negro areas of town. Nashville had its Rocktown, Black Center, and Black Bottom; Montgomery, its Baguehomma and Peacocks Tract; Richmond, its Jackson Ward and Byrd Island; and Raleigh, its Hungry Neck and Hell's Half Acre.[30]

City directories for Atlanta and Richmond in 1891 and for Montgomery in 1895 provide the surest guides for a re-creation of residential patterns. By those dates segregation was firmly established.[31] The residences for blacks and whites for those years were plotted on a map. In each case the great majority of linear blocks were either all-white or all-black. The second greatest group were those whose residents were from 90 to 99 percent of one race, unanimity being prevented by no more than one or two members of the opposite race. In those less frequent instances where 11–29 percent of the residents were black, the figure was usually under 20 percent and often under 15 percent. By far the smallest number of blocks were 30–69 percent black, especially those less than 49 percent. In other words, the decided tendency was away from truly mixed blocks. Truly integrated arrangements were unstable and occurred in changing neighborhoods. Once a block became more than 20 percent black, it was on its way to the predominant pattern of segregation. And this was at a time when the percentage of blacks in the three cities ranged from 40 percent to 59 percent.

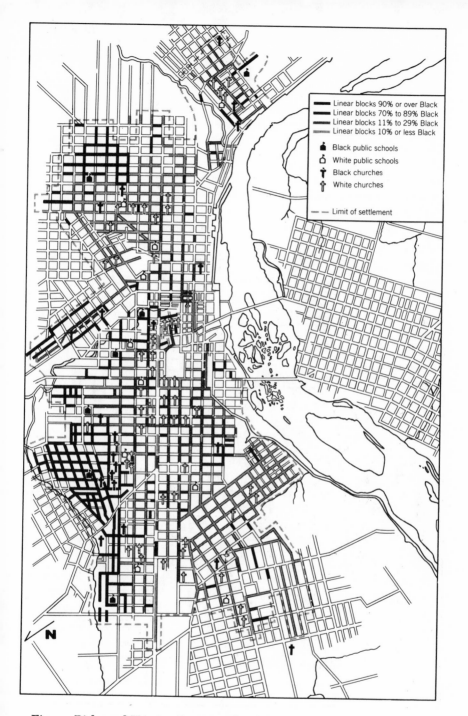

N

Fig. 1   Richmond Housing Patterns, Churches, and Schools, 1891

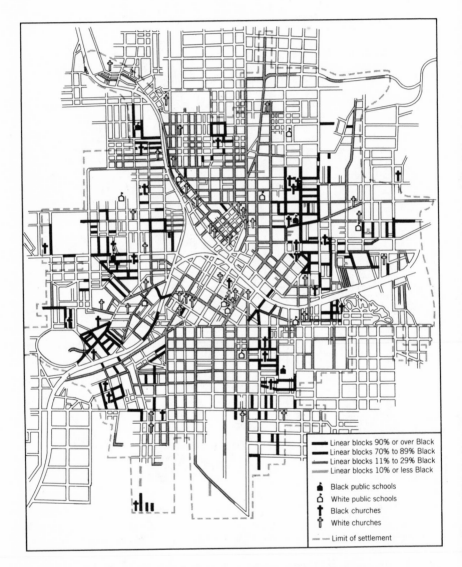

Fig. 2   Atlanta Housing Patterns, Churches, and Schools, 1891

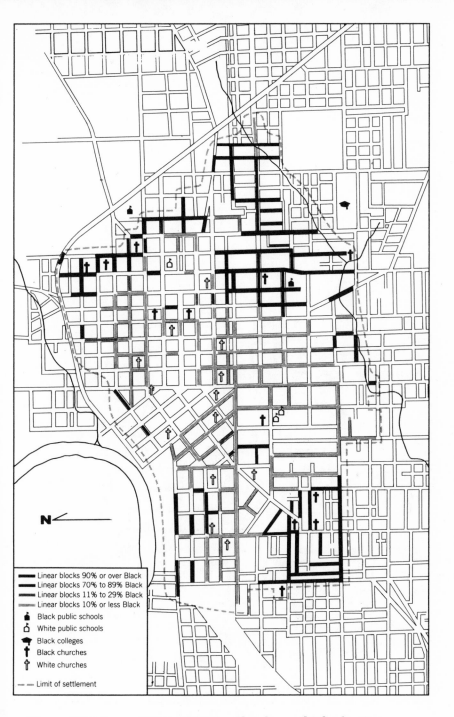

N

Linear blocks 90% or over Black
Linear blocks 70% to 89% Black
Linear blocks 11% to 29% Black
Linear blocks 10% or less Black
Black public schools
White public schools
Black colleges
Black churches
White churches

Limit of settlement

Fig. 3   Montgomery Housing Patterns, Churches, and Schools, 1895

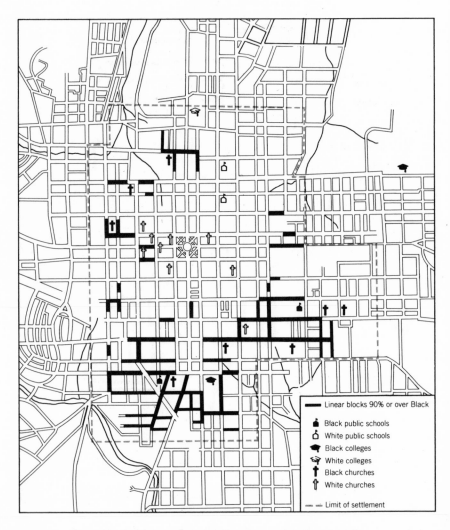

Fig. 4   Raleigh Housing Patterns, Churches, and Schools, 1886

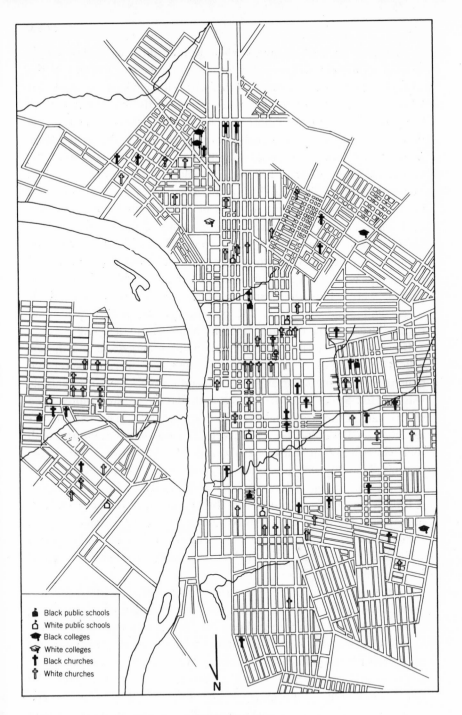

Fig. 5 Nashville Churches and Schools, 1890

That there were a few blocks where at least three out of ten people were of a different race was due largely to the lack of mobility of the white residents. Most of these whites were either widows or unskilled laborers, frequently of foreign stock. Many of the widows had been trapped in changing neighborhoods, while the workers gravitated to these areas because of the cheap housing and proximity to factories, railroads, or saloons. A closer examination reveals that even in the temporary stage of racial balance, intrablock patterns of segregation existed. Although the reliability of the Atlanta directory is limited by the chaotic numbering system used in the city, the order in which names appear conveys an idea of the grouping of races within blocks. On Beach Street, for example, there were nine unskilled laborers; the names of five blacks were grouped together followed by the names of four whites with a space in between. On Venable, eight of the first nine persons were white, the next four black, then six white, one black, seven white, and one black. The presence of two or three vacancies further attests to the change which the block was undergoing.[32]

Because of the accuracy of its house-numbering system and the excellent organization of its directory, Montgomery provides better evidence of an alternating arrangement on certain blocks. A clear example was on Holt Street between Herron and Clay where five whites lived on one side of the street and five blacks on the other. This pattern was repeated on Randolph between North Decatur and Bainbridge with four whites and four blacks living across from one another. The situation on Randolph one block east suggests the next step: there were eight Negroes on one side, six whites and two vacancies on the other. A further variation was present on Hilliard between Houston and Pelham, where Numbers 2, 4, 8 were vacant, Number 6 occupied by an Italian laborer, Numbers 20 and 24 occupied by a white widow and a white laborer, and the rest of the block, including number 22, occupied by thirteen Negroes.[33]

As was already true in 1870 and 1880, grocers joined widows and unskilled laborers to comprise almost the entire number of whites living on black streets. Often foreign-born, they frequently lived sandwiched among blacks as the lone Caucasians on Negro streets. On one block of West Leigh in Richmond's Jackson Ward, there were forty-three Negroes and a white grocer on the corner; on the corner across the street was another white grocer in the midst of fifty-one blacks. Repeated on blocks throughout the ward, this scene was also evident in the concentration of blacks in other parts of the city.[34] Though not as common as in Richmond, the same pattern was found elsewhere. On a block of Bainbridge Street in Montgomery, there was one white grocer on the corner and twenty-two blacks on the rest of the street; on Day Street between South Holt and Godfrey, twenty Negroes and one grocer on the corner; on Dorsett between Luckie and Jeff Davis, twenty blacks and the ubiquitous grocer on the corner of Davis.[35]

Most of these groceries were small frame dwellings which sold meat, vegetables, and liquor. Frequently there was a small saloon attached. As a rule, the owner lived in the rear, although in Montgomery there was a tendency toward absentee proprietors. Many of the grocers, such as Mrs. Mary McManus of Nashville, erected small shanties on their property and rented to blacks.[36] According to Richard Wright, Jr., son of the Georgia black educator and politician, the first white he remembered seeing while growing up in Augusta was the president of Atlanta University; the second was "Schwartz who ran the corner store and sold liquor to our people." Lest there be any doubt as to the respectability of the place, Wright added that "my father warned me not to enter this store unless my mother sent me."[37]

The opposite practice of blacks living in the midst of a white majority reflected the persistence of the antebellum pattern. After the war many freedmen remained to serve their former owners as servants or to do odd jobs for the white neighbors. The tradition against sleep-in help led many of these individuals to move into former slave quarters or to build shanties in alleys behind the whites' houses.[38] Thus, the entries in city directories for fashionable streets such as Franklin, Grace, and Governor in Richmond; Lawrence and Washington in Montgomery; or Peachtree, Washington, and Capitol in Atlanta contain a sprinkling of blacks; the designations of "rear" or "½" suggest the relative status of the occupants. Sometimes the directories listed no occupation for the Negroes; other times, simply "laborer." More often they were listed as cooks, drivers, waiters, and, especially in Montgomery, laundresses and domestics. Obviously these blacks and whites did not live next to one another as neighbors, but rather in an employer-employee relationship.[39]

On occasion, however, Negroes did live among well-off whites as neighbors rather than servants. The Reverend Richard Smith of the C.M.E. Church in Atlanta and the Reverend J. E. Rawlins of Richmond lived on the same blocks as prosperous whites. In Montgomery Ann

Hale, widow of the city's wealthiest Negro, lived among whites on Washington Street.[40] Sometimes a successful small businessman or a Negro skilled laborer lived with whites of a similar status, but such situations were infrequent and frowned upon.

Whatever the cause of Negro sections, economic realities rather than political, moral, or aesthetic considerations determined their locations. Blacks tended to be poor and for this reason found shelter where it was available, preferably near their jobs. In Atlanta, as well as the other four cities, there was a "cluster of negro cottages fronting the cemetery."[41] Land near the cemeteries was undesirable because of the drainage problems and offensive odors; whites generally spurned industrial sites for the same reasons. Nashville's Rolling Mill Hill was the site of numerous houses "occupied almost altogether by colored people."[42] Atlanta's Lousy Flat, adjacent to the ice mill, was another black area. An *Atlanta Constitution* reporter noted that the houses "are scattered on all sides of the ice mill and the occupants can easily hear every pulsation of the engine which makes the ice." Another "nest of negro huts occupied by a multitude of negroes" appeared "just beyond the rolling mills near the old slaughter pen." The city's notorious Beaver Slide, "the filthiest place in Atlanta," was sandwiched between a coffin factory and a large planing mill.[43] And in all the cities pockets of blacks found shelter along the railroad tracks, especially adjacent to the railroad yards. In Nashville a sizable number lived under the Nashville, Chattanooga, and St. Louis trestle on Crawford Street.

Although poor whites could be found near industrial and other unpleasant sites, the alleys and rear dwellings of the cities were almost entirely the province of the blacks. Not every city had a place named Hayti Alley as Raleigh did, but the conditions that produced the name were present in alleys everywhere. They were filthy narrow places, often open sewers, and the breeding grounds of disease and crime. Some were in the downtown area behind leading hotels such as Richmond's Exchange Hotel or Raleigh's Maxwell House; others intersected some of the most fashionable neighborhoods where many blacks lived in former slave quarters. Wherever they appeared, they presented municipal officials, in the words of Nashville's Board of Health, with "the greatest of all city cankers." After compiling a census of alley dwellings, concentrated mainly in the four most populous Negro wards, the Board concluded that "the alleys in Nashville were never intended for resident houses. And almost without exception the houses upon these alleys, now used for tenements, were built for cattle, and not for men."[44]

Not only did blacks live in quarters meant for cattle, but they attempted to survive in low-lying areas of the city subject to frequent flooding and better suited for fish than people. The banks of Bacon's Branch and Shockoe Creek in Richmond, Wilson Spring and Lick Branch in Nashville, and Jeannetta Ditch and Cypress Pond Creek in Montgomery were all centers of Negro habitation. Indeed, the easiest way to locate Negro settlements in a Southern city at the end of the nineteenth century was to find the lowest spots. A housing map could be made from a topographical map, after allowances had been made for alleys and industrial sites.

Within a few years after the war, the nuclei of Atlanta's twentieth-century Negro districts had already been formed. These areas were located in the valleys and bottoms of the six wards, the same wards in which the whites lived along the ridges and atop the hills. The sole exceptions were the areas around the black colleges, especially Atlanta University, which was located on some of the highest land in the city. More typical, however, were the low ground along the Tanyard Branch in the Fifth Ward and the valley east of Capitol Avenue along Fraser, Martin, and Terry, which included the Peasville, Summer Hill, and Peopleton Negro settlements (now the site of the Atlanta Stadium and an interstate highway network). There was also a major concentration of blacks along Decatur Street east of Pratt in Butler Street Bottoms. As the elevation increased on both sides of Butler, the numbers of blacks declined until on the higher streets of Courtland and Jackson there were totally white blocks or, as a white resident of the area crudely phrased it, there were many whites "who reside upon the picturesque heights above the reach of de African scent."[45]

During an 1873 overflow of the Cumberland River which inundated the lower end of Nashville, visitor Edward King reported that "houses were set afloat, negroes were driven from the cabins to the streets, and poverty and distress were great."[46] Evacuation of homes that bordered Wilson Spring, Lick Creek, and the Sulphur Spring was almost an annual occurrence.[47] Hardest hit, however, was the area known for obvious reasons as Black Bottom, where "negroes of the poorest class" lived. There was a natural boundary to this area in the form of higher ground and, "further south, and beyond the hill, some of the best families of Nashville . . . [had] their residences."[48] Working-class whites also lived nearby, but whatever their financial situation or the condition of their homes, whites were spared the major hazards to health and comfort Negroes faced in the Bottom. In 1883 the *Nashville Banner* reported that Black Bottom contained numerous "deep vacant lots . . . which have suffered so much from inundation and have consequently been comparatively worthless to their owners." The following year witnessed a repetition of the familiar scene.

> The lower places in Black Bottom, fed by Wilson Spring Branch, are covered with water to the depth of several feet. The bottom between Cherry and Summer streets, opposite the Negro Pearl School building, is a perfect lake of water. . . . The low places between Cherry and College streets are covered with water. An alley running parallel with and between these two streets, resembles a canal, being covered with water to the depth of three feet for 200 yards. The low grounds between the river front and South Market street are flooded, the water surrounding several houses.[49]

Clearly the residences of blacks in the Southern cities were confined to the least desirable locations. The fact that these sites were scattered throughout the city accounted for the seeming dispersal of the Negro population; the undesirability of the sites and their proximity to unskilled jobs accounted for the concentration of the Negroes within them. But what of the houses themselves? Were they large enough, did they provide sufficient shelter, did they possess conveniences? In short, were they adequate for the maintenance of health and well-being? For a very small part of the Negro community, they were; for the vast majority, however, they could be termed substandard at best.

Some Negroes had prospered and found suitable dwellings comparable to those of most whites. In 1884 the Montgomery *Colored Citizen* expressed pride in the almost exclusively black section known as Peacocks Tract. "It contains over two thousand nice houses and lots, bought and paid for by the colored people. It is laid off in beautiful streets and squares, and its inhabitants are some of our oldest and best citizens."[50] The house of Henry Harding, perhaps Nashville's wealthiest black, bore testimony to the great strides some blacks had made. It was fully carpeted, well furnished, and graced by pictures, paintings, and mirrors on the walls of its large rooms.[51]

Atlanta Negroes made the most progress in the accumulation of real property. Visiting the city in 1868, David Macrae found that 220 Negroes had already built houses. After a Southern inspection tour the following year, a representative of the Freedmen's Union Commission concluded that in the Georgia capital "the colored people are more prosperous and hopeful than in many places. They are turning their thoughts very much to buying land and building houses." In 1883 Professor W. H. Crogman of Clark University told a Northern audience that these early efforts had borne fruit.

> You would be pleased as well as surprised to see the number of comfortable homes the colored people now own in some parts of the city of Atlanta—homes with front yards and shrubbery and croquet wickets sticking up in the grass. Here and there, too, you will find one who is tired of living on the first floor, and so has built him a little two story house.[52]

A few like barber Albert Nash did even better. On a large corner lot he erected a handsome three-story frame house with front and rear porches. Surrounded by attractive foliage, it had the rare advantage of a concrete foundation. It was set on ground higher than the street and was enclosed by a lovely stone wall. A successful merchant, John Schell, had an even more impressive three-story house with a gabled roof and large porch.[53] Other leaders of the Negro community including Carrie Steele Logan (founder of the Negro orphanage), Bob Steele (barber), and David T. Howard (undertaker) had their houses built by the Atlanta Building and Loan Association, a white-owned organization. Run by Joel Hurt, the city's leading builder, it listed among its customers not only prominent citizens such as Henry W. Grady and Hoke Smith, but also many white people of small means and "worthy members of the Negro race."[54] Enough substantial houses had been constructed on Wheat Street so that by 1884 one of the city assessors called it "the fashionable avenue of the colored population." It contained the most valuable house owned by a Negro, a two-story structure worth $3,500.[55] Regardless of the condition of these houses, even the best were still confined to the black areas of the city. As the *Constitution* pointed out, "whenever the rains are unusually heavy Wheat Street suffers severely. Wednesday afternoon it was flooded and the residents were to long for boats."[56]

The majority of blacks, however, enjoyed neither adequate housing nor pleasant surroundings. Exact figures for the composition of the Negro housing market cannot be ascertained without detailed investigation of deeds and building maps, most of which are no longer extant. There is, however, valuable information that varies in quality and quantity for selected cities.

In 1877 the Nashville Board of Health conducted the most thorough survey taken during the period. It reported that the city's blacks "reside mainly in old stables, situated upon alleys in the midst of privy vaults, or in wooden shanties a remnant of war times, or in huts closely crowded together on the outskirts." Almost 60 percent of the white-occupied houses were of brick with an additional 38 percent of frame construction; less than 3 percent (75 residences) were classified as "shanties." Of the 1,352 Negro-occupied buildings, 40 percent were of frame construction and 25 percent of brick; almost 32 percent (431 residences) were "shanties." Less than 50 percent of the white dwellings were one-story, an almost equal number had two stories, and approximately 10 percent had three stories; Negro houses were overwhelmingly one-story (77 percent) with all but seven of the remainder two-story. Although more than a third of the white houses had wet or dry cellars, this was true of less than 6 percent of those occupied by blacks. In other sanitary features as well, Nashville's whites enjoyed a great advantage. In the entire city there were 332 bathtubs, all but one in white homes; this was also true for 459 of the 462 water closets in houses and 117 of the 120 water closets in yards. Negroes held their own with whites only when the numbers of pitts, boxes, and surface privies were tabulated.[57]

Less exact statistics tell the same story for other cities. Although conducted in 1910, a survey by the British Board of Trade in Atlanta accurately described conditions in the city twenty years earlier.

> The typical dwellings of the coloured people contain two or three rooms . . . the whole building . . . consists of one story, built of wood on brick piles. As a rule in the case of two room dwellings there is no entrance lobby, the front room being entered direct from the street. A water supply is seldom provided in the house. A standpipe is placed in the yard and usually serves a number of dwellings. The sanitary conveniences are also grouped together in the yard and shared in common by several tenants. The yards attached to a group of these dwellings are not as a rule fenced off. In many instances the houses look as though built upon a piece of wasteland, with all its inequalities unlevelled, and the yards of the houses are often not to be distinguished from the surrounding plots. The practice of building these little "shacks" on brick piles dispenses with the need for a specially prepared foundation.

The report then briefly treated the three- and very rare four-room vari-
ations of this layout. The whites, on the other hand, frequently had
four-, five-, and six-room cottages. The report concluded that among
workers of similar grades and earnings, "the standard of housing
among the negroes is in general much lower than among the whites."[58]

An 1874 census of Richmond revealed that in Jackson Ward, which
was 70 percent Negro, wooden houses outnumbered brick by three to
one. In the three largest white wards, however, brick houses outnumbered those of wood by as much as four and one-half to one. According
to an 1887 report of the city scavenger, Richmond blacks also experienced the same lack of sanitary facilities as their Atlanta and Nashville
counterparts.[59]

For most blacks the discomforts of poor living conditions were miti-
gated by the freedom which they enjoyed. A Nashville reporter concluded after a tour of the Negro areas in 1872 that for the residents
"to get a house, no matter how small a scale, elevates them to a dignity
and position, and entitles them to be looked up to and venerated ac-
cordingly. They therefore sacrifice everything in the way of good
homes as servants to encompass this end." This desire to be master in
their own homes was noted by an Atlanta real estate agent sixteen
years later. "There is great demand . . . among the colored population
for small houses," he said. "The demand is greater than the supply
and they just take anything in the shape of a small house they can
get." Most of these were rentals. Of the 5,039 houses in Richmond in
1866, 4,671 were owned by whites and only 368 by Negroes.[60] As the
period progressed, more blacks became property owners, but the majority were still renters. In a canvass of a Nashville Negro district conducted in 1896, 77 of the 145 homes were rented, 61 were owned, and
7 were being bought in monthly installments.[61]

Everywhere blacks took what housing they could get. "No one who
has occasion to pass out South Summer Street has failed to notice the
old frame rookery, which stands, ready to topple over from age and
decay, on the side of the Wilson Spring Branch," observed the Nashville *Republican Banner* in September 1872. "It is two stories high,
with a basement. It has been divided and subdivided until it has
grown as checkered as the career of its hundred colored tenants who
manage barely to eke out a precarious existence." Home to many was
a single room; if they were fortunate, it contained only one family.
"Not houses but rooms contain each a family" remarked the Raleigh

News and Observer about the lower-class black sections of its city. An Atlanta Negro, a cripple named George Robinson, lived with his wife and handicapped five-year-old son in one room of a two-room structure, while two black women occupied the other.[62] On South High Street in Nashville, just beyond Ash, there was a row of three small double tenement houses, all occupied by Negroes. In the northern half of the third house lived a woman, her two younger brothers, her son, and a male boarder. Another Nashville house on Summer Street, described as "a first class rat harbor," had four rooms, each containing a different Negro family.[63]

Unsanitary housing meant high mortality rates. Although there was a decline in the official death rate for blacks during the period, at best it only kept pace with the dip in the death rate of whites and the gap between the two groups remained about the same.[64] Poor living conditions not only took their yearly toll in deaths from the constant companions of consumption and pneumonia, but periodically the black areas were ravished by epidemics of cholera, smallpox, and, to a lesser extent, yellow fever. Whites also contracted these diseases, but in far fewer numbers. To plot the appearance of these maladies is to pinpoint the Negro areas of the city. In 1882, for example, an outbreak of smallpox in Nashville was limited mainly to the "areas outside the city limits and in localities peopled almost entirely by colored people."[65] That same year in Atlanta an especially serious outbreak of smallpox was confined primarily to Negro sections such as the notorious Beaver Slide, a group of four old ill-ventilated and filthy shanties in the rear of the equally unsanitary Willingham Building on Ivy Street.[66]

Vaccination could prevent smallpox; cholera, on the other hand, posed a greater threat because only healthful surroundings could provide immunity. It is not surprising, therefore, that the cholera outbreak in Richmond in 1866 began in a Negro area near the Lancasterian schoolhouse and adjoining Shockoe Creek Bridge. According to a contemporary account, the creek, "although a running stream, is yet a depository of dead cats and dogs, while grass and weeds grow and decay upon its banks."[67] There was a great loss of life, but nothing compared with the epidemics Nashville faced. During an outbreak in 1866, the victims were mainly from the black settlements in the vicinity of Lick Creek, Brooks Alley, and the outskirts of town.[68] In 1873 the dreaded disease killed approximately nine hundred people, probably two-thirds of them black. According to a physician, the cholera appeared first in the

Negro section "known as Wilson Spring neighborhood, a bed for all epidemics that reach Nashville." The *Republican Banner* noted six days later that although South Nashville had become comparatively free of it, the epidemic "has followed the course of the western depression and now prevails along the Lick Branch bottom more than anywhere else." The chief sufferers were "principally among colored people and those persons who have already been pretty badly used up by habitual dissipations."[69]

The newspapers, boards of health, and public officials decried the unsanitary conditions under which blacks lived and urged an immediate improvement. "Certainly the African race whose splendid labor has both before and since the days of revolutionary strife, done so much for the United States and whose excellent temper was so admirably displayed in days of bloodshed and devastation," argued the Nashville Board of Health in a survey of housing conditions, "deserve better of the American people than to be allowed to perish in the stables and hovels of cities."[70] In the minds of most whites the solution was to get the blacks out of the cities and onto the farms where healthful conditions prevailed; short of this, some effort should be made to rid these areas of their worst slums.

Few of the critics were solely motivated by concern for the blacks, for the realities of urban life meant that what adversely affected one neighborhood might eventually threaten the entire city. A letter writer to the *Montgomery Daily Advertiser* voiced his dismay in 1865 at the influx of Negroes to the city and their crowding together in unsanitary quarters.

> If an epidemic should break out anywhere among them, it would spread over this city with a most terrible fatality to white and black. It is almost or quite impossible to keep the city in a proper sanitary condition; and it will be almost a miracle if we should escape. Everything demands that these idle, lazy, thieving negroes should be perforce placed out in healthy districts and made to work.

The following year the *Richmond Dispatch* under the heading of "The Hot Beds of Disease in Richmond" described some of the worst houses in the city, practically all of them occupied by blacks. Included were a house in Exchange Alley inhabited by more than one hundred Negroes and the rooms over Ruskell's Stables on Wall Street, "densely packed with negro men, women and children." More than twenty years later in 1887 the *Nashville Banner* echoed this fear of the possible effects upon the whole city of disease-prone black neighborhoods. Typically it singled out Black Bottom, which whites living on higher ground had to pass on the way to the business district. The absence of sewer connections and the resultant filth and stagnant water surrounding numerous Negro shanties led the reporter to conclude that "if the city should be visited by any epidemic this neighborhood will prove a most potent help to its spreading." One man was heard to say that "if the South Nashville streetcars don't take to running faster, we will all take malaria in passing through."[71]

Despite such fears, the municipal governments did little to provide those public services that would have ameliorated the situation. Nashville's Black Bottom was not alone in lacking adequate sewers, although such facilities were necessary to receive the drainage from higher ground. A Nashville sanitary survey taken in 1877 disclosed 425 instances of sewage drainage for white-occupied houses and only 15 for blacks, 45 examples of surface sewage for whites and 6 for blacks, and 25 subterranean outlets, all of them for whites.[72] For years residents of Atlanta's Fourth Ward, which contained the largest number of Negroes, suffered because of the lack of a sewer in the vicinity of Butler Street, one of the lowest points in the city and entirely Negro. In 1890 the issue finally surfaced, thanks to pressure from white residents affected by the unpleasant consequences.[73] According to the *Atlanta Constitution,*

> There are probably more reasons for building a sewer along the Butler street branch than in any other portion of the city where there are no sewers. The branch is in the bottom of a deep valley and drains most of the fourth ward, the residents of which complain that this open branch, with its constantly moving charge of impure matter, is very unhealthy and injurious to the ward. . . . It will be for the benefit of the whole city and may save in the prevention of disease, much more than it will cost.

After almost a year of lobbying, the extension was finally authorized, but the date of actual construction is not known.[74]

The cities dragged their feet in providing other needed improvements to Negro neighborhoods. Voicing a complaint common to most Southern Negro communities, Richmond's *Virginia Star* bemoaned the lack of streetlights and free water. The absence of adequate water was of special concern. In accounting for a Negro death rate nearly two and one-half times greater than that of the whites as late as 1885, Atlanta

Mayor Hillyer told the Council that improvement would follow "if good clear water were supplied to all the lower levels of the city, where so many of the colored people live, and their contaminated wells were all filled up and obliterated." Nothing was done, however, and the city even refused to remove contaminated water. Three years after the mayor's plea Fifth Ward voters protested about the "dozen pools of green water" in May's Alley and accused their white councilman of ignoring their part of the ward in favor of a white section.[75]

There were pools of water in May's Alley because the alley was not paved. This was true of all alleys as well as the streets on which blacks lived. "One of the leading thoroughfares is in the rear of the fourth ward," reported the *Atlanta Constitution*, "and is called 'Mudhole street.'" "M.K.B." complained in an 1889 letter to the *Constitution* about West Hunter Street from Atlanta University to downtown. Although hundreds of people used it on their way to work, it was "utterly without sidewalks" and the street itself was "made up of ditches and gullies."[76]

Other public services and conveniences found in white sections were absent. An *Atlanta Constitution* reporter who interviewed the president of Atlanta University in 1887 commented that Mitchell Street was very nice, but it "would be far more picturesque and pleasant with a street car line traversing its many graceful grades." This area of Negro settlement, he said, also should have paved sidewalks instead of the "red and yielding loam." Writing in the third person about his ordeal to reach the campus from the center of town, he observed that "five-ten-fifteen minutes rolled on and the reporter found himself panting for breath at the foot of the last long hill which leads to Atlanta University. . . . Five more 'toiling moments'" passed before he reached the school, although he needed "a brief blowing spell [which] pulled himself together for a last supreme effort." Allowing for overdramatization, the sizable black population living in the area clearly faced great difficulty in traveling to jobs, schools, or even downtown. Even when streetcar service existed, it was unsatisfactory. As of 1900, Richmond's Jackson Ward had twenty-minute service on a single-track line; nearby white areas had five- and ten-minute service on double-track lines.[77]

Black neighborhoods also lacked adequate fire protection. In 1887 a fire destroyed Union Hall, one of the main buildings of Atlanta's Spelman College, causing $15,000 damage. Although the fire department "responded promptly," a two-mile run over rough roads made it impossible to reach the scene in time to do more than keep the fire from spreading to the adjoining buildings. The chief engineer of the Richmond Fire Department suggested building a small firehouse in Jackson Ward because of "the rapid increase of frame buildings, which are highly inflammable."[78] Yet no action was taken. Nor was there any positive reply to requests by residents and the Board of Health for the construction of a park in Jackson Ward, even though all the other wards had at least two while Jackson had none.[79]

Despite frequent pleas by both concerned blacks and whites to improve the conditions in the Negro sections of the cities, there was little progress by the end of the period. The major response was an early form of urban renewal which, even then, took the additional form of Negro removal. "Six or eight negro shanties situated on South Cherry street near the corner of Franklin, have been torn away and a lumberyard taken their place," reported Nashville's *Daily American* in 1878. A decade later the *Nashville Banner* observed that "General Thruston is building three handsome brick cottages on Summer street, below Line, to take the place of some old shanties once occupied by negroes." In 1875 the Richmond City Council voted to buy the area on Chimborazo Heights "where negroes live in squalid filth" and turn it into a public park. Atlantans provided a fitting climax to the period as Negro shanties on Foster Street became the main casualty of the opening of Edgewood Avenue in the mid-1880s to provide easier access to the center of the city from white suburban developments. A more positive approach to the problem was taken by Nashville with its periodic annexations of surrounding localities, partly caused by the desire to bring these areas under the control of the Board of Health.[80]

Long before the end of the century, housing for most Southern urban Negroes meant inadequate shelter, disease-ridden environments, and residential segregation. The mass of substandard housing was left untouched to fester and blot the face of the urban centers. For the most part Negro shanties were out of sight "in the least frequented portions of the city," according to the Montgomery city physician.[81] Only when the whites had to pass on the way to work, such as the case with Nashville's Black Bottom, was the civic conscience aroused. Whether under the Radicals or the Redeemers, the situation was little changed.

II

FROM EXCLUSION TO SEGREGATION

Segregated job opportunities and housing generally constituted set-backs for blacks. Nevertheless, segregation in other areas of Southern life ironically often signified an improvement, for what it replaced was not integration but exclusion. The pattern was clearest in welfare services, education, and militia service, but also was present in a variety of public accommodations and institutions of the black community.

Segregation was neither a tactic invented by the Redeemers to punish blacks nor the result of a bargain between Democrats and Populists in the 1890s to forestall Negroes from becoming a pivotal force in Southern politics. It was the Northerners in the form of the U.S. Army, the Freedmen's Bureau, and Republican politicians who together with their Southern allies inaugurated much of the segregation. White Republicans, elected largely by Negro votes, wanted to improve the lives of their chief supporters; but, as was true of their Northern predecessors, the major concern was an end to exclusion. Integration was rarely considered, although blacks were promised facilities equal to those of whites.

Many Republicans were Southerners who still believed in Negro inferiority; most Northerners had never been free from such prejudice either. Nor were the realities of power lost on these men. Strongly anti-Negro mountain whites in North Carolina, Tennessee, and Alabama formed a major part of the Republican coalition and integration would have constituted an obvious affront, costing many votes. Similarly, if the Republicans elsewhere were to stay in power, allies needed to be attracted from among independents, former Whigs, and even Democrats. The professed policy of separate but equal had the benefit of minimizing white hostility while still presenting the blacks with a significant improvement over their treatment at the hands of earlier administrations.

Negroes themselves favored this policy over exclusion. Along with their white allies, they believed, or at least hoped, that separate treatment could be truly equal. Protests against segregation were primarily confined to the area of public accommodations where from 1875 to 1883 blacks had the law on their side. Equal access rather than integration was their chief aim. As a result, they convinced any doubting whites that they too wanted segregation. Their decision to form separate churches immediately after the war further strengthened this impression.

6

Health and Welfare Services and Correctional Institutions

The poor living conditions and low-paying jobs of the black migrants created unprecedented health and welfare problems for white urban dwellers. Before the Civil War public officials had been spared the burden of supporting large numbers of ill and indigent blacks: slave welfare had been the responsibility of the master, while free Negroes had been left to fend for themselves. The growing number of ante-bellum local institutions such as orphanages, hospitals, and almshouses or state facilities such as insane asylums and institutions for the blind, deaf, and dumb were limited, with few exceptions, to whites. Even jails and penitentiaries contained few Negroes, since punishment generally came from the lash of the master or the public whipper.[1]

Emancipation left open the questions of who would assume the responsibility for the needy and criminal freedmen and on what basis. In other words, would the antebellum policy of exclusion be retained and, if not, what would replace it? Conflict arose between those who favored public responsibility for the care of the indigent or ill blacks and those who denied the necessity of such action. At various times from 1865 to 1890 missionary societies, the Freedmen's Bureau, the United States Army, Southern whites, and the Negroes themselves shouldered the burden. What finally emerged was a shift from a policy of exclusion to one of segregation. Integrated access to services was rarely considered and even less often permitted. By 1890 the announced goal of the Southern welfare policy was the acceptance of blacks in institutions on the basis of separate but equal treatment.

Public affirmations aside, however, the system in reality rarely functioned on a basis other than separate but unequal treatment.

The beleaguered cities, short of funds sufficient to perform even their normal services and in any case determined to perpetuate antebellum welfare policy, initially sought to evade the responsibility of providing food and shelter to needy blacks. A Montgomery newspaper during the summer of 1865 urged citizens to aid the suffering poor in their midst, but emphasized that "our remarks are in behalf of the destitute *white* population; the Freedmen's Bureau will doubtless look after the destitute freedmen." Within two years the county built a poorhouse solely for the use of white paupers.[2]

The Bureau, with the aid of the Army and Northern benevolent societies, at first did care for these Negroes and by so doing paved the way for the adoption of segregated facilities by municipal administrations. During the extremely cold Richmond winter of 1866–1867, the American Missionary Association processed an average of one hundred black applicants for relief each day. These individuals were given sticks of wood and a small amount of meal immediately. If they required further assistance, they were referred to the Bureau.[3] Beginning in 1868, the Bureau used the same procedure in its soup kitchens in the Alabama towns of Montgomery, Mobile, Huntsville, and Selma.[4] The Bureau and the societies also cooperated in the founding of orphanages for blacks in Richmond, Atlanta, and Nashville[5]; and in all the cities, the combined Northern forces temporarily dispensed clothing to destitute blacks.[6]

It proved difficult to transfer the responsibility for poor Negroes from federal to local officials. This shift is obscure in most cities, but in Richmond it can be clearly traced in the City Council minutes. In November 1865 the Council received a letter from the Assistant Commissioner of the Freedmen's Bureau in Virginia informing it to make provisions for 260 Richmond black paupers then under the Bureau's care. A month later whites were forbidden from turning out their infirm former slaves until local authorities made arrangements for their support. Yet as of May 1866, the Richmond City Council had not moved in this direction. It instead notified the Bureau that supervision of the freedmen would be undertaken only after a corresponding transfer of authority in judicial matters. Besides, added the Council, "the colored population has . . . been increased by a vast influx from the surrounding country" and the city was "having trouble providing for the white poor." In August 1867 General John Schofield, the state military commander, ordered Virginia overseers of the poor and superintendents of the almshouses "to receive and provide for all indigent colored people now in the charge of the Freedmen's Bureau." This time the Council objected on the ground that it had to assume responsibility for nonresidents and in any case, the strain on the treasury meant that it had only inadequate facilities. After further footdragging, the Council appropriated money for the task in the fall. In January 1868 the first blacks finally entered the almshouse.[7]

Similar negotiations occurred elsewhere. The Bureau had to prod Nashville officials by giving $1,000 for the care of the sick in return for a guarantee that they would admit Negroes to the poorhouse. But, while federal authorities were cajoling or forcing local governments to accept blacks in their almshouses, segregation had become a reality. Nor was this situation altered once municipalities assumed jurisdiction. As the first Negro paupers entered the old Nashville poorhouse in August 1866, the white paupers moved into new quarters. A similar situation occurred in Richmond two years later.[8]

In addition to permitting blacks in the almshouses, municipal administrations gradually provided other assistance. Out-relief consisting of fuel or food became available once the cities abandoned reliance on the Freedmen's Bureau. An 1866 Atlanta ordinance established a sliding scale of fees to be given the marshal or deputy marshal for distributing rations to whites, blacks, and black insane. During the same year the North Carolina legislature gave local justices of the peace the power to elect "two distinct and independent courts of wardens" for the poor, one for blacks and one for whites.[9]

The cities could not afford to neglect a second responsibility—the burial of black paupers. Since antebellum times three cities—Nashville, Raleigh, and Richmond—had by ordinance enforced racial segregation in their municipal cemeteries. Montgomery and Atlanta had *de facto* rather than *de jure* segregation. With the end of the war, these practices continued and much of the cities' aid to the Negroes consisted of burying their paupers. In Montgomery, for example, from December 1866 to April 1877, all but 6 of the 136 paupers interred in Potter's Field were black. In Atlanta five randomly chosen months for the years 1868 to 1872 disclose 21 white pauper burials as compared to 129 for blacks.[10]

Whites pointed to the seeming degeneration among Negroes as

proof that life in the country as a slave was superior to life in the city as a free man. According to the *Montgomery Daily Ledger,* freedom was "prejudicial" to the health of Montgomery Negroes:

> When slaves, they could be up early and late, labor hard, expose themselves in all kinds of weather and seldom complain or take to their beds. Now they seem unable to perform half the labor to which they have been accustomed, the least exposure throws them.

Nor could the freedmen count on the supervision and help that they allegedly received as slaves. The newspaper later pointed to the case of a Negro mother who climbed into an abandoned dump cart after giving birth to a child on the ground. After she died from lack of care, hogs came along and ate her infant. The editor charged the Freedmen's Bureau with criminal negligence and claimed that such a thing would never have occurred under slavery. A black woman found dead of starvation in the streets of Richmond prompted a similar reply by the *Richmond Dispatch.* A few days later the newspaper observed that the winter closing of the tobacco factories would especially hurt the black worker because, in contrast to the pre-Civil War days, "he is only employed when he is wanted."[11]

Ill Negroes may or may not have been able to count on their "friends" in the countryside, but they could expect little from the Conservative governments brought into power by Presidential Reconstruction. Despite their need for medical care, blacks continued to be largely excluded from local hospitals. Richmond's public dispensary and system of city physicians inaugurated in 1867, for example, was solely for the benefit of indigent whites.[12]

The Freedmen's Bureau and the Army once again countered exclusionary policies with segregated facilities. In Nashville, despite the opposition of neighbors, the Bureau converted two buildings near the penitentiary into freedmen hospitals. During an 1865 epidemic in Montgomery, the Assistant Superintendent of Freedmen offered to accept at the army hospital "all cases of small pox without distinction of color, for treatment." He added, however, that "Should tents be used, a separate tent will be assigned to white patients, and every effort made for their comfort." During the same year, a white woman and her two sick children were refused entrance to the army hospital in Atlanta because it was only for blacks. No other local facility was available so they had to be sent to Chattanooga.[13]

Mental illnesses also plagued the former slaves so the Bureau entered this area of health care as well. Virginia, which alone among the five states had provided for Negroes in its antebellum insane asylums, was one of two to admit them during Presidential Reconstruction. Before the war Negroes—or "as many of them as can be accommodated after all the white insane applying for admission"—were assigned rooms in the basement of the Eastern Lunatic Asylum at Williamsburg. In 1865 the Freedmen's Bureau cared for sick and insane blacks in a former Confederate army hospital near Richmond. Four years later the state's military commander made the institution a state asylum. The Bureau continued to pay its expenses through the following February when control was turned over entirely to the reorganized state government. The few Negro insane in the Williamsburg asylum were transferred to the hospital and nonresidents were sent to the Freedmen's Hospital in Washington, D.C.[14]

Ignoring Virginia's "conditional" policy, Tennessee's leading Radical journal boasted in 1866 that "Tennessee has the honor of being the first state to make special provision for her insane colored people."[15] A Republican legislature had just authorized the Tennessee Hospital for the Insane to construct quarters for the Negro insane in Nashville "so as to keep them secure and safe, and yet separate and apart from the white patients." The first blacks moved into a three-story brick building near the structure for the whites in 1868. About the same time the Republican-controlled North Carolina legislature set aside separate quarters for Negroes at the state insane asylum in Raleigh and founded the Negro department at the Institution for the Blind, Deaf, and Dumb.[16]

There were fewer public facilities on the local level, but in those that existed, the same pattern was evident. Montgomery Radicals, for example, operated a city hospital divided into white and black wards, while the Radicals in charge of the county government appropriated 75 cents per day for each inmate of the segregated county poorhouse and hospital. Radicals retained segregated cemeteries in all five cities and in Raleigh took steps to make the segregation even more pronounced. In 1868 the City Council opened a separate city graveyard for Negroes. Blacks could still be buried in their section of the old cemetery, but lot prices were lower in the new one so as to attract more customers.[17]

The Republicans did make an important break with past practice. Even though segregated, some public institutions were opened to blacks for the first time. In other instances such as the Richmond and Nashville almshouses or the Virginia insane asylum, the Radicals administered segregated institutions that the military had forced upon the postwar Conservative governments.[18] The justification, it must be remembered, was equal access. But the Republicans were in power for such a short period that they had time to institute merely a small portion of the welfare apparatus freedmen needed. When the Republicans surrendered office, only Richmond and Montgomery had public hospitals; only Richmond provided for its Negro orphans. Certain state institutions continued to exclude Negroes, and relief and medical aid were still less available for blacks than for whites. Therefore, it was the Redeemers, many of them former slave owners and veterans of the Confederate Army, who determined the quality and quantity of welfare facilities for blacks during the largest segment of the period.

Many of the Redeemers had taken part in the first postwar white governments that had excluded Negroes from health and welfare services. Since 1867 the quality of life for most urban blacks had improved little. Despite pleas that they return to the countryside,[19] the number of urban blacks increased each year. Democratic officials frequently called attention to the miserable living conditions of the Negroes in seeking to account for their high death rates. Sometimes they hedged and blamed the "inherent weaknesses" of the race, a subtle way of extolling the virtues of slavery.[20] But the head of the Richmond Board of Health put the blame for the high mortality rate squarely where it belonged. It was not due to "race constitutional defects," he said. The main causes were poverty and overcrowding.[21]

The search for a solution to this problem of needy blacks divided the Redeemers. Some felt that to provide services would encourage the influx of more Negroes to the cities, whereas by providing fewer ones, many of the blacks already there would return to the land. Few expressed such views openly, preferring instead to oppose new facilities because of alleged lack of funds. Much of the opposition only can be inferred from the defeats suffered by proponents of greater aid to Negroes. In 1881 the president of the Richmond Board of Health urged city officials to provide more help since "the care and the protection of the colored race now rests on us." Five years later he pointed to the "legion of old colored midwives" who practiced almost exclusively on the blacks. The resultant high Negro infant mortality, he said, "appeals to our liberality to furnish physicians to attend the indigent class."[22]

Nevertheless, the Redeemer city councils sometimes reverted to the practice of excluding Negroes from poor relief or medical assistance. Some public services were abolished, thus depriving whites as well as blacks of their benefits. In such instances the Negroes were worse hit since the whites usually found succor elsewhere. When Montgomery's Democrats won full control of the city government in 1875, the newly elected mayor closed the public hospital as part of his retrenchment program.[23] In similar fashion the Redeemer state legislature closed the Freedmen's Hospital established by the Radicals near Talladega.[24] In Nashville, where the Democrats accused Republican Mayor Thomas A. Kercheval of using poor relief as a device to attract Negro voters to his party, the Redeemers abolished the system of municipal out-relief. After Kercheval regained power, the Democratic-controlled Council thwarted his efforts to reestablish the old system of public charity.[25] Throughout the rest of the period the city expected the county asylum and private relief organizations to bear the welfare burden.

Concern over the possibility that undeserving blacks would benefit from public assistance was as much a factor as the political considerations. Newspapers were especially conscious of the allegedly great number of blacks who, though able to work, preferred to beg. "There are a number of trifling negroes who, constitutionally opposed to work, are commencing the winter campaign by the usual programme of living on charity," the *Nashville Banner* charged. Referring to a recent distribution of alms, the *Atlanta Constitution* noted that in the crowd were a number of blacks "in good health, strong of limb, and more comfortably dressed than some of the whites who were dispensing charity." The newspaper was happy to report that they "were properly dealt with," but it was upset that "the negroes . . . disgrace themselves by such exhibitions." In 1888 Atlanta abolished the office of Warden of the Poor and turned over the job of dispensing out-relief to a member of the police force to assure that applicants would receive careful scrutiny.[26]

Not only were Negroes cut off from certain services they had previously received, but they continued to be excluded from many of the older welfare facilities. In addition, several new institutions which opened during Reconstruction were only for whites. Perhaps because

HEALTH AND WELFARE SERVICES

they had educational as well as welfare functions, orphanages would not accept blacks even on a segregated basis. Davidson County (Nashville) supported three orphanages; Richmond had contributed to four since antebellum times; Fulton County (Atlanta) contributed to at least two others.[27] Despite receiving public tax money, all of them were restricted to whites. The same was true of the all-white state orphanages founded in Georgia in 1869 and in North Carolina in 1872 and the state-supported Alabama Baptist Orphans Home established in 1870.[28] Both the city and state governments went even further, however, and generally refused to provide public funds for Negro orphans housed in separate institutions. Two private facilities, Richmond's Friends Asylum for Colored Orphans and Atlanta's Carrie Steele Orphan Home, and the state-run North Carolina Colored Orphan Asylum, founded in 1887, were the sole exceptions.[29]

Officials were even more intransigent with regard to supporting Negro "fallen" or destitute women. Although Richmond, Nashville, and Atlanta made generous appropriations to private institutions which cared for white women, they made no provisions for blacks. Once again a minority of Redeemers attempted to broaden the scope of such concern. When a special committee of the Atlanta City Council advised that $50 per month be given both to the Home for the Friendless and to the Women's Christian Home, one member objected to the racially restricted character of the aid. The chairman of the committee replied that, "whenever the negroes get up a home of their own, I will be willing to help them."[30] The period closed without any such black facility.

Negroes also continued to be barred from most local hospitals. This was especially true of private institutions. All of those in Richmond during the 1870s and 1880s were strictly for whites. In Atlanta the city government paid private hospitals to take care of indigent patients. Finding facilities that would accept Negroes proved difficult, however, and for several years blacks did not receive similar benefits. "There has been no place for the sick of our colored population," wrote the mayor in 1881, "and I have been compelled to resort to private parties to furnish places and nurses for them." Sometimes the municipal officials contributed even more directly to exclusionary practices; the public hospital in Raleigh, for example, admitted only whites.[31]

Nonetheless, despite an occasional reversion to the policy of exclusion or its continuation where the Radicals had left it undisturbe~

Redeemers' most frequent response to the legacy of Radical rule was to endorse the shift from exclusion to segregation. It must be remembered, however, that the Redeemers were not a monolithic group, even within a given city or city council. Whether due to fear of Northern intervention if Negroes did not receive adequate attention or because of paternalistic or political impulses, some Democrats supported aid to blacks and publicly reaffirmed the Radical principle that separate treatment was to be equal treatment. When plans were made in 1876 for the opening of a Jim Crow institution for Georgia's Negro deaf and dumb, the legislature ordered that "the present Board of Trustess [of the white institution] will act for this colored institution and conduct it, in all respects as the present one of the whites is conducted."[32] The annex of Atlanta Hospital to be completed in 1880 was for Negro patients, "who will receive every attention bestowed on the whites." And the final justice: "Every grave which the keeper has dug," read a Richmond ordinance, "whether for the body of a white or colored person, shall be at least six feet deep."[33]

But the implementation of plans for Negro accommodations frequently met with delays, and, in cases such as the Atlanta Hospital, never came to fruition. In explaining why Negroes were still barred from the Georgia Institution for the Deaf and Dumb in 1873, the Board of Commissioners stated that "it was incompatible with the general school law that blacks and whites should be educated together." They felt that it was now time to spend $6,000 for the separate accommodation of blacks. Money was finally appropriated in 1876 for a Negro department to be opened when there were ten or more applicants. The bill provided that the Negro division

> shall, in all respects, be conducted separate from the other institution; . . . the funds appropriated for its use to be a separate fund; the teachers and all other employees to be as distinctly separate as though the two institutions were in different towns.

Yet the school did not open until March 1882. Four months earlier the Negro department of the Georgia Academy for the Blind had opened in Macon in separate quarters far apart from the whites. The existence of the Macon facility was due in part to the urging of the superintendent of the Academy, first expressed in 1880, that "all those reasons which move us to educate the blind of one race are equally strong in the case of the other."[34]

The exchanges between the state legislature and the principal of the Alabama Institution for the Deaf and Dumb and Blind even more graphically demonstrate the split among public officials and the reluctance of legislators to accept obligation for the care of black dependents. In his annual report for 1884, the principal sadly observed that he could "hardly see how the state can afford longer to *neglect entirely* the colored deaf and dumb and blind youth growing up in our midst." His pleas continued in subsequent reports and his report for 1890 termed a Negro department "*a great public need*" and appealed for "justice [for] these unfortunate classes." Two years later the legislature finally responded with an appropriation of $12,000. Placed in charge of the principal of the white school but with a separate staff of white teachers, the new department opened in January 1892. In Virginia care for this disadvantaged group was not seriously considered until 1896; and it was not until September 1909 that the Virginia School for the Colored Deaf and Blind Children belatedly opened outside Newport News.[35]

Whenever possible the Redeemers fortified the separation initiated by the Radicals. Negroes who had occupied the six lower wards of the main building at the Alabama insane asylum during Reconstruction were moved by Redeemers into separate quarters nearby. North Carolina Redeemers immediately sought to transfer the blacks at the Raleigh asylum to one to be built in Wilmington. After delays due to a shortage of funds, the Negro institution was finally built in Goldsboro in 1880. And in both Raleigh and Atlanta, Redeemer councils passed stricter regulations regarding separation of the races in the cemeteries.[36]

Segregation was also present in welfare services and institutions established after Redemption. During the winter of 1874, for example, the Richmond office which handed out food and fuel to the poor was open to whites in the morning and to blacks in the afternoon; during the rest of the year, whites got aid on Thursdays and blacks on Fridays. In response to a serious outbreak of smallpox in 1881, Atlanta officials instituted a system of compulsory free vaccinations with separate downtown offices for each race. The state of Tennessee added a Negro department when it assumed direction of the privately-run all-white Tennessee Industrial School in 1887.[37]

Although most of Atlanta's hospitals would admit only indigent white patients referred by the city, the local government finally convinced the Ivy Street Hospital and Providence Infirmary to accept indigents of both races. A possible reason for the change in policy of these two hospitals was their connection with the Southern Medical College which used charity patients "for the promotion of medical teaching."[38] Once admitted the Negroes were treated in segregated wards. Indeed, segregated facilities had been included in every plan for a public hospital in Atlanta since the early 1870s. In 1888 a group of physicians urged that while "equal provision" should be made for whites and blacks, there should be widely separate wards and entrances for each race.[39] The new institution, named after Henry W. Grady, opened with its segregated wards and entrances in 1892. It followed by two years the opening of Nashville's segregated municipal hospital.[40]

The Redeemers moved in the same direction in correctional institutions. It is not necessary to adopt completely the view that nineteenth-century orphanages, insane asylums, hospitals, poorhouses, and other welfare institutions were the products of the same desire for social control that produced prisons to see the similarities shared by all of these facilities.[41] Clearly all reflected the growing trend toward confinement as a means of dealing with pressing problems and achieving rehabilitation. They were also linked by a shift from exclusion to segregation in their response toward blacks.

Confinement of blacks in penitentiaries and local jails was largely a postwar development for in antebellum times Negro criminals were more likely to be whipped than incarcerated. "Before the emancipation of the slaves," wrote the governor of Tennessee in 1875, "there were never more than 15 or 20 colored convicts [in the state penitentiary] while now there are 505 colored convicts and only 380 whites."[42]

As a result of the influx of black prisoners, social control became as much a problem within the correctional institutions as in the outside world. A committee of the Georgia legislature recommended in 1866 that Negro and white convicts receive equal punishment, but added that "under no circumstances should a social equality be recognized—not even in the worst cases of felony."[43] Nevertheless, segregation was possible only if there was sufficient space. When room was limited, blacks and whites were confined together despite the desires of law enforcement officials.[44]

One way to prevent the mixture of the races at small penitentiaries was to lease out black prisoners. This plan had the added advantages of providing favored employers with cheap labor and the state government with extra revenue.[45] But this inhumane and corrupt system came under increasing criticism.

The need for segregation was uppermost in the minds of Georgia officials who sought alternatives to the lease system. In 1875 the Keeper of the Penitentiary proposed substituting the islands off Savannah as penal colonies. "It would be my policy," he averred, "to separate the whites and blacks, working them on distinct farms." The lease system was kept, however, and after a trip to one of the camps, the keeper reported approvingly that in the barracks "the white men sleep to themselves on one side of the building."[46] Most of the camps were in fact composed exclusively of Negroes so that intra-camp segregation was usually unnecessary. Laws passed in 1888 and 1890 decreed that white and black prisoners were not to work or be confined together, adding legal sanction to customs and attitudes already governing behavior.[47]

Although males were segregated in Alabama state prison camps by 1882, because of overcrowding, white women convicted of adultery with Negroes occupied the same cells as Negro women. The warden complained, calling for the complete segregation of prisoners in one large prison. By 1884 the two main prison camps for leased convicts had separate quarters for the races; in at least one of them two rows of tubs stood in the newly erected bathhouse—one side for blacks and the other for whites. Six years later Wetumpka Prison where nonleased convicts were confined had a different building for each race.[48]

Integration was more common in local jails and workhouses. But as in the state prisons, whether or not segregation was employed depended mainly on the size of the facility; whether or not segregation appeared in descriptions of jails depended on the observer. In Richmond, for example, neither the City Council minutes nor the yearly reports of the various city departments concerning the jail mention racial separation, yet an inspection committee appointed by the Hustings Court in 1882 reported that the races occupied cells on the opposite sides of the building. Accounts for subsequent years continued to note this arrangement as well as the existence of Jim Crow bathtubs by 1889.[49] Questions remain about the nature of pre-1882 policy.

No matter how much officials desired segregated quarters, integration in small jails was often unavoidable. Not until the end of the period, for example, did the construction of large jails in Atlanta and Nashville assure racial segregation.[50] By 1889 the Fulton County jail as well as the Atlanta city jail was segregated; plans drawn the following year for a new stockade for county chain gang convicts included separate bathtubs for whites and blacks. By 1890 Raleigh also had a segregated jail, workhouse, and chain gang camp.[51]

In Montgomery, where segregation seems to have been most successfully enforced, racial mixing of convicts could not always be prevented. Segregated quarters were assigned as early as 1865 and retained by a Radical jailer.[52] Overcrowding, however, meant that an occasional white was incarcerated with blacks. Even after the passage of state laws prohibiting the confining together of black and white prisoners, the *Montgomery Daily Advertiser* complained in 1885 that at the county jail "the arrangements for keeping the races separate are far from what they should be."[53] The shift from exclusion to segregation finally became complete that summer as plans were announced for a new jail, one that had solitary cells "for both male and female—whites and blacks separate."[54]

Although orphanages and industrial schools occasionally received young offenders, there were no reformatories during the period. It is important to note, however, that as in these other institutions, it was expected that, when built, the reformatories would be segregated.[55]

The Redeemers thus continued the policies practiced by the Freedmen's Bureau, the U.S. Army, and the Radicals, but Negroes were still often left to fend for themselves. Confronted by exclusion or insufficient attention, blacks sought to fill voids left by governmental neglect. Such attempts at self-help further strengthened the system of segregated welfare care.

Negro societies were the core of the self-help effort. Secret fraternal societies like the Masons or Odd Fellows performed welfare as well as social functions. More important, however, were the numerous benevolent societies. Some like the Independent Order of Good Samaritans, the Daughters of Samaria, or the Richmond-based United Order of True Reformers were national organizations with branches throughout the South. Others were local in origin and frequently church affiliated. In return for small monthly dues, members were entitled to sick benefits and, if necessary, burial fees. One of the first, the Nashville Colored Benevolent Society, was organized in 1865 by twelve Nashville blacks. Another, located in Atlanta, had as its motto: "We assist the needy; we relieve our sick; we bury our dead."[56]

As the years passed and the Negroes accumulated more money, the societies and their services to the black community multiplied. They proved invaluable during Nashville's cholera epidemic of 1873, although their treasuries were virtually depleted as a result. In that year the Colored Benevolent Society had twenty-seven branches throughout Tennessee with a membership of 2,000. In its annual report of 1881, the Ladies' Benevolent Society No. 1 claimed 440 members, 207 of whom had been assisted and 11 buried; $1,528.25 had been paid for the sick, $330 for funerals, $30.50 for charity, $96 for secretary and rent. Still left in the fund after these expenditures was $1,603.50.[57] Clearly the resources of such individual societies were not great, but when considered together, they helped to soften the impact of exclusionary practices.

The sick benefits were greatly welcomed by Negroes who could not afford the premiums of large insurance companies (whose policies were in any case rarely available to them)[58] and who could expect little aid from the city governments.[59] An even more important reason for the popularity of these organizations were the burial benefits. After his trip through the South, the Englishman William Dixon concluded that "one thing only in the future weighs sufficiently on a Negro's mind to shape his action. He is very anxious about his funeral." Dixon was told by his hotel waiter in Richmond that "Every culled person is a member of two or three [burial] societies. . . . When he die, dey have all big sight." The *Nashville Banner* marveled that "singular as it may appear the colored people have a great horror of being buried by the county, or even of receiving a coffin for that purpose. They will submit to all sorts of privations to bury their dead independently." Although some were critical of the lavish funerals with brass bands, handsome hearses and coffins, and the spectacle of the society's members decked out in the finest uniforms, to the poor Negro and his family this was a brief time when he would be someone important. Faced with the alternatives of the involuntary donations of their bodies to the local medical school or paupers' burials in an unkempt potter's field where body snatchers preyed, it is not surprising that many blacks contributed their pennies so that, in places like Atlanta, they could have funerals that ranged in price from $7 to $45 instead of the $1.83 burial accorded the indigent.[60]

Many of the societies had their own cemetery plots in the municipal graveyards. In 1883, for example, Atlanta's Odd Fellow lodges claimed this benefit as one of their major attractions for prospective members. Nashville's Colored Benevolent Society went even further. "[F]eeling the great necessity that exists for a separate and properly enclosed burial place," the society founded the Mount Ararat Cemetery on the outskirts of the city in 1869. In Richmond, where blacks were excluded from the two best cemeteries and allotted an unfenced portion of Shockoe Cemetery, Negroes had organized six private cemeteries by 1880.[61]

Beginning in 1878 Atlanta Negroes had petitioned the city government to purchase a site for a black cemetery. In 1884 the city stopped selling lots in the municipal graveyard and allowed the private white-owned West View Cemetery to open. In return for Council approval, the company agreed to bury paupers of both races and guaranteed that separate ground would be set apart for Negroes. The terms for the incorporation of West View convinced the blacks that the city had no intention of establishing a separate Negro cemetery; therefore, a black company founded South View Cemetery and petitioned the Council for the right to bury Negro paupers. Finally in 1888, over the vigorous objections of West View's directors who disliked losing the business, the city acceded to the requests of the Negro firm.[62]

Black philanthropic organizations modeled after those of the white community also aided the Negro poor. Black clergymen organized the Nashville Provident Association in 1865. On the first day they raised over $500 with which they established a wood depot and later a soup kitchen. The Colored Home Mission Society No. 1 of East Nashville fulfilled a similar function of distributing supplies and clothing to the needy.[63] The most important organization of this type was the Colored Ladies Relief Society, an off-spring of the Nashville Ladies Relief Society. The white-run N.L.R.S. had been especially active during the severe winter of 1884 in distributing food, fuel, and clothing to the city's poor. Yet its aid was highly selective. "You know we never help negroes," said one of its leaders in 1886, "unless they are very old people or sick."[64] And as a "scientific charity," it carefully distinguished among the deserving and undeserving poor. Soon after, the society decided "to let the colored people manage the taking care of their own people." In December 1886 the Colored Ladies Relief Society was organized with thirty members, each of whom paid dues of either $3 per year or 25¢ per month.[65]

In addition to individual donations from both blacks and whites, the

C.L.R.S. received $318.95 of the $1,000 appropriated to the Nashville Relief Society by the County Court in 1887. Later in the year, however, its president told a reporter, "We have no money and no way to get it." Thanks to the support of white and black businessmen, the society continued to provide relief. Its April 1890 report of activities for the previous six months disclosed that between 500 and 1,000 people had received assistance which included almost 1,000 bushels of coal and other provisions.[66]

In two cities Negroes resorted to private means to get the benefits denied them by the public hospitals. In 1885, seven years after the founding of the Hospital of St. John's Guild for destitute whites, the Leonard Medical Hospital opened in Raleigh under the management of Shaw Institute, a local black college. Raleigh Negroes received free medicine from the city, but nonresidents had their board and medicine paid by their own counties. The black community of Montgomery, refused admittance to the Montgomery Infirmary, founded the James Hale Infirmary. Named after a prominent local black, financed largely by his widow, and run by his son-in-law, Dr. C. N. Dorsette, the institution provided indispensable services for blacks well into the twentieth century. Blacks should not only build churches and houses, Mrs. Hale said, but "homes for the orphans, the poor and the aged of our race, and also infirmaries and hospitals where the lame, sick, and injured can be cared for."[67]

Negro orphaned and dependent children fared worst at the hands of public officials. After the Freedmen's Bureau and Northern societies closed their facilities, blacks were turned back on their own resources. Negro churches and benevolent societies supported many children and placed them with private families. Benefits such as one given in Nashville by Central Tennessee College's Centennial Singers brought in needed funds. But more was necessary, and blacks turned increasingly to the organization of their own asylums. Failure was often the result. In 1873 a group of Negroes organized the Colored Ladies House of Industry of Nashville to give "moral and religious instruction" to more than 300 homeless black youths and to train them in "industrial habits and pursuits." The year before another group had established the People's Orphan Association, but there is no evidence that either institution ever went into operation. Montgomery blacks were similarly thwarted in their efforts to start an orphanage.[68]

Two institutions for Negro girls were eventually founded in Nashville and Montgomery,[69] but the greatest advances in the care of dependent black children came elsewhere. Continual requests from Negroes led the Richmond City Council in 1867 to authorize the use of a lot for the erection of a black asylum. After much haggling, the city added $500 to the $6,250 raised by the Society of Friends and the orphanage opened two years later as the Friends Asylum for Colored Orphans. Its trustees included five Quakers and several representatives of local Negro churches. As with the five white institutions in Richmond, in return for yearly appropriations the orphanage accepted five children per year referred by the municipal government. Atlanta's Carrie Steele Orphan Home, built on land the city donated, was founded in 1890 by Carrie Steele Logan, a former slave who worked as a stewardess at the railway depot. Its board of trustees was composed entirely of religious, business, and educational leaders of black Atlanta. Some Northerners and local whites contributed funds, but most of the support came from Negroes in the form of provisions or in amounts of money ranging from 10 cents to 50 dollars.[70] Whites were pleased since, said a supporter, "an orphan's home would prove a blessing to the hundreds of negro children who are growing up in Atlanta without discipline or instruction and from whose ranks the chain gang is being filled." Besides, added another, "it is the intention of the people interested in the home to take the little negro waifs and make good servants of them."[71] To Negroes the asylum was a way of reducing suffering, but to whites it was a way of achieving control over a new generation of blacks who did not know their proper place.

The interest in Negro orphanages or cemeteries suggests that blacks were less concerned with encouraging integration than with ending exclusion. For the most part Negro leaders left unchallenged the existence of segregation in welfare facilities.[72] This attitude did not indicate passivity, however. Where blacks were barred, they requested the establishment of Negro departments or separate institutions. The petitions of blacks for a Negro division at the Georgia Academy for the Blind played a key role in its formation; and it was a Nashville black legislator, T. A. Sykes, who introduced the bill providing segregated accommodations for blacks at both the Tennessee School for the Blind in Nashville and the School for the Deaf and Dumb in Knoxville. W. H. Young, one of the two Negro justices on the Davidson County Court, opposed appropriations for two white orphanages and a mission home for fallen white women because Negroes in similar circumstances were denied aid. He advocated a home for black fallen women and the construction of a Negro reformatory. He received encouragement from the *Nashville Banner,* which argued that "public aid from the treasury of state, county, or city should be rendered to all alike."[73]

Once access to a service was attained, blacks sought greater influence in its management. In response to conciliatory feelers from the local Democratic administration, the *Richmond Planet* called for black supervision of the Negro almshouse and for a black physician to care for its inmates. A group of Atlanta blacks petitioned the City Council in 1889 to appoint a Negro named Ashbury as one of the city physicians and to turn over all black patients to him. In North Carolina James H. Harris, a Negro former state legislator and Raleigh councilman, insisted that blacks be appointed to the boards of all state institutions where blacks were housed. The reason was simple. "No one," he said, "can enter so fully into the sympathy of the negro's condition as the negro himself."[74]

Calls for increased Negro participation bore little fruit. Their major impact was to convince whites that blacks were satisfied with the status quo—that is, segregation. Despite opposition, however, there were a few Negro administrators. Alfred Menefee, a Nashville politician, served as one of the county poorhouse commissioners in 1869. Raleigh's George W. Brodie was a director of the North Carolina Insane Asylum, and, as late as 1877, James H. Harris was a member of the Board of the North Carolina Institution for the Deaf and Dumb and Blind. Under the Readjusters in Virginia, a leading Richmond city councilman was selected as vice president of the Board of Directors of the Negro insane asylum. When the Tennessee Industrial School opened in 1888, T. A. Sykes, a former North Carolina and Tennessee state legislator and Davidson County magistrate, was placed in charge of its Negro department. And in Alabama a board of six prominent blacks advised the all-white Board of Trustees of the Asylum for the Deaf and Dumb and Blind.[75] But such appointments were infrequently made and for real control over their own welfare, the Negroes had to be content with their benevolent societies, cemetery associations, and with such institutions as the James Hale Infirmary, the Carrie Steele Orphan Home, and the Friends Asylum for Colored Orphans.

In seeking separate institutions, Negroes and their white allies evidently believed that such facilities could be made equal. The white Democrats who overthrew the Radicals proclaimed that the blacks would receive equal treatment. But how did the record of segregation square with the rhetoric of equality?

Occasionally whites and blacks did receive comparable treatment. The ideal came closest to realization in the institutions for the care of the blind, deaf, and dumb. Speaking before a Senate committee in 1880, James O'Hara, a black future Congressman from North Carolina, compared the care given to both races in his state's institution. "They have the same kind of provisions, meats, vegetables, and fruits; the same bedding and furniture, carpets, pianos, etc., all the same in both institutions, without distinction at all."[76] In 1882 the trustees of the Georgia Asylum for Deaf and Dumb in an evaluation of the program for Negroes noted that "the quality of food and clothing furnished is the same as that supplied to the whites." As late as 1887, per capita expenditure for provisions at the Academy for the Blind was only $5 greater for the white department.[77] City and county facilities sometimes also accorded Negroes a fair share of their services. Figures available for the Richmond municipal hospital, in-relief at the almshouse, and out-relief distribution indicate a rough parity in the numbers of both races being cared for.[78]

Despite these few examples, the principle of separate but equal flourished more in theory than in practice. Blacks still were not permitted in certain hospitals, state asylums, and orphanages. Even where public officials provided for their care, the belief in Negro inferiority that had once underwritten the policy of exclusion now led to an inequitable administration of separate facilities.

Discrimination was evident in admission policies. Destitute Negroes were more likely to receive hospital care than their more well-off brothers. The latter, unlike comparable whites, were not provided with facilities they could afford. Selectivity in the care of the insane posed a similar problem. In Alabama and Tennessee, for example, white patients at the state asylum were of three types—paying, indigent, and criminal—whereas only the latter two classes of blacks were present. Despite a long list of Negroes waiting to get into the state asylums, local authorities paid more attention to the smaller number of needy whites. The Davidson County Poorhouse and Asylum for many years admitted only white insane. By the early 1880s, it had begun to admit blacks, but in 1884, a typical year, there were 60 white inmates and only 25 blacks.[79] As elsewhere, the majority of black insane were confined in jails or left to wander the streets.

In other institutions as well, the number of white inmates grew while the Negro waiting lists mounted. The Tennessee Industrial School in 1890 had 25 black students and 165 whites; in the same year the Georgia Institution for the Deaf and Dumb had 26 Negroes and 75 whites. Blacks had the same problem getting poor relief commensurate with their needs. In 1884 the Davidson County Asylum had 174 white inmates and 101 Negroes. Atlanta officials during 1887 gave out-relief to 310 whites and only 177 blacks. And although Richmond authorities dispensed equal amounts of out-relief to members of both races, many more black than white applicants were denied aid.[80]

Reports seldom contained breakdowns of expenditures by race, but, when given, they generally revealed inequality. In Virginia per capita expenditure at the all-Negro Central Lunatic Asylum in the mid-1870s was about $177 annually, as compared to $191 at the all-white Eastern Lunatic Asylum. By 1889 Central was receiving $127.91 per inmate, while appropriations at the three white asylums ranged from $151.20 to $236.04. The North Carolina asylum for the Negro insane erected in 1881 cost $152,000; the older one for whites in Raleigh cost $350,000 and the new one in Morgantown, though still incomplete in 1884, was already in excess of the latter figure.[81]

Locally, the picture was the same. Although the Friends Asylum for Colored Orphans in Richmond received as much public money as the largest recipient among the white asylums, the total for the four white institutions was far larger. In 1885 white patients sent by the Atlanta City Council to Ivy Street Hospital cost the city 75 cents per day, while Negro patients cost less than 25 cents. And when Fulton County officials finally erected new poorhouse facilities in 1889, they expended $8,000 for a one-story brick building for whites—and $1,500 for six double wooden cottages for blacks on the other side of the woods.[82]

Insufficient funds meant poorer facilities. In many instances white accommodations were also in unsatisfactory condition, but when money became available they were the first to be rehabilitated or replaced. Many of the Jim Crow quarters were unsuited for their purposes, inadequately equipped, and usually overcrowded. "Our colored department is in need of shop rooms and some repairs and extensions," complained the head of the Tennessee Industrial School in 1888. Two years later the director of the School for the Blind echoed: "The houses occupied by the colored pupils are ill adapted for a school —they were originally residences and are situated on a busy thoroughfare."[83]

The Negro insane were especially ill housed. In Georgia the Negroes occupied a building described as "insecure and not adapted for the purposes for which . . . it is now used." The superintendent of the Alabama asylum reported in 1884 that, while there was enough room for the white insane "for several years to come," the blacks were so crowded that each of their two small buildings immediately needed a second story. The legislature took no action and in desperation he carried his fight to the pages of the Atlanta Constitution in 1885. It was not until 1888, however, that a new structure for 200 patients opened. In the interim two brick buildings had been erected to provide accommodations for an additional 300 whites.[84]

The pattern found on the state level was duplicated in the cities: inferior accommodations, advocacy by certain whites of needed improvements, and a long lag in implementation. Conditions at the Richmond almshouses were typical. The white almshouse was a three-story brick building; the Negro one, though normally containing more inmates, was of smaller wooden construction. In 1876 the mayor drew attention to one of the results of this discrimination, the much higher mortality rate among Negro inmates. Although there were 35 more whites than blacks, 125 blacks had died but only 34 whites. In 1883 the Superintendent of Public Charities pointed to the need for new quarters: "The building now used for the inmates . . . is totally unfit for the purpose, not having been erected for an almshouse and only selected for temporary use for the said institution, is therefore wanting in nearly every appliance and convenience; and I do not believe that it can be made suitable." In comparison to the steam-heated white almshouse, the Negro department was warmed by stoves; sexes were separated at the former, but not at the latter.[85] To these and other inadequacies was added the deplorable condition of the Negro hospital, a facility which, though located in the almshouse, also served as the only hospital available to Negroes of all classes. "It is hoped that at an early day, we may be provided with one for the colored as well arranged as that for the white department," wrote the almshouse physician in 1887. Despite such pleas, a new almshouse for the Negro paupers was not built until 1908.[86]

Blacks in Atlanta were no more fortunate. Not only did Negro paupers lack adequate poorhouse facilities, but they and their better-off brothers lacked equal hospital accommodations. In 1896 a Negro critic pointed out that in Atlanta,

> there is not a decent hospital where colored people can be cared for. At the Grady Hospital, which takes about $20,000 of the city's money annually to run it, is a small wooden annex down by the kitchen, in which may be crowded fifty or sixty beds, and that is all the hospital advantages 40,000 colored citizens have. But, on the other hand, our white friends, with a population of about 70,000, have all the wards and private rooms in the entire brick building at this hospital, together with a very fine hospital here, known as St. Joseph's Infirmary.[87]

Poor health care combined with unsanitary living conditions and inadequate diet to produce high mortality rates among blacks. In 1875 the white mortality rate in Nashville was 25.78 per 1,000; for blacks, it was 49.69. Each successive year the numbers changed, but the essential relationship remained. By 1890 the figures were 13.52 and 25.03 respectively. Black children suffered the most. Deaths under five years of age usually constituted about one-third of the total deaths, while among Negroes they were never less than 40 percent. The great number of unreported deaths, always greater among the Negroes and especially among the children, made both the death rate of blacks and the percentage of deaths of the children even worse than the official statistics indicated.[88] Mortality figures in other cities followed the same pattern.[89]

Aside from the periodic epidemics, the chief killers of the blacks were consumption and pneumonia, both diseases largely due to substandard shelter and unhealthy surroundings. Discounting stillbirths, in every year it was consumption first and pneumonia second that accounted for the difference between white and Negro death rates. In 1890, for example, white deaths from consumption in Atlanta numbered 80 and black, 136; those from pneumonia, 46 and 89 respectively.[90] Tabulation of the Montgomery death rates is difficult because of the poor system of reporting and the mistaken estimates of the population, but it seems that the white rate was always at least half of the black. Again the same two killers hit Negroes harder. Between December 1875 and May 1877, for example, there were 12 white deaths from consumption and 13 from pneumonia, as compared to 34 and 27 deaths from those diseases among the blacks.[91]

Treatment in correctional institutions produced similar results. Living quarters and hospital facilities for blacks were grossly inferior. Seeking to account for the high number of consumptive deaths among Negro convicts at the North Carolina penitentiary, the prison doctor speculated that one cause might be "the unhealthy cell arrangement . . . built only for temporary use and . . . deficient in almost every element of comfort."[92]

Death rates within the penitentiary were significantly higher than for whites, but separate treatment was especially unequal outside the walls. In 1879 all but 15 of the 222 Virginia convicts hired out were black. Of the 15 who died, 14 were Negroes. By 1885 all 211 leased convicts were blacks. As of October 1, 1890, leased Georgia convicts included 140 white males, no white females, 1,478 black males, and 48 black females. Referring to the high death rate among Negro convicts, the head of the prison system had earlier observed:

> I feel confident that the casualties would have been fewer if the colored convicts were property having a value to preserve. Then the proprietors would look after them with commendable care and not leave them, as leasees have too often done, to the ignorance, inattention or inhumanity of irresponsible hirelings.[93]

Blacks were not only more likely to be hired out, but those who remained within the penitentiary were denied an equal opportunity to improve themselves. After an 1880 tour of the North Carolina penitentiary, a member of a respected Raleigh Negro family charged that the white prisoners stayed in the shops and made shoes or did other light work while the Negroes were confined to the rock pile. Another Raleigh black decried the fact that whites were able to learn a trade in prison, whereas Negroes were restricted to unskilled labor gangs. By 1890 white prisoners made up 40 percent of the nonleased male convicts, but only 15 percent of those leased out.[94]

Equal treatment was missing in death as in life. Negro sections of municipal graveyards contradicted claims by city boosters of the park-like beauty of their cemeteries. To an *Atlanta Constitution* reporter in 1884, the little hillside in Oakland Cemetery where the blacks were buried looked less like a burial ground than a newly planted potato

patch, "a dreary spot, devoid of shrubbery" with graves so close together "that it is about impossible to step among them without step-
ping on [one]." The area was littered with whiskey bottles, toys, iron
bureaus, and other uncollected debris. In 1877 the superintendent of
Richmond's Shockoe Cemetery complained about the portion allotted
to the Negro poor. It was ill-fitted for a burial ground, he charged,
being an unenclosed field and "its now overcrowded condition renders
it impossible to make any interment therein without disturbing some
previous burial, thus making it both repulsive and inhumane."[95]

By 1890 white Southerners had been forced to accept responsibility
for providing public and private welfare care for blacks, although there
were still many institutions which refused to admit Negroes. Negro
blind, deaf, and dumb were excluded from the Alabama and Virginia
asylums; numerous local hospitals would accept white charity patients
but not middle-class blacks; the black community was left to contend
with its dependent children. New institutions like Richmond's Virginia
Home for Incurables, opened in 1894, were still being founded "for
whites only."[96] On the other hand, Virginia and Alabama finally provided for Negro deaf, dumb, and blind; hospitals like Richmond's Retreat for the Sick, opened only to whites since its founding in 1877,
eventually provided separate wards for black patients[97]; and in 1900
Virginia accepted support of the previously privately-run Virginia
Labor School of the Negro Reformatory, eleven years after it had
opened the Laurel Industrial School for white boys.[98]

These facilities founded after 1890 were segregated, but such action
marked a continuation of past practices. For in the years after the Civil
War segregation became the norm in Southern welfare policy. What it
replaced was not integration, which rarely existed, but exclusion, a
policy that had been formulated in antebellum times and was only
reluctantly modified by the first postwar Conservative governments.

7

Education

In education as in welfare services, the antebellum South had been a hostile environment for blacks. Laws prohibited slaves from receiving an education, while few free Negroes had either the time or the opportunity to seek schooling. Of the more than 116,000 students in North Carolina in 1860, only 133 were black; this was also true of only 152 of Tennessee's more than 160,000 students.[1] As a result, the Negroes who flocked to the postbellum cities, like those left behind, were largely illiterate.

By 1890 four major decisions had been made concerning public education in the South. The first involved the very acceptance of state-supported public school systems. The second and third meant that blacks as well as whites were to be among the students, although the two races would be strictly segregated. And the final decision, well on its way to widespread implementation, was that blacks rather than whites would teach the black pupils.

Throughout the period, no matter who was in control politically, urban Negroes had access to schools to a far greater degree than rural blacks. Many came to the cities specifically because of the opportunities for education. Originally under the missionaries sent by the Northern benevolent societies, later under the first systems of public education established by the Republicans, and finally under the paternalistic eyes of the Redeemers, they experienced one of freedom's main benefits. But, because the distinction between blacks and whites was never forgotten, the best that realistically could be hoped for was a policy of separate but equal treatment. It did not take long for even this hope to be shattered.

As towns fell under the control of Union forces, representatives from Northern philanthropic societies arrived to bring education and religion to the enthusiastic freedmen. Aided by the Freedmen's Bureau, these societies, particularly the American Missionary Association (AMA) and the American Freedmen's and Union Commission (AFUC), played the leading role in educating the freedmen during the first half decade after the war. It was a formidable task, made even more so by the presence of local hostility to their efforts. There were several reasons for this opposition. One was that poor whites were allegedly "ignored." "At the same time," wrote an Atlanta teacher, Southerners "are too proud to confess that the whites need or would accept our charity." The resistance of other residents was due to the belief that Negroes had no place in school. "Hoeing, ploughing, spinning, and sewing are more necessary now to the negro than the singing of 'emancipation' hymns or the study of that multiplication table and alphabet which are supposed to be the panacea for all the ills that negro flesh is heir to," the *Richmond Dispatch* argued. "The negro must *work* or *starve* and this he will eventually find out in spite of all the 'strong minded females' in Yankeedom." A Richmonder succinctly expressed this view by exclaiming, "the idea of a darkey's going to school!"[2]

The most opposition was due to Southern white unwillingness to surrender control over the freedmen in this sensitive area to the bearers of an alien ideology. The teachers were thought to be in collusion with political carpetbaggers who told the blacks that white Southerners were their worst enemies. According to the *Atlanta Constitution*, one of the region's moderate newspapers,

> In ninety-nine cases out of a hundred, the negroes that are taught by these teachers have exemplified their lessons by hostility to their old masters, by voting and talking against him [sic], and by banding in secret leagues for Radical purposes. And the teachers, immediately on their arrival in a community, have sought out the members of the Radical party, affiliated with them, espoused their doctrines and zealously inculcated them varying their advocacy by liberal abuse of rebels.[3]

Considering such feelings, it is not surprising that the first Northern teachers to arrive in Raleigh in 1865 were told "we don't want nigger teachers" and were denied lodging in the white community. They finally found rooms in the house of a mulatto woman. A year later the Freedmen's Bureau still found it "utterly impossible" to secure rooms with white families for the teachers, even though many of the citizens desperately needed the additional income. "The feelings of the community, with very few exceptions are hostile to your Association and its schools," wrote the Superintendent of Freedmen's Schools in Richmond to Lyman Abbott, General Secretary of the AFUC, in 1866.

> This is a safe inference from the increasing slanders and ridicule of the public press, the universal "cold shoulder" of the clergy . . . the words and acts of children, young men, and women on the street, meant to be insulting and finally, the occasional destruction of a school house or assault upon a teacher.

The message was clear to a Raleigh teacher who found a note on her doorstep depicting a skull and crossbones and the outline of a coffin.[4]

The taunts of local residents did not deter the Northerners. At times the teachers seemed to thrive on them. "The opposition to our work in this place is very great," wrote a Raleigh teacher. "So in proportion rises our anxiety and desire for great success." One of her colleagues, described by a friend as "a real missionary," rejoiced, "this is a good time and I'm in it. I do enjoy life and labor here very much and bless the Yarmouth people for sending me." When hostility became too pressing, the teachers could draw on the expansive reservoir of Northern support. Nonetheless, the pressure and the warm climate took its toll, and most teachers returned home during the summer vacations. As a Raleigh teacher expressed it, "the sun is becoming allied with the 'rebs' to drive us North." Many did not return in the fall. There was a high turnover rate and very few lasted more than two years. As veterans left, however, new recruits flocked southward to take their places.[5]

Many of the teachers came with the hope of teaching whites and blacks in the same schools. As a representative of the AMA later said, when explaining his son's enrollment at Atlanta University, "under existing circumstances his presence there bears plain witness to a faith in the divine doctrine of a universal human brotherhood." Most officials soon realized that the mixing of the races would be harmful to their main objective of educating Negroes. In a letter to the Reverend Lyman Abbott, R. M. Manly, the moving force for the education of the freedmen in Richmond, advised against seeking integration since "in my opinion, the whites will not attend school with the blacks." Abbott received a similar opinion from General Clinton B. Fisk, Assistant Commissioner of Freedmen for Kentucky and Tennessee, who wrote from Nashville:

> You cannot gather the whites and blacks into the same school. Both races rebel against it. Separate schools under the same organization can be successfully conducted. I know of no successful experiment of mixing them in the same school. I do know of signal failure.

There is no record of blacks having opposed the presence of whites in their classrooms, but the same statement could not be made of whites. As late as 1867, five white children attended one of the Negro schools in Raleigh, but pressures from the white community proved too great. Reporting the exodus of the whites from his classes, the teacher sadly observed, "Most of them go without any schooling at all rather than bear up against the ridicule that meets them for going to a Freedmen's school."[6]

The teachers came south for a variety of reasons. It seems clear, however, that hostility toward the South or crass political motives carried little weight. The majority were imbued with strong antislavery beliefs, humanitarian impulses, and burning religious fervor. Much like the late-nineteenth-century settlement house workers and the first batch of Peace Corps volunteers, they saw the downtrodden and sought to help. Some, like a teacher at Atlanta's Storrs School, were perhaps atoning for past sins. "I am ashamed everyday to think I was ever guilty of being a democrat," she wrote in 1870, "and ask God [to] forgive me for ever having sympathy, in the least, with them who would keep these people in slavery." As for the typical reason, Raleigh's Lucy Dow expressed it best: "Our great hope lies in the children. They must be taught habits of industry, economy, personal and household cleanliness and much more besides book learning."[7]

Finding such ardor not easily dispelled, white Southerners sought to stifle Northern efforts by discouraging Negro participation. Shunning the burning of buildings and the attacks on pupils or teachers found in some other cities and especially in the countryside, local residents adopted a variety of less violent tactics. According to a society official, Raleigh whites announced that "no man, woman, or child . . . shall attend school and remain in their employ." Lucy Chase bore witness to the seriousness of such threats in Richmond. "Many of our children have been driven from their homes because they came to school; and, in some instances, *whole families* have been turned into the streets because they were represented in the classroom." White ministers in Richmond's Negro churches also discouraged school attendance and in Raleigh some inventive whites told Negro children that Northern teachers were responsible for the sudden increase of sickness in the city.[8]

Nevertheless, it proved extremely difficult to dampen the Negroes' drive for education. Freedmen viewed education as the key to social, economic, and political mobility and they demonstrated an intense desire to enjoy its fruits. "I look for, but do not find any diminution of interest," wrote a Richmond teacher in 1866. "Everybody wants to learn to read." At about the same time in Raleigh teachers were finding "a surprising thirst for knowledge among the colored people."[9]

This interest of the freedmen encouraged the representatives of the benevolent societies and the Freedmen's Bureau to proceed with the formation of schools. To some extent the freedmen had laid the groundwork for these efforts. The first three teachers sent to Raleigh by the AMA in July 1865 assumed control of a school for Negro children that had been established and taught by blacks at an African Methodist Episcopal church. The AMA teachers who arrived in Atlanta during the same year found a small school organized by two ex-slaves in the basement of an old church. Although determined to contribute to the education of their race, the blacks realized their need for additional help. They shouldered part of the burden such as paying the board of AMA instructors in Atlanta and contributing money to the fuel fund of the New England Branch of the Freedmen and Union Commission (NEBFUC) school in Richmond, but their meager resources permitted little more.[10]

At first there was great reliance on Negro churches. By 1864 classes were being held in five Nashville churches. A similar situation existed in Richmond where instruction began within fourteen days after the city's occupation by federal troops in 1865. Out of desperation anything with a roof was sought for educational purposes. Federal authorities brought a railroad car from Chattanooga to Atlanta to serve as a school; a hotel dining room was pressed into service in Raleigh; and in Montgomery the Fitz and Frazier slave auction mart with the old sign still on the door became a school for freedmen, several of whom had once been sold there. Richmond Negro schools in 1866 were "mostly in garrets, or down in vaults; poor rooms, with scant supplies of benches, desks and books."[11]

Conditions improved with the increased activity of the Freedmen's Bureau and the missionary societies. Between 1865 and 1870 the Bureau supplied most of the buildings. These facilities consisted of confiscated Confederate property, rented dwellings, and new construction. The new structures were generally of a modest two-story frame variety. The most important primary schools were the Johnson and Washington schools in Raleigh, the Swayne School in Montgomery, and the Summer Hill and Storrs schools in Atlanta. In the case of Storrs, $1,000 of the $6,000 building costs came from the Reverend H. M. Storrs's congregation in Cincinnati. The remainder was paid jointly by the Bureau and the AMA. The Bureau also helped launch several of the institutions of higher learning founded before 1870. It gave $18,000 for construction of the Freedmen's Aid Society's Central Tennessee College in Nashville, donated over $6,000 to the Freedmen's Commission of the Protestant Episcopal Church's St. Augustine's College in Raleigh, and provided the AMA's Fisk University in Nashville with its first building, a former army hospital.[12]

As fast as accommodations could be found, eager adults and children filled them to capacity. Shortly after federal forces occupied Nashville in 1862, there were 1,200 students in the freedmen schools. Half of these attended miscellaneous private institutions, while the rest, mostly children of contrabands, went to the schools of the United Presbyterian Freedmen's Mission under the direction of the Reverend J. G. McKee. By 1867 schools run by four societies served approximately 3,000 students with an additional 250 being taught in private schools. An estimated 1,000, however, could not be accepted. In Montgomery the AMA's Swayne School had begun in October 1866 with an enrollment of 210; after eight months the number had grown to 700. High enrollments necessitated maximum utilization of available facilities. At Atlanta's Storrs School, for example, the regular school for children was held from 9:00 to 2:00; afterward, there was an adult school composed mostly of married women; and from 7:00 to 10:00 an evening school was conducted for 100 men.[13]

The religious motivation of many of the teachers and the fervent Protestantism of the societies—whether denominational or nondenominational—meant that religion, morality, and temperance formed the framework for the curriculum. News of religious revivals in teachers' letters matched reports of academic progress. Montgomery's W. T. Richardson spoke for most when he noted that in addition to stressing academic skills, "We have endeavored also . . . to inculcate moral and religious instruction; hoping thereby to elevate the minds and reach the hearts of our pupils." When a Richmond church housing a Negro school burned down, one of the teachers reported that the church members, "realizing that the interests of religion and education are inseparably united," decided to rebuild immediately. The freedmen were also warned of the dangers of liquor and urged to forsake its temptation.[14] The linking of religion, morality, and education suggests that the Yankees in their own way were as concerned as Southern whites with the need to regulate behavior within the Negro community.

A surprising number of students had some preparation for school. Lucy Chase, surveying her thousand Richmond students in 1866, found eighty good readers, two hundred good spellers, and one hundred who knew the alphabet. Of the remainder, many had picked up one or two letters from hidden books for "in spite of the rigid laws against teaching the negroes, nearly every colored family in Richmond has one or more members who can read." In Nashville many of the first students were contrabands who had learned to read as soldiers. Others had benefited from the antebellum private schools run by blacks like the evangelist Daniel Wadkins. The famous Negro tutor John Chavis left Raleigh blacks both a legacy of interest in education and students who could teach others.[15]

Yet in all the cities such students were in the minority. Most of the freedmen were learning the alphabet or studying the first primer, while the more advanced moved on to geography and arithmetic. Writing was reserved for the most advanced. Music and special exercises also helped to keep the interest of the students. Religious hymns and patriotic songs such as "Jesus Loves Me" and "Rally Round the Flag, Boys" were especially popular with both the freedmen and their teachers.[16]

Although some scholars have argued that the teachers were political arms of the Republican Party,[17] the evidence for these five cities suggests otherwise. No doubt the political views of the teachers at times influenced discussions of the freedmen's rights. The naming of schools after Abraham Lincoln and hanging pictures of Lincoln and Charles Sumner in prominent places also gave a political tinge to education;

but with the exception of John Silsby in Montgomery and R. M. Manly in Richmond, none of the teachers played an active role in political campaigns.[18] The instructors, of course, were ardent patriots; one Richmond teacher raised the U.S. flag over her school so that former Confederates drilling nearby would at least be exercising within sight of the Stars and Stripes. There seems, however, to have been little explicit intrusion of politics into the classroom. A Raleigh teacher noted with approval in 1866 that there were Thanksgiving services in all the churches, "but as far as I have learned the preachers were very careful to make no allusion to the state of the country." After seven years of teaching in Raleigh, Louise Dorr wrote that "in my own school slavery or the war is never spoken of, unless it be by some chance visitor who contrasts the privileges of the present with those of the past. I believe in taking things as they are and not as they were or might have been."[19] Such abstractions as equal rights may have been discussed, but the instructors were in no sense arms of the Union League or of the Radicals in Congress.

Negroes of all ages were drawn to the schools. Each teacher seemed to have at least one overaged student who walked long distances to school, worked hard, and triumphed over all obstacles. Lizzie Leonard of Raleigh told of a thirty-year-old man who, though living three miles away, had not missed a class. Six other men walked the same distance to her night school. Especially eager were the 175 adults at the NEBFUC night school in Richmond. Although most of them worked all day, they were "as enthusiastic, and express as much delight in learning to read, as a child with a new toy or story book." But education was more than a toy; it was symbolic of emancipation. To a student at Richmond's Lincoln Industrial School the meaning was clear:

> I am highly animated to think that slavery is dead, and I am my own woman, and hope, with the assistance of God, to remain a free woman until I die. And now I thank God that I have the opportunity to read and to write, and also my children. I often look back at the time when I was locked up in jail, and put upon the auction-block and sold to the highest bidder and now we have a nice time with Miss Forrester.[20]

The best hope for the race lay with its youngsters, and even adults who were too busy working to attend classes made certain to send their offspring. The parents took pride in their children's accomplishments and urged the teachers to use strong discipline, including whipping, in order that the benefits of education not be lost. J. W. Duncan reported from Richmond that

> The parents are delighted with the idea of their children learning to read, and many take great pleasure in visiting the schools, and asking the teacher to pay 'ticular pains to our children, as we wish them to get all the learning they can, 'caus you know Miss, I's got no learning myself consequently I know how much I loses without it.

As one Raleigh mother expressed it, "It does me good to see my color coming up."[21]

For all these students the religious side of the curriculum had left its imprint. "I came here a stranger, I am an orphan and without a relative. . . . I felt alone in the world, but now I feel that I have Christ for my friend, and I shall never want for a place to go for sympathy." Above all there was the linkage between education and religion, knowledge and morality that the benevolent societies instilled in their pupils. Wrote a Montgomery girl to her teacher: "I am going to try and learn as much as I can this year. . . . I wish I could teach the heathen all I know myself . . . so that they can follow the Savior too, and obey his commandments. I join the Normal class this week so I can learn to teach others."[22]

According to most contemporaries, the blacks made excellent progress. The teachers thought them attentive, hard working, and quick to learn. Joseph M'Kelvey reported about his Nashville students in 1865: "Their advancement was rapid. Several who did not know a letter when [I] first met with them [in April] by the first of June could read short sentences without hesitation." Some white instructors, however, found that while the freedmen did very well in geography and spelling, they lagged behind in mathematics and in dealing with abstract concepts. This weakness was usually attributed to the lack of earlier training. B. L. Canedy, who had taught in white schools in Boston for fifteen years and the Richmond Negro schools for five years, thought her black pupils "slower" because "they were wholly destitute of mental training till after the war." With time she felt they would be "as good scholars as the white children." Her colleague, Miss Howe, was less restrained and stated that her pupils in Maine had never learned as fast as the freedmen in Richmond. Additional praise appeared in the comments of Freedmen's Bureau officials and the assortment of foreign visitors who toured the schools. Their remarks cannot

always be taken at face value for it is difficult to know what they expected to find, but nevertheless, they presented a uniformly favorable
picture.[23]

Even Southern whites found much to praise in the schools, though
they were still unhappy about the dominant role played by the Northerners. After witnessing closing exercises at the Nashville Negro
schools, "Uncle Job" wrote:

> The success of this school exhibition shows that colored children,
> as well as colored men, learn the drill very rapidly. Habituated to
> obedience, they learn with marvelous speed, both in camp and in
> school, and as the men have made excellent soldiers, so the children
> bid fair to make excellent scholars.[24]

Future praise from white Southerners would be couched in the same
terms. No matter what a freedman did he would still be essentially the
perfect imitator, good at following, but less adept at reasoning for himself. Nevertheless, such indications of learning left the white man's
traditional image of the Negro somewhat tarnished.

Any change in the white man's perception of blacks caused by these
institutions was of secondary importance to the fact that the graduates
and even the nongraduates were able to teach others. This proved
particularly significant for the rural Negroes who had less contact with
Northern societies. To some extent the black emissaries to the surrounding countryside helped to redress this initial neglect. An AMA
teacher in Atlanta told of a student who roomed in the capital and
walked six miles every day to teach in a rural school. In Raleigh the
Washington and Lincoln schools had produced five teachers by 1867.
And by 1871 fourteen of the students who had been educated by the
NEBFUC in Richmond were teaching in the vicinity. The pioneer
among the society's Negro teachers had been Peter Woolfolk, who was
given his own class after graduating from the society's normal school
in 1868. He was frequently visited by officials who remarked favorably
on his ability.[25]

Despite their normal school divisions, however, the primary schools
could not meet the pressing need for able teachers. The societies realized this and soon founded more advanced institutions. Though called
colleges or universities, at first they were little more than high schools.
Prior to 1870 most of them had primary and secondary departments
which permitted poorly prepared students to work their way up to

collegiate or normal school divisions. Although the main objective was to prepare teachers, the institutions also sought to graduate educated preachers, and several contained industrial departments where men learned farming or skilled trades and women mastered domestic skills. Several institutions were founded in rural areas or smaller towns, but, as with the primary schools, the benevolent societies concentrated most of their efforts in the larger cities where the impact could be greater and more visible. The result was so successful that no city tour for important visitors was complete without an inspection of "the colored college."

The two most influential schools were Atlanta University and Nashville's Fisk University, both founded by the American Missionary Association. Though overshadowed by the AMA, other societies produced an array of Negro colleges before the end of the century. Each of the five cities with the exception of Montgomery became sites for these colleges. (See Table 6.) These schools together with Morris Brown in Atlanta and the State Normal School in Montgomery made significant contributions to Negro life. The teachers they produced staffed public schools throughout the South; their preachers served in countless churches; other graduates went into business and law; and, at Meharry Medical College of Central Tennessee College and the Leonard Medical School of Shaw Institute, black doctors learned how to treat the ills of their people. Then, too, they provided a new generation of educated blacks, ready and able to form a racial elite. In the 1890s when the lines were drawn among blacks for and against the policies of Booker T. Washington, that leader's severest critics would come from the faculties of Virginia Union, Atlanta University, and Fisk. At the center would be W. E. B. Du Bois, a graduate of Fisk and a teacher at Atlanta University.

By 1870 the organizations had shifted their priorities with the intent of improving their advanced schools while turning over primary education to Southern officials. From the beginning the societies had expected public authorities to assume responsibility in this area[26]; instead, the whites during Presidential Reconstruction had dragged their feet. Although prompted largely by anti-Negro attitudes, the delay was due partly to the disrepute in which public education had long been held in the South. Alone among the five cities, Nashville had operated a public school system before the war, but its pupils were considered charity cases. On the state level only North Carolina made any

Table 6

School	City	Sponsor	Date Founded
Shaw Institute	Raleigh	American Baptist Home Mission Society	1865
St. Augustine's College	Raleigh	Protestant Episcopal Church	1867
Central Tennessee College	Nashville	Freedmen's Aid Society of M.E. Church	1866
Nashville Normal and Theological Institute (Roger Williams University)	Nashville	American Baptist Home Mission Society	1866
Fisk University	Nashville	American Missionary Association	1866
Meharry Medical College	Nashville	Freedmen's Aid Society of M.E. Church	1876
Atlanta University	Atlanta	American Missionary Association	1865
Atlanta Baptist Seminary (Morehouse College)	Atlanta	American Baptist Home Mission Society	1867 (moved from Augusta 1879)
Atlanta Baptist Female Seminary (Spelman College)	Atlanta	American Baptist Home Mission Society	1881
Clark University	Atlanta	Freedmen's Aid Society of M.E. Church	1869
Gammon Theological Seminary	Atlanta	Freedmen's Aid Society of M.E. Church	1883
Morris Brown College	Atlanta	Georgia A.M.E.	1881
State Normal School for Colored Children (Alabama State University)	Montgomery	State of Alabama	1874 (moved from Marion 1887)
Hartshorn Memorial College	Richmond	American Baptist Home Mission Society	1883
Richmond Theological Seminary (Virginia Union University)	Richmond	American Baptist Home Mission Society	1865

significant antebellum progress in the field of public education. Whatever had been done, of course, had been strictly for whites. After the
war, Negroes complicated the problem.

The initial Southern response was to ignore the blacks and to move
haltingly toward the education of white children at public expense.
Georgia enacted legislation in December 1866 which permitted public
education for whites but did nothing to make it a reality. Meanwhile,
under the administration of Governor Jonathan Worth, North Carolina
abolished its state-supported public schools to prevent the enrollment
of blacks.[27] But a growing clamor that whites commonly went without
schooling while blacks received excellent education from Northern in-
vaders had its effect. In February 1867 North Carolina Conservatives
reinstituted a system of public education for white children between
the ages of six and twenty-one. And in Atlanta, the Committee on Public Schools of the City Council in November 1869 urged the opening
of public schools for whites. They admitted it would be wise for the
Board of Education to provide for blacks as well, but "the wants of
the white children are more immediate and pressing." As late as February 1872, all 1,200 pupils in Atlanta's public schools were white.[28]

Unlike other states, Tennessee early went on record in favor of education for children of both races. An 1866 statute authorized public
schools for all youngsters, but required that the races be taught separately.[29] As in Georgia, passage of the law did not mean that the
schools were built or that provisions were made for both races. Such
action, although limited, was taken on the state level because at the
time Tennessee was the only Southern state in which the Republicans
were in control of the government. Tennessee Republicans thus expressed the policy later to be followed by members of the party throughout the South: exclusion would be replaced, but by segregation rather
than integration.

Nashville, however, was still in the hands of Conservatives who,
while providing schools for the whites, used the existence of freedmen
schools to defend the absence of public facilities for Negroes. By the
summer of 1867 the city fathers were ready to change their policy.
Several factors, mostly negative, influenced this decision: the dislike of
having blacks educated by Northerners, the fear that impending Republican control of the Council would result in integrated schools, and
the possibility of noneducated Negroes becoming "thieves and scoun-
drels." Soon after, the Board of Education informed the Assistant Com-

missioner of the Freedmen's Bureau of the city's decision to educate blacks. Though the schools would be separate, selection and certification of teachers, grading of pupils, and the rest of the organization would be "in all the respects the same" as the whites received. In a swipe at the societies, the Board also stated that "nothing of a sectional, political or partisan nature in social or religious matters shall be inculcated in these schools." In order to house these students the authorities relied on the federal government and the benevolent societies. The two original schools, Bell View and Lincoln, which opened in September 1867 and the two that opened the following year, McKee and the Gun Factory Building, were either rented or purchased from the Northerners and all had previously been freedmen schools.[30]

Elsewhere Negro public education was absent until Congressional Reconstruction brought Republican governments to power. The Reconstruction constitutions of Alabama (1868), Virginia (1868), North Carolina (1868), and Georgia (1868) acknowledged for the first time the state's obligation to educate blacks. Although Negroes were to be educated at public expense, the Republicans, if indeed they desired otherwise, were careful not to go entirely against the grain of Southern opinion. Negro education was to be equal to white education, but it was to be separate. The constitutions did not specify either segregation or integration, but the laws passed by Republican-controlled legislatures clarified any possible ambiguity.

On its concluding day members of the North Carolina Constitutional Convention sought to allay white fears about integrated schools. Part of a resolution proposed by a Negro member and unanimously adopted stated that "it is the sense of this convention that the interests and happiness of the two races would be best protected by the establishment of separate schools." The school law drafted in 1869 clearly enunciated the principle of separate but equal education. Similarly, Georgia guaranteed separate schools in 1870. Its statute ordered that local officials "shall provide the same facilities for each [race], both as regards school houses and fixtures, and the attainments and abilities of teachers, length of term-time, etc." In Alabama, however, mixed schools with "the unanimous consent of the parents and guardians of such children" (an unlikely possibility) were permitted by an 1868 law.[31]

Individual cities proceeded at different speeds to make public education a reality. Everywhere the Radicals prodded others to action and the former missionary society schools served as the nuclei for the new black systems. Richmond public schools actually antedated the beginning of the state system. Although the state constitution had made no mention of racial segregation in public education, the Radical-controlled Richmond City Council clearly spelled out its segregated policy in an 1869 ordinance. During the first year of operation, the Freedmen's Bureau contributed most of the buildings rent free and supplied without charge two-thirds of the furniture, while the Northern societies provided the teachers and paid half their salaries. The Board of Education appropriated $15,000 each for the white and black institutions. At the end of the year the Bureau stopped paying the rent and sold all its property, much of it to the city. The societies sold other freedmen schools such as Bakery and Navy Hill. Still others, like the Richmond Colored High and Normal School, were not turned over completely until 1876.[32]

The Raleigh school system did not officially begin until 1877. Prior to that date in the case of the Johnson School and until 1875 for the Washington School, the city's two main Negro educational facilities received most of their funds from the AMA and remained under its direction. Once the system began, the whites were taught in the old public schoolhouses while the Negroes continued to meet in churches and the buildings erected by the Freedmen's Bureau and benevolent societies.[33]

Frequently the system of dual support for the Negro public schools persisted several years after the initiation of the citywide school system. A source of continual dispute, however, was the composition of the teaching staffs. As late as 1882, the AMA contributed almost $3,000 to the Montgomery Negro schools. Until 1884 the society made available the Swayne School building and nominated its teachers who were paid by the Board of Education. Disagreements over hiring practices resulted in the school's finally being turned over to the city. In Atlanta Radicals led by Negro former councilman William Finch secured Negro schools in February 1872. One of them, Summer Hill, was made available free of charge by the Northern Methodist Missionary Society, with the city assuming the cost of its support. This arrangement continued until the Board of Education voted to purchase the building and the lot in 1876. The other school, Storrs, was loaned free of charge by the AMA which nominated the teachers whose salaries were paid by the Board. As in Montgomery, disputes raged over who would have the final authority in hiring the faculty and in 1878 the agreement was terminated. Storrs then became a private school which enjoyed an excellent reputation among members of the black community.[34] Although the schools themselves did not always provide a continuity with the original period of missionary fervor, some of the teachers stayed to teach in the public schools after the phasing out of the missionary endeavors.[35]

Urban Redeemers greeted this continuing link with mixed emotions. On the one hand, the supply of rent-free buildings was attractive to officials chronically plagued with monetary worries; on the other, as long as this tie persisted, whether, through instructors or money, there existed a formidable alternative to Southern white control over black minds. One of the first orders of business for the Redeemers, therefore, was to hire only residents as teachers. In addition to weeding out the Northerners, this would supply jobs to local whites who were unable to secure positions in the white schools.[36]

Nashville authorities unsuccessfully sought to discourage Northern teachers by telling them their schools might not resume after the 1869 Christmas vacation; the following summer the Board of Aldermen unanimously passed a bill providing that public school teachers had to reside permanently within the city. Shortly thereafter the Richmond City Council refused an offer of the Friends Freedmen Association of New York to provide twelve instructors and to pay one-fourth of their salaries. At the end of the academic year the Board of Education also decided that all teachers had to be permanent residents. One of the two dissenting votes came from R. M. Manly, head of the Richmond Education Association which ran the Colored High and Normal School.[37]

But the Redeemers had to tread carefully. Upon their return to power they found the lines on education firmly drawn. They might trim at the edges, but they had to respect the ground rules of the basic Radical policy as expressed in state constitutions, educational statutes, and city ordinances. The threat of federal intervention still hung over their heads and conscious of this fact, they announced that the gains won by the blacks would not be jeopardized. The shift from exclusion to segregation would be maintained, but, more important, the Radical policy of separate but equal treatment would be continued.[38]

Such assurances occurred at the same time that Redeemers eliminated all legal loopholes in the system of segregated schools. As a result, the principle of separate but equal was frequently written into the statutes. An 1872 Nashville ordinance required that "the same rules, laws, and regulations" should apply to white and black schools "and the same penalties shall be incurred by the superintendents, teachers or other parties for violating the provisions of such laws."[39] More often, however, the focus was on separation. Redeemer constitutions specifically provided for segregated schools, although this sanction marked no deviation from previous practice.[40]

The professed ideal of separate but equal schools came under serious attack only once during the period. In 1874 the U.S. House of Representatives passed a civil rights bill which prohibited separate schools. Southern officials and their supporters feared that passage of this measure would threaten the very foundations of the public school systems for whites and Negroes alike. Writing of his efforts to dissuade government officials from support of the educational provision of the bill, Barnas Sears, General Agent of the Peabody Fund, noted:

> My first aim was to see its friends and induce them to omit the clause altogether, or to require only *equal privileges* of education without mixing the two races in the schools. I think I convinced them all that the bill would overthrow the state systems of free schools and leave both blacks and poor whites who are now provided for by them most chiefly, destitute of schools altogether, as private schools would be substituted for public schools.[41]

John Fleming, Tennessee State Superintendent of Schools, was typical of officials who shared Sears's fears. Arguing that the proposed law conflicted with state statutes and the beliefs of Tennesseans, Fleming pointed out that "the school is too close to the family circle not to be subject, in a great degree, to social laws and influences." The public school was a new and fragile institution, "dependent upon continued popular favor for support, and in our present stage of progress like tender plants that require gentle handling and tender culture." The integration of the races would "utterly destroy the whole fabric." Nor was there any reason to change the system, he continued, since the only distinction between the white and black schools involved separation and not unequal education. In an effort to influence Congress, Fleming sent a circular to the state's local boards of education and county superintendents instructing them not to negotiate any new contracts with either black or white teachers until action on the bill was completed.[42]

By complying with this directive, the Nashville Board joined cities elsewhere in anticipating the worst from the proposed legislation. The Richmond Board of Education postponed purchasing a Negro schoolhouse it was then renting because of the "uncertain and perhaps *fatal future*" of the public school system. Atlanta's superintendent was equally pessimistic. He felt it unwise to "make any change or extension of the schools" for if mixed schools were to be required, "we should be compelled to abandon our present public schools, and reorganize our educational interests on some narrow interests."[43]

The Redeemers could also count on the support of white Republicans. According to the *Nashville Bulletin*,

> the passage of the mixed school provision will be simply disastrous, not only to Tennessee, but to the whole South. It will be the destruction of the public school system and no greater calamity could befall the people of the Southern States, and more especially the colored race. Social matters are beyond the reach of congressional legislation. If equal facilities are provided for colored schools and the education of colored children, the object of the law is accomplished and the desired results are secured . . . it is not a question of mixed or separate schools, but it is a question of whether we shall have separate schools or none at all.

These sentiments were warmly endorsed by Dr. W. P. Jones, the Republican state senator for the city. He argued that there should be no objection to separate schools since "the range of study, the scholastic period, and the distribution of school money [are] as liberal as to white children." And in Alabama the Republican State Platform of 1874 declared that "the republican party does not desire mixed schools or accommodations for colored people, but they ask that in all these advantages they shall be equal."[44]

The efforts of the Southern Redeemers, the Peabody Fund, and the Southern Republicans who did not want to alienate potential white voters helped to strike the school clause from the final version of the Civil Rights Bill. They were aided by Northerners who also did not relish the prospect of integrated schools. Separate facilities were to be a fact of life; the hope for Negroes lay in the attainment of equality within the confines of segregation.

With the last formidable threat to separate schools defeated, the cities proceeded to expand and improve their accommodations for whites and blacks. Municipal officials, though conscious of certain inadequacies in the Negro schools, were fond of proclaiming the essential equality of both sets of institutions. In 1883 the Raleigh Township School Committee reported that "no distinction is made in the city between grades, length of session, or salary of teachers, between white and colored schools. Both races have equal facilities and the same course of study." In his 1891 report Atlanta's Superintendent of Schools claimed that Negroes and whites enjoyed "equal accommodations." "The same course of study, the same curriculum and [the] same laws," he said, "are given them [blacks] as are given the white race. Atlanta has been liberal to her colored population."[45]

Despite Redeemer assurances to the contrary, an ever-widening gap in the distribution of funds for the two races came to replace the Republicans' relatively equal treatment. The differences ranged from the expenditure per enrolled child in Richmond during 1890–1891 of $10.25 for whites and $9.50 for blacks to the $5.58 per white child and $3.47 per black youngster in Montgomery in 1880, the last year for which figures are available. The sums for the Alabama capital represented an investment of $1.17 for each white of school age and only 44¢ for each Negro.[46]

Conditions in the schools reflected these differences. In every city there was a shortage of space for blacks. Whereas during the 1875 academic year Richmond educators lacked accommodations for 117 more white than Negro students, in 1888 600 Negroes and only 200 whites were denied entrance. Worse still, from the standpoint of the blacks, the whites would soon have seats, thanks to the opening of additional rooms in Springfield and Elba schools, while the blacks would have to wait until funds for new facilities were available "in the near future."[47]

Such announcements about finding accommodations for the Negroes "in the near future" came to have a hollow ring. When more room was planned for whites, it was sought through the erection of new buildings. When dealing with black needs, however, officials preferred renting or subdividing older buildings; if they decided upon new construction, they carefully chose sites which hindered the dispersal of Negroes. Authorities often delayed improvements for blacks while better provisions were made as quickly as financially possible for whites. And with occasional exceptions such as the Moore Street School in Richmond or the Gray Street School in Atlanta, both built after 1887, the Negro schools were generally older, less favorably located, and of inferior construction.[48] In 1876 the Richmond Superintendent recommended closing the Navy Hill School since it was in bad repair and "very unfit for school purposes"; in 1891 the building was still in use. By 1891 only two of the six Negro schools were in "good" or "very good" condition as compared to nine of the ten for whites. The Cemetery Hill School completed in Montgomery in 1887 was a frame building that provided blacks with "greater school facilities and much more comfort than they have had heretofore." On the other hand, a white school opened the previous year was an "elegant and commodious brick building" with a capacity of 405 students, more than twice that of the Negro school. The Lawrence School built for blacks in 1890 indicated Nashville's attitude toward black needs. In an age when wooden schools were anachronistic and when several hundred black students were without accommodations, the city erected a one-story five-room frame structure with seats for only 214.[49]

The principle of separate but equal also went largely unheeded in the number of advanced grades available to Negro pupils. With the exception of Raleigh, all the cities had high schools for their white children at an early date, but only Richmond and Nashville had established such facilities for their blacks by 1890. And in Nashville the high school was organized by adding grades to a grammar school, thus seriously increasing overcrowding.[50] Even more damaging was the absence of completely graded grammar schools. In Raleigh in 1884 only Johnson offered classes in all seven grades like the white institutions. After it closed in 1885, Negro students were limited to the first five grades. In Richmond, where black students received the best treatment, eight of the nine white elementary schools in 1891 offered classes in one of the two highest grades as compared to four of their seven Negro counterparts.[51]

In frustration some blacks turned to private black schools; others sought to spur local lawmakers to improve the quality of Negro public education. Rather than push for an end to segregation, the blacks fought for the ideal of truly equal, though separate, Negro schools. Most of the limited improvements can be traced directly to those pressures. In January 1874 the Nashville Board of Education acknowledged that "the colored people are demanding more convenient accommodations in the central and western portions of the city." Nine months later the Board's request for additional facilities for blacks in West Nashville was approved by the Board of Aldermen.[52] Petitions from Atlanta Negroes in 1880 and 1888 led the Board of Education to construct the Houston Street and Gray Street schools.[53]

More often the petitions were tabled, bottled up in committee, or rejected outright. Twice during 1873 Atlanta officials cited a lack of funds in rejecting black pleas for additional schools. A petition signed by seventy-seven Richmond Negroes in 1878 complained that all the Negro schools "lie within a space of five blocks by fifteen . . . and that long since the seating capacity of these has been entirely exhausted." Students had to travel great distances to attend Valley School, which was practically inaccessible during the winter months. The Board's proposal to enlarge Valley was therefore seen as unsatisfactory. When the petitioners called for new schools in Church Hill and Rocketts, the Board responded that it sympathized heartily with the desire for more accommodations, but due to a lack of funds they could take no action.[54]

Two years later a different group of thirty-four Richmond Negroes reiterated the call for increased accommodations in the eastern section of the city. The plans to enlarge Valley still had not been implemented and the petitioners took the opportunity to criticize further the site and to endorse again a policy of dispersal rather than concentration. Of particular concern was the location of the school, which was not only at a great distance from the prospective pupils but was "in a bottom near a creek into which the filth of the other side of the city is drained." The petition was tabled. Responding to pressure from white parents, the Board subsequently abandoned its efforts to sell an east end white school site in order to help meet black needs. Montgomery Negroes who underwent similar experiences with their petitions finally got their Board to erect a new building in 1888, but only after raising $500 toward its construction.[55]

Blacks were more successful in deciding who would teach their children. The Redeemers initially chose to staff the black schools with white teachers, although replacing any remaining Northerners with Southerners. Increasingly, however, blacks challenged this policy by pushing for the appointment of Negroes. More petitions were presented to boards of education and city councils on this matter than on any other matter of concern to Negroes. Although such petitions appeared as early as 1869 in Nashville and 1873 in Atlanta, the great increase in the movement for black faculties came after 1875. This was due in part to the failure of the Civil Rights Act of that year to forbid segregated schools. This omission convinced Negroes that segregated schools would be a long-term reality. Then, too, the growing number of graduates from black colleges provided a pool of candidates who were ready to teach and who clearly had no chance of teaching white children.[56] Thus, less than five months after passage of the Civil Rights Act, four Negroes petitioned the Richmond Board of Education. In general their approach and tone would be followed in countless subsequent petitions in Richmond and elsewhere: they profusely thanked whites for what good had been done, but respectfully asked that further improvement be bestowed through the appointment of black teachers.[57] But moderation meant little to white teachers. In 1877 a white veteran of the missionary movement in Raleigh complained to the governor that "there was an attempt made by certain of the colored people to throw out all the northern teachers from my school . . . and to put all colored teachers in."[58] The effort was thwarted, but there as elsewhere it did not signal any loss of Negro interest in the matter.

By 1881 the Colored Press Association convention in Louisville went on record calling for Negro staffs in Negro schools. The following year Richmond's black newspaper, the *Virginia Star*, led the fight to have Richmond's young blacks "instructed by those who have their interests at heart." A letter praising the newspaper's position revealed that segregated schools were not seen as a betrayal of Negro rights. Although the writer called for the end of the ban against intermarriage and the end of segregation in churches, he cited the major need in school policy as the hiring of black teachers in the black schools.[59]

The Civil Rights Act and the growing pool of job applicants help to account for the call for black teachers, but there were other reasons as well, among them the attitudes and qualifications of the white teachers. In cities such as Nashville certain white teachers forbade their Negro pupils to recognize them in public.[60] Of greater consequence was the fact that after the Northern societies surrendered their power to appoint the faculties, the Negro schools served as the dumping grounds for the rejects from the white institutions. For the 1871–1872 session, the Richmond Board of Education needed twelve teachers for the white and fifteen for the Negro schools. Those individuals with the highest scores on the teacher's examination were sent to the white schools. Those with the next highest scores were assigned to the black schools if they were willing to teach black children. Since many whites refused to work with blacks, the remaining positions had to be filled with applicants "whose standard was lower than heretofore enumerated." Throughout the period it seemed that any incompetent white teacher ended up in a Negro school. M. C. P. Bennett, having failed to gain reappointment to the white schools, argued her case in a series of four letters to the Richmond Board in 1876 and was finally assigned to a black institution.[61]

But black teachers were seen as preferable to even qualified whites. Some blacks wanted Negro teachers because they would mingle socially with the families of the pupils, assisting in the "elevation of the race." Rising black pride led others to reject the notion that black graduates of Fisk, Central Tennessee, Atlanta, and Howard were unable to match whites in the classroom. Most would have agreed with James H. Harris, Raleigh's leading Negro politician, who called for the hiring of black teachers because only a black could truly understand the problems of other blacks.[62]

Individual school boards and city administrators reacted differently to the requests for black instructors. From the beginning of its public school system, Richmond assigned Negro teachers to Navy Hill, a black school under the direction of a white principal. The other cities, however, proved more reluctant to hire blacks. One of the major obstacles was the possibility that this step would lead to integrated faculties. Even after it was decided to permit the entry of Negroes into the system, qualification examinations and teacher preparation classes were held at different hours or even days for the two races. By the end of the period, only Raleigh still had integrated staffs in Negro schools. Montgomery had permitted this practice in the AMA Swayne School, but after the school became totally subject to public decisions in the mid-1880s, only blacks were employed. The three other cities avoided racial mixing, with the exception of one year at Atlanta's Storrs School. Richmond, however, believed it was necessary to have white principals in control of the Negro teachers and continued this policy into the twentieth century. Atlanta and especially Nashville, on the other hand, turned schools over to black faculties only when there were enough qualified applicants to fill all the positions including that of principal.[63]

The problem of securing a sufficient number of competent Negroes to staff an entire school was the most frequent of the many excuses offered to forestall black requests. Sometimes the boards simply explained that it was inadvisable to take such action at that time or that the plan constituted an unnecessary experiment. Unstated was the feared loss of control over the Negro students. On one occasion the Richmond Board refused on the unsupported ground that most of the black parents preferred white teachers and that acquiescence would serve only to further extend the color line in race relations. Another consideration, whether explicit or implicit, was never absent from the minds of board members. "I am perfectly willing for colored teachers to have colored schools," said an Atlanta Board member, "but the colored schools in Atlanta have been served faithfully by white ladies, all of whom except one, are southern born. I am not willing to see them turned off without notice."[64]

By the time black instructors were finally given control of Negro schools, this problem of what to do with the white teachers had been settled by their retirement or reassignment to newly built white schools.[65] There were other factors as well which accounted for the final surrender of the city boards to the wishes of the Negroes. Clearly the unending array of petitions played an important role as did the pressure brought by Negro politicians such as J. C. Napier, the prominent lawyer and Nashville city councilman. Perhaps foremost in the minds of many whites was the matter of economy. Unlike the calls for better schools, the issue of black teachers found white and black aims in agreement. As a member of the Atlanta Board of Education pointed out, rather than increasing the financial burdens of the local boards, it was cheaper to hire black teachers.[66] The comparative salaries of blacks and whites bore him out.

Even though it was sometimes unclear if the discrepancy between the salaries of whites and blacks was a reflection of a difference in ability or merely due to prejudice, by 1891 every city had a widening gap in the salaries paid to the two sets of instructors.[67] Due to the lingering influence of the missionary societies and the continued employment of whites in the Negro schools, the salaries for teachers in the respective schools were initially comparable and at least theoretically based on merit. As late as August 1874, the salaries of teachers (all of whom were Caucasian) in Atlanta's white and Negro schools were similar, although the staffs in the black schools were already earning somewhat less. By 1891, however, when all the principals and teachers in the Negro institutions were black, the gap in salaries had become a chasm. Negro principals earned $650 annually; only one of the thirteen white principals received such a small amount, with all but three of the remaining being paid more than $1,200. One teacher in each black school made $400 and the others, either $350 or $375; in the white schools the lowest salary was $500 and most of the instructors earned at least $550.[68] A majority of the Negro faculty members were graduates of Atlanta University and by no means unqualified to take over instruction of their race; certainly the best among them were better than the worst among the white teachers. The Board of Education saw an easy way to save money, regardless of whether or not the reductions were merited.

Atlanta seems to have been in the middle in its attitude toward salaries of black and white employees in Negro schools. The scant information available for Raleigh suggests that teachers of white pupils enjoyed a slight edge, though not as great as in Atlanta.[69] The more extensive data for Richmond suggests the same pattern. Due largely to the salary equalization efforts of the Readjuster-controlled Board of Education in 1883, teachers in the white schools made only slightly more than their black counterparts in the black institutions and there was clearly an effort to reward on the basis of qualifications.[70] Nashville, however, which maintained a roughly equal pay scale throughout most of the 1880s, moved haltingly in the direction of inequality with the appearance of its first salary schedule for white schools in 1889. Black protests resulted in an upward revision of the schedule for Negro schools, but in December 1891 a minimum difference of at least $5 per month between white and black teachers still reflected the new double standard; the monthly gap between white and black administrators now ranged from $40 to $100.[71]

Montgomery officials had no compunction against furthering the divergence of salaries in their two sets of schools. While the arrangement with the AMA was in force, the wages were approximately the same. By 1875, however, the white school principal was earning $150 per month and the staff members between $50 and $75; the Negro school principal received $100 and his teachers, $35 to $60 with only one in the highest category. By 1880 the average white school's teacher was making $60 per month and his Negro school counterpart, $49. Ten years later the white teachers had maintained their earlier salary, but individuals in black schools (by now all Negroes) had been reduced to $38. By 1893 no black teacher was making more than $320 per year, while the lowest salary for whites was $400.[72]

Ironically, the shift from white to black teachers was made easier by the earlier neglect of black facilities. When new schools for blacks were finally opened in the 1880s, it seemed natural to appoint Negroes because of black requests, the absence of white teachers to be displaced, and the lower salaries of blacks. Such considerations, for example, accounted for the appointment of blacks to the Knowles School in Nashville and the East End School in Richmond.[73] Yet the innovation would have still been impossible had there not been competent Negroes available to fill the positions. Favorable reports coming from other cities about the quality of black appointees led an Atlanta Board of Education member to base part of his support on the precedents set in Augusta, Savannah, and Macon. The existence of growing numbers of such qualified individuals by the late 1880s thus nullified the charge that inexperienced or incompetent blacks would be replacing whites. Whereas in 1884, only 5 of the 24 Negro applicants passed Nashville's teacher's examination, by 1887, this was true of 19 of 42. More significant, two of the top three scores, including the highest, were achieved by Negroes. Seventh in the city was a young Fisk student named W. E. B. Du Bois.[74]

Despite such arguments in favor of the black requests, the transition was a slow process, usually spread over several years and confronted by staunch resistance. The Pearl School, the last black facility in Nashville to be staffed by Negroes, had to wait until 1887. In that year Summer Hill School achieved the same distinction in Atlanta, thanks only to the tie-breaking vote of the president of the Board of Education. In Richmond, black teachers were placed in all the Negro schools only after the Readjuster governor appointed a new Board of Education. The Board hired Negro principals and teachers for every black school except the high school. When the Democrats returned to power, they replaced the principals with whites, but retained the black instructors. The Colored High and Normal School, however, remained entirely in the hands of whites until 1924.[75]

Having finally acted, the boards of education seemed pleased with the performances of the black faculty members. "I believe the Board found the key to the problem of the education of our colored population when competent colored teachers were put in charge of Houston Street School," wrote the Atlanta Superintendent of Education in 1881. They "have demonstrated the fact that they understand their own race, and can discipline and teach to the satisfaction of their patrons." His counterpart in Montgomery reported that the Negro instructors "have done very well," although he modified his praise by observing that "it would not be very easy to find teachers among the blacks that would succeed better."[76]

Satisfaction with the new system was partly due to the fact that most of the new faculty members were considered "safe"; the boards and the white citizens at-large felt that the students would not be exposed to ideas that would threaten the status quo in race relations. When the Atlanta school board initially considered the appointment of Negro teachers in 1877, one of the requirements was that they be natives of the South and residents of Georgia; ten years later one of the main arguments in favor of turning the last school over to black instructors was the existence of a sufficient number of competent graduates of Southern institutions. In 1887, 24 of the Negro teachers employed by the city had received their training at Atlanta University; by 1910 more than three-quarters of the faculty members in the black schools were its alumni.[77] Indeed, not only did most of the teachers graduate from neighborhood colleges or normal schools, but many came up through the local public school system. Of the 84 Negro instructors employed by the Richmond school system in 1890, 80 had attended the Negro high school, as compared to only 87 graduates of the white high school among the 154 teachers in the white schools.[78]

Blacks were less successful in securing appointments to local boards of education. Demands such as those made by two Atlanta Negroes, politician C. C. Wimbish and R. H. Carter, principal of the Houston Street School, at the Georgia Educational Convention for Colored Men held in 1883 bore little fruit; nor were the numerous petitions any more effective.[79] The contrast with requests for black teachers was marked, for much more was at stake. As the *Richmond Dispatch* put it, blacks should not be allowed to exercise control over white children, teachers, and taxpayers. It also feared that mixed schools would result and besides, it said, "where and when did the negro become possessed of the notion that he was the equal of the white man."[80]

Only when Republicans or Readjusters, as in Richmond, were in power did Negroes have the opportunity to serve on local boards. Alfred Menefee served in Nashville in 1867, Richard Forrester and R. A. Paul in Richmond in 1883, and Holland Thompson in Montgomery from 1870 to 1873. Along with their white Republican colleagues, they lost their positions when the city councils reverted to Democratic control.[81] The boards on which these men served were the most favorable to the cause of Negro education. The Readjusters during their brief hegemony in Richmond, for example, not only appointed black principals and teachers to all the Negro grammar schools, but added needed

classroom space by making Moore Street Industrial School, a previously private Negro institution, a part of the public system and by constructing a twelve-room building in the neglected eastern part of the
city. In the long run the Board had the greatest influence on the decision of its successors to accord blacks the best treatment of any of the
five cities. Of all the Negro members, however, the most influential
in the five capitals (and perhaps in the entire South) was Holland
Thompson. Montgomery's two-term state legislator and four-term city
councilman, Thompson was appointed to the city's first school board
by the Republican Council of which he was a prominent member. He
was instrumental in helping to organize the system and in defending
the right of Negro schools to equal appropriations.[82]

Given the general inclination of whites to neglect the Negro public
schools in order to fund the white schools, the blacks made the best
of their predicament. Despite overcrowded classrooms, poorer equipment, and often inferior teaching, Negro children maintained in most
of the cities the same or even a better attendance record than their
white counterparts. In Richmond throughout the late 1870s and 1880s,
the percentage of Negro attendance based on enrolled students was
normally 1 percent or 2 percent higher than whites, although both
were approximately 95 percent. In 1890 the figures were 96.5 percent
for blacks and 92.9 percent for whites.[83]

Clearly Negro interest in education had not diminished. Besides
general comments by visitors and officials, however, there are little
more than occasional rates of promotion or examination scores to
evaluate the success of this education. Even these statistics can be
misleading given the differences in teaching, testing, grading, and the
possible desire of both black and white instructors to show better performances from their students. Nevertheless, the figures deserve some
mention. The fragmentary evidence suggests an edge in favor of the
whites that was narrowing as the period progressed. Whereas the
average final grade in Nashville schools in 1873 was 60 percent for
Negroes and 73 percent for whites, by 1890 the respective statistics
were 66 percent and 72 percent. Throughout the early years in Richmond, final examination averages for whites were 4 to 11 percent
higher than those for blacks, but during the 1880–1881 academic year,
the Negroes actually scored higher by a margin of 82.5 percent to 80.3
percent; five years later they still enjoyed a slight lead of 85.7 percent
to 85.4 percent. Rates of promotion in Richmond, especially in the

higher grades, were still decidedly in favor of the whites with the figures for the lowest grade in 1890 being 82.1 percent for whites and
76.3 percent for blacks; for the high schools they were 65.4 percent
and 52.3 percent respectively.[84]

Regardless of statistics, the quality of the graduates produced by
these Negro schools attests to their educational contribution. In Richmond during the period under discussion the graduates included Maggie L. Walker, who became one of the wealthiest black women in the
country, secretary-treasurer of the Independent Order of Saint Luke,
founder of St. Luke's Penny Savings Bank, and a member of the
Board of Directors of the N.A.A.C.P.; James Hugo Johnston, the future president of Virginia State University; and John Mitchell, Jr.,
later editor of the *Richmond Planet,* banker, city councilman, and a
leading militant force in national Negro affairs.[85] When the great number of teachers, ministers, and professionals is added to these individuals, it is clear that the black public schools, despite all odds against
them, played an important role in the lives and advancement of Negroes.

The schools, however, did not reach all segments of the black community. An English visitor correctly pointed to the forces working
against education, even in Richmond. Though somewhat overdrawn
and marred by an underestimation of the desire of blacks for education and the effects of inadequate school facilities, the picture would
hold for the entire urban South. It would also apply to the white poor.

> Two Negro parents out of three neglect to send their little folks to
> school. They will not take the pains. School hours are fixed, school
> habits orderly; and Negroes find it hard to keep fixed hours and to
> maintain order in their cabins. If their imps go to school, they must
> be called bedtimes, and must be washed and combed. Clothes need
> making and mending. Meals must be cooked, and the youngsters must
> be sent out early. Children bring home slates and books, and want a
> quiet corner for their evening tasks. But where, in the filthy cabins of
> Jackson's Ward, are they to find quiet nooks? And then though
> schools are free, books and slates cost money; and the dollars spent on
> books and slates are so much taken from the margin left for drams
> and gurds. Improvident fathers find the cost of school a burden; in-
> dolent mothers find the worry of school a great addition to their cares.
> Such parents sicken at the efforts to be made, a strain from dawn to
> dusk; a self denial from year to year; and in their indolent selfishness,
> they let their children loiter in the lanes and wallow in the styes [*sic*].

Available statistics for the lower class suggest that Negroes were less likely to be literate than whites. Of 18 white pauper children in the Richmond almshouse in 1874, 8 could read; only 2 of the 14 Negro children could. The figures among white men were 45 out of 59; among black men, 8 out of 68. Of 2,898 whites arrested in Nashville in 1890, 2,788 could read and write, but this was true of only 925 of the 2,987 blacks. Citywide census data for Nashville, Richmond, and Atlanta reflect a similar gap between Negro and white literacy.[86]

In short, the benefits of education were unevenly distributed. As in other areas, treatment of blacks varied from city to city. Negroes fared best in Richmond, where the number of blacks on the City Council and the Readjuster Board of Education helped to defend their rights. In Montgomery and Atlanta, on the other hand, where Negro political power was weakest after Reconstruction, their situation was especially inferior to whites. For a brief time during Reconstruction blacks enjoyed equality in appropriations in the five capitals, but they were still denied adequate facilities. Under the Redeemers this earlier parity was destroyed until even in Richmond by the late 1880s the gap between black and white schools was widening. The protests from urban blacks thus resulted primarily in the replacing of white instructors with blacks. This early display of black power had its cost, however. Blacks accommodated themselves to the system of segregated schools and produced a group with a vested interest in its continuation. And they also made it easier for whites to discriminate. Segregation had replaced exclusion, but nowhere did the principle of separate but equal constitute anything more than empty rhetoric.

8

Public Accommodations

Race relations in public accommodations were relatively fluid. Unlike welfare and education, *de jure* segregation was not widespread until after 1890. As a result, there was a degree of integration throughout the period not matched in other aspects of Southern life. Nevertheless, *de facto* segregation generally prevailed. And, again, what it ordinarily replaced was not integration, but exclusion, although the roots of this shift often lay in the antebellum period.

Before the war blacks, except for servants, had been excluded from restaurants, hotels, and parks. They were also barred from many theaters and shows, though managers sometimes provided segregated sections. Steamboats and railroads segregated those few blacks who traveled as paying passengers, while in New Orleans the use of separate streetcars for blacks superseded earlier exclusion.[1]

Southern whites continued these policies during the years 1865 to 1867. Some places of amusement continued to exclude blacks; others retained their earlier pattern of segregated seating, as did those in New Orleans; and still others—for example, those in Nashville, Montgomery, and Richmond—opened their doors to freedmen for the first time, although also on a segregated basis. Traveling circuses, which were especially popular with blacks, went so far in Montgomery as to establish separate entrances for the races.[2] The states of Texas, Mississippi, and Florida passed laws to strengthen existing segregation on public conveyances. Savannah officials closed their city parks from fear that blacks would have to be admitted. Meanwhile, the leading white res-

182

taurants and hotels continued exclusion. But the postwar shift was already evident in the decision of Nashville streetcar owners to provide segregated cars for the previously excluded blacks.[3]

As in education and welfare, Republicans were either unwilling or unable to end segregation in most forms of public accommodation. The Republican-controlled legislature in North Carolina was so averse to the idea of forced integration that, in 1870, it defeated a proposal to assure Negroes the same facilities as whites on steamboats and railroads. Even the spate of antidiscrimination laws passed elsewhere, often over the objections of white Republicans, seem to have had little effect on the pattern of segregation in public conveyances. If they accomplished anything, it was to encourage the railroads and steamboat companies to provide supposedly equal—though separate—accommodations for blacks.[4] Despite the passage of the 1866 Civil Rights Act, a British traveler who extensively toured the South during 1867–1868 concluded that "there are 'nigger cars' open, of course, to white people and often used as smoking cars, but to which all coloured passengers have to confine themselves."[5] Vernon Lane Wharton concluded about Mississippi's antidiscrimination railroad act passed in 1870 that "In spite of its stringent provisions, the law had almost no effect."[6] As demonstrated by the numerous suits by blacks against Southern railroad companies, with few exceptions the best that blacks could hope for were segregated accommodations the equal of the whites. Blacks, for example, were forced to ride on the platforms of cars between Montgomery and Union Springs, Alabama.[7]

The Reconstruction governments had a greater impact on traveling arrangements in streetcars. This feature of urban life presents the most problems for anyone interested in tracing the evolution of patterns of segregation. Historians generally agree that *de jure* segregation was a product of the 1890s.[8] The extent of prior *de facto* segregation remains uncertain, however, partly because of the character of the streetcar system itself. It would be a simple matter if there had been different cars for the two races either run separately or in tandem, but the presence of one car without racial designation could still mean either that blacks had been excluded or that they had been segregated within that car. Another difficulty in considering the streetcar arises from its staggered appearance in Southern cities. The New Orleans system, for example, dates from the antebellum period, while Richmond's began operating in 1865, Atlanta's in 1871, and Raleigh's in

1886. Each line might have been segregated from its inception, and thus it cannot be assumed that, because Louisville or New Orleans apparently desegregated their cars before 1870, subsequent lines in other cities followed their example. The same is true within each city—because segregation was discontinued on one line does not necessarily mean that it was not resumed until the appearance of Jim Crow legislation, nor does it mean that other companies in the city did not initiate *de facto* segregation. What is clear is that in many cities the initial Republican contribution was to force streetcar companies to admit black riders.

Richmond provides an early example of the change in streetcar policy. Prior to May 1867, Richmond Negroes were initially excluded from using the cars and then permitted to ride on the outside. In April of that year four blacks staged a sit-in and were forcibly ejected from a car by a policeman. City officials ruled that, as a private concern, the railway company could establish its own regulations, but they were overruled by federal military authorities, who directed that the cars must carry all passengers able to pay the fare. Nevertheless, General John Schofield permitted the substitution of segregation for exclusion. Sources differ as to whether there were alternate cars for each race, with the Negro car distinguished by a black ball on its roof, or whether those cars with a white ball were solely for white women and their escorts. In either case, segregation remained in force even after Radical Republicans gained control of the city administration.[9]

This transition from exclusion to segregation, with perhaps an intermediary stage of riding on the platforms of the cars, was repeated in other cities. Negroes in Nashville, Charleston, and Mobile were among the many who won the right to ride in the streetcars under civilian Republicans or military authorities. As late as 1871, however, Maria Waterbury, a Northern teacher, found that a Mobile streetcar contained an iron lattice dividing the car racially. When a woman took her servant into the white end of the car, the conductor stopped the vehicle and moved the black woman into her "proper place." In New Orleans the question remains as to the presence of segregation when blacks finally rode in the same cars as whites.[10]

Republicans had less effect on racial patterns in a wide variety of other public accommodations. Exclusion remained the rule in the best restaurants and hotels as well as in many theaters, such as the Mobile Opera House.[11] Judging from the recurring use in newspaper adver-

tisements of the words "gentlemen" and "ladies" to describe the patrons of skating rinks or to such phrases as "the management reserve
[sic] the right to refuse admission or use of skates to any objectionable
person," this new craze must have been another form of recreation initially denied blacks. Nevertheless, blacks did enjoy many forms of
segregated recreation. Newspapers were filled with advertisements
or news accounts concerning "negro barrooms," "negro brothels," and
"negro billiard parlors."[12] Montgomery boasted a "colored skating
rink," Nashville had a "colored fairgrounds," and New Orleans and
Nashville had Negro grandstands at the local racetracks. Negroes
in Montgomery went to picnics at Lambert Springs and the Cypress Pond, while whites went to Oak Grove and Pickett Springs. And
most of the theaters, including many previously closed to blacks, provided segregated seating in the galleries.[13] There is also evidence that
Republican politicians observed the color line. At the 1869 constitutional convention in South Carolina, white delegates occupied the
front rows while the blacks filled in the seats at the rear of the hall; in
the courtroom of the Radical Circuit Court judge in Richmond, whites
sat on the west side and blacks on the east; and in 1868 North Carolina Republicans divided the gallery of the Senate into three sections:
one for whites, one for blacks, and one for both races. Republican
Governor Robert Scott of South Carolina sought to make amends to
that state's blacks because none had been invited to the annual governor's ball in 1869. He held open house every Thursday, but "only
Negro politicians called at that time."[14]

Although the Republicans supported segregation during and after
Reconstruction, they did urge "equal treatment" for blacks. During
debates on Congressional civil rights legislation, for example, Senator
Joshua Hill of Georgia and Representative Alexander White of Alabama argued that separate provisions for blacks in public carriers,
places of amusement, hotels, and restaurants were not a violation of
civil rights if the accommodations were equal to those of whites.[15] The
Alabama Republican Party in its 1874 platform declared that "the republican party does not desire mixed schools or accommodations for
colored people, but they ask that in all these advantages they shall be
equal." Tennessee's 1881 statute which provided for separate but equal
accommodations on railroad cars was signed by a Republican governor; and it was a Republican-controlled Georgia legislature that passed
an 1870 statute requiring "like and equal accommodations in public

transportation." Alabama Republicans unsuccessfully pushed for such a measure and then congratulated those railroads which voluntarily provided separate but equal accommodations.[16] The Republican legacy to the Redeemers therefore consisted of the seemingly mutually exclusive policies of segregation and equality.

Given the opposition of Southern whites, it seems unlikely that the Republicans, even had they wanted to, could have forced integration on the South. Conditions in the region at the end of Reconstruction were revealed in the reaction to the civil rights agitation that culminated in the Civil Rights Act of 1875.[17] Commenting on an early version of the Civil Rights Bill, the *Nashville Union and American* observed that its sponsor, Charles Sumner, wanted blacks to be on an "equal footing" with whites in all activities. "This is a bold step for Mr. Sumner to take," the editor said, "but he is fanatic enough to do it." As the bill neared final passage, other newspapers echoed the fear that it would drastically change the pattern of Southern life. In February 1875 the *Atlanta Constitution*—though thankful for the final version's omission of cemeteries and schools—concluded that "its other provisions are all that the most revolutionary white villain or the densest negro brain could desire." After passage of the act, Raleigh's *Daily Sentinel* argued that "if the principles of the Republicans succeed, the negro will be forced upon . . . [the white man's] wife, and his daughter, on the cars, steamboats, in public inns, at hotel tables, and in theatres and other places of amusement."[18]

Once passions cooled, the Southern press reassured its readers that either the law quickly would be declared unconstitutional or else the Democrats would repeal it when they won their expected victories in the 1876 presidential and Congressional elections. Referring to the statute as a "dead letter," the *Atlanta Constitution* pointed out that "it gets a judicial cuff whenever it appears in the courts, no matter whether the judge be a republican or democrat."[19] The paper was correct. Federal courts in Atlanta, Richmond, and Savannah upheld the right of railroads and steamboats to provide separate accommodations for the races just as they could for members of the two sexes.[20]

Whites defended segregation as an indispensable device for the control of "uppity blacks." Since the end of the war the Democratic press had encouraged fears of disorder or racial conflict that would result from nonobservance of the color line. But in the final analysis social equality meant to white Southerners the specter of miscegenation, intermarriage, and amalgamation that would inevitably follow any departure from segregation or exclusion. "The whole people of this state are not ready to accept the perfect social and political equality of the blacks with them," wrote the *Nashville Union and American* in opposing passage of the Fourteenth Amendment.

> They are not prepared to admit the Negro . . . to indiscriminate mingling in the social circle, at church, in the ball room, in the theatre, in the concert hall, in railroad cars, in the parlor, and at hotels and watering places. They have not yet satisfied themselves of the superiority of the theory of miscegenation and the improving results of amalgamation; and are not, therefore, ready to open the doors of marriage between the races, either by legal enactment or in the more solemn form of constitutional provision.[21]

This linking of civil rights with social equality and intermarriage was also present in remarks made to David Macrae by a Southerner who argued that political equality would lead to social equality,

> for if . . . I sit side by side in the Senate, House, or on the judicial bench, with a colored man, how can I refuse to sit with him at the table? What will follow? . . . If we have social equality we shall have intermarriage, and if we have intermarriage we shall degenerate; we shall become a race of mulattoes; . . . we shall be ruled out from the family of white nations. Sir, it is a matter of life and death with the Southern people to keep their blood pure.

This opinion was offered before a number of Southern clergymen, who heartily endorsed it. Macrae concluded that "this seemed to me everywhere the dread that lies deepest in the Southern heart, and gave most fury to its [integration's] opposition." Montgomery Congressman Hilary A. Herbert also believed that Negroes wanted the promise allegedly made them by Radicals of "absolute and complete social equality, equal rights not only in public conveyances, hotels and theatres, but also in the relations of marriage."[22]

Bothered little by the Civil Rights Act even before its official demise in 1883, the Redeemers occasionally returned to exclusion or instituted segregation in those few cases where there had been integration. Whereas Hamilton Park and Angelo's Hall in Jackson, Mississippi, for example, had been used by whites and blacks on separate occasions under the Republicans, by 1890 both facilities were closed to blacks.[23] The basic response of the Redeemers, however, was to continue already existing segregation.

White opinion was not unified, but most Redeemers also adopted the rhetoric of the Republicans' separate but equal commitment. Despite the failure to honor this pledge, in several instances the Redeemers actually moved beyond their predecessors to provide segregated, if unequal, facilities in areas previously characterized by exclusion. Some whites even distinguished between segregation and discrimination. Thus a Tennessee law prohibited "discrimination" in any place of public amusement which charged a fee, but nevertheless maintained that this provision did not outlaw "separate accommodations and seats for colored and white persons."[24]

As early as 1872, Atlanta's Union Passenger Depot had a "Freedmen's Saloon" and at least by 1885 Nashville's Union Depot had "a colored passenger room." In 1885 Austin, Texas, was among the many Texas cities required by law to have separate waiting rooms for both races.[25] It is not known what facilities existed for blacks before the appearance of these Negro waiting rooms. The experiences of Montgomery and Raleigh, however, are instructive. The new Union Depot in Montgomery was described in 1877 as having "a ladies' waiting room" and a "gents' waiting room"; the original plans for the Raleigh Union Depot in 1890 included a "ladies' waiting room" and a "gentlemen's waiting room." Although there was no reference to a Negro waiting room, the use of the words "gents," "gentlemen," and "ladies" rather than "men" and "women" suggests the exclusion of blacks. If so, then the mention of three waiting rooms at the Montgomery Depot in 1885—one each for "ladies," "gentlemen," and "colored people"—and the revised plans for the Raleigh Depot which contained a separate waiting room for blacks suggest further evidence of the shift from exclusion to segregation.[26]

Segregation persisted or replaced exclusion in theaters. For the most part blacks were confined to separate galleries. In Richmond, however, thanks to the 1875 Civil Rights Act blacks won access to a segregated portion of the once all-white dress circle.[27] Most restaurants and hotels continued to exclude blacks, as did the better barrooms. Some bars catering to whites charged blacks outrageous prices or doctored their drinks; less subtle was the sign over the bar of a Nashville saloon in 1884: NO DRINKS SOLD TO COLORED PERSONS. In 1888 the *Atlanta Constitution* reported that of Atlanta's sixty-eight saloons, five served blacks and of those only two definitely served both races.[28] On those instances when blacks were admitted to primarily white restaurants, bars, and

hotels, they were carefully segregated. Albert Binersch operated a restaurant in the rear of a Nashville saloon and served "responsible and
well behaved colored people" in his kitchen; the Planters Hotel in
Augusta, Georgia, seated blacks at separate tables in the dining room,
while the St. Charles, the only Richmond hotel to accept a black delegate to the 1886 Knights of Labor convention, gave him second-class
quarters and seated him at a table in the dining room farthest from the
door and behind a screen; and in answer to the Civil Rights Act, Montgomery's Ruby Saloon set up "a small counter" apart from the main
bar for black customers.[29] Such examples probably marked only a transitory stage on the way to total segregation in separate establishments.

The With the exception of New Orleans, athletic events were rigidly segregated. Most cities had at least two black baseball teams, and, since
there were no games between organized teams of blacks and whites,
there were city championship games for each race.[30] Prostitution also
suffered the effects of segregation. Even in New Orleans, houses of
prostitution offering white and black women to a mixed clientele had
become a rarity by 1880. Atlanta had separate blocks for white and
black prostitutes. When two well-dressed mulattoes sought admission
to a brothel on Collins Street that served only whites, they were driven
off by gunfire. Nashville's Lone Star brothel, on the other hand, had its
ground and upper floors occupied by white prostitutes and its basement by blacks.[31] If taken to court, the prostitutes would likely have
found the spectators racially separated, and perhaps, like the procedure
in Savannah's Mayor's Court in 1876, they would have sworn on a
Bible set aside for their particular race.[32]

The situation in parks was more complex. There were few formal
parks and pleasure grounds in antebellum cities and blacks were excluded from those which existed.[33] It was not until the mid-1870s, in
most cases after Republicans had relinquished control of local governments, that the park movement began to affect Southern urban life.
Most of these new parks were privately owned, often by streetcar companies, which used them to encourage traffic on their lines, but munici-
pally-owned parks became common by the 1880s.

As already mentioned in the case of Jackson's Hamilton Park, blacks
increasingly were barred from many parks. Sometimes, as in the case
of Nashville's Spring Park, this can be surmised only from the language
of the local press. In other cases speculation is unnecessary. In 1881
an Atlanta black brought suit against the city for being ejected from

City Hall Park because of his color. Six years later blacks taking the street railway to Ponce de Leon Springs were informed "politely but forcibly" by policemen that they would not be admitted; in 1890 blacks were excluded from the city's Inman Park. Already Atlanta blacks had begun to gravitate to the grounds and woods around Clark University, leading the *Atlanta Constitution* to call for construction of a park for them in that area.[34] Then, too, in most Southern cities blacks and whites continued to frequent separate picnic groves, while the large all-white cemeteries served as parks for whites.

Nevertheless, the existence of separate parks for whites and blacks as a general phenomenon seems to have been the product of the post-1890 period. As of 1882, Nashville's Watkins Park was visited by "persons of all shades and sizes." As late as 1890, blacks and whites were invited to watch a Negro militia company drill in Atlanta's Piedmont Park and on Independence Day, blacks were among the mostly white crowd which enjoyed the facilities at the city's Grant Park. Montgomery's Highland and Raleigh's Pullem Park were apparently open to blacks and whites.[35]

In the absence of separate parks, segregation within the grounds became the norm. Although blacks enjoyed access to Atlanta's Ponce de Leon Springs until the late 1880s, the two races entertained themselves at separate dancehalls and refreshment stands. Blacks attending the two free concerts given at Nashville's Glendale Park were barred from the new pavilion, while those visiting Raleigh's Brookside Park could not use the swimming pool.[36] And when a new zoo opened in Atlanta's Grant Park, it contained eight cages occupying the center of the building and stretching from one end to the other. An aisle seven feet wide was railed off on each side of the row of cages: one for blacks, the other for whites. "There is no communication between them," the *Atlanta Constitution* observed, "and two large double doors at each side of the building serve as entrance and exit to the aisles."[37]

Segregation also seems to have been the rule at expositions and fairs. Nashville Negroes had their own fairgrounds, purchased by a black organization.[38] Blacks could attend certain functions at the white fairgrounds but specifically which functions and at what times is not always clear. Negroes, for example, were barred from the interstate drill competition held in 1883. But again admittance of both races went hand-in-hand with segregation. There was a special gate provided for blacks in the Exposition Building at a Nashville fair in 1875; there was a "colored people's saloon" in addition to the main grandstand saloon at the 1871 Georgia State Fair in Macon; and at the Southern Exposition held in Montgomery in 1890 the two races ate in separate restaurants.[39]

The situation in public conveyances is still less easily discernible, and there seems to have been a greater divergence in practice. As under the Republicans, steamboats remained the most segregated form of travel. Although Virginia did not pass a law requiring the racial separation of passengers on steamboats until 1900, the *City of Richmond* in service to Norfolk since 1880 had from its inception "a neat and comfortable dining room for colored passengers in the lower cabin."[40] George Washington Cable discovered in 1887 that Louisiana Negroes had to confine themselves to a separate quarter of the boats called the "Freedman's bureau." And to Frederick Douglass it seemed the Negro ironically had more freedom on steamboats as a slave since "he could ride anywhere, side by side with his white master. . . . [A]s a freedman, he was not allowed a cabin abaft the wheel."[41]

Although there was greater integration in train travel, blacks were generally confined to the smoking and second-class cars, though occasionally they were provided with separate first-class accommodations the equal of white passengers. During her trip through the United States in 1883, Iza Duffus Hardy was especially struck by the variety of methods used on trains to keep Negroes "in their place." On the train leaving Charleston, Negroes were in a separate second-class car, although they did pay a lower fare than whites. At Savannah on the Florida Express, the Negroes rode in the forward part of the smoking car nearest the engine. Somewhat farther south Hardy found a car labeled "For Coloured Passengers" which she discovered "was in every respect exactly like the car reserved for us 'white folk,' the same velvet seats, ice water tank; every comfort the same—and of course, the same fare." As opposed to this rare instance of a first-class car, the car assigned to Negroes in Charleston was described by her traveling companion Lady Duffus Hardy as "seedy looking." The association of Negroes with smoking cars was very pronounced. While traveling on the Central Railroad in Georgia eight years earlier, Alexander Stephens and two other noted Georgians were ejected from a first-class Negro car because they had seen blacks in it and had assumed it was a second-class car where they could smoke.[42]

The first-class cars for Negroes on the Central Railroad reflected an effort by certain railroads and sympathetic whites to provide separate but equal accommodations for blacks able to afford first-class rates.[43] As early as 1870, the Orange Railroad passenger trains in Virginia had a special car exclusively for Negroes where smoking was prohibited. A regular smoking car was to be used by both blacks and whites. In 1885 a Louisville and Nashville train running between Montgomery and Mobile had a first-class coach "specially provided for colored people." In the opinion of the *Atlanta Constitution*, it "was as good in every sense as the [white] car. . . . There was no smoking or disorder permitted." In a case involving alleged discrimination on an Alabama railroad in 1887, the Interstate Commerce Commission held that different cars for the races indeed could be used provided that the accommodations were equal and that Negroes paying first-class fare received first-class facilities.[44]

In only one area of Southern life was the shift to segregation relatively incomplete by 1890. August Meier and Elliott Rudwick have argued that segregation in streetcars "declined after being instituted in many places prior to and just after the Civil War."[45] There is certainly evidence to support the contention that streetcars were the most integrated Southern facility. Referring to the color line, the Nashville *Daily American* observed in 1880 that "in Tennessee there is such a line, as every man, white and black, well knows, but on our street cars the races ride together without thought of it, or offensive exhibition, or attempt to isolate the colored passenger." Ten years later, when there was a rumor that the president of one of Richmond's street railways had been asked to provide separate cars for black passengers, the *Richmond Planet*, a Negro newspaper, expressed surprise and counseled against the plan since "we do not know of a city in the south in which discrimination is made on the street cars." And in 1908 Ray Stannard Baker sadly concluded that "a few years ago the Negro came and went in the street cars in most cities and sat where he pleased, but gradually Jim Crow laws or local regulations were passed forcing him into certain seats at the back of the car."[46]

Segregation, however, may have been more prevalent than these accounts would indicate. In Richmond and Savannah segregated streetcars persisted at least until the mid-1870s.[47] But segregation on horse cars could be inconvenient and expensive to maintain. Because the horses could pull only one rather small car at a time, the segregation of passengers required either the use of an entirely separate car and horse for blacks or else limiting them to a portion of the already crowded cars open to whites. This problem was remedied by the appearance on Southern streets at the end of the 1880s of the dummy streetcar and the later electrification of the lines. The steam-driven dummy derived its name from the attempt to disguise the engine as a passenger car in order to cut down on noise and to avoid frightening horses. Since it had two cars, or else a single car larger than that pulled by horses, segregation of the races was easier.

In 1886 Montgomery initiated dummy service with the forward cars reserved for whites and the rear cars for blacks.[48] Two years later the dummy was also responsible for the first clear indication of segregation in Atlanta. The dummy service, begun by the Metropolitan Street Railway Company in September 1888, included two cars in addition to the engine—one painted yellow for whites, the other red for blacks. Likewise, the first documented case of segregation in a Nashville streetcar after 1867 was contained in an 1888 report about a Negro minister's sermon. It simply noted that "in a sermon Sunday night, [the minister] attacked the management of the dummy line for insisting that he should move to another car or get off." This incident serves not only as an example of streetcar segregation, but as a demonstration of the difficulties involved in researching the subject, for neither the *Nashville Banner* nor the *Daily American*—the two leading dailies in the city—carried a news account of the episode and the latter did not even mention the sermon. During the following two years, however, the newspapers reported additional instances of blacks being told to go to separate cars.[49]

The period of seeming flexibility came to an end with the passage of statutes enforcing segregation. Both blacks and the streetcar companies often objected to these Jim Crow measures.[50] But what were they protesting? Was it segregation or legal segregation that blacks were against? Did the owners object to any form of racial separation or simply to one that made them supply additional cars, usually an unprofitable venture? The fact that many Nashville blacks would have settled for separate cars in 1905 as long as there were black fare collectors suggests that the boycotts were not simply against segregation.[51] The twentieth-century practice of dividing streetcars into black and white sections lends credence to the view that white owners were objecting less to the initiation of segregation than to the legal requirement for more cars. As the *Richmond Planet* noted, Southern managers realized that "separate cars would not pay and what was worse there would be more trouble on account of it."[52] Thanks to the co-operation of local officials the managers could handle the "trouble"; financial aspects were another matter.

Then, too, why would streetcars be immune from segregation, given its prevalence in most other areas of Southern life? One answer, of course, is that they were not. But if they were, then why? The answer would seem to lie less with the absence of white hostility than in the circumstances in which streetcars operated. The resistance of white managers might be a reason, but as important was the greater leverage blacks exercised over streetcar policy as compared, for example, to railroad policy. Clearly boycotts presented a more serious threat to a local streetcar line than they did to a railroad, which drew passengers from many communities. In addition, boycotts could be better organized because of the existence of alternative means of transportation. Whether by using hacks, private carriages, or simply walking, Negroes could still go about their business without the streetcars.

Both white Republicans and Redeemers came to embrace the shift from exclusion to segregation in public accommodations. But what helped to assure this shift was the attitude of the blacks themselves.

Blacks on occasion did criticize segregation. During Richmond's celebration of the passage of the Fifteenth Amendment, a Negro minister, the Reverend J. Sella Martin, was accused by the *Richmond Dispatch* of saying that "the negroes must claim the right to sit with the whites in theatres, churches, and other public buildings, to ride with them on the cars, and to stay at the same hotels with them." Similarly, after Tennessee passed its Jim Crow law in 1881, the Reverend W. A. Sinclair of Nashville argued that "no man of color [should] ride in a car simply because it is set apart and *labeled* 'exclusively for negroes,' but rather let every individual choose of the regular coaches the one in which to ride." Six years later when Charles Dudley Warner asked a group of leading Nashville black businessmen, "what do you want here in the way of civil rights that you have not?" the answer was, "we want to be treated like men, like anybody else regardless of color. . . . We want public conveyances open to us according to the fare we pay; we want the privilege to go to hotels and to theatres, operas and places of amusement . . . we cannot go to the places assigned us in concerts and theatres without loss of self respect."[53]

Negroes sometimes opposed segregation by deeds as well as by words. As noted earlier, by 1870 Charleston, New Orleans, Richmond, Mobile, and Nashville were among several cities to experience challenges to the policies of exclusion or segregation on their streetcars.[54] Suits also were brought against offending railroad companies.[55] Challenges to segregation, however, were most pronounced after passage of the 1875 Civil Rights Act. But for the most part blacks failed in their attempts to break down the racial barriers in theaters, hotels, restaurants, public conveyances, and bars.[56] More isolated and equally unsuccessful attempts occurred with decreasing frequency in subsequent years.[57] The few successes were due to special circumstances. During his visit to Atlanta in 1877, for example, Lieutenant Henry O. Flipper, a native of the city and the first Negro graduate of West Point, was invited by a white officer into Schumann's Drugstore for a glass of soda water. Flipper later told a large crowd of blacks that "I know it is not a usual thing to sell to colored people, but we got it." When he added that before coming to the meeting he and J. O. Wimbish, a Negro politician, had joined another white officer for a drink of soda at Schumann's, the crowd, appreciative of the difficulties, loudly applauded.[58]

Despite this opposition to segregation, the majority of blacks, including their leaders, focused their attention elsewhere. The failure of a sustained attack on segregation perhaps resulted from the lack of support from their white allies and the courts. There were other reasons as well. Five prominent Nashville blacks, for example, argued that Negroes would not use passage of the Civil Rights Bill "to make themselves obnoxious" since they had too much self-respect to go where they were not wanted. Besides, they added, such actions would lead only to disturbances and they wanted as little agitation as possible.[59] Bishop Henry M. Turner echoed this view in 1889, telling a reporter that "I don't find much trouble in traveling at [sic] the south on account of my color, for the simple reason that I am not in the habit of pushing myself where I am not wanted."[60] A similar attitude might have governed the response of "several really respectable colored persons" in Charleston to the attempt of a Negro to buy a ticket for the orchestra or dress circle of the Academy of Music in 1870. Calling the move a cheap political trick, they "avowed their willingness to sit in the places provided for their own race when they visited the Academy."[61]

Economic pressures also led blacks to accept segregation. Negroes who relied on a white clientele were especially reluctant to serve members of both races. Shortly after the passage of the Civil Rights Act two Negro barbers in Edgefield, across the river from Nashville, refused to serve black customers. The previous year a Negro delegation had been ejected when it demanded shaves at the shop of a black barber in Chattanooga. Asked if their money was not as good as a white man's, the barber, fearful of the loss of his white customers, answered, "Yes just as good, but there is not enough of it."[62] Both whites and blacks understood the focus of economic power. In 1875 the *Nashville Union and American* listed twelve blacks who had been testing compliance to the Civil Rights Act. The fact that "most of them got their reward by losing their situations" helps explain why there were not more protesters.[63]

Other blacks sought to work out an equitable arrangement within the confines of a segregated order. They accepted segregation per se because it was seen as an improvement over the policy of exclusion and because they believed, or at least hoped, that separate facilities could be equal. A rider on the Nashville streetcar set apart for blacks in 1866 did not complain about the segregation, but threatened a boycott unless the company protected black passengers from abusive whites who forced their way into the car and used obscene language in front of black women. A Norfolk, Virginia, Negro observing that the city was building a new opera house suggested that "colored theatre-goers . . . petition the managers to give them a respectable place to sit, apart from those of a lewd character." To Atlanta's C. H. J. Taylor writing during a period of racial tension in his city, it seemed that whites and blacks should "travel each in their own distinct path, steering clear of debatable ground, never forgetting to render one to the other that which equity and good conscience demands [sic]." And when William H. Councill, Negro principal of the Alabama State Normal School, brought suit against the Western and Atlantic Railroad on the ground that despite his possession of a first-class ticket, he was ejected from the first-class car and removed to the Negro car, he admitted the right of the company to classify passengers by race, but maintained it was the duty of the railroad to furnish equal facilities and conveniences for both races.[64]

In other ways as well blacks seemed to provide support for white claims that they really preferred segregation. When blacks ran their own railroad excursions or benefit concerts, they provided segregated facilities for their white friends. And when the white community per-sisted in its policy of exclusion, blacks responded as they had in the areas of education and welfare, by opening their own hotels, ice cream parlors, and skating rinks.[65] Part of this response was an accommoda-tion to white prejudice; but it was also related to the development of a group identity among blacks. Though it cannot be equated with the racism of whites, by moving in this direction, blacks themselves con-tributed to the emergence of the separate black and white worlds which characterized Southern urban life by 1890.

The separation of the races was accomplished largely without the aid of statutes as long as both races accepted its existence. As early as 1866, an English traveler, William Dixon, noted that the Negro in Richmond, regardless of his legal rights, knew "how far he may go, and where he must stop." He also knew that "habits are not changed by paper law." In 1880 two of the Negro witnesses testifying before a Congressional committee pointed to this difference between the power of law and the power of custom. When asked if there were any laws in Alabama applied solely to one race, James T. Rapier answered: "Cus-tom is law in our country now, and was before the war." Asked again if there were any discriminatory provisions in the constitution or state statutes, he replied, "None that I know of; but what we complain of is the administration of the law—the custom of the country." James O'Hara of North Carolina agreed: "These are matters [segregation in public accommodations] that are and must be regulated purely by prejudice and feeling, and the law cannot regulate."[66]

When integration did occur, it was only at the initiation of whites and was confined as a rule to the least desirable facilities—cheap, in-ferior restaurants, second-class and smoking cars on trains. Whites were there because they chose to be; blacks were there because they had no choice.

9

More Than Religion: The Urban Church

The coming together of Negroes, whether slave or free, for religious purposes was one of the few permissible gatherings for antebellum blacks. This seemingly noncontroversial practice aroused ambivalent feelings among some whites. Although religion was thought a useful tool in making the Negroes better satisfied with their lot in life, anything that brought blacks together in great numbers held within it the seeds of insurrection. A compromise was usually achieved, therefore, in which religious services were permitted with white supervision. Negroes had special places in white churches, commonly in the gallery, or, if they worshiped in separate buildings, white ministers served the congregation.

After the war, urban Negroes established their own churches free from white interference. These institutions immediately became the centers of Negro urban life. At one time or another they functioned not merely as houses of worship, but as school buildings, lecture halls, meeting houses, and entertainment centers. "They had many and varied programs for the young and old alike," remembered a Montgomery Negro. These city churches were better than those in the country, she maintained, because "they could touch people more often than just once or twice per month which was customary in rural churches." As the *Atlanta Constitution* noted, "the colored man not only takes his spiritual information but also his special information from the pulpit of the church which he attends."[1]

These churches under the strong leadership of charismatic pastors

198

helped to shape the lives of their members. In doing so they exercised a measure of internal social control. These churches were not always, as some scholars have suggested, entirely independent institutions. As in other areas, here, too, blacks often depended on the support of whites for financial assistance and other forms of encouragement. The whites in turn were careful to help those pastors and churches which served the interests of the larger community. In these years, therefore, was established the twentieth-century pattern of the black ministry, furnishing both the most militant and the most accommodating of the race's leaders.

Many of the postwar black churches had antebellum roots. Though most had been under the guidance of white ministers, there were some examples of autonomous black congregations. Nashville's First Colored Christian Church was organized in 1824 and apparently run entirely by Negroes. It had over 300 members by 1866, thanks to the aggressive leadership of Elder Peter Lowery. Although Richmond's Fifth Colored Baptist Church was not openly organized until December 1865, its members had been meeting clandestinely since 1860. The group, gathered together by John Harris, a slave born in Africa, prayed in a small shed. The fear of discovery led them to move their meeting place several times, but they finally bought a stable on Main Street where the church was officially organized under the leadership of the Reverend Charles Bowe.[2]

More common were those Negro congregations which seceded from white churches after the war. Conducted in the basements of the white churches or in separate buildings, their antebellum services had given both slaves and free Negroes a feeling of religious unity and independence which they eagerly pursued once given the opportunity. Negro assistants often were permitted to preach and conduct services and when the time came, these men led their fellows out of the white churches. The most famous example was Richmond's First African Baptist Church. When the white congregants of the First Baptist Church moved into a new structure in 1841, they turned over the old building to the black members. In order to allay fears that the separate congregation would add to the threat of insurrection, services were held only during the day and were conducted by the Reverend Robert Ryland, the pastor of the white church and the man largely responsible for the new arrangement.[3] In 1846 the Negroes paid $5,902.08 to the former owners for the property, $2,752 of which was donated by the white citizens of Richmond. Even after the sale, the free Negro members did not hold the deed and were not allowed to act as trustees of the church in legal matters. The original membership of 1,708 slaves and free Negroes grew to 2,650 by 1855.[4]

After the war the white congregants continued to sponsor the church and some Negroes were reluctant to break the ties. Ryland, however, resigned as pastor, expressing the opinion that the Negroes "would naturally and justly prefer a minister of their own color." The deed was transferred to the blacks in 1866 and James Henry Holmes became the first Negro pastor in 1867, a post he held until his death in 1901. A former slave who had been baptized by the Reverend Ryland, Holmes had been a deacon of the church from 1856 to 1865 and since 1865 had served as assistant minister. Under his leadership the church paid off its debt and became the largest congregation in the United States with a membership of 5,000.[5]

The antebellum Baptists gave their Negro congregants more freedom over their own religious life than did the other denominations. In addition to the First African, three other Negro Baptist churches in Richmond began as separate antebellum congregations within a white church. Similar occurrences were so frequent in other Virginia cities that it helped account for the predominance of Baptists among the Negroes of the state.[6] The First Colored Baptist churches in Montgomery, Raleigh, and Nashville followed the same pattern. Often the white mother church aided in the organization of the separate congregations. White members of Richmond's Second Baptist Church had their slaves build a brick chapel for black members after the blacks expressed a desire to worship separately. Shortly thereafter a group of thirty-five free Negroes became owners of the property. After the Negro members of Montgomery's First Baptist Church complained about having to worship in the basement, the whites gave their black brethren a church site and helped them build a new sanctuary in 1867.[7]

Negro members of antebellum Methodist congregations also enjoyed considerable religious independence. St. Paul's A.M.E. Church in Raleigh began in 1848 as a separate congregation of free Negroes and slaves and was placed in charge of the white pastor of the parent church. Nashville blacks affiliated with McKendree Church worshiped in a separate chapel near the railroad. In 1865 they became officially independent and joined the African Methodist Episcopal Church as

St. John's Chapel. From 1832 to 1852 free Negroes and slaves who belonged to Montgomery's Court Street Methodist Church sat in the galleries during the regular services. Dissatisfied with this arrangement, 451 Negro members convinced the whites to let them erect their own building. They reconstructed an old frame church previously used by the congregation, moved it to a new site on Holcombe Street, and named it Old Ship. Because the whites regarded the endeavor as a home mission project, they still provided the preachers. In 1862, however, a bishop of the M.E. Church South appointed a slave preacher named Allen Hannon as pastor. In January 1866 the white church relinquished ownership of the lot and the building for $1. Under the leadership of the Reverend Hannon, the church then became affiliated with the A.M.E. Zion Church.[8]

Whites in other denominations maintained a tighter hold over their black congregants during the antebellum period and were less inclined to let their Negro followers secede from their control even after emancipation. Southern Presbyterians looked with particular disfavor at the spectacle of independent black congregations freed from white guidance and discipline. "We hardly know what to say, think, or hope; the [black Presbyterians] are disinclined to hear the word of God from us, and are led astray by superstitious leaders," said an Alabama preacher in 1868. "Almost universally they prefer separate organizations and preachers of their own color," said another the following year. "Freedmen manifest a strong disposition to go to themselves and love preachers of their own color," wrote a third in 1870. White Presbyterians could still take heart from an 1880 report which asserted that "the Montgomery church keeps its hold upon the colored people who appreciate our distinctive doctrines, government and mode of worship." A few Negroes continued to attend services at the First Presbyterian Church and occupied their traditional seats in the former slave balcony. Even they longed for a church of their own and during the mid-1880s, they petitioned to organize a separate church and to have a Negro minister. The white members financed the erection of the First Colored Church and the congregation welcomed its first black pastor. All the Negro members of the old church except the sexton became members of the new church.[9]

Episcopalians experienced a similar problem. Their learned, highly-disciplined, and staid services drove away some former Negro mem-

bers, and, of greater import, they were reluctant to allow those that
remained the freedom of separate churches. Before the war black
members of St. John's Episcopal Church in Montgomery had worshiped in a small brick building on church grounds. In 1869 the
building was torn down and the Negroes thereafter sat in the church
balcony. Deprived of their wish to have their own congregation, the
number of Montgomery's black Episcopalians steadily declined.[10] The
worshipers in Richmond and Nashville were more fortunate. Richmond's St. Phillip's Episcopal Church was organized for antebellum
Negroes under the tutelage of the rector of the white St. James Episcopal Church. By 1861 the congregation had its own building and by
1866 became totally independent. White Episcopalians in Nashville
moved more slowly in the direction of establishing separate Negro
bodies, but by 1890 they also were committed to this policy.[11]

The Northern missionaries who came south with the advancing
Union troops also started Negro churches. Northern Methodists in
Nashville founded Clark Chapel in 1865 and Thompson Chapel ten
years later. Both were connected with Central Tennessee College
which itself grew out of a school for blacks established in the basement
of Clark Chapel. Raleigh's St. Augustine's Episcopal Church was
founded in 1868 by the Reverend J. Brinton Smith of the Protestant
Episcopal Church, a white Northerner who was the first president of
St. Augustine's College. Across town the Reverend Henry M. Tupper,
president of the American Baptist Home Mission Society's Shaw Institute, organized the Second Baptist Church Colored. Northern representatives of the American Missionary Association founded Congregational churches in each of the five cities. The most important were
in Atlanta and Nashville, where they were able to draw on the students
at Fisk and Atlanta universities.[12]

Although the churches founded by the Northerners began with
white pastors, by the end of the period blacks generally had taken their
place. This was not true of the Congregationalists who persisted in the
use of white clergymen. Although their congregations were usually
composed of both races, it seems that racial segregation was practiced
in the seating arrangement. The Catholics, though making less headway among the blacks, followed the Congregational pattern. The
church in Raleigh reserved special seats for Negroes, as did the one in
Richmond during the first postwar years. In 1885, however, Richmond
Catholics strengthened the barrier of segregation by establishing St.

Joseph's Church. Though led by a white priest, it was the first in the state solely for Negro Catholics.[13]

Such efforts to keep whites in charge of black congregations or to interest the freedmen in services that departed from the emotion-laden Methodist or Baptist tradition were generally unsuccessful. Negroes clearly preferred their own churches where they were in control. Throughout the postwar period the trend in black religious life was toward the formation of a growing number of churches under black elders and pastors of the African Methodist and, especially, the Baptist faith.

Many of the postbellum churches were the result of secessions from older Negro congregations. This trend was already apparent during antebellum times. Whites founded Richmond's Ebenezer Baptist Church in 1858 to house the overflow of the membership at the First African Church. Out of this congregation in turn came Shiloh Baptist Church (1867) and St. John's (1870). Overcrowding, doctrinal disputes, convenience, or personality clashes accounted for most of the defections. Usually the pattern of withdrawal and re-formation was accomplished under the leadership of a discontented elder or minister. While serving as the minister of the Second Colored Baptist Church, the Reverend William Troy of Richmond disagreed with the elders over policy and led a group of members to found Sharon Baptist Church. But Troy soon ran into trouble again and therefore left that church with a band of followers to organize Moore Street Baptist. No other clergyman could match the peripatetic Troy, but everywhere new congregations emerged from the divisions of the old. By 1885 there were four Negro churches in Raleigh which had sprung from the First Baptist Colored Church, although about 1,000 of the city's 1,500 Negro Baptists still belonged to the mother institution. Even more numerous were the six offspring of Atlanta's Mt. Zion Baptist Church. In Montgomery the Dexter Avenue Baptist Church, later made famous as Martin Luther King, Jr.'s, first pastorate, was formed in 1877 by seceders from the First Colored Baptist Church. Although the congregational organization of the Baptist churches made them more susceptible to the formation of new branches, other denominations were also affected. The Leigh Street Methodist Episcopal Church in Richmond, for example, was founded by a group that withdrew from the Bethel A.M.E. Church in order to affiliate with the newly formed Colored Methodist Episcopal Conference.[14]

Other churches continued to be formed throughout the period. Many grew out of informal prayer meetings when members decided to buy some land and erect a house of worship. Still others were composed of new residents or former members of white churches. Whatever the origins or the denominational affiliation, blacks saw the churches as a sign of their freedom; the invisible church of slavery had become visible. Most of the buildings were of wood and some congregations met in stables or in meeting halls. Jones Church in Atlanta, for example, was an "old frame building with walls almost as thin as an egg shell. The thin walls [had] many larger openings in them through which a man [could] thrust his hand."[15] But the chief aim of the blacks was clear. Because of their symbolic value, the churches became a testament not only to the religious faith of the Negroes but to their material progress. To trace the move of a church from its original building to another larger and more attractive one is to trace "the progress of the race."

A railroad boxcar was the initial home for Atlanta's First Colored Baptist Church, commonly known as Friendship Baptist. Begun in 1868 with 25 members, the congregation grew to 1,500 by 1882 and occupied a handsome wooden building which was part of the church's $35,000 worth of property. At the time this valuation was greater than eleven of the city's white churches. Ten years later there were 2,500 members and $60,000 worth of property, making it the second strongest, numerically and financially, of any Negro Baptist church in the state.[16] By 1892 Richmond blacks could boast of several large brick Greek Revival and Gothic churches with handsome columns and expensive interior woodwork. But one of the most beautiful churches in the entire region was the First Colored Baptist in Nashville. After twice rebuilding and enlarging the frame structure inherited from its white mother church, the congregation built a magnificent new edifice of brick and stone at a cost of about $25,000. It had a slate roof, an ornate front with a one-hundred-foot spire, and an auditorium that seated 1,500 persons. It was "a splendid house of worship beautifully painted and elegantly frescoed," wrote a local observer.

> The pulpit is handsomely carpeted, with a painting in the rear representing the river Jordan in majestic flow. The splendid pipe organ, which cost upwards of $1000, is placed to the right of the pulpit, and the organist and choir discourse music of which no church in the city would be ashamed.[17]

Church leaders were proud of the fact that they had paid off much of the debt incurred in supporting and building these structures. They were especially pleased that a large share of the money had come from the black community, a fact duly noted by whites. When discussing the church facilities of Macon and Atlanta during a trip through the South in 1870, J. W. Alvord reported that "the Freedmen give more liberally for church purposes than even towards the support of their schools." Twenty years later the *Nashville Banner* noted that blacks contributed more to their churches than whites "in proportion to their property and earnings." In addition to collecting regular dues, the churches used a variety of means to attract funds. A favorite technique was to hold a fair or carnival. In 1874 Nashville's First Colored Baptist Church resorted to a "Grand Rally" on behalf of the proposed new building in which every member was expected to donate at least $1 toward its erection. In an effort to get funds to pay for the Mt. Zion A.M.E. Zion parsonage, the Reverend T. A. Weathington preached a sermon on charity which brought $64, exceeding his goal of $40.[18]

Even though Negroes also aided congregations other than their own,[19] both blacks and whites realized that the black community lacked the wealth to support adequately its rapidly proliferating number of churches. Many whites therefore continued the pattern of assistance to Negro churches so evident immediately after emancipation. Some were influenced by paternalism, others by sincere good wishes for the welfare of blacks. A third motivation was the omnipresent desire for social control. Thus the *Atlanta Constitution*, one of the most important forces urging interracial religious cooperation, urged white financial aid for a C.M.E. church because "their [the denomination's] influence has been wonderfully conservative between the races."[20]

For their part blacks actively sought white aid. Newspapers frequently carried the pleas of ministers for white support. On one occasion, the Reverend Morris Hamilton of Nashville's St. Paul's Chapel A.M.E. appealed largely to the city's white population for a needed $4,000. On another, the Reverend E. R. Carter called upon white friends in Atlanta to help his church raise $600 for the construction of an old-age home. Besides appealing for outright donations, Negroes also invited whites to their church services and benefit activities. "Reserved seats will be kept for white friends, who are respectfully invited," said a notice for a fund-raising meeting of Nashville Negroes. In 1875 the Centennials, a Negro singing group patterned after the

Fisk Jubilee Singers, gave a concert at the Nashville Opera House "before the white people" to reduce the debt of the First Colored Baptist Church.[21]

Despite white assistance, the church was the only institution over which the blacks exercised effective control. For this reason it became the hub of Negro urban life. In the words of W. E. B. Du Bois, "the church became the center of economic activity as well as of amusement, education and social intercourse."[22] The religious function, of course, was central, but in the early postwar years the Negro church exercised a wide-ranging influence on the lives of Negroes that transcended the narrow bounds of scripture.

Negroes as a group were zealous churchgoers. Unlike white churches which generally had two services on Sunday, many black churches had three services, each lasting more than two hours and featuring a fire and brimstone sermon. Atlanta's Friendship Baptist held three services each weekday in addition to its Sunday meetings. Members came to praise God, to be swept up in the religious fervor in order to forget everyday burdens, and to meet friends. Bertha McClain of Montgomery's Old Ship A.M.E. Zion acknowledged that one of her reasons for attending church was "to hear the people mourn and shout." Seeking to "arouse an emotional feeling in his flock," the preacher told the congregation about "the long white robes and golden slippers after death which made them feel like they did not need any of those things here." Visitors to Richmond churches saw ample evidence of emotional behavior. "The white visitor," wrote Edward King about Richmond's First African Baptist,

> unobtrusively seating himself in one of the rear pews can look over a vast congregation of blacks listening with tearful and rapt attention to the emotional discourse of their preacher, or singing wild hymns as they are read out, line by line, by the deacon. The singing is one of the most remarkable features in all the African churches in Richmond; everyone joins in it, and it is not uncommon to see the churches so crowded that the doors are blockaded, the worshippers obstructing even the sidewalks, as they unite with enthusiasm in the simple yet really beautiful service.[23]

In his tour of the South, William Wells Brown found the tendency toward "outward demonstrations, such as, shouting the loud 'amen,' and the most boisterous noise in prayer" to be one of the weaknesses of his people. He praised the excellent church structures in all the cities he visited but deplored what went on inside. After attending services in Nashville's St. Paul's A.M.E., "a building that the citizens may well be proud of," he sadly reported that "the meeting was kept up till a late hour, during which, four or five sisters becoming exhausted, had fallen upon the floor and lay there, or had been removed by their friends." That evening he attended services at the First Colored Baptist Church where he was appalled by the response provoked by the pastor. Seeking to start the congregation "to shouting," the pastor had taken from his pocket a letter that represented the deeds of a person to be weighed after death.

> For fully ten minutes the preacher walked the pulpit, repeating in a loud, incoherent manner, "And the angel will read from this letter." This created the wildest excitement, and not less than ten or fifteen were shouting in different parts of the house, while four or five were going from seat to seat shaking hands with the occupants of the pews. "Let dat angel come right down now an' read dat letter," shouted a Sister, at the top of her voice. This was the signal for loud exclamations from various parts of the house. "Yes, yes, I want's to hear the letter." "Come, Jesus, come, or send an angel to read the letter." "Lord, send us the power."

What made the spectacle even more shameful, according to Brown, was that "this was one of the most refined congregations in Nashville."[24]

Still, depending on the congregation, the denomination, or the circumstances of the service, the visitor might have found the services little different from the majority of white ones. The urban churches as a whole were certainly more disciplined than their rural counterparts. This was especially true of the churches founded by the Northern missionaries representing the Congregational sect. "Our people are improving in their ways," wrote an AMA representative from Richmond in 1865. "On the Sabbath they give earnest attention and have given up their moanings, whinings, and shakings. I can now talk more plainly to them than I dared when I first came here. I speak against indulging in 'dancing praises' and holding meetings till late into the night." Even the Baptist and Methodist congregations, especially those that catered to the growing middle class, often drew white praise. A Richmond reporter visiting the First African Baptist in 1874 condescendingly remarked that "the church is not, as I suspected it might be, a mob. It is thoroughly organized. . . . The discipline is strict." The *Atlanta Constitution*, reporting about services at Atlanta's Third Baptist, also noted that "the quietness and attention of the congregation was a source of general remark."[25]

As the period progressed and both the ministers and their charges secured additional education, more worshipers turned to less emotional services. Professor W. H. Crogman of Clark University told of an old-fashioned preacher who decried the fact that Atlanta's twenty-five Negro public school teachers no longer attended his church, preferring instead "that fashionable church on the next street." The clergyman felt it was a sign that the younger generation was less devout, but Crogman disagreed.

> With their enlarged intellectual life, they [young Negroes] are naturally craving for a higher order of pulpit instruction. Their fathers were satisfied to be made happy. The children, of necessity less emotional and excitable, desire to have their reason appealed to as well. They expect to be instructed and helped and strengthened. The pulpit that cannot supply this demand will not hold the rising generation.

During his tour of Southern cities in 1891, Samuel J. Barrows found the same trend. Although "the old time preacher" could still be found in many communities because the former slaves were "loath to give up the hysteric emotionalism of revival preaching," the "younger and progressive Negroes [were] breaking away from it and demanding preachers whose intelligence and education secure respect."[26] Nevertheless, the number of blacks who sought more decorous forms of worship was in the minority. They were limited to the better educated and to those seeking to improve their status both in their own eyes and in the eyes of whites.

These services were not the ones commonly reported in local newspapers. Whites apparently preferred reading about incidents which suggested that blacks were more interested in raising Cain than in hearing about him. The *Atlanta Constitution* reported that for several weeks a boisterous crowd of young Negroes had disrupted services at Summer Hill Methodist Church. The previous day when two ushers had sought to take two of the group to jail, they were attacked by the rest of the mob and severely beaten. In Montgomery a Negro minister had to ask the captain of the city's night police to address his congregation on the need to maintain order.[27]

These disturbances convinced whites that, although religion could be useful in keeping blacks in their place, it also contained the seeds of disorder, disorder which could impinge upon the lives of whites. "The negro church is a nuisance! and the authorities should see that the noise they [the blacks] make, not only on Sunday but daily, be stopped; God is not deaf!" said the *Montgomery Mail*.

Revivals were special sources of disruption. Many Negroes seemed to lose interest in all else but religion. Even the members of the most sedate congregations were caught up in the religious fervor. A member of Richmond's First African Baptist noted that his church "was considered the most sacred or most aristocratic of our many temples of worship. Though of Baptist denomination, no shouting, hysterics or religious frenzies were tolerated. Ordinarily its members were considered to be 'too classy' for such undignified emotional demonstrations." But when a revival was underway, "the bars were let down, and no one was restricted as to manner of expression, when 'God spoke peace' to his soul." At such times "the children prayed all around the school yards, on the hillsides, in the streets. Adults, more courageous, occasionally went out to the graveyard in efforts to secure immediate communion with the Holy Spirit."[28]

There was no time limit to these revivals. One at Atlanta's Wheat Street A.M.E. Church was still going strong after two weeks. The doors of the sanctuary remained open continuously and the building was packed at all hours. Many of the members spent several days and nights inside. One Negro said that he had not seen his wife for five days since she left for the revival. A white man reported that his cook had gone to the meeting when it opened and after four days he was forced to hire a replacement. A second complained that his washerwoman had "gone crazy with the prospect of religion" and he had been unable to get any clothes washed for two weeks. "Revivals may be very good in their way," the *Atlanta Constitution* commented in expressing the chagrin of the white community, "but when our cooks and washerwomen throw down their work and hurry off to the church to spend the week, they get to be a nuisance."[29]

It was frequently impossible to determine where religious functions diverged from social ones. Baptisms, expressly religious acts, were remembered by Bertha McClain as "quite a unique affair in those days when people did not have many attractions of entertainment for young or old." In every town hundreds of blacks and whites lined the banks of rivers or creeks to watch the hymn-singing candidates in white robes or with white handkerchiefs on their heads march to the water to be submerged. A typical revival might see as many as two hundred baptisms.[30]

Sunday School classes, weekly prayer meetings and Bible groups, lectures, and concerts provided further opportunities for the congregations to meet at the church. "As psychologists would now say," wrote Wendell Dabney about week night Sunday School practice at Richmond's First African Baptist, "the motivating impulse arose [more] from love of sociability, than [from the] desire to learn the Sunday School lessons. Many a marriage grew from the sentiment that circulated so freely in those Thursday night Sunday School meetings." Because the church building was frequently the only available hall in the neighborhood, it hosted a number of guest speakers. In order to encourage public attendance these talks were either free or had a small admission charge. Although the sermons on Sundays often concerned abstract moral discussions or dissections of the Bible, church lectures instilled racial pride by acquainting the blacks with the accomplishments of the race and the rights of citizenship. In 1865 Nashville's Negroes were apprised of their new rights and responsibilities in a series of lectures given at St. John's A.M.E. In later years the building hosted talks on "The Negro and His Peculiarities" and "The Progress of the Negro Race." Richmond Negroes attending an address at Ebenezer Baptist heard "A Historical Glance at the Colored Man in Africa—his victories—glorious achievements in war, architecture, society, intellect and religion."[31] Seated in an impressive building erected largely through their own efforts, surrounded by well-dressed and well-mannered members of their race, and listening to a catalog of advances made by other Negroes, the black audience must have found these evenings a reassuring experience.

The size, financial resources, and frequent communal activities of the Negro churches encouraged functions other than those of a religious or social nature. One concern was the care of the sick and needy. Congregations formed themselves into numerous benevolent societies that assumed responsibility for orphans, old people, and the infirm. Most of these services were limited to members of the church, yet as in the case of Montgomery's James Hale Infirmary, founded by persons connected with Old Ship A.M.E. Zion, the facilities were open to the entire black community. The Negro branches of the Y.M.C.A. owed their existence to the unified efforts of the local black churches. This was also true of the many local relief societies. A notice for the reorganization meeting of the Nashville Colored Ladies Relief Society announced that "every church is requested to send representatives" and "all pastors are requested to bring this matter before their congregations." After the society was reorganized, ministers were asked to take up collections for its benefit. Negro clergymen in Atlanta distributed charity certificates redeemable for food or fuel from local relief organizations.[32]

The Negro church was also influential in the field of education. An important reason for the education of blacks, whether in the minds of the former slaveholders, the Northern missionaries, or the blacks themselves, was to enable them to read the Bible. Then, too, the church buildings often provided the classrooms. The missionaries who came south frequently found classes already in session in many church buildings. They continued this trend so that as of October 1866, for example, two of the three missionary schools in Richmond were held in churches. Many institutions of Negro higher education, including Fisk, Central Tennessee, and Hartshorn Memorial, began in the basements of Negro churches. In Atlanta the Bethel A.M.E. congregation was instrumental in founding Morris Brown College, and the Old Ship and First Baptist congregations in Montgomery were responsible for the moving of the State Normal School for Colored Children to the capital.[33] In every city churches at one time or another served as temporary facilities for Negro public schools; and while white colleges or public schools held their graduation exercises in the local theaters, black ceremonies took place in the churches.

The church also had an economic dimension. On one level it was a place to gather support for a particular economic enterprise. For example, in Nashville when the Freedmen's Bank was under attack in 1874, the local Advisory Board, itself composed of at least one minister, saw to it that "steps were taken to bring the interests of the bank before the colored people through the churches." On another level the benevolent societies spawned by the churches frequently evolved into insurance organizations and then into full-fledged businesses. Then, too, there were few boards of Negro companies that did not contain one or more clergymen. Special expositions held in the churches also stimulated the drive for the race's economic improvement. One such demonstration was held in 1886 at Nashville's St. John's A.M.E. Church. Organized by the pastor, the Reverend George W. Bryant, and directed by leading members of the congregation, it featured exhibits of handicrafts, needlework, dental work, quilts, medicines, and furniture to illustrate the great progress of the race.[34]

One final role of the church, the political, is difficult to evaluate. Again, the presence of the church as a convenient meeting place was central. Churches hosted protest meetings, political rallies, and, in the case of Richmond's First African Baptist, even a constitutional convention. Ministers often took stands on key issues, both as individuals and as leaders of their congregations, though frequently they were arrayed on opposite sides of a given issue. On occasion they ran for and held elective office, but more often they preferred to make known their views as nonoffice seekers. No campaign took place without several of them using their considerable oratorical powers to good partisan advantage.

The interest of these preachers and their congregations was most intense in the frequent prohibition campaigns that dominated the political scene by the mid-1880s. Congregations formed temperance societies and whites enlisted black ministers to preach to both races in the cause of reform. On election day members of most churches marched to the polls under the leadership of their pastor to cast their votes against the whiskey evil. Feelings ran high on this issue. After the spirited Atlanta campaign of 1887, three members of the Colored Congregational Church were expelled for working for the antiprohibition forces. The Lloyd Street Colored Church, Big Bethel, and Allen's Temple all considered punitive action against their members who voted wet, while Friendship Baptist limited its acts of censure to the officers who had deserted the cause.[35]

In whatever realm the church exercised influence, the minister played a dominant role. From him the congregation received its spiritual guidance, its moral leadership, and at times its political direction. In many cases he had founded the church, or, if not, his position in the community had much to do with attracting new members. He was enlisted to take part in economic and social welfare ventures. As much as anyone, he influenced a significant segment of the black community. Clearly the whites believed this to be true and did not hesitate to assign him important tasks.

During a serious smallpox outbreak, the *Atlanta Constitution* asserted that it was "the duty of the colored ministers to advise their people to be vaccinated." The newspaper also felt that the clergymen could end the alleged problem of unemployed able-bodied blacks who sought free handouts. "Here is the chance for the negro preachers [to] . . . teach their congregations that it is disgraceful for those who are able to obtain work to accept charity." In a letter to the *Nashville Banner*, a citizen recommended the seating of twelve Negro ministers on the platform during an evangelical meeting. The blacks, he wrote, "are largely led by their pastors, perhaps more so than whites." With their aid the cause of "temperance, Christian work, and the Christian life" would be furthered.[36]

Who were these men on whom so much seemed to depend? Judging from fragmentary biographical material, they were a diverse group of different ages, backgrounds, and denominations. Their salaries in the five cities ranged from less than $400 per year to approximately $1,500 with added fringe benefits.[37] At first they were mainly uneducated former slaves who had acted as class leaders or assistant pastors in antebellum Negro churches. Several remained in charge of their congregations into the late years of the century. Others were replaced, often by a new breed of clergyman who had graduated from a local Negro college or seminary. Graduates of these schools were more likely to gravitate to the more fashionable and wealthy pulpits, leaving preachers of the old style in charge of the poorer congregations where services were more emotional. Churches of the latter type seem to have been composed almost entirely of lower-class Baptist and A.M.E. members. For their pastors, preaching was likely to be a part-time occupation. As the *Atlanta Constitution* pointed out, "there are about fifty colored 'local preachers' in Atlanta, who follow various occupations and preach whenever it is necessary."[38] Their more successful colleagues, however, enjoyed prominence in the community, lived a middle-class life, and were often among the richest Negroes of the area.

John Jasper of Richmond was the most famous of the old-style preachers who emerged from slavery without an advanced education but with considerable personal gifts sufficient to build and lead an important congregation. Jasper was born a slave in 1812 and worked as a house servant, field hand, and coal mover. The son of a slave preacher, he experienced conversion in his midtwenties, joined the First African Baptist Church, and became a roving minister. Along with a fellow pastor and nine other former members of the First African, he started a church on Brown's Island in the James River in September 1867. The members, then as later, were primarily former slaves, most of whom were from the country and derisively called "corn field niggers." After three years of moving from one inadequate building to another, the congregation—thanks to Jasper's shrewd bargaining—became permanently settled in a remodeled chapel to which was added a handsome annex.

The Sixth Mount Zion Baptist Church, as it was called, gained national prominence in 1878 when Jasper delivered an energetic defense of a literal interpretation of the Bible entitled "The Sun Do Move and the Earth Am Square." Thereafter no visit to Richmond was complete without attendance at a Jasper service. Many local whites, sitting in seats reserved for them, also enjoyed the spectacle of the minister who was noted for "fervid zeal, gifted imagery and colorful oratory." By 1887 Jasper estimated that he had preached the popular sermon one hundred times and had rejected requests to give it throughout the United States and Europe. He himself had less than seven months of schooling and maintained that "I never wrote a sermon in my life."[39]

Jasper seems to have been held in higher repute by whites than by "higher-class" Negroes, who felt that his efforts actually lowered the dignity of the race and confirmed white charges of black ignorance. Soon after Jasper first gave his sermon, the *Virginia Star*, which he had earlier attacked, warned that "Brother John will find that either [the] stopping of the *Star* or the moving of the sun is a task that demands more moral and intellectual strength than he possesses." Regardless of his detractors, Jasper could point to a record of accomplishment: he was a celebrity; his church was debt free with more than 2,000 members and a nationally known choir. When he died in 1901, the Richmond press gave his funeral extensive coverage.[40]

The first two pastors of Montgomery's First Colored Baptist Church also made significant contributions to black religious life despite the lack of formal education. Nathan Ashby was born in Virginia in 1810. He was sold to traders and brought to Alabama where in 1842 he purchased his freedom for $900. Although a carpenter by trade, he had preached to other Negro members of the First Baptist Church on Sunday afternoons in the basement of the white church. After years of service as an unordained assistant pastor of the Negro church before it became an independent body, he was ordained in 1867 by the white minister. He helped build the church's first house of worship and became president of the Alabama Baptist Convention that was founded in the new building.[41]

Less is known about the background of his successor, James A. Foster, but it was evidently similar to Ashby's. There is no indication that he had any formal education, yet he filled the pulpit for twenty years until his death in 1891. During his pastorate he served as the third president of the State Convention, trustee of both the State Normal School and the Swayne School, moderator of the Spring Hill Association, life member of the American Baptist Home Mission Society, and one of the original incorporators of Selma University. By 1950 the State Convention which he and Ashby had founded contained 2,292 churches and 401,000 communicants and had property valued at over $2,100,000. In the same year the National Baptist Convention, which was also founded in the church, had a membership of more than 4,385,200 communicants in 24,953 churches; its property was valued at $117,470,546.[42] By then the church that these two individuals had built had long been one of the city's most important and would soon have in its pulpit a young minister named Ralph David Abernathy.

Although a majority of the Negro pastors by 1890 still had no more than a basic education, a growing number, especially among the young divines, possessed at least some years of collegiate theological training, if not a degree. This change was most evident among the Baptists as the products of Roger Williams, Atlanta Baptist Seminary, Richmond Theological Seminary, and Shaw Institute received pulpits. Many of their students were in charge of congregations while still taking courses. The availability of these schools also enabled local churches to send their pastors for additional study. Finally, adult Negroes already engaged in other occupations in these cities took advantage of the facilities to enter the ministry.[43]

One of the best examples of the new generation of black clergymen was the Reverend E. R. Carter, the second pastor of Atlanta's prestigious Friendship Baptist Church. Born in Athens, Georgia, in 1859, evidently of slave parents, he entered Atlanta Baptist Seminary in 1879. His first charge was a church at Stone Mountain at a salary of $8 per month. Called to Friendship in 1882, he expanded the membership, eliminated the debt, and became a major figure both in the black community and in Atlanta at large. He edited the Negro Baptist newspaper of Georgia and served as Grand Worthy Chief Templar of the state, vice president of the Georgia State Baptist Sunday School Convention, and a member of the Centennial Committee of

Colored Baptists. Considered a scholar of Greek, French, and He-
brew, he made two trips to Europe and a third to the Middle East, one
trip paid for by a grateful congregation.[44]

Despite close ties with the white community,[45] Carter was a strong
advocate of equal rights. In his study of Atlanta's black community,
entitled *The Black Side*, Carter thanked whites for their help, but
made it clear that more assistance was needed and that previous accomplishments had been made despite intense opposition. Upon
returning from Europe in 1888, he did not mince words when asked
by a *Constitution* reporter what pleased him about England. "The
thing that I liked the most was the absolute freedom," he said. "I
never felt that I was free until I got on England's soil. I never smelt
anything like race prejudice."[46]

Walter H. Brooks was another well-educated young man who entered the ministry. The son of a white businessman and a slave, he was
born in Richmond around 1850. During the war he worked in the local
manufacturing firm to which he and his mother had been sold. After
the war he briefly attended a primary school taught by a Northern
missionary and then received further schooling in Rhode Island and
at Lincoln University in Pennsylvania. Upon graduation in 1872, he
entered Lincoln's theological seminary where he was converted to
Presbyterianism and became an elder of the church. Within a year he
changed his mind and was baptized. He continued his education and
finally returned to Richmond where he became a member of the First
African Baptist. As a result of political connections, he secured a position as clerk in the post office before joining the American Baptist Publication Society in 1874. Two years later he was ordained and in 1877
became pastor of the venerable Second Colored Baptist Church. While
in Richmond he supported the Funders in Virginia political campaigns
to the chagrin of other black leaders, but partly redeemed himself by
being in the forefront of those calling for more black teachers in the
city's public schools.

Brooks received national attention in 1880 when he became the first
Negro delegate to address the all-white Baptist General Association.
According to a white observer, "his oratory is not of that over-fervid
style believed to be so common among colored speakers. His logic . . .
is as clear and incisive as his English is correct, which is saying very
much." In that same year he left his pastorate to do field work for the
American Baptist Publication Society, but two years later he returned

to the pulpit as head of Washington, D.C.'s prestigious Nineteenth Street Baptist Church. In this capacity he became a leader of the city's temperance movement. His widespread fame resulted in the awarding of honorary D.D. degrees from Roger Williams College and the State University of Louisville. By that time he had returned to Lincoln to complete a Master of Arts degree, thus giving him an impressive array of academic honors. Educational achievement was no doubt an important reason for his advancement, but he also aided his career by marrying the daughter of the Reverend James Henry Holmes, the former slave preacher who served as pastor of the First African Baptist for thirty-four years, a marriage that symbolized the shift of leadership in the Negro church from the first generation of black clergy to the second.[47]

Many other members of the new generation of educated clergy figured prominently in the affairs of their communities.[48] But perhaps H. H. Proctor of Atlanta's First Congregational Church best personified the new trends in the composition of the Negro clergy. Born in 1868 and graduated at the head of his class at Fisk in 1891, he was also an alumnus of Yale Divinity School. In 1894 he became the first black minister of the Congregational Church which, severing its ties with the AMA, became self-supporting. By the beginning of the twentieth century it was one of the few churches in the city free of debt. With a membership of 500 it was also the largest black Congregational church in the country.[49]

Scholars have generally concluded that, whether educated or not, the Negro clergy of this period was a force for accommodation rather than protest.[50] In fact, a given minister's role varied according to his age, denomination, general background, and personality. In addition, individual pastors may have taken an accommodationist position in one set of circumstances and a protest stance in another. Then, too, a specific action such as calling for black teachers in separate but equal schools often contained elements of both protest and accommodation.[51]

The Reverend W. H. Tillman was representative of those ministers who might be termed accommodationists. Respected among Negroes, he was pastor of Atlanta's prestigious Wheat Street Church and served on the Executive Board of the Baptist State Convention; admired by the white community from which he frequently sought funds, he urged his congregation to follow the lead of Southern whites. In 1889 he used the pages of the *Atlanta Constitution* to publicly condemn militant blacks for disturbing interracial peace by holding "indignant meet-. ing[s]." The Reverend L. Gardner of Atlanta's Wood's Chapel demonstrated a similar sensitivity to white feelings. In a special Wednesday sermon in 1875 he urged his congregants to be kind to whites and accept the Civil Rights Bill "properly like wise men." Negroes must not force themselves on anybody's company or in any house or place where they were not wanted because such an action would be uncivil and violate the other individual's rights.[52]

Negro ministers did not always function as the force for social control assigned to them by whites. Whites were no doubt taken aback by E. R. Carter's remarks about racial prejudice. The Reverend Preston Taylor of Nashville also must have confused white observers, for he seemed all that whites could have expected in a black clergyman. Though born a slave in 1849, he proved that this was no bar to success. After serving in the Union Army, he worked as a laborer and then became minister of the Christian Church in Mt. Sterling, Kentucky. During a pastorate that lasted fifteen years, his congregation became the largest of that denomination in the state and he was chosen as the church's general evangelist for the United States. Among his accomplishments, he founded the Christian Bible College, a Negro college in New Castle, Kentucky. After coming to Nashville, he assumed the pulpit of the Gay Street Church, one of the largest and wealthiest in the city and became a state officer of the Colored Masons and Colored Odd Fellows.

Taylor, like many of his colleagues, felt that, even if pastors were otherworldly in their sermons, they could accumulate worldly goods. In 1888 he began an undertaking business which grew into one of the most successful black enterprises in Nashville. Soon after, he served as pastor of the Lee Avenue Christian Church. A staunch prohibitionist, he was a speaker frequently called upon by whites to influence his people. In short, few individuals better represented the ideal of a Negro community that was apart from white society yet available to that white community when black help was needed. But, despite his acceptance of segregation as pastor of a Negro church and owner of a Negro mortuary, he objected to the seating of blacks in the gallery of the Opera House. When the choir of his church was requested to entertain there, he refused to sanction the performance and denounced the members who accepted the discrimination. Twenty years later he helped lead a black streetcar boycott after the passage of a Jim Crow statute.[53]

The Reverend George W. Bryant of Nashville's highly regarded St. John's A.M.E. was another minister who could be useful to whites in such matters as prohibition, but who had a mind of his own and a sharp tongue to match. Little is known of his prepastorate years except that he was born in 1850 and earned both M.D. and D.D. degrees. Active in political affairs, he became chaplain of the Negro military companies of Tennessee in 1885. Although his political activities caused large segments of the white community to view him with suspicion, in 1885 he was appointed to the finance committee of the Citizens Reform Association and was the main Negro speaker of the forces seeking to keep the municipal reform administration in power. He had objected to the all-white ticket proposed by the opposition, and, though successful in getting a Negro added, he still supported the reformers. In urging the substitution of a black he had said:

> We are no longer the wards of any political party; we have paid that last debt of gratitude; we stand as untrammeled freemen, and I tell you that the party which recognizes our rights, our manhood, privileges as citizens, will get our votes. We will cling to those who treat us best.

Although white Democrats often called for such nonpartisanship, it nonetheless sounded too independent to some of them. Nor was this his only "transgression." At a meeting in St. John's that condemned the 1886 massacre of Negroes at Carrollton, Mississippi, Bryant said that, if such violence continued, it would cause the rising generation to revert to the Mosaic disposition and demand an eye for an eye.[54]

Other Negro clergy asserted their independence of whites and pushed for equal rights. Many supported the Republican Party to the dismay of most white Southerners. A few, like Augusta's Henry M. Turner and Nashville's Luke Mason, were very active in party affairs and were elected to office. More common were nonpartisan forms of protest. Atlanta's J. S. Flipper decried the "whining, suppliant way of asking for anything by the colored people" and refused to be used by whites in the 1887 local option campaign. Nashville's W. A. Sinclair consistently challenged segregated railroad accommodations. And at least by 1905 Mason was engaged in social protest. He joined Preston Taylor and Bishop Evans Tyree as one of the leaders of the Nashville streetcar boycott.[55]

Clearly the black ministers represented a cross-section of backgrounds and attitudes. What they seem to have shared was a commanding presence, eloquent use of language, and driving ambition that enabled them to overcome the twin obstacles of poverty and slavery. They were, above all, strong men; but their positions were frequently fragile, a fact which is too often overlooked. Many who chose not to engage in politics in the outside world nevertheless owed their ministerial success to political maneuvering within the narrower religious world of the black church and conference. Every minister had to be sensitive to the feelings of the congregation and especially of the elders or trustees. In addition, whereas Baptist ministers had to contend solely with the local government of the church, members of other denominations, such as the various branches of Methodism, had to contend with the bishops and State Conference. The practice of rotating clergy in these faiths frequently made it difficult for pastors to exercise the freedom and the power enjoyed by their Baptist counterparts.

The most noteworthy case of a clergyman being deposed by his flock occurred in Nashville in 1887. The Reverend R. T. Huffman of the First Colored Baptist was charged with committing "seduction, abduction, and bastardy" against a young member of the church. At first he was found innocent by a court of twenty-two members and elders who decided that the girl had been intimate with many men and these specific charges could not be substantiated. Its decision was ratified by the congregation by a vote of approximately 200 to 75. Nevertheless, the father of the girl brought the case to court and there followed a week-long trial. The pastor was again found innocent but only after much debate among the jury. As expected, the case received much publicity before, during, and after the verdict was rendered.[56]

George T. Robinson, the editor of the *Tennessee Star*, and J. C. Napier mobilized the disenchanted members of the First Baptist. With the support of the most prominent members of Nashville's black community, they held several anti-Huffman meetings. According to a resolution, these individuals took action because "the moral teachings and the influence of the public schools, all institutions of learning, and the home training of our young people is [sic] being perverted by the teachings and example of R. T. Huffman." The pastor of such an important church clearly had a great responsibility, and even the suggestion of improper behavior was undesirable. "It is repugnant to our sense of decency and respect," resolved another meeting, "and we deem it a terrible calamity to our community to be afflicted with immoral, low, vicious and *even suspicious* preachers." Such men, it was argued, lowered the status of the race and "we feel called upon to meet the danger with prompt and stern means, such as his guilt demands and its heinousness justifies." Such action included mobbing the minister at church, verbally assaulting him in the press, and, in one case, initiating a scuffle during which a pistol was fired. Despite this harassment, Huffman, a preacher of the old style for thirty years, refused to resign. He charged that the moral issue was fraudulent and that the friction within the church was caused by the officers who had allegedly misappropriated funds. Eventually, however, Huffman fled the city. In choosing a successor, the congregation typically selected a representative of the new breed of educated clergy. Upon returning to Nashville, Huffman demonstrated that there was still room in the Negro community for an old-fashioned preacher. He became pastor of the Mt. Olive Baptist Church, a new congregation composed of lower-class blacks, many of whom had followed him out of the First Baptist.[57]

Few fights between pastors and their congregations contained the dramatic impact or received the attention from both whites and blacks as did the Huffman scandal; however, Atlanta's famous Big Bethel A.M.E. periodically erupted in confrontations involving pastors, elders, and members that made good copy for the newspapers. There was an incident in 1874 involving the locking out of the pastor, the Reverend W. D. Johnson, by fifteen congregants after he had suspended one prominent member and expelled another.[58] Most of the difficulties centered around W. J. Gaines, twice pastor of Big Bethel, later presiding elder, and eventually bishop of the A.M.E. church.

In another series of incidents highlighted by major disturbances in 1881 and 1885, Gaines's control of the church was challenged by dissident members led by William Finch, himself an ordained minister, as well as a successful tailor and former city councilman. At one time Finch, after quitting the church over a disagreement with Pastor Gaines, called his opponent "the Right Reverend Caesar Gaines," a man "who while pretending to serve the father of truth is really serving Satan." Despite the criticism, Gaines succeeded in retaining power. In 1885 as presiding elder, he and Bishop Henry M. Turner forced the congregation to accept a pastor whom many members felt incompetent, bypassing a former minister who was the popular choice. According to Dr. Roderick D. Badger, a Negro dentist and one of the race's wealthiest citizens, "Gaines tries to own the church and the people, and some

of us feel that we don't belong to him." Several members were expelled
because of the matter, including Badger, who was accused by Gaines
of "sowing seeds of dissension and . . . [of] using indecent language
to a committee sent to reprove him." The pastor whom Gaines backed,
however, served only a short time and was replaced by J. S. Flipper.
The congregation, despite the denomination's hierarchical authority,
had won a contest of wills against Turner and Gaines, two of the most
powerful clerics in the entire church.[59]

In numerous other cases disenchanted congregations drove powerful clergymen from the pulpit. When not dismissed, others had to fight
charges of moral laxity or, as in the case of two Nashville ministers,
misappropriation of funds.[60] Sometimes dismissals were made over
matters of church practice, but often the true reason involved a power
struggle between the trustees or elders and the pastor. Preston Taylor
in Nashville, for example, was charged by his church's Board of Elders
with instituting objectionable innovations in the services. As soon as
they notified Taylor that his contract would not be renewed after January 1888, he allegedly "began preaching against the well-established
authority of the official elders . . . and so influenced a portion of the
congregation that when his term had expired he had brought about
great confusion and disturbance among the members." Taylor and his
supporters disrupted two meetings called to take action against him.
As a result, a suit was instituted in Chancery Court to prevent him
from occupying the pulpit. The proceedings had a familiar outcome:
Taylor and many of his parishioners left the congregation and organized the Lee Avenue Christian Church.[61]

Political disagreements also contributed to antagonism between the
pastor and his flock. William B. Derrick, one of the most distinguished
members of the Virginia Conference of the A.M.E. and a future bishop,
was forced to leave his Richmond pulpit after he supported the Democrats in the fight over readjustment of the state debt. After an election
in Atlanta in 1884, a number of Negro preachers who had sided with
the Bourbon candidate came under attack from their congregations.
One of them, the Reverend G. W. Martin, was actually grabbed by a
mob while preaching a sermon. At other times the pressure was more
subtle. Despite his obvious qualifications, the Reverend George W.
Bryant was requested to resign in 1886 by both Boards of Stewards of
his church. He took a poll of the congregation and, finding only twenty
in favor of his leaving, decided to stay. The next day, however, he

changed his mind in order "to live at peace with all men, especially with the church." No reason was ever given for the opposition of the boards, although Bryant's political activity was probably an important factor. The previous year he had been hung in effigy for his role in the municipal campaign. The disruption of Atlanta congregations became such a serious problem in 1884 that the Wheat Street Baptist Church proudly proclaimed in the *Constitution* that

> to [the] praise and credit of this congregation of colored Christian people, in the city, let it be stated, with emphasis that, while other flocks of this race have been torn asunder by mistaken and disappointed politicians, they with one accord, held a business meeting on Friday night last, in which there was exhibited by the entire membership, the most commendable order, and fraternal feeling during the whole conference. Not the slightest discourtesy, towards their beloved pastor, was even hinted at.[62]

What these cases suggest is that Negroes came to expect more from their pastors as the period progressed. The ministers no longer exercised complete control over their flocks, if indeed they ever had. Perhaps as their influence and power in the outside community diminished, blacks became more eager to exercise it within the few areas that remained. Not only did the churches compensate for the deprivations of the world by promoting the benefits of the afterlife, they also provided opportunities to forget the absence of secular political power through the substitution of church government.

The churches were the single most important institutions in the lives of the urban Negroes. Of prime importance was their position as the hub of their congregants' segregated lives. The exclusion of blacks from white churches and the setting up of separate black congregations, begun during the antebellum period, was institutionalized in the postbellum years. By 1890 integrated churches or black congregations served by white ministers had practically vanished. As Bishop J. W. Hood of the A.M.E. Zion Church wrote in 1882, "God has raised up an effective colored ministry who could not have been employed without congregations of their own people." Whites interpreted such remarks and increasing racial separation as further evidence that Negroes truly preferred a segregated existence. "It has never yet been possible to hold whites and blacks in a common church," the *Atlanta Constitution* claimed. "Split after split has occurred where this was tried, confer-

ence after conference has divided, and the African Methodist Church
. . . is a striking example of how the masses of negroes feel about it."
The few exceptions merely proved the point for

> the man who goes from one of these chill and quiet [mixed] churches
> into Big Bethel or Friendship and sees thousands of colored folks,
> earnest and happy and responsive, taking religion hot from the lips
> of one of their own race can not doubt that mixed churches are
> doomed by the voluntary action of the negroes themselves, who pre-
> fer to worship in their own temples, with their own people and under
> the inspiration of their own preachers.[63]

Whites, of course, would not have welcomed any other arrangement. In 1874 a Presbyterian congregation in Nashville strongly objected to its minister's proposal that a separate section of the church
be reserved for blacks who wanted to attend services. This opposition
emerged despite the fact that those few Negroes who chose to attend
were among the most well mannered and wealthy of the race. One of
the critics pointed out that, if the church were crowded, whites would
either have to enter the black section or stand. He also argued that
"the disagreeable scent of the blacks" and their emotional attitude toward religion "would shock any congregation of this enlightened age."
Referring to other members, he concluded that,

> besides this, there are a great many persons who are naturally preju-
> diced against the negro, and these persons would never attend the
> church where they were given special privileges. My opinion is that
> it is best to let the negro worship in his own way, for when you go
> mixing the races in religion, or anything else, there will be trouble.

Another opponent stated the issue more bluntly. "Do the citizens of
Nashville intend to see their wives and fair daughters seated by repre-
sentatives of a race who have always been considered our slaves?"
Mixing white and black, he concluded, was like mixing oil and water.[64]

As a result, it was decided by both blacks and whites that the races
would worship separately. Because a similar decision had been made
by whites and a number of blacks for other facets of urban life such as
education, welfare, and entertainment, it was natural that the churches
and their ministers should become, to mix metaphors, both magnets for
Negroes and anchors of their communities. Indeed, because churches
gravitated to areas of dense black population and thereby encouraged
still more Negroes to settle nearby, they, along with the schools, contributed to the development of *de facto* housing segregation. In short,

they functioned as town halls and community centers as much as houses of worship. To lead these concentrations of Negro dwellers, no one was better suited or more willing than the pastors who exercised considerable power in the black sector and also acted as emissaries between the racially separate worlds of the urban South.

10

Division and Unity: The Black Community

Throughout the period from 1865 to 1890 Southern urban centers were divided into separate black and white worlds. Negroes and whites had their own schools, churches, welfare institutions, fraternal organizations, public accommodations, and neighborhoods. Yet, as in the white world, the black portion of the community contained subcommunities composed of people who, though sharing a common racial designation, differed according to their origins, interests, and accomplishments. Divisions among urban Negroes were even more significant than those existing among whites; often they rivaled those between whites and blacks. The differences, whether in choice of church affiliation, occupation, politics, or recreational activities, brought the various groups into frequent conflict. At times the result was a degree of internal social control that united the community and strengthened it in its dealings with whites. More often conflict weakened the community by sapping its strength in internecine warfare that hindered racial unity and common effort.

A visitor to one of the cities during the period might easily have concluded that only the distinctions between whites and blacks really mattered. Typically the visitor's tour would include attendance at a Negro church service, a trip to the local black college or public school, and an inspection of factories or other businesses where the races were rarely employed in comparable positions. While in town he or she might observe one of the frequent parades organized by the various

226

Negro societies. If the city directory were examined, the visitor would find the schools, benevolent societies, military companies, and residents identified or perhaps even listed by race. Visitors could easily learn "where the niggers live," where they were buried, and what political party they voted for. The reverse side of the coin worked for whites as well. In short, it apparently made sense to talk of "Black Atlanta" or "White Nashville."

The black fraternal and benevolent societies gave a special flavor and unity to Negro urban life. Given the restrictions imposed by whites on social activities and welfare aid for blacks, each black organization was forced to play a number of roles. Whereas the major objective of the benevolent societies was to provide aid to needy brethren, the fraternal or secret societies sought primarily to improve the social life of blacks. Yet, just as the benevolent societies fulfilled an important social role through their many meetings, parades, and fairs, the secret orders also provided for their members' welfare. Raleigh's Excelsior Lodge No. 21 of Colored Masons, for example, aided needy members, their widows, and their orphaned children.[1] The organization of such groups followed quickly after the end of the war. The charter members were usually prominent blacks; and their presence, combined with the widespread interest in such activities, assured that the endeavors would succeed.

A Nashville lodge of Colored Masons was organized in January 1866. By 1870 there were two lodges of Colored Odd Fellows in Atlanta and both Masonic and Odd Fellow lodges in Richmond.[2] Richmond had more than thirty secret societies by 1866. Eight years later a partial list of groups appearing in the *Richmond Dispatch* included six lodges of Colored Masons, six lodges of Odd Fellows, six councils of the Order of Rechabites, seventeen divisions of Sons of Temperance, six sections of Cadets of Temperance, twenty-three lodges of Good Samaritans, twenty-five female benevolent orders, and forty miscellaneous associations. Membership ranged from 16 to 360. Even a small town like Raleigh had two lodges of Colored Masons, seven lodges of Good Samaritans, and a society of Colored Odd Fellows in 1886. In Nashville in 1890 an estimated "one-half of the colored males" belonged to secret or benevolent organizations.[3]

Military companies fulfilled the same social functions as the societies. Their drills, parades, and campouts provided release from the everyday pressures of earning a living and fostered a sense of camaraderie. Persons with economic or political ambitions could make potentially valuable contacts because the officers were business and political leaders in the black community. Many young men of different backgrounds grasped the opportunity to associate with them and to wear a fancy uniform.

These volunteer companies bore further witness to the shift from exclusion to segregation. State militia units had excluded blacks prior to Reconstruction. In North Carolina, Alabama, and Tennessee the Republicans quickly enlisted blacks to help defend their governments, although in North Carolina and perhaps elsewhere they established separate white and Negro companies, each under their own officers. Black companies persisted in the three states after Redemption, and Georgia and Virginia Redeemers finally endorsed the new policy by permitting segregated units. Nashville, Richmond, and Atlanta each had as many as four companies, the latter city's with a total membership of almost 200 men in 1891. All were closely supervised by the officers of white companies, who not only acted as judges during the drills, but often provided financial support.[4]

The largely voluntary fire companies followed the same pattern. Although neither Atlanta nor Richmond had black firemen, Radicals in Raleigh and Nashville initiated the shift from exclusion to segregation. By 1869 Raleigh Republicans organized the all-Negro Victor Hand Engine Company and soon added the Bucket and Ladder Company. Nashville, the only city with an antebellum ordinance prohibiting black firemen, established an all-Negro Hook and Ladder Company under the Radicals, although it had a lower status than the five all-white units. Not until 1885 did a reform administration elected with Negro support finally provide for the first black engine company. Montgomery Negroes, on the other hand, had served together with whites in two of that city's three volunteer engine companies from September 1864 to December 1866. At the end of 1866 the Conservatives brought all the Negroes together in a separate unit called the Grey Eagle Company. This segregated arrangement was continued throughout the subsequent period of Republican control.[5]

Parades were among the most popular activities of the Negro societies, fire brigades, and military companies. The opening of a new meeting hall, anniversaries of societies, or funerals brought out the members in all their splendid finery. Urban blacks also turned out in large numbers for celebrations of the Fourth of July, anniversaries of the passage of the Thirteenth, Fourteenth, and Fifteenth amendments, the adoption of the Civil Rights acts, and, of course, Emancipation Day. "Today bids fair for a 'glorious Fourth' for the boys and the niggers," wrote an unsympathetic white Atlantan in 1884. "Since the war the 4th of July has been preeminently niggers' day in the South, the white folks having lost their zeal for it in the war to a great measure." As the years passed, Southern whites celebrated Independence Day as before, but few whites joined blacks on their other special days.[6]

The 1868 Emancipation Day procession in Nashville included the military companies, Sons of Relief, Barbers Association, Mutual Relief, Mechanics Association, and Equal Rights League. Twenty-two years later the Atlanta commemoration of emancipation disclosed the existence of an even more developed separate black community. Led by a brass band, four Negro military companies and a delegation from various societies marched in a procession to the Lloyd Street Methodist Church. The program at the church included prayers by several ministers, reading of the Emancipation Proclamation by the Reverend W. J. Gaines, singing by students of four local black colleges, a eulogy of Lincoln, and a reading of an essay on "The Race Problem." After the services, Smith Easley, a local black politician, introduced to the large gathering several resolutions condemning recent lynchings in the state.[7]

On selected occasions blacks joined in white-organized celebrations. The 1875 Richmond procession honoring Stonewall Jackson was typical. The white groups formed the front line and the blacks brought up the rear, "distinct from the white procession, separately organized and under separate control." The other cities followed similar procedures, providing more evidence of a separate black community with institutions and organizations that, while mirroring those of the white community, had to be kept apart from it. In Nashville, for example, the long parade held in honor of President Grover Cleveland during his visit in 1887 was divided into seven sections: the first five containing important whites and their organizations, the last two, their black counterparts. Two years earlier a similarly segregated parade had preceded the laying of the cornerstone of the new capitol in Atlanta.[8]

Most other forms of recreation for blacks took place within the bounds of the black community. Excursions were one of the most popular means of amusement. Commencing soon after the war, these railroad trips provided enjoyment and were visible symbols of the blacks' new freedom. To judge by the frequent mention of individuals who missed the return train, they were also used as a cheap method of moving to a new town. The 1886 excursion organized by the Reverend T. R. Rogers from Montgomery to Atlanta cost $2 per person. The frequency of trips and the great number of people involved, however, led a critical Montgomery bishop to estimate that $24,000 annually was spent in Montgomery for such sojourns. During a typical trip, a thousand Negroes arrived in Atlanta from Athens. They were entertained by Negro military companies, were honored by a lengthy procession, and were guests at a military drill and fire company contest. When the excursion was repeated the following month, the visit included a park outing with drills, a shooting contest, and a baseball game.[9]

Local outings were equally popular, especially on holidays like the Fourth of July and Emancipation Day. Picnics were organized by the basic institutions of the black community—the church, the school, the benevolent society or secret order, and often the political party. Sometimes they were held in parks where whites also gathered, but more often they took place in clearly identified black picnic groves or black-owned Colored Fairgrounds. These fairgrounds also hosted annual fairs at which Negroes viewed examples of the race's progress, listened to speeches, and watched horse racing.[10]

Such institutions as the schools, churches, and orders gave physical expression to the idea of a uniform black community. Their existence encouraged the development of segregated neighborhoods; by serving a variety of needs they functioned as the centers of black urban life. Schools and churches traditionally hosted special activities such as fairs, dances, and lectures. Other buildings were constructed in order to have sufficient meeting places for the proliferating number of societies. The Odd Fellows halls in Nashville, Richmond, and Atlanta, the Masonic halls in Richmond and Raleigh, the Good Samaritan halls in Atlanta and Richmond, and the True Reformers Hall in Richmond, valued at $20,000, were impressive symbols of the black community and were utilized by organizations other than those responsible for their construction. During its brief existence, the Freedmen's Bank contributed rooms in its buildings for the use of local Negro groups. In several instances successful blacks rented out their own facilities. Most noteworthy was Montgomery's Dorsette Hall which also housed Dr. C. N. Dorsette's office and drugstore. The Odd Fellows met there and a longtime Montgomery black resident remembered it as the place for "all outstanding entertainments for Negroes such as weddings, banquets and dances."[11]

By the last decade of the century, each city had its centers of black life. In the Second and Fourth wards in the southern part of Raleigh were found the city's two Negro grade schools, six of the nine black churches, the Institution for the Colored Blind and Deaf and Dumb, one of the city's two black colleges, the Colored Masonic Hall, and most of the Negro hotels and businesses. By 1895 Richmond's Jackson Ward, which as early as 1880 had been termed "the Black Belt," contained almost half of the capital's Negroes, eleven meeting halls for blacks, ten Negro churches, the black almshouse, and five of the seven Negro public schools. In a two- or three-block section centered around Atlanta's Wheat Street were the homes and businesses of the black community's leaders, most of its notable churches, its best public schools, and such important meeting places as the Good Samaritan Building, the Odd Fellows Hall, and the Schell Opera House and Hall.[12]

Ironically, old slave market locations often became centers of Negro life. It is not known if this was due to the relative unattractiveness of the area or to a reluctance on the part of whites to identify with the vestiges of the tragic past. But the evidence is there. Down the street from the Nashville branch of the Freedmen's Bank were the remains of a former slave mart. Before the war the 200 block of Dexter Avenue in Montgomery was the hub of the slave trade. There was one slave market on one side, two on the other, and a fourth one block away. During the postwar period the block contained Dorsette Hall (possibly housed in one of the old markets), the engine house of the Negro fire company, the meeting place of the Colored Masons, the Negro publishing firm of R. R. Morris and T. A. Weathington, the confectionary shop of a prominent merchant, a Negro boarding house, the store of a Negro house painter, and the Dexter Avenue Church.[13]

In addition to the organizations, common activities, and physical symbols, the fledgling black press seemed to confirm assumptions about black unity. Only a smattering of issues from the period has survived and many of the names are now unknown, but it is clear that each city supported, if only briefly, a surprising number of editorial endeavors. Two of the most successful were Richmond's *Virginia Star* and *Richmond Planet*. Though less successful, Atlanta could boast of the *Appeal, Weekly Defiance,* and *Pilot;* Montgomery had the *Weekly*

Advance, Herald, and *Colored Citizen;* Raleigh supported the *Journal of Freedom* and *Weekly Republican.* Nashville, however, was breeding ground for the most newspapers. Among them were the *Colored Tennessean, Pilot, Planet, Fisk Expositor, True Republican, Star,* and *Free Lance.* Editorial policies differed according to political and social philosophies, but every one of these publications served as organs "through which they [blacks] could voice their sentiments at all times and on all questions."[14] Regardless of editorial stands, all the newspapers displayed a rabid boosterism that celebrated every sign of black success and encouraged the race toward further progress. Perhaps most important, the newspapers served as town criers, announcing events of special importance to Negroes, thus strengthening belief in the presence of a separate black world within the larger urban society.

The editors, all of whom were active in political life, tended to be professionals or businessmen. Some were Democrats. C. H. J. Taylor, an Atlanta lawyer and former minister to Liberia, briefly published the *Appeal* at the end of the 1880s. In Montgomery another Negro lawyer, James A. Scott, an officer of the National Colored Press Association, published and edited the *Weekly Advance,* described by him in 1881 as "the only straight-out Democratic paper published in the South that is edited by a Negro." But the great majority of proprietors were staunch Republicans. Nashville's *True Republican,* edited by the Oberlin-educated lawyer Samuel Lowery, was the voice of the anti-Brownlow Negro wing of the Republican Party; W. A. Pledger, one of Georgia's most powerful Negro politicians, was behind the Atlanta *Weekly Defiance.* The most famous editor was John Mitchell, Jr., of the *Richmond Planet.* Born a slave shortly before the end of the war, he was educated in a black church school and then graduated first in his class from the Richmond Colored High and Normal School. After becoming editor of the *Planet* in 1884, he served several terms as a Republican city councilman and was active in state and national Republican politics.[15]

Since there are few extant runs of individual newspapers, it is difficult to piece together editorial policies and to assess the stands taken on many issues. From fragmentary evidence, however, it seems that on occasion the Republican papers took militant and aggressive positions which angered whites. The *Weekly Defiance,* for example, although "extensively read by the colored people of Atlanta" and published intermittently throughout the 1880s, did not come to the attention of most whites until 1885. In that year the *Constitution* reported that "for some time past the paper has been making use of some very strong language. Its editor has been assaulting the police department, the courts and the chaingang lessees." The *Weekly Defiance* had chastised local officials for unequal enforcement of the laws and had urged selective boycotts of white merchants who had allegedly insulted blacks. Two libel charges against co-editors Alonzo W. Burnett and W. A. Pledger resulted from articles criticizing two prominent whites. The first originated from the claim that a local installment furniture dealer had donated $371 to the Y.M.C.A. "to clear his conscience up for the robbery committed on poor negroes."[16]

The second libel suit was brought after a charge that G. W. Adair, Atlanta's leading realtor, had told Henry A. Rucker that Rucker would have to relocate the business he had just purchased from a white man. Editor Pledger claimed that Rucker, who had previously lost his position in the revenue service, allegedly for racial reasons, was again being discriminated against because of his color. After Rucker was forced to sell his business at a loss, Pledger urged blacks to "leave this old skunk [Adair] to himself to stink himself to death."[17] A similar lack of deference toward whites caused J. C. Duke of the *Herald* to flee Montgomery. His articles about the lynchings of blacks for alleged sexual affronts to white women had concluded with the suggestion that white women were perhaps attracted to Negro men.[18]

Few black editors were so bold, but many others envisioned their roles, at least in part, as defenders of Negro interests. "On behalf of five millions of colored people we appeal to the white people of the South for simple and pure justice," wrote the editor of the *Virginia Star* in 1882 in a major statement of policy.

> No candid white person in the South will deny that the colored people have been denied their civil and political rights. For are they not as a class excluded from our juries, from holding office, aye, from teaching their own children in the capacity of public free school teachers. . . . God for some good and sufficient reason has cast our lots together in this country. . . . Both races are proud of and love this country and neither will be driven from it.

The two races should be friends, but "bad men both white and colored will not permit us to be." According to the editor, the solution was simple.

Give us our rights which belong to us. Give us fair and living wages for a fair day's work. Treat our women with the respect due to their sex. Open the doors of lucrative business to our young men and women. Assist and encourage us to educate our children and bring them up in refinement whenever our means will admit of it. In short, let them open their hearts and treat us kindly; we have done nothing to entitle us to any other kind of treatment.[19]

Fighting for the interests of the race merged easily into calls for blacks to assert themselves, as in John Mitchell's crusade against lynchings in the pages of the *Richmond Planet*. While this was more of a Southern than a local problem, Richmond Negroes could not fail to be impressed with Mitchell's frequent entreaties to protect themselves. "Colored men stand up and be counted. Defend your homes against the midnight assasin [*sic*], above all protect your women," ran one editorial. Each issue contained the number of lynchings to that date in a column headed by a drawing of whites shooting at a Negro hanging from a tree. Frequent gun advertisements appeared, and, lest the meaning be lost, Mitchell proclaimed that "there is no use talking, a Winchester rifle in your house and a man there who knows how to use it will bring respect from white folks and the colored ones too, for that matter. Great is the Winchester rifle." The matter of securing respect from the white press led the *Virginia Star* to urge a boycott of all newspapers which denigrated Negroes.

The paper that teaches your son that he is not, after years of Christian training and mental discipline, the equal of a white youth of the same status is not fit to be on your family table. The paper that tells your cultured and virtuous daughter who may be crowned with the noblest attributes of a lofty womanhood, that she would degrade and lower the morals of white women of the same purity and breadth of character ought not to be placed in her hands. It ought only be used to wrap up pitch, its only equal in its tendency to defile.[20]

No matter what the white men did, the black editors were confident that racial pride and unity would bring advancement. "Every Negro that do [*sic*] not possess race pride and manhood enough to aid in elevating the race," argued Montgomery's *Herald*, "should be taught to keep still and not try to keep others from elevating them because perhaps he is unable or too mean to do so." When spirits flagged, the newspapers were there to urge continued effort with the prospect of eventual triumph. "Every man should be glad that he is a Negro," wrote John Mitchell in 1890. "The very oppression which is being forced upon him like a pall is working wonderful results, trying him in the furnace of fire and bringing him out a new race regenerated and redeemed. Who wouldn't be a Negro!" To those who believed that Negroes could not thrive in freedom and had no history to be proud of, Mitchell echoed other editors in stating that "you may say what you will the Negro is here to stay. Nothing goes on without him. He was in the Revolutionary War, the War of 1812, the Mexican War, the War of Rebellion, and will be in every one that will take place in this country. Great is the Negro!"[21]

In its role of booster, the Negro press was ever conscious of upwardly mobile blacks who could serve as inspirational figures for the less fortunate. Not all of these individuals were well-known, but each of them had overcome the odds against success. The *Colored Citizen,* for example, singled out Montgomery's Alonzo Davis. Instead of continuing to pay "a heavy rent," Davis had invested $750 in a piece of land and "built not a little house." In case the message was too subtle, it was clearly enunciated later in the article. "What he had done every man now paying out his money for rent might do." The *Richmond Planet* celebrated the achievements of the race in more abstract terms.

> Every time we see a Negro physician, it does us good. When we see a Negro pharmacist, it goes still better. When we see Negro lawyers, professors, bank presidents, inventors, machinists, skilled mechanics as well as linguists, we grin as much as our mouth will allow and shout—the Negro is coming.[22]

As cheerleader for the black community, the Negro press also urged the support of black business and professional men. Although some of the newspapers, especially Democratic publications like Montgomery's *Weekly Advance,* featured notices by white businessmen, the majority contained mostly Negro advertisements. Pleas throughout the papers asked readers to patronize members of their own race. The advertisements, of course, were a means of communication between disparate members of the black community, the sellers and the consumers. In fact, a major function of the black press was to serve as a medium for the exchange of economic, political, and social information among Negroes. Frequently the white newspapers proved too expensive for such messages or on occasion even refused to permit their publication. One Montgomery black subscribed to the *Colored Citizen* because of an unsuccessful attempt to get the *Montgomery Daily Advertiser* to publish

New Year's calls for Negro women. Arguing that since only bad things about Negroes were written in the white press—"how near they [Negroes] resemble a mule or a hog, or how many or what ones are in jail"—the subscriber concluded that the best place for announcements was in the black newspapers.[23]

A typical issue of Montgomery's *Colored Citizen* listed church services, mentioned the next meetings of the Odd Fellows Damon Lodge 2068, Messiah Household of Ruth, and the Grey Eagle Fire Company, and commented favorably about both an enjoyable "calico reception" given at the Knights of Wisemen's Hall and a reunion of Knights of Wisemen addressed by prominent blacks. Such events might receive at best one line in the white press; here they received lengthy treatment. Another item in the *Weekly Advance* reflected the frequent merging of the functions of town crier and race booster. It announced the commencement of the second annual industrial fair in Montgomery and urged: "Let every colored man, woman and child go to work and make the fair a credit to the race."[24]

There were other forms of communication. In the first days of freedom, notices frequently appeared in Nashville's *Colored Tennessean* requesting information concerning sold relatives. Letters such as the one in the *Virginia Star* criticizing white press coverage disseminated views on the problems of the day. The *Weekly Defiance* chronicled the whereabouts of prominent Atlanta blacks and black visitors to the city. And finally there were the want ads. "Colored Men and Women can find employment by calling at this office" ran a notice in the *Virginia Star* by J. P. Justis, Employment and Emigrant Agent. "Women will be sent to New York or other northern cities, where they can get high wages without paying anything in advance."[25]

Despite the varied functions of the black publications, they had only limited success in the five cities. "Most colored papers *start* (after great advertising) with a boom, then 'peter out,'" Atlanta's Reverend E. R. Carter sadly concluded in 1894. The pattern by then was all too familiar. A group of "prominent Negroes" would get together, put out a newspaper, appeal for black support, and within a year dissolve the enterprise because of internal squabbles, financial problems, or lack of support from the community. Often failure was due to all three. A few lasted more than a year or two, but only the *Richmond Planet* managed to publish continuously for more than a decade. Even the *Virginia Star*, described by a white visitor as "a very credible publication," was constantly threatened with failure and was reduced to pleading with its readers for backing. "Colored men! You say you are as good as white men. If white men support scores of newspapers in this state, can you not support one? If you cannot, you do not prove that you are as good as white men." Within six years the paper was dead, part of its demise attributable to competition from the new *Richmond Planet*. The formation of so many journals within each city undermined the prospects of success for any, given the meager resources of the black reading public. Mergers were thus a frequent occurrence, but even they did not prevent financial ruin. Most disheartening to editors were the "social parasites," subscribers who did not pay their bills.[26]

The difficulties Negro publications encountered emphasized the weaknesses within the black community. Although there were advertisements from black businessmen and some whites in the Negro papers, the white press was the favorite medium for members of both races. Many of the most successful blacks still served a white clientele as barbers, restaurateurs, or livery operators and patronized those publications their clients read. Other individuals like job-seeking domestics also relied on the white press. In addition to suffering from inadequate advertising revenue, the black newspapers were plagued by the high rate of illiteracy within the community. Added to the large numbers unable to read were even larger numbers who could not afford or did not want to support a newspaper. Despite such unpromising prospects, new enterprises were continually launched, adding the burden of extra competition to the already sizable obstacles for success.

The problems of the Negro press in these cities suggest a greater failure: the inability to form a community more noteworthy for its similarities than its differences, more significant for its unity than its divisions. White observers frequently made this point, usually by emphasizing the economic differences among blacks. Writing of conditions among Negroes in Southern cities at the end of 1874, Nashville's *Republican Banner* observed that

> the negro we usually come in contact with is the thrifty and cleanly [*sic*] barber or dining room servant, and even sometimes, the banker or merchant. He is generally improving his opportunity but, unfortunately, he cannot be taken as the representative of the indolent and shiftless hundreds of thousands whose highest ambition is a drink of raw singlings and a fiddle and dance. The latter kind, when found in the country, always have a grassy crop. When in the city, they divide

their time between their low dance houses and the workhouse, and there is no one who deplores their miserable way of living, as the negro who reflects on to-morrow, and makes himself a smooth and sensible way in the world.[27]

In 1881 Noble Prentis, a Northern traveler who toured North Carolina, South Carolina, Georgia, Virginia, and Tennessee, spending most of his time in major cities, endorsed the widespread view that "the colored race in the South has divided into two classes—one moving upward and the other down. The former class are acquiring property and consideration; the latter are in danger of being swept from the earth by their own vices." Southerners publicized differences among Negroes as a means of lecturing them on the best ways to advance. After presenting interviews with the wealthiest blacks in the city, the *Atlanta Constitution* observed "that the negro, so long as he follows with sober thrift and industry his different pursuits, is at home with white friends in the South."[28]

By the 1890s most successful blacks were concentrating more on economic activities than politics and seeking to improve themselves through thrift and accommodation. In each city the members of this fledgling middle class formed a group separate from the black masses. Differences existed among them, yet their way of life distinguished them from the rest of their race. They were better fed and housed, had more money, entertained themselves differently, and belonged to different organizations and churches.

Social activities present the clearest difference. There were many areas of common interest, such as parades, picnics, church services, and fraternal orders. Circuses, the theater, and public amusements also attracted individuals from both groups. Still, members of the rising middle class had their own activities not shared by the lower class.

A more extensive educational background stimulated interest in the formation and support of literary and debating societies as well as the black press. By 1880 interested Richmond Negroes could join one of several literary clubs or attend one of their many public programs. According to the *Richmond Dispatch*, the Excelsior Literary Organization was the oldest in the city and had a "flourishing limited membership of 25." But there were also the Tea Rose Lyceum (later renamed the Garrison Lyceum in honor of William Lloyd Garrison), the Acme Lyceum, Dumas Reading Club, Institute Lyceum, Alpha Lyceum, Temperance Reading Club, and the Education and Historical Associa-

tion. Subjects for consideration during the period included black jour-
nalism and Communism. On one occasion the Young Men's Valley Debating Club argued the question "Which was the greater general, R. E.
Lee or Stonewall Jackson?" Topics before Atlanta's Negro societies
included prospects for women's suffrage, the condition of Negroes in
the South, the relative status of Indians and blacks, and "Who deserves
the more honor, Columbus for the discovery or Washington for the defense of America?"[29]

Out of these literary societies grew the first attempts to establish libraries for urban blacks, who were denied access to those "public libraries" run by private white associations. The members of Nashville's
Chautauqua Literary and Scientific Circle in 1884 unsuccessfully
sought to form a public library, appealing to both races to donate
books.[30] Negroes in Atlanta made more progress, though in the end
they too failed. In 1879 a group of young Odd Fellows, "representing
the best class of colored citizens of Atlanta," held a meeting to organize
the state's first Negro library association, but it was not until the following year that the Reverend Joseph Wood and his Summer Hill Methodist Church congregation opened the city's first Negro library with
three hundred books. The *Atlanta Constitution* urged white citizens to
support this effort because it demonstrated the interest of blacks in
self-improvement. In 1881 the *Constitution* noted that three hundred
of "our best colored citizens" enjoyed a lecture on "The Importance of
Reading" by Professor W. H. Crogman for the benefit of the Abyssinian Library. The library was prospering and had recently received an
engraving of Abe Lincoln to match the one it owned of George Washington. A few months later, however, the officers including President
Wood and David T. Howard, a successful young businessman, found
it impossible to maintain the facility solely on the regular dues of members. Fund-raising events followed, but the library was forced to close.
Three years later a new round of benefits began in an unsuccessful attempt to reopen it.[31]

The "respectable element" in black society also attended public lectures, supported glee clubs, and organized drama clubs. These included a lecture by George T. Downing on "The Life and Times of
Charles Sumner" given at Richmond's Sharon Baptist Church and
J. M. Whitehead's speech on "The Past, Present and Future of the
African Race of the United States" given at Montgomery's First Colored Baptist Church. Other events took place at the Negro colleges

which invited the community to frequent "evenings of entertainment." Such evenings at Fisk or Central Tennessee College might include performances by the Jubilee or Centennial Singers, solos by wives of leading black citizens, recitations of poems, musical performances, and assorted readings.[32] Often these concerts were fund-raisers either for the colleges themselves or for other community enterprises such as welfare institutions or, as in the case of Atlanta, the Negro library.

Much of the entertaining among black society was done in the home. Such a preference, of course, was natural to people who had accumulated money and property, but to many whites this was simply another instance of Negroes copying the behavior of white society. A bitter white Montgomery resident noted that the tradition of "open house" on New Year's Day was falling into disfavor among whites, although "the negroes imitating the whites, as so many apes would do, called upon their dusky friends in large numbers."[33]

Such disdain obscured the fact that by the end of the century there existed a fairly homogeneous black elite that exercised leadership in political, social, and economic matters. In the first years after the war this group consisted mainly of former slaves. Their number included small businessmen and artisans who catered primarily to white customers, ministers of the leading churches, and some politicians. By 1890 an increasing number were professionals and businessmen with black clientele who, for the most part, were better educated and more successful than their predecessors.

According to August Meier and David Lewis, Atlanta Negroes during the period had already established a well-defined upper class centered around the First Congregational Church, Atlanta University, and a dozen social clubs.[34] Other churches such as the Friendship Baptist contributed members as well. Whatever its makeup, there is little question as to the existence of an elite in Atlanta and the other cities. The 1877 wedding of Peter McMichel, the Negro janitor of the Georgia Senate, was attended by members of the legislature and "the select portion of the colored society of the city." A Raleigh newspaper reported that an identifiable black "aristocracy" had arisen by 1881 in the North Carolina capital. "At their fashionable weddings the array of silks, white kid [gloves] and jewelry is gorgeous." A longtime Negro resident of Richmond remembered that his city "was a real center for society. . . . The Negroes formerly owned by the old aristocracy trained their own children as they formerly trained those of their mas-

ters. In consequence they acquired a culture sadly lacking in many of
the black and white college graduates of the day." Wealth added to
their status. "Thousands of dollars were represented in the little clan
of families [Bowlers, Keenes, Forresters, Brooks, Matt Hopes, Dave
Perkins, Randolphs, Dabneys]. They lived downtown. There were social clubs galore and at their entertainments no outsider was permitted
to participate."[35]

Nashville's interlocking black leadership was typical. Whether in
fraternal organizations, political rallies, business ventures, or social
gatherings, the same names continually reappear. Among the officers
of the state Masonic society elected in 1871 were two Nashville barbers, Nelson Walker and S. R. Walker, the Reverend N. G. Merry
of the First Colored Baptist Church, and William A. Sumner, the leading businessman. Two years later when a group of Nashville Negroes
met to condemn the seizure of the *Virginius* and the execution of its
crew by the Spanish government, William Sumner served as chairman,
while Nelson Walker was the chief speaker. Others taking an active
part were B. J. Hadley, politician and saloon owner, Alfred Menefee,
and Abram Smith, the latter two both lawyers and leading Republicans. Following the death of William Lloyd Garrison in 1879, local
blacks held a memorial meeting under the chairmanship of Menefee.
On the committee of arrangements were J. C. Napier, the city's most
influential black, and local leaders such as W. H. Young, R. D. Campbell, J. J. Curry, and G. W. Shaffer. Four days later, when a chapter of
the Colored Knights Templar was founded, the organizers included
Shaffer, S. R. Walker, Lewis Winter, the wealthy dry-goods merchant,
and Lyttleton Jones, another prominent barber. In 1887 the Independent Order of Immaculates listed Dr. W. A. Hadley as national president, Dr. R. F. Boyd, physician and businessman, as treasurer, and a
lawyer, A. B. Bradford, as secretary.[36]

On special occasions which required the appearance of the city's
black leadership, many of these same prominent individuals were present. At the banquet given for future Virginia Congressman John Mercer Langston in 1885, speakers included J. C. Napier (his son-in-law),
W. H. Young, and S. R. Walker, while in the audience were Lyttleton
Jones, W. A. Hadley, and A. B. Bradford. Among the other people in
attendance were Henry Harding, the wealthiest black in the city, J. H.
Dismukes, law partner of W. H. Young, T. A. Sykes, former North
Carolina and Tennessee state legislator, George T. Robinson, lawyer

and editor of the *Tennessee Star*, and S. H. Sumner, evidently related to William Sumner who had died by this date.[37]

These men and their wives socialized with each other as well. Unlike those in Montgomery, the white newspapers in Nashville listed the names and addresses of Negro women who would be receiving New Year's visitors. For 1880 the list included the daughters of the Reverend N. G. Merry and the wife of Henry Harding. Three years later many of the same women attended a gathering in honor of John Mercer Langston and his wife. The affair, graced by the presence of "the elite of colored society" dressed in silk, cashmere, and satin, featured vocal and instrumental music by guests. Most of the same people, among them Mr. and Mrs. Lyttleton Jones, Mr. and Mrs. T. A. Sykes, B. J. Hadley, and J. H. Keeble, were present in 1885 at a party given by the Ugly Club at the residence of the J. C. Napiers to honor two members of the Jubilee Singers. Six weeks earlier the Napiers, Sykeses, and Keebles had been present along with Mr. and Mrs. J. H. Dismukes, Mrs. S. H. Sumner, and J. B. Bosley at a reception given by the Joneses.[38]

Perhaps the high point of black social life came in 1878 with the marriage of J. C. Napier's sister. The ceremony, in the home of Napier's father, was attended by members of the Negro aristocracy, the Fisk faculty, and many Fisk pupils. Circulating about the home with its "large double parlors" were Negro men "neatly attired, while the dresses of the women were of the most elegant and expensive character, made after the latest fashions." The white Reverend H. S. Bennett of Fisk performed the ceremony. According to the *Daily American* reporter, the elegantly dressed bride "would attract attention by her style and *distingué* air" in any assemblage. Among the many presents was a gift from P. B. S. Pinchback, the black former lieutenant governor of Louisiana.[39]

Another way to document the existence of a black elite is to note the varied connections of its members. The Nashville lawyer and businessman J. C. Napier was active in both St. Paul's A.M.E. and the First Colored Baptist, a state and city officeholder, a member of the state Republican Executive Committee, the president of the Negro branch of the Y.M.C.A., and a member of several temperance and fraternal societies. N. P. Vandervall, a grocer, was a longtime member of Richmond's prestigious First African Baptist, in which he filled every position but pastor; he also belonged to the Mechanics Society and Union

Friendship Society, served as treasurer of a local Odd Fellows lodge, sat on the City Council for six years, and was a trustee of the Negro orphanage, the Odd Fellows Hall, and the Union Burial Ground. Robert Steele, Atlanta's leading barber catering to whites, was an elder at Bethel A.M.E. Church, a trustee of the Carrie Steele Orphan Home (run by his mother), and a member of both the Masonic Lodge and the Afro-American Historical Society.[40]

The lives of such people were far removed from the experiences of the majority of urban blacks, especially those lowest in economic and social standing. Although the poorest Negroes shared many of the same recreational activities, they usually participated with friends of their own economic stratum. They also found alternate and less respectable means of entertainment so that it is possible to reconstruct a social world for the lower classes which bore little resemblance to that of their more successful brethren. Indeed, this demi-world resembled that of poor whites more than that of better-off blacks. Of course, not only lower-class blacks participated in disreputable activities, but such behavior was more typical of their way of life.

At the center of this world, according to most observers, were the infamous gambling and whiskey dens. Nashville's "White Castle," located in the midst of Hell's Half Acre, caused the *Nashville Banner* to complain in 1890 that

> for over twenty years . . . the two story frame tenement on the west side of McLemore street, just south of where the railroad trestle skirts Sulphur Spring bottom has been a notorious resort. The lowest negroes of both sexes have congregated there, sometimes living there in numbers for which three or four times as large a domicile would have been none too large on sanitary grounds alone. Innumerable shooting scrapes, bloody cutting affrays, gambling and other offenses have been committed within its walls, and criminals have been located and arrested there by the police.

The Ant Hole in Atlanta was "a negro den . . . which gave the police no small amount of trouble." Located in a room under the building at the corner of Ivy and Decatur, it "was certainly one of the worst places in the city. Negroes of the very worst type congregate there and play cards, smoke and drink. It was a fit place to bear a harvest of criminals and doubtless many daring crimes had their conception there." In the same vicinity behind the notorious Willingham Building was the Beaver Slide—so named because the great amount of passing in and out resembled a beaver slide on the banks of a creek. It consisted of a succession of small one-story houses containing filthy sleeping rooms and small businesses.[41]

Impromptu dances were a basic feature of lower-class social life. Evenings of paydays and Saturday nights were popular times. Whether held in public halls, bars, or homes, there was an admission charge of between a dime and a quarter. Inside there was drinking, dancing, and brawling which often resulted in the summoning of the police. Negroes were frequently joined both at these dances and in their dives by lower-class whites. In March 1866 the Raleigh *Tri-Weekly Standard* reported that a police raid of "a mixed ball at the Bake House" resulted in several arrests. Four years later a barroom run by a Negro policeman near the railroad tracks was doing a thriving business as a rendezvous for "a motley crowd of blacks and whites." Because in every city most saloonkeepers were white, the great majority of these Negro dens were owned, if not operated, by whites. "The city papers everywhere," reported the *Montgomery Daily Advertiser* in 1865, "are complaining of the disgusting negro balls and check apron hops, which are gotten up by mean white men." When Richmond police raided the Good Idea, "a negro gambling saloon," in 1870, they arrested ten Negroes and the white owner.[42]

Blacks of this class had other forms of amusement which set them apart from others of their race. Judicial proceedings served as a form of free theater. Henry Douglas who had escaped from the Nashville workhouse, for example, was recaptured a few days later sitting among spectators in the Criminal Court. During an 1882 smallpox epidemic, Atlanta Negroes who flocked to witness trials in the Recorder's Court were informed that they would be unable to attend until they were vaccinated. Within thirty minutes, according to the police commissioners, "no less than a dozen came back with smiling faces and a bare arm showing the fresh sore." As one of the commissioners said, "I knew it would work before I begun, for the negroes in Atlanta would rather miss church or a circus than police court." Wakes were also the occasion for much socializing, though at times with dire results. In at least one instance so many mourners were jammed into a rickety structure that the shanty collapsed.[43] Other activities included attendance at circuses, parades, and baseball games, especially those involving black teams.

Lotteries (or, as they later would be called in the North, "numbers" or "policy") were already a part of black urban life in the emerging Southern ghettoes. Whites ran the action, largely for Negro customers. As early as 1866, the *Richmond Dispatch* reported that a white man had been arrested for selling Negroes tickets for the Kentucky state lottery. Fifteen years later an *Atlanta Constitution* reporter sought to expose Atlanta's illegal vendors of lottery tickets. The first place he visited was a little shoe shop on Ivy Street at the rear of the Southern Hotel. The room was "full of negro men and women with one or two worthless white men." One blind Negro told him, "I dreamed that 14, 12, 23 and 63 were going to win, but they wouldn't let me play on 'em, my folks wouldn't, and sure enough they did come." Daily drawings of numbers took place at 12:30 P.M. in Mobile, and vendors at various places in the city got telegrams from the Willingham Building telling the results. "I'll try 7, 13, 25, 63 Monday," said the blind man. "I've dreamed about 'em three times now." When the reporter went to the Willingham Building, he found "a nest of darkeys" playing cards, drinking, and having "a general carousal." He was told that the proprietors had become frightened and had quit the lottery business a day or two before. If they had closed, it was only temporarily. Later in the year a white man was arrested for running a lottery in an office on Ivy Street near the Willingham Building, Ant Hole, and Beaver Slide.[44]

To the more prominent Negroes, their lower-class brothers presented at best a form of embarrassment. Worse still, they damaged the race's chances of further success, for their activities could be used by unfriendly whites to tar all blacks. Examples of crime, vice, and ignorance led to generalizations about "the negro." Often the middle class sought to lend a helping hand to improve the lot of the less fortunate; at other times they called upon the local authorities to protect them from encroachments of the "criminal elements." Increasingly, however, they tried to discipline these individuals themselves and thus to attain a degree of internal social control. Such attempts clearly reveal the class splits among blacks and the commitment upon the part of racial leaders to ameliorate differences so that the entire community would profit.

Influential blacks advocated a policy of self-improvement and self-betterment. In expressing their faith in self-help and by reminding their audience of the need to be hard-working, clean-living, and upstanding citizens, they echoed the sentiments of both their allies and detractors among the whites. At an 1865 Nashville barbecue attended largely by blacks, John Lawrence, a white army chaplain and later head of the Tennessee Board of Education, urged that the Negroes use their freedom wisely. According to the local Republican newspaper which endorsed his views, Lawrence "called attention to the need of improvement in the dwellings of the colored people, urging them to industry and economy, not for the purpose of spending their savings in showy jewelry and high colored ribbons, but to purchase for themselves comfortable homes and lands in the country."[45]

Two months earlier these same themes had been fully developed in an "Address to the Colored Americans of the State" written by the business committee of a convention of blacks held in the city. The committee (dominated by Nashville Negroes) reminded its audience that "as freedmen you are now called upon to so conduct yourselves in all occupations, and under all circumstances, as to cause the enemies of our race to blush for shame, and cause our friends throughout the world to rejoice." Blacks should adhere to the principles of "industry, education, economy and Christianity." Or as a Montgomery Negro expressed it, "Let us use well the advantages of our churches and schools and we shall lay the foundations for our permanent progress in everything that is good." Even the militant John Mitchell stressed these themes and counseled his *Richmond Planet* readers that "we are on trial and must be careful as to how we conduct ourselves."[46]

In their efforts to reduce the disorder found in the lower-class tenements and dives, "respectable" blacks enlisted the support of city officials. In 1881 the *Atlanta Constitution* reported that "the leading colored citizens of the city" had inaugurated a reform movement. They planned to present a petition to the grand jury calling for abatement of the various Negro dens which had "become the headquarters of the idle and vicious of the race." They also intended to visit the city judge to call attention to "another evil that sadly needs the attention of the authorities," the large number of black vagrants.[47]

The conflict between these two main groups of the black community was most evident in Nashville. After a brawl had broken out among some Negroes at the Memorial Day observance in the city's National Cemetery in 1874, the *Republican Banner* reported that

> some of the better class of colored men expressed great indignation at the disreputable conduct of those engaged in the fight. They say it looks like the negroes cannot come together without fighting or

quarreling; and that those of them who are disposed to conduct themselves as good citizens, have to bear the brunt of such trifling rascals.

A few months later the killing of a black after a "fancy ball" led "the
better class of negroes" under the leadership of Alfred Menefee, a
Republican officeholder, lawyer, and fixture of black society, to draft
a petition urging the suppression of "immorality." The petitioners
argued that, "if we desire to rise to eminence as a race of people, we
must suppress these fandangos, breakdowns and late festivals, and insist upon taking colored women of ill-fame off the streets at night."
Not only were such activities disgraceful and injurious to the reputation of the black community, but if allowed to continue "many of the
rising generation will be led astray, when they should pursue a path of
high moral rectitude." At another meeting the following month the
group thanked the municipal authorities for acting on their complaints
and announced their determination to "do everything in our power to
put all species of crime beyond the reach of the rising generation, and
endeavor ourselves to lead exceptionable lives." In 1886 at the height
of agitation over disorder in Black Bottom, many of the same citizens
gave their support to the recently organized all-white Law and Order
leagues in order to remind the whites that not all Negroes were criminals. As a young black complained, "the white people make no distinction between the different classes of negroes whereas we make
several distinct grades."[48]

The middle-class blacks also cooperated with elements of the white
community that favored temperance or prohibition. After the 1882
convention of the Georgia W.C.T.U. rejected black participation on
the ground that "it is best to keep the colored work separate from the
white," some blacks formed a separate temperance group.[49] Nashville,
where J. C. Napier, Dr. R. F. Boyd, and the Reverend Preston Taylor
supported the movement, also had separate organizations. T. A. Sykes,
however, served on the State Temperance Executive Committee and
addressed both white and black audiences. The presence of such important Negroes drew many blacks to the cause of temperance, but
proponents feared that their influence would not extend to the class
most in need of reform. When a "well known colored man" was asked
about the Negroes' view of the movement in Nashville, he replied:

The better class approve it and will support it, but many of our people are easily influenced, and, of course, will be induced to oppose it.

We very much fear that should the question ever come before the people that the weaker of our race will be unduly influenced to cast their ballots against it.[50]

The middle-class blacks sought other ways to close the gap between themselves and the masses. Organizations such as the Colored Ladies Relief Society of Nashville tried not only to provide food and fuel to the poor but to improve their morals. Nashville's Negroes sought to reform Hell's Half Acre through the construction of a manufacturing plant that would employ about two hundred of "the idle and shiftless blacks" of the neighborhood. Planned as a reformatory and industrial institution, the Reverend Preston Taylor spearheaded the effort with the backing of his Gay Street Christian Church; however, insufficient funds led to the project's eventual failure. A similar fate met Peter Lowery's Tennessee Manual Labor University. Lowery argued that such an institution would help disadvantaged Negro youths who "become subjects of roving and vice." To control this "lawless class," Lowery proposed industrial education, which would "cultivate the intellect, morals and skilled industry of the hands to fit and qualify them for good and useful citizenship." Despite the fund-raising efforts of black leaders Alfred Menefee, William Butler, and Monroe Jamison, whites showed little interest in this attempt by blacks to discipline the unruly elements within their midst.[51] Negroes were more successful in organizing separate branches of the Y.M.C.A. in each city. Those founded in Richmond and Nashville in 1876 were the first of their kind in the South.[52] These organizations not only served as social centers for prosperous middle-class Negroes but gave them a chance to seek the reformation of their erring brethren.

Class cleavages had clearly emerged by 1890, but there were other sources of division as well. Color was sometimes a factor, especially in influencing the choice of a mate. Mixed marriages involving blacks and mulattoes were relatively rare. A study of 102 prominent male Negroes revealed that all but eleven married women of the same racial designation; nine of these, including three city councilmen, were blacks who followed the well-known pattern of "marrying lighter." Reflecting the makeup of the Negro elite in Montgomery, in twenty-one of the thirty-three marriages that matched mulattoes or blacks, both partners were black; in Nashville, on the other hand, where there was no intermixture, seventeen of the twenty-three marriages united mulattoes.[53]

Nonetheless, whatever may have been the case in other cities, these five cities provide little evidence of color as a badge of special status. According to the *Atlanta Constitution,* the color line was commonly drawn between blacks and quadroons in cities, especially in Augusta and Savannah where "there are society divisions of the most pronounced characteristics among negroes." But no mention was made of Atlanta.[54] And in each of the five cities there were enough mulattoes and blacks scattered throughout the social structure to make generalizations based on color unreliable. One of the wealthiest members of the largely black Montgomery elite was the mulatto contractor James Hale. The merchant Henry Harding and barber Lyttleton Jones and their black wives were only two of Nashville's blacks who gained entry into the primarily mulatto upper crust of that city's Negro community. Though more evidence is needed, it seems that wealth and cultural attributes were more important than color in gaining social acceptance or political leadership. The only indication of overt color prejudice within any of the five communities occurred in Nashville. A Blue Vein Society, formed by some light-skinned Negroes, was the subject of a passionate attack by the Reverend Thompson of the city's elite St. John's A.M.E. Church and evidently did not become an important factor in Negro life.[55]

While color may have produced some friction, other divisive forces were more evident. For example, splits arose among individuals seeking leadership positions. Often such conflict took place between recognized groups such as between politicians and preachers; more often it emerged within such groups. Sometimes prospective leaders squared off against one another for personal reasons, although more often they disagreed over substantive issues, such as the black response to segregation or prohibition. Even the generation gap took its toll.[56]

Emigration also sparked disagreement. Blacks had to weigh the relative merits of staying in the cities or leaving in search of better opportunities. Among the alternatives were a return to the countryside, migration to the North, or foreign colonization, especially to Africa. Although the debate over migration attracted the greatest interest during the exodus to Kansas and Indiana at the end of the 1870s and during the back-to-Africa movement in the 1890s, urban Negroes discussed the topic throughout the period.

Local newspapers carried the advertisements of labor agents in the market for black workers. The *Richmond Dispatch* reported that, during a two-week period in 1870, 250 Virginia Negroes had been transported by steamer to New York and then to Boston under the auspices of a Boston company. These blacks were hired in many parts of New England, chiefly as cooks, housemaids, and dining-room servants. Later issues of the newspaper included repeated advertisements by J. P. Justis of Richmond. "Colored women—I wish to hire six or eight good cooks, washers, and ironers to live with private families in New York. Wages $12 to $16 per month." "Wanted—Twenty-five coal miners for Indiana and Illinois mines (all colored)." Other agents advertised for Negroes to do farm or railroad work in the Southern states.[57]

It is difficult to gauge the extent of black migration from the cities. A number clearly went to Northern cities as the *Richmond Dispatch* pointed out. No strangers to urban life, they differed from later migrants who tended to come directly from the countryside.[58] The lure of Midwestern farm land attracted others. During 1876 Nashville's *Daily American* reported that about ninety Negroes, "chiefly from this city," had left on a steamer for Kansas. They said they wanted to get employment and to flee from political oppression. Three years later at the height of the exodus, the newspaper noted that on one day about fifty Negroes had departed for Kansas in the morning and an additional one hundred had left in the afternoon.[59]

A few prominent black leaders encouraged emigration. Two days after the election of a Conservative city ticket in 1869, a group of Nashville Negroes led by defeated council candidate Randall Brown met to discuss the possibility of moving to the Western territories. Little came of this effort, but six years later interest revived. Citing the recent lynchings of two local blacks, discrimination in the courts, arbitrary enforcement of the vagrant act, and lack of support by the Republican Party, a statewide emigration convention met in Nashville. Local blacks dominated the meeting, but their pleas of "on to Kansas" were as unsuccessful as they had been in 1869.[60]

Agitation in favor of migration resumed with a new intensity in the spring and summer of 1879. A debate was held at Nashville's Liberty Hall on the question "That the Negroes Ought Not to Migrate from the Southern States." Black lawyer and politician W. H. Young spoke in the negative. His statement that he would like to see all Negroes move to Kansas and leave none in the South was loudly applauded, while the promigration crowd constantly interrupted his opponent's remarks. Young began publication of the *Emigration Herald* in which he reported that "we are now organizing an emigration club, and making preparations to emigrate to Kansas without suffering." The next month an emigration circular listed bad economic conditions and the desire for land as reasons for the movement. Other blacks, however, were motivated by discrimination in the schools, in the courts, and at the ballot box.[61]

In 1880 William H. Ash, a "prominent and influential man from Montgomery," returned to the Alabama capital after a tour through southern Kansas to see how blacks were managing. His impressions were favorable and he predicted that a thousand Negroes would emigrate there from Montgomery and Madison counties the following spring. He cited Democratic exclusion of blacks from representation in all public affairs as a major reason for the proposed exodus. He and James T. Rapier, a black former Congressman and Montgomery federal officeholder, had purchased sections in a Kansas county to sell at low rates and on long terms to settlers. Ash's idea was ridiculed by the Negro editor of the *Weekly Advance*, who sarcastically envisioned every black leaving Alabama and moving to Kansas.[62]

In fact, most Negro leaders attacked the various migration schemes. During the 1870s racial leaders in Nashville and Atlanta were especially active in combatting such movements. The Reverend Daniel Wadkins, who had previously branded Randall Brown "a mule stealing refugee from the penitentiary," announced his opposition to migration at the Emigration Convention held in Nashville in 1875. Three months later that body reconvened to hear the report of H. A. Napier, who had been sent to examine conditions in Kansas. Napier admitted that life was good there, but emphasized that each settler needed more than $1,000. This disclosure buttressed the arguments of the antimigration forces. They succeeded in getting the report adopted over the protests of the most ardent migrationists, who maintained that little capital was required.[63] When growing numbers of Negroes were leaving Atlanta in the early 1870s, George McKinney, a black businessman, charged that certain whites around the depot were giving Negroes $2.50 to go west. In a letter to the *Atlanta Constitution*, he assured his fellow blacks that "we had best remain where we are known" since "the laws of Georgia are just and equal."[64]

An Atlanta black was hired in 1875 to investigate the living conditions in Mississippi. Upon his return he advised Negroes against emigration, but he guaranteed the fairest accommodations for those who still wanted to leave. The following year the *Constitution* happily reported the proposed formation of an Anti-Emigration Club by local blacks. The club aimed to find the causes for and to devise the means of checking heavy migration. In addition to forestalling emigration by showing that work was harder and less rewarding in the new cotton states than in Georgia, the club was planning an employment bureau for Negro farm hands, servants, and skilled laborers.[65]

By the late 1880s depressed economic conditions and increased discrimination in the migration areas of the Midwest and Deep South caused growing numbers of potential emigrants to look toward foreign countries. During 1888 at the height of interest, South American nations were especially popular as proposed destinations. J. C. Napier, previously in favor of emigration to Kansas, charged that supporters of foreign migration were either enemies of the people or misguided friends. "The colored people of Nashville will work on in this city," he said, "believing they can accomplish more here than elsewhere." J. H. Keeble, politician and editor of the *Free Lance*, told his readers under the headline "It is Right to Stay Here" that the Negro press firmly believed that "this country is as suitable for the negro as for whites, and urges that we stay."[66]

It is impossible to know for certain what motivated the opponents of emigration. Most probably they acted out of the sincere belief that the blacks were better off where they were. Nonetheless, self-interest was also a factor, for without the black masses the positions of Negro politicians, professionals, and businessmen would be seriously undermined.[67] Unless they wanted to follow their clients (as some of the politicians and ministers did), their continued success depended upon discouraging prospective emigrants. In this struggle the middle class was once again arrayed against large numbers of the working and lower classes.

This conflict was especially strong during the appearance of a back-to-Africa scheme in Atlanta in 1890. The strains it caused further testify to the fundamental disunity within the black community. In the fall of 1890 representatives of the Congo Steamship Company and the Congo Land Improvement Company began selling tickets to the Congo for $1. More than three hundred black Atlantans took advantage of the offer, causing leaders to mobilize to expose the plan as a fraud. The opposition to the company was led by the Reverend E. R. Carter, C. C. Wimbish, Republican politician, and Joseph McKinley, one of the city's richest Negro businessmen. Frequent meetings of "exodusters," most of them servants, were held at Schell's Hall under the aegis of John T. Schell, one of the few "respectable" individuals involved in the endeavor.[68] A black critic expressed little fear of the emigration ever taking place since he was convinced the proposal was fraudulent, but he thought it might prove a useful lesson to certain members of the race. A few "men with more property than education and sense" were involved, but, he said, "as a rule only the worst element are backing this movement, and if they should get out of the country this city would be well rid of them. They are the scum of the city and I have no use for them."[69]

The editor of the *Southern Appeal*, a Negro Democratic paper, took the threat more seriously, however, and issued a stern warning against emigration. In doing so he revealed the concern of many blacks who relied upon the trade of their race and who felt that migration would help neither those who left nor those who stayed behind. Only in his praise for the white Southerner did he significantly differ from other critics of the movement.

> Negroes must learn that there is no Eldorado nowadays. If there was the white man would have found it long ago. If he, with his energy, wealth, and progress, has not found Africa to be an Eldorado, why in the name of common sense can we expect to go there with a dollar, and find a country where bread grows on trees and syrup runs all over the country in rivers? To go to or return from Africa would doubtless cost about $300. How many of these enthusiasts have that with which to return if they are disappointed? And can you so conceal it that it cannot be stolen from you? If not don't go!

Besides, all past efforts at emigration even within the United States had failed and had resulted in "the poor, disappointed negroes" returning to the South, "which is the best place for them after all." Soon after the crisis passed, it was officially announced that the Congo Company was indeed a fraud.[70] If anything, the disclosure reinforced the gap which existed between members of the lower class who had been gullible enough to believe in the scheme and those of the middle class who had sought to discredit it.

By 1890 there existed a definable black community. Its areas of concentration could be plotted on a map, its leaders identified, and its progress since emancipation assessed. Yet it was not monolithic. It was divided by class differences which affected political, social, economic, and even religious life. This is not surprising. Every ethnic group has faced this problem to a greater or lesser degree. The conflict between German and East European Jews, Northern and Southern Italians, and Protestant and Catholic Irish and Germans also calls into question the idea of intragroup harmony. Blacks could even less afford this handicap. Indeed, as the period progressed, it seemed that the divisions widened and that new ones arose to further weaken the blacks' ability to meet the hostile white world with a unified voice.

III

FROM EXCLUSION TO EXCLUSION:
THE ROLE OF BLACKS
IN URBAN POLITICS

As in the antebellum period, postbellum urban white Southerners were obsessed with disciplining their cities' growing black populations. Some of the attempts to improve discipline have already been discussed. Whites viewed public education as an opportunity for increased control; blacks were confined to certain jobs to protect white workers and provide a surplus of cheap labor; compulsory vaccination, enforcement of sanitary regulations, and admittance of blacks to hospitals helped control the serious health threat untreated freedmen posed; segregation within schools, churches, welfare facilities, militia companies, and public accommodations restricted opportunities for meetings between the races and thus reduced the possibility of either amalgamation or conflict; and in many instances, especially in schools, efforts were made to keep whites in positions of authority for as long as possible.

The blacks themselves turned their attention to internal discipline. The preachers and school teachers encouraged their charges to live righteous, moral, and temperate lives, to be well mannered, trust in God, and work hard. Blacks organized themselves in benevolent societies, literary societies, and social clubs, all of which advocated service to the black community and were dedicated to the improvement of the race. Their leaders worked with whites to reduce tensions and increase benefits for blacks. Above all, those in positions of leadership, themselves members of a growing middle class, decried the excesses of lower-class blacks whose actions threatened the advancement of the race.

Whites were not satisfied. In one area in particular they felt that blacks, be they middle or lower class, had to be "put in their place." In the interest of harmony among whites and in order to assure the success of white policies in other areas of urban life, black political rights had to be abridged. Negro participation in the political life of the antebellum South had ceased with the disfranchisement of Tennessee and North Carolina free Negroes in 1834 and 1835. Although most Southern whites accepted the abolition of slavery, few of them advocated full political rights for the freedmen. Despite white opposition, however, blacks won the right to vote and hold office in 1867; and throughout the remainder of the period, white Southerners struggled with the reality of the Negro voter. Once again their aim was to develop a system that would minimize the effects of the Negroes' new freedom. Not until after 1890 did the South decide on the path of wholesale *de jure* disfranchisement. In the interim, the idea of controlling the black vote, especially on the local level, remained the central consideration in Southern politics. The important question in the political history of urban Negroes during the period 1867 to 1890 was not merely whether or not they could vote, but what power their vote might have.

11

From Reconstruction to Redemption

After the war the immediate political problem for most Southern whites was to prevent the enfranchisement of the freedmen. Their opposition proved successful under Presidential Reconstruction, but black suffrage and officeholding became a fact of life under Congressional Reconstruction. With the indispensable help of the new black voters, Republicans won control of four of the five cities. In the fifth—Atlanta—four of ten councilmen were Republican and the mayor was an Independent. Conservatives and Democrats were determined to "redeem" their cities for the forces of "white supremacy." By 1875 this process of redemption was completed in the last of the cities. It had been accomplished by a mixture of fraud, intimidation, and, most important, legislative manipulation. The result was a severe weakening of black political influence and power almost two decades before the enactment of widespread disfranchisement legislation.

Between the end of the war and the beginning of Congressional Reconstruction in March 1867, elections were held first under the antebellum charters, constitutions, and statutes and then under new laws which perpetuated the ban against Negro suffrage and officeholding. The first postwar election in Raleigh occurred in January 1866, when the white citizens under the provisions of the prewar charter went to the polls to choose from a list of white candidates. This after all was the way it had been since 1835. Because the new charter issued in March 1866 retained the bars to Negro participation in government, the January 1867 municipal election found the pattern of the past undisturbed. Nashville's first postwar city canvass in September 1866 was conducted under the Suffrage Act of 1865, which also restricted political rights to whites. Under such conditions it is not surprising that in Nashville and Raleigh, as well as in the other three cities, the vic- torious candidates were former Confederates and/or Conservatives.[1]

To these newly elected officials and their supporters, the idea of Negro suffrage was anathema. At the core of their opposition was the belief in white supremacy and the impossibility of sharing power with blacks. "One or the other must win—white *or* black; not white *and* black," argued a Montgomery voter. "There can be no co-rulers of black and white—no more than white and black can live in the same house or sit at the same table." Announcing both its and the Demo- cratic Party's opposition to Negro suffrage, the *Atlanta Constitution* contended that the Negro was regarded as "inferior by nature to the white race—as even below the Indian, and with less claim than the latter to the franchise." According to a Richmond state legislator, the belief in black inferiority was so firmly entrenched in the minds of white Southerners that any attempt to force Negro suffrage would lead to widespread violence between the races in which the freedmen would suffer most. Nor would the condition of the Negroes be altered by improved education or economic advancement since "you would have to change their skin before you can do it. . . . The condition is annexed to the color."[2]

If given the vote, opponents charged, the blacks would be unable to use it wisely and would fall under the control of the Radicals, under- mining the political life of the region. An Atlanta physician asserted that blacks would elect "the most unreliable class of men," a situation that would lead to lower "moral and political standards." Even worse, according to others, the awarding of the suffrage would open the door to additional changes in interracial contact. The *Montgomery Daily Ledger* declared that the South could not give in to the "fanaticism of New England" for that would be a first step toward "social equality." If blacks could vote, then they also would be eligible to hold office. To make Negroes Congressmen, governors, or judges, charged the *Atlanta Constitution*, would be "to degrade . . . [the white] race by elevating an inferior above it." To do so, argued the *Montgomery Daily Adver- tiser*, would be "to consent to our own degradation, and the overthrow of all true republicanism in the system of government instituted by our fathers for our benefit and protection in common with the white men of the North."[3]

In the minds of most whites the interest blacks devoted to politics distracted them from more necessary tasks. Similarly, political marches and demonstrations disturbed the peace of the community and heightened white fears of insurrection. The spectacle of "Radical negroes" coming into Raleigh for a political barbecue in 1868 brought alarm to local residents. "They are marching through the town with music while I write," reported one woman. "I very much fear there will be a disturbance of some kind." When she resumed the letter the following morning, she noted with some exaggeration, "it was hard getting any sleep last night—the Darkies were serenading [Governor] Holden . . . there seem to be *thousands* here." She not only typified the reaction of the whites to threatened disorder, but her additional comment that the black workmen "have stopped work today to attend the Radical Barbeque [*sic*]" drew attention to another aspect of the problem: the interruption of everyday affairs. Earlier in the year Drury Lacy, another resident of Raleigh who described himself as "still a Rebel," drew a similar conclusion about a celebration following a Radical political victory. Then he got to the heart of his feelings and his fears. "Next winter we shall have an increase of house-breaking, robbing, and burning, for they will have nothing to eat or drink." The letters of Sallie Munford Talbott to her husband during the 1867 fall campaign in Richmond told of "election riots and disturbances" caused by "the crowds of darkies" that prevented her from visiting relatives.[4]

The former Confederates were not alone in seeking to maintain white supremacy. Many white Unionists and Republicans initially urged caution in the granting of even limited suffrage to blacks. Speaking at a Union rally in May 1865, William Holden, editor of Raleigh's *Daily Standard* and soon to be named Provisional Governor of North Carolina, referred to whites as the "governing and self-governing race." The 1865 suffrage act in Tennessee which restricted voting to whites was signed by the state's leading Unionist, Governor William Brownlow. The *Nashville Daily Press and Times* was among the many Unionist newspapers to support this restriction. In an editorial on "The Status of the Negro," the Republican editor S. R. Mercer argued that "it is a good maxim to 'make haste slowly.' We mean that measures to the

end of making the negroes citizens, with all the rights and immuni-
ties of white men, while yet they are unprepared for an intelligent exercise of the privileges of citizenship, is too hasty."[5]

These political leaders subscribed to the common belief in the un-
readiness of blacks for the suffrage; they also feared that the endorsement of the franchise for the freedmen would undermine rather than
strengthen the Unionist cause in the South. In testimony before the
Joint Committee on Reconstruction, Milton J. Saffold, a Montgomery
Unionist, argued that with government protection loyal white men and
Northern immigrants could form a strong Union Party. But although
he had "no prejudice whatever against qualified negro suffrage," he concluded that

> if you compel us to carry through universal suffrage of colored men
> over twenty-one years of age, without qualification, it will prove quite
> an incubus upon us in the organization of a national Union party of
> white men there; it will furnish our opponents with a very effective
> weapon against us.[6]

Segments of the Negro population also at first assigned a lower pri-
ority to gaining the vote than to receiving guarantees on landowning,
legal rights, and education. According to August Meier, this attitude
was prevalent among the black masses, although their leaders were
more concerned with enfranchisement. Even conventions called by
Negro leaders in North Carolina and Alabama in 1865 and 1866, however, stressed educational and economic needs over political rights.[7]
Travelers in the South during the first months after the war reported
similar views among individual blacks.[8]

The early mixed reaction to the necessity of universal male suffrage
quickly vanished as blacks came to realize that in the vote lay the key
to better education, fairer justice, and equal treatment. The Nashville
Negroes who comprised the State Equal Rights League in June 1866
called for passage of the Fourteenth Amendment and the making of
"sufficient changes in the Constitution of this State to strike every ves-
tige of injustice from it, and guarantee equal political rights to our
race, in the Elective Franchise." To Montgomery's leading black politician, Holland Thompson, it was obvious by March 1867 that blacks
required the vote to assure the "speediest elevation" of the race.[9]

Blacks were not alone in agitating for the suffrage. As early as the
fall of 1865, a representative of the Northern Freedmen's Society had

warned during a trip to Nashville, "I regard the prospects of 'recon-struction' in this city, if we leave the negro out of our plans (an infat-uation that should not be indulged in for a moment) as slim indeed."[10] After the passage of the Black Codes and the election of former Con-federates to Congress, state offices, and city halls throughout the South, most white Republicans came to agree. They soon realized that only through the enfranchisement of Negroes would their party be able to win elections in the South and thus preserve Republican dom-ination of the national government.

The enfranchisement of the freedmen without qualification was ac-complished with the passage of the Reconstruction Acts and the ad-vent of military rule. In April 1867, for example, the Raleigh charter was amended so that any twenty-one-year-old male citizen could vote and hold office provided that he met a minimum residence require-ment. Similar changes occurred in the other cities, although in Nash-ville and Atlanta the process took longer. Atlanta officials did not ac-knowledge the right of Negroes to vote in local elections until the passage of a special ordinance in November 1868; a state Supreme Court decision of June 1869 conferred the right to hold office. Ten-nessee blacks were enfranchised in February 1867, but a section of the law which withheld the right to hold office or sit on juries was not removed until twelve months later.[11]

Despite such delays, by 1868 white Southerners were forced to ac-cept Negro suffrage. "The Radical Congress at Washington has put us all under Military government again, and General Pope is our ruler," complained an Atlanta businessman. "We are invited to form new State constitutions giving to the negroes the right of suffrage, and I suppose we shall *have to do it.*" The old arguments against enfran-chisement, including the freedmen's lack of formal education and po-litical experience, were again made in the press. An Atlanta editor claimed that the removal of white control had left the Negro "to fol-low, in a great measure, the sensual and selfish instincts of his nature." He summarized the problem as he saw it and called attention to its widespread implications.

> As an integral element of the body politic, with equal and co-ordinate privileges with the white race, the tendency of this relation is neces-sarily to deteriorate the whole. Hence, society in the South has a double task to perform—to preserve its own normal condition, and to resist the aggressive and corrupting tendencies of social and political

equality with the blacks. How to accomplish this essential result, and preserve the desired amity between the races is *the* great problem of the day.[12]

The impact of Negro suffrage first was evident in the elections for delegates to the state constitutional conventions. Thanks to the disfranchisement or nonregistration of many former Confederates, black voters were usually in the majority. In Raleigh where Negroes comprised a slight majority of the residents, there were 847 registered whites as compared to 1,267 blacks. In Richmond the figures were 6,120 blacks and 5,063 whites. In Nashville, located in a state which was not under military rule and did not draw up a new constitution until 1870, registrants in the fall of 1867 numbered 8,056 blacks and 2,151 whites. Only in Atlanta did the white registrants outnumber the black and in that case merely by 1,765 to 1,621.[13]

The edge in Negro enrollment was reflected in the selection of several black delegates to the conventions—Lewis Lindsay and Joseph Cox of Richmond, Peyton Finley of Montgomery, and James H. Harris of Raleigh. Not only were whites faced with the "ignominy" of being represented by Negroes, but, as residents of capitals where the proceedings were held, they encountered black representatives from other parts of the state. Samuel P. Richards of Atlanta, whose city selected an all-white delegation, nevertheless could not accept the new order of things.

> The Menagerie Convention has been in operation—that is, *showing*—for two weeks now and except as a great show have accomplished nothing at all but to spend our money at the rate of $2000 per diem. It makes me feel wolfish every time I think about those niggers there pretending to make laws for Georgia white men. It is too great a burlesque on law and order.[14]

The governments established under these new constitutions helped inaugurate the shift from exclusion to segregation in education, welfare, militia service, and public accommodations. But what did they mean to blacks in terms of elective and patronage positions? The evidence for the five cities supports the recent revisionist studies which refute the traditional image of black control. The blacks, however, did receive a greater share of the offices than either before or after the Republicans were in power.

James T. Rapier from Montgomery's district was the only black to represent these cities in Congress, but several served in state legislatures. Wake County elected three blacks including James H. Harris, one of the state's most important black politicians; between 1868 and 1876 Montgomery chose ten black legislators, four of them for two or more terms.[15] When the Radicals controlled the county governments in Nashville, Montgomery, and Raleigh, Negroes served as commissioners and justices of the peace; in Nashville they also held the position of county jailer.

But it was in the city councils that blacks made their greatest impact during their few years of ascendancy. Two of the four Radical councilmen elected in Atlanta in 1870 were black, including William Finch. Four blacks, but never more than two at a time, served on the Montgomery Council between 1868 and 1875. The most noteworthy, grocer Holland Thompson, was one of three aldermen chosen for the Board of School Commissioners, one of three appointed to fix rates of assessment on personal property, and one of two who prepared the new City Code. He and Finch were largely responsible for the inauguration of their cities' Negro schools. The sole Negro elected to the Nashville Board of Aldermen during Mayor A. E. Alden's victorious campaign in 1867 was disqualified because of Tennessee's bar on Negro officeholding; following its repeal, however, one of the ten new aldermen and at least six of the twenty council members chosen during Alden's reelection bid in 1868 were black. Two of the nine-man Raleigh Board of Commissioners appointed by military authorities in 1868, including James H. Harris, were also Negro.[16] From the first municipal election in 1869 through 1875, blacks won no less than three and as many as five of the commission seats.

Along with their white allies, black politicians made certain that blacks enjoyed patronage appointments ranging from municipal offices to jobs as common laborers. At one of its first meetings, the Radical Council in Nashville unanimously resolved at the urging of Mayor Alden's spokesman that "in electing officers of the Corporation of Nashville, this Board will recognize no distinction in color, race or previous condition." One week later the mayor removed the white guards at the almshouse and replaced them with three Negroes.[17] Other blacks were appointed city sexton and assistant street overseer, the latter job created especially for a Negro. Raleigh blacks fared best in patronage largely because of the length of Radical control and its secure base. Doc Chavis was city pump contractor during the period of great expansion in the town's water works. Norfleet Dunston, a shoemaker by trade and a politician by profession who served several terms as alderman and county justice of the peace, was appointed township tax receiver in 1872 and often drew extra pay as a registrar. Positions as election officials meant an extra $3 to $8 per day and were rarely awarded to blacks, but exceptions occasionally were made also in Montgomery and Nashville.[18] In all the cities when the Radicals were in power, the mass of blacks benefited from increased employment in construction work.

The most noteworthy form of patronage was the appointment of Negroes to the fire and police departments. Even here, black regular policemen were found only in Montgomery and Raleigh, the two cities where Radical influence was greatest. Atlanta and Richmond, in which Radicals exercised the least power, not only refused to appoint black policemen, but rejected black firemen as well. Nashville and Raleigh Radicals established separate black fire companies, while their Montgomery counterparts retained the segregated unit inherited from their predecessors.

In seeking to rid the cities of Republican control, local Conservatives and Democrats depended upon support from the newly redeemed state governments. Indeed, favorable action on the part of state legislators was the single most important factor in the triumph of urban Redeemers. The cities were the creation of the states and in the political sphere, as in so many other aspects of urban life, final power rested with the legislators. And since the five cities were all capitals, state officials had a special interest in them. Forced to spend part or all of the year there, the officials were greatly concerned with controlling their Negro populations. While in other cities the primary thrust for enlisting the state government in ousting the Radicals came from the permanent residents, in these five cases the impetus came from both residents and state representatives.

Assisted by sympathetic governors, the state legislators arranged for the direct removal of opposition officeholders, altered the ways in which local officials were elected, rearranged political boundaries through judicious gerrymandering, and legislated new requirements for voting. These maneuvers gave the local Conservatives and Democrats great leverage. For this reason, there was less need to resort to the more generally publicized tactics of fraud, intimidation, and violence. Not that these illegal measures were totally absent. Especially good use was made of them in Richmond and Montgomery; but even in these cities they complemented the legal tactics of Redemption.

The most blatant lawful technique was simply to remove Radicals from office and either appoint their replacements or provide for new elections. The military established the precedent for such action during Congressional Reconstruction. In 1868 Commanding General John Schofield ousted the ex-Confederates and appointed George Chahoon mayor of Richmond along with an all-white and largely Republican City Council. They served until March 1870, when the newly elected Conservative state legislature passed the Enabling Act which declared vacant all municipal offices. Under the terms of the act, moderate Republican Governor Gilbert Walker appointed Conservatives to the City Council. The Council in turn chose as mayor Henry K. Ellyson, publisher of the rabidly Democratic *Richmond Dispatch*. Chahoon and his colleagues refused to acknowledge the legality of the legislation and barricaded themselves inside the police station. Special police chosen by Ellyson laid siege to the station and federal troops were finally brought in after pitched battles between Ellyson and Chahoon supporters. The turmoil ended with the army in control and the opposing claimants agreeing to let the state Supreme Court of Appeals settle the matter. In the interim both parties had access to public buildings. For more than a month the city had a dual government: one recognized by U.S. Circuit Court Judge John Underwood, a staunch Radical, and the other by Governor Walker. Not unexpectedly the state court, composed entirely of Conservatives, found the Enabling Act constitutional and declared Ellyson the rightful mayor.[19]

Tennessee state officials played a similar role in disposing of Nashville's Radical Mayor A. E. Alden. On the strength of a four to one margin of black over white registrants, Alden and his entire ticket had been elected in September 1867. Representing the wing of the Republican Party controlled largely by Northern federal officeholders, Alden was opposed by a band of "home-grown" Radicals led by his mayoral opponent, H. S. Scovel, and S. R. Mercer of the *Nashville Daily Press and Times*. Both wings of the Republican Party actively courted the Negro vote, although Alden was far more successful. "While many of our race and color 'entered devious paths and fainted by the wayside,'" Alden told the Council in his inaugural address, "our colored friends with a true unflinching patriotism worthy of imitation, declared their loyalty at the ballot box almost unanimously."[20]

Alden continued to court Negro voters through adroit use of patronage and as his reelection campaign approached, allegedly brought in Negroes from as far away as Kentucky to cast votes for him in return for money or jobs. Again Alden defeated a native Republican, this time by a vote of 1,839 to 1,336, an increase in the total number of ballots cast of over 500 despite a decline in the city's population. Though its charges must be weighed carefully, the opposition press seems to have been correct in attributing victory to the flagrant use of repeaters, the denial of the suffrage to legal voters, and other fraudulent practices. Helping also to assure victory was the appointment by Alden of all the election judges and clerks, many of them city employees with a clear stake in an Alden win.[21] Whether legal or illegal, the Negro voters were the key to victory. And it seemed that Nashville could expect several more years of Alden rule. Yet, because of alleged excessive spending ascribed to corruption, local citizens succeeded in getting the Conservative legislature to place the city in receivership. Alden was removed from office in June 1869, and in the subsequent municipal campaign the Conservatives swept every ward.[22]

Redeemer legislatures also undermined local Radical strength by changing the procedures for selecting officials. Democratic strength in Atlanta, for example, was due only in part to the greater number of white than black voters. Even more important was the method used to elect members of the City Council. During the first two municipal elections in which blacks were permitted to vote, the entire electorate chose the mayor and each of the ten councilmen (two from each ward). Despite splits in their party, the Democrats won complete victories in both elections.[23] In October 1870 the Republican state legislature replaced the general ticket arrangement with a ward election system. This change, while doing little to improve the prospects of electing a Republican mayor, helped the Republicans in council races due to their slim majorities in the Third and Fourth wards, where Negroes were concentrated. The tactic bore fruit two months later when the Republicans elected four of the ten aldermen, including two blacks from the Third and Fourth wards.[24]

The *Atlanta Constitution* made the usual complaints about "the stupendous Radical frauds," including the use of illegal Negro voters made possible by both a weak registration law and the practice of allowing voters to cast ballots in any ward. The Republican *Daily New Era,* on the other hand, claimed with more evidence that the key to the council races was the change in the election law, which ended city-wide selection of aldermen.[25] Without it, all the Radicals would have been defeated since Democrats who voted for the Independent mayoral candidate would not have supported Radical councilmen.

In light of these facts, the *Constitution* concluded that "the necessity of changing back is therefore apparent."[26] Soon after the Democrats regained control of the legislature, they repealed the new law and Atlanta reverted to the old system. In December 1871 the entire Democratic municipal ticket was swept into office, ending Atlanta's brief flirtation with Radical and Negro officeholders. According to the *Constitution,* the victory was "largely due" to the Fulton County (Atlanta) delegation in the legislature which changed the voting procedure. Although President U. S. Grant carried the city in 1872, the Republican Party had been destroyed as a major contender in local elections. The Republican challenger for mayor in that year was soundly defeated and in 1873 the Democratic candidate ran unopposed, as was largely true of the Democratic slate of aldermen.[27] In future years black aldermanic candidates occasionally were the leading vote-getters in their home wards but were smothered by the white Democratic votes their opponents gathered in other wards.[28]

The Tennessee and North Carolina legislatures also interceded to rob Radicals of their local gains. Nine weeks after the Conservatives in Nashville swept the city in the 1869 municipal election, the transfer of power was completed. The new Conservative state legislature abolished the Republican-controlled Board of County Commissioners and replaced it with the old General Court made up of locally elected justices of the peace. The Court, dominated by Conservatives, discharged all Republican appointees of the commissioners and reinstated previous officeholders. County government in Raleigh's Wake County was likewise redeemed by the North Carolina legislature. Empowered by the 1875 Redeemer Constitution, the legislature transferred the right of electing justices of the peace for counties, cities, and towns from the people to themselves. The justices were now to appoint the county commissioners who had been popularly elected in the past (always Republicans in Wake), removing still other offices from the grasp of the Negro and white Republicans. Earlier the legislature had helped to redeem the city of Raleigh itself. An act of February 16, 1875, gave a drastically altered Board of Aldermen the power to choose the previously popularly elected mayor.[29]

What made the election of the mayor by the Raleigh aldermen such a victory for the Democrats was the use of a third device employed by state legislatures to ensure acceptable councils—gerrymandering. Gerrymandering in its various forms was the most effective tactic used by sympathetic legislatures both to redeem the cities and to keep them in the hands of white Democrats. Without this technique, Redemption of Raleigh would have taken many more years. The tenacity of Raleigh Radicalism was due to the presence of a significant number of white Republicans (as in Nashville) plus the relative parity in the number of white and Negro voters (as in pre-1875 Montgomery). Then, too, the white Conservatives were less inclined to use the tactics of violence and fraud Richmonders employed, and, due to Republican strength in the state government, they were unable, as had Atlanta, to count on help from that sector until 1875.

In their frustrating attempts to oust the Radicals between 1869 and 1875, the Democrats raised the specter of black rule and tried to rally the "good" whites to throw out the "bad" scalawags, carpetbaggers, and Negroes. Despite this tactic, in 1872 when there were more white than Negro registered voters for the first time since the war, the Republicans again won the office of mayor and captured seven of the nine positions on the Board of Commissioners. The Democratic *Daily News* conceded that its party neither campaigned hard nor got out the vote in contrast to the Republicans who did both. As opposed to the other cities, there was no cry of fraud or intimidation. Charges of Democratic apathy again were leveled by the *Daily Sentinel* when the Negroes regained the lead in registered voters the next year. The Republicans achieved a complete sweep in the 1873 election and the newspaper sadly concluded that "the white people are satisfied with things as they are."[30]

The Democrats returned stronger in 1874 and elected four of the nine commissioners, but still lost the mayoralty by 300 votes. One of the four Democrats narrowly won election, while the five Republicans won handily. The following year despite an all-out attack based on the racial issue by the two Democratic newspapers, the county Republican slate of delegates to the Constitutional Convention won overwhelmingly with Raleigh again leading the way.[31]

In short, Raleigh Democrats simply did not have enough white votes. Nor did their feeble attempts to attract black voters make much headway against the Radical tide. It was at this point that salvation came instead from a *deus ex machina* in the form of the legislature's new Raleigh election law. Until February 1875, Raleigh had been divided into three wards: Eastern, Middle, and Western. The Middle Ward included the business district and many of the city's finest homes; it was the Conservative stronghold from 1865 to 1875. After the enfranchisement of Negroes, the two other wards were solidly Republican. With the exception of the Republican sweep in 1873, when a black was narrowly returned as one of the Middle Ward's aldermen, all of the Negro aldermen came from the Western and Eastern wards.

The same 1875 act which gave the aldermen power to elect the mayor divided the city into five wards. Even though the Middle Ward contained less than one-third of the population of either of the other wards under the old system, its southern boundary was shortened in order to exclude a large number of Negroes. Despite the fact that the ratio of its population and voters to those of the Eastern and Western wards had been declining each year, the ward, now called the Third, was to have five aldermen whereas each of the other four would have only three. The Eastern Ward was irregularly divided into two wards, the First and Second, so as to assure Conservative control of the former. Under the old system the Republicans invariably sent three commissioners from the eastern part of the city; after redistricting, the Democrats and Republicans each sent three aldermen.[32]

A similar arrangement was made for the city's western sector. In 1874 the Western Ward contained 295 registered whites and 369 registered Negroes. As was true of the Eastern Ward, the whites were concentrated in the north and the blacks in the south. Judiciously separated into the Fourth and Fifth wards in 1875 with no regard to size of population or geographical boundaries, the old Republican ascendancy was now destroyed. For the 1875 elections the Fourth Ward had 47 white and 221 black voters; the Fifth had 299 white and 242 black. The latter Negro figure is misleading, however, since many of the blacks flooded the ward to register after the new lines had been drawn.[33]

Assured of five votes from the Third Ward and three from the First, Democrats needed to capture only one of the aldermanic races in the sole contested ward, the Fifth, to control the Council and therefore elect the mayor. In fact, the Democrats never failed to return the full slate. Even though the Republicans could count on electing six aldermen (at least half of them black), they had no chance of recapturing control of the city. They continued to receive a majority of the votes cast in local elections—Hayes and Garfield carried the city as well—but the Democrats had finally found a way to cope with the Negro vote. No wonder when announcing the return of eleven Democratic and six Republican aldermen in May 1875, the *Daily Sentinel* could gloat that "the long looked for time has come at last and Raleigh is in the hands of her good and true."[34]

In three of the remaining cities (Atlanta did not need such assistance), gerrymandering also kept the capitals free from Radical control. Closest to the Raleigh model was Richmond's similar attempt to nullify the Negro vote by isolating it within a portion of the city. Earlier Radical gerrymandering necessitated such action. Mayor Chahoon's administration had annexed two heavily Negro areas on the outskirts of Richmond and had carved the city into five wards—Monroe, Clay, Jefferson, Marshall, and Madison—replacing the previous three-ward alignment. Large segments of black voters were intentionally included in each ward.[35] Thus, although Conservatives retained control of the Council in the municipal election of May 1870, the first since the Radicals had been removed from office, all fifteen victorious Conservatives had been involved in close campaigns, the largest margin of victory being 45 votes. At that time in only one ward did the whites outnumber the blacks by more than 300 voters, and even there the edge was only 1,701 to 1,330.[36]

Taking advantage of the concentration of black population in the northern portion of the city, the new Council created a sixth ward irregularly carved out of the upper areas of four of the original five. This became the famous Jackson Ward, the center of Black Richmond for the remainder of the century. Although the charter required that each ward have as nearly as possible an equal number of voters, by 1874 Jackson had a population of 11,806 while only two of the other wards had more than 9,100. More to the point, 70 percent of Jackson was black as compared to 44 percent of the ward with the next highest black concentration.[37] In effect the Conservatives gave the Republicans five seats on the Council and three positions as justices of the peace in return for guaranteed possession of the remaining twenty-five seats and fifteen justiceships. In succeeding years Conservatives were free to offer occasional challenges in Jackson Ward, while the Republicans rarely contested elections in Conservative bailiwicks. After the establishment of a bicameral city legislature in 1874, white Conservatives or Democrats regularly held at least twenty-five of the thirty council posts and fifteen of the eighteen aldermanic seats.

The Tennessee legislature likewise endorsed Nashville's plans to limit the number of black council candidates. Local Democrats proved incapable of preventing the Republican leader, Thomas A. Kercheval, from winning two one-year and six two-year terms as mayor from 1872 to 1887. Nevertheless, in none of his terms did he ever have with him a majority of either of the city's two legislative bodies. Taking advantage of Kercheval's first defeat in 1874, the new mayor and City Council pushed through a redistricting bill approved by the state legislature which made it all but impossible for the Republicans to elect representatives from any but two or three wards.[38]

But it was in Montgomery that the technique of gerrymandering was used to its fullest advantage. Rather than seeking to confine Republican and Negro influence, local Democrats and their friends in the legislature sought to eliminate it altogether. Not until 1875, after a hiatus of seven years, did Montgomery elect an entire Democratic slate of mayor and City Council. Even then several of the races were close and victory was due to a crippling split among white Republicans and the defection of an estimated 450 blacks. The Republicans had previously rebounded from an 1871 defeat to regain control of the Council and drastic action was required in 1875 if the Democrats were to prevent another comeback. Allegedly as part of a retrenchment program, the new mayor called upon the Redeemer legislature to reduce the boundaries of the city so as to exclude an "unprofitable portion of its territory" where the city spent far more in providing services than it received from taxes. The resulting legislation approved the suggested change, but extended the police jurisdiction of the city one mile beyond its limits to include these retroceded areas and guaranteed the former residents all privileges to Swayne School which they had previously enjoyed.[39]

It is at this point that the mayor's intent becomes clear for Swayne was one of the city's two Negro schools. Nowhere else is there any indication that the excluded inhabitants were primarily black, but in fact the area was taken from the solidly Negro portions of the Fourth and Fifth wards, the two bastions of Republican support. What was presented as an economy measure was actually a thinly veiled effort to minimize the effects of black suffrage. And it was successful. After the 1877 municipal election when the law became effective, the Republicans never seriously challenged for control of the city and no more blacks sat on the City Council. As the *Daily Advertiser* stated, the victory "wipes out Radicalism entirely from our city politics."[40]

Gerrymandering was clearly the most effective technique in controlling the Radicals, yet it was made even more effective by legislative changes in the requirements for voting. Although this fourth legal device in support of the Conservatives became most significant later in the century, it was already being put to good use in the earlier period, especially in Montgomery. In 1871 the Democrats in Montgomery had captured nine of the twelve council seats although the Radicals had elected their mayoral candidate. The Democratic Council immediately sought to tighten voting requirements. Under the Republicans, state law had permitted the voter to cast his ballot at any polling place within his county of residence, and according to a staunch Democrat, "negroes soon began to tramp from place to place to cast their ballots at different boxes on the same day." Another law had made it a crime punishable by a fine of not less than $3,000 to challenge voters.[41]

A new charter secured by the Democrats in February 1872 dealt a severe blow to Republicans. The registration book for each ward had to be closed ten days before the election. In order to vote in a local election a person had to be a resident of the state for six months, the city for three months, and the ward for fifteen days.[42] Despite such obstacles, the Republicans managed to win back control of the Council and reelect their mayor in the next election. In March 1875, therefore, even tighter restrictions were added after the *Montgomery Daily Advertiser*, speaking for local Democrats, pleaded that "if the Legislature does not come to the aid of the negro dominated communities then there is no help for this portion of Alabama."[43] The residency requirement was increased to five months in the city and three months in the ward. And in order to vote, a certificate of registration had to be surrendered at the polling place which, thanks to another new section, had to be in the voter's home precinct. Throughout the process, both at registration and voting, officials (generally Democrats) had the right to challenge voters. Further undermining the Republicans, a provision shifted election day from the regularly scheduled December date to May 1875, although victorious candidates were not to take office until December 1875. The Redeemers thus hoped to capitalize on the momentum generated by their statewide victories in the 1874 fall elections and, more important, sought to prevent nonresident Republi-

cans from meeting the residency requirements in time for the municipal election.[44] One of the effects of the laws was immediately obvious
to the English author, Charles Nordhoff, who passed through Montgomery during the election swept by the Democrats. He noted that

> in this place Democrats bought up, at two dollars a piece, the regis-
> tration certificates of [over two hundred] colored men . . . and
> these were carefully retained, except in cases where it was quite cer-
> tain that the original holder would vote the Democratic ticket.[45]

In most of the five cities, and generally in the rest of the urban
South, the legal techniques already described were sufficient to defeat
the white Republicans and the new black voters. Yet Democrats and
Conservatives in each city relied to varying degrees on the extralegal
tactics of intimidation, fraud, and violence to obtain or hold power.
Nowhere, however, were they employed as consistently as in Richmond.

As already noted, Richmond Conservatives secured office through
the state's replacement of Chahoon's Radical Administration and once
in power they gerrymandered the city to ensure domination of the City
Council. Nonetheless, without the resort to illegal activities they would
not have triumphed in the critical municipal elections in 1870 nor
would they have continued their firm hold on the office of mayor.

In May 1870, a month after Chahoon had been removed from office,
he renewed his contest with Mayor Ellyson in another municipal election. Other city officials and the entire City Council were to be elected
at the same time. Realizing the importance of the Negro vote, the Conservatives sought to neutralize it.[46] In order to encourage whites to
register there were separate places for the two races in each precinct.[47]
Committees of young white men were appointed to canvass the city
and weed out instances of fraudulent registration by blacks. They frequently had Negro and white Radicals arrested for allegedly giving
false information or interfering with officers in the conduct of their
duty. Invariably the charges were later dismissed, but often not until
after the election, thus costing the Radicals needed votes.[48]

On election day separate voting lines were used for each race,
a practice which, though inherited from the military authorities, was
now used to limit the number of Negro voters.[49] The predominantly
Conservative officials at the polls also harassed many blacks. Although
Richmond's Conservatives were clearly better organized than their

counterparts in the other four cities—in addition to their fraudulent voting inspectors, they enjoyed formidable press support, used primaries to select their candidates, held nightly ward club meetings, had poll watchers, and provided transportation to the polls—Chahoon won by a majority of 283 votes and carried with him the rest of the general ticket. The Conservatives, however, captured fifteen of the twenty-five council seats. The *Richmond Dispatch* was consoled by the Conservative council victories and the fact that Republicans had elected justices of the peace in only two wards.[50]

The Conservatives, however, were not ready to settle for a partial victory. Despite the fact that even the *Dispatch* did not question the validity of Chahoon's triumph, the official count of the ballots by the Conservative-dominated Board of Election Commissioners reversed the original tabulation and declared Ellyson the winner by a slim margin of 29 votes with the rest of the Conservative general ticket winning by 33 to 172 vote majorities. The action followed the disclosure that the ballots from the Third Precinct of Jefferson Ward allegedly had been removed from their box by a group of "ruffians" who attacked the persons carrying them to City Hall for the official count. Although the tally had been placed on the poll books, the commissioners decided to throw out the precinct's results.[51]

The Radicals had been "counted out." Alone among the four precincts in the ward, the Third had more black than white voters; indeed, it had the largest number of Negro voters of any precinct in the city. Whereas in the first count Chahoon had carried Jefferson Ward by 1,916 to 1,802, the official tabulation without the Third Precinct gave Ellyson a 250 vote victory, sufficient to account for his margin in the entire city. The elimination of the precinct's votes also meant victory for the ward's five Conservative council candidates and their three running mates for justices of the peace. The Radical council delegation was therefore reduced to the five from Monroe Ward and a sixth from Marshall Ward. Similarly, only three of the fifteen justices of the peace were Republican compared to the original six. Another result was that all the justices and councilmen were white.[52]

The Radicals challenged the right of the commissioners to throw out ballots in Jefferson Ward in the face of the judges' sworn statements that the poll books were correct. To the dismay of the *Dispatch*, the Conservative judges on the Hustings Court agreed that the original vote total should have been accepted and acknowledged that had the votes from the Jefferson precinct been counted, the Republicans clearly would have won the election. As a result of numerous irregularities at the polling places, the judges ordered a new election. In the meantime, however, the recently sworn-in officials remained in office. Another concession to the Conservatives was even more significant. Despite the fact that the Election Commission's decision had affected the council race from Jefferson Ward, only the races for citywide offices would be repeated. Then, too, another registration drive held before the special election enabled the Conservatives to increase the white majority over black voters to 1,036.[53]

On election day Conservatives once again delayed and interfered with the casting of Negro votes, especially in Jefferson Ward. A Republican charged that, although the Second Precinct in Jefferson Ward had approximately 900 registered voters, only a few more than 700 ballots were cast and at the time of closing more than 150 Negroes were waiting to vote. In the Third Precinct over 300 blacks allegedly were left in a similar position. Thanks to the existence of separate lines for the races, white Conservatives sped through the polls. Even with such ploys and increased registration, the Democratic mayoral candidate won by only 189 votes. On the same day the incumbent Republican Congressman, Charles H. Porter, was defeated by his Conservative opponent despite the presence of U.S. troops and federal deputy marshals who arrested several Conservative judges for election irregularities.[54]

The effects of Redemption on local elective and patronage jobs were not uniform. In 1872 Sampson W. Keeble, a Nashville barber and former slave, became the first black in Tennessee to be elected to the General Assembly. Another Nashville Negro, T. A. Sykes, later served in the Tennessee House. Aside from these two and an occasional county officer such as magistrate or constable, after Redemption elected Negro officials were found only in the city councils of Richmond, Raleigh, and Nashville. Among those serving several terms on predominantly Democratic councils were Richmond's Josiah Crump, John H. Adams, and John Mitchell, Jr.; Nashville's J. C. Napier; and Raleigh's Norfleet Dunston, James H. Harris, and James H. Jones. For the most part they were placed on minor committees, with the notable exception of Dunston, who served on the Finance Committee. Sometimes blacks had no committee assignments. In 1889, for example, the only members of Raleigh's Council without assignments were black, although other aldermen served on two committees. More typical was the situation on the Richmond Council. Blacks were on committees dealing with Lunatics, Markets, the Fire Department, Cemeteries, Relief of the Poor, and Accounts and Printing. None ever served on the major committees of Finance, Retrenchment and Reform, and Board of Public Interests.[55]

The power and influence of Negro councilmen among white Democratic majorities was therefore limited. In Nashville Napier and Thomas Griswold met continued defeat in their efforts to get Negro policemen. Richmond members were equally unsuccessful in achieving one of their major goals, the purchase of land for a city park in Jackson Ward; only the election of independent councilmen enabled them to move ahead with their plans for a Negro armory. In the three cities the councilmen secured better school facilities for their race only when the regular Democratic ranks were diluted by other whites elected with black support. For the most part, Negro influence on the councils was restricted to helping constituents in minor ways. Norfleet Dunston was instrumental in improving the condition of Raleigh's Negro cemetery. Griswold and Napier succeeded in getting streets in Nashville's black neighborhoods graded and repaired. They also influenced the decision of the Board of Health to deny a permit for the construction of a pork packing plant near Fisk University. Richmond blacks did better. They brought about improved streets and better lighting in Jackson Ward, the dispensing of coal to the Negro poor, the opening of the first black night school, and the appropriation of money for the Negro militia companies.[56]

On occasion blacks also received patronage jobs dispensed by local Democratic administrations. Although Raleigh and Montgomery lost their black policemen, black firemen remained in the three cities that had them.[57] Nashville Negroes, who retained potent leverage in local elections until the end of the period, fared best in the area of job opportunities at the hands of the Democrats. Blacks served as jail guards, stable keepers, city porters, notaries public, and election officials.[58] In Raleigh Stewart Ellison, a former Republican state legislator and city councilman, was appointed city jailer in 1887. John E. Williams served as clerk of the Superior Court from 1881 to 1885 due to the sponsorship of a leading Raleigh Democrat. The Republican councilman Norfleet Dunston continued to benefit from the use of his shoe shop as a polling place.[59] Atlanta's Mitchell Cargill was the recipient of a different kind of patronage. An undertaker, he frequently received the bodies of Negro paupers for burial. Not only did he get a fee, but he evidently had an illegal arrangement with a local medical college which paid him for his corpses. In a more direct form of assistance, the Atlanta City Council selected S. H. Jackson as janitor, "an office just created in answer to a numerously signed petition by colored people."[60]

Urban blacks were also given a few jobs by state and national Democratic administrations. Nashville barber Lyttleton Jones was made a porter by the Speaker of the Tennessee House. Three Negroes including Conservative Issac Hunter from Richmond served on the eleven-man Board of Directors of the Central Lunatic Asylum. In North Carolina the new Democratic administration's appointment of black magistrates and support of black militia companies led the Republican *Raleigh Register* to conclude that "everything heretofore done by the Republicans and denounced as putting the negro above the white man, has been done by the Democrats since the last election." During President Grover Cleveland's first administration, there were still Negro post office workers and in Raleigh Stewart Ellison filled a government contract for carpentry on a building worth $300,000.[61]

Nevertheless, as might be expected, state and federal patronage for blacks was greatest when the Republicans enjoyed power. Negroes in each city served in the post offices, customhouses, and revenue offices. No black was ever appointed postmaster, but several served in lesser positions. In 1882, for example, eight of Richmond's eighteen letter carriers were Negro, as was everyone in the mailing department except the chief. Under the Cleveland administration, however, only two black employees in the mail department were retained.[62]

The number of black postal workers in Atlanta also fluctuated with the national fortunes of the Republicans. In 1875 two of the six carriers were black. Both were actively engaged in Republican politics and one of them, C. C. Wimbish, was an important party leader. Seven years later one-fifth of the thirty-five postal workers were Negro. In the late 1880s five blacks served as clerks under a Democratic postmaster, but, as the *Atlanta Constitution* was quick to point out, each of them was segregated from the white co-workers. Upon the return of the Republicans in 1889, the appointment of a black as clerk in the registered letter department caused a furor. A white man and his daughter immediately resigned from the department on the ground that the woman should not be brought into such close contact with a Negro.

The new Republican postmaster pointed out that the black's desk was separated from the whites by a brick wall and that he had been given that position deliberately to keep him away from the public. Despite these measures, both the black clerk and his political sponsor were burned in effigy, and two of the signers of the postmaster's bond withdrew their names. At the time there were four regular and five substitute Negro carriers. In addition there were seven black postal clerks on trains running out of Atlanta. Henry H. Craig, Montgomery state legislator and city councilman, served in a similar capacity on the Montgomery and Westpoint Railroad.[63]

Other Negroes were employed in the Treasury Department. N. H. Alexander held the $3,000 job of receiver of the land office in Montgomery. J. C. Napier and T. A. Sykes, Nashville's two most important black politicians, both served two terms as Internal Revenue gaugers, while Negro former Congressman James T. Rapier served five years as Internal Revenue collector in Montgomery. O. M. Stewart, editor of the *Virginia Star,* spent at least one year as gauger in Richmond at the same time that S. B. Clarkson was one of the four deputy collectors of revenue. Other Richmond black politicians served as assistant assessor (Landon Boyd) and janitor of the customhouse (Lewis Lindsay and Joseph Cox). Raleigh state legislator James H. Young was rewarded with the job of deputy collector of revenue and later special inspector of customs. Political leaders among Atlanta's Negroes used the Treasury Department largess to compensate for the lack of local and state patronage. W. A. Pledger was appointed surveyor of the customhouse in Atlanta; C. C. Wimbish, who had been a mail carrier, moved up to Pledger's customs' post in 1888.[64]

The most successful aspirant to office in the Treasury Department was Henry A. Rucker. A light-skinned former slave born in 1852, Rucker had been taken to Atlanta at an early age. After graduating from Storrs School, he attended Atlanta University through the sophomore year. He left in 1880 to assume the position of storekeeper and gauger in the Internal Revenue Service. In that year he was a delegate to the first of several Republican National Conventions that he would attend. A promotion to a clerkship in the office of collector soon followed. Rucker, like Richmond's Clarkson, suffered from Grover Cleveland's two victories, but in 1897 President William McKinley appointed him Collector of Internal Revenue for the state of Georgia. Other Negroes achieved appointment to lesser though not insignificant posts. John Oliver, already the recipient of local patronage as the first black notary public appointed in Virginia, was by 1870 deputy U.S. marshal for Richmond. Jack Heard, an Atlanta Negro, served as bailiff in his city's federal courtroom.[65]

State patronage was limited to only a few years, mainly during Reconstruction. Jackson McHenry, narrowly defeated for the Atlanta City Council in 1870, served as janitor for the Finance Committee of the Reconstruction legislature at $30 per month. John R. Casswell, later elected Wake County commissioner, became night watchman at the North Carolina Institution for the Deaf and Dumb and Blind in 1868. R. A. Paul, commander of one of Richmond's Negro militia companies and a member of the Board of Education, served as messenger for Readjuster Governor William Cameron whom he helped elect. About the same time Tennessee's newly elected Republican governor appointed Nashville minister Daniel Wadkins as chaplain of the state penitentiary. A former political associate of Wadkins, James H. Sumner, had served as doorkeeper of the House of Representatives under the previous Republican governor.[66]

With Democrats in control of city and state governments and occasionally the national government as well, there were considerably fewer elected and appointed black officeholders. The Negro voter remained but his vote bought him far less than it had under the Republicans. Yet in Nashville, Raleigh, and Richmond, the specter of Negro councilmen continued to haunt local whites. For in those cities, as elsewhere, Redemption had only meant containment of black suffrage—not its destruction. And, not surprisingly, blacks soon sought to expand their options within the limits set by whites.

12

The Search for Alternatives
to One-Party Allegiance

Many whites were dismayed by what they considered excessive numbers of Negro officeholders, especially under Republican administrations. In contrast, most blacks felt that they had been denied their share of the jobs. Dissatisfaction with the Republicans led to bitter intraparty feuds between blacks and whites. And, while the mass of blacks remained deeply committed to the Republican Party, on occasion even the most loyal party members considered the merits of endorsing Independent or even Democratic candidates. Often they did so, but as the period waned, so too did the options open to black leaders and their followers.

The chief targets of black displeasure were the white federal officeholders who controlled local, state, and national patronage. In 1873 a conference of Richmond blacks protested against the "feudalistic" attitude of the state's Republican leaders who used the Negro vote without giving blacks a share of the political gains. Seven years later, during the height of the Readjuster movement in the city, two of its Negro leaders demanded that black Republicans rather than the local customhouse clique should be the recipients and dispensers of local and federal favors. In 1881 Negro Republicans unsuccessfully urged Senator William A. Mahone to replace the white Superintendent of Mails in the Richmond post office for, among other reasons, "we have among our own people those who . . . have the competency to fill this position." Negroes of Marshall Ward were still complaining in

1890 that they had been ignored by the leaders of Richmond's Republican Party. Of the six residents of the ward who held federal jobs, only one, a boatman, was black—and now he had been removed.[1]

Atlanta Negroes, led by W. A. Pledger, pushed through a resolution at the 1880 State Convention calling for blacks to get three-fourths of the patronage jobs. Two years later the patronage policies of the Garfield administration so upset Jackson McHenry that in answer to a question as to whether the party had forgotten the Negroes, he remarked, "Seems so! Let 'em go ahead, though and make all their trades and bargains they want to—we'll try and see 'em when they try to deliver the goods." In 1889 Pledger and McHenry led a delegation of Atlanta blacks to see President Benjamin Harrison in an unsuccessful effort to get more appointments. The following year Moses H. Bentley, a former chairman of the Republican County Committee, considered deserting the local Republican candidate for state senator due to the meager allotment of jobs to blacks.[2]

Nashville's political leaders, the most successful and sophisticated among those in the five capitals, were even more determined to receive proper recognition. At frequent protest meetings during the 1870s and 1880s, blacks demanded a larger share of the offices. The desired jobs were not forthcoming and consequently black delegates to the 1890 Republican County Convention defeated a resolution backed by white officeholders endorsing the administration of President Harrison.[3]

Negro Republicans also objected to frequent white Republican efforts to keep them off party tickets. Richmond blacks were dismayed in 1870 by the all-white Republican city slate. "Colored men have been betrayed and can not trust the men who want to make them their tools," charged one of the leaders of a protest meeting. At the 1872 Davidson County Republican Convention, Nashville Negro Councilman John McGowan led an unsuccessful attempt to nominate a black for Congressman, threatening that unless this were done, the Negroes would withdraw from the party. In 1876 when the white Republican editor of the *Nashville Bulletin* argued that the party could be successful without blacks, a Negro leader angrily responded that, rather than seeking to exclude his people, the Republicans should reward them for past contributions. "The time has now come," he asserted, "when colored Republicans must share a part of the positions. . . . *If a people are truly represented it is by their own race.*" And in the fall elections of that year T. J. Bell, a black lawyer, announced as an independent candidate for the state legislature in order to protest the failure of white Republicans to place any Negroes on the ticket. Under pressure from more conservative black leaders, however, he withdrew a week later.[4]

In Atlanta Moses H. Bentley went through with his similarly motivated independent campaign for Congress in 1876. "For eleven years," he said, "the colored people have been hitching up the horses for white men to ride into office." Three years later Bentley proposed two resolutions at a National Colored Conference held in Nashville. The first called for proportional distribution of Congressional seats among whites and blacks: blacks should have at least two of the positions in states with eight or nine Congressmen and one in states with three or four representatives. The second resolution called for a rotation between blacks and whites in all state legislative districts represented by whites.[5]

In 1890 a group of Richmond Negro leaders unsuccessfully sought to free themselves from James Bahen, a white Republican who "virtually controlled politics in the [Jackson] ward."[6] Bahen was a forty-two-year-old grocer who lived in the heart of Jackson Ward, almost entirely surrounded by blacks. He was the most important among the German, Irish, and Italian grocer-saloonkeepers "who not only got most of the colored voters' cash, but trained them in the way they should go when casting their ballots."[7] Little is known about Bahen, but fragmenatry evidence suggests he headed an effective political machine. In 1882 he first won election to the Common Council together with four first-time Negro victors. The five of them defeated two tickets, one of Democrats and the other of the ward's Negro Republican incumbents. The top vote-getter among the defeated Republicans, despite the fact that he and his running mates were longtime councilmen, received only 41 votes while Bahen and his slate got over 300. Bahen was continually reelected to the Council, soon moving up to the Board of Aldermen. Resentful of his power, Negroes led by John Mitchell, Jr., offered an independent Republican ticket in 1890. It was similar to the regular one except for the substitution of blacks for Bahen, two other whites, and two of their black supporters. Nevertheless, Bahen easily beat back the challenge.[8]

The high point of resentment against white Republican control of the nominating process occurred in 1888 when Nashville Negroes forced the nomination of W. H. Young for Congress. Young, a promi-

nent black attorney, politician, and magistrate, had been criticizing
the white stranglehold on offices since the presidential campaign of
1880. As editor of the Nashville *Herald and Pilot*, he had half-heartedly
supported Garfield after his favorite, Grant, was defeated for the nomination. His support was so lukewarm that he was accused of backing
the Democratic candidate and for the rest of the decade there were
doubts as to his party loyalty.[9] White Republicans were also upset by
his speech as temporary chairman of the 1888 County Convention. He
had charged Republicans with ignoring Negroes in Davidson County,
and concluded that if blacks tolerated this neglect any longer they
were "great fools." White Republicans and Democrats viewed him as
a rabble-rouser and decried his nomination for Congress.[10] A majority of the white delegates left the hall as his nomination became assured and the *Nashville Banner* accurately prophesied that he had no
chance of winning the election since "the white voters of his party will
be as active in knifing him as the most partisan democrats." One delegate spoke for most of his white colleagues when he said that he "would
never have anything to do with them [Negro representatives] again."[11]

Other Negroes also discovered that, even if they got on the ticket,
they could not count on the same degree of support that whites received. After the defeat of a Raleigh black for the state legislature in
1880, a local Negro newspaper concluded that "there is no use in dis-
guising the fact; the Negro voters of Wake County have been sold out
by some of their pretended white friends." Whether victorious or not,
nominated blacks invariably ran behind their running mates. In 1872
Sampson W. Keeble and his white running mate Captain James Ready
were elected to the General Assembly from Davidson County. In the
city of Nashville, however, Keeble trailed Ready by 500 votes and received 300 less than went to President Grant on the same day. The
election of magistrates four years later demonstrated another reason
for Negro dissatisfaction. Due to the crowded field in the at-large contest for the twenty justice of the peace positions in the city and to bloc
voting by blacks, Keeble finished twentieth, a few votes ahead of
Ready. The latter, a staunch Republican and former city chairman of
the party, nevertheless demanded a recount which showed him the victor. Yet Keeble had already been certified as elected and had been
sworn in. Ready then proceeded to carry the case through the courts
in an unseemly attempt to deprive a fellow Republican of office. Similar treatment contributed to John Mitchell's decision to withdraw from

Richmond's Congressional contest in 1890. Although nominated, he claimed that he was being boycotted by white party managers. For the first time since Reconstruction, the Democratic Congressional candidate ran unopposed.[12]

Negroes found some solace in intraparty activities, although here too key positions of power usually went to whites. James H. Harris, J. C. Napier, W. A. Pledger, and Henry A. Rucker were among the handful of blacks to serve as delegates to Republican National Conventions.[13] Pledger served one term (rather than the customary two) as chairman of the Executive Committee of the Georgia Republican Party, Napier served several terms as one of the four officers on the Tennessee State Committee, and Josiah Crump served on the Virginia State Committee.[14] Locally Negroes sometimes headed county committees. W. D. Moore, Moses H. Bentley, and Jackson McHenry were among the Atlanta blacks handed this largely honorary prize, while J. H. Keeble and C. O. Harris filled the same positions in Nashville and Montgomery respectively.[15] More often, especially during the early postwar years, this post was entrusted to white federal officeholders.

At local nominating conventions for the legislature and Congress, Negroes generally were either in the majority or had rough parity with whites. Black representatives from Davidson County to the 1867 Congressional Nominating Convention, for example, comprised 58 of the 101 members; there were only 4 white delegates at the 1880 Congressional Nominating Convention in Richmond. As a rule, though, the whites still exercised more power. At the 1867 Montgomery meeting called to select delegates to the Union Republican State Convention, there were 11 whites and approximately 70 blacks in attendance. A slight majority of black representatives were chosen, but by a committee of three whites and two blacks. At such conventions a Negro was usually named as temporary chairman who then made way for a white permanent chairman, although a black was ordinarily given the position of permanent secretary.[16]

Regardless of who occupied the major offices, Negroes coalesced around the competing factions of whites. The whites controlled access to elective and appointive office and blacks had to side either with the primarily Northern white federal officeholders or with the Southern whites who sought a greater share of patronage and power for themselves. As a rule, the majority of Negroes supported the Northern men, while their fewer, though often more prominent, brothers backed the "home-grown" Republicans. Indicative of this trend was the 1870 Congressional Convention held in Richmond. Twenty-three of the thirty delegates were black and the majority lined up behind the incumbent white Congressman Charles H. Porter, the candidate of party boss Sam Maddox and Joseph M. Humphreys, Collector of Customs. They beat back the opposition of native Richmond whites who later charged that the convention had been rigged in favor of the "custom house ring." A city Republican Club organized by anti-Porter forces two weeks later included as officers at least four Negro politicians who regularly opposed the white carpetbaggers—Ben Scott, Cornelius Harris, Peter Randolph, and C. T. Payne.[17]

Such divisions among blacks weakened their bargaining power with white leaders. Ten years after the 1870 debacle Richmond's Madison Ward Republicans were sharply divided between those supporting "National Republicans" and those favoring the "local Customs House people." The leaders of the former faction again included C. T. Payne and Cornelius Harris. When the "National Republicans" gained control of the Congressional Nominating Convention that year, Lewis Lindsay's slate of delegates from Clay Ward lost a credentials battle against a rival slate of "National Republicans."[18]

At the core of the disagreement among Richmond Negroes was the scramble for the meager patronage available to blacks. Similar motivation produced conflict in other cities as well. Nashville politicians, T. A. Sykes and J. C. Napier, were constantly at odds. And in 1889 when Jackson McHenry and C. C. Wimbish were appointed janitors (watchmen) of the U.S. Court Building in Atlanta, Henry A. Rucker contested their selection because he had not been consulted. During the County Convention held the previous year, Wimbish and McHenry forces had challenged Rucker-backed delegations and both had supported the rival white leaders in the district.[19]

White members of the uneasy Republican coalition struggled to maintain power while holding on to Negro support. Many of them were Southerners who still believed in Negro inferiority, while others were prejudiced Northerners. Above all, they feared that prospective white supporters would turn away from the party if it had too many black officeholders. As the period progressed, white Republicans were faced with the realization that they could not win without the Negro vote, but such support ironically made it increasingly difficult to attract the white voters indispensable for final victory. Thus for the white Republicans as well as the white Democrats, the Negroes had to be disciplined and kept in their place lest they prove detrimental to the larger goals.

The Republican appeal for the black vote, first forged during Reconstruction, kept alive the threat of reenslavement by the Democrats. The exhortation of Raleigh's *Daily Standard* in the 1868 gubernatorial election was echoed throughout the period.

> Colored men your own liberties and lives are at stake, as well as the liberties and lives of the great body of the whites. The same leading rebels who fought four long years to keep you in slavery are still engaged in rebellion. They hope so to manage things as to make slaves of you again. *Be sure to go to the polls and vote.*

In 1871 a Montgomery resident told a Senate committee about a friend whose former slaves had come back to him after the Republican defeat in the local election. "Well, massa, what house must I go into?" asked one. "I understand that the democrats have succeeded, and that we are slaves again."[20]

In addition to raising fears of reenslavement, Republicans sought the votes of blacks with the aid of bribes, picnics, parades, and free whiskey, the same devices used by Democrats to attract immigrant voters in the North. Some whites promised Negroes a larger role in party affairs. Soon after the *Nashville Daily Press and Times* called for greater representation of blacks in city politics, the State Central Committee added a committee of two Negroes from Nashville and one from each Congressional district to "participate . . . with us concerning measures for the benefit of our common cause." In the first election after the ban on black officeholders was lifted, one of the three Davidson County commission seats was assigned specifically to a Negro. In another instance a white member of the Republican City Executive Committee asked that his place be taken by a black since the Republicans of his ward were "mostly colored" and he thought they should be represented by a member of their own race.[21] As part of the heated rivalries among whites throughout the period, efforts were frequently made to increase Negro patronage. In 1880 Colonel J. E. Bryant, locked in a bitter struggle with the officeholding faction led by Atlanta postmaster John Conley, charged that an insufficient number of blacks had been appointed to key positions in the post office. A Montgomery

Republican argued in an 1884 letter to the *Colored Citizen* that the Half Breed sector of the party was seeking "to put negroes down as hewers of wood and drawers of water, cast them out of office, give them a certain amount of education but keep them down as an inferior class of people." On the other hand, the Stalwarts, of which he was one, were "different men," he claimed.

> They want to see the negro advance, they want to see you hold offices such as you are competent of holding, they want to see you educated, they want to see you have equal rights, socially, morally and politically. . . . We have to support stalwarts at home to elect such men as assure your rights.[22]

Despite these scattered efforts, white Republicans for the most part sought to restrict or even eliminate black officeholding. In 1870 the Atlanta *Daily New Era* used the appointment of Hiram Revels to the U.S. Senate from Mississippi as the occasion to warn against Negro officials. Instead of running for office, it said, Negroes should support white Republicans. Black politicians would not be competent to confront Democrats in Congress and Republicans needed the ablest men in the legislative branch to best protect the rights of blacks. Besides, it continued, if Negro representatives ran for office, white politicians would refuse to join the ticket, thus further weakening the party. Despite Nashville Mayor Thomas A. Kercheval's heavy dependence on Negro votes for his numerous victories, on two occasions he blocked the addition of blacks to his council slate: the first time in 1874 on the ground that opponents would use their presence to discredit him, the second time in 1887 because he felt that Negroes could no longer be elected to public office.[23]

Still another technique used to attract black voters was a defense of their political and civil rights. The Republicans constantly reminded Negroes that they were responsible for removing restrictions on black legal rights, instituting universal black male suffrage, organizing Negro militia units, inaugurating Negro public education, opening state and local welfare institutions to them, and pressing for their admittance to public conveyances and accommodations. Yet, as already demonstrated, whites were conscious of the need to maintain support among both blacks and whites. Under such circumstances the policy of separate but equal facilities was developed.

White Republicans included a few egalitarians like the Reverend

James Hunnicutt of Richmond. A few others, including Atlanta's Colonel A. E. Buck, commander of a Negro regiment during the war, R. M. Manly of Richmond, a former representative of Northern philanthropic societies, and John Lawrence, judge of the Freedmen's Bureau Court in Nashville, were truly interested in the rights of Negroes.[24] The rest, especially among scalawags, were concerned mainly with the offices the black vote could supply and had no strong commitment to equal rights. North Carolina Governor William Holden, though a Unionist, had been an early opponent of Negro suffrage. The same was true of L. H. Chandler, the Radical candidate for commonwealth attorney in the 1870 Richmond municipal election.[25] Montgomery's Radical city marshal in 1871 was a former professional Negro hunter and its chancellor had voted for an antebellum statute that would have made every free Negro a slave unless he left the state.[26] The lack of support given the 1875 Civil Rights Act by white Republicans was indicative of their attempt to avoid alienating white voters.

The pressures involved in holding together a white-black coalition proved too much for many of the white Republicans. The early postwar numerical advantage of black over white voters vanished, thanks to the drop in Negro registration and the enfranchisement of more former Confederates, especially after the Amnesty Act of 1872. White Republicans, therefore, became more interested in attracting greater white support, even at the cost of alienating the blacks. This movement was given further impetus in the 1880s by the patronage policies of the Chester Arthur and Benjamin Harrison administrations. But at its core was the unmistakable fact that identification with Negroes was guaranteeing Republican defeat. "I see but one way now to get the better of the bloodthirsty Bourbon Democrats," wrote W. M. Smith to William A. Mahone following the Republican-Readjuster defeat of 1883, and "that is to draw a *color line* under the name of the *white man's liberal party of Virginia*. I have introduced the subject to several very intelligent negroes and they say that the negroes will rally to any liberal party led by you."[27]

Other whites did not bother to consult their black brethren. On the day before the convening of the District Republican Convention in Atlanta to select delegates to the National Convention of 1884, several white Republicans, all former state and federal officeholders, issued a call for a special meeting to consider the relationship between the party and the Negroes. In their view the blacks were selling their votes to the highest bidders, and therefore they favored the formation of a totally white Republican Party in Georgia as the only way to win elections. After a series of meetings, Jonathan Norcross, one of the men, changed his mind and sought to include blacks who sympathized with "Whig Republicans." He endorsed a racially mixed delegation for the National Convention, but defeated in his efforts, he went as part of the all-white contingent. William Markham, another of the insurgents, was among several Atlanta Republicans who later challenged Colonel A. E. Buck's continued support of Negroes for federal posts. Markham's faction urged the appointment of whites to attract Democrats to the party. In the words of A. B. Carrier, a well-known insurance man, "I am a republican in national politics, but I am a white man and for the white man's party." Another in the group castigated Buck in a letter to the *Atlanta Constitution* and charged that the Republican Party in the state was a "negro party."[28]

Similar strains were tearing apart Nashville's Republican coalition. In August 1886 the *Nashville Banner* reported that a group of county Republicans were planning to form a "whites only" club. This action was largely in response to the independent stance of local Negroes. As a black politician asserted, "the negro is in the national republican party to stay, but in local elections they [*sic*] are independent." This policy was not surprising since local elections were conducted on a nonpartisan basis. In 1888 the real source of white annoyance became clear. Blacks ignored white directives and nominated W. H. Young for Congress. Within a month five prominent Republicans applied for a charter for the Central Republican Club of Tennessee. Its stated aim was to bring together those Republicans who had previously taken no part in party affairs. In practice, its membership was limited to white Republicans, including J. R. Dillan, chairman of the State Republican Committee.[29]

Within this divisive context local Republicans met to nominate candidates for the county legislative ticket. The convention became a battleground between the Negroes, eager to press their new found political power, and the frustrated whites, convinced of the need to keep the blacks in their place. The whites were in an especially difficult situation. On the one hand, Negroes complained about having to vote for white candidates and demanded a fair share of the offices; on the other, as recent city and legislative elections had demonstrated, they were sure losers as candidates.

The fight between blacks and whites commenced with a struggle over the position of temporary chairman, previously an uncontested Negro office. This time a white candidate opposed two blacks. The black vote split, allowing the white man to win a plurality. He needed a majority, however, and a run-off between him and the leading black resulted in a tie with each getting only the votes of his race's delegates. In the end the white vice chairman broke the tie by voting his color. A similar division marked the race for permanent chairman, although everyone agreed on a Negro for secretary.

The conflict was renewed with an attempt to nominate Tip Gamble, president of the Central Republican Club, for the state senate. In an-swer to Negro complaints, Gamble claimed that he could win the race because of his white contacts, while a black man would lose because black voters could be bought off or counted out. In the end another white was nominated, since, as Gamble admitted, "we know we could not elect a candidate without the assistance of the colored vote." In protest every white nominated for the house seats refused to run. Gam-ble and his supporters then nominated blacks for these positions. Ac-cording to the *Nashville Banner*, "they were determined to make the ticket as black as possible." Led by J. C. Napier, the Negroes also de-clined. Finally the white candidates who had already accepted a place on the ticket for senator and joint senator withdrew and the conven-tion adjourned in chaos. After several unsuccessful efforts at compro-mise, a ticket with six whites and one black was selected; a motion to accept it by acclamation was defeated with all but six Negroes voting against it on the ground that two of the candidates were members of the Central Republican Club.[30]

Nor were the wounds healed by the campaign, especially after W. H. Young's sound defeat. At the 1890 county legislative conven-tion, S. R. Walker, a longtime Negro leader, opposed E. S. Ashcraft, a charter member of the Central Republican Club, for the position of permanent chairman. Walker was easily turned back as white Repub-licans solidified their hold on the party machinery.[31]

Given the realities of intraparty strife and at times the presence of outright hostility, blacks weighed the various political alternatives. To-ward the end of the period a number of them espoused a philosophy later identified with Booker T. Washington. In a paper entitled "Is It a Desirable Thing for a Colored Man to Enter Politics?" given at a meeting of Nashville's St. Paul's Historical and Literary Society in

1889, R. A. Sealy argued in the negative. Blacks should leave politics, he said, and concentrate on acquiring wealth and education in order to gain all the rights and privileges of whites. The previous year the Reverend C. N. Grandison of Clark University had told an Atlanta Emancipation Day rally, "Don't bother yourself about politics but fit yourself for the enjoyment of the rights and duties of citizenship."[32]

For most blacks, however, politics was still a field worth pursuing. For some it meant a means of securing their full rights; for others, political patronage or elected office; for still others, a guaranteed two dollars and free whiskey for their vote on election day. Since the motivation varied so much, this commitment to politics did not assure unity among Negroes. Increasingly, they split as to the merits of sticking with the Republicans, seeking to play an independent role in the balance of power, or going over to the Democrats.

Leaders frequently were divided on important issues and in election campaigns. The contest over the proposed annexation of a Nashville suburb in 1880, for example, found J. H. Burrus, Republican politician, educator, and member of the area's school board, in opposition; William Butler, a local Republican justice of the peace, led the proponents. Seven years later Nashville Negro leaders actively campaigned against each other during both a mayoral election and a bond issue referendum. Then too there were disagreements between leaders and their followers. After J. C. Napier pledged to the Republican gubernatorial candidate "the unanimous support of the colored voters of Davidson," a Negro writing to the *Nashville Banner* pointed to Napier's recent failures to get his candidates elected either in the municipal campaign or at the County Convention. Napier could not deliver on his pledge, the writer argued, because "the distribution of 'loaves and fishes' had not seemed equitable to the 'colored voters'" and "they have come to the conclusion that wisdom demands that they look more strictly into the character of men asking public suffrage than to the political badge those men wear."[33] Finally there were the splits within the black community that reflected its class differences. "The respectable element of the colored population are raising a big kick about the way the negroes sold out at the polls," reported the *Nashville Banner* after a typical election. Division among blacks was so great that debate over the advisability of running two Negroes for the Atlanta City Council in 1887 allegedly led one black to assert that "I don't believe in putting any colored man in the council. If we give the office to any nigger it will only split up the colored folks. Keep the niggers out of offices of that kind and we can keep the people together."[34]

Some blacks felt that what was needed was an independent stance in order to force concessions from both major parties or from independent candidates. Such a philosophy seemed most plausible in local contests. "Viewing the situation of affairs in Georgia, and from a standpoint that our people have suffered long from misrule and bad government under the republican party, a change must ensue," declared the Atlanta *Weekly Defiance* in 1882.

> Some coalition or combination must be effected in local affairs so as to give us at least a dog's showing. . . . We cannot stultify ourselves; we cannot longer follow republicans that have claimed that name solely for office; on the contrary, we must follow those who will be found giving us recognition immediately, and then we will be found doing the duty of citizens and statesmen.

During the city election in 1887, Fifth Ward Negroes came together determined to delay their endorsements in order to "look to their best interest." Similar advice came from a Montgomery Negro. "It seems that the white Republicans on all occasions especially in conventions are opposed to negro supremacy," he wrote to the *Alabama Enterprise* in 1886.

> I heartily favor the calling of a colored man's convention, and let the convention see if the colored people can't organize some plans by which the negro can receive the proper recognition from the white race, not only politically but morally and socially.[35]

Nashville Negroes demonstrated the most active and sustained interest in casting their votes selectively. Partially this was due to the high level of intelligence and political sophistication among the leaders, but it was also due to the nonpartisan local elections common in the 1870s and 1880s. Upset over the lack of white Republican support for the Civil Rights Bill in 1874, John McGowan, a Negro former councilman, concluded that blacks had been deserted "by weakneed [sic] white men of the Republican party, pretended friends of the negro." The black reply to such treatment should be selectivity in voting. As disillusionment with the Republicans grew, blacks indicated that their only loyalty was to their race. "I repeat frankly that I offer my vote to the highest bidder," stated one, "not for money, but the greatest measure of justice."[36]

Nashville blacks used an independent stance to best advantage during the 1883 municipal campaign. That election was the first after a single chamber council had replaced the bicameral body. The councilmen were elected at-large from the city's fourteen wards with no two coming from the same ward. A mayor was also selected, but real power rested with a three-man Board of Public Works chosen by the Council. Reform elements in the city coalesced in an effort to oust the allegedly corrupt Republican Mayor Thomas A. Kercheval and his crew of ward bosses. Organizing themselves as the Citizens Reform Association, they charged that financial mismanagement was responsible for the poor condition of the streets and the inadequacy of the water works system. In an attempt to deprive Kercheval of the majority of Negro votes which had keyed his previous victories, they awarded two of the ten council positions on the slate to blacks, J. C. Napier and C. C. Gowdey, both former councilmen. Negro leaders such as W. F. Anderson and W. H. Young quickly fell in behind the ticket and sought to convince the black masses that Kercheval had used them in the past solely for his own ends. Both major newspapers, the *Nashville Banner* and the *Daily American,* supported the movement and applauded Negro participation. The publications and the reformers frequently reminded black voters that Kercheval was running on an all-white ticket, while T. G. Ryman, one of the reformers, had declined nomination in order to permit Gowdey's selection. Urging that blacks support the slate, Ryman reminded them that "for the first time since your freedom . . . the best white citizens offer you fair representation in our city affairs and in an honest reform movement."[37]

Despite Kercheval's efforts to hold on to his Negro supporters, there were enough defections to carry the reformers into office. Many whites bypassed Napier and Gowdey, both of whom, though victorious, finished at least 500 votes behind their running mates. Their white allies readily acknowledged the pivotal role of the blacks in the victory. "Kercheval could not and did not control the colored vote," proclaimed the *Nashville Banner.* "The intelligent colored men of the city voted for Phillips [the reform candidate] and the straight ticket."[38] Young, Anderson, and the white leader Colonel A. S. Colyar were named as the three people most responsible for the triumph.[39] A month later a group of thirty businessmen presented Young with a gold watch and chain in honor of his service. In his first speech after the victory, Colyar told an audience: "In the name of the suffering taxpayers of this city, I

take occasion . . . to thank the colored men who in such large numbers came to their relief."[40]

Negroes had won two council seats and other favors soon followed.
New mayor Hooper Phillips, a Democrat, insisted that the City Council
"urge the Board of Public Works, in making their appointments, to act
in a spirit of fairness and justice, giving to the colored people of our
city a fair and equitable representation to which they are so justly entitled."[41] Blacks did not get all they wanted—there were no appointments to the police department, for example—but gains were made.

Over the strong opposition of local residents and insurance under-
writers, the members of the newly created East Nashville Fire Company were all Negroes, the first to serve in the regular fire department.
As further reward for a job well done, Gowdey was appointed its captain. Before he left the Council to take his new post, however, he aided
the Negro residents of his ward by sponsoring resolutions authorizing
the Board of Public Works to give free water to needy persons and requesting the Board to place a free public hydrant at the corner of Lincoln Alley and Vine Street for the "benefit of the poor people in that
locality," all of whom were black. W. F. Anderson also enjoyed the
Board's largess as he was appointed one of the two bridge watchmen.
Napier meanwhile used his position on the Council to secure construction of the first two brick schoolhouses for blacks. Twenty-five years
later he wrote to a white leader of the movement that he had always
regarded the Citizens Reform Association as

> the salvation of Nashville and its taxpayers. Further than this, it did
> more to unite and bring together the *better classes* of white and
> colored people than anything that has occurred since the Civil War.
> The colored people of Nashville are still enjoying many benefits that
> resulted from this movement.[42]

Yet, as with most reform movements of the day, it was short-lived.
In 1885 the mayoralty and five of the council seats were again at stake.
The reformers made a serious mistake in nominating Major A. W.
Wills, a Republican, for mayor, although four of the five council nominees were Democrats. The fifth and lone black was J. C. Napier, who
had been elected to one of the five short terms in 1883. Opposing these
men were Kercheval and his slate of five candidates which this time
included a Negro, the Reverend Luke Mason, a longtime foe of Napier.
Once again both groups solicited the votes of blacks. The most heated

fight was in the Fourth Ward where Negroes comprised a majority of the voters, but throughout the city "the feature of the contest [was] the great fight over the colored vote." W. H. Young was again the major speaker on the reform side, though now he shared the spotlight with T. A. Sykes and the Reverend George W. Bryant. These three men were also among the few blacks on the campaign and finance committees. In his most reported speech Young claimed that the reform administration had employed over 2,000 Negroes, and, unlike the situation under Kercheval, there were no kickbacks from wages. "Kercheval said his hands were tied when you used to go to him for a favor. I tell you he never will get them loose enough to do anything for the colored man." Besides, said Young, the reform movement had paid off $160,000 of debts incurred by Kercheval and now had a $130,000 surplus in the treasury.[43]

Fraud and bribery characterized the election on both sides. Kercheval made his usual good use of black paupers brought in from the countryside and illegally naturalized foreigners; the reformers had a bank near the polls where they purchased votes for two dollars. And in the Sixth Ward there were six more ballots in the box than the number of voters. The Negro vote split, although an observer calculated that a majority of black ballots went to Wills. In reporting voting activity before noon, the *Nashville Banner* mentioned groups of 24, 35, and even 111 Negroes marching to the polls and voting as a bloc. The final tally reflected both white dissatisfaction with the previous reform administration and the absence of a Democrat at the head of the ticket. Kercheval emerged victorious as did four of his five running mates. Mason was the sole loser and finished at the rear of the pack within 33 of Napier, almost 250 behind the eighth place finisher.[44] The election was also a verdict against Negro aspirants to public office and reflected displeasure with such reform administration contributions as the Negro fire company and the increased support for black schools. Negro backing was not enough to elect blacks to office and division in their ranks made it risky to rely on them to help an entire ticket.

Nashville blacks nevertheless remained interested in keeping their political options open. An 1886 meeting at St. John's A.M.E. Church brought together the city's black leaders who urged independent use of the ballot to right wrongs. They wanted industrial schools to overcome union resistance to Negro apprentices, access to the jury box, opportunity to become clerks in stores in which they spent their money, better press treatment, and, of course, a fair share of the offices. As they pointed out, not one of the nearly fifty public servants employed at the courthouse was black. The remedy, they declared, was a united black vote tied not to party but to interest.[45]

In 1887 this discontent was institutionalized with the formation of the Tammany Club of Nashville under the leadership of George T. Robinson, a recent Fisk graduate and editor of the *Tennessee Star*. The objective was to use the Negro vote to wring concessions from competing whites. "Well, sir," Robinson told a reporter who asked for specifics,

> the only things that we have yet received have been a few positions in the fire department and several subordinate positions. Here's what we want: We want negroes on the police force, negroes in the City Council, negroes on the Board of Education, negroes on the Board of Public Works, and negroes wherever white men are. These things we propose to demand before we cast our votes. . . . We have between 2500 and 3000 voters in this city, out of a total between 9500 and 10,000 voters and we want our share of the officers and positions. . . . We are not going to draw the race line, but we are going to do like the Irish.[46]

In the subsequent nonpartisan election the club failed to get J. B. Bosley placed on the all-white ticket chosen by the Knights of Labor, but saw him picked for the opposition ticket as councilman from the Fourth Ward. Due to ticket splitting by some whites and a less than expected black turnout, Bosley went down to defeat, although less than 100 votes shy of victory.[47]

Other independent coalitions also met largely with failure. Atlanta and Richmond Negroes comprised a significant portion of their counties' Greenback vote in the 1878 state and local elections, but the Democrats still won easily. In Nashville Randall Brown temporarily left the Republican Party to become one of the three members of the Greenback's county platform and resolutions committee. Despite the presence of a full and active Republican ticket, the Greenback Party ran second to the Democrats in the election, carrying with it perhaps half the Negro vote. Running as a Greenback for state representative, J. B. Bosley outpolled the only Republican Negro in the race, the well-known Sampson W. Keeble, by more than 350 votes.[48]

Of greater significance were independent movements joined by Richmond Negroes in the 1880s. In the 1886 municipal campaign blacks actively supported a workingmen's coalition party led by the Knights of Labor. Although the Democrats captured every citywide office except city sergeant, the reformers swept five of the six wards, so that the new Board of Aldermen had only nine Democrats out of eighteen and the Common Council, nine of thirty. Negro leaders were especially interested in the equalization of wages for white and black laborers. It is uncertain whether or not they succeeded. The one tangible benefit they received was the appropriation of $4,000 for the purchase of a site for the Negro armory in Jackson Ward. Black councilmen had been trying unsuccessfully for seven years to get these funds. The action was taken, however, only days before the council members came up for reelection.[49]

The Readjuster movement headed by William A. Mahone produced the most important independent effort involving Richmond Negroes. In 1880 Negroes such as Cornelius Harris, R. A. Paul, and Ben Scott prevented the nomination of regular Republican candidates so that the Readjuster-Republican coalition could challenge the Democrats on even terms. Harris urged blacks to stand solidly behind the Readjusters whose success, he claimed, would "assure us the peaceful enjoyment of those rights and privileges promised by our Constitution and our laws." Especially useful was O. M. Stewart's *Virginia Star*.[50]

Although unable to defeat the Democrats in municipal elections, the Readjuster total from the city, consisting largely of Negro votes, contributed to the party's victorious gubernatorial campaign in 1881 and enabled the party's candidate from Henrico County to be returned to the General Assembly in 1883. As one of his first actions in office, the new governor, William Cameron, declared vacant the seats of the Richmond Board of Education. As two of the new appointees, he chose R. A. Paul and Richard Forrester, two Negro leaders in the reform movement. They served for only one year but were instrumental in improving black education.[51]

The Readjusters had only a brief period of control, and, like the Greenbackers and assorted local independent movements throughout the period, they were plagued by white desertions due to the active participation of Negroes as voters and candidates. Some blacks in desperation turned to the tactic of all-Negro tickets in an effort to make clear their determination to solidify the black vote and free it from the control of whites. Yet the tactic was self-defeating. Negro registration was steadily declining and even where it was still significant, whites had found ways of limiting its impact. Thus for the 1886 legislative elections, an all-Negro slate composed of three of Atlanta's most prominent figures received less than 130 votes against the white Democratic total of almost 900. Four years later when white registration was 4,165 and black was 587, an all-Negro municipal ticket drew 317 votes to almost 3,000 for their white opponents. Nevertheless, during the same period, Nashville, Richmond, and Raleigh Negroes considered similar steps.[52]

One other alternative remained. "There is no reason why the colored vote should be solidly republican," remarked W. A. Pledger during one of his periods of disenchantment with the party. "There is every reason why it may become largely democratic." Other Republican Negro politicians and journalists made similar statements from time to time. After Grover Cleveland's first presidential victory, Atlanta's Jackson McHenry joined Pledger in urging a "wait and see" policy as far as Democratic intentions were concerned, while noting that "it will be time enough for us to choose between the two great parties which we will support in the future." To admit the possibility of a choice was significant; on occasion McHenry and friends Moses H. Bentley and George McKinney went further and campaigned for Redeemer gubernatorial candidates in Georgia like Alfred H. Colquitt, Alexander Stephens, and John B. Gordon.[53] During a Montgomery election campaign, the *Colored Citizen* reminded its readers that

> the colored man, while he is a republican, should not let his party zeal blind him to his own highest interest. Some of the democrats nominated by the county convention are among the best friends that the colored people have in the democratic party.

A few years later the Republican editor of the *Herald* pledged his support and that of his Montgomery readers to the incumbent Democratic mayor if he would end police persecution of blacks. Nashville Negroes in 1885 also held out the prospects of their vote if Democrats assured them equality before the law. When large numbers of blacks protested against Republican treatment by voting Democratic in the county elections the following year, the *Nashville Banner* reported that one Democratic worker felt "the colored voter is now a permanent part of the democratic party in the county."[54]

This statement was overly optimistic, but in every city Democrats could count on some Negro votes. Some individuals no doubt were driven into the party out of fear for their jobs or personal safety. Others came out of thankfulness for favors done by white Democrats. "Two or three hundred colored men, more or less, would be in a suffering condition today, were it not for the noble generosity and magnanimity of the merchants of Commerce and Court streets," ran the appeal by an organizer of Montgomery's Colored Men's Greeley and Brown Club. He singled out Negro bricklayers, railroad hands, and barbers who "should not fight the breast that gives us milk."[55] Some remained true to the party of their former masters. Elias Polk of Nashville was described as "the old body servant of ex-President Polk and a prominent local politician of Democratic principles." Wash Terry said he always voted Democratic since he was "taught by instinct and by my white friends that it was right." Caesar Shorter had been a slave of former Alabama Governor John Shorter whom he described as "a good master." After a brief period as a Republican, he left the party when convinced that the Union League sought to turn members against their former owners. His allegiance to the Democrats was strengthened by his repeated appointments as porter at the state capitol.[56]

For most blacks, the determining factor was the failure of the Republicans to deliver what was expected of them. Thus they turned to the Democrats for negative rather than positive reasons. Meeting to choose delegates to a state convention of black Conservatives in 1867, Nashville Negroes charged that Radicals were not their friends because the Radical franchise act had excluded blacks from juries and public office. Among the delegates was the Reverend Daniel Wadkins, elected councilman but denied his seat because of the act. Another was Joseph Williams, "the fearless and eloquent orator," an organizer and speaker for the Democrats not only in Nashville but throughout the South. The Reverend J. W. Dungee had been a leading Republican in Richmond, but left the party in 1876 after it nominated for mayor a former Congressman who had voted against the Civil Rights Act.[57]

The two most articulate Negro Democrats were newspaper editor James A. Scott of Montgomery and attorney C. H. J. Taylor of Atlanta. During the 1880 presidential election, Scott's editorials in the *Weekly Advance* gave detailed reasons why Negroes should transfer their allegiance to the Democrats. First were listed the weaknesses of the Republican Party. It was no longer the party of Lincoln, Sumner, and other great figures.[58] It had failed to implement its early promises: land was not given to blacks and offices went to Northern whites in-

terested only in securing the Negroes' votes rather than promoting
their welfare. Republican administrations were marked by corruption, the most serious resulting in the fall of the Freedmen's Bank.
The Democrats, on the other hand, were pictured as worthy individuals. Their governments were honest and had reduced the public debt.
Black rights had been left undisturbed.

> The negro still casts his vote, unmolested; he still sits in the jury box;
> he still exercises every political right that he ever had, and without
> interference or hindrance; his children have good schools to attend
> free; he still makes his contracts and is master of himself.

By claiming that blacks were better off under the Democrats, Scott
sounded like a white Southerner defending his region's treatment of
blacks. He had decided that Negroes would have to live with the
Southern whites without much help from fickle white Republican
friends interested only in using the Negroes. Voicing another refrain
commonly heard from white Democrats, he declared, "we go to them
[the Democrats] in trouble and distress, and are always treated kindly,
they are all in all to us, and why should we oppose them in politics?"
In short, "colored men have everything to gain by being Democrats
and nothing by being Republicans. What affects their white employers
or landlords is necessarily felt by them. Their interests and the interests of the white men of the South are identical."[59]

While not taking such partisan positions, C. H. J. Taylor voiced similar sentiments. Before arriving in Atlanta around 1889, he had practiced law in the North and had edited the Kansas City *World*. He
briefly served as Minister to Liberia under President Cleveland in 1887
and was a delegate to the 1888 Democratic National Convention. In
one of his first acts after moving to the city, he contributed five dollars
toward construction of the Georgia Confederate Home. A few months
later he issued a glowing tribute to the memory of Henry W. Grady.[60]

Taylor had a strong aversion to local Negro Republican politicians,
partially because of his elitist philosophy. In 1890 he planned a convention of conservative blacks to seek the best means "for real betterment of our condition, as it relates to our material interests." Each delegate, he said, "will be able to read and write, own property and have
standing among the decent people of the community where he lives."
Delegates would be appointed rather than elected. "This was done not

to stifle free speech among the race, but knowing my people as I do, should the delegates be elected, the most unfit persons in a majority of cases would be selected." Among those invited were Negro Democrats James Monroe Trotter, J. C. Mathews, and George T. Downing. Earlier Taylor had joined several of these men as a minority faction at a National Convention of Colored Men called by P. B. S. Pinchback. Speaking for this group, he expressed opposition to the Force Bill, defended treatment of Negroes by Southern whites, and urged blacks to "do your own thinking about how you shall exercise your suffrage." And, as he urged his race on another occasion, "adopt a consistent conservative course remembering always that your interests are identical with your white neighbors and that what benefits the one, benefits the other."[61]

Yet despite discontent over party policies, the Republican Party continued to be seen as the natural home of the Negro voter. This view was most marked in national elections, though true to a lesser extent on the local scene as well. When Nashville's Pearl School was dismissed in the afternoon of election day 1884, its seven hundred pupils paraded the streets with Blaine and Logan badges pinned to their clothes; gaily dressed Negro women wearing Republican buttons accompanied them. During the 1889 state political campaign in Virginia, black ministers, including most of Richmond's clergy, sent out a signed circular urging Negroes to vote for the Republican Party "and to do all in your power to instruct our people to help the ticket." In an interview the Reverend Richard Wells said he believed that no Negro should be a Democrat and asserted that he knew of none in his congregation.[62]

Most Negroes simply could not bring themselves to trust the Democratic Party. Despite Senator Charles Sumner's endorsement of Horace Greeley in 1872, leading Nashville Negroes reaffirmed their support of President Grant on the ground that the party of Greeley was still the same party of Seymour and, they said, the record of the "Democratic Party for nearly half a century has been one of opposition to every measure calculated to benefit the black man, politically or socially." In 1885 after a series of favorable articles in the *Daily American*, several Negro leaders expressed approval of the treatment accorded them in the press and by President Cleveland, but maintained that more proof of Democratic sincerity was required; until then they would remain Republicans. "It will take some time for that paper [the *Daily American*] to convince us it means to do justice," wrote another black man. He felt Democrats were just after Negro votes. Although this was true also of the Republicans, "still we prefer the party that has done the most good for the negro."[63]

13

Resolving the Uncertainties: Toward Elimination of the Black Vote

Redemption had been accomplished in the five cities, but the Negroes still had the vote. As long as sizable numbers exercised their right of suffrage, particularly on the side of Republicans or independents, whites could never feel totally in control. The logical response was disfranchisement. This final step would not be taken until Southerners were certain that there would be no interference from the North. Meanwhile, the Redeemers opted for what might be termed piecemeal or *de facto* disfranchisement. A number of tactics were devised to rid the cities of Negro officeholders and reduce the possibility that black votes could be used to challenge the Democratic establishment. Paradoxically, such devices were used at the same time that Democrats were making appeals for the black vote. Rather than attempting to win over the existing voters, these policies aimed at reducing the number of votes the Negroes could throw into battle.

Democrats proclaimed that the white Southerner was the Negro's best friend and that the true interests of blacks lay in voting Democratic. Thus appeals were made to attract black voters to the party, although on white terms. Throughout the period, white Democrats unsuccessfully sought to combine a belief in black inferiority with a pledge of fair treatment for blacks. In an 1889 editorial the *Atlanta Constitution* provided an excellent example of this schizophrenic approach. According to the newspaper, the South had two obligations in her dealings with the Negroes. First, she must maintain the political, as well as the social, integrity of the white race. . . . She must determine that, at all hazards, she will prevent the domination of the black race, that was once put in domination over us. That the white race shall control, and that neither through division in our ranks, nor through the power or money of others, shall the control of blacks be re-established.

But, continued the editor,

there is another duty that is pressing. We must hold the friendship and the confidence of the negro. We must convince him that he, most dependent on the bounty and protection of the government, will find that most fully guaranteed, when the property and intelligence of the south are in full control. . . . We must show that we deserve what we ask for, and without which our very best efforts will be weakened and our vindication postponed.

Or, in the words of a Lynchburg, Virginia, lawyer: "The negroes must understand that we will give them perfect equality before the law, and treat them with justice and fairness and liberality, but that they are not fit to rule us, and that we will die before they shall do so."[1]

Democratic newspapers initially opposed to Negro suffrage now sought black votes. During the 1868 presidential election, the *Atlanta Constitution* assured blacks that the Democratic Party was interested in their well-being and was not going to reenslave them. Examples of Negroes working for the party were featured in news stories and blacks were invited to march in Democratic processions. The *Montgomery Weekly Advertiser* appealed to Negroes to support their "true friends" by working to defeat the state's new constitution in 1867, a document guaranteeing universal black manhood suffrage. And in the midst of the 1870 legislative elections in Virginia, the *Richmond Dispatch* called upon Negroes to throw off the yoke of "unprincipled and incompetent" strangers and return to the Southern white Conservatives, "their only true friends."[2]

In each city beginning with the 1868 campaign, Negro Democratic clubs were organized during presidential elections. "If the Republicans don't mind, the negroes will all become Democrats," needled Nashville's *Daily American*. And as the period progressed, some newspapers saw definite advantages to Negro suffrage, if the Democrats could control it. "Whatever we thought of this new political element [Negro voting] three or four years ago," said Nashville's *Republican Banner* in 1872, "the ballot in the hands of the colored voter is by no means regarded as the greatest evil that could have befallen the South. We believe with the *Mobile Register* that our section gains in political weight thereby, and that some of these days the Radicals will wish they had let Sambo alone." By the end of the 1870s, the *Atlanta Constitution* was predicting that the Republicans would soon seek to disfranchise the blacks, since the Southern Democrats were winning their votes.[3]

Democrats used a variety of means to attract black support. A speaker at an Atlanta University rally in 1870 encouraged his colleagues to seek out Negroes. "Every white man knows that among colored men there is someone that he can influence that is under some obligation to him." Votes from blacks were publicly praised and future rewards implied. After Negroes had contributed to the unsuccessful efforts to defeat Nashville's incumbent Radical Mayor A. E. Alden in 1868, a citizens meeting urged that whites "remember gratefully the colored people who nobly tried to relieve them in the late municipal elections." A decade later, when sizable defections from the Radical candidate allowed one of the city's leading Democrats, E. A. Stahlman, to win reelection to the City Council, he thanked "the intelligence and worth" of the blacks who had supported him and said that "whenever it is in my power to serve you consistently, such service will be cheerfully rendered."[4]

Appeals to patronize Negro party workers were another way support was acknowledged. The *Montgomery Daily Advertiser*, for example, mentioned Levi Floyd as the driver of Hack No. 4, "a good democrat and deserving of all patronage"; its weekly version described Tom Gorham as "our popular colored friend" whose barbershop deserved to be frequented.[5] Similarly the few Negro Democratic newspapers were supported by "those who want to see the negro vote taken from the bondage of republican partisans."[6] After the 1880 state and presidential campaign, the Alabama chairman of the Democratic and Conservative Party praised the contributions of the *Weekly Advance*, edited by James A. Scott, and concluded that it was "not only our duty, but a privilege that we should avail ourselves of, to do everything we can to support and maintain the paper."[7]

As already noted, even after Redemption, Democrats tolerated Negro elected officials and gave blacks some local, state, and federal jobs. But the concessions granted Negro officeholders, the awarding of patronage, the organization of black campaign clubs, and the appeals of newspapers and party leaders did little to sway the mass of black voters.

Some whites attributed this phenomenon to pressure rather than to choice. Montgomery's James H. Clanton testified that

> there is constant intimidation at the polls. . . . They [blacks] form a line, and put their sentries at the gate to examine every negro's ticket as he comes in. . . . They had to run the gauntlet as they went to vote; as they passed by this colored captain he took their tickets and examined them; if it was a democratic ticket he would take it and give them a republican ticket for it. . . . The man in line would have to pass on or be stamped to death.

Other Negroes were threatened if they voted Democratic and sometimes party workers were attacked. The *Republican Banner* charged that during the 1868 presidential election Nashville policemen guarding the polls tore up the ballots of two prospective Democratic voters. After the presidential campaign twelve years later, a group of Nashville black Republicans stoned the house of Lyttleton Jones, president of the Colored Hancock and English Club, and tore down the iron rooster on the barber pole in front of his shop. Citing an attack on a Negro Democrat, the *Atlanta Constitution* lamented the frequency of such occurrences and asserted: "Democrats will see that colored men are protected in the exercise of their suffrage. They have a perfect right to vote the democratic ticket, if they want to." That blacks wanted to do so was clear to the Southern press. "If left free and without fear," said the *Richmond Dispatch* about its city's Negroes, "naturally the colored voter would exercise his own discretion and follow the instincts of his own judgement."[8]

Continued black resistance led many Democrats to take an even more paternalistic tone and to demean the sophistication of black voters. If only they knew what was best for them! The local press was especially dismayed that blacks blindly followed the lead of "outsiders." "It was once, perhaps, natural that the negro should have voted the Republican ticket, as it was that party which gave him his freedom," stated the Nashville *Republican Banner* during a heated campaign in 1874. "It is strange though, at this late day, that the negro should cast his vote for a man whom he never saw, in preference to a conservative who has perhaps done him personal favors, yet we have seen this done time and again." The *Richmond Dispatch* lamented that the typical black "recognizes the white Democrats as his friends during 364 days of the year. On the remaining day he is a Republican and votes as his masters tell him to vote." The *Atlanta Constitution* was especially troubled by this phenomenon and made the most consistent effort to attract Negro support to the Democratic Party.[9]

Although white Democrats couched their language in terms of "voting intelligently"—following interests rather than prejudices—when they spoke of Negroes failing to vote wisely, they really meant that blacks were not choosing Democrats. "As long as the negroes keep up the race or color line—and they seem inclined to keep it up indefinitely— they can make no real progress," argued the *Atlanta Constitution*.

> It is as easy for a black man to win the respect and confidence of his neighbors as it is for a white man to accomplish that result. The conditions are precisely the same, provided the black man is sensible enough to forget the fact of his color when he goes to the polls and vote in favor of the party best calculated to further his own material interests and the interests of his neighbors.

In 1874, when "quite a respectable number of the more intelligent and well-meaning colored resident voters" cast their ballots for the Democratic candidate for county chancellor, the Nashville *Republican Banner* took this as a sign of growing political maturity. In 1890 the *Richmond Dispatch* was still arguing that the Southern white was the Negro's best friend. Like other newspapers, it suggested that blacks eschew politics—which meant, of course, switch party allegiance. "Let him [the Negro] break the shackles which he allows to bind him to the Republican party, and he will not long afterwards have anything but good words and kind feeling for the superior race."[10]

The use of such phrases as "superior race" reveals that the blacks, even after joining the party, were not to be treated as equals. Although on occasion Democratic journals defended full participation of Negroes in party affairs,[11] for most Democrats blacks had proved themselves fit only to vote for white Democratic candidates. Once again, at best, segregation was to replace exclusion.

Blacks were caught in the middle, with both parties interested in their support but neither willing to give them what they wanted in return. As the *Nashville Banner* expressed it: "The political parties want the votes of the negroes, but do not want to divide the honors."[12] The clearest expression of antagonism to the idea of Negroes within positions of power came from the *Richmond Dispatch*. In 1870, at the same time that its editorials and news columns were urging blacks to vote for the Conservatives, "their true friends," the newspaper featured numerous articles attacking fraudulent voting by Negroes and referred to the Radicals as a party of ignorant blacks and mean whites. When a Negro Radical ran against a white Conservative to fill a vacancy in the House of Delegates, the editor urged Conservatives to vote against him not so much because he was a Radical as because he was a Negro.

> Upon what principle, upon what ground of reason and propriety, should the idea prevail of allowing this city to be represented by a negro? Who founded this Government? Who are the responsible people dwelling on the land now? Are these originators of Government— are these owners of all the property and possessors of all the wisdom and experience essential to government—to give place now to African slaves of yesterday? Ignorant, inexperienced, incompetent beings, who have no acquirements, no experience, no wisdom, to fit them for lawmaking or mending, and who are irresponsible and relieved by destitution from the oppression of misgovernment. . . . It becomes the duty of the whites to protect the Commonwealth. This protection is not only necessary for them, but for the negroes. This land is not ready for barbarism, and we must fight barbarism to the end.[13]

A decade of appeals to the blacks for their vote did nothing to change the *Dispatch's* view. "The Conservative party is a white man's party," it stated in 1880 at the height of the Readjuster movement. "It avows its opposition to mixed marriages, to mixed schools and to a mixed police. If any negro votes for our ticket, he will do it with the distinct understanding that he is not to be put into any of these offices." Three years later the editor endorsed the following resolution passed at a meeting of the state's leading Conservatives: "We are in favor of granting and securing to the colored people all of their just rights, and of treating them not only with justice, but with kindness and forbearance, but they must know that they are to behave themselves, and *keep in their proper places.*" According to the *Dispatch,* this meant that "negroes are not to be placed in any office in which they would be the official superiors of the whites. . . . It means that the whites are the superior and governing race."[14]

Such statements were not the only inconsistencies within the Democratic campaign to attract black voters. Among the placards and transparencies displayed in a Conservative procession the night before the 1874 Davidson County elections were "negro equality the downfall of public schools. We won't mix," "uphold social distinction," and "no civil rights for us." Eight years later, while Nashville newspapers were urging Negroes to support the independent Democratic county ticket, whites greeted Negro candidates attempting to speak at a Democratic rally with cries of "he's a coon," and "down with the nigger." Not surprisingly, Negro Democrats brought up the rear of the mammoth victory procession held in 1884 to celebrate the election of Grover Cleveland.[15]

If segregation was the rule in processions, exclusion became the most common policy in primaries and nominating conventions. Indeed, the white primary which became the staple of statewide politics in the 1890s was developed in the Southern cities during the 1870s. While the *Atlanta Constitution* was appealing for Negro support in 1876, the Democratic City Executive Committee decided to continue its ban on Negro voters in the upcoming primary since, in the words of one member, "if you let in that element you let in one that can be almost entirely controlled by whiskey and money." Although six Richmond blacks served as delegates to the 1870 Conservative nominating convention for Congressman, this practice soon ended. In 1877 the *Richmond Dispatch* strongly endorsed the City Conservative Committee's decision to institute a white primary for the selection of candidates. "To open the ballot box to negroes is to open it to fraud," it noted. There were few Negro Conservatives and in any event, "we beg to be excused from entering into a scramble with darkies as to who shall be the white people's candidate for Governor." In Montgomery the Negro Republican editor of the *Herald* taunted local black Democrats about the presence of similar restrictions in the Alabama capital.[16]

Clearly, then, despite their talk of wanting blacks, white Democrats were willing to do little to attract them. Those who sincerely wanted the black vote felt that they would get it because the Negroes would realize that Southern whites were their true friends. These whites did not make the task of discovery easier, however, since they simply reverted to their paternalistic claims of knowing what was best for the blacks. But there was another side to the failure of the Democrats to entice more Negroes: many Democrats preferred to have the blacks as Republicans.

It was quite taxing to be both the party of white supremacy and the party of equal treatment. Thus the *Dispatch* seems to have welcomed indications that the black vote was unattainable. Using the Civil Rights Act as an excuse, an 1875 editorial announced an end to appeals apprising Negroes of their real friends. Previous appeals had proved fruitless as blacks continued to vote for "strangers without character" rather than Southern white Democrats. "Now it is far wiser . . . to make no more appeals and no more concessions." During the following year's mayoral campaign, one issue contained two laudatory stories about prospective black Democratic voters, but an editorial in the same issue proclaimed:

> The parties here are *fortunately for us* divided by the color line. We would not have it otherwise. The temptations which a large vote of Conservative negroes could offer to our candidates would be demoralizing. It is better as it is. The fact being, then, as we have stated it, it remains only for the voters to decide whether they will vote for the candidates of their own race or those of the colored people.

The fact that after the election the *Dispatch* acknowledged that a significant number of blacks had voted for the Conservative mayor, a development likely at the time of the pre-election editorial, makes it clear how the Democrats themselves drew the color line and used it for their own advantage.[17] Without the great majority of blacks in the Republican Party, this tactic, of course, would have been impossible.

Few elections took place in any city without the Democratic press injecting the racial issue and urging defeat of the "infamous" Negro-carpetbagger coalition. Independent movements such as the Readjusters and the Greenbackers, as well as local independent candidates, were tarred with the brush of Negro equality. In order to stir up white voters during the 1881 municipal campaign, the *Atlanta Constitution,* announcing that Negroes in the Fourth Ward had nominated a noted black minister for councilman, warned that the whites would have to choose "their best man" or else lose the ward. There was, of course, no chance that the Negro would be elected, as was confirmed by the 34 votes he received. During the 1884 presidential and Congressional elections, Nashville's two most rabid Democratic newspapers sought to fan rumors that the Republicans would swear in two hundred Negro deputy marshals for duty on election day.[18]

The *Richmond Dispatch* was most prone to use evidence of black support as a means to discredit opponents. Under the headline "The Negroes Did It," an 1879 editorial attributed the Readjuster victory in the state elections solely to the black vote. During municipal elections the following year, readers were told that "if you want to see negro policemen on our streets, and negroes asserting their equality in every public building, stand idly by and allow the city government to pass into the hands of the Readjusters." The city's Democratic leadership took a similar stance. Asserting that the character of Richmond would change if the Readjusters were elected, a party circular of 1889 predicted not only political disaster, but social chaos as well. Among other changes to be expected, "negroes would certainly become more impudent on the streets than ever."[19]

Along with appeals to defeat candidates who relied upon black votes went constant pleas for intraparty harmony. Thanks to the measures that either brought about or accompanied Redemption in each city, under usual circumstances there was no longer a chance for a "negro victory." But since significant numbers of blacks still exercised the franchise, struggles between opposing factions within the Democratic Party might permit the black vote to decide elections, either by supporting one of the Democrats or by backing a Republican. The presence of competing slates of Democrats in Nashville, for example, enabled the Republicans to elect a Congressman in 1870, a mayor and two state legislators (one a Negro, Sampson W. Keeble) in 1872, four more state legislators (including T. A. Sykes) and the governor in 1880. No wonder that the Democratic newspapers constantly urged party members to reconcile their differences and unite behind a single candidate.[20]

Richmonders heard similar pleas from their newspapers. Urging on the party faithful during the 1870 elections, the *Richmond Dispatch* emphasized that "union and harmony" were the key to victory and that "the public welfare is superior to all personal considerations." Five years later an all-out effort was made to discourage fragmentation of Democratic voting strength. True to the fears of the *Dispatch*, independent white Democratic candidates "sought . . . the votes of the inferior race to defeat their fellow citizens and brothers." The independents were pictured as traitors to their race; issues dividing the bolters from the regular slate were passed over and all attention focused on the racial issue in order to firm up the ranks.[21]

The *Atlanta Constitution* voiced the same sentiments during the 1878 municipal elections. To prevent William Finch from defeating his five white opponents for alderman and the Republican candidate for mayor from winning against two Democrats, the whites would have to agree on one candidate for each position. The whites did not heed this advice, however, and instead bid for the Negro vote. The newspaper charged that on voting day each faction bribed blacks with money and whiskey and concluded: "It is demonstrated that the negro, when he is divided between democrats, is an exceedingly unruly and boisterous element in our politics." According to a prominent Democrat, after Alexander Stephens defeated a Republican-endorsed independent Democrat for governor in 1882, "this thing of begging or buying negro votes won't do. It degrades the white man, it influences the negro with an undue sense of importance and it debauches our whole political system."[22]

White Democrats therefore sought to tighten the discipline within their party. In some cases candidates confronted by a serious Republican threat agreed that the weaker man would bow out. When Negro carpenter Mitchell Cargile, described by the *Atlanta Constitution* as "one of the most popular and exemplary colored men in the city," ran for the Council in the Third Ward, one of his white opponents withdrew on the afternoon of the election and threw his support to the remaining white candidate. By 1882 Nashville Democrats also had learned to avoid costly divisions. The races for county offices were three cornered (all whites), except the one for county register. J. H. Burrus, a popular Negro Republican, was running and Democrats agreed on a single challenger lest the position be lost to a black. Two years later the Democratic County Executive Committee nominated candidates for the first time for the positions of magistrate and constable in order to prevent C. C. Gowdey or some other black from consolidating the Negro vote while the usual proliferation of white candidates split the Democratic vote.[23] Citywide primaries became popular in an effort to fight out party differences before the general election. As noted earlier, these primaries soon became restricted to whites so that Negro voters could be bypassed entirely.

The whites were largely successful in preventing blacks from exercising leverage in regular elections. When a Republican candidate was running against a Democrat, the former had little chance of victory unless the race took place in Richmond's Jackson Ward, in Raleigh's Second and Fourth wards, or in Nashville. Even when the Democrats were split, Republicans could never seriously challenge for control of an entire city, thanks to the gerrymandering that had guaranteed the continuation of Redemption. The Negroes, however, could still threaten the established order in a special kind of election involving the explosive issue of prohibition that surfaced in Southern cities during the 1880s. Prohibition divided communities and parties nearly down the middle and thus encouraged pursuit of the black vote. Coming after many years of division among whites in local elections, the prohibition campaigns convinced whites of the need to eliminate black suffrage. Perhaps more than any other factor it set the stage for the decision to push for complete disfranchisement of the Negroes several years before the Populist-Bourbon split, commonly cited as the reason for Negro disfranchisement.[24]

Prohibition became the chief issue in Atlanta politics after the Georgia legislature passed a statewide local option law in August 1885. Counties could now hold referenda on whether to remain wet or go dry. Fulton County held a referendum in the fall of 1885; another occurred two years later; and until 1888, the fight over prohibition dominated municipal elections. Interest in the issue is evident from the registration figures for the November 1885 local option referendum. Whereas the total for the previous legislative election had been 3,947 registrants, the referendum produced 7,213, "by far the largest registration ever known in the city." Whites in the evenly divided wet and dry camps had to seek allies among the 3,134 black voters.[25]

Prohibitionists found eager supporters among the city's black clergy. W. J. Gaines, Henry M. Turner, and E. R. Carter were in the forefront of the dry forces, preaching in their churches, forming prohibition clubs, and addressing mass meetings. The three men were among the white and black leaders who addressed a massive segregated tent meeting of 4,000 Negroes and 2,000 whites. Carter told the audience that liquor was responsible for all the Negro's ills, including rheumatism, consumption, poverty, and ignorance. In order further to encourage Negro prohibitionists, the White Young Men's Prohibition Club offered the Colored Y.M.P.C. $285 in prizes to be distributed to Negro ward clubs with the largest enrollments. And like the antiprohibitionists, the pros often paid the poll taxes of black supporters and supplied them with refreshments on election day.[26]

The antis found their Negro allies among the political leaders. The election graphically exposed the tensions within the black community between the politicians and the preachers. "No minister has the right to dictate to us how we shall vote and how we shall pray," declared W. A. Pledger in one of his many attacks on Negro clergymen in general and the Reverend Carter in particular. Such men had no business meddling in politics—a view echoed by James B. Parker, who charged black pastors with allowing their churches to become headquarters for the drys while white churches remained neutral.[27] Pledger based his opposition to prohibition on the ground that it was bad for the economic interests of the city and especially for the blacks employed in the restaurants, bars, hotels, and as hackmen. Besides, not only would the city lose revenue and the blacks their jobs, but prohibition could not work. "The rich will have it [liquor] by the barrel and the poor will get it from illicit dealers . . . yet the great amount of tax and license will be gone and free schools shut down."[28]

On the night before the election both groups sought to prevent defections among their black supporters. Friendship Baptist, Butler Street Baptist, and Wheat Street Baptist churches held elaborate dinners for prohibitionists and kept on late into the night with speeches and tableaux in order to keep them away from the antis. Meanwhile, the antis fed large numbers of their supporters, supplied them with beer, and kept them overnight at the West Point depot. On election day each side marched their well-drilled supporters to the polls in long lines. The wets carried the city by 2,624 to 2,303, but returns from the outlying districts allowed the drys to carry the county by 216 votes. According to observers, the victory was due to the Negro votes.[29]

Prohibition emerged again as the sole issue of the 1886 municipal campaign. Once more it seemed that the Negroes would be called upon to settle the dispute. At first, prohibition and antiprohibition forces prepared to nominate candidates for election. Thanks to the efforts of William Finch, both E. R. Carter and W. J. Gaines were appointed to the committee of twenty-five chosen to select candidates favorable to the drys. In turn Moses H. Bentley and Alonzo W. Burnett were chosen to represent the blacks on the slate-making committee of the wets. Negroes, though happy about this representation, were reported to be interested in having members on the City Council itself. Whether true or not, the rumor led the whites temporarily to set aside their quarrel and draw up a compromise ticket chosen by a committee of fifty whites. The ticket was opposed at a mass meeting by blacks, Knights of Labor, and hardline antis and pros, but in the end they had no choice but to endorse it. Thus once again blacks had been thwarted in their efforts to secure greater representation through the use of their political strength.[30]

It was easier for whites to compromise on candidates than for them to reach accord on the issue of prohibition itself. The following year when there was another referendum on local option, both sides again solicited Negro votes. This campaign was even more intense than the previous one. Registration increased 1,357 over the 1885 total and for an entire month the *Atlanta Constitution* devoted half of its columns to prohibition-related matters.[31] This time most of the city leaders endorsed prohibition. With the exception of Pledger, influential politicians such as Jackson McHenry, Smith Easley, and C. C. Wimbish joined the Reverend Carter and the Reverend Gaines at the head of the black drys. Even Moses H. Bentley made the switch, giving as his reason the great benefits that prohibition had brought to the Negroes. McHenry gave the same reason, but it is more likely that he was influenced by the attitudes of Colonel A. E. Buck and J. E. Bryant. These two white Republicans were his chief patrons in the party (as was true for Wimbish, Bentley, and Easley as well), and both had been ardent proponents of prohibition in 1885. Similar consideration moved Bentley, although the promise of leading prohibitionists to frequent his barbershop was also an important factor. Whatever the reasons, Pledger was left as the only major black figure siding with the antis. He renewed his charges against the Negro preachers and argued that Negroes had been unjustly punished for violations of the liquor law while whites had easily evaded it. For the most part blacks in the opposing camps attacked each other's white allies, charging them with buying their Negro supporters.[32]

The election resulted in a solid defeat for the drys with all but one precinct in the county voting against continuing the experiment. Most Atlantans blamed the blacks for the defeat. Although it seems that the masses did desert their leaders to give a majority of their votes to the wets, the *Constitution* correctly pointed out that the largest white precinct gave as great an antiprohibition majority as did the two strongest Negro wards.[33]

Subsequent efforts to revive the issue met with little success, in part due to the black presence. In 1888 an antiprohibition municipal ticket sought to enlist Negro support against the Conservative ticket composed of pros, antis, and neutral candidates. Party regulars, however, aided by the *Atlanta Constitution*, spread a rumor that blacks had been promised two council positions, five places in the fire department and two on the police force, one driver's job for the police wagon, and one sanitary inspector's post. This charge discredited the party in the eyes of most whites. Negroes in turn found that the antis would make no firm concessions, so they endorsed the Conservatives. Two years later when prohibitionists rekindled interest in local option, they avoided a renewed contest for Negro votes, since in the words of a local judge, "This is a white man's country, and it is to the interest of both races that white people should rule it."[34]

The central role of blacks in prohibition campaigns also upset whites in other cities. The United States Senate Judiciary Committee reported that the "race war" in Jackson, Mississippi, in 1888 was due to bad feelings produced by a local option election.[35] There were no disturbances in any of this study's five cities, but discontent was evident. Commenting on the victory of Atlanta drys in 1885 in the midst of Richmond's own local option campaign, the *Richmond Dispatch* concluded that "wouldn't it be an unfortunate condition of things to have such a law forced upon white men by negro votes?" Nonetheless, the blacks still had to be cajoled and shortly before the Richmond election, an Atlanta observer concluded that "in Richmond as in Atlanta the colored man is the much badgered factor. His vote will weigh more than it ever did before." Unlike the Atlanta elections, however, the black vote was not decisive. Although "the negroes voted almost solidly against prohibition," so did the whites and three of the white wards returned greater majorities for the wets than did Jackson. In contrast to the pattern in Atlanta, the Reverend John Jasper delivered his church to the wets.[36] Raleigh, on the other hand, had instituted prohibition in 1886 by a slim margin of 60 votes despite the opposition of the black masses.[37]

In 1887 Nashville voted on a prohibition amendment to the state constitution. As in Raleigh and Atlanta, the black preachers urged support for the drys. Once again both groups of whites appealed to the Negro voters. Entreaties were made in the newspapers, segregated mass meetings were held, and on election day there was dispensing of food, money, and, in the case of the wets, whiskey. In the end Nashville blacks voted overwhelmingly against prohibition. Thanks to wet majorities in four of the wards with the largest black population, the amendment was defeated in the city by 1,400 votes.[38] The *Daily American* subsequently concluded that in order for reforms such as prohibition to be enacted in Tennessee, blacks would have to be excluded from political life.[39]

For many other white Southerners besides the *Daily American* editor the prohibition campaigns of the late 1880s were the last straw. Democratic entreaties to the black voter had been rebuffed; independent candidates threatened to divide the whites and lead to increased Negro influence; and now special issues such as prohibition further encour-

aged pursuit of the black votes. An increasing number of whites therefore joined their fellow Democrats who had long been calling for still
firmer limitations on black suffrage.

"We do not deny that we use every means, not actually violent, at
our disposal to neutralize the Negro vote," admitted a Montgomery
leader in 1880, who believed that black control meant financial ruin.[40]
These efforts were thought especially necessary on the local level
where, in the words of a Richmond resident in 1886, "we 'live and move
and have our being.' . . . It is true in national affairs their [Negro]
vote or influence does not count or amount to much, but we are more
concerned for our home rule than for national control."[41] In order to
achieve the required control over the black voter, the same techniques
utilized to bring about Redemption were continued and, where possible, expanded. They can be divided into three broad categories. In
ascending order of subtlety, they are violence and intimidation, manipulation of voting procedures and outright fraud, and the use of laws to
alter voting requirements, redraw boundaries, and change the form of
government. Together with the white primaries, these devices finally
brought an end to Negro interference in the political realm.

Only in Richmond was there extensive use of threatened or actual
violence. Elections for the most part were relatively peaceful affairs in
the other four cities, but in the Virginia capital local thugs and policemen discouraged Negro voters, provoked them into fights so they could
then be arrested, and caused their arrest on charges of illegal voting—
charges inevitably dropped once the polls closed. Although true in all
precincts with significant numbers of black votes, Jackson Ward was
the focal point for these kinds of activities. After registration for an
important election, the *Richmond Planet* concluded that the four to six
"burly policemen" present at each precinct in the ward "were there
simply to overawe the voters and to make them submit to any outrage
the registrar and challenger saw fit to impose on them." A longtime
resident remembered one election when the activities of "the ward
bruisers" in "challenging and impeding voters" led to a riot after the
polls closed. The extent of interference with black voters is evident
from the *Richmond Dispatch*'s account of the various Democratic
workers in the ward during a typical election in 1888. The story matter-
of-factly noted that one worker was "arrested once and was bailed,"
another "had many colored voters arrested and he himself was arrested
twice and bailed," and a third "was characteristically energetic and was

twice arrested but the warrants were withdrawn." Such behavior had earlier necessitated Readjuster Governor William Cameron's remaining in Richmond on election day in 1883 "to prevent or suppress the organized lawlessness."[42]

The more common form of intimidation, however, was the use of financial pressure. Montgomery's white employers used their authority either to get blacks to vote Democratic or to keep them from the polls.[43] Republican newspapers carried stories about Negroes losing their jobs because of their party allegiance. Other blacks were reminded of debts to Democratic storekeepers at election times. Two grocer-saloonkeepers in Jackson Ward, for example, "catered almost entirely to the negro trade, and won many votes for white candidates for city office."[44]

Saloonkeepers were also in a position to control Negro voters by dispensing free drinks. The buying of votes either through liquor, jobs, or money was one of the examples of fraudulent practices used by both the Republicans and the Redeemers.[45] Yet after Redemption the Democrats had a decided edge due to their control of the election machinery. A Virginia law passed in 1875 required that local courts appoint three election judges and two clerks for each voting place. "Whenever it is practicable to do so," the judges were to be members of different parties, "but no election shall be deemed invalid where the . . . judges shall not belong to different political parties." Since Conservatives or Democrats controlled local courts throughout the period, at least two of the judges and often both clerks in each precinct were members of the majority party. Often, as in the case of the 1875 legislative elections, there were one independent and two Conservative judges at each precinct, thus leaving out the Republicans entirely. Only in 1883, thanks to Readjuster intervention, did the Republicans have a majority of the judgeships in each precinct and a three to two edge on the Board of Elections.[46]

Handicapped in this manner in most elections, white Republicans and their Negro allies were open everywhere to Democratic fraud and manipulation. On the simplest level was ballot-box stuffing and the disregarding of Republican ballots. Hilary A. Herbert who represented Montgomery in the United States Congress during the 1870s and 1880s noted that "a portion of the negro vote . . . had been suppressed" during some of his races. Acknowledging this disregard of black votes, the *Colored Citizen* observed that "a nomination in Montgomery by the democrats is an election; the remainder is mere form." During the 1888 Congressional race, Richmond Republicans registered a rare triumph over such vote stealing. Republican John W. Wise contested the election against the longtime Democratic incumbent on the ground that 400 Jackson Ward Negroes were prevented from voting. Wise was seated in 1890 by a straight party vote of Congress and the grand jury of the U.S. Circuit Court indicted six election officials, all but one of them Democrats, for fraud and intimidation of voters in Jackson's First and Second precincts.[47]

More often, illegal tactics fed the Democratic majorities. During the 1875 legislative elections, for example, the results from the First Precinct of Jefferson Ward gave the Democratic candidates approximately 400 votes and the Independents, about a dozen. Yet there were 614 registered white and 265 black voters, of whom, according to the books, 279 whites and 105 Negroes actually voted. Even though more than 100 witnesses testified that they had voted for the Independents, a jury took twenty minutes to find the chief judge not guilty of fraud. Regarding the elections in Jackson Ward, C. A. Bryce remembered that two ex-Confederate soldiers serving as election officials "worked hard all day long on election days to suppress the black and tan vote and count in anything just so it had a white hide and posed for a Conservative."[48]

Democrats also made use of their control of city councils, boards of elections, and judges to regulate voting procedures at the polls. Charles Nordhoff discovered in 1875 that "in some cities, for instance, as in Atlanta and Savannah, insufficient voting boxes are provided, and the negro voters are crowded out and prevented from casting their full vote." Richmond made especially effective use of this tactic, thanks to the concentration of blacks in Jackson Ward. John Mitchell, Jr., in the pages of the *Richmond Planet* and in the City Council sought unsuccessfully to secure an equitable number of precincts in Jackson. In 1876, for example, although Jackson cast twenty-seven more votes than the next largest ward in the presidential election, it had only three precincts, while three of the remaining five wards had four; four years later its three precincts were among the five in the city out of a total of twenty-one, with over 3,500 voters. By 1890 the number had been increased to four, but by then two smaller wards had five precincts.[49]

Not only were there fewer polling places in Jackson Ward, but the Democratic judges used tactics of delay and frequent challenges on technicalities to decrease the numbers actually voting. These efforts were aided by the use of separate voting lines for each race. Since few whites were Republicans, fewer blacks were Democrats, and whites were greatly outnumbered, all the Democratic votes in a precinct could be cast easily while the Negro line was held up for challenges. As a result, the closing of the polls found several hundred Negroes still waiting to vote.[50] Although Conservatives argued that the practice originated during Military Reconstruction and maintained that no discrimination was intended, the figures told the true story. In the critical 1889 state election when William A. Mahone ran for governor, the black vote in Jackson was 2,000 less than those registered in 1887.[51]

Separate lines, registration books, and ballot boxes were also used in Atlanta; Raleigh; Augusta, Georgia; and Norfolk, Virginia; but nowhere was interference as extensive as in Jackson Ward.[52] In addition to the techniques mentioned, Richmond Democrats switched polling places on the mornings of the elections, changed the names of streets so that people registered according to the old names would be disfranchised, and, in some cases, bribed the precinct leaders to substitute Democratic tickets for the Republican ones they were supposed to give illiterate voters. In short,

> the elections held in this ward were always stormy and unfair and characterized by cheating, delaying, intimidating and purchasing of votes. Everything that could be done to impede the negro vote was done. . . . It was well understood that the blacks had to be beaten by hook or by crook—they knew what to expect and they knew who was putting the thing on them but they could not prevent it.[53]

Most whites, if at all possible, preferred to avoid such blatant fraud. Writing after his city had been "buried under a negro majority of 524" in 1885, a Petersburg, Virginia, white called upon the state legislature to amend the city's charter. Other cities had been freed from Negro rule, he wrote, but due to the large number of blacks, "it is impossible for the Democratic party here to win in an election. Not since 1871 have they won at any time *except by fraud committed under the leadership of the champion of a 'free ballot' and a fair count.*" He decried the fact that fraud was necessary, but the only other way to win an election would be if the white Democratic legislators provided some appropriate statutes. Such action was needed in order to end the "degradation of political bondage to an inferior race."[54] As earlier noted, white Democrats in Atlanta, Montgomery, Raleigh, and Richmond used similar relief from their state legislators either to bring about Redemption or to entrench themselves more firmly once they gained office.

The legislatures continued to help as the years passed and as the Negroes continued to present political problems. Negro justices of the peace, a feature of Nashville political life between 1868 and 1876, practically disappeared after 1876 when the city shifted from the ward to at-large elections. Then in 1883, when it seemed that Negroes had assured themselves of regularly electing two black councilmen from the Fourth Ward and often one from the Sixth, a new charter provided for at-large elections. With the exception of J. C. Napier's and C. C. Gowdey's brief terms as reform aldermen, the change meant no more Negroes on the Council. Annexations could also be manipulated for racial purposes. The area which Montgomery had retroceded in 1877 was kept outside the city despite its increased tax base in order to eliminate additional black voters. Ward boundaries as well were adjusted with racial factors in mind. In 1889 the Tennessee legislature passed a redistricting bill for Chattanooga's wards aimed at giving three wards to the Negro Republicans and the other five to the Democrats. Jackson, Mississippi, Democrats who finally ousted their Republican mayor in 1888 secured an amended charter in 1890 which included "changes [in the] wards so as to give perpetual control of the board of aldermen to the white people."[55]

The legislatures aided the cause of *de facto* disfranchisement even more through changes in the qualifications for voting. Georgia whites manipulated registration requirements to discourage Negro voters. The fact that registration was usually held some weeks or even months before elections capitalized on the lack of interest among voters and the insufficient information available to them. The procedure also required potential voters to miss part of a day's work and travel across the city to register at one of the few authorized places. Soon after the Georgia General Assembly passed a more stringent registration law in 1884, the *Atlanta Constitution* reported that future elections would most probably be "more certain and reputable than they have been at any time since the war." Lest there be any doubt as to the main targets of the law, the newspaper noted following the first elections held under it that "quite a number of ignorant negroes" were not permitted to vote since they had not previously registered. Many blacks attempting to register had been turned away when they could not prove that they had paid all of their city, county, and state taxes plus the one-dollar poll tax instituted since the adoption of the 1877 state constitution. The requirements of paying the poll tax and presenting the receipt at the polls had been used to disqualify Negro voters since Redemption.[56]

Other taxes had to be paid as well. At a typical election in 1876 prepared lists of Negro voters who had paid their taxes were carefully checked "for almost every darkey who presented himself." A similar search was not made for whites. After the 1882 gubernatorial election, it was alleged that 1,500 citizens, including "some men of the highest responsibility," had voted without having paid taxes. The new 1884 law provided even greater opportunity for discrimination because of the cumulative nature of its tax payment requirement. As a *Constitution* reporter observed, no one was certain just what was required of the voters or how payment was to be proved; therefore, "some pay [the poll tax] for a year or two preceding; but not a man has paid back to 1877."[57]

By 1890 the practice of separate registrations for local and state elections had further complicated the entire process and the toll extracted upon the Negro community was evident in the registration figures. An estimated two-thirds of the 3,074 registered voters for the 1884 elections were white, for as the *Constitution* noted, "the colored voters are in a large majority on the defaulter's list."[58]

In 1876 the Democratic legislature of Virginia amended the constitution to include, among the disqualifications for voting, failure to pay the poll tax and conviction for certain misdemeanors, among them petit larceny, a frequent charge against blacks. As a result of the 1876 amendment, Richmond whites came close to nullifying the Negro vote, even in Jackson Ward. Realizing the significance of the constitutional change, the *Virginia Star* urged its readers during the 1878 municipal campaign to "go down to the collector's office . . . and pay your head tax. . . . Don't lose the only ward we have by neglecting this duty."[59]

Despite such appeals, the act had its intended effect: white eligible voters outnumbered blacks in all the wards including Jackson. Considering the excess of white votes and continued Conservative control of the election machinery, the outcome of the elections was predetermined. The Conservatives' three candidates for justices of the peace won handily as did all but one of their council nominees. The Republicans had been so discouraged that they ran no slate for mayor or for council seats in wards other than Jackson. During the state elections held the following year, the Conservative legislative ticket ran unopposed and only 91 votes were cast in Jackson Ward. The *Richmond Dispatch* saw the amendment as the key to white control of the city and therefore urged its readers to oppose the Readjusters who were pledged to end the poll tax.

> We would like for the regular Democratic speakers to press home upon the Independent candidates for electors and for Congress these questions: 1) Would it not be better for Virginia if none but white men had the right to vote? 2) If so, and it being out of the power of any State to deprive negroes of the right to vote, or to discriminate between them and white men as to that right, does not sound policy require the true sons of Virginia to keep the capitation tax in force as a means of rendering a great evil less than it would be under a suffrage restricted by no qualifications?[60]

The Readjusters, who already controlled the state house, won the legislature in 1882 and immediately repealed the tax. The difference was apparent in the 1883 legislative campaign. Jackson Ward Republicans, who had rebounded from their initial defeats to win back control of the ward in 1880 with small majorities, now outpolled their opponents in the old manner, 1,710 to 676. Richmond whites would have to wait twenty more years for a return to the conditions of 1878–1879. As late as 1888, there were still 6,431 registered Negro voters compared to 10,071 whites.[61]

By 1890, however, Nashville whites had used the state legislature to bring permanent relief from future interference of black voters. In none of the cities during the period was the Negro vote as actively pursued in local elections. Rather than eliminate blacks as a factor as in Montgomery and Atlanta or confine their influence to ward elections as in Raleigh and Richmond, local whites had permitted the Negroes to determine not only council but mayoral contests as well. Tennessee instituted a poll tax in 1870, but proof of its payment was only briefly a requirement for voting. Thus in 1887 the *Nashville Banner* remembered that, while it had once been the case, failure to pay the tax no longer disqualified a person from casting a ballot. The law had been changed in 1873 because the tax tended to be paid just before the election by candidates or representatives of the political parties. Now that payment was not required for voting there was a great problem collecting it from among the propertyless classes and especially, according to the *Banner*, from "a large bulk of the colored population." In 1890 the state legislature took advantage of this situation to once again make payment a requirement for voting. The tax of two-dollars per head proved too expensive for the Republican politicians. In the first election after its passage Republicans helplessly watched the Democratic organization pay the taxes of their supporters and dispense the receipts.[62]

The poll tax was the *coup de grace* to Nashville's Republicans and to the black voters. Their position had already been undermined by new voting and registration laws passed by the Democratic legislature in 1889. The acts were clearly aimed at Republican strength among Negroes in the state's urban areas since they applied only to cities of 9,000 and counties of 70,000 people—Nashville, Memphis, Chattanooga, Knoxville, and their counties. As the *Nashville Banner* claimed, the object was "to practically exclude the vote of the illiterate negroes in the cities and counties where the law applies." The election law required the use of a complicated nonpartisan Australian ballot with candidates for each office listed alphabetically. Aid in marking ballots was prohibited unless election officials decided help was needed "by reason of blindness or other physical disability." This gave discretion to Democratic officials who might (and in fact did) use this loophole to assist illiterate white voters while illiterate blacks were effectively disfranchised. Ballots marked incorrectly were disqualified, opening another avenue for fraud. According to the editor of the *Memphis Avalanche*, "we have the australian ballot system in Memphis, and through it many negroes, not being able to read, are only expedients and amount to very little."[63]

The effects of the new election laws were immediately obvious in the 1889 municipal contests in Nashville. "The majority of unregistered citizens are . . . negroes, who, on account of ignorance, or prejudice, or suspicion, or indifference would not secure certificates," reported the *Nashville Banner* after the completion of the registration a month before the election. In the election itself, the number of Negro voters declined greatly and the Republicans were soundly defeated despite the use of dummy tickets and tags. The first device allowed illiterate voters to memorize the order of candidates; the second had slats cut out in such a way that only the names of Republican candidates were visible when the tag was laid on the ballot. Not only did many of the registered blacks, themselves a small percentage of the eligible voters, fail to turn out, but Negro ballots were probably prominent among the large number the election officials threw out.[64]

The poll tax, required for the first time in Nashville in 1890, solidified the Democratic position. Only 1,225 blacks bothered to register for the county election as compared to 5,641 whites. Since payment of the poll tax was not required until election day, these figures do not reflect the even smaller number of black voters. The *Banner* estimated that no more than 500 Negroes in the entire county actually voted, the number from Nashville being less than half that figure. Whereas the two previous county elections had brought out between 14,700 and 15,600 voters, this campaign produced 6,500. Although the state and Congressional elections came three months later, the law required a new registration. This time only 733 blacks and 4,000 whites signed up. The Republican gubernatorial candidate drew a meager 387 votes, placing him third behind the Democrat and Prohibitionist. In the Fourth Ward which had given the Republicans 316 votes in the last election before the new laws, there was a *total* of only 120 votes cast. Without exaggeration the *Nashville Banner* could conclude:

> The election and poll tax laws of Tennessee seem to have solved the race problem by relegating the negro vote to the limbo of impecuniosity and indifference. . . . Very many of the registered negroes did not pay their poll taxes and it is said some who paid sold their certificates of registration. In fine . . . the negro vote, which has usually been large in this county, dropped out of sight. . . . If such laws as have the effect in Tennessee of reducing the vote of the lower classes to a minimum were in operation in Mississippi, Alabama and other states of the further South, there would perhaps be little of the race problem.[65]

The kind of laws mentioned by the *Banner* did indeed spread to the rest of the South, but not until the next decade would they be found in all the states.[66] Meanwhile, in Montgomery, Nashville, and Atlanta the end to Negro influence had come by 1890. Richmond and Raleigh would have to wait until the new century to banish black officeholders, but, with the exception of Raleigh's brief experience with Fusion in the 1890s, Negro influence had been successfully isolated.[67]

Although the blacks kept the vote after Redemption in all the cities, the disfranchisement of the last decade of the nineteenth and first decade of the twentieth century was the logical culmination of white thinking since the onset of Reconstruction. While already limited, the political power Negroes exercised under Radical administrations was systematically pared away by the Redeemers. There was simply no place for the black voter in the Southern way of life. However the Negroes chose to exercise the franchise, they would have met disapproval from the Democrats. If they voted Republican, they would have been accused of ingratitude, ignorance, and bloc voting. If they divided their votes among Republicans and Democrats, then Democrats would be competing against Republicans for their votes. Even if they all voted Democratic, there would be competition among white Democrats for their ballots. As the Southern press stressed on numerous occasions, blacks should never be able to exercise a pivotal role in politics. Hence at the core was not the issue of how the Negroes voted but the fact that they could vote; it was Negro suffrage per se that was the problem. As a disquieting force in Southern politics, whites believed blacks had to be disciplined. Through the use of legal and illegal techniques, this job had largely been accomplished in the Southern cities by 1890.

EPILOGUE
Race Relations and Social Control

In each of the five cities during the first twenty-five years after the war, blacks successfully built communities around their own churches, schools, welfare institutions, societies, and businesses. They were, however, victims of increasing discrimination which undermined early gains and restricted future opportunities for advancement.

Especially affected by continued white hostility were the Negroes in Atlanta and Montgomery, where the black vote had ceased to be a factor in the regular elections since the mid-1870s. At least partially because of the absence of black officeholders in these two cities, there was also far greater disparity in the level of educational and welfare services made available to blacks in comparison to whites. Furthermore, Atlanta was the only city to have not even one black judge, policeman, or fireman, and Montgomery blacks faced the worst housing conditions.

It is not entirely clear why these two cities provided such particularly uncongenial environments for blacks. The percentage of Negroes evidently was not the deciding factor. Although Montgomery had the largest percentage of blacks throughout the period, Raleigh followed close behind and Atlanta's percentage was similar to that of Richmond or Nashville. Nor was the length of Republican municipal control especially important. Atlanta never was in Republican hands, while urban Redemption took the longest to accomplish in Montgomery and Raleigh. Even economic success does not account for the differences, for while Montgomery blacks were the least prosperous, Atlanta blacks merited favorable comparison with those of Nashville and Richmond.

It would seem that the persistence of black political power, as weak as it would become, was the factor that accounted for the better overall conditions for blacks in Nashville, Raleigh, and Richmond. But what accounted for the continued black political presence after Redemption in these cities? To a large extent this was a reflection of political realities in Tennessee, North Carolina, and Virginia in which the Republican Party or strong independent movements prevented the Democrats from totally destroying local Republican influence or from totally ignoring black interests after Redemption. Furthermore, unlike Georgia and Alabama, these three states were among the most moderate in the South in terms of their racial attitudes, thus reflecting the broader differences between the Upper South and Lower South.

The backdrop provided by whites thus accounts for some of the advantages of blacks in three of the cities; however, it is no coincidence that unlike Atlanta and Montgomery, Nashville, Raleigh, and Richmond also had prosperous free Negro communities during the antebellum period. Often highly respected by whites, representatives of this group such as J. C. Napier later used their ties with white leaders to good effect. Even when those ties did not exist, the former free Negroes still provided an indispensable and disproportionate share of postbellum black leadership in the three cities. Only a closer examination of the continuities in leadership from the antebellum to the postbellum black communities will provide enough evidence to support a firm conclusion, but it appears that the strength of the antebellum black community of a particular city was a critical factor in the pattern of subsequent race relations in that locale.[1]

These points of divergence among the five cities are important, but they are more differences of degree than kind. It is therefore the shared elements within Southern urban race relations that reveal the most about the impact of Congressional Reconstruction and the extent of segregation in the South prior to 1890. Everywhere the white desire to control the lives of blacks clashed with the black hope of finally enjoying the fruits of freedom. Driven by fears about the consequences if blacks were not "kept in their place," whites had helped establish a new pattern of race relations in the urban South by 1890. That it was one not solely their creation, nor one that entirely satisfied them, was due to Northern "interference" and to the determination of the blacks. These common aspects of Southern black urban life also suggest a new framework in which to consider the change after 1890 from a system of *de facto* to *de jure* segregation.

Since the appearance in 1955 of C. Vann Woodward's *The Strange Career of Jim Crow*, extensive research has been undertaken to uncover the origins of racial segregation in the South. Woodward challenged the traditional view that the restrictive Jim Crow codes were the product of the immediate post-Reconstruction period. Emphasizing the legal side of segregation, he has argued that the separation of the races was an outgrowth of forces operating in the last decade of the nineteenth and the first years of the twentieth century. He has since modified his original position, but the existence of a law enforcing segregation remains his key variable in evaluating the nature of race relations. Because of the alleged absence of these statutes, Woodward is convinced that "forgotten alternatives" existed in the period between Redemption and the full-scale arrival of Jim Crow.[2]

Although George B. Tindall had in part anticipated Woodward's arguments in his book about South Carolina Negroes, it is "the Woodward Thesis" over which historians have chosen sides. Charles E. Wynes, Frenise A. Logan, and Henry C. Dethloff and Robert P. Jones have explicitly declared their support for Woodward, even though much of their evidence points in the opposite direction; the same is true of John W. Blassingame's and Dale A. Somers' more recent implicit endorsements. On the other hand, in his study of South Carolina blacks, Joel Williamson, unlike Woodward, emphasized customs rather than laws and saw segregation so entrenched in South Carolina by the end of Reconstruction that he referred to the early appearance of a "duo-chromatic order." Vernon Lane Wharton's earlier account of Mississippi reached a similar conclusion for that state and has been used to support the arguments of Woodward's critics. Richard C. Wade's work on slavery in antebellum Southern cities, Roger A. Fischer's studies of antebellum and postbellum New Orleans, and Ira Berlin's treatment of antebellum free Negroes also call into question Woodward's conclusions.[3]

The debate has been fruitful, shedding needed light on race relations in the postbellum South. But the emphasis on the alternatives of segregation or integration has obscured the obvious "forgotten alternative" which was not integration, but exclusion. The issue, therefore, should not be merely when segregation first appeared, but what it replaced.

For in the beginning—which is to say before the Civil War—blacks were excluded from the franchise, militia companies, schools, and most hospitals, asylums, and places of public accommodation. The first postwar governments during Presidential Reconstruction generally sought to continue the antebellum policy of exclusion. Nevertheless, by 1890, before the resort to widespread *de jure* segregation, *de facto* segregation had replaced exclusion as the norm in Southern race relations. In the process the stage of integration had been largely skipped. This shift from exclusion to segregation occurred thanks to the efforts of white Republicans, who initiated it; blacks, who supported and at times requested it; and Redeemers, who accepted and expanded the new policy once they came to power.

If segregation is viewed as an improvement for blacks, then the Republicans are seen in a new perspective. The older school of Reconstruction history, heavily influenced by W. A. Dunning and his students, saw the Republicans as trying to "Africanize" the South.[4] Subsequent national and state studies by revisionists stressed the accomplishments of the Reconstruction regimes and emphasized the positive qualities of white Republicans.[5] Recently, however, the Republicans have come under attack again, but this time because they did too little to help the blacks. Scholars such as Forrest G. Wood and Lawrence J. Friedman argue that the Republicans shared the racist attitudes of the Redeemers, especially in their support of segregation.[6] Yet the differences between most Republicans and Democrats were real and of great importance.

Republicans were clearly more committed than Democrats to Negro suffrage and officeholding. And while it is true that the Republicans, either because of prejudice, political considerations, or constitutional principles, did not insist on integration, they did challenge the old policy of exclusion. That they sought to replace it with separate but equal treatment is less a condemnation of their own narrow visions than of their times and of the staunch opposition they faced. Certainly the blacks who supported the shift from exclusion to segregation recognized the difference between the two parties.

Any definitive explanation of why white Republicans accepted a primarily segregated society in the South must await further study. It does seem, however, that some so-called carpetbaggers came South with hopes of achieving an integrated society and continued to work for it; a much larger number, though, came with that goal but finding the task too difficult, settled for the more attainable goal of separate but equal treatment for blacks; still others evidently arrived already committed to the latter policy. On the other hand, there is no question that native white Southern Republicans were less wedded to the concept of equal rights. From the beginning they, like most white Democrats, were at best interested in replacing exclusion with segregation and were more than willing to minimize the impact of black voters and officeholders. As other scholars have suggested, the so-called scalawags were the weakest link in the fragile Southern Republican coalition.[7]

But why was there an increase in *de jure* segregation after 1890? This question does not concern Professor Woodward's critics who are content merely to document the existence of widespread *de facto* segregation prior to 1890. Professor Woodward asks why after a period of racial flexibility did white Southerners decide to segregate the races rigidly in the final decade of the nineteenth century. His answer is that there was an erosion of Northern opposition to such action, a weakening of white conservative determination to ensure fair treatment of blacks, and an end of hopes by white radicals for a biracial coalition. Given the extent of *de facto* segregation, however, a better question might be, why after 1890 did Southern whites find it increasingly necessary to substitute a *de jure* system? For as Gilbert Thomas Stephenson pointed out for train travel, "the Jim Crow laws . . . coming later did scarcely more than to legalize an existing and widespread system."[8]

In approaching the subject in this manner, one acknowledges that for many years prior to 1890 racial separation by custom did exist, despite the fact that blacks were enfranchised; and this undermines Woodward's contention that proscription, segregation, and disfranchisement were post-1890 developments inextricably linked together. Furthermore, because white conservatives and their Populist opponents had embraced segregation long before 1890, their "capitulation to racism" can be overstated. One is therefore left with the conclusion that the withdrawal of Northern opposition was mainly responsible for the passage of Jim Crow statutes.

While essentially correct, such a view treats Southern blacks as objects rather than as subjects of history. Black attitudes were perhaps as important as anything else in explaining the timing of the decision to legalize what previously had been left to custom. In other words, black resistance might have prompted the final step in the longstanding effort of whites to control the region's black population. Proof for such a hypothesis, of course, goes beyond the scope of this study, but the years prior to 1890 contain some suggestive evidence.

By 1890 a new generation had emerged, especially in the cities. Like youth in general, they tended to be impatient; born in freedom they had no fond memories of slavery or attachments to the past as did some of their older relatives. Following the path suggested by whites, many of them attained a high degree of education, led moral lives, and were regular churchgoers. Nonetheless, despite their behavior and achievements, they were subjected to the same indignities as their less successful black brothers.

Beginning in the 1870s, the apparent dissimilarity between generations of blacks increased white concern over the maintenance of social control. Soon after passage of the 1875 Civil Rights Act, the *Richmond Dispatch* reported the attempt of James Ellis, a mulatto waiter, to gain access to the parquet of the Richmond Theatre. The test of the law ended unsuccessfully as Ellis returned to the Negro gallery after the audience physically threatened him. The significance of the action was not lost on the reporter, who noted that Ellis was the son of Caesar Ellis, "who has been for thirty or thirty-five years a trusted servant of the *Whig* [a local newspaper] and greatly respected in this community."[9] The refusal of members of the new generation to abide by the old standards of behavior was also evident in the exclusion of a Clark University student in 1890 for what the white president considered improper conduct. The student, A. L. Smith, had supported an extremely critical obituary of Jefferson Davis, written by the editor of the school newspaper. Soon after the obituary appeared, Smith defied the president's attempt to censor a speech in which he stated that all whites stood together, were opposed to blacks, and had "their heels on black necks." In covering the story, the *Atlanta Constitution* strongly endorsed the policy of weeding out radical students.[10]

Young Nashville Negroes most visibly challenged the inequities caused by racial prejudice and *de facto* segregation. In 1888, for example, college students were discussing such controversial topics as "The Riot at Wakalak, Mississippi" in which whites killed several Negroes and "The Unsolved Problem," which also referred to the sensitive issue of race relations. "Our ladies are dragged about by the roughs and plugs on the Dummy Lines and our most cultured gentlemen are assigned special places in the car, like hogs," complained the *Nashville Tribune*, edited by Fisk University graduates. Despite such treatment, continued the article, "we charter cars and take our picnics on them. This is cur-like; licking the hand that smites us. . . . We must first respect ourselves if we [w]ould have people respect us."[11]

Similar prodding came often from the Fisk University newspaper, whose editors included W. E. B. Du Bois. The *Fisk Herald* also drew attention to the generational differences among both blacks and whites. One article in 1889 accounted for the wave of riots and disturbances directed against blacks by pointing both to the "younger whites who are even more hostile and bitter than the older ones" and to "the younger Negroes [who] are ignorant of the so-called instinctive fear of their fathers . . . [are] prone to brood in bitterness and suppressed rage over their wrongs, [and] are more sensitive to injustice and quick to resent." Earlier the newspaper had carried a lead article entitled "Who Are We?" "We are not the Negro from whom the chains of slavery fell a quarter of a century ago, most assuredly not," nor the Negroes "who imperfectly exercised the right of suffrage during the 'Period of Reconstruction.'" In explaining who they were, the author spoke for a special class born after slavery, subscribers to the ideal of democracy and self-help, men who had followed established rules for success.

> Many of our men—and these are they who are the objects of apprehension—have spent years in such institutions as Fisk University, whose atmosphere is permeated with ideas of religion, morality and liberty, who have imbibed these principles and are today instilling them into other minds. It can be truly said that we who have learned what the privileges and responsibilities of citizenship are, have no desire to see the South ruled simply by majorities. At the same time it need not be expected that we will contend for anything less than our actual desserts in the functions of government. If we cannot perform these functions as well as the average Southerner then the great educational forces now operating in our midst are here to no purpose.

This last sentence summarized the frustration and anger of the new generation. And to those older blacks who counseled patience and gradual improvement, these persons responded, "we are now qualified, and being the equal of whites, should be treated as such."[12]

Some made known their displeasure through actions as well as words. In 1889 a group of well-dressed, quiet, young black women tried to gain access to the white car of a Nashville dummy line. When asked whether blacks often demanded equal rights of this kind, a white pas-

senger responded, "Oh, no, as a rule the negroes are right obedient.
. . . They know they have to be."[13] After a young Negro clergyman,
W. A. Sinclair, had unsuccessfully sought entrance to a first-class railroad car for a female friend in 1881, he wrote to the *Daily American*
asking that the editor explain this discrimination. Referring to people
of his class, he said:

> They are peaceable, industrious, civil; they are amassing property,
> and many are educated, refined and cultivated; their strides in the
> march of progress are so rapid and wonderful as to call forth the high-
> est encoimums [sic] from the best men of the South. How is it that
> they are thus outraged, and denied privileges paid for and the more
> favored element of the community sits in silence with eyes, ears and
> mouths closed?[14]

Sinclair failed to realize that for most whites the distinctions among
Negroes were unimportant. The only difference that mattered was between blacks and whites. And because people like Sinclair would not
recognize *de facto* segregation, doubt remained as to the possibility of
keeping Negroes fully "in their place" without resort to additional laws.

At the same time, white Southerners had to contend with other forms
of black assertiveness including their insistence on voting independently, protesting unequal justice, and calling for control over their own
education. But most threatening was an increasing tendency among
lower-class blacks to use physical means in resisting local white policemen. August Meier and Elliott Rudwick have chronicled the tendency
toward retaliatory violence by blacks against police in the early twentieth century.[15] While lacking the intellectual defense given it after the
turn of the century, the pattern of such violence already existed in the
postbellum years.

From almost the moment of emancipation, blacks in cities across the
South had had their clashes with the police, particularly over the arrests of other blacks.[16] With the growth of segregated neighborhoods,
the likelihood of such incidents increased since the white policemen
now faced the possibility of being surrounded by large groups of
blacks. According to newspaper accounts, Atlanta was the city most
troubled by warfare between Negroes and the police. Although an attempt by a group of blacks to rescue a prisoner from two policemen in
1868 resulted in a riot which left a policeman injured, a Negro killed,
and two others wounded, such incidents were not common in Atlanta
until the 1880s.[17] Three years of this decade in particular witnessed

enough conflicts to lead the *Atlanta Constitution* to fear for the security of the city.

In 1881 a Negro allegedly pushed a white woman off the sidewalk in an effort to get into the memorial exercises for President James Garfield. When he resisted arrest, he was clubbed. A crowd of his friends gathered and prepared to free him. More police were called. Since "there was a general resistance . . . several bloody heads were the result." Two hundred blacks followed the officers to the station where another fight ensued. Soon after the crowd had dispersed, it attempted to free a second Negro who also had been arrested. The *Constitution* took the occasion to issue a stern reprimand, although it did not blame all blacks for the incident. "The negroes participating in the difficulty were of that class which frequent every southern town. . . . The affair is as much regretted by the better class of colored people as by the whites."[18] The newspaper was especially sensitive to the outbreak because two months earlier a large group of Negroes had stoned a policeman, and two of the blacks had resisted arrest with drawn guns. Nor could the paper be cheered up by the advice given to local blacks by a Negro newspaper. After cataloging a list of grievances against the police, the editor of the Atlanta *Weekly Defiance* asked, "Are we going to be murdered like dogs right here in this community and not open our mouths?" The choice was either to leave Atlanta or else "something must be done and that soon."[19]

In August 1883 a mob of blacks rescued a young boy from the police, who were taking him to the station house. The chief of police made it clear that this was not an isolated incident. "This thing is becoming too common. Almost every day something of the kind occurs. The negroes, whenever an arrest is made in an 'out of the way' part of the city, try every way to obstruct the officers. They even follow the officers all the way to the station house abusing them." A week later a black man accused of raping an elderly Negro woman was freed by his friends from the custody of a white man who had captured him. A *Constitution* editorial urged a tougher policy on the part of the police and contrasted the behavior of the white and Negro communities, this time not being careful to differentiate among blacks.

> When a white criminal is pursued and arrested, we never hear of the white people surrounding the officers of the law and attempting a rescue. But the conditions are all changed when the criminal is a negro. The moment that a negro steals, or robs, or commits some other crime,

his person seems to become sacred in the eyes of his race, and he is
harbored, protected and deified. If he is captured, resists an officer
and is shot, as he should be, and as a white criminal would be, immediately the leading negroes drum up a mass meeting and proceed
to pass a string of senseless but sympathetic resolutions, after a series
of harangues that would be a discredit to the Zulus.[20]

Judging from the coverage in the *Constitution,* relations between
police and blacks improved somewhat during the next few years. By
the summer and fall of 1888, however, confrontations once again became common. After reporting several incidents that had almost resulted in riots on the Fourth of July, the *Constitution* noted that "the
negroes had an idea that they owned the town yesterday and went just
as far as they dared in their efforts to release almost every negro who
was arrested." At the end of the month another disturbance occurred
when an escaped Negro was arrested on Decatur Street near Ivy, close
to the notorious Willingham Building, the capital of Atlanta's demi-
world. The police were forced to take refuge from a large mob in the
office of a coal yard. The crowd was finally dispersed through the arrest
of two of its leaders and the appeals of Alonzo W. Burnett, the editor
of the *Weekly Defiance* and an unsuccessful aspirant for a position on
the police force. A week later a Negro cut a white man's face with a
saber during an Odd Fellows procession. A policeman standing nearby
served him with a warrant but did not make an arrest since according
to the *Constitution,* "it might have provoked a riot, as the negro that
did the cutting was inclined to be boisterous and his colored brothers
were rather decided in their expressions of sympathy."[21]

This was not an isolated example of the effective use of intimidation
by blacks against white policemen. In October a mob in Summer Hill
freed a Negro arrested for drunkenness. Alonzo Burnett again calmed
the crowd but was prevented from calling a patrol wagon. The police
were thus isolated and a compromise was reached when the brother of
the prisoner said he would get him sober and produce him in court the
following morning. By the next day, there had been no arrest, and no
one could find either the prisoner or his brother. Alleged members of
the mob were later brought to trial but were freed for lack of evidence.[22] By 1895 the problem of Negro resistance to arrest was so serious that it was a subject brought up in interviewing prospective policemen. An exchange reported in the *Atlanta Constitution* suggests not
only the concern of the police over this matter, but the extent to which

Negro intimidation had been successful. One of the police commissioners asked an Irish applicant, "What would you do in case you tried to arrest a couple of niggers on Decatur street and they started to fight you?" The Irishman replied: "What wud you do and what wud any sensible man do? Blow your gong and run like the virry divil!"[23]

Given white fears generated by black resistance in word and deed at the end of the 1880s, it is not surprising that Southerners were quick to seize the opportunity presented by the North's defection from the fight for equal rights. It was the opening they had been looking for since the Civil War and such limited flexibility in race relations as there had been would now be eliminated. It might very well have been that in the minds of whites, black assertiveness had left them no choice.

Notes

PREFACE

1. Bureau of the Census, *Negro Population 1790–1915* (Washington, D.C., 1918), pp. 33, 90–92.
2. For a convenient introduction to the controversy, see Joel Williamson (ed.), *The Origins of Segregation* (Lexington, Mass., 1968).
3. Vernon Lane Wharton, *The Negro in Mississippi 1865–1890* (Chapel Hill, 1947).
4. Carl Bridenbaugh, *Cities in the Wilderness: Urban Life in America 1625–1742* (New York, 1938); Richard C. Wade, *The Urban Frontier: Pioneer Life in Early Pittsburgh, Cincinnati, Lexington, Louisville, and St. Louis* (Chicago, 1964); Kenneth W. Wheeler, *To Wear a City's Crown: The Beginnings of Urban Growth in Texas, 1836–1865* (Cambridge, Mass., 1968). A notable exception is Richard C. Wade, *Slavery in the Cities: The South 1820–1860* (New York, 1964).
5. See, for example, John W. Blassingame, *Black New Orleans 1860–1880* (Chicago, 1973); Robert E. Perdue, *The Negro in Savannah 1865–1900* (New York, 1973); Joel Williamson, *After Slavery: The Negro in South Carolina During Reconstruction, 1861–1877* (Chapel Hill, 1965); George Brown Tindall, *South Carolina Negroes 1877–1900* (Columbia, 1952). The only previous multicity examination of race relations during the period is Zane L. Miller, "Urban Blacks in the South, 1865–1920: An Analysis of Some Quantitative Data on Richmond, Savannah, New Orleans, Louisville, and Birmingham," in *The New Urban History: Quantitative Explorations by American Historians*, ed. Leo F. Schnore (Princeton, 1975), pp. 184–204. Despite its title, Miller's essay focuses on the post-1890 period.

1. THE URBAN SOUTH

1. Computed from U.S. censuses 1860 and 1890 and T. Lynn Smith, "The Emergence of Cities," in *The Urban South*, eds. Rupert B. Vance and Nicholas J. Demerath (Chapel Hill, 1954), p. 33.

2. This overview of postbellum urbanization is documented in Howard N. Rabinowitz, "Continuity and Change: Southern Urban Development 1860–1900," in *The City in Southern History: The Development of Urban Civilization in the South,* eds. Blaine A. Brownell and David R. Goldfield (New York, 1977), pp. 92–122, 204–209.

3. Bureau of the Census, *Report on the Social Statistics of Cities. Part II. The Southern and the Western States* (Washington, D.C., 1887), 157–58.

4. Sidney Andrews, *The South Since the War: As Shown by Fourteen Weeks of Travel and Observation in Georgia and the Carolinas* (Boston, 1866), p. 339.

5. *Ibid.,* p. 340.

6. Milledgeville *Federal Union,* February 12, 1867, quoted in Franklin M. Garrett, *Atlanta and Environs: A Chronicle of Its People and Events* (3 vols.; New York, 1954), I, 768; Andrews, *South Since the War,* p. 340; Edward King, *The Southern States of North America* (London, 1875), p. 350.

7. Andrews, *South Since the War,* p. 341; John Stainback Wilson, *Atlanta As It Is* (New York, 1871), p. 5; George Augustus Sala, *America Revisited: From the Bay of New York to the Gulf of Mexico and From Lake Michigan to the Pacific* (5th ed.; London, 1885), p. 264.

8. John Richard Dennett, *The South As It Is: 1865–1866,* edited with an introduction by Henry M. Christman (reprinted; New York, 1967), pp. 267–68; Adelaide L. Fries (ed.), "The Elizabeth Sterchi Letters," *Atlanta Historical Bulletin,* V (July 1940), 200; Sir George Campbell, *White and Black: The Outcome of A Visit to the United States* (London, 1879), p. 369.

9. Robert Somers, *The Southern States Since the War 1870–1871,* Introduction and Index by Malcolm C. McMillan (reprinted; Tuscaloosa, Ala., 1965), p. 93; King, *Southern States of North America,* p. 350; *Atlanta Constitution,* March 25, 1889.

10. Bureau of the Census, *Ninth Census: Population* (Washington, D.C., 1872), I, 102; Bureau of the Census, *Eleventh Census: Population* (Washington, D.C., 1893), I, Part I, 527.

11. G. Mildred Thompson, *Reconstruction in Georgia: Economic, Social, Political, 1865–1872* (reprinted; Gloucester, Mass., 1964) is the standard Dunningite treatment of the period. An able revisionist study is Alan Conway, *The Reconstruction of Georgia* (Minneapolis, 1966).

12. John W. Reps, *Town Planning in Frontier America* (Princeton, 1965), pp. 222–23; Elizabeth D. Reid (ed.), *From Raleigh's Past* (Raleigh, 1965), pp. 1–6.

13. Richard Yates, "Governor Vance and the End of the War in North Carolina," *North Carolina Historical Review,* XVIII (October 1941), 328–31 contains a good account of the negotiations and the aftermath of the surrender in the city; Dennett, *South As It Is,* p. 148.

14. Campbell, *White and Black,* p. 304; Raleigh *Daily Constitution,* July 9, 1875, quoted in Sarah McCulloh Lemmon, "Raleigh—An Example of the New South?" *North Carolina Historical Review,* XLIII (July 1966), 265; Raleigh *State Chronicle,* February 2, 1888; April 17, 1890, quoted *ibid.,* pp. 266, 273.

15. For a general survey, see Lemmon's study, which is marred, however, by the author's unanalytical approach to the concept of the New South and by her failure to consider the status of Raleigh Negroes.

16. Bureau of the Census, *Census, 1870,* I, 225; Bureau of the Census, *Census, 1890,* I, Part I, 546.

17. North Carolina also underwent a relatively long period of Radical influence. Although the Democrats recaptured control of the state legislature in 1870,

they did not gain a two-thirds majority until 1874, and there was a Republican governor until 1876. The standard work by another Dunning student is J. G. de Roulhac Hamilton, *Reconstruction in North Carolina* (reprinted; Gloucester, Mass., 1964).

18. Bureau of the Census, *Social Statistics of Cities*, Part II, 199–200; H. G. Mc-Call (comp.), *A Sketch, Historical and Statistical of the City of Montgomery* (Montgomery, 1885), pp. 6, 10.

19. (W. Corson), *Two Months in the Confederate States Including A Visit to New Orleans Under the Domination of General Butler* (London, 1863), pp. 118–19.

20. Dennett, *South As It Is*, p. 293; Henry Deedes, *Sketches of the South and West: or Ten Months Residence in the United States* (London, 1869), pp. 142–43.

21. Whitelaw Reid, *After the War: A Tour of the Southern States 1865–1866*, edited with an introduction by C. Vann Woodward (reprinted; New York, 1965), pp. 374–75; Somers, *Southern States*, p. 173.

22. McCall, *Sketch of Montgomery*, pp. 40, 51–60; Bureau of the Census, *Social Statistics of Cities*, Part II, 200; Bureau of the Census, *Census, 1870*, I, 81; Bureau of the Census, *Census, 1890*, I, Part I, 524.

23. Testimony of Judge William Smith, in U.S. Congress, 39th Cong., 1st Sess., *Report of the Joint Committee on Reconstruction* (Washington, D.C., 1866), Part III, 11; testimony of General A. L. Chetlain, *ibid.*, 149.

24. The standard account, by another Dunning student, is W. L. Fleming, *Civil War and Reconstruction in Alabama* (reprinted; Gloucester, Mass., 1949).

25. For background on the founding and early development of Richmond, see Bureau of the Census, *Social Statistics of Cities*, Part II, 79–80.

26. Emory M. Thomas, *The Confederate State of Richmond: A Biography of the Capital* (Austin, 1971), *passim*.

27. Reid, *After the War*, p. 355; David Thomas, *My American Tour: Being Notes Taken During A Tour Through the United States Shortly After the Close of the Late American War* (Bury, 1868), p. 197; Captain George W. Pepper, *Personal Recollections of Sherman's Campaigns in Georgia and the Carolinas* (Zanesville, Ohio, 1866), pp. 449–50.

28. Bureau of the Census, *Social Statistics of Cities*, Part II, 80–81.

29. Richmond, *Report of the Geodetic and Topographic Survey of Richmond, Virginia* (Richmond, 1923), p. 5; Bureau of the Census, *Census, 1870*, I, 280; Bureau of the Census, *Census, 1890*, I, Part I, 557.

30. The Republicans experienced even greater difficulties at the state level. By the time Virginia was readmitted to the Union in 1870, it already had been redeemed. The standard account is Hamilton James Eckenrode, *The Political History of Virginia During the Reconstruction* ("Johns Hopkins University Studies in Historical and Political Science," Vol. XXII, Nos. 6–8; Baltimore, 1904). But see also Jack P. Maddex, Jr., *The Virginia Conservatives 1867–1879: A Study in Reconstruction Politics* (Chapel Hill, 1970).

31. For the founding and early history of the city, see the brief sketch by Anson Nelson, a prominent local businessman, in Bureau of the Census, *Social Statistics of Cities*, Part II, 151–53. See also John Wooldridge (ed.), *History of Nashville, Tennessee* (Nashville, 1890); W. W. Clayton, *History of Davidson County,'Tennessee* (Philadelphia, 1880).

32. J. C. Guild, *Old Times in Tennessee* (Nashville, 1878), pp. 495–96.

33. James B. Craighead to George Rainsford Fairbanks, July 25, 1865, George Rainsford Fairbanks Mss., Southern Historical Collection, University of North

NOTES TO PAGES 16–21

Carolina Library, Chapel Hill. These are copies of the original papers which are located at the University of the South, Sewanee, Tennessee.

34. *Nashville Banner*, March 25, 1881; Alexander K. McClure, *The South: Its Industrial, Financial, and Political Condition* (Philadelphia, 1886), p. 136; Noble L. Prentis, *Southern Letters* (Topeka, 1881), p. 36.

35. Bureau of the Census, *Census, 1870*, I, 262; Bureau of the Census, *Census, 1890*, I, Part I, 555; on annexations, see Bureau of the Census, *Social Statistics of Cities*, Part II, 153; *Nashville Banner*, March 11, 1890.

36. King, *Southern States of North America*, pp. 727–28; Bureau of the Census, *Social Statistics of Cities*, Part II, 153; Prentis, *Southern Letters*, pp. 44–45.

37. Nashville *Republican Banner*, June 5, 1873; letter of "A.F." to a friend in Ohio, reprinted in *Nashville Banner*, July 10, 1890. See also Nashville *Republican Banner*, June 7, 1873.

38. This was true for the state as well. See Thomas B. Alexander, *Political Reconstruction in Tennessee* (Nashville, 1950).

2.   BLACK MIGRANTS AND WHITE CITIES

1. Richard C. Wade, *Slavery in the Cities: The South 1820–1860* (New York, 1964), p. 243 and *passim*.

2. Bureau of the Census, *Negro Population 1790–1915* (Washington, D.C., 1918), pp. 26–27. The undercounting of blacks limits the reliability of both the city directories and the censuses. Both sources tended to miss large numbers of poor people, especially poor blacks. Part of the reason was black suspicion of the information gatherers. According to an Atlanta resident, "there is one thing with which directory men and census men have to contend here in the South and that is the antipathy of the negro to being put on any list. In the mind of the average negro, the question of taxation looms up most prominently. Now, I have eight negroes in my employ. To my certain knowledge not more than one or two of them have been taken in the census; and you can't get them to send in their names, . . . they . . . believe that this means to get on the tax lists" (*Atlanta Constitution*, June 20, 1890).

3. *Nashville Dispatch*, August 16, 1865; V. T. Barnwell (comp.), *Barnwell's Atlanta City Directory and Stranger's Guide* (Atlanta, 1867), p. 16; W. R. Handleiter (comp.), *Handleiter's Atlanta City Directory* (Atlanta, 1870), p. viii.

4. *Montgomery Daily Ledger*, October 25, 1865; letter to the editor, Mobile *Nationalist*, February 15, 1866; Myrta Lockett Avary, *Dixie After the War. An Exposition of Social Conditions Existing in the South During the Twelve Years Succeeding the Fall of Richmond* (New York, 1906), p. 190; *Richmond Dispatch*, March 15, 1866.

5. Richmond *Times*, June 14, 19, 1865, quoted in Alrutheus Ambush Taylor, *The Negro in the Reconstruction of Virginia* (Washington, D.C., 1926), pp. 105–106.

6. Circular reprinted in *Montgomery Daily Advertiser*, September 9, 1865.

7. Nashville, Minutes of the Nashville Board of Aldermen, June 23, 1863, Office of the Metropolitan Clerk, Davidson County Building and Nashville City Hall, Nashville; J. W. Clark to his brother, January 31, 1864, John R. Peacock Col-

lection, Southern Historical Collection, University of North Carolina Library, Chapel Hill.

8. Copy of the report in *Nashville Daily Press and Times*, October 18, 1865. See also *Nashville Dispatch*, August 16, 1865, for support of Fisk's policy.

9. *Nashville Daily Press and Times*, January 19, 1866.

10. Circular of O. O. Howard to Assistant Commissioners of the Freedmen's Bureau, February 1866, reprinted in *Richmond Dispatch*, February 26, 1866. For the action of the military in Atlanta, see Atlanta, Minutes of the Atlanta City Council, October 4, 1865, Office of the City Clerk, Atlanta City Hall. See also *Daily Atlanta Intelligencer*, August 27, 1865.

11. C. B. Berry, *The Other Side: How It Struck Us* (New York, 1880), pp. 90–91; George Rose, *The Great Country; Or, Impressions of America* (London, 1868), p. 153. For the reaction of Richmond authorities, see Richmond, Minutes of the Richmond City Council, May 14, 1866, Archives Division of the Virginia State Library, Richmond (for years after 1866 the minutes are located in the Office of the City Clerk, Richmond City Hall). See also *Richmond Dispatch*, August 16, 1866.

12. Raleigh *Weekly Progress*, September 26, 1867.

13. Testimony of Henry M. Turner, in U.S. Congress, 42nd Cong., 2nd Sess., *Testimony Taken by the Joint Select Committee to Inquire Into the Condition of Affairs in the Late Insurrectionary States* (Washington, D.C., 1872), VII, 1040 (hereafter cited as *KKK Hearings*). For instances of Alabama Negroes who fled to Montgomery for protection, see the testimonies of James H. Alston, *ibid.*, IX, 1016–22; Henry Giles, *ibid.*, 1009–16; Smith Watley, *ibid.*, 1004–1009. Among those Georgia Negroes who testified that they came to Atlanta for the same reason were Daniel Lane, *ibid.*, VII, 653–55; Warner Davis, *ibid.*, 727–30; Alexander Hinton, *ibid.*, 684–87; Warren Jones, *ibid.*, 689–92; Hannah Flournoy, *ibid.*, 532–35. For a white man's view of Negroes leaving Warren County for Atlanta because of "disturbances," see the testimony of John C. Norris, *ibid.*, VI, 207. George Burnett, a white resident of Atlanta, had a similar view, but a dissent can be found in the testimony of William Burnet of nearby Decatur (*ibid.*, 69; *ibid.*, VII, 998–99). Two white residents of Montgomery, however, emphasized the security of blacks in their city as compared to the situation in the rural areas of the state. See the testimonies of Samuel F. Rice, *ibid.*, VIII, 493 and Willard Warner, *ibid.*, 31. Blacks continued to find better treatment in cities. See, for example, testimony of Benjamin Singleton, in U.S. Senate, 46th Cong., 2nd Sess., *Report and Testimony of the Select Committee of the United States Senate to Investigate the Causes for the Removal of the Negroes from the Southern States to the Northern States* (Washington, D.C., 1880), Part III, 385.

14. Testimony of Henry M. Turner, in *KKK Hearings*, VII, 1040.

15. Testimony of Charles Wallace Howard, *ibid.*, 837; testimony of William Burnet, *ibid.*, 998.

16. *Nashville Union and American*, November 27, 1870; Sarah G. Follansbee, "Journal," Alabama Department of Archives and History, Montgomery; *Nashville Daily Press and Times*, January 29, April 28, 1866. For the mustering out of the 100th U.S. Colored Infantry, see *ibid.*, January 4, 1866.

17. J. G. McKee to the Reverend Dr. J. B. Clark, January 15, 1866, American Missionary Association Archives, Amistad Research Center, Dillard University, New Orleans; *Athens Banner Watchman* editorial reprinted in *Atlanta Con-*

stitution, January 24, 1887. The reasons given by Ray Stannard Baker for the cityward migration of Southern blacks during the first decade of the twentieth century were thus true for the pre-1890 period as well. He discovered that the two main causes were "the lack of schooling in the country" and "the lack of protection." See Ray Stannard Baker, *Following the Color Line* (reprinted; New York, 1964), p. 101.

18. According to the *Memphis Argus,* for example, "Saturday night, Sunday and Sunday night were periods of unusual lawlessness among the negro population. Fighting, shooting and drunkenness were the general order" (September 26, 1865).

19. J. W. A. Sanford to his son, December 19, 1889, John William Augustine Sanford Papers, Alabama Department of Archives and History. See also *Atlanta Constitution,* December 21, 1871.

20. *Atlanta Constitution,* July 5, 1878. William Nixon, a Negro servant whose obituary was carried in the *Nashville Banner,* October 13, 1888, was one of the many blacks who migrated by way of an excursion. He had come to town from Shelbyville to see the state fair and had decided to stay.

21. *Daily Atlanta Intelligencer,* February 7, 1867.

22. W. H. Crogman, "The Negro Problem," a speech delivered at Chautauqua, New York, August 1885, reprinted in the author's *Talks for the Times* (Atlanta, 1896), pp. 252–53. There is another source of additional black population which merits mention. Nashville, Richmond, and Raleigh were the sites of state penitentiaries and large numbers of convicts remained in these cities after they were released. See, for example, letter of "Citizen" to the editor, Nashville *Daily American,* December 22, 1876, which attributes much of the city's crime to the fact that "a large proportion of the population are ex-convicts."

23. *Montgomery Daily Ledger,* September 23, 1865; *Atlanta Constitution,* February 14, 1871; Nashville *Republican Banner,* February 19, 1873; August 20, 1875. See also *Montgomery Daily Ledger,* September 4, 1865; *Atlanta Constitution,* May 13, 1876; *Montgomery Daily Advertiser,* July 21, 1865; November 17, 1880; *Nashville Dispatch,* August 12, 1865; *Nashville Daily Press and Times,* November 28, 1865; *Nashville Union and American,* October 21, 1869.

24. *Atlanta Constitution,* January 24, 1884; Raleigh *Daily Sentinel,* April 24, 1866.

25. Guion Griffis Johnson, "Southern Paternalism toward Negroes after Emancipation," *Journal of Southern History,* XXIII (November 1957), 483–509; *Atlanta Constitution,* February 2, 1881; *Nashville Banner,* September 22, 1883; May 2, 1887; Richmond, *Amended Charter and Ordinances* (1871), p. 14; *Richmond Dispatch,* November 9, 1883. *Richmond Dispatch,* May 26, 1883, had already observed that a Negro was "nothing but a grown child unable to take care of himself." See also *Montgomery Daily Advertiser,* May 7, 1868.

26. See Howard N. Rabinowitz, "The Search for Social Control: Race Relations in the Urban South, 1865–1890" (2 vols.; unpublished Ph.D. dissertation, University of Chicago, 1973), I, 57–82.

27. *Montgomery Daily Ledger,* September 2, October 25, 1865; Avary, *Dixie After the War,* p. 194; *Daily Atlanta Intelligencer,* July 7, 1866.

28. Testimony of Charles Wallace Howard, in *KKK Hearings,* VII, 833, 835; F. Barham Zincke, *Last Winter in the United States: Being Table Talk Collected During a Tour Through the Late Southern Confederation, the Far West, the Rocky Mountains, etc.* (London, 1868), p. 72; *Savannah Tribune,* August 17, 1889.

29. *Nashville Banner,* April 8, October 31, 1881.

30. *Montgomery Daily Ledger*, September 21, 1865; *Richmond Dispatch*, February 23, 1866; *Nashville Banner*, January 1, 1889. For an extended discussion of the alleged advantages of slavery over freedom, see *Nashville Dispatch*, July 29, 1865.

31. Baker, *Following the Color Line*, p. 44; *Atlanta Constitution*, October 22, 1878.

32. *Ibid.*, December 16, 1884; September 27, 1879. For a similar treatment accorded a deceased Richmond black "who has under all circumstances preserved the kindly relations which existed between white and colored people of Virginia in the olden time," see *Richmond Dispatch*, June 8, 1870.

33. *Atlanta Constitution*, March 7, 1880. The *Richmond Dispatch*, July 26, 1866, joyously noted that despite the influence of the Freedmen's Bureau, prominent whites leaving the city for nearby watering places were accompanied by "clean-looking negro servants, who follow their masters or mistresses with . . . as much respect as ever."

34. *Atlanta Constitution*, March 14, 1890. It was a common view that rural Negroes were better workers. According to the *Montgomery Daily Advertiser*, June 18, 1867, "away from the towns, where political agitators do not drive the idea of work out of their heads, the freedmen are working unusually well, and our exchanges speak uniformly of the kind feeling existing between employees and employers." See also *Richmond Dispatch*, December 27, 1865.

35. See, for example, *Atlanta Constitution*, April 24, December 8, 1878. Uncle Remus tells his first story about Brer Rabbit in the July 20, 1879, issue, but it is told to a young white boy on the back porch of an Atlanta home, not in the countryside. Harris continued to write about Remus's experiences in the city until the appearance of "Brer Rabbit, Brer Fox, and the Tar Baby" in the November 16, 1879, issue. From then on there is no mention of the urban environment. For the Jubilee Singers, see Nashville *Daily American*, August 6, 1888.

3. JUSTICE

1. Ira Berlin, *Slaves Without Masters: The Free Negro in the Antebellum South* (New York, 1974), *passim*.

2. Nashville, *A Digest of the General Laws of the Corporation of Nashville* (1865), p. 81; Richmond, Minutes of the Richmond City Council, October 25, 1865, Archives Division of the Virginia State Library, Richmond (for years after 1866 the minutes are located in the Office of the City Clerk, Richmond City Hall); Atlanta, Minutes of the Atlanta City Council, July 14, 1865, Office of the City Clerk, Atlanta City Hall.

3. Atlanta City Council Minutes, January 5, 1866.

4. Testimony of Colonel Eliphalet Whittlesey, in U.S. Congress, 39th Cong., 1st Sess., *Report of the Joint Committee on Reconstruction* (Washington, D.C., 1866), Part II, 182.

5. Testimony of Colonel Orlando Brown, *ibid.*, 127.

6. Raleigh *Daily Standard*, July 18, 20, 24, 1865.

7. *Ibid.*, September 27, 1865; *Montgomery Daily Ledger*, September 2, 1865.

8. *Montgomery Daily Ledger*, September 9, 1865; Franklin M. Garrett, *Atlanta and Environs: A Chronicle of Its People and Events* (3 vols.; New York, 1954), I, 677.

9. Letter of B. L. Canedy, May 27, 1865, in *The Freedmen's Record*, I (July 1865), 116. The military also forbade Negroes from carrying weapons (*Richmond Dispatch*, December 18, 1865).

10. John Richard Dennett, *The South As It Is 1865–1866*, edited with an introduction by Henry M. Christman (reprinted; New York, 1967), p. 270. For other attacks on blacks by soldiers, see *Atlanta Constitution*, November 20, 1868; *Richmond Dispatch*, December 13, 1865; June 4, 1866. In the district which included Mobile, the commanding general of white troops ordered the enlisted men kept in camp at night unless given special permission to leave because of "repeated complaints . . . in regard to acts of violence and robbery committed by enlisted men of their commands upon negroes" (*Mobile Advertiser and Register*, January 5, 1866).

11. *Nashville Daily Press and Times*, August 24, 1865; January 18, March 13, April 10, 1866; letter of General Clinton B. Fisk, quoted in *The American Missionary*, X (February 1866), 40.

12. For laws in Virginia, Alabama, and Georgia, see Gilbert Thomas Stephenson, *Race Distinctions in American Law* (New York, 1910), pp. 239, 242, 245. An 1865 Tennessee statute permitted Negro testimony in all cases (*ibid.*, p. 244); North Carolina permitted black testimony in cases involving only whites if both parties gave their consent (North Carolina, *Public Laws* [1866], p. 102).

13. North Carolina, *Public Laws* (1866), p. 102; testimony of Nedom Angier, in U.S. Congress, 42nd Cong., 2nd Sess., *Testimony Taken by the Joint Select Committee to Inquire Into the Condition of Affairs in the Late Insurrectionary States* (Washington, D.C., 1872), VII, 1064 (hereafter cited as *KKK Hearings*).

14. North Carolina, *Public Laws* (1866), p. 102.

15. J. G. de Roulhac Hamilton, *Reconstruction in North Carolina* (reprinted; Gloucester, Mass., 1964), p. 156; North Carolina, *Ordinances Passed by the North Carolina State Convention* (1865–1866), p. 39.

16. North Carolina, *Public Laws* (1866), p. 101. Former slaves cohabiting together as husband and wife had to register their marriage before September 1, 1866 (*ibid.*, pp. 100–101). This date was extended to January 1, 1868, by the General Assembly on March 4, 1867 (*ibid.* [1866–1867], p. 93). In other states slave unions simply were sanctified as marriage by law. See Stephenson, *Race Distinctions in American Law*, pp. 69, 73–74.

17. Georgia, *Laws* (1865–1866), p. 241.

18. See, for example, Stephenson, *Race Distinctions in American Law*, p. 42; *Nashville Daily Press and Times*, April 26, 1866; Atlanta, *Code* (1866), p. 10.

19. Stephenson, *Race Distinctions in American Law*, p. 53. The North Carolina apprentice law also gave preference to former owners (North Carolina, *Public Laws* [1866], p. 100).

20. Raleigh, *Ordinances* (1867), pp. 25, 39, 51; North Carolina, *Public Laws* (1866), p. 100.

21. Richmond *Times*, June 21, 1865; Writers Program of the Works Progress Administration in the State of Virginia (comp.), *The Negro in Virginia* (New York, 1940), p. 224.

22. *Nashville Daily Press and Times*, October 6, 11, 17, 20, November 21, 1866.

23. Raleigh *Daily Sentinel*, October 18, 1875; Atlanta City Council Minutes, February 2, 1885.

24. *Nashville Union and American*, April 22, 1870; Nashville *Republican Banner*, February 12, 1871; Nashville *Daily American*, April 15, 1879; *Nashville Banner*, February 8, 1888.

25. *Atlanta Constitution*, November 4, 1877; January 9, 1888.

26. Bureau of the Census, *Eleventh Census: Population* (Washington, D.C., 1893), I, Part II, 634, 696, 718.

27. North Carolina, *Public Laws* (1876–1877), p. 227; on Lockhart, see J. H. Chataigne (comp.), *Raleigh City Directory 1875–1876* (Raleigh, 1875), p. 10; R. H. Whitaker, *Whitaker's Reminiscences: Incidents and Anecdotes* (Raleigh, 1905), p. 242.

28. *Richmond Dispatch*, January 28, 1870.

29. See, for example, *ibid.*, May 27, 1876; May 27, 1882.

30. *Nashville Union and American*, November 2, 1869; Nashville *Daily American*, August 4, 1876; *Nashville Banner*, August 6, 1888; April 1, 1889.

31. *Nashville Union and American*, December 11, 1869; January 22, August 9, 1870; Nashville *Daily American*, April 8, 1877.

32. Stephenson, *Race Distinctions in American Law*, p. 249.

33. WPA, *Negro in Virginia*, pp. 226–27.

34. C. Mildred Thompson, *Reconstruction in Georgia: Economic, Social, Political, 1865–1872* (reprinted; Gloucester, Mass., 1964), p. 177; *Montgomery Weekly Advertiser*, September 10, October 8, 1867; Order of General Edmund Canby, printed in Raleigh *Daily Standard*, September 24, 1867.

35. North Carolina, *Public Laws* (1868), p. 11; *Atlanta Constitution*, February 24, 1869; Raleigh *Daily Standard*, December 29, 1869.

36. Quoted in *Richmond Dispatch*, October 30, 1875.

37. *Nashville Union and American*, March 6, 1875; letter of "A Well Wisher" to the editor, Nashville *Daily American*, June 15, 1878. See also *Richmond Dispatch*, March 11, 25, 1880.

38. See, for example, *Richmond Dispatch*, August 27, 1870; March 11, October 4, 1875; *Atlanta Constitution*, March 11, 22, 1873; Nashville *Daily American*, April 12, 1877; May 25, 1878; September 23, 1879; *Nashville Banner*, September 18, 1882; September 8, 1885; March 21, 1890; *Montgomery Daily Advertiser*, November 4–5, 1890.

39. *Montgomery Daily Advertiser*, March 1, 1876. For the effects of the new law, see *ibid.*, February 20–21, 1877.

40. North Carolina, *Public Laws* (1876–1877), p. 228. See also for Richmond, Sir George Campbell, *White and Black: The Outcome of A Visit to the United States* (London, 1879), p. 301; for Atlanta and other Georgia cities, see testimony of John H. Christy, in *KKK Hearings*, VI, 245; *Atlanta Constitution*, December 19, 1873; Charles Nordhoff, *The Cotton States in the Spring and Summer of 1875* (New York, 1876), p. 102. Even while jury selection was in the hands of Wake County Radicals, Raleigh Negroes had suffered discrimination, but it grew worse under the Redeemers. See Wake County, Minutes of the Wake County Board of Commissioners, March 4, September 5, 1871, North Carolina Department of Archives and History, Raleigh; Raleigh *Daily Sentinel*, December 7, 1875; testimony of John O. Kelly, in U.S. Senate, 46th Cong., 2nd Sess., *Report of the Select Committee of the United States Senate to Investigate the Causes for the Removal of the Negroes from the Southern States to the Northern States* (Washington, D.C., 1880), Part I, 249–50 (hereafter cited as *Report on the Removal of Southern Negroes*); *Raleigh Register*, February 27, 1884.

41. Nashville *Republican Banner,* February 8, 1872; May 21, 1875; *Nashville Banner,* March 1, 1884; April 23, 1886.
42. *Richmond Dispatch,* March 27, April 10, 1880; January 3, 29, May 7, 1885. The final jury for the Cluverius trial contained six whites from Richmond and six from Alexandria (*ibid.,* May 12, 1885).
43. *Atlanta Constitution,* July 3, 8, 1880; August 26, 1884; March 26, 1889.
44. *Montgomery Daily Advertiser,* March 23, 1880; July 21, 1885; March 11, 18, 25, April 1, July 29, November 25, December 3, 1890; *Nashville Banner,* December 26, 1885; May 3, 1886; Raleigh *News and Observer,* September 23, December 5, 1890; Stephenson, *Race Distinctions in American Law,* p. 271.
45. Atlanta City Council Minutes, September 6, 1867; for later efforts, see *Atlanta Constitution,* April 2, 1885; March 26, 1889.
46. Montgomery, Minutes of the Montgomery City Council, August 15, 24, 1868, Alabama Department of Archives and History, Montgomery; Montgomery, *Message of the Mayor and Reports of the Various City Officers and Standing Committees of the City Council for the Term Ending April 30, 1877* (Montgomery, 1877), p. 26. Negro policemen had actually been removed by the lame-duck Republican administration as a temporary measure when the force was reduced for economic reasons. Their Redeemer successors restored the force to its original size by hiring additional whites (*Montgomery Daily Advertiser,* June 15, September 7, 1875; January 11, 1876).
47. Raleigh *Daily Sentinel,* July 25, 1868; August 21, 1875; Raleigh *Daily Standard,* July 27, 1868; L. Branson (ed.), *The North Carolina Business Directory 1872* (Raleigh, 1872), p. 219.
48. *Nashville Union and Dispatch,* October 15, 1867; *Nashville Banner,* February 15, 29, 1884. For other attempts to place Negroes on the force, see Nashville *Republican Banner,* November 29, 1873; Nashville *Daily American,* March 26, June 1, 1880. There were, however, two Negro politicians who were elected as county constables. See, for example, Nashville *Republican Banner,* July 1, 1871; August 3, 1872; Nashville *Daily American,* August 6, 1880; *Nashville Banner,* August 8, 1882.
49. Montgomery City Council Minutes, August 15, 24, 1868. Several Republicans were also among those councilmen who blocked an effort to assign one Negro and one white policeman to each beat (*Montgomery Daily Advertiser,* August 25-26, 1868).
50. Nashville *Daily American,* October 30, 1875; November 15, 1878; January 1, 1880; Helen G. Edmonds, *The Negro and Fusion Politics in North Carolina 1894-1901* (Chapel Hill, 1951), pp. 126, 130; Mobile *Nationalist,* July 4, 1867.
51. Richmond City Council Minutes, April 6, 1866; Richmond, Report of the Chief of Police, *Annual Reports of the City Departments of Richmond, Virginia, for the Year Ending January 31, 1873* (Richmond, 1873), p. 294; *ibid.,* 1876-1877, p. 11; *ibid.,* 1885, p. 10; *ibid.,* 1890, p. 12; Raleigh, *Annual Reports of the Mayor and Officers of the City of Raleigh for the Year Ending February 28, 1891* (Raleigh, 1891), p. 34; Montgomery, *Annual Reports,* 1889-1890, p. 34.
52. See, for example, Henry Deedes, *Sketches of the South and West: or Ten Months Residence in the United States* (London, 1869), pp. 143-46; *Richmond Dispatch,* August 3, 1866; *Atlanta Constitution,* January 13, 1878;

Montgomery *Alabama State Journal*, September 24, November 18, 1873; January 7, 29, 1874.

53. *Richmond Planet*, August 9, 1890; Savannah *Colored Tribune*, April 22, 1876.

54. *Atlanta Constitution*, December 9, 1873; May 25, 1877.

55. *Nashville Banner*, May 16–17, 1887; *Atlanta Constitution*, August 13, 15, 1872; *Montgomery Daily Ledger*, September 14, 1865.

56. *Nashville Banner*, July 26, 1890.

57. Testimony of James H. Clanton, in *KKK Hearings*, VIII, 242. Acts of violence were most common on Saturday nights and holidays, especially Christmas Day. See, for example, *Atlanta Constitution*, December 27, 1878; December 26, 1885. A Nashville grand jury stated clearly that the victims of crimes committed by blacks "are chiefly among our colored population" (*Nashville Banner*, November 14, 1890).

58. *Atlanta Constitution*, June 24, 1869; Tennessee, *Constitution* (1870), Art. 11; North Carolina, *Constitution* (1875), Art. 14, sec. 8; WPA, *Negro in Virginia*, p. 237.

59. *Atlanta Constitution*, May 10, 1878; Stephenson, *Race Distinctions in American Law*, pp. 273–74.

60. Nashville, *Annual Reports of the City of Nashville for the Year Ending October 1, 1880* (Nashville, 1880), p. 26; *ibid.*, 1884–1885, p. 62; *ibid.*, 1888–1889, p. 76.

61. Nashville *Daily American*, February 27, 1877.

62. See, for example, Nashville *Tennessee Tribune*, September 18, 1871, and, though coming under earlier antimiscegenation legislation, *Nashville Daily Press and Times*, July 6, 1865; March 3, June 29, 1866.

63. *Atlanta Constitution*, August 17, 1888.

64. See, for example, *Atlanta Constitution*, September 27, 1876; letter of "South Nashville" to the editor, Nashville *Daily American*, March 12, 1879. Arrest figures from Nashville, *Annual Reports*, 1880–1881, p. 32; *ibid.*, 1889–1890, p. 60; Atlanta City Council Minutes, January 5, 1891. The large number of black females arrested also contributed to the fact that more blacks than whites between the ages of ten and thirty were arrested while the reverse was true for those over thirty. For the arrest record of Lizzie Patterson, Atlanta's most notorious black streetwalker, see *Atlanta Constitution*, June 28, 1876; January 5, 1877; July 16, 1883.

65. See, for example, *Atlanta Constitution*, January 25, 1874; *Nashville Banner*, May 12, 1890.

66. On Kercheval's role, see Chapter 12; for Atlanta's containment policy toward vice, see *Atlanta Constitution*, August 11, 1887.

67. Atlanta police captain quoted in *Atlanta Constitution*, December 8, 1883.

68. See, for example, *Atlanta Daily Sun*, February 8, 1871; Atlanta City Council Minutes, March 15, 1872; *Atlanta Constitution*, September 13, 1877; May 28, 1880; April 15, 21, 1881; Nashville *Republican Banner*, December 22, 1874; Nashville *Daily American*, November 21, 1878; *Nashville Banner*, August 9, 1882; March 27, 1884.

69. Nashville *Republican Banner*, June 9, 1875 (italics added).

70. *Nashville Banner*, September 8, 11, 13, 1886.

71. *Atlanta Constitution*, July 29, 1885.

72. *Ibid.*, January 27, September 23, 1881; February 22, 1879; *Richmond Dispatch*, August 5, 1875. It is likely that most of the 120 persons arrested for

"suspicion" in Montgomery in 1887 were Negro (Montgomery, *Annual Reports, 1886–1887*, p. 31).

73. Richmond, *Annual Reports, 1873–1874*, p. xiv.

74. Nashville *Daily American*, March 2, 1879.

75. Newspapers which reported court cases were often inconsistent in labeling the races of defendants. This made it difficult to compare sentences assessed to whites and blacks. Take, for example, the *Nashville Banner*, May 12, 1890. At the beginning of one column on page 8 under the heading of "The Criminal Court," the cases of seven separate defendants were described, giving the name, charge, background information, and decision of each. All defendants were identified as "colored." Just below this account under the heading of "Cases in the Courts" were listed the decisions reached in the cases heard in the Criminal, Chancery, and Circuit Courts. The same seven defendants appeared here as appeared in the more detailed descriptions in the other column, but this time only four of them were identified as "colored."

76. *Atlanta Constitution*, May 10, 14–15, 1872; Montgomery *Herald*, August 6, 1887. See also testimony of John O. Kelly, in *Report on the Removal of Southern Negroes*, Part I, 250; *Nashville Banner*, November 23, 1885; Nashville *Daily American*, November 11, 1879; *Atlanta Constitution*, February 26, 1882; December 4, 13, 1889.

77. *Atlanta Constitution*, August 22, 1884; letter of the chief of police to the editor, Nashville *Daily American*, August 21, 1880.

78. *Richmond Dispatch*, April 23, June 7, 1870; August 2, 1875; February 20, 1880; July 30, 1866.

79. *Montgomery Daily Ledger*, December 6, 1865; Campbell, *White and Black*, p. 360. See also *Montgomery Daily Advertiser*, November 12, 1865; *Montgomery Daily Ledger*, January 8, 1866; *Mobile Advertiser and Register*, quoted in Mobile *Nationalist*, June 28, 1866.

80. *Richmond Dispatch*, December 11, 1866; January 1, 1872; January 1, 1873; Montgomery, *Annual Reports, 1886–1887*, pp. 25–31 (the Atlanta Police Court Docket for 1871–1872 revealed that, though more whites than Negroes were arrested, there were more Negroes on street duty since whites were better able to pay fines [Alexa Wynelle Benson, "Race Relations in Atlanta, As Seen in a Critical Analysis of the City Council Proceedings and Other Related Works, 1865–1877" (unpublished M.A. thesis, Atlanta University, 1966), p. 56]); *Atlanta Constitution*, November 20, 1875; September 14, 1881.

81. Wake County, Minutes of the Wake County Superior Court, 1866–1868, p. 102, North Carolina Department of Archives and History; *Montgomery Daily Ledger*, December 30, 1865; *Montgomery Daily Advertiser*, January 5, 1866.

82. *Montgomery Daily Advertiser*, April 23, 1867; Alabama, *Biennial Report of the Inspectors of the Alabama Penitentiary for the Two Years Ending September 30, 1884* (Montgomery, 1884), p. 50; Alabama, *Biennial Report of the Inspectors of Convicts for the Two Years Ending September 30, 1886* (Montgomery, 1886), pp. 211–12.

83. *Atlanta Constitution*, October 18, 1883.

84. *Montgomery Daily Ledger*, December 8, 1865.

85. *Atlanta Constitution*, March 22, 1876.

86. Richmond *Virginia Star*, December 14, 1878; resident quoted in C. B. Berry, *The Other Side: How It Struck Us* (New York, 1880), pp. 98–99; *Richmond*

Dispatch, November 16–17, 1866; February 6, January 14, 1880; whipper quoted in *Atlanta Constitution*, November 20, 1878.

87. Testimony of John C. Norris, in *KKK Hearings*, VI, 212.

88. Nashville *Republican Banner*, March 26–28, 1872. Jones was probably innocent. He had been identified by the dying man but only through the aid of moonlight in a darkened room. The man's wife had been unable to make a positive identification.

89. *Ibid.*, May 1, 1875; quotation *ibid.*, May 2, 1875. See also *Nashville Union and American*, May 2, 1875.

90. Nashville *Republican Banner*, May 19, 23, July 15, 1875.

91. Nashville *Daily American*, June 10, 13, 26, 1877.

92. *Nashville Banner*, May 16, 1881; September 7, 1882; *Atlanta Constitution*, August 31, 1876.

93. Montgomery *Colored Citizen*, April 26, 1884; Montgomery *Alabama Enterprise*, July 10, 1886; *Richmond Planet*, August 25, 1888. See also *Savannah Tribune*, September 28, 1889.

94. *Nashville Daily Press and Times*, June 17, 1866; *Nashville Banner*, March 14–15, 20, 1889; *Atlanta Constitution*, July 23, 1885; February 16, 1884; June 16, 1882.

95. *Richmond Dispatch*, May 28, 1866; May 9, 14, 1867; for the circumstances of the Atlanta killing and subsequent accounts of the inquest and trial, see *Atlanta Constitution*, May 23, June 9, 24, December 17, 19, 1885.

96. *Atlanta Constitution*, June 20–21, 23–24, 1885; Raleigh *News and Observer*, August 3, 5–6, September 24, 1890; January 9, 11, 1891. For additional cases in which policemen charged with brutality against blacks were exonerated, see Atlanta City Council Minutes, May 17, 1867; *Atlanta Constitution*, February 18, March 16, 1880; July 31, 1887. Between 1872 and 1890 at least two Negroes confined to local correctional institutions were the victims of unprovoked murders by guards who went unpunished (Nashville *Daily American*, March 17–22, 1876). Referring to the second murder, the *Nashville Banner* asked: "Will any sensible man say there was excuse for the shooting down of this man, convicted criminal though he was?" (October 10, 1884). The coroner's jury, however, found it to be a case of justifiable homicide (*ibid.*, October 11, 1884).

97. *Atlanta Constitution*, February 12, 1890. An Atlanta Negro newspaper, the *Weekly Defiance*, unsuccessfully sought the dismissal of a local policeman who used for "rifle practice" a fleeing Negro arrested for disorderly conduct (October 22, 1881). No action was taken against a Richmond policeman, who severely wounded a Negro attempting to flee with several chickens (*Richmond Dispatch*, April 20, 1875).

98. Montgomery City Council Minutes, February 22, 1870; *Nashville Union and Dispatch*, January 21, 1868; *Nashville Daily Press and Times*, May 7, 1868. Blacks also won damage suits filed against the cities. See, for example, *Nashville Banner*, February 19, 1885; Atlanta, Report of the City Attorney, *Annual Report of the Officers of the City of Atlanta for the Year Ending December 31, 1889* (Atlanta, 1890), p. 60; Atlanta City Council Minutes, January 6, 1890.

99. *Richmond Dispatch*, April 20, 1875; *Atlanta Constitution*, October 31, 1883; April 24, 1886; Montgomery *Colored Citizen*, April 12, 5, 1884.

100. Nashville *Republican Banner*, April 24, May 30, 1872; Nashville *Daily American*, May 26, 1890 (italics added); *Nashville Banner*, May 22, 1890.

101. *Richmond Dispatch,* April 3–4, July 10–14, 1888. For other examples of light sentences for unprovoked attacks on blacks, see *Nashville Banner,* June 28, 1887; *Nashville Daily Press and Times,* July 27, 1866; Benson, "Race Relations in Atlanta," p. 55; *Atlanta Constitution,* November 27–29, 1879.
102. *Atlanta Constitution,* October 8, 1870.
103. *Ibid.,* August 23–25, October 31, 1883; August 26, 1876.
104. See, for example, *ibid.,* October 7, 1871; August 13, 1879. For police complaints about loopholes in the vagrancy laws, see *ibid.,* September 17, 1885; Nashville, *Annual Reports,* 1880–1881, p. 35.
105. *Richmond Dispatch,* June 8, 1866; *Nashville Banner,* June 24, 1890; *Atlanta Constitution,* August 28, 1879.
106. *Atlanta Constitution,* June 28, 1882; June 27–29, 1883; *Atlanta Republican* quoted *ibid.,* June 28, 1882.
107. *Ibid.,* June 20, July 8, 1885; March 5–6, 1886. Burnett also had been charged with libel by another white businessman. His co-editor, W. A. Pledger, eventually was tried in that case and was fined (*ibid.,* November 29, 1885).
108. Letter of Thomas W. Wrenne to the editor, *Nashville Banner,* July 7, 1880; letter of John Harris to the editor, Nashville *Daily American,* July 10, 1880; letter of "C.E." to the editor, *ibid.,* August 17, 1885.
109. *Atlanta Constitution,* October 11, 1878; Nashville, *Annual Reports,* 1882–1883, p. 4; *Nashville Banner,* May 27, 1890.
110. *Atlanta Constitution,* July 19, 1883.

4. THE NEW ECONOMIC STRUCTURE

1. Richard C. Wade, *Slavery in the Cities: The South 1820–1860* (New York, 1964); Ira Berlin, *Slaves Without Masters: The Free Negro in the Antebellum South* (New York, 1974).
2. Monroe N. Work (comp.), "Some Negro Members of Reconstruction Conventions and Legislatures and of Congress," *Journal of Negro History,* V (January 1920), 117; Luther Porter Jackson, *Free Negro Labor and Property Holding in Virginia 1830–1860* (reprinted; New York, 1969), pp. 138, 142–43, 146, 151, 153, 155–58, 161–62. In the other Virginia cities the largest property-producing occupation was the livery business. Small shopkeepers, including grocers, confectioners, barkeepers, and restaurant proprietors, also were well represented (*ibid.,* pp. 155–58).
3. Morris Raymond Boucher, "The Free Negro in Alabama Prior to 1860" (unpublished Ph.D. dissertation, Graduate College of the State University of Iowa, 1950), pp. 495–96.
4. *Nashville Banner,* January 18, 1890.
5. Work, "Some Negro Members of Reconstruction," 118.
6. I have used the job classification system devised by Alba M. Edwards as modified by Kenneth L. Kusmer. See Kenneth L. Kusmer, *A Ghetto Takes Shape: Black Cleveland, 1870–1930* (Urbana, 1976), Appendix I. Unlike Kusmer, in Tables 2–4 I have computed percentages on the basis of the classifiable occupations rather than the total work force.
7. Grigsby Hart Wotton, Jr., "New City of the South: Atlanta, 1843–1873" (unpublished Ph.D. dissertation, The Johns Hopkins University, 1973), p. 321; Frenise A. Logan, "The Economic Status of the Town Negro in Post-Reconstruction North Carolina," *North Carolina Historical Review,* XXXV (Octo-

ber 1958), 448; Sir George Campbell, *White and Black: The Outcome of A Visit to the United States* (London, 1879), p. 378.

8. See the picture of Negro workers at the Compress and Storage Company in *Artwork of Montgomery, Alabama* (Chicago, 1894), Part VII; Nashville employers mentioned in Alrutheus Ambush Taylor, *The Negro in Tennessee 1865–1880* (Washington, D.C., 1941), p. 141; Richmond Chamber of Commerce, *The Advantages of Richmond, Virginia as a Manufacturing and Trading Centre* (Richmond, 1882), p. 26; factory owner quoted in David Macrae, *The Americans at Home* (2 vols.; Edinburgh, 1879), I, 152. See also William Robertson and W. F. Robertson, *Our American Tour: Being a Run of Ten Thousand Miles from the Atlantic to the Golden Gate in the Autumn of 1869* (Edinburgh, 1871), p. 116; William Saunders, *Through the Light Continent* (London, 1879), p. 72; Campbell, *White and Black*, pp. 294–98; Alrutheus Ambush Taylor, *The Negro in the Reconstruction of Virginia* (Washington, D.C., 1926), p. 119.

9. Campbell, *White and Black*, p. 388; Noble L. Prentis, *Southern Letters* (Topeka, 1881), p. 47.

10. Clinton B. Fisk quoted in J. T. Trowbridge, *The South: A Tour of Its Battlefields and Ruined Cities* (Hartford, 1866), p. 288; Robert Somers, *The Southern States Since the War 1870–1871*, Introduction and Index by Malcolm C. McMillan (reprinted; Tuscaloosa, Ala., 1965), pp. 14–15.

11. *Nashville Daily Press*, April 10, 1865; *Montgomery Daily Ledger*, August 14, 1865; *Atlanta Constitution*, August 11, 1889.

12. *Atlanta Constitution*, September 7, 1890; *Richmond Dispatch*, November 6, 1887.

13. Advertisements found in *Nashville Daily Press and Times*, October 4, 1865; *Richmond Dispatch*, January 22, 1875; *Nashville Banner*, November 10, 1888 (see also *Richmond Dispatch*, June 8, 1870; *Nashville Banner*, March 25, 1887); for complaints about black domestic help, see *Montgomery Daily Ledger*, August 8, 1865; *Richmond Dispatch*, December 27, 1865; *Nashville Banner*, September 24, 1881; March 15, 1883.

14. Robert Shields Crump, "Yesterdays: Memories of an Earlier Richmond," annotated with a foreword by Elizabeth Hawes Ryland, p. 68, Valentine Museum, Richmond; for the black share of Atlanta's skilled workers in 1890, see Table 4; for 1870, see Wotton, "New City of the South," p. 321. Although Wotton and I used slightly different classification systems, it is unlikely that this significantly affected the comparison between 1870 and 1890.

15. Letter of "Parent" to the editor, *Atlanta Constitution*, August 7, 1887; Alexander K. McClure, *The South: Its Industrial, Financial and Political Condition* (Philadelphia, 1886), p. 80; Henry W. Grady, *The New South* (New York, 1889), pp. 249–50; Ray Stannard Baker, *Following the Color Line* (reprinted; New York, 1964), p. 29.

16. Campbell, *White and Black*, p. 316; Lady Duffus Hardy (Mary McDowell), *Down South* (London, 1883), p. 51. It is quite possible that the two "whites" that Campbell saw were actually mulattoes.

17. Taylor, *Negro in Tennessee*, p. 145; W. E. B. Du Bois (ed.), *The Negro Artisan* ("Atlanta University Publications," No. 7, ed. W. E. B. Du Bois; Atlanta, 1902), p. 148; Nashville *Daily American*, October 15–16, 1879.

18. *Nashville Banner*, April 23, 1886.

19. Bureau of the Census, *Eleventh Census: Population* (Washington, D.C., 1893), I, Part II, 634, 718; Du Bois, *Negro Artisan*, pp. 136–37.

356

NOTES TO PAGES 71–76

20. *Nashville Banner*, December 6, 13, 1890; Du Bois, *Negro Artisan*, p. 155; *Richmond Dispatch*, January 2, 1888.

21. Wake County, Minutes of the Wake County Board of Commissioners, September 21, 1869, North Carolina Department of Archives and History, Raleigh; Somers, *Southern States*, pp. 17–18; testimony of John O. Kelly, in U.S. Senate, 46th Cong., 2nd Sess., *Report of the Select Committee of the United States Senate to Investigate the Causes for the Removal of the Negroes from the Southern States to the Northern States* (Washington, D.C., 1880), Part I, 246 (hereafter cited as *Report on the Removal of Southern Negroes*); Samuel P. Richards, "Diary," July 19, 1884, Atlanta Historical Society (see also entries for January 31, February 22, 1873; May 2, 1877; November 1, 1883); *Daily Atlanta Intelligencer*, June 3, 1870; North Carolina, *First Annual Report of the Bureau of Labor Statistics for Year Ending 1887*, comp. W. N. Jones (Raleigh, 1887), p. 169 (all the car builders, carpenters, and watchmen were white; all the brakemen, black); Atlanta, Minutes of the Atlanta City Council, May 7, 1888, Office of the City Clerk, Atlanta City Hall.

22. Boyd quoted in James T. Haley (comp.), *Afro-American Encyclopedia or, the Thoughts, Doings and Sayings of the Race* (Nashville, 1896), p. 68; J. W. Gibson and W. H. Crogman, *Progress of A Race or The Remarkable Advancement of the American Negro* (rev. ed.; Atlanta, 1902), pp. 306–307.

23. *Atlanta Constitution*, March 10, 1877; Nashville *Daily American*, December 9, 1880.

24. *Atlanta Constitution*, February 23, 1883; *Nashville Banner*, October 30, 1885.

25. *Nashville Daily Press and Times*, December 4, 1866.

26. Nashville *Republican Banner*, February 22, March 12, 1871; *Nashville Banner*, June 13, 1881.

27. *Richmond Dispatch*, May 6, 16, 1867; May 6, 1872; June 25, 1875.

28. *Atlanta Constitution*, July 29, 1881; May 4, 1883; *Richmond Dispatch*, May 5–6, 1875.

29. *Atlanta Constitution*, May 22, 1872.

30. *Ibid.*, July 29, 26, 1881.

31. *Ibid.*, August 3, 1881.

32. *Ibid.*, July 26, August 3, 1881.

33. *Ibid.*, July 30, 29, 1881; Atlanta City Council Minutes, August 15, 1881.

34. See, for example, the remarks of E. M. Garrett, Superintendent of Richmond Public Schools, in Richmond, *Fourteenth Annual Report of the School Board and Superintendent of Public Schools for the Scholastic Year Ending July 31, 1882* (Richmond, 1882), p. 45; *Nashville Banner*, September 24, 1883; *Atlanta Constitution*, April 29, May 31, 1885. For a thoughtful critique of the idea that Booker T. Washington was responsible for the popularity of industrial education among blacks, see August Meier, *Negro Thought in America 1880–1915* (Ann Arbor, 1966), especially pp. 85–99.

35. Lowery quoted in *Nashville Daily Press and Times*, February 12, 1867. Lowery was an antebellum free Negro farmer and livery-stable keeper in Davidson County who had amassed $15,000 in real property by 1860 (J. Merton England, "The Free Negro in Ante-Bellum Tennessee," *Journal of Southern History*, IX [February 1943], 53).

36. Richmond, Minutes of the Richmond Board of Education, September 1, 28, 1882; September 27, 1883, Richmond Board of Education Building (for the early history of the Moore Street School, see *Richmond Dispatch*, July 12, 1875); *Atlanta Constitution*, December 14, 1883.

37. W. H. Crogman, *Talks for the Times* (Atlanta, 1896), p. 110; *Richmond Planet*, February 21, 1885.

38. Charles M. Wallace, *The Boy Gangs of Richmond in the Dear Old Days* (Richmond, 1938), pp. 97–98; *Daily Atlanta Intelligencer*, July 14, 1866. Most of these people were recent migrants from rural areas where "the farmer is greatly in need of their labor" (*ibid.*). For more on peddlers, see *Montgomery Daily Ledger*, September 6, 1865; *Nashville Union and Dispatch*, May 18, 1867; letter of "Citizen" to the editor, *Montgomery Daily Advertiser*, June 6, 1874; *Nashville Banner*, March 14, 1883.

39. Raleigh *Weekly Progress*, February 7, 1867 (one statute required that in a business transaction involving the sale of articles worth more than $10 in which one of the parties was a Negro, the exchange had to be witnessed by a white who could read and write [North Carolina, *Public Laws* (1866), p. 100]); *Atlanta Constitution*, August 24, 1880; *Richmond Planet*, June 16, 1886.

40. *Branson's and Farrar's North Carolina Business Directory 1866–1867* (Raleigh, 1867), pp. 108–109; *Raleigh Directory 1886* (Raleigh, 1886), pp. 133–60; William J. Divine (comp.), *Richmond City Directory 1866* (Richmond, 1866), pp. 175–202; J. H. Chataigne (comp.), *Chataigne's Directory of Richmond for 1891* (Richmond, 1891), pp. 724–26, 734, 736, 739, 744, 752, 770–71.

41. W. E. B. Du Bois (ed.), *The Negro in Business* ("Atlanta University Publications," No. 4, ed. W. E. B. Du Bois; Atlanta, 1899), pp. 7, 68; H. G. Saunders (comp.), *R. L. Polk & Company's Atlanta City Directory 1891* (Atlanta, 1891), pp. 1121–99; C. J. Allardt (comp.), *Montgomery City Directory for 1891* (Montgomery, 1891), pp. 211–52. For the unsuccessful effort of one shop to rely on white rather than black barbers, compare advertisements for Gallagher and Connell in *Montgomery Daily Advertiser*, August 26, 1875 and February 6, 1876. For a similar attempt in Raleigh, see Raleigh *News and Observer*, September 5, 1890.

42. Allardt, *Montgomery Directory, 1891*, pp. 220, 226, 232, 248–49; Chataigne, *Richmond Directory, 1891*, pp. 735–36, 751, 754, 757, 779. For Negro complaints of discrimination in the awarding of liquor licenses in Atlanta, see Atlanta *Weekly Defiance*, October 8, 1881.

43. Nashville *Daily American*, January 2, 1878. There were no Negro renters the following year, but Smith was back in 1880 (*ibid.*, January 2, 1879; January 2, 1880).

44. Ross A. Smith (comp.), *The Montgomery City Directory for 1880–1881* (Montgomery, 1880), p. 217; Allardt, *Montgomery Directory, 1891*, pp. 240–41.

45. Nashville *Colored Tennessean*, August 12, 1865; July 18, 1866; Montgomery *Herald*, October 16, 1886; *Richmond Dispatch*, April 16–17, 1890. See also *Richmond Planet*, August 25, 1888.

46. *Fisk Herald*, V (May 1887), 10; Richmond *Virginia Star*, November 18, 1882. Eight years later one of the partners was still in business, though barred from the meetings of his fellow bookdealers because of his race (*Richmond Planet*, September 13, 1890). See also E. R. Carter, *The Black Side: A Partial History of the Business, Religious, and Educational Side of the Negro in Atlanta, Georgia* (Atlanta, 1894), pp. 133, 152–54.

47. *Nashville Union and American*, September 29, 1870; Taylor, *Negro in Tennessee*, pp. 157–58, 240; *Nashville Banner*, October 28, 1884 (for a typical Nashville fair, see, for example, Nashville *Republican Banner*, September 24,

1874); Frenise A. Logan, "The Colored Industrial Association of North Carolina and Its Fair of 1886," *North Carolina Historical Review*, XXXIV (January 1957), 58; Montgomery *Weekly Advance*, September 3, 1881; *Atlanta Constitution*, July 22, 1887; January 28, 1888.

48. *The National Freedman*, I (August 15, 1865), 242.

49. *Nashville Banner*, May 18, 1882; *Atlanta Constitution*, January 3, 1878; for the dedication of the publishing firm's four-story building, see *Nashville Banner*, January 21, 1889.

50. Taylor, *Negro in Virginia*, p. 131; *Richmond Dispatch*, January 1, 1878; January 1, 1879; Richmond *Virginia Star*, May 11, 1878; *Richmond Dispatch*, February 11, 1880; *Nashville Banner*, December 18, 1888; February 23, 1889; Nashville *Republican Banner*, March 16, 1872; *Atlanta Constitution*, May 11, 1890; Carter, *Black Side*, p. 63.

51. W. E. B. Du Bois (ed.), *Economic Co-operation Among Negro Americans* ("Atlanta University Publications," No. 12, ed. W. E. B. Du Bois; Atlanta, 1907), p. 136; Carl R. Osthaus, *Freedmen, Philanthropy and Fraud: A History of the Freedman's Savings Bank* (Urbana, 1976), *passim*, and especially Chapter 4. Practically all scholars except Osthaus refer to the Freedmen's Bank. The same was true of most contemporaries. The official name, however, was National Freedman's Savings and Trust Company. I have therefore used Freedman's in the official title of the bank but have otherwise used Freedmen's Bank.

52. Address of the Advisory Committee printed in *Nashville Daily Press and Times*, June 19, 1866.

53. *Atlanta Constitution*, January 19, 1870; Du Bois, *Economic Co-operation*, p. 136; *Richmond Dispatch*, January 2, 1873.

54. *Atlanta Constitution*, June 18, 1882; Nashville *Republican Banner*, November 25, 1871. All the banks accepted deposits of as little as five cents.

55. Osthaus, *Freedmen, Philanthropy and Fraud*, pp. 166–72 and *passim*.

56. Nashville *Republican Banner*, July 3, 1874; Richmond *Virginia Star*, December 14, 1878.

57. For the development and impact of the order and its bank, see Writers Program of the Works Progress Administration in the State of Virginia (comp.), *The Negro in Virginia* (New York, 1940), pp. 292–93; Gibson and Crogman, *Progress of A Race*, p. 240; Du Bois, *Economic Co-operation*, pp. 101–104; Abram L. Harris, *The Negro as Capitalist: A Study of Banking and Business Among American Negroes* (reprinted; Gloucester, Mass., 1968), pp. 62–74.

58. Baker, *Following the Color Line*, p. 40; Saunders, *Atlanta Directory*, 1891, p. 41; Florence Brine, "Interview of David Howard," 1940, Atlanta Historical Society; *Atlanta Constitution*, August 23, 1890; Gibson and Crogman, *Progress of A Race*, p. 280.

59. G. F. Richings, *Evidences of Progress Among Colored People* (10th ed.; Philadelphia, 1903), pp. 541–42; Charles Octavius Boothe, *The Cyclopedia of the Colored Baptists of Alabama* (Birmingham, 1895), p. 226; Gibson and Crogman, *Progress of A Race*, p. 242.

60. W. N. Hartshorn, *An Era of Progress and Promise 1863–1910: The Religious, Moral and Educational Development of the American Negro Since His Emancipation* (Boston, 1910), p. 439.

61. *Richmond Dispatch*, October 20, 1866.

62. *Atlanta Constitution*, November 24, 1877; I. W. Avery (ed.), *City of Atlanta*

("World's Fair Series on Great American Cities"; Louisville, 1892), pp.
158–59. Bentley was one of the few blacks to be discussed who had entirely
urban antecedents. A native of Macon, he was raised in Savannah and came
to Atlanta in the early 1870s.

63. Among other signs of affluence, Keeble had a $100 watch (Nashville *Republi-
can Banner*, October 18, 1871). Walker engaged in frequent real estate trans-
actions. See, for example, Taylor, *Negro in Tennessee*, p. 165. Patterson was
probably the Negro barber mentioned as having accumulated between
$75,000 and $100,000 by 1891 in Samuel J. Barrows, "What the Southern
Negro Is Doing for Himself," *Atlantic Monthly*, LXVII (June 1891), 810.
For Lyons, see *Atlanta Constitution*, December 18, 1887.

64. Celestine Sibley, *Peachtree Street USA: An Affectionate Portrait of Atlanta*
(New York, 1963), pp. 91–92.

65. *Atlanta Constitution*, February 21, 1878; Nashville *Daily American*, April 24,
1886.

66. Bureau of the Census, Manuscript Census Schedules, Population, 1870,
Tennessee, Davidson County, City of Nashville, Ward 4, p. 15; testimony of
Kelly, in *Report on the Removal of Southern Negroes*, Part I, 251.

67. *Atlanta Constitution*, June 6, 1887; *Nashville Banner*, August 28, 1890.

68. Hartshorn, *Era of Progress and Promise*, p. 460; Carter, *Black Side*, pp. 207–
208; Baker, *Following the Color Line*, p. 41.

69. Du Bois, *Negro Artisan*, pp. 143–44. See also *Nashville Banner*, July 6, 1886;
May 14, 1889; Haley, *Afro-American Encyclopedia*, pp. 210–11.

70. *Atlanta Constitution*, June 2, 1882.

71. Bureau of the Census, Manuscript Census Schedules, Population, 1870, Ala-
bama, Montgomery County, City of Montgomery, Ward 4, p. 41; Reverend
J. Van Catledge, "Short History of Old Ship," in *Souvenir Program of the
One Hundredth Anniversary of the Old Ship African Methodist Episcopal
Zion Church 1852–1952* (Montgomery, 1952), pp. 6–7; *Montgomery Daily
Advertiser*, January 14, 1885.

72. *Atlanta Constitution*, August 31, 1890, contains biographical sketches of the
three men. For additional information on Tate and Crumbley, see Carter,
Black Side, pp. 20, 60–63.

73. Haley, *Afro-American Encyclopedia*, pp. 205–206; Richings, *Evidences of
Progress Among Colored People*, p. 272; *Nashville Banner*, June 29, 1889.

74. *Nashville Banner*, December 16, 1886; March 9, 1888; Bureau of the Census,
Manuscript Census Schedules, 1870, Nashville, Ward 4, p. 67; rents and loans
owed Harding listed in "Inventory of Henry Harding's Estate," Davidson
County (Tennessee) Will Book 29 (1886–1888), pp. 623–24, Microfilm Copy,
Tennessee State Library and Archives, Nashville.

75. *Savannah Tribune*, December 1, 1888; Gibson and Crogman, *Progress of A
Race*, p. 301; Richings, *Evidences of Progress Among Colored People*, p. 274.

76. *Atlanta Constitution*, June 25, 1874; March 10, 1882; March 12, 1886.

77. Richings, *Evidences of Progress Among Colored People*, pp. 489–90.

78. Untitled article by Jane Taylor Duke, *Richmond News Leader*, April 15,
1938.

79. *Ibid.*; WPA, *Negro in Virginia*, p. 298; Bureau of the Census, Manuscript
Census Schedules, Population, 1870, Virginia, Henrico County, City of
Richmond, Jefferson Ward, p. 152.

80. Du Bois, *Negro in Business*, pp. 25, 30, 35–36, 68; Baker, *Following the
Color Line*, p. 41. When white residents of a fashionable Atlanta neighbor-

hood objected to the construction of shanties nearby, the *Atlanta Constitution* reported, "It is believed to be the purpose of the owner of the shanties to rent them to negro shopkeepers, as they are nothing more or less than stalls" (August 23, 1889). Blacks were less likely than whites to own their stores. A Nashville survey in 1877 discovered 605 brick stores and 103 frame stores owned by whites and only 14 brick shops and 4 frame shops owned by blacks (Nashville, *Second Annual Report of the Nashville Board of Health for the Year Ending July 4, 1877* [Nashville, 1877], p. 108).

81. Du Bois, *Negro in Business*, p. 71; Great Britain, Board of Trade, *Cost of Living in American Towns: Report of an Enquiry by the Board of Trade into Working Class Rents, Housing and Retail Prices Together with Rates of Wages in Certain Occupations in the Principal Industrial Towns of the United States of America* (London, 1911), p. 58.

82. Bureau of the Census, *Census, 1890*, I, Part II, 634, 718, 696; Logan, "The Economic Status of the Town Negro," 450.

83. Gibson and Crogman, *Progress of A Race*, p. 570; Nashville *Republican Banner*, March 2, 28, 1872; for Ewing, see brief sketch in Gibson and Crogman, *Progress of A Race*, p. 575.

84. Gibson and Crogman, *Progress of A Race*, pp. 564–67; D. W. Culp (ed.), *Twentieth Century Negro Literature or A Cyclopedia of Thought on the Vital Topics Relating to the American Negro* (Atlanta, 1902), p. 108. McElwee represented a district outside of Davidson County.

85. Richings, *Evidences of Progress Among Colored People*, p. 268; Hartshorn, *Era of Progress and Promise*, p. 415; Gibson and Crogman, *Progress of A Race*, pp. 567–69.

86. *Atlanta Constitution*, April 14, December 22, 1888.

87. Montgomery *Herald*, July 3, 1887; Richings, *Evidences of Progress Among Colored People*, pp. 496–97.

88. Nashville *Daily American*, February 27, 1880.

89. Haley, *Afro-American Encyclopedia*, pp. 59–62, 226; Richings, *Evidences of Progress Among Colored People*, pp. 266–67; Gibson and Crogman, *Progress of A Race*, p. 588.

90. Carter, *Black Side*, pp. 134–38. The third alumnus was Dr. Albert Owen Lockhart (*ibid.*, pp. 128–30).

91. *Atlanta Constitution*, July 14, 1882; March 1, 1884; August 31, December 28–29, 1890; Bureau of the Census, Manuscript Census Schedules, Population, 1870, Georgia, Fulton County, City of Atlanta, Ward 4, p. 88.

92. Haley, *Afro-American Encyclopedia*, p. 76.

93. Montgomery *Colored Citizen*, April 12, 1884; Montgomery *Herald*, October 16, 1886; Van Catledge, "Short History of Old Ship," p. 10; Barrows, "What the Southern Negro Is Doing for Himself," 809, 813. Dorsette was an associate of Booker T. Washington and aided him in his unsuccessful attempt to prevent the moving of the State Normal School for Colored Children to Montgomery in 1887. See Louis R. Harlan, "Booker T. Washington in Biographical Perspective," *American Historical Review*, LXXV (October 1970), 1595–96.

94. Haley, *Afro-American Encyclopedia*, pp. 75–76.

95. Carter, *Black Side*, pp. 130–33.

96. *Atlanta Constitution*, February 10, 1869; August 7, 1873; Georgia, *Report of the Comptroller General of the State of Georgia for the Year Ending September 30, 1886* (Atlanta, 1886), pp. 125–29; *ibid.*, 1889–1890, pp. 128–32, 104.

97. *Atlanta Constitution*, August 22, 1875; August 24, 1880.

98. Taylor, *Negro in Virginia*, p. 135; Haley, *Afro-American Encyclopedia*, p. 212.

99. *Montgomery Daily Advertiser*, September 28, 1878.

100. Taylor, *Negro in Tennessee*, p. 167; *Nashville Banner*, December 18, 1886.

101. *Nashville Banner*, January 18, 1890.

102. Richmond, *Annual Reports of the City Departments of Richmond, Virginia, for the Year Ending December 31, 1890* (Richmond, 1891), p. 26; Taylor, *Negro in Virginia*, p. 135; *Nashville Banner*, December 18, 1886.

103. Richard J. Hopkins, "Occupational and Geographic Mobility in Atlanta 1870–1896," *Journal of Southern History*, XXXIV (May 1968), 200–13. See also Richard J. Hopkins, "Status, Mobility and Dimensions of Change in a Southern City: Atlanta 1870–1910," in *Cities in American History*, eds. Kenneth T. Jackson and Stanley K. Schultz (New York, 1972), pp. 216–31. For similar conclusions about Negro mobility in another Southern city, see Paul B. Worthman, "Working Class Mobility in Birmingham, Alabama 1880–1914," in *Anonymous Americans: Explorations in Nineteenth Century Social History*, ed. Tamara K. Hareven (Englewood, N.J., 1971), pp. 172–213.

5. NEGRO HOUSING AND NEIGHBORHOODS

1. Richard C. Wade, *Slavery in the Cities: The South 1820–1860* (New York, 1964), pp. 55–79.

2. See, for example, Karl E. Taeuber and Alma Taeuber, *Negroes in Cities: Residential Segregation and Neighborhood Change* (Chicago, 1965), pp. 43–53.

3. Bureau of the Census, *Eleventh Census: Population* (Washington, D.C., 1893), I, Part I, 579.

4. Mary Winfield Scott, *Old Richmond Neighborhoods* (Richmond, 1950), pp. 245, 257, 260, 285–86, 295, 299.

5. *Ibid.*, pp. 250, 255, 258, 300, 289, 295.

6. *Richmond Dispatch*, July 29, 1880.

7. C. A. Bryce, "Good Old Days When Jackson Ward Was a Political Battleground," *Richmond Times Dispatch*, May 8, 1921.

8. J. H. Chataigne (comp.), *Chataigne's Directory of Richmond for 1891* (Richmond, 1891), *passim*.

9. Carle Boschen, Untitled Reminiscence #2, p. 7, in "Richmond Reminiscences," Valentine Museum, Richmond.

10. R. A. Brock, *Richmond as a Manufacturing and Trading Centre* (Richmond, 1880), p. 30. See also *Montgomery Daily Ledger*, August 18, November 8, 1865; letter of Joseph M'Kelvey, quoted in Western Freedmen's Aid Commission, *Second Annual Report of the Western Freedmen's Aid Commission* (Cincinnati, 1865), p. 35.

11. See, for example, *Richmond Dispatch*, March 24, 1866; *Montgomery Daily Ledger*, August 15, 1865.

12. *Raleigh Directory 1880–1881: Being a Complete Index to the Residents of the City. Also a Classified Business Directory*, comp. Charles Emerson & Company (Raleigh, 1879), p. 34; E. Y. Clarke, *Atlanta Illustrated* (3rd ed.; Atlanta, 1881), p. 138; *Atlanta Constitution*, January 2, 1878.

13. Dr. John M. Woodworth, "Narrative of the Cholera Epidemic of 1873 in the

United States," in Nashville, *Third Annual Report of the Nashville Board of Health for the Two Years Ending December 31, 1879* (Nashville, 1880), p. 80; Nashville *Republican Banner*, June 30, 1872.

14. Nashville *Republican Banner*, July 2, 1873.
15. Eugene M. Mitchell, "Queer Place Names in Old Atlanta," *Atlanta Historical Bulletin*, I (April 1931), 29. Referring to the Summer Hill School, the *Atlanta Constitution* noted that "the patronage of this school extends throughout one of the thickest colored quarters in the city" (June 28, 1879).
16. *Atlanta Constitution*, May 9, 1887.
17. Montgomery *Alabama State Journal*, August 18, 1872, quoted in American Missionary Association, *Twenty-Sixth Annual Report of the American Missionary Association and Proceedings at the Annual Meeting Held at Racine, Wisconsin, October 30 and 31, 1872* (New York, 1872), p. 33; the Reverend G. W. Andrews quoted *ibid.*, 1873, p. 32.
18. Nashville *Republican Banner*, April 27, 1873.
19. Montgomery *Alabama State Journal*, August 18, 1872, quoted in AMA, *Annual Report*, 1872, p. 33; *Atlanta Constitution*, June 10, 1881; Josephus Daniels, *Tar Heel Editor* (Chapel Hill, 1939), p. 304; Writers Program of the Works Progress Administration in the State of North Carolina, *Raleigh, Capital of North Carolina* (Raleigh, 1942), p. 58.
20. Nashville *Colored Tennessean*, March 24, 1866; *Nashville Banner*, June 9, December 20, 1888.
21. *Atlanta Constitution*, March 9, 1887.
22. *Nashville Banner*, December 18, 1888; February 23, September 21, 1889.
23. *Savannah Tribune*, April 6, 1889.
24. See Roger L. Rice, "Residential Segregation by Law, 1910–1917," *Journal of Southern History*, XXXIV (May 1968), 179–99.
25. *Nashville Daily Press and Times*, June 27, 1865; *Nashville Banner*, September 21, 1889. On another occasion the *Nashville Union and American* reported that "several small houses in respectable localities have been torn down by their owners within the past few days, because of objections urged against them by insurance companies and decent people living near them. They were in most cases occupied by disorderly negroes and were therefore a source of constant annoyance as well as dangerous to more valuable property adjoining. Costly experience has taught the importance of abating such nuisances" (July 28, 1869). On the other hand, Atlanta officials rejected the petition of Charles Hickett *et al.*, which called for the removal of shanties on McDaniel Street occupied by "filthy negroes" (Atlanta, Minutes of the Atlanta City Council, April 16, May 7, 1888, Office of the City Clerk, Atlanta City Hall). Interestingly, housing notices in local white newspapers rarely included racial restrictions. Unlike employers in help wanted advertisements, who frequently specified race, homeowners and landlords evidently felt that readers understood that offers were only for whites.
26. Copy of the order in Reconstruction Folder, "W" File, Division of Military Records, Alabama Department of Archives and History, Montgomery; *Montgomery Daily Ledger*, August 15, 25, 1865.
27. Raleigh *Daily Sentinel*, March 25, 27, 1875.
28. Bureau of the Census, Manuscript Census Schedules, Population, 1870, Georgia, Fulton County, City of Atlanta; Virginia, Henrico County, City of Richmond; Alabama, Montgomery County, City of Montgomery; *ibid.*, 1880; discussion with John Martin, Yale University graduate student, Atlanta,

Georgia, August 1968. Linear blocks are "facing sides of a block-long street segment" (Taeuber and Taeuber, *Negroes in Cities*, p. 222).

29. *Atlanta Constitution*, July 20, 1881; for Darktown and Peasville, see Mitchell, "Queer Place Names," 29; for Jenningstown, see *Atlanta Constitution*, September 25, 1875.

30. Peacocks Tract, for example, contained only six white families amid more than five hundred Negroes (Bureau of the Census, Manuscript Census Schedules, 1880, Montgomery, Second Ward, pp. 1–9, 12, 55–56).

31. H. G. Saunders (comp.), *R. L. Polk & Company's Atlanta City Directory 1891* (Atlanta, 1891); Chataigne, *Richmond Directory, 1891; City Directory of Montgomery 1895* (Montgomery, 1895). I chose these three cities and years because of the nature of the sources. Prior to these dates, the directories listed residents alphabetically. After these dates, names were arranged alphabetically and by street address. The addition of the second section made it possible to plot on a map in a reasonable amount of time all the inhabitants mentioned. This was not the case for Nashville or Raleigh. Directories for Nashville, at least until 1900, were arranged only alphabetically. Raleigh directories also were arranged alphabetically, but as of the 1886 edition there were separate sections for blacks and whites. Because of the small population of the city in 1886, it was possible to map the homes of black residents. Their heavy concentration on certain streets and their complete absence from numerous others suggest that a plotting of white residents would reveal the same pattern found in Richmond, Montgomery, and Atlanta. See *Raleigh City Directory 1886* (Raleigh, 1886). For a useful introduction to housing patterns in Nashville during this period which supports many of my findings for Atlanta, Richmond, and Montgomery, see James F. Blumstein and Benjamin Walter (eds.), *Growing Metropolis: Aspects of Development in Nashville* (Nashville, 1975), Chapters 1–3.

32. Saunders, *Atlanta Directory, 1891*, pp. 128, 283. See also *ibid.*, pp. 181–82, 272, 281–82.

33. *Montgomery Directory, 1895*, pp. 93, 115. Samuel J. Barrows, a New England reformer and future U.S. Congressman who visited the city in 1891, noted that "in some of the streets, the whites occupy one side, and the blacks the other. Occasionally the colors alternate, like the squares on a checkerboard" (Samuel J. Barrows, "What the Southern Negro is Doing for Himself," *Atlantic Monthly*, LXVII [June 1891], 809). For additional examples of groupings of blacks and whites, see Chataigne, *Richmond Directory, 1891*, pp. 883–84; John M. Marshall, "Residential Expansion and Central-City Change," in Blumstein and Walter, *Growing Metropolis*, p. 38.

34. Chataigne, *Richmond Directory, 1891*, p. 944. See also *ibid.*, pp. 867, 913–14, 942–43, 1054. For previous years, see, for example, Bureau of the Census, Manuscript Census Schedules, 1870, Richmond, Clay Ward, pp. 5, 23–26; Marshall Ward, pp. 57–74; Monroe Ward, pp. 128–33, 138–48; *ibid.*, 1880, Jackson Ward, First Precinct, pp. 14–18, 20–24.

35. *Montgomery Directory, 1895*, pp. 68, 82, 87. For a similar pattern in 1880, see Bureau of the Census, Manuscript Census Schedules, 1880, Montgomery, Second Ward, pp. 31–33; Fourth Ward, pp. 55–61.

36. *Nashville Banner*, December 13, 1888. See also *Atlanta Constitution*, December 12, 1876.

37. Richard R. Wright, Jr., *87 Years Behind the Black Curtain: An Autobiography* (Philadelphia, 1965), p. 69.

38. Great Britain, Board of Trade, *Cost of Living in American Towns: Report of an Enquiry by the Board of Trade into Working Class Rents, Housing and Retail Prices Together with Rates of Wages in Certain Occupations in the Principal Industrial Towns of the United States of America* (London, 1911), p. 56.
39. See, for example, Chataigne, *Richmond Directory, 1891,* pp. 921, 923–25, 929; *Montgomery Directory, 1895,* p. 123; Saunders, *Atlanta Directory, 1891,* p. 125.
40. Saunders, *Atlanta Directory, 1891,* p. 142; Chataigne, *Richmond Directory, 1891,* pp. 961–62; *Montgomery Directory, 1895,* p. 123.
41. *Atlanta Constitution,* September 20, 1876.
42. Nashville *Republican Banner,* November 27, 1873.
43. *Atlanta Constitution,* April 14, 1886; September 10, 1881; April 7–8, 1882.
44. Board of Health quoted in Nashville *Daily American,* October 4, 1876. See also *Richmond Dispatch,* March 26, 1866.
45. The quotation is from *Atlanta Constitution,* June 19, 1868. The sketch of Negro areas is based upon residential maps drawn from the listings in Saunders, *Atlanta Directory, 1891,* interviews of Franklin M. Garrett, Director of the Atlanta Historical Society, in August 1968, and Mr. Garrett's *Atlanta and Environs: A Chronicle of Its People and Events* (3 vols.; New York, 1954), I, 741. Today the surest way of finding the turn-of-the-century Negro areas of these cities is to trace the routes of the new interstate highways.
46. Edward King, *The Southern States of North America* (London, 1875), p. 726.
47. See, for example, Nashville *Republican Banner,* April 10, 1872; December 5, 1873; February 24, April 16–18, 1874; *Nashville Banner,* January 13, 1882; April 6, 1886; February 3, 1887.
48. *Nashville Banner,* June 25, 1883.
49. *Ibid.,* March 1, 1883; February 4, 1884.
50. Montgomery *Colored Citizen,* April 5, 1884. Samuel J. Barrows was impressed by the number of excellent homes owned by Negroes which he saw during his trip to the city in 1891. "The interiors of these homes, especially of the younger and more progressive people, are comfortably and tastefully furnished. The rooms are as high as those of their white neighbors, well carpeted and papered, while the piano or the cabinet organ suggests loftier musical tastes than that of the plantation banjo. . . . It is estimated that there are from 250 to 300 pianos and cabinet organs in the homes of colored people in Montgomery" (Barrows, "What the Southern Negro Is Doing for Himself," 809).
51. "Inventory of Henry Harding's Estate," Davidson County (Tennessee) Will Book 29 (1886–1888), p. 624, Microfilm Copy, Tennessee State Library and Archives, Nashville. See also *Nashville Banner,* April 25, 1883.
52. David Macrae, *The Americans at Home* (2 vols.; Edinburgh, 1870), II, 56; New England Branch of the Freedmen's Union Commission, "Report of the Committee to Inspect the Freedmen's Schools," in *The Freedmen's Record,* V (August 1869), 30; W. H. Crogman, "The Negro's Needs," a speech delivered in Henry Ward Beecher's church, October 14, 1883, reprinted in the author's *Talks for the Times* (Atlanta, 1896), p. 146.
53. For pictures of both houses, see J. W. Gibson and W. H. Crogman, *Progress of A Race or The Remarkable Advancement of the American Negro* (rev. ed.; Atlanta, 1902), pp. 275, 278.
54. Sarah Simms Edge, "Joel Hurt," *Atlanta Historical Bulletin,* IX (April 1955), 67.
55. *Atlanta Constitution,* March 1, 1884. For floor plans, detailed descriptions, and

pictures of the "better housing" owned by Atlanta blacks, see W. E. B. Du Bois (ed.), *The Negro American Family* ("Atlanta University Publications," No. 13, ed. W. E. B. Du Bois; Atlanta, 1908), pp. 64–68, 74–80, 91–96.

56. *Atlanta Constitution*, June 25, 1886.

57. Nashville, *Report of the Board of Health*, 1876–1877, pp. 108–10.

58. Great Britain Board of Trade, *Cost of Living in American Towns*, pp. 56–58. See also the housing survey for Atlanta in 1900 and the floor plans, detailed descriptions, and pictures of substandard housing in Du Bois, *The Negro American Family*, pp. 58–60, 73–74, and especially 86–90. Du Bois concluded that "a third of the black population is poorly housed and . . . a fifth very poorly" (*ibid.*, p. 60). For a picture of typical Negro slum housing in Montgomery, see *Artwork of Montgomery, Alabama* (Chicago, 1894), Part XII.

59. *Richmond Dispatch*, January 1, 1875; Richmond, Report of the City Scavenger, *Annual Reports of the City Departments of Richmond, Virginia, for the Year Ending December 31, 1887* (Richmond, 1888), p. 94.

60. Nashville *Republican Banner*, January 2, 1872; *Atlanta Constitution*, September 4, 1888; *Richmond Dispatch*, October 2, 1866.

61. Gibson and Crogman, *Progress of A Race*, pp. 305–306. Of the 77 who rented, 12 paid above $6 per month, 18 paid $6, 20 paid $5, and 27 paid less than $5. The highest monthly payment made by those who bought homes was $12; the lowest, $5.

62. Nashville *Republican Banner*, September 15, 1872; Raleigh *News and Observer*, August 10, 1890; *Atlanta Constitution*, July 23, 1887.

63. *Nashville Banner*, July 11, 1887; May 25, 1882 (see also *ibid.*, June 25, 1883); Nashville *Republican Banner*, January 2, 1872; Nashville *Daily American*, July 20, 1876.

64. See Chapter 6.

65. *Nashville Banner*, June 26, 1882. Cf. Nashville, Report of the City Health Officer, *Annual Reports of the City of Nashville for the Year Ending October 1, 1888* (Nashville, 1888), p. 10.

66. Atlanta City Council Minutes, April 5, 1882; Atlanta *Christian Index and Southern Baptist*, May 11, 1882. See also *Atlanta Constitution*, April 18, 1882, for the outbreak of smallpox in a two-story frame house in the rear of the Gate City Hotel which was "occupied by negroes . . . very much crowded and . . . a very dangerous place for any contagious disease to make its appearance."

67. *Richmond Dispatch*, August 8, 16, 1866.

68. See *Nashville Daily Press and Times*, September 1866, *passim*.

69. Nashville *Republican Banner*, June 8, 14, 1873; physician quoted *ibid.*, June 11, 1873. For the number of deaths and their locations, see *ibid.*, June 8–July 1, 1873.

70. Nashville, *Report of the Board of Health*, 1876–1877, p. 24.

71. *Montgomery Daily Advertiser*, August 5, 1865; *Richmond Dispatch*, May 9, 1866; *Nashville Banner*, July 4, 1887.

72. Nashville, *Report of the Board of Health*, 1876–1877, p. 110.

73. *Atlanta Constitution*, October 1, 1890.

74. *Ibid.*, January 19, October 7, 1890. See also *ibid.*, September 28, 1890.

75. Richmond *Virginia Star*, November 18, 1882; Atlanta, Message of the Mayor, *Annual Report of the Mayor and Officers of the City of Atlanta for Fiscal Year Ending December 31, 1885* (Atlanta, 1886), p. 22; *Atlanta Constitution*, November 22, 1888. Negro households in Nashville also had more primitive

means of water supply than their white counterparts. The conditions were made even worse by the poor provisions for sewage disposal. Whereas 2,773 white households relied on hydrants, 218 on wells, 239 on springs, and 76 on cisterns, the corresponding figures for black households were 604, 140, 548, and 8. In other words, almost 42 percent of the blacks used the often contaminated springs, a source used by less than 8 percent of the whites (Nashville, *Report of the Board of Health*, 1876–1877, p. 109).

76. *Atlanta Constitution*, February 6, 1879; October 25, 1889. As late as February 1900, Butler north of Wheat Street, Old Wheat, Fraser south of Woodward, and practically the entire area around Atlanta University were among the great majority of Negro residential streets still unpaved. With few exceptions, paving in the city was limited to business streets and white residential areas. See paving map in *Foote and Davis Directory of Atlanta for 1900* (Atlanta, 1900).

77. *Atlanta Constitution*, December 23, 1887; Richard Mendales, "Sic Transit Richmond" (unpublished report for The Twentieth Century Urban Negro Project, Center for Urban Studies, University of Chicago, 1969).

78. *Atlanta Constitution*, June 25, 1887; Richmond, *Annual Reports*, 1885–1886, p. 8. Fire was an especially serious threat to the black-occupied homes because they were more likely to be of wood. If Nashville was representative, blacks also resorted to more primitive and more dangerous (and less efficient) forms of heating and lighting. All but 16 of the 1,331 black households included in the 1877 Board of Health survey were lighted by coal oil as compared to only 1,912 of the almost 3,200 white households. And whereas 590 black households used wood fireplaces for heat, this was true of only 61 white households (Nashville, *Report of the Board of Health*, 1876–1877, p. 109).

79. Richmond, Report of the Board of Health, *Annual Reports*, 1879–1880, p. 12. Negroes in all cities were also plagued by inadequate garbage collection. Pointing to the poor sanitary condition of a certain area, the *Nashville Banner*, April 13, 1883, noted that "it is almost entirely inhabited by negroes, and being in a retired region, it is claimed does not receive the attention it should."

80. Nashville *Daily American*, March 2, 1878; *Nashville Banner*, April 9, 1887; *Richmond Dispatch*, October 18, 1875; *Atlanta Constitution*, February 23, 1890; for the relation of public-health concerns to annexation, see Nashville *Republican Banner*, December 19, 1877.

81. Montgomery, Report of the City Physician, *Annual Message of the Mayor of Montgomery and Reports for the Various City Officers and Standing Committees of the City Council for the Fiscal Year Ending April 30, 1877* (Montgomery, 1877), p. 53.

6. HEALTH AND WELFARE SERVICES AND CORRECTIONAL INSTITUTIONS

1. See, for example, Richard C. Wade, *Slavery in the Cities: The South 1820–1860* (New York, 1964), pp. 267–69; Ira Berlin, *Slaves Without Masters: The Free Negro in the Antebellum South* (New York, 1974), pp. 321–27.

2. *Montgomery Daily Ledger*, August 15, 1865; *Montgomery Weekly Advertiser*, April 9, 1867.

3. Letter of the Reverend W. D. Harris, February 1, 1867, in *The American Missionary*, XI (March 1867), 50–51.

4. Montgomery, Minutes of the Montgomery City Council, February 24, 1868, Alabama Department of Archives and History, Montgomery.

5. *Richmond Dispatch*, October 23, 1866; *The American Missionary*, XI (February 1867), 29; J. W. Alvord, *First Semi-Annual Report on Schools and Finances of Freedmen* (Washington, D.C., 1866), p. 7.

6. See, for example, letter of L. E. Williams, April 14, 1866, in *The National Freedman*, II (May 1866), 146–47; letter of W. T. Richardson, Superintendent of Schools for the Cleveland Aid Commission, July 1, 1867, in *The American Missionary*, XI (September 1867), 206.

7. Colonel O. Brown to the Overseer of the Poor, November 20, 1865, in Richmond, Minutes of the Richmond City Council, November 27, 1865, Archives Division of the Virginia State Library, Richmond; *Richmond Dispatch*, January 1, 1866; Richmond City Council Minutes, May 14, 1866; August 17, 1867; March 31, 1868 (for years after 1866 the minutes are located in the Office of the City Clerk, Richmond City Hall). In July 1868 the Council, due to "heavy drafts upon the City Treasury," was forced to ask the Bureau to help in providing for the Negro destitute (*ibid.*, July 1, 14, 1868). Money that had been earmarked for the blacks was not being used, however, and the Bureau pressured the Council into spending it (*ibid.*, November 20, December 1, 1868).

8. Alrutheus Ambush Taylor, *The Negro in Tennessee 1865–1880* (Washington, D.C., 1941), p. 35; *Nashville Daily Press and Times*, August 6, 1866; Richmond City Council Minutes, March 31, 1868.

9. Atlanta, *Revised Code* (1866), p. 61 (see also the modification of this law [*ibid.* (1868), p. 74]); North Carolina, *Public Laws* (1866), pp. 102–103.

10. Montgomery, *Message of the Mayor and Reports of the Various City Officers and Standing Committees of the City Council for the Term Ending April 30, 1877* (Montgomery, 1877), p. 52; Atlanta, Minutes of the Atlanta City Council, June 5, July 3, 1868; July 9, 1869; August 4, 1871; August 3, 1872, Office of the City Clerk, Atlanta City Hall.

11. *Montgomery Daily Ledger*, October 3, 12–13, 1865; *Richmond Dispatch*, October 4, 17, 1866.

12. Richmond City Council Minutes, February 18, March 11, 1867.

13. *Nashville Daily Press and Times*, April 13, 1867; letter of C. M. Buckley, in Montgomery City Council Minutes, September 30, 1865; Atlanta City Council Minutes, September 29, 1865.

14. Dr. William Francis Drewy, *Historical Sketch of the Central State Hospital and the Care of the Colored Insane of Virginia 1870–1905* (Richmond, 1905), n.p. During the 1840s Dr. Francis T. Stribling, the head of the Western Lunatic Asylum, had unsuccessfully called for an asylum exclusively for the Negro insane.

15. *Nashville Daily Press and Times*, August 6, 1866.

16. Tennessee, *Acts* (1865–1866), c. 4, sec. 22; Tennessee, *Report of the Board of State Charities of Tennessee to the Fifty-Third General Assembly* (Nashville, 1903), p. 22; Raleigh *Daily Sentinel*, March 18, 1875; L. L. Polk (comp.), *Handbook of North Carolina Embracing Historical and Physiographical Sketches of the State with Statistical and Other Information Relating to Its Industries, Resources and Political Conditions* (Raleigh, 1879), p. 182.

17. Montgomery City Council Minutes, October 5, 1868; March 18, 1872; Montgomery *Weekly State Journal*, July 28, 1871; Raleigh, *Amended Charters and*

Ordinances (1867), p. 46; *ibid.* (1873), pp. 31-32. See also Richmond, *Amended Charter and Ordinances* (1867), pp. 91-92; Nashville, *Amended Charter, Acts of the General Assembly and Ordinances* (1868), p. 60. The segregation in Atlanta and Montgomery continued to be *de facto*.

18. Republicans played a similar role in states and cities not selected for intensive examination. In Mississippi, Republican state governments in 1870 and 1871 maintained wards for Negroes in charity hospitals established in Vicksburg and Natchez. In 1870 the Radicals made provisions for separate and allegedly equal treatment of blacks in the state insane asylum. Radicals also opened the doors of the Institution for Deaf and Dumb to blacks, evidently on a segregated basis. See Vernon Lane Wharton, *The Negro in Mississippi 1865-1890* (Chapel Hill, 1947), pp. 266-68. In South Carolina Radicals provided segregated quarters for blacks in the state insane asylum and orphanage. They also admitted them to the Institution for the Deaf and Blind, but closed the facility when whites withdrew. See Joel Williamson, *After Slavery: The Negro in South Carolina During Reconstruction 1861-1877* (Chapel Hill, 1965), pp. 281, 290-91, and George Brown Tindall, *South Carolina Negroes 1877-1900* (Columbia, 1952), pp. 278, 280-81.

19. See, for example, *Nashville Union and American*, November 27, 1870; James S. Hinton, a Negro member of the Indiana Canal Commission, quoted in Nashville *Daily American*, April 5, 1876; *Huntsville Gazette*, February 10, 1883.

20. See, for example, Report of the President of the Atlanta Board of Health, in Atlanta City Council Minutes, January 1, 1883; Nashville *Daily American*, April 29, 1876.

21. Richmond, *Annual Report of the Board of Health of the City of Richmond for the Year 1883* (Richmond, 1884), p. 6.

22. *Ibid.*, 1881, p. 6; *ibid.*, 1886, pp. 6-7.

23. Montgomery, *Annual Reports*, 1876-1877, p. 14; *ibid.*, 1884-1885, pp. 55-56.

24. *Montgomery Daily Advertiser*, January 27, 1875.

25. See, for example, Nashville *Daily American*, October 28, November 24, 1875, for a good summary of the controversy.

26. *Nashville Banner*, November 23, 1882; *Atlanta Constitution*, January 9, 1884; Atlanta, Report of the Council Committee on Relief, *Annual Report of the Officers of the City of Atlanta for the Year Ending December 31, 1889* (Atlanta, 1890), p. 34.

27. On Davidson County, see, for example, Nashville *Republican Banner*, January 5, 1871; on Richmond, see Jane Taylor Duke, "The Richmond Home for Boys 1846-1855," pp. 16, 20, Virginia State Library; *Constitution and By-Laws of the Female Humane Association of the City of Richmond with a Sketch of the Association* (Richmond, 1898), *passim;* on Fulton County, see *Atlanta Constitution*, February 12, 1889.

28. *Atlanta Constitution*, April 10, 1869; North Carolina, *Report of the Board of Public Charities of North Carolina* (Raleigh, 1891), pp. 12-14; *Montgomery Daily Advertiser*, January 20, 1870.

29. *Charter and By Laws of the Friends Asylum for Colored Orphans* (Richmond, 1883), *passim;* Richmond City Council Minutes, July 1, 1866; July 8, 1867; December 31, 1868; *The Carrie Steele Orphan Home of the City of Atlanta* (Atlanta, 1893), *passim;* Wiley Britton Sanders, *Negro Child Welfare in North Carolina* (Chapel Hill, 1933), p. 72.

30. *Atlanta Constitution*, April 2, 1889.

31. Valedictory of Mayor Calhoun, in Atlanta City Council Minutes, January 3, 1881; Raleigh, *Annual Reports of the Mayor and Officers of the City of Raleigh for Fiscal Year Ending April 30, 1884* (Raleigh, 1884), pp. 12–13.

32. Georgia, *Report of the Board of Trustees and Other Officers of the Georgia Institution for the Education of the Deaf and Dumb for the Year Ending June 30, 1876* (Atlanta, 1876), p. 7. The possibility remains, however, that this injunction concerning the conduct of the institution was meant to apply merely to administrative procedures rather than being a call for equal treatment.

33. *Atlanta Constitution*, May 2, 1880; Richmond, *Ordinances and Amended Charter* (1867), p. 93.

34. Georgia, *Report of the Institution for the Deaf and Dumb*, 1872–1873, pp. 8–9; *ibid.*, 1875–1876, p. 6; Georgia, *Report of the Board of Trustees of the Georgia Academy for the Blind for 1883* (Atlanta, 1884), p. 11; *ibid.*, 1880, pp. 14–18.

35. Alabama, *Annual Reports of the Alabama Institution for the Education of the Deaf and Dumb and Blind for 1883 and 1884* (Montgomery, 1884), pp. 11–12; *ibid.*, 1889–1890, pp. 7–8; *ibid.*, 1891–1892, p. 11 (see also *ibid.*, 1885–1886, pp. 21–22; *ibid.*, 1887–1888, p. 9); Virginia, *First Annual Report of the State Board of Charities and Corrections to the Governor of Virginia for the Year Ending September 30, 1909* (Richmond, 1909), p. 169; Writers Program of the Works Progress Administration in the State of Virginia (comp.), *The Negro in Virginia* (New York, 1940), p. 343.

36. Alabama, *Seventh Annual Report of the Officers of the Alabama Insane Hospital for the Year 1867* (Tuscaloosa, 1867), p. 9; *ibid.*, 1871, p. 8; *ibid.*, 1883–1884, p. 16; Polk, *Handbook of North Carolina*, pp. 181–82; Raleigh *Daily Sentinel*, March 18, November 3, December 8, 1875; *Visitors Guide to the North Carolina Exposition and Raleigh, 1884* (Raleigh, 1884), p. 15; Raleigh, *Amended Charter and Ordinances* (1876), pp. 96–97; Atlanta City Council Minutes, September 13, 1867; January 3, 1873; April 2, 1877; Atlanta, *Code* (1886), p. 156.

37. Richmond, *Annual Reports of the City Departments of Richmond, Virginia, for the Year Ending January 31, 1874* (Richmond, 1874), p. 11; *Atlanta Constitution*, January 13, 1882; Tennessee, *Report of the Board of State Charities*, 1903, p. 33; Tennessee, *First Biennial Report of the Tennessee Industrial School for the Period 1887–1888* (Nashville, 1888), p. 22.

38. Atlanta City Council Minutes, February 4, 1884; July 16, 1888; Atlanta, *Annual Report*, 1889, p. 35; *Atlanta Constitution*, September 28, 1884. The Negro fear of medical schools was a standing joke in Southern newspapers. According to the *Atlanta Constitution*, "a medical student can do more to scare a negro than a score of policemen" (January 2, 1880). The January 8, 1880, issue added, "It is said that after dark, a darkey can't be found within a mile of any medical college in the city." See also *Nashville Banner*, December 29, 1882.

39. Atlanta, *Annual Report*, 1888, pp. 41–45. See also *Atlanta Constitution*, January 27, 1872.

40. Writers Program of the Works Progress Administration in the State of Georgia, *Atlanta: A City of the Modern South* ("American Guide Series"; New York, 1942), p. 76. For a floor plan of the hospital, see *Atlanta Constitution*, December 7, 1890; Nashville, *Reports of the City of Nashville for the Year Ending October 1, 1889* (Nashville, 1889), p. 33. Before the Nash-

ville city hospital was opened, indigent blacks received publicly-supported segregated treatment at the University Hospital and at the Hospital of the Good Shepherd. As was true in Atlanta, both were affiliated with medical schools. See Nashville, *Report of the Nashville Board of Health for the Two Years Ending December 31, 1878* (Nashville, 1879), p. 103; *Nashville Banner,* January 8, 14, 1888; March 30, 1889.

41. David J. Rothman, *The Discovery of the Asylum: Social Order and Disorder in the New Republic* (Boston, 1971).

42. Tennessee, *Message of John C. Brown, Governor of Tennessee, to the Thirty-Ninth General Assembly of the State of Tennessee, January 4, 1875* (Nashville, 1875), p. 19.

43. Quoted in Atlanta *Daily New Era,* November 20, 1866. For segregation at the South Carolina penitentiary at this time, see Williamson, *After Slavery,* p. 281.

44. This was true even during the post-1890 period when penal segregation is generally acknowledged to have become pervasive. The Code of Laws and Regulations for the Penitentiary System of Tennessee in 1896, for example, called for the separation of white and black convicts, but added that this should be done "only as far as practicable" (Tennessee, *Report of the Warden, Superintendent and Other Officers of the Tennessee Penitentiary for the Year Ending December 31, 1896* [Nashville, 1897], p. 13). See also Frank William Hoffer, Delbert Martin Mann, Floyd Nelson House, *The Jails of Virginia: A Study of the Local Penal System* (New York, 1933), p. 112.

45. Though elsewhere a postwar phenomenon, by 1858 Virginia already had turned to the lease system as a substitute for the exclusion of blacks or their confinement with whites (Berlin, *Slaves Without Masters,* pp. 323–24).

46. Georgia, *Reports of the Principal Keeper and Officers of the Georgia Penitentiary for Year 1875* (Atlanta, 1876), pp. 10–12; *ibid.,* 1878–1880, p. 4.

47. Amanda Johnson, *Georgia as Colony and State* (Atlanta, 1938), p. 668; Gilbert Thomas Stephenson, *Race Distinctions in American Law* (New York, 1910), p. 146. Jim Crow hospital arrangements were present by 1888 (Johnson, *Georgia,* p. 668).

48. Alabama, *Biennial Report of the Inspectors of the Alabama Penitentiary for the Two Years Ending September 30, 1882* (Montgomery, 1882), pp. 19–21; *ibid.,* 1882–1884, pp. 22, 27, 201, 264; Alabama, *First Biennial Report of the Inspectors of Convicts from October 1, 1888 to October 1, 1890* (Montgomery, 1890), p. 5. See also *ibid.,* 1884–1886, p. 17, for a call for the use of entirely separate prisons to prevent any contact between the races. Separation at Wetumpka had been impossible earlier since the prison had only one usable cell block. Separate hospital quarters for the races are mentioned in Alabama, *Report of the Penitentiary, 1882–1884,* p. 27. For segregated cells, hospitals, or prayer meetings in other state penitentiaries, see North Carolina, *Biennial Report of the Board of Directors, Architect and Warden, Steward and Physician of the North Carolina State Penitentiary for the Two Years Ending October 31, 1880* (Raleigh, 1880), p. 46; *ibid.,* 1882–1884, p. 17; Tennessee, *Report of the Penitentiary, 1878–1880,* pp. 15, 30; *Nashville Union and American,* December 15, 1870; *Nashville Banner,* April 3, 1885; Roger A. Fischer, *The Segregation Struggle in Louisiana 1862–77* (Urbana, 1974), p. 84.

49. Hustings Court Order Books, No. 13, pp. 60, 367; *ibid.,* No. 16, p. 241; *ibid.,* No. 17, pp. 137–39; *ibid.,* No. 24, p. 163, Richmond City Hall.

50. Atlanta, *Annual Report,* 1889, p. 159; *Nashville Banner,* August 30, 1890.

For complaints about the confining together of some black and white prisoners due to a lack of room, see Nashville *Daily American*, October 13, 1887.

51. *Atlanta Constitution*, June 11, 1889; January 9, 1890; Raleigh *News and Observer*, March 29, 1890.

52. *Montgomery Daily Ledger*, August 29, 1865; Montgomery *Daily State Sentinel*, July 22, 1867.

53. Stephenson, *Race Distinctions in American Law*, p. 146; *Montgomery Daily Advertiser*, February 26, 1885. See also *ibid.*, September 26, 1871.

54. *Ibid.*, July 11, 1885. A similar progression had perhaps taken place by 1875 in Orleans Parish Prison in New Orleans (Fischer, *Segregation Struggle*, p. 84).

55. Montgomery residents showed an early interest in establishing a house of correction for black youths (*Montgomery Daily Advertiser*, April 14, 1880). During 1889, four years before the passage of a state law requiring the racial separation of young offenders, Atlanta citizens proposed building a segregated reformatory (*Atlanta Constitution*, December 21, 1889).

56. Excelsior Lodge No. 21 of Colored Masons (Raleigh), Minutes, 1875–1886, North Carolina Department of Archives and History, Raleigh. See, for example, entries for January 24, September 25, 1876; Taylor, *Negro in Tennessee*, p. 157; *Atlanta Constitution*, June 13, 1871.

57. Nashville *Republican Banner*, July 20, April 13, 1873; *Nashville Banner*, September 9, 1881. For the role of benevolent societies in Atlanta, see *Atlanta Constitution*, November 13, 1883, and W. E. B. Du Bois (ed.), *Economic Co-operation Among Negro Americans* ("Atlanta University Publications," No. 12, ed. W. E. B. Du Bois; Atlanta, 1907), p. 95.

58. See Walter B. Weare, *Black Business in the New South: A Social History of the North Carolina Mutual Life Insurance Company* (Urbana, 1973).

59. See *Richmond Planet*, December 6, 1890.

60. William Hepworth Dixon, *White Conquest* (2 vols.; London, 1876), II, 166; *Nashville Banner*, January 8, 1885; *Atlanta Constitution*, November 13, 1883. See also George Sala, *America Revisited: From the Bay of New York to the Gulf of Mexico and From Lake Michigan to the Pacific* (5th ed.; London, 1885), pp. 206–207.

61. *Atlanta Constitution*, November 13, 1883; *Nashville Daily Press and Times*, March 17, 1869; Richmond, *Amended Charter and Ordinances* (1867), pp. 91–92; Bureau of the Census, *Report on the Social Statistics of Cities. Part II. The Southern and the Western States* (Washington, D.C., 1887), 82.

62. On the early calls for a Negro cemetery, see Atlanta City Council Minutes, February 18, March 14, 18, 1878; on South View, see *ibid.*, August 15, September 6, 1886; Atlanta, *Annual Report*, 1888, p. 46; for the opening of West View, see *ibid.*, 1884, p. 18; for the reaction of its officials to South View, see Atlanta City Council Minutes, May 7, 21, 1888. Among the officers of South View were two prominent Negro undertakers, David T. Howard and Mitchell Cargill (*Atlanta Constitution*, March 17, 1886). See also the call of Holland Thompson, one of Montgomery's two black aldermen, for a separate black graveyard to replace the poorly maintained portion of the Montgomery cemetery reserved for Negroes (Montgomery City Council Minutes, May 3, 1869).

63. *Nashville Daily Press and Times*, December 16, 1865; *Nashville Banner*, January 28, 1888. The N.P.A. aided both whites and blacks.

64. Quoted in *Nashville Banner*, November 20, 1886. On earlier activities of the society, see *ibid.*, January 11, 1884.

65. *Ibid.*, November 27, December 10, 1886.

66. *Ibid.*, January 9, November 29, 1887; April 8, 1890. See also *ibid.*, January 16, 1888.

67. Raleigh, *Annual Reports*, 1883–1884, pp. 12–13; "Circular Letter Addressed to Various Counties by President [Henry M.] Tupper of Shaw Institute," *ibid.*, 1884–1885, pp. 16–17 (unlike the white hospital, the black hospital and its dispensary were open for only part of the year); C. J. Allardt (comp.), *Montgomery City Directory for 1891* (Montgomery, 1891), p. 16; Charles Octavius Boothe, *The Cyclopedia of the Colored Baptists of Alabama* (Birmingham, 1895), p. 59; Mrs. Hale quoted in J. W. Gibson and W. H. Crogman, *Progress of A Race or The Remarkable Advancement of the American Negro* (rev. ed.; Atlanta, 1902), pp. 480–81.

68. Nashville *Daily American*, January 30, 1876; Nashville *Republican Banner*, November 5, 1873; August 8, 1872; *Montgomery Daily Advertiser*, September 23, 1873; Montgomery *Herald*, September 25, October 16, 1886.

69. For the institution for dependent black girls in Nashville run by Julia G. Thomas, see William Wells Brown, *My Southern Home, or the South and Its People* (Boston, 1880), p. 219; for the Montgomery Industrial School for Negro Girls, see Ruth McAllister Vines, "The Contributions of Negroes in Providing School Facilities in the Montgomery, Alabama City Schools" (unpublished M.A. thesis, State Teachers College at Montgomery, 1943), p. 16, and W. N. Hartshorn, *An Era of Progress and Promise 1863–1910: The Religious, Moral and Educational Development of the American Negro Since His Emancipation* (Boston, 1910), p. 357.

70. *Friends Asylum for Colored Orphans, passim;* Richmond City Council Minutes, July 1, 1866; July 8, 1867; December 31, 1868; E. R. Carter, *The Black Side: A Partial History of the Business, Religious, and Educational Side of the Negro in Atlanta, Georgia* (Atlanta, 1894), pp. 35–37. See also *The Carrie Steele Orphan Home, passim.*

71. *Atlanta Constitution*, March 16, 1887; Colonel Albert Howell quoted *ibid.*, December 1, 1889. The Leonard Street Home for Negro female orphans was also founded in 1890 by an English woman, L. M. Lawson. The children were mainly from the Atlanta slums and had been abandoned by their parents. See Hartshorn, *Era of Progress and Promise*, pp. 373–75; W. E. B. Du Bois (ed.), *Efforts for Social Betterment Among Negro Americans* ("Atlanta University Publications," No. 14, ed. W. E. B. Du Bois; Atlanta, 1909), p. 78. Although both Du Bois and Hartshorn state that the home opened in 1890, the *Atlanta Constitution*, June 7, 1889, noted that a black orphan school was operating on Leonard Street with S. L. Grant, a white woman, as matron. The roots of Miss Lawson's institution therefore probably go back at least to 1889.

72. Joel Williamson suggests the same policy on the part of Negroes in South Carolina (Williamson, *After Slavery*, p. 281).

73. Georgia, *Report of the Academy for the Blind*, 1880, p. 18; Tennessee, 42nd General Assembly, *House Journal* (Nashville, 1881), p. 5; *Nashville Banner*, January 9–10, 1884. The *Banner* correctly noted that Young "had objected to any discrimination in public favors." The support of black women and children in separate institutions would not have been seen by him as "discrimination," providing the appropriations were equal.

74. *Richmond Planet*, June 12, 1886; petition of H. M. Turner *et al.*, in Atlanta

City Council Minutes, February 4, 1889 (a second petition was presented the following June and like the first, it was buried in committee [*Atlanta Constitution*, June 18, July 9, 1889]); Harris quoted in *Raleigh Register*, March 27, 1878.

75. *Nashville Daily Press and Times*, January 8, 1869; Raleigh *Daily Sentinel*, November 3, 1875; State of North Carolina Appointment Certificate, June 1, 1875, in James H. Harris Papers, North Carolina Department of Archives and History; Drewy, *Historical Sketch*, n.p.; Tennessee, *Report of the Tennessee Industrial School*, 1887–1888, p. 22; Alabama, *Reports of the Institution for the Deaf and Dumb and Blind*, 1890–1892, p. 22.

76. Testimony in U.S. Senate, 46th Cong., 2nd Sess., *Report and Testimony of the Select Committee of the United States Senate to Investigate the Causes for the Removal of the Negroes from the Southern States to the Northern States* (Washington, D.C., 1880), Part I, 55 (hereafter cited as *Report on the Removal of Southern Negroes*). For the years 1872–1873, $5,000 was spent for repairs on each of the two buildings; during 1874–1876, $3,500 more was spent on the Negro than on the white building. Well into the 1890s whatever differences there were in the improvements favored the Negro department. See North Carolina, *A Statistical Record of the Progress of Public Education in North Carolina, 1870–1906*, comp. Charles L. Coon (Raleigh, 1907), pp. 19–21.

77. Georgia, *Report of the Institution for the Deaf and Dumb*, 1881–1882, p. 7; Georgia, *Report of the Academy for the Blind*, 1886–1887, p. 8. The amounts were $42 for whites and $37 for blacks.

78. Richmond, *Annual Reports*, 1872–1873, pp. 319, 322, 325; *ibid.*, 1873–1874, pp. 38, 44; *ibid.*, 1874–1875, p. 40.

79. See, for example, Alabama, *Report of the Alabama Insane Hospital*, 1888–1890, p. 11; Tennessee, *Report of the Central Tennessee Hospital for the Insane for the Two Years Ending January 1, 1875* (Nashville, 1875), p. 19; Report of the Commissioners of the Asylum to the County Court, reprinted in *Nashville Banner*, July 7, 1884.

80. Tennessee, *Report of the Tennessee Industrial School*, 1889–1890, p. 26; Georgia, *Report of the Institution for the Deaf and Dumb*, 1890, pp. 20–21; Report of the Commissioners of the Asylum to the County Court, reprinted in *Nashville Banner*, July 7, 1884; Atlanta, *Annual Report*, 1887, p. 35; Richmond, *Annual Reports*, 1876–1877, pp. 45–47. By the mid-1880s a pattern emerged in which three to four times as many blacks as whites were annually being refused aid. The high rejection rate reflected the widespread belief that charity only encouraged idleness among blacks and led to their concentration in cities. See, for example, letter to the editor, *Richmond Dispatch*, October 24, 1874; interview of City Warden of the Poor in *Atlanta Constitution*, December 7, 1890; *Nashville Banner*, January 25, 1882; January 14, 1884.

81. Virginia, *Reports of the Board of Directors and Medical Superintendent of the Central Lunatic Asylum of Virginia for the Years 1875 and 1876* (Richmond, 1876), p. 8; Virginia, *Annual Report of the Virginia Eastern Lunatic Asylum for the Year Ending September 30, 1877* (Richmond, 1877), p. 17; Virginia, *Reports of the Central Lunatic Asylum, 1888–1889*, p. 38; Virginia, *Annual Report of the Board of Directors and of the Superintendent of the Western Lunatic Asylum of Virginia for the Fiscal Year 1889–1890* (Richmond, 1890), p. 18 (a year later the figure for the Negro asylum had dropped

to $115.65 [Virginia, *Reports of the Central Lunatic Asylum, 1889–1890*, p. 36]); Polk, *Handbook of North Carolina*, pp. 181–82; *Visitors Guide to the North Carolina Exposition of 1884*, p. 15.

82. In 1876 Friends and St. Joseph each got $1,000; Richmond Male Asylum and the Female Humane Association, $750; and St. Paul's Church Home, $500. Richmond, *Annual Reports*, 1875–1876, p. 175; Atlanta, *Annual Report*, 1885, p. 54; *Atlanta Constitution*, April 12, 1889.

83. Tennessee, *Report of the Tennessee Industrial School*, 1887–1888, p. 18; Tennessee, *Biennial Report of the Trustees and Superintendent of the Tennessee School for the Blind, January, 1891* (Nashville, 1891), p. 5.

84. Georgia, *Report of the Trustees, Superintendent, Resident Physician and Treasurer of the Lunatic Asylum of the State of Georgia, from January 1, 1870 to October 1, 1871* (Atlanta, 1871), p. 5; Alabama, *Report of the Alabama Insane Hospital*, 1882–1884, p. 16; *Atlanta Constitution*, December 29, 1885; Alabama, *Report of the Alabama Insane Hospital*, 1886–1888, pp. 23–24. By 1890 there were 913 white and 331 Negro patients (*ibid.*, 1888–1890, p. 11).

85. Richmond, *Annual Reports*, 1875–1876, p. xiii; *ibid.*, 1882–1883, pp. 6–7. At the Montgomery city hospital whites were also separated according to sex, but blacks were not (Montgomery *Alabama State Journal*, July 26, 1873).

86. Richmond, *Annual Reports*, 1887, p. 6; Virginia, *Report of the State Board of Charities and Corrections*, 1908–1909, p. 107. Nashville Negroes were somewhat more fortunate. After a committee investigating the county poorhouse reported in 1874 that the black facilities were "inferior in every respect to the white quarters," authorities promptly prepared to build a new institution (Nashville *Republican Banner*, January 24, 1874). It was finally opened two years later, but even these new quarters were inferior to those of the whites.

87. Quoted in Gibson and Crogman, *Progress of A Race*, p. 314. Blacks had long realized the need for adequate hospital facilities, but at least two efforts by Negroes to start a hospital failed. See *Atlanta Constitution*, December 23, 1887; May 21, 1890.

88. For death rates of blacks and whites from 1875 to 1888, see Nashville, Report of the City Health Officer, *Annual Reports*, 1887–1888, p. 108; for 1890 figures, see *ibid.*, 1889–1890, pp. 113–15.

89. See, for example, Richmond, *Annual Reports*, 1875–1876, p. 92; *ibid.*, 1877–1878, p. 30; *ibid.*, 1881–1882, p. 6; *ibid.*, 1886–1887, p. 5; Raleigh, *Annual Reports*, 1889–1890, p. 124.

90. Atlanta, Report of the Superintendent of Health, *Annual Report*, 1890, pp. 121–24. Board of Health Report, *ibid.*, 1891, pp. 218–19, contains a summary of death rates and a breakdown by age for the period 1880–1891. For the typical division by disease, see *ibid.*, 1890, pp. 529–30; *ibid.*, 1884, p. 138.

91. Montgomery, *Annual Reports*, 1876–1877, pp. 52–53. To some extent the main sources of inaccuracy in the city's health data cancel out one another. The underreporting of black deaths serves to lower the black death rate. But while population estimates used to compile the death rates undercount the blacks, they grossly overestimate the white population, thus reducing the white death rate. For example, in 1885 the city physician estimated that the city contained 12,000 whites and 11,000 blacks; however, the U.S. Census of 1880 had found 6,782 whites and 9,931 blacks and the Census of 1890 was to find 8,892 whites and 12,987 blacks (*ibid.*, 1884–1885, p. 54; Bureau of the Census, *Tenth Census: Population* [Washington, D.C., 1883], I, 96; Bureau of the Census, *Eleventh Census: Population* [Washington, D.C., 1893], I,

Part I, 540). The miscalculations by local authorities were products of a booster spirit. By understating the Negro population and overestimating the white population (and thus lowering its death rate), officials hoped to attract more whites to the city.

92. North Carolina, *Report of the Penitentiary, 1878–1880*, p. 146.

93. Virginia, *Annual Reports of the Board of Directors of the Virginia State Penitentiary for the Year Ending September 30, 1879* (Richmond, 1880), p. 23; *ibid.*, 1884–1885, p. 10; Georgia, *Reports of the Penitentiary, 1888–1890*, p. 3; *ibid.*, 1875, p. 16. It is worth noting that the counties containing Georgia's five largest cities, including Atlanta, contributed almost 30 percent of the state's prison population while having no more than 13 percent of Georgia's population.

94. Testimony of Charles Otey, in *Report on the Removal of Southern Negroes*, Part I, 130–31; testimony of John O. Kelly, *ibid.*, 250; North Carolina, *Report of the Penitentiary*, 1888–1890, p. 40.

95. *Atlanta Constitution*, December 24, 1884; Richmond, *Annual Reports*, 1876–1877, pp. 2–3.

96. (Charles Poindexter [ed.]), *Richmond, Virginia: Her Advantages and Attractions* (Richmond, 1895), p. 122.

97. The first mention of "two wards upon the grounds comfortably fitted up for such colored patients, male and female, as the Managers may consider it proper to receive" occurs in Retreat for the Sick, *Sixteenth Annual Report of the Retreat for the Sick 1892–1893* (Richmond, 1893), p. 1. A black annex "furnished exactly like the white wards" was added to the Old Dominion Hospital around 1895 (Poindexter, *Richmond*, p. 124). The Richmond Eye, Ear and Throat Institute had separate quarters for blacks by 1885, as did the Medical College Free Dispensary by 1882. See *Richmond Dispatch*, March 22, 1885; Richmond *Virginia Star*, December 9, 1882.

98. Virginia, *Biennial Report of the Prison Association of Virginia for Years 1896–1897* (Richmond, 1897), p. 8; Virginia, *Report of the State Board of Charities and Corrections*, 1908–1909, p. 161.

7. EDUCATION

1. Bureau of the Census, *Eighth Census: Vital Statistics* (Washington, D.C., 1864), pp. 507–508.

2. Letter of E. B. Adams, Agent of American Freedmen's and Union Commission for Georgia, undated, in *The American Freedman*, I (June 1866), 44; *Richmond Dispatch*, May 8, 1866; Richmonder quoted in letter of Lucy Chase, April 29, 1865, in *The Freedmen's Record*, I (June 1865), 98–99.

3. *Atlanta Constitution*, May 1, 1869.

4. Report of the Reverend G. W. Hawkins, in *The National Freedman*, I (September 15, 1865), 276; testimony of Colonel Eliphalet Whittlesey, in U.S. Congress, 39th Cong., 1st Sess., *Report of the Joint Committee on Reconstruction* (Washington, D.C., 1866), Part II, 183; letter of R. M. Manly, April 13, 1866, in *The American Freedman*, I (August 1866), 181; skull and crossbones incident reported in W. N. Hartshorn, *An Era of Progress and Promise 1863–1910: The Religious, Moral and Educational Development of the American Negro Since His Emancipation* (Boston, 1910), pp. 88–89.

5. Letter of M. E. Jones, undated, in *The National Freedman*, I (September 15, 1865), 263; letter of Lucy Dow, November 24, 1866, in *The Freedmen's Record*, III (January 1867), 4; letter of T. N. Chase, October 1, 1871, in *The American Missionary*, XV (December 1871), 283–84; unsigned letter from Raleigh, June 14, 1866, in *The Freedmen's Record*, II (July 1866), 133; conclusions about turnover based on correspondence in American Missionary Association Archives, Amistad Research Center, Dillard University, New Orleans, and the lists of teachers contained in the following publications: *The American Missionary*, *The American Freedman*, *The Freedmen's Record*, and *The National Freedman*.

6. Letter of the Reverend Evarts Kent, Pastor of the Colored Congregational Church, to the editor, *Atlanta Constitution*, July 20, 1887; letter of R. M. Manly, April 13, 1866, in *The American Freedman*, I (August 1866), 76; letter of General Clinton B. Fisk, April 23, 1866, quoted *ibid.*, p. 71; report of F. P. Brewer, in *The American Missionary*, XI (March 1867), 52.

7. Unsigned letter, undated, in *The American Missionary*, XIV (January 1870), 7; letter of Lucy Dow, November 29, 1866, in *The Freedmen's Record*, III (January 1867), 5. For a specific denial that the teachers came south "to fill the minds of our pupils with hatred," see letter of MBS (Mary B. Slade), *ibid.*, VII (January 1871), 98.

8. Letter of the Reverend William G. Hawkins, Corresponding Secretary of the Freedmen's Relief Association, July 19, 1865, in *The Natio.:al Freedman*, I (August 1865), 22; letter of Lucy Chase, April 29, 1865, in *The Freedmen's Record*, I (June 1865), 98; letter of J. M. Duncan, June 9, 1865, in *The American Missionary*, IX (August 1865), 172; letter of Adeline Harris, undated, in *The National Freedman*, I (September 15, 1865), 262. Opposition from white preachers was quickly surmounted due to the exodus of blacks from white churches. Economic pressure was more difficult to overcome. Ellen Ellis, a former dressmaker, reported that since her white customers in Richmond had learned that she had enrolled at the Northern-run Lincoln Industrial School, "they will not now, on any terms, give me employment again" (letter of Ellen Ellis, March 25, 1867, in *The Freedmen's Record*, III [April 1867], 106).

9. Letter of B. L. Canedy, November 7, 1866, in *The Freedmen's Record*, II (December 1866), 210; testimony of Colonel Eliphalet Whittlesey, in *Joint Committee Report on Reconstruction*, Part II, 190. For the continued faith of blacks in the power of education, see Charles Nordhoff, *The Cotton States in the Spring and Summer of 1875* (New York, 1876), p. 100; William Saunders, *Through the Light Continent* (London, 1879), pp. 84–85; "Richmond Public Schools," *Frank Leslie's Illustrated Newspaper*, XXVIII (July 21, 1883), 354; Montgomery *Alabama Guide*, October 1884; speeches of Atlanta Negro leaders Jackson McHenry and C. C. Wimbish in *Atlanta Constitution*, March 26, 1884; September 16, 1890; *Richmond Planet*, July 27, 1889.

10. Letter of the Reverend W. G. Hawkins, undated, in *The National Freedman*, I (September 15, 1865), 276; Franklin M. Garrett, *Atlanta and Environs: A Chronicle of Its People and Events* (3 vols.; New York, 1954), I, 741–42; *The American Missionary*, XI (October 1867), 224; letter of Horace W. Hovey, December 5, 1866, in *The Freedmen's Record*, III (January 1867), 21. See also letter of Harrison Leland, July 3, 1865, in *The Freedmen's Record*, I (August 1865), 133.

11. The Reverend Lewis Pettijohn to Mr. Jocelin, February 15, 1864, AMA Ar-

chives; excerpt from Richmond *Republic*, May 30, 1865, reprinted in *The American Missionary*, IX (July 1865), 153; Garrett, *Atlanta and Environs*, I, 741–42; letter of Harrison Leland, July 3, 1865, in *The Freedmen's Record*, I (August 1865), 133; extract from report of J. W. Alvord, July 1, 1868, in *The American Missionary*, XIII (January 1869), 4; Richmond quotation from William Hepworth Dixon, *The New America* (2 vols.; 6th ed.; London, 1867), II, 329. Richmond Theological Seminary, founded by the American Baptist Home Mission Society, began in Lumpkin's Jail, originally a jail for slaves waiting to be sold at auction (R. A. Brock, *Richmond as a Manufacturing and Trading Centre* [Richmond, 1880], p. 28).

12. *The American Missionary*, XI (February 1867), 28–29; Wallace P. Reed, *History of Atlanta, Georgia* (Syracuse, 1889), p. 325; John Wooldridge (ed.), *History of Nashville, Tennessee* (Nashville, 1890), p. 429; Cecil D. Halliberston, *A History of St. Augustine's College 1867–1937* (Raleigh, 1937), pp. 1–2; *Nashville Daily Press and Times*, December 29, 1865.

13. The Reverend David Chapman, Army chaplain stationed in Nashville, to George Whipple, November 18, 1863, AMA Archives; *Nashville Daily Press and Times*, June 14, 1867; letter of W. T. Richardson, Superintendent of Schools for the Cleveland Aid Commission, July 1, 1867, in *The American Missionary*, XI (September 1867), 205–206; report of Superintendent E. A. Ware, *ibid*. (May 1867), 97–98.

14. Letter of Richardson, July 1, 1867, in *The American Missionary*, XI (September 1867), 205–206 (he added: "It may seem to some that religious instruction is distinct from the general work of education; but we have no such warrant from our great teacher"); letter of John Walker, March 31, 1866, in *The National Freedman*, II (April 1866), 120. On one occasion the Reverend W. D. Harris reported from Richmond that 112 had taken the pledge (*The American Missionary*, X [April 1866], 75). See also remarks of F. P. Brewer, *ibid*., XI (July 1867), 159.

15. Lucy Chase quoted in *The American Freedman*, I (May 1866), 29; G. W. Hubbard, "History of the Colored Schools in Nashville," mentioned in *Nashville Republican Banner*, June 2, 1874; John Hope Franklin, *The Free Negro in North Carolina 1790–1860* (Chapel Hill, 1943), pp. 169–74. Franklin points out that a large number of North Carolina free Negroes received an informal education. In 1850 43 percent of the free Negro adults were literate. Ten years later the number in schools had declined greatly, but the literacy rate was higher.

16. Letter of Lucy Dow, November 24, 1866, in *The Freedmen's Record*, III (January 1867), 4; for the use of music, see, for example, letter of J. W. Duncan, June 9, 1865, in *The American Missionary*, IX (August 1865), 171. For a description of a typical day in the freedmen schools throughout the South, see Henry Lee Swint, *The Northern Teacher in the South* (Nashville, 1941), pp. 80–82.

17. See, for example, Swint, *The Northern Teacher*, pp. 140–42.

18. On Silsby, see Loren Schweninger, "The American Missionary Association and Northern Philanthropy in Reconstruction Alabama," *Alabama Historical Quarterly*, XXXII (Fall and Winter 1970), 149, 154–55. Manly served as clerk in the Richmond Office of Internal Revenue (*Richmond Dispatch*, July 2, 1875).

19. David Thomas, *My American Tour: Being Notes Taken During a Tour Through the United States Shortly After the Close of the Late American War* (Bury, 1868), p. 198; letter of Lizzie Leonard, December 4, 1866, in *The*

Freedmen's Record, III (January 1867), 8; Louise Dorr to Governor Zebulon Vance, August 17, 1877, (North Carolina) Governors' Papers, North Carolina Department of Archives and History, Raleigh. Referring to the Northern teachers in general, Dorr added, "We have no time for politics. Our work is too absorbing." See also *Atlanta Constitution,* June 29, 1871.

20. Letter of Lizzie Leonard, December 4, 1866, in *The Freedmen's Record,* III (January 1867), 7–8; letter of Horace W. Hovey, February 2, 1867, *ibid.,* III (March 1867), 41; letter of Fanny Jackson, Richmond student, March 22, 1867, *ibid.,* III (April 1867), 106. See also David Macrae, *The Americans at Home* (2 vols.; Edinburgh, 1870), II, 65–66.

21. Letter of J. W. Duncan, June 9, 1865, in *The American Missionary,* IX (August 1865), 171; mother quoted in letter of Lizzie Leonard, undated, in *The Freedmen's Record,* III (March 1867), 36.

22. Atlanta student quoted in letter of Carrie Gordon, May 17, 1870, in *The American Missionary,* XIV (September 1870), 196; letter of Fanny Wilson, January 21, 1869, *ibid.,* XIII (April 1869), 91.

23. Joseph M'Kelvey remarks in Western Freedmen's Aid Commission, *Second Annual Report of the Western Freedmen's Aid Commission* (Cincinnati, 1865), pp. 35–36; Miss Canedy quoted in Macrae, *Americans at Home,* I, 139 (see also letter of Horace W. Hovey to Ednah D. Cheney, Secretary of Freedmen's Aid Society, March 16, 1867, in *The Freedmen's Record,* III [April 1867], 63–64); Miss Howe quoted in Thomas, *My American Tour,* p. 199. For a typical foreigner's view, see *ibid.* See also letter of General Rufus B. Saxton, June 19, 1867, in *The American Missionary,* XI (September 1867), 193.

24. *Nashville Daily Press and Times,* December 27, 1865.

25. Letter of "A[n Atlanta] Teacher," September 23, 1870, in *The American Missionary,* XIV (November 1870), 247; J. W. Alvord, *Fourth Semi-Annual Report on Schools and Finances of Freedmen* (Washington, D.C., 1868), p. 17; letter of B. L. Canedy, March 4, 1871, in *The Freedmen's Record,* VII (April 1871), 111; for Woolfolk's performance, see letter of "EDC," October 17, 1868, *ibid.,* IV (November 1868), 175–76. Woolfolk became a prominent figure in Negro political and economic circles.

26. See, for example, letter of the Reverend D. Burt, Superintendent of Education of the Freedmen's Bureau in Tennessee, to the editor, *Nashville Union and Dispatch,* October 29, 1867.

27. Georgia, *Laws* (1866), p. 59; North Carolina, *Public Laws* (1866), p. 87; for Worth's position, see his letter to William A. Graham, January 12, 1866, in J. G. de Roulhac Hamilton (ed.), *Correspondence of Jonathan Worth* (2 vols.; Raleigh, 1909), I, 467.

28. North Carolina, *Public Laws* (1866–67), pp. 17–20; Atlanta, *Report of the Committee on Public Schools to the City Council of Atlanta, Georgia* (Atlanta, 1869), p. 11; Atlanta, Minutes of the Atlanta Board of Education, January 30, 1872, Atlanta Board of Education Building. For the support of the Peabody Fund for a system of white-only education, see letter of Barnas Sears, general agent of the fund, to the Committee on Public Schools, reprinted in *Atlanta Constitution,* November 2, 1869. For complaints of Atlantans that black children were better off than whites, see letter of Elizabeth Sterchi to Bishop George F. Bannson, January 14, 1869, in Adelaide L. Fries (ed.), "The Elizabeth Sterchi Letters," *Atlanta Historical Bulletin,* V (April 1940), 202; letter of W. L. Mansfield to the editor, *Atlanta Constitution,* April 15, 1869. Even by the end of the period many Georgians felt that Negroes had an unfair ad-

vantage over whites, thanks to the support of Northern philanthropists. See, for example, remarks of the chancellor of the University of Georgia, *ibid.*, July 26, 1889; letter to the editor, *ibid.*, August 25, 1889. For additional examples of the relationship between the freedmen's schools and the formation of white-only public schools, see excerpt from the Report of the Freedmen's Bureau's Superintendent of Schools, in *The American Missionary*, XI (November 1867), 248; Raleigh *Daily Sentinel*, October 29, 1866.

29. Tennessee, *Laws* (1865–1866), p. 65.

30. I. M. Hoyt, Secretary of the Board, to Major-General Carlin, July 27, 1867, in Nashville, Minutes of the Nashville Board of Education, July 27, 1867, Box 25, in J. Emerich Nagy Collection on the Nashville Schools, Tennessee State Library and Archives, Nashville; for the schools, see *ibid.*, September 4, 1867; April 1, 1868, Box 25; debate over organization of Negro schools reported in full in *Nashville Daily Press and Times*, June 14, 1867.

31. Marcus C. S. Noble, *A History of the Public Schools of North Carolina* (Chapel Hill, 1930), pp. 296, 314–15; Georgia, *Acts and Resolutions* (1870), p. 57; Alabama, *Acts* (1868), p. 148.

32. Richmond, *Amended Charter and Ordinances* (1869), p. 251; Richmond, Minutes of the Richmond Board of Education, September 30, 1869; January 16, May 22, 1871, Richmond Board of Education Building; Richmond, *Third Annual Report of the Richmond Public Schools for the Scholastic Year Ending July 31, 1871* (Richmond, 1871), p. 7; *ibid.*, 1876–1877, pp. 222–23; *ibid.*, 1875–1876, pp. 68–70.

33. Raleigh, *Annual Reports of the Mayor and Officers of the City of Raleigh for Fiscal Year Ending April 30, 1884* (Raleigh, 1884), pp. 54, 56. For the background of the 1877 state act which provided for a system of city graded schools supported by special local taxes, see Charles L. Coon, "The Beginnings of the North Carolina City Schools 1867–1887," *South Atlantic Quarterly*, XII (July 1913), 239, 243. Until 1877 the only public revenue given local schools came from a statewide common school fund.

34. Dr. Fred L. Brownlee, Executive Secretary of the AMA, to Ruth McAllister Vines, July 1, 1943, in Ruth McAllister Vines, "The Contributions of Negroes in Providing School Facilities in the Montgomery, Alabama City Schools" (unpublished M.A. thesis, State Teachers College at Montgomery, 1943), p. 21; Montgomery, Minutes of the Montgomery Board of Education, September 16, 1879; June 5, 1882, Montgomery County Board of Education Building, Montgomery; transfer of control of Swayne to the city mentioned in H. G. McCall (comp.), *A Sketch, Historical and Statistical of the City of Montgomery* (Montgomery, 1885), p. 20; Atlanta Board of Education Minutes, December 30, 1871; January 25, 30, 1872; December 13, 1876; for friction between the Atlanta School Board and the AMA, see *ibid.*, July 5, 1872; July 24, August 28, 1873; July 27, 1876; July 1, 3, August 22, 1878; for Storrs, see *Atlanta Constitution*, June 28, 1879; untitled article by Ella E. Roper, in *The American Missionary*, XLIV (July 1890), 212–14; American Missionary Association, *44th Annual Report of the American Missionary Association and Proceedings of the Annual Meeting held at Northampton, Massachusetts, October 21–23, 1890* (New York, 1890), p. 53.

35. All but Nashville's Teresa McKeon remained in the Negro schools. At first she taught in black schools, but in 1881 she was teaching fourth grade at the white Hume School. Eight years later she was one of the school's two principals (*Nashville Banner*, September 10, 1881; September 7, 1889).

36. When the Atlanta Board of Education terminated its agreement with the AMA, a letter from "Many Citizens" in the *Atlanta Constitution*, August 29, 1877, rejoiced: "It is neither just nor patriotic to tax southerners for the education of the colored people among us, and then employ northern teachers, while there are so many southern men and women who need the situations, who are amply qualified and better understand the idiosyncrasies of the African race."

37. J. W. Alvord to O. O. Howard, January 26, 1870, in J. W. Alvord, *Letters from the South Relating to the Condition of Freedmen Addressed to Major General O. O. Howard* (Washington, D.C., 1870), p. 32; Nashville, Minutes of the Nashville Board of Aldermen, July 28, 1870, Office of the Metropolitan Clerk, Davidson County Building and Nashville City Hall, Nashville (this motion had been tabled on June 23, 1870); Richmond Board of Education Minutes, August 8, 1870; June 12, 1871.

38. See, for example, the report on the hygiene of the public schools in Nashville, *Third Annual Report of the Nashville Board of Health for the Year Ending December 30, 1878* (Nashville, 1879), pp. 260–61; Virginia, *Annual Report of the Superintendent of Public Instruction for the Year Ending July 31, 1881* (Richmond, 1881), pp. 124–25; Atlanta, Report of the President of the Board of Education, *Seventh Annual Report of the Atlanta Board of Education for School Year Ending August 31, 1878* (Atlanta, 1878), pp. 7–8.

39. Nashville, *Ordinances and Miscellaneous Laws* (1872), p. 170. See also Georgia, *Laws* (1886–1887), pp. 73–74.

40. Georgia, *Constitution* (1877), Art. 8, sec. 1; Tennessee, *Constitution* (1870), Art. 11, sec. 12; Alabama, *Constitution* (1875), Art. 13, sec. 1; North Carolina, *Constitution* (1875), Art. 9, sec. 2. Virginia did not frame a new constitution until 1902. It too included a ban on coeducation of the races already contained in earlier school statutes (Virginia, *Constitution* [1902], Art. 9, sec. 140; Virginia, *Code* [1873], c. 78, sec. 58; Virginia, *Laws* [1881–1882], p. 37; *ibid.* [1895–1896], p. 352).

41. Barnas Sears to the Honorable Robert Winthrop, January 8, 1874, Jabez Lamar Monroe Curry Letters, Alabama Department of Archives and History, Montgomery. In addition to defending segregation, the Peabody Fund contributed unequally to the support of white and black schools. In 1877 the two Negro schools in Raleigh received a total of $500; the white school which had about one hundred more students received $1,000 (North Carolina, *Report of the Superintendent of Public Instruction of North Carolina for 1877* [Raleigh, 1878], p. 34). Six years earlier the fund had decided to give Negro schools two-thirds as much as white schools of the same size. The reason given was that "it costs less to maintain schools for the colored than for the white children" (quoted in Horace Mann Bond, *The Education of the Negro in the Social Order* [New York, 1934], p. 131).

42. Tennessee, *Annual Report of John M. Fleming, State Superintendent of Public Instruction for the Scholastic Year Ending August 31, 1874* (Nashville, 1875), pp. 26–27, 29; the circular reprinted *ibid.*, p. 28.

43. Alfred Moses to R. M. Manly, Secretary of the Richmond Educational Association, December 19, 1873, in Richmond Board of Education Minutes, December 20, 1873; Atlanta, *Annual Report of the Board of Education*, 1873–1874, pp. 18–19.

44. *Nashville Bulletin*, May 7, 1874, reprinted in Nashville *Republican Banner*, May 8, 1874; letter of W. P. Jones to the editor, *Nashville Bulletin*, reprinted in Nashville *Republican Banner*, May 29, 1874; Alabama platform quoted in

Atlanta Constitution, August 23, 1874. Senator William G. Brownlow was another Tennessee Republican who opposed the mixed school clause of the Civil Rights Bill: "Let the colored people have their own schools and churches and the white people have theirs. Let the colored people have a fair divide of the school fund and they will find their own teachers and preachers" (quoted *ibid.,* February 15, 1874). Republicans reacted in a similar fashion elsewhere. The Republican Superintendent of Public Instruction in North Carolina wrote to one of the state's senators: "No legislation in favor of mixed schools has ever been attempted in this state. Public sentiment on this subject is all one way. Opposition to mixed schools is so strong that if the people are free to choose between mixed schools and no schools, they will prefer no schools" (North Carolina, *Report of the Superintendent of Public Instruction,* 1873–1874, p. 64).

45. Raleigh, *Annual Reports,* 1883–1884, p. 51; Atlanta, *Annual Report of the Board of Education,* 1891, p. 277.

46. Richmond, *Annual Report of the Public Schools,* 1890–1891, pp. 38–39; Alabama, *Report of the Superintendent of Education of the State of Alabama for School Year Ending September 30, 1880* (Montgomery, 1880), p. 28. Under the Radicals in 1870–1871, Montgomery had spent $11.51 on each white and $11.44 on each black student (Montgomery, Minutes of the Montgomery City Council, September 4, 1871, Alabama Department of Archives and History).

47. Richmond Board of Education Minutes, November 25, 1875; September 24, 1888. The excess of rejected black over white applicants was already evident in the 1877–1878 school year when 150 white and 525 black children were initially denied admission to the public schools because of insufficient space. It was expected that at least 40 of the whites would be accepted later in the year (*ibid.,* September 27, 1877).

48. For an extended discussion of the Gray School, see E. R. Carter, *The Black Side: A Partial History of the Business, Religious, and Educational Side of the Negro in Atlanta, Georgia* (Atlanta, 1894), pp. 224–26; on the Moore Street School, see Richmond, *Annual Report of the Public Schools,* 1890–1891, p. 44.

49. Richmond, *Annual Report of the Public Schools,* 1875–1876, p. 367; *ibid.,* 1890–1891, pp. 84–85; Montgomery, *Annual Message of the Mayor of Montgomery and Reports for the Various City Officers and Standing Committees of the City Council for the Fiscal Year Ending April 30, 1887* (Montgomery, 1887), p. 57; Nashville, Lawrence School Notes, Box 57, Nagy Collection. The way in which a new Negro school was furnished ten years earlier also demonstrated the attitude of whites and was perhaps a regular procedure for black schools. According to the Nashville *Daily American,* November 1, 1879, "All the furniture for it was obtained from the various other school buildings in the city, and has not cost the city a cent." By 1890 Negro school property owned by the city of Montgomery was valued at $2,500; the white property, $41,000. Between 1876 and 1890 the value of Negro school property in Richmond increased from $60,000 to $123,000 at a time when white property grew from $167,400 to $267,700. In 1892 Atlanta's five Negro schools were valued at $62,250 and the thirteen white schools at $319,530 (Montgomery, Finance Committee Report, *Annual Reports,* 1889–1890, p. 20; Richmond, *Annual Report of the Public Schools,* 1875–1876, p. 36; *ibid.,* 1890–1891, p. 44; Atlanta, *Annual Report of the Board of Education,* 1892, pp. 26–27).

50. See, for example, Nashville Board of Education Minutes, September 29, 1884; June 29, 1885; September 15, 1886, Box 26, Nagy Collection. In Richmond the high school program of whites was more rigorous and extensive than that

of the blacks. For the schedules of students, see Richmond, *Annual Report of the Public Schools*, 1879–1880, pp. 41, 43; *ibid.*, 1890–1891, pp. 56, 61.

51. Raleigh, *Annual Reports*, 1885–1886, p. 87. Expressed another way, 7.6 percent of the enrolled white students and 4.5 percent of the enrolled black students in Richmond were in the two highest grammar school grades (Richmond, *Annual Report of the Public Schools*, 1890–1891, pp. 36–37). By the end of the period, Richmond and Atlanta also operated night schools only for whites.

52. Nashville Board of Education Minutes, January 6, 1874, Box 26, Nagy Collection; Nashville Board of Aldermen Minutes, October 20, 1874. Typically the new accommodations were to be in a rented rather than in a specially constructed building.

53. Atlanta Board of Education Minutes, April 29, September 3, 1880; March 22, November 22, 1888.

54. *Ibid.*, January 3, October 28, 1873. For similar rejections in Atlanta, see *ibid.*, October 30, 1875; June 26, 1880. The Richmond petition and the Board's response can be found in Richmond Board of Education Minutes, February 28, 1878.

55. Richmond Board of Education Minutes, March 25, June 30, September 23, October 6, 1880; for petitions of Negro churches to have their buildings used as public schools, see Montgomery Board of Education Minutes, February 7, August 14, 1876; for the role of Negro contributions in 1888, see Vines, "The Contributions of Negroes," p. 21. For evidence of continued difficulty in getting positive responses to petitions in Nashville, see letter of W. H. Young to the editor, *Nashville Banner*, November 29, 1889.

56. See, for example, letters of the Reverend L. M. Hapgood to the editor, *Nashville Banner*, May 23, June 13, 1883; account of a black protest meeting, *ibid.*, June 9, 1883; interview of the Reverend W. J. Gaines in *Atlanta Constitution*, June 16, 1887.

57. Richmond Board of Education Minutes, June 24, 1875.

58. Louise Dorr to Governor Zebulon Vance, August 17, 1877, (North Carolina) Governors' Papers. The prominent Atlanta Negro, the Reverend W. J. Gaines, also expressed dissatisfaction with his city's Northern teachers (interview in *Atlanta Constitution*, June 16, 1887; letter to the editor, *ibid.*, June 21, 1887). For friction between Northern teachers and Montgomery blacks, see separate letters of the Reverend and Mrs. G. W. Andrews to the Reverend M. E. Strieby, June 17, July 11, 1875, AMA Archives. For additional petitions requesting black teachers, see Atlanta Board of Education Minutes, August 22, 1874; April 27, July 10, 1876; June 13, 1878; Nashville Board of Education Minutes, March 6, April 3, 1877; June 12, 1883, Box 26, Nagy Collection. At a meeting called to draw up the June 12, 1883 petition, W. H. Young, a black lawyer and politician, proposed that if the petition were rejected, blacks should withdraw their children from the schools. More moderate leaders prevailed, however, and Nashville was spared what would have been one of the first Southern school boycotts (*Nashville Banner*, June 12, 1883).

59. Colored Press Association resolution in Montgomery *Weekly Advance*, September 3, 1881; Richmond *Virginia Star*, November 18, 1882; letter of "F" to the editor, *ibid.*, December 16, 1882. See also *ibid.*, December 9, 1882. In a similar manner, the editor of the Montgomery *Alabama Guide*, October 1884, recommended Tuskegee Institute because "the school is managed and controlled by our race."

60. William Wells Brown, *My Southern Home, or the South and Its People* (Bos-

ton, 1880), p. 215. See also interview of a white teacher in *Nashville Banner*, January 29, 1884.

61. Richmond Board of Education Minutes, September 5, 1871; for Mrs. Bennett, see especially *ibid.*, September 21, 26, 1876.

62. Nashville *Daily American*, April 7, 1877; Brown, *My Southern Home*, p. 215; *Raleigh Register*, March 27, 1878.

63. For separate examinations and teacher preparation classes, see, for example, Nashville Board of Education Minutes, June 15, 1887, Box 26, Nagy Collection; Atlanta, *Annual Report of the Board of Education*, 1884, p. 17; Atlanta Board of Education Minutes, October 9, 1877; Montgomery Board of Education Minutes, August 19, 1882; Richmond Board of Education Minutes, September 7, 1870; for the shift in Swayne School faculty, compare the lists of teachers in Joel Davis (comp.), *Montgomery Directory 1883–1884* (Montgomery, 1883), p. 22, and C. J. Allardt (comp.), *Montgomery City Directory for 1888* (Montgomery, 1888), p. 16; for the position on all-black staffs, including principals, see, for example, Nashville Board of Education Minutes, November 5, 1878, Box 26, Nagy Collection.

64. Richmond Board of Education Minutes, June 30, 1880; Atlanta school board member quoted in *Atlanta Constitution*, June 25, 1887.

65. See, for example, the decision to turn over Nashville's Bell View School to black teachers in Nashville Board of Education Minutes, June 12, 1883, Box 26, Nagy Collection.

66. For Napier's role, see, for example, accounts of the Nashville Common Council meetings in the Nashville *Daily American*, August 29, 1879; *Nashville Banner*, May 26, 1882; Atlanta school board member remark in Atlanta Board of Education Minutes, July 26, 1877. The first black teacher was hired to teach at Montgomery's Swayne School because an extra teacher was needed and the Board of Education could not afford to pay the regular salary. See letter of J. M. McPherron to E. M. Cravath, February 4, 1874, AMA Archives.

67. At the same time pupil–teacher ratios were higher in the black schools. Again the differences were least in Richmond and greatest in Montgomery. For the 1890–1891 school year, the ratio in Richmond was 39 : 1 in the white schools and 43 : 1 in the black schools (Richmond, *Annual Report of the Public Schools*, 1890–1891, pp. 5–6). For the 1885–1886 school year in Montgomery, the ratios were 42 : 1 and 73 : 1 respectively (Montgomery, *Annual Reports*, 1885–1886, pp. 76–77).

68. Atlanta, *Annual Report of the Board of Education*, 1873–1874, pp. 6–7; *ibid.*, 1891, pp. 267–71. Summer Hill School provides an excellent example of the impact on salaries produced by the shift to black teachers. See especially *ibid.*, 1885, p. 5; *ibid.*, 1887, p. 148.

69. This was due primarily to the large number of whites teaching Negro pupils. In the white Centennial Graded School one teacher received $50 per month and the others $40 per month; in the Negro schools two teachers received $30 and the rest, $40 (Raleigh, *Annual Reports*, 1883–1884, pp. 52–57).

70. Richmond, *Annual Report of the Public Schools*, 1874–1875, p. 351; *ibid.*, 1890–1891, pp. 38–39; Richmond Board of Education Minutes, July 1, 1881; July 26, 1883; September 25, 1884; September 24, 1888.

71. Nashville, Salary Schedules, Box 51, Nagy Collection.

72. Montgomery City Council Minutes, December 5, 1870; Montgomery Board of Education Minutes, December 31, 1875; July 1, 1893; Alabama, *Report of the Superintendent of Education*, 1879–1880, p. 19; *ibid.*, 1890–1891, p. 162.

73. Nashville Board of Education Minutes, October 7, 1879, Box 26, Nagy Collection; Richmond, *Annual Report of the Public Schools*, 1881–1882, p. 22.

74. Atlanta Board of Education Minutes, July 26, 1877; Nashville Board of Education Minutes, May 26, 1884; May 30, 1887, Box 26, Nagy Collection. For charges that unqualified blacks would replace qualified whites, see Nashville *Daily American*, May 26, 1880; *Nashville Banner*, June 11, 1883.

75. Nashville Board of Education Minutes, June 14–15, 1887, Box 26, Nagy Collection. The change was made at Summer Hill because the performance of blacks in that year's teacher's examination could not be ignored (*Atlanta Constitution*, June 25, 1887. The next day, when the time came to elect the Negro teachers, two councilmen were still in opposition. One said he wanted "no niggers" in the school [*ibid.*, June 28, 1887]. The chief stumbling block had been the absence of available positions for the white teachers); Richmond Board of Education Minutes, March 7, June 28, 1883; June 26–27, 1884. The Readjusters, however, were dedicated to the principle of separate (though equal) schools. See *ibid.*, March 7, 1883.

76. Atlanta, *Annual Report of the Board of Education*, 1880–1881, p. 8; Montgomery Board of Education Minutes, June 8, 1889. See also Richmond Board of Education Minutes, June 26, 1884; October 26, 1885.

77. Atlanta Board of Education Minutes, October 2, 1877; June 25, 1887; *Atlanta Constitution*, December 23, 1887; Hartshorn, *Era of Progress and Promise*, pp. 88–89.

78. Richmond, *Annual Report of the Public Schools*, 1889–1890, p. 13. See also Nashville *Daily American*, October 10, 1879; Carter, *Black Side*, pp. 101–103, 240. Even "home-grown" talent could prove difficult. See, for example, accounts of the disciplinary problems at the Colored High and Normal School in Richmond Board of Education Minutes, December 28, 1885; July 2, 1886. School officials also had difficulties with individual black teachers and principals. A. A. Graves, a graduate of Atlanta University and principal of Atlanta's Gate City School, resigned after school children were dismissed for a celebration to honor Jefferson Davis (Carter, *Black Side*, pp. 232–36). Graves's successor, L. M. Hershaw, was fired after making a speech in which he criticized Southern educational policy toward Negroes and unfavorably compared the region to the North. He was reinstated after writing a contrite apology. See *Atlanta Constitution*, July 26, August 30, 1889. Daniel B. Williams, a Richmond teacher, was dismissed after a clash with his white principal over the school's promotion policy. He was encouraged to re-apply for his position by the Board of Education and having done so, saw his request unanimously denied (Richmond Board of Education Minutes, February 22, March 22, 1883).

79. See *Atlanta Constitution*, December 14, 1883, for the remarks of Wimbish and Carter. Petitions calling for black representation on boards of education are mentioned in Nashville Board of Aldermen Minutes, November 21, 1876; Atlanta, Minutes of the Atlanta City Council, December 5, 1887, Office of the City Clerk, Atlanta City Hall.

80. *Richmond Dispatch*, May 26, 1883; see also *ibid.*, May 25, 1883.

81. *Nashville Union and Dispatch*, December 17, 1867; Nashville Board of Aldermen Minutes, October 30, 1869; William Asbury Christian, *Richmond: Her Past and Present* (Richmond, 1912), pp. 382, 387; Montgomery City Council Minutes, September 19, 1870; January 10, 1873. There may have been a second Negro who served on the Montgomery Board of City School Commis-

sioners. See Howard N. Rabinowitz, "Half a Loaf: The Shift from White to Black Teachers in the Negro Schools of the Urban South, 1865–1890," *Journal of Southern History*, XL (November 1974), pp. 593–94, footnote 116.

82. For the role of the Readjusters, see, for example, Richmond Board of Education Minutes, September 23, 1883; for Holland Thompson's role, see, for example, Montgomery City Council Minutes, September 5, 1870.

83. See, for example, Richmond, *Annual Report of the Public Schools*, 1881–1882, 1883–1884, 1886–1887, 1889–1890. See also Montgomery, *Annual Reports*, 1889–1890, pp. 82–83.

84. Nashville, Statistical Tables 1854–1886, Box 51, Nagy Collection; Nashville, *Annual Report of the Board of Education of Nashville for Scholastic Year 1889–1890* (Nashville, 1890), p. 36; Richmond Board of Education Minutes, June 7, 1872; Richmond, *Annual Report of the Public Schools*, 1880–1881, p. 53; *ibid.*, 1885–1886, p. 23; *ibid.*, 1890–1891, pp. 32–33.

85. *Richmond Times Dispatch*, August 20, 1933.

86. William Hepworth Dixon, *White Conquest* (2 vols.; London, 1876), II, 170; Richmond, *Annual Reports of the City Departments of Richmond, Virginia, for the Year Ending January 31, 1874* (Richmond, 1874), p. 31; Nashville, *Reports of the City of Nashville for Year Ending October 1, 1890* (Nashville, 1891), p. 59; Bureau of the Census, *Negro Population 1790–1915* (Washington, D.C., 1918), p. 435. Much of the Negro illiteracy can probably be attributed to the large number of migrants from rural areas where educational opportunities for blacks were limited.

8. PUBLIC ACCOMMODATIONS

1. Richard C. Wade, *Slavery in the Cities: The South 1820–1860* (New York, 1964), pp. 266–71; Ira Berlin, *Slaves Without Masters: The Free Negro in the Antebellum South* (New York, 1974), pp. 321–27; Roger A. Fischer, *The Segregation Struggle in Louisiana 1862–77* (Urbana, 1974), p. 13.

2. Dale A. Somers, "Black and White in New Orleans: A Study in Urban Race Relations, 1865–1900," *Journal of Southern History*, XL (February 1974), 25; Whitelaw Reid, *After the War: A Tour of the Southern States 1865–1866*, edited with an introduction by C. Vann Woodward (reprinted; New York, 1965), p. 377; *Montgomery Daily Ledger*, November 20, 1865; for segregation in theaters, see *Nashville Daily Press*, January 30, 1865; *Montgomery Daily Advertiser*, October 24, 1865; *Richmond Dispatch*, November 7, 1866. For additional examples of segregated seating at circuses, see Raleigh *Daily Standard*, March 3, 1866; *Richmond Dispatch*, October 6, November 7, 1866; *Nashville Daily Press*, April 3, 1865.

3. Texas, *General Laws* (1866), p. 97; Mississippi, *Laws* (1865), pp. 231–32; Florida, *Laws* (1865), p. 24; Robert E. Perdue, *The Negro in Savannah 1865–1900* (New York, 1973), p. 22; letter of "A Colored Man" to the editor, *Nashville Daily Press and Times*, June 4, 1867.

4. "A Bill to Protect the Rights of Citizens Traveling in Public Conveyances," February 21, 1870, (North Carolina) Legislative Papers #836, North Carolina Department of Archives and History, Raleigh. For laws passed elsewhere, see Joel Williamson, *After Slavery: The Negro in South Carolina During Re-*

construction 1861–1877 (Chapel Hill, 1965), pp. 279–80, 357; Vernon Lane Wharton, *The Negro in Mississippi 1865–1890* (Chapel Hill, 1947), p. 231; *Cong. Globe,* 42nd Cong., 2nd Sess., pp. 429–34 (January 17, 1872).

5. David Macrae, *The Americans at Home* (2 vols.; Edinburgh, 1870), II, 219. See also Two Englishmen (Alexander Rivington and Harris Rivington), *Reminiscences of America in 1869* (2nd rev. ed.; London, 1870), p. 220.

6. Wharton, *Negro in Mississippi,* p. 231. Louisiana's law was equally ineffective with regard to steamboats and railroads. Significant integration in trains, however, may have been secured through the use during the chartering process of written and verbal pledges to provide "equal accommodations" to members of both races (John W. Blassingame, *Black New Orleans 1860–1880* [Chicago, 1973], pp. 190–94).

7. Letter of "CBL" to the editor, *Montgomery Daily Advertiser,* November 8, 1871. For examples of suits, see *Atlanta Constitution,* April 12, May 19, 1871; *Richmond Dispatch,* May 24, 1876; Nashville *Daily American,* May 16, 1879.

8. Roger A. Fischer, "A Pioneer Protest: The New Orleans Street Car Controversy of 1867," *Journal of Negro History,* LIII (July 1968), 232–33; Marjorie M. Norris, "An Early Instance of Non-Violence: The Louisville Demonstrations of 1870–1871," *Journal of Southern History,* XXXII (November 1966), 487–504; August Meier and Elliott Rudwick, "A Strange Chapter in the Career of 'Jim Crow' [Savannah]," *The Making of Black America,* Vol. II: *The Black Community,* eds. August Meier and Elliott Rudwick ("Studies in American Negro Life Series"; New York, 1969), pp. 14–19; August Meier and Elliott Rudwick, "Negro Boycotts of Jim Crow Street Cars in Tennessee," *American Quarterly,* XXI (Winter 1969), 755–63; August Meier and Elliott Rudwick, "The Boycott Movement Against Jim Crow Streetcars in the South, 1900–1906," *Journal of American History,* LV (March 1969), 756–75.

9. Writers Program of the Works Progress Administration in the State of Virginia (comp.), *The Negro in Virginia* (New York, 1940), pp. 241–42. Alexander Wilbourne Weddell, *Richmond, Virginia in Old Prints 1737–1887* (Richmond, 1932), p. 234, and the WPA study, p. 242, mention that Negro cars had black balls on top; *Richmond Dispatch,* May 9, 1867, refers to a ladies' car as a "ball car." See also *ibid.,* January 29, 1870.

10. Letter of "A Colored Man" to the editor, *Nashville Daily Press and Times,* June 26, 1866; *ibid.,* June 18, 25, 28, 1867; Mobile *Nationalist,* July 25, 1867; April 29, 1870; for Charleston, see *ibid.,* May 9, 1867; Maria Waterbury, *Seven Years Among the Freedmen* (2nd rev. ed.; Chicago, 1891), pp. 115–16; Fischer, "A Pioneer Protest," for example, never confronts the basic distinction between exclusion and segregation.

11. Mobile blacks were not admitted to the Opera House until 1885 and then only because of a deal with vote-seeking white reformers who allowed blacks to use the facility for a private gathering (Charles Dudley Warner, *Studies in the South and West with Comments on Canada* [New York, 1889], pp. 14–15). For the exclusion of blacks from hotels, see *Montgomery Daily Advertiser,* February 26, 1873; Montgomery *Alabama State Journal,* March 7, 1873; *Atlanta Constitution,* October 7, 1868.

12. For skating rinks, see *Montgomery Daily Advertiser,* March 12, 1870; Montgomery *Alabama State Journal,* April 9, 1872; *Atlanta Constitution,* December 21, 1869; October 18, 1871; *Nashville Union and American,* June 7, 1870; for barrooms, etc., see *Daily Atlanta Intelligencer,* July 14, 1870; *Nashville Daily Press and Times,* February 1, 1868; Montgomery *Daily State Sentinel,* July 3,

1867; *Montgomery Daily Advertiser*, March 9, 1871; Montgomery *Republican Sentinel*, October 31, 1872.

13. Montgomery *Alabama State Journal*, April 6, 1873; Nashville *Republican Banner*, March 2, 1871; Blassingame, *Black New Orleans*, p. 185; Nashville *Republican Banner*, March 8, April 13, 1871; for picnics, see, for example, *Montgomery Daily Advertiser*, May 4, 29, June 3, July 6, 1869; May 28, 1870; Montgomery *Alabama State Journal*, July 5, 31, 1869; May 8, 17, June 11, 1872; for theaters, see, for example, advertisements in *Atlanta Constitution*, January 21, 1871; Raleigh *Daily Standard*, October 15, 1869; *Richmond Dispatch*, May 3, 1869; *Nashville Union and American*, January 25, 1871; *Montgomery Daily Advertiser*, January 30, 1872.

14. Williamson, *After Slavery*, pp. 293–94; *Richmond Dispatch*, May 9, 1867; North Carolina, *Senate Journal*, p. 41 (July 1868). Democrats also practiced segregation at their rallies. For the presence of separate speakers' stands and dinner tables at a Democratic barbecue, see *Montgomery Daily Advertiser*, August 16, 1868.

15. *Cong. Globe*, 42nd Cong., 2nd Sess., p. 241 (December 20, 1871); *Cong. Record*, 43rd Cong., 2nd Sess., III, Part 2, 939 (February 3, 1875); *ibid.*, Part 3, Appendix, 15 (February 4, 1875). For the opposition of Tennessee white Republicans to national civil rights legislation, see Nashville *Republican Banner*, May 8, September 10, October 1, 1874. For further support of the contention that, with the exception of a few Radicals, Congressional Republicans sought to end exclusion and unequal treatment of blacks rather than segregation per se, see Alfred Avins, "Racial Segregation in Public Accommodations: Some Reflected Light on the Fourteenth Amendment From the Civil Rights Act of 1875," *Western Reserve Law Review*, 18 (May 1967), 1251–83.

16. Montgomery *Alabama State Journal*, August 23, 1874; Stanley J. Folmsbee, "The Origin of the First 'Jim Crow' Law," *Journal of Southern History*, XV (May 1949), 235–47; Georgia, *Laws* (1870), p. 398; for the attempt to pass civil rights legislation in Alabama, see Montgomery *Alabama State Journal*, February 25, March 1, 7, 9–10, April 8, August 14, 1873; for Alabama Republican support of separate but equal treatment, see *ibid.*, January 27, 1872; May 29, June 6, 14, 30, July 11, 1874; Montgomery *Weekly State Journal*, December 11, 1869; March 18, 1870; Mobile *Nationalist*, April 18, 1867.

17. For earlier opposition to prospective state civil rights acts, see *Montgomery Daily Advertiser*, August 13, 1868; December 7, 1869; July 4, 1873; Blassingame, *Black New Orleans*, pp. 183–84, 190–91; Williamson, *After Slavery*, p. 280.

18. *Nashville Union and American*, April 19, 1870; *Atlanta Constitution*, February 6, 1875; Raleigh *Daily Sentinel*, August 2, 1875.

19. *Atlanta Constitution*, April 3, 1875. See also *ibid.*, March 27, 1875; October 16, 1883; *Richmond Dispatch*, March 10, 1875; Nashville *Republican Banner*, March 2, 1875; *Nashville Banner*, October 18, 1883; *Montgomery Daily Advertiser*, October 23, 1883. Even if the law did not alter Southern life, the potential for more rigid enforcement always existed and whites therefore rejoiced when the U.S. Supreme Court declared it unconstitutional in 1883. See, for example, *Richmond Dispatch*, October 14–21, 1883; *Atlanta Constitution*, October 16, 21, 1883.

20. *Atlanta Constitution*, January 28, 1876; *Richmond Dispatch*, May 24, 1876; Savannah case reported in Nashville *Daily American*, May 16, 1879.

21. *Nashville Union and American,* June 27, 1866.
22. Macrae, *Americans at Home,* II, 19; Hilary A. Herbert, "Grandfather's Talks About His Life Under Two Flags," pp. 291–92, Southern Historical Collection, University of North Carolina Library, Chapel Hill.
23. Wharton, *Negro in Mississippi,* p. 232.
24. Tennessee, *Laws* (1885), pp. 124–25. See also *Atlanta Constitution,* July 25, 1887; Henry W. Grady, *The New South* (New York, 1889), p. 246.
25. *Atlanta Constitution,* January 25, 1872; *Nashville Banner,* December 15, 1885; Lawrence D. Rice, *The Negro in Texas 1874–1900* (Baton Rouge, 1971), p. 147. Segregation in Nashville waiting rooms was probably in force much earlier than 1885. The fact that in 1873 the city's Louisville Depot had a "gentlemen's sitting room" rather than a "men's" waiting room suggests the existence of a Negro waiting room or else the absence of any provision for black passengers (Nashville *Republican Banner,* November 14, 1873).
26. *Montgomery Daily Advertiser,* February 14, 1877; October 17, 1885; Raleigh *News and Observer,* April 24, October 31, 1890. For segregated waiting rooms at Atlanta's new East Tennessee, Virginia and Georgia Railroad Station, see *Atlanta Constitution,* March 23, 1884. For the existence of a "white waiting room" at Nashville's Lincks Depot, see letter of Mrs. N. J. Stith to the editor, *Nashville Banner,* August 27, 1890. Segregation was also practiced at small town stations. See, for example, the situation in Huntsville, Alabama, reported in *Huntsville Gazette,* June 19, 1886; McDonough, Georgia, reported in *Atlanta Constitution,* October 18, 1890; and Columbia, Tennessee, reported in Nashville *Daily American,* June 30, 1877. The Columbia station, erected two years after the passage of the Civil Rights Act, is another indication of the slight impact of the law, as was the continued segregation in Atlanta's Union Depot in 1882 (*Atlanta Constitution,* December 28, 1882).
27. Atlanta *Weekly Defiance,* October 8, 1881; *Atlanta Constitution,* September 23, 1874; October 27, 1877; Nashville *Republican Banner,* November 8, 1873; Raleigh *News and Observer,* January 11, 1891; *Richmond Dispatch,* December 9, 11, 1875. John Blassingame reports that after being confined to the Jim Crow section of the St. Charles Theatre following the war, New Orleans blacks finally gained the right to sit in the Dress Circle as a result of the Civil Rights Act. He does not mention if they were segregated as in Richmond. He also points out that after vacillating between segregation and integration, the New Orleans Opera House was finally forced to accept integration by the Civil Rights Act. There is no indication as to how long this policy persisted, but whatever its length, it clearly departed from the provisions elsewhere in the South (Blassingame, *Black New Orleans,* pp. 186–87).
28. *Nashville Union and American,* March 16, 1875; *Nashville Banner,* November 3, 1884; *Atlanta Constitution,* February 18, 1888. The Atlanta saloons that served blacks were located on Decatur Street in the heart of the city's vice district. Under fear that the Civil Rights Act of 1875 would force black guests upon them, white hotels in Augusta, Georgia, and Chattanooga, Tennessee, gave up their public licenses and became private boardinghouses (*Atlanta Constitution,* March 7, 9, 1875). A black who sought lodging at a Nashville boardinghouse was told by the proprietor, "I don't board your kind" (*Nashville Union and American,* March 11, 1875). John Blassingame concluded that even in New Orleans white hotel and restaurant owners were among the staunchest foes of the Civil Rights Act (Blassingame, *Black New Orleans,*

p. 196). See also Fischer, *Segregation Struggle*, p. 142; Charles E. Wynes, *Race Relations in Virginia 1870–1902* (Charlottesville, 1961), p. 76.

29. Nashville *Daily American*, June 13, 1883; *Atlanta Constitution*, March 9, 1875; *Richmond Dispatch*, October 7, 1886; *Montgomery Daily Advertiser*, May 12, 1875. The situation in New Orleans again seems to have been atypical in that a number of the leading restaurants were integrated. Even so, by 1874 former lieutenant governor P. B. S. Pinchback was refused service at Redwitz's saloon (Blassingame, *Black New Orleans*, pp. 188–89). White teachers at Negro colleges were severely criticized for eating at the same tables with their students (*The American Missionary*, XX [February 1876], 36; Charles Nordhoff, *The Cotton States in the Spring and Summer of 1875* [New York, 1876], p. 106).

30. For segregated baseball, see *Atlanta Constitution*, May 31, 1886; August 11, 1887; *Nashville Daily Press and Times*, March 24, 1868; *Nashville Banner*, July 6, 1881; September 2, 1887; Sarah McCulloh Lemmon, "Entertainment in Raleigh in 1890," *North Carolina Historical Review*, XL (October 1963), 334. Atlanta also maintained segregation in its frequent walking races (*Atlanta Constitution*, July 6, 1884). For the situation in New Orleans, see Somers, "Black and White in New Orleans," pp. 34–35, 39–41.

31. Fischer, *Segregation Struggle*, p. 151; H. G. Saunders (comp.), *R. L. Polk & Company's Atlanta City Directory 1891* (Atlanta, 1891), pp. 150, 245; *Atlanta Constitution*, July 31, 1888; Nashville *Daily American*, March 28, 1877. It is not known whether or not the Lone Star also had a mixed clientele.

32. Savannah *Colored Tribune*, July 15, 1876. Jim Crow Bibles were present by 1868 in some Virginia courts (Macrae, *Americans at Home*, I, 146–47).

33. Wade, *Slavery in the Cities*, p. 267.

34. *Nashville Banner*, June 16, July 7, 1883; Atlanta, Minutes of the Atlanta City Council, January 2, 1882, Office of the City Clerk, Atlanta City Hall; letter of "X.L.F." to the editor, *Atlanta Constitution*, July 19, 1887; *ibid.*, July 1, 1890; for interest in a park near Clark University, see *ibid.*, March 24, 1889.

35. *Nashville Banner*, October 16, 1882; *Atlanta Constitution*, July 5, 10, 1890; *Montgomery Daily Advertiser*, June 3, 1890; Raleigh *News and Observer*, July 21, 1889. Highland Park had its name changed to Oak Park during the 1890s and was one of those affected by the trend toward separate parks for the races. A local Negro resident remembered that the only blacks admitted by that time were nurses with white children (Bertha Thomas McClain, *Montgomery Then and Now as I Remember* [Montgomery, 1960], p. 23).

36. *Atlanta Constitution*, July 19, 1874; *Nashville Banner*, May 22, 1888; Raleigh *News and Observer*, May 4, June 13, 1890. In 1878 a resident of Nashville suggested that the city was missing something that no European or American town should be without—a pool. Of course, it would be "regulated by statutes" and accessible only to whites (letter of Professor E. A. Wagner to the editor, Nashville *Daily American*, May 23, 1878).

37. *Atlanta Constitution*, April 4, 1890. It is not known if Negroes had been permitted in the old building and, if so, under what conditions.

38. Nashville *Republican Banner*, March 2, 1871.

39. *Nashville Banner*, May 25, 1883; Nashville *Republican Banner*, May 20, 1875; *Atlanta Constitution*, October 19, 1871; letter of C. A. Stack to the editor, *Montgomery Daily Advertiser*, November 5, 1890.

40. Gilbert Thomas Stephenson, *Race Distinctions in American Law* (New York,

1910), p. 215; *Richmond Dispatch,* August 27, 1880. The dining room for whites was described as "elaborate."

41. George Washington Cable, "The Negro Question," in Arlin Turner (ed.), *The Negro Question* (reprinted; Garden City, 1958), p. 129; Frederick Douglass, "The Color Line," *North American Review,* CXXXII (July 1881), 576. See also Raleigh *News and Observer,* May 4, 1890.

42. Iza Duffus Hardy, *Between Two Oceans or Sketches of American Travel* (London, 1884), pp. 306–307; Lady Duffus Hardy (Mary McDowell), *Down South* (London, 1883), p. 85; Stephens incident reported in Nashville *Republican Banner,* May 11, 1875. For further examples of the confinement of blacks to smoking cars, see letter of H. S. Bennett to the editor, Nashville *Daily American,* March 23, 1879; W. H. Crogman, "The Negro's Claims," a speech delivered in Henry Ward Beecher's church, October 14, 1883, reprinted in the author's *Talks for the Times* (Atlanta, 1896), p. 191; *Atlanta Constitution,* April 10, 1889.

43. For examples of Redeemer newspaper concern for truly equal separate accommodations, see *Montgomery Daily Advertiser,* February 21, March 8, 1873; *Richmond Dispatch,* October 14, 1870; *Atlanta Constitution,* October 16, 1883; January 1, 1885; Nashville *Daily American,* October 3, 1881; July 30, 1885.

44. Excerpt from *Lynchburg News,* reprinted in *Richmond Dispatch,* April 8, 1870; *Atlanta Constitution,* June 15, 1885; December 4, 1887. See also David G. McComb, *Houston: The Bayou City* (Austin, 1969), p. 160.

45. Meier and Rudwick, "A Strange Chapter in the Career of 'Jim Crow,'" p. 15.

46. Nashville *Daily American,* April 11, 1880; *Richmond Planet,* December 27, 1890; Baker, *Following the Color Line* (reprinted; New York, 1964), p. 31. See also Hardy, *Between Two Oceans,* p. 316; letter of "M" to the editor, Nashville *Republican Banner,* November 18, 1874; Warner, *Studies in the South and West,* p. 291.

47. For Richmond, see the remarks of Negro Congressmen Joseph Rainey and Richard Cain, *Cong. Record,* 43rd Cong., 2nd Sess., pp. 955, 957 (February 3, 1875). According to Meier and Rudwick, Savannah streetcars were desegregated in 1872 ("A Strange Chapter in the Career of 'Jim Crow,'" p. 16). Other evidence suggests that this change did not occur until sometime after 1875. See Perdue, *Negro in Savannah,* p. 34; Nordhoff, *The Cotton States,* p. 106.

48. Letter of Eliza Bowers to the editor, *Atlanta Constitution,* July 28, 1889. Miss Bowers, an Atlanta white, remembered entering the Negro car in Montgomery by mistake three years earlier.

49. Franklin M. Garrett, *Atlanta and Environs: A Chronicle of Its People and Events* (3 vols.; New York, 1954), II, 175; *Nashville Banner,* May 1, 1888. For subsequent incidents in Nashville, see, for example, *ibid.,* May 26, June 9, 1890. See also the statement by Atlanta Mayor W. F. Slaton in which he remembered being ejected from the Negro car on the Nashville dummy even though there were only a few people in it while the white car was "packed full" (*Atlanta Constitution,* August 6, 1889).

50. Meier and Rudwick, "Boycott Movement Against Jim Crow Streetcars in the South," 757.

51. Meier and Rudwick, "Negro Boycotts in Tennessee," 761.

52. *Richmond Planet,* December 27, 1890.

53. *Richmond Dispatch,* April 22, 1870; letter of W. A. Sinclair to the editor,

Nashville *Daily American,* October 4, 1881; Warner, *Studies in the South and West,* pp. 116–17. See also Savannah *Colored Tribune,* March 25, 1876.

54. Memphis was another. See *Nashville Union and Dispatch,* December 19, 1867.

55. In addition to those already mentioned, see *Atlanta Constitution,* April 12, May 19, 1871; Blassingame, *Black New Orleans,* pp. 191–92.

56. See, for example, Blassingame, *Black New Orleans,* pp. 185–86; Nashville *Republican Banner,* March 13–14, 1875; *Nashville Union and American,* March 13–14, 1875; *Atlanta Constitution,* March 6, 9–10, 1875; Raleigh *Daily Sentinel,* March 6, 1875; *Richmond Dispatch,* March 9–10, 1875; *Montgomery Daily Advertiser,* March 6, 13–14, 1875.

57. For "testing" on railroads, see Nashville *Daily American,* October 2–3, 5, 1881; *Nashville Banner,* September 30, October 7, 1881; *Atlanta Constitution,* August 9, 1889; for an attempt to buy soda water at a Nashville shop that served only whites, see *Nashville Banner,* October 3, 1881; for attempts to sit in white sections of theaters, see *Atlanta Constitution,* September 28, 1881; *Nashville Banner,* April 17, 1887; for an attempt to integrate a Nashville streetcar, see Nashville *Daily American,* July 20, 1889.

58. *Atlanta Constitution,* July 10, 1877.

59. Quoted *ibid.,* March 6, 1875.

60. Quoted *ibid.,* January 7, 1889.

61. *Charleston News,* January 10, 1870, reprinted *ibid.,* January 14, 1870. Implicit here is support for Roger Fischer's contention that many blacks accepted segregation out of a belief that the ultimate reward was not worth the effort needed to secure it (*Segregation Struggle,* pp. 86–87).

62. *Nashville Union and American,* March 9, 1875; excerpt from *Cincinnati Commercial,* reprinted in Nashville *Republican Banner,* June 17, 1874.

63. *Nashville Union and American,* March 11, 1875. For the threat of economic retaliation against protesters, see Nashville *Republican Banner,* March 11, 1875; Montgomery *Alabama State Journal,* March 13–14, 1875; *Montgomery Daily Advertiser,* March 24, 1875. The fear of economic retaliation led Elias Napier, a prosperous livery-stable owner in Nashville, to announce publicly that he was not one of a group of Negroes who had sought admission to a white restaurant. "I do not wish myself on any man," he wrote, "and as for civil rights, I want all to know that I was opposed to the passage of the civil rights bill from the first" (letter of Elias Napier to the editor, Nashville *Republican Banner,* March 11, 1875).

64. Letter of "A Colored Man" to the editor, *Nashville Daily Press and Times,* June 26, 1866; letter of unidentified Norfolk Negro to the editor, Richmond *Virginia Star,* March 27, 1880; letter of C. H. J. Taylor to the editor, *Atlanta Constitution,* August 15, 1889; Councill incident reported *ibid.,* July 24, 1887. For additional evidence of black interest in separate but equal accommodations in public conveyances, see letter of State Senator Ragsdale to the editor, *Richmond Dispatch,* July 4, 1870; Montgomery *Alabama State Journal,* July 26, 1869; Montgomery *Weekly State Journal,* December 16, 1870; *Montgomery Daily Advertiser,* June 2, 1885; McComb, *Houston,* p. 160; Avins, "Racial Segregation," 1280.

65. For excursions and concerts, see *Atlanta Constitution,* November 6, 1875; June 16, September 1, 1877; September 9, 1890; Raleigh *News and Observer,* January 12, August 14, 1890; *Montgomery Daily Advertiser,* July 21, 1885; for hotels and boardinghouses, see J. H. Chataigne (comp.), *Chataigne's Direc-*

tory of Richmond for 1891 (Richmond, 1891), p. 1031; Richmond *Virginia Star,* December 14, 1878; December 9, 23, 1882; *Richmond Planet,* June 12, 1886; *Atlanta Constitution,* March 10, 1882; *Nashville Union and American,* September 14, 1873; Montgomery *Weekly Citizen,* August 2, 1884; J. H. Chataigne (comp.), *Raleigh City Directory 1875–1876* (Raleigh, 1875), p. 133; for ice cream parlors, see Montgomery *Herald,* July 23, 1887; *Fisk Herald,* VII (May 1890), 16; Atlanta *Weekly Defiance,* October 8, 1881; for skating rinks, see *Atlanta Constitution,* April 23, 1885; Montgomery *Alabama State Journal,* April 6, 1873; *Huntsville Gazette,* January 23, 1886.

66. William Hepworth Dixon, *The New America* (2 vols.; 6th ed.; London, 1867), II, 332–33; testimony of James T. Rapier, in U.S. Senate, 46th Cong., 2nd Sess., *Report and Testimony of the Select Committee of the United States Senate to Investigate the Causes for the Removal of the Negroes from the Southern States to the Northern States* (Washington, D.C., 1880), Part II, 476–77; testimony of James O'Hara, *ibid.,* Part I, 57.

9. MORE THAN RELIGION: THE URBAN CHURCH

1. Bertha Thomas McClain, *Montgomery Then and Now as I Remember* (Montgomery, 1960), p. 28; *Atlanta Constitution,* June 18, 1882.
2. *Nashville Daily Press and Times,* July 13, 1866; Works Progress Administration, Historical Records Survey of Virginia, Division of Professional and Service Projects, "Negro Baptist Churches in Richmond," 1940, p. 19, Valentine Museum, Richmond.
3. *Ibid.,* p. 13. Robert Ryland mentions two incidents which aroused white suspicions about the dangers of having a distinct Negro church. In one instance a female member of the church murdered her master, mistress, and their infant child. Both she and her husband (another church member who was evidently innocent) were executed. On another occasion the church came under attack when it was discovered that letters of escaped slaves were being sent to members from the North and being distributed in church. The letters urged the slaves to escape and told them how to do so (Robert Ryland, "Reminiscences of the First African Baptist Church in Richmond, Virginia," *American Baptist Memorial,* Parts I–IV (September–December 1855), 262–66, 290–92, 322–27, 353–56).
4. Luther Porter Jackson, *Free Negro Labor and Property Holding in Virginia 1830–1860* (reprinted; New York, 1969), pp. 161–62; Ryland, "Reminiscences of the First African Baptist," 264. According to Jackson, the members of the First African contributed toward the construction of meeting houses for Negro communicants in several other Virginia cities.
5. Writers Program of the Works Progress Administration in the State of Virginia (comp.), *The Negro in Virginia* (New York, 1940), p. 250; Ryland quoted *ibid.,* p. 248; WPA, "Negro Baptist Churches in Richmond," pp. 13–14; R. A. Brock, *Richmond as a Manufacturing and Trading Centre* (Richmond, 1880), pp. 38–39.
6. The three other antebellum Richmond congregations were the Second African Baptist, Ebenezer Baptist (or Third African Baptist), and Fourth Baptist. There is disagreement as to the founding date of the first two. According to

Alrutheus Ambush Taylor, Ebenezer was founded in 1855; Luther Jackson says it was 1856; and the WPA workers claim it was 1858. The WPA study says that the Second African was organized in February 1846, while Jackson claims its origin was in 1847. Only the WPA work discusses the Fourth Baptist which was founded in 1859. Taylor mentions the activities of Negro Baptists in other ante-bellum cities and is the source for the conclusion about the predominance of Baptists among Virginia Negroes (Alrutheus Ambush Taylor, *The Negro in the Reconstruction of Virginia* (Washington, D.C., 1926), pp. 18–19, 186; Jackson, *Free Negro Labor and Property Holding*, p. 162; WPA, "Negro Baptist Churches in Richmond," pp. 15, 18).

7. WPA, "Negro Baptist Churches in Richmond," p. 15; Alfred Lewis Bratcher, *Eighty-Three Years: The Moving Story of Church Growth* (Montgomery, 1950), pp. 7–9. The property for Ebenezer Baptist was purchased for the new congregation by the Reverend Ryland. Six years later the Negroes repaid the $8,100 purchase price to Ryland and evidently became owners of the building (Jackson, *Free Negro Labor and Property Holding*, pp. 161–62).

8. John Hope Franklin, *The Free Negro in North Carolina 1790–1860* (Chapel Hill, 1943), pp. 176–77; *Nashville Daily Press and Times*, July 21, 1866; letter to the editor, *ibid.*, August 4, 1866; M. P. Blue, *Churches of the City of Montgomery, Alabama* (Montgomery, 1878), pp. 14, 20; Reverend J. Van Catledge, "Short History of Old Ship," in *Souvenir Program of the One Hundredth Anniversary of the Old Ship African Methodist Episcopal Zion Church 1852–1952* (Montgomery, 1952), pp. 5–7.

9. James W. Marshall, "Presbyterian Church in Alabama," 35 vols., IV, 1871; VII, 1791; IV, 1886, Alabama Department of Archives and History, Montgomery; (first name not given) Fitzgerald, "One Hundred Thirty-Fifth Year of the First Presbyterian Church, Montgomery, Alabama," p. 4, Alabama Department of Archives and History. For a picture of the slave balcony located on the left side of the building, see *A History of Montgomery in Pictures* (n.p.), p. 50.

10. Mattie Pegues Wood, *The Life of St. John's Parish: A History of St. John's Episcopal Church from 1834–1955* (Montgomery, 1955), *passim;* Glenn N. Sisk, "Negro Churches in the Alabama Black Belt 1875–1917," *Journal of the Presbyterian Historical Society*, XXXIII (June 1955), 90. On one occasion, according to Mrs. Wood, the minister Dr. Stringfellow was interrupted during his sermon with a loud "amen" from the Negro gallery. Moments later came a second and then a third "amen." Stringfellow called out "be quiet up there!" which was answered by "I'se got religion!" The minister sternly replied, "this is no place for that!" and continued his sermon (Wood, *St. John's Parish*, p. 89). Though perhaps apocryphal, something like this confrontation could very well have taken place between believers in two very different forms of religious expression.

11. Reverend Bowyer Stewart, *The Work of the Church in the South During the Period of Reconstruction* (Milwaukee, 1913), pp. 50–59; Ulrich Troubetzkoy (ed.), *Richmond: City of Churches: A Short History of Richmond's Denominations and Faiths* (Richmond, 1957), p. 16; *Nashville Banner*, June 29, 1889; July 28, 1890.

12. John Wooldridge (ed.), *History of Nashville, Tennessee* (Nashville, 1890), p. 503; Cecil D. Halliberston, *A History of St. Augustine's College 1867–1937* (Raleigh, 1937), p. 7; L. Branson (ed.), *The North Carolina Business Directory 1869* (Raleigh, 1869), p. 152; Thomas H. Martin, *Atlanta and Its Build-*

ers (2 vols.; Atlanta, 1902), II, 565–66; W. W. Clayton, *History of Davidson County, Tennessee* (Philadelphia, 1880), p. 340.

13. For the existence of segregation in Raleigh's Congregational Church, see Wilmoth Annette Carter, "The Negro Main Street of a Contemporary Urban Community" (unpublished Ph.D. dissertation, University of Chicago, 1959), p. 112; on the issue of a Negro minister for Montgomery's Congregational Church, see letter of E. C. Stickel to the Reverend M. E. Strieby, May 28, 1877, American Missionary Association Archives, Amistad Research Center, Dillard University, New Orleans; for segregation among Catholics, see Raleigh *Daily Standard,* September 7, 1869; Troubetzkoy, *Richmond: City of Churches,* p. 29; William Wells Brown, *My Southern Home, or the South and Its People* (Boston, 1880), pp. 207–208; *Richmond Dispatch,* November 24, 1885. For at least part of the period, however, Nashville's black Catholics were not segregated (Nashville *Republican Banner,* November 13, 1875).

14. WPA, "Negro Baptist Churches in Richmond," pp. 15–17, 19, 25, 39–40; A. J. Rogers (comp.), *A Brief History of the Formation and Growth of the First Baptist Church of Raleigh, North Carolina* (Raleigh, 1927), p. 6; *Raleigh Register,* May 6, 1885; E. R. Carter, *The Black Side: A Partial History of the Business, Religious, and Educational Side of the Negro in Atlanta, Georgia* (Atlanta, 1894), pp. 57–60; Charles Octavius Boothe, *The Cyclopedia of the Colored Baptists of Alabama* (Birmingham, 1895), p. 60; Troubetzkoy, *Richmond: City of Churches,* p. 45.

15. *Atlanta Constitution,* December 19, 1885.

16. Carter, *Black Side,* pp. 21, 243–44; *Atlanta Constitution,* August 27, 1882; I. W. Avery (ed.), *City of Atlanta* ("World's Fair Series on Great American Cities"; Louisville, 1892), p. 155. Although Avery and Carter (the church's minister) list 1868 as the date of the organization, a plaque at the church gives the date as 1862. It is probable that the founders began meeting clandestinely at the earlier date.

17. WPA, "Negro Baptist Churches in Richmond," *passim;* Clayton, *History of Davidson County,* p. 323; Nashville *Republican Banner,* December 18, 1874; quotation in *Nashville Banner,* February 15, 1887.

18. J. W. Alvord to O. O. Howard, January 21, 1871, in J. W. Alvord, *Letters from the South Relating to the Condition of Freedmen Addressed to Major General O. O. Howard* (Washington, D.C., 1870), p. 24; *Nashville Banner,* March 10, 1890; Nashville *Republican Banner,* August 23, 1874; Montgomery *Herald,* February 19, 1887. See also *Nashville Union and American,* December 29, 1870; Nashville *Daily American,* April 22, 1877. Some blacks, however, felt that too much was being spent on churches. The money could better be used for the purchase of land and homes and for the construction of schools. See, for example, speech of Joseph T. Wilson before the Colored Men's Convention, *Richmond Dispatch,* April 16, 1890.

19. Willis Grandy Briggs, "Raleigh Fifty Years Ago," Raleigh *News and Observer,* October 20, 1935, in Willis Grandy Briggs Collection, Southern Historical Collection, University of North Carolina Library, Chapel Hill; *Nashville Banner,* August 14, 1883.

20. *Atlanta Constitution,* July 12, 1882. See also *ibid.,* August 5, 1868; February 15, 1881. Nonfinancial assistance included the use of white arbitration committees to settle factional disputes within Negro churches. See, for example, Nashville *Daily American,* April 7, 1877; *Atlanta Constitution,* December 26, 1884.

21. Nashville *Republican Banner*, May 12, 1871; *Atlanta Constitution*, January 26, 1890; *Nashville Banner*, June 12, 1885; Nashville *Daily American*, October 29, 1875; for additional appeals for white financial aid, see *Montgomery Weekly Advertiser*, April 16, 1867; Montgomery *Daily State Sentinel*, May 31, 1867; Raleigh *News and Observer*, April 2, 1890; *Atlanta Constitution*, November 9, 1881; Nashville *Republican Banner*, December 18, 1874; Nashville *Daily American*, January 12, 1879; *Nashville Banner*, January 2, 1886; June 18, July 6, August 10, 1887; October 15, 1888; June 4, 1890. The impact of such aid remains a subject for further investigation. It is doubtful, however, that there were many cases comparable to the Opelika, Alabama, Negro church that was allegedly "captured" by the Democrats in the 1875 elections through a moderate subscription to the church fund. See Charles Nordhoff, *The Cotton States in the Spring and Summer of 1875* (New York, 1876), p. 92.
22. W. E. B. Du Bois (ed.), *Economic Co-operation Among Negro Americans* ("Atlanta University Publications," No. 12, ed. W. E. B. Du Bois; Atlanta, 1907), p. 24.
23. Church notice in *Atlanta Constitution*, June 17, 1883; McClain, *Montgomery Then and Now*, p. 29; Edward King, *The Southern States of North America* (London, 1875), p. 630.
24. Brown, *My Southern Home*, pp. 191–93.
25. Richmond missionary quoted in *The American Missionary*, IX (December 1865), 270; Richmond correspondent of the *Watchman and Reflector*, quoted in Taylor, *Negro in Virginia*, p. 187; *Atlanta Constitution*, April 18, 1871. David Macrae concluded about another Richmond church: "The service was very much like that of a white congregation, saving in one or two particulars." The major difference was in the fervor of the singing (David Macrae, *The Americans at Home* [2 vols.; Edinburgh, 1870], II, 98).
26. W. H. Crogman, "Christian Scholars for Negro Pulpits," a speech delivered at Gammon Theological Seminary, December 23, 1893, reprinted in the author's *Talks for the Times* (Atlanta, 1896), pp. 305–306; Samuel J. Barrows, "What the Southern Negro is Doing for Himself," *Atlantic Monthly*, LXVII (June 1891), 813.
27. *Atlanta Constitution*, August 15, 1874; *Montgomery Daily Advertiser*, March 26, 1867. For other examples of church disturbances, see *Atlanta Constitution*, June 18, September 24, 1886; May 9, 1887; *Nashville Banner*, September 21, 1882; March 16, June 28, December 21, 1886; April 9, 1887; June 28, 1890; Montgomery *Daily State Sentinel*, October 16, 1867.
28. *Montgomery Mail* quoted in Mobile *Nationalist*, May 24, 1866; Wendell P. Dabney (ed.), *Maggie L. Walker: Her Life and Deeds* (Cincinnati, 1927), pp. 30–31. For the effects of two of Richmond's revivals, see *Richmond Dispatch*, April 15, 1878; May 13, 1889.
29. *Atlanta Constitution*, May 29, 1878.
30. McClain, *Montgomery Then and Now*, p. 30. See also *Nashville Union and American*, April 9, 1870; Nashville *Republican Banner*, April 18, 1875; *Richmond Dispatch*, May 13, 1889.
31. Dabney, *Maggie L. Walker*, p. 31; *Nashville Daily Press and Times*, November 15, 1865; *Nashville Banner*, August 6, 1885; January 25, 1886; Richmond *Virginia Star*, August 27, 1881.
32. *Nashville Banner*, September 29, November 8, 1887; *Atlanta Constitution*, January 6, 1881. The president and vice president of the Board of Trustees of the Carrie Steele Orphan Home were ministers (*Atlanta Constitution*, July 2,

1889). Three of the four members of the Board of Directors of the James Hale Infirmary were also ministers (C. J. Allardt [comp.], *Montgomery City Directory for 1891* [Montgomery, 1891], p. 16).

33. *Richmond Dispatch,* October 23, 1866; Bratcher, *Eighty-Three Years,* pp. 14–15; Van Catledge, "Short History of Old Ship," p. 7.

34. Nashville *Republican Banner,* March 27, 1874 (the two blacks serving on the Executive Committee of the Atlanta Freedmen's Bank in 1870 were clergymen [Atlanta *Daily New Era,* January 19, 1870]); *Nashville Banner,* January 1, 1886. An economic function of a different sort was provided by Richmond's First African Baptist, whose officials set up the equivalent of an employment bureau. See *Richmond Dispatch,* January 24, 1866.

35. *Atlanta Constitution,* December 14, 25, 1887.

36. *Ibid.,* May 10, 1882; January 9, 1884; *Nashville Banner,* February 2, 1886.

37. See, for example, Montgomery *Colored Citizen,* May 17, 1884; *Richmond Planet,* February 21, 1885; interview of the Reverend J. S. Flipper in *Atlanta Constitution,* November 16, 1887.

38. *Atlanta Constitution,* August 17, 1877. Many of these individuals preached to unorganized groups in the surrounding countryside. For one such figure in Montgomery, a former slave preacher named Jacob Belser who worked as a pressman and huckster, see Montgomery *Daily State Sentinel,* May 30, June 28, July 30, 1867.

39. WPA, "Negro Baptist Churches in Richmond," pp. 36–38; Jasper interview in *Richmond Dispatch,* reprinted in *Atlanta Constitution,* June 14, 1887; for impressions of visitors to Jasper's church, see Brown, *My Southern Home,* p. 205; Anthony Quinton Keasby, *From the Hudson to the St. John's* (Newark, N.J., 1874), p. 10.

40. Richmond *Virginia Star,* May 14, 1878; WPA, *Negro in Virginia,* pp. 250–51.

41. Boothe, *Cyclopedia of Colored Baptists of Alabama,* pp. 111–14; Bratcher, *Eighty-Three Years,* pp. 13–14.

42. Boothe, *Cyclopedia of Colored Baptists of Alabama,* pp. 141–43; Bratcher, *Eighty-Three Years,* pp. 13–14. For Nelson G. Merry and Randolph Bartholomew, two Nashville counterparts of Jasper, Ashby, and Foster, see Howard N. Rabinowitz, "The Search for Social Control: Race Relations in the Urban South, 1865–1890" (2 vols.; unpublished Ph.D. dissertation, University of Chicago, 1973), I, 449–50.

43. For the central role of Atlanta Baptist Seminary, see biographies of selected preachers in Avery, *City of Atlanta,* p. 157; Carter, *Black Side,* pp. 84–85, 89–94, 96–101, 114–16, 218–20, 316–19.

44. Carter, *Black Side,* pp. 244–46, 255. Carter replaced the deceased Frank Quarles, an uneducated former slave who founded Friendship in 1868 and became the city's leading black divine. For Quarles, see *Atlanta Constitution,* May 28, 1871; December 6, 13, 1881; Carter, *Black Side,* p. 29.

45. Avery, *City of Atlanta,* p. 155; *Atlanta Constitution,* November 12, 1887.

46. See especially Carter, *Black Side,* pp. iii–iv; *Atlanta Constitution,* September 9, 1888.

47. White observer quoted in *Nashville Banner,* September 22, 1888; biographical material drawn from D. W. Culp (ed.), *Twentieth Century Negro Literature or A Cyclopedia of Thought on the Vital Topics Relating to the American Negro* (Atlanta, 1902), p. 315; Taylor, *Negro in Virginia,* pp. 160–62, 170, 268; WPA, *Negro in Virginia,* p. 249.

48. See, for example, Rabinowitz, "Search for Social Control," I, 453–55, 457–58.
49. W. N. Hartshorn, *An Era of Progress and Promise 1863–1910: The Religious, Moral and Educational Development of the American Negro Since His Emancipation* (Boston, 1910), p. 459; Martin, *Atlanta and Its Builders*, II, 565–66; *Nashville Banner*, September 12, 1890.
50. For a discussion of protest and accommodation as the two major alternatives characterizing black thought at the turn of the century, see August Meier, *Negro Thought in America 1880–1915* (Ann Arbor, 1966), pp. 69–82 and *passim*.
51. The participation of ministers in school protests is documented in Chapter 7, but see also the call for a mass meeting to be held at Nashville's St. Paul's A.M.E. in order to protest inadequate school facilities. Five of the eight signatories of the petition were ministers (*Nashville Banner*, November 3, 1888). The following year each clergyman was requested to give "wide circulation through his pulpit" to a similar meeting to be held at St. John's A.M.E. (*ibid.*, December 9, 1889).
52. Carter, *Black Side*, pp. 246–50; Avery, *City of Atlanta*, p. 158; letter to the editor, *Atlanta Constitution*, October 27, 1889; Gardner quoted *ibid.*, March 21, 1875. For the views of two Nashville Negro ministers, C. S. Smith and C. O. H. Thomas, who urged patience, hard work, and morality instead of protest, see Nashville *Daily American*, June 10, 1877; June 1, 1879.
53. William J. Simmons, *Men of Mark: Eminent, Progressive and Rising* (Cleveland, 1887), pp. 296–301; James T. Haley (comp.), *Afro-American Encyclopedia or, the Thoughts, Doings and Sayings of the Race* (Nashville, 1896), p. 220. Taylor served as president of the Union Transportation Company of Nashville, which was organized in 1905 as part of the unsuccessful boycott (August Meier and Elliott Rudwick, "Negro Boycotts of Jim Crow Street Cars in Tennessee," *American Quarterly*, XXI [Winter 1969], 762). Taylor died an extremely wealthy man. See his will, Davidson County (Tennessee) Will Book 47 (1930–31), pp. 399–403, Microfilm Copy, Tennessee State Library and Archives, Nashville.
54. *Nashville Banner*, August 20, September 25, 1885; March 26, 1886. The protest meeting was chaired by a minister and Bryant was joined on the seven-man resolutions committee by still a third clergyman.
55. For Turner, who also spent some time in Atlanta, see Simmons, *Men of Mark*, pp. 805–19; for Mason, see *Nashville Banner*, June 12, 1887; June 9, 18, 1888; Meier and Rudwick, "Negro Boycotts in Tennessee," 762; for Flipper, see *Atlanta Constitution*, June 20, November 17, 1887; for Sinclair, see Nashville *Daily American*, October 4, 1881; December 5, 1883.
56. *Nashville Banner*, October 5–6, 8, 18, 27, 1886.
57. Resolutions *ibid.*, December 21, November 3, 1886 (italics added); for the countercharge of Huffman, see *ibid.*, December 22, 1886; for the dénouement, see *ibid.*, October 15, 1887. For the background and activities of Huffman's replacement, the Reverend M. W. Gilbert, who led a successful fight to exclude Huffman from membership in the National Association of Colored Baptists, see Rabinowitz, "Search for Social Control," I, 468–69.
58. *Atlanta Constitution*, August 9, 1874.
59. Letter of William Finch to the editor, *ibid.*, December 18, 1881 (see also *ibid.*, December 27, 1881; January 1, 1882); Badger and Gaines quoted *ibid.*, July 9, 1885; final controversy *ibid.*, July 8–9, 1885.

60. For charges of financial impropriety, see *Nashville Banner*, February 13, June 28, 1886; for moral laxity, see *Atlanta Constitution*, May 15, 1884; *Richmond Dispatch*, November 21, 1866; April 13, 1880.

61. *Nashville Banner*, March 7, 1888; July 21, 1890.

62. Simmons, *Men of Mark*, pp. 88–96; Taylor, *Negro in Virginia*, p. 181; *Atlanta Constitution*, December 5, 1884; Bryant quoted in *Nashville Banner*, August 25, 1886, but see also *ibid.*, August 21, 31, 1886; October 13, 1885 (after leaving Nashville, Bryant became pastor of a Knoxville, Tennessee, church but was soon dismissed [*ibid.*, September 27, 1887]); announcement by Atlanta congregation in *Atlanta Constitution*, December 7, 1884. For the conflict between the deacon of a Montgomery Negro Methodist church and its pastor resulting in a "terrible state of confusion, bordering on chaos," see *Montgomery Daily Advertiser*, March 5, 1880.

63. Letter of J. W. Hood to the General Conference of the M.E. Church South, reprinted in *Nashville Banner*, May 15, 1882; *Atlanta Constitution*, June 16, 1887.

64. Letters to the editor, Nashville *Republican Banner*, March 28–29, 1874.

10. DIVISION AND UNITY: THE BLACK COMMUNITY

1. Excelsior Lodge No. 21 of Colored Masons (Raleigh), Minutes, 1875–1886, North Carolina Department of Archives and History, Raleigh.

2. *Nashville Union and Dispatch*, January 7, 1868; *Atlanta Constitution*, April 30, 1872; *Richmond Dispatch*, June 18, 1870; June 5, 1875.

3. Writers Program of the Works Progress Administration in the State of Virginia (comp.), *The Negro in Virginia* (New York, 1940), p. 292; *Richmond Dispatch*, January 1, 1874; *Raleigh City Directory 1886* (Raleigh, 1886), pp. 18–19; *Nashville Banner*, January 18, 1890. See also *Atlanta Constitution*, August 24, 1880; *Montgomery Daily Advertiser*, August 22, 1890.

4. Otis A. Singletary, *Negro Militia and Reconstruction* (Austin, 1957), pp. 5, 11–15, 21; for lists of companies and their officers, see, for example, Nashville *Daily American*, December 11, 1875; April 3, 1877; Ross A. Smith (comp.), *The Montgomery City Directory for 1880–1881* (Montgomery, 1880), p. 252; H. G. Saunders (comp.), *R. L. Polk & Company's Atlanta City Directory 1891* (Atlanta, 1891), p. 1210; (J. H.) Chataigne and (B. W.) Gillis (comps.), *Richmond City Directory for the Year Beginning February 1, 1877* (Richmond, 1877), p. 39; for ties with the white companies, see, for example, *Atlanta Constitution*, March 14, May 22, 1879; May 8, 1890.

5. L. Branson (ed.), *The North Carolina Business Directory 1869* (Raleigh, 1869), p. 152; L. Branson (ed.), *North Carolina Business Directory 1872* (Raleigh, 1872), p. 230; Nashville, *Digest of General Laws* (1865), p. 41; *Nashville Union and Dispatch*, October 23–25, 1867; Nashville *Republican Banner*, December 22, 1874; January 19, 1875; *Nashville Banner*, November 8, 1884; January 14–15, September 5, 1885; Montgomery, Minutes of the Montgomery City Council, September 5, 1864; March 5, December 3, 1866; February 18, 1867; January 4, 1869, Alabama Department of Archives and History, Montgomery; *Montgomery Weekly Advertiser*, June 18, 1867.

6. Samuel P. Richards, "Diary," July 4, 1884, Atlanta Historical Society. See also *ibid.*, July 4, 1889.

7. *Nashville Daily Press and Times,* December 30, 1868; *Atlanta Constitution,* January 2, 1890. For additional accounts of black celebrations of special occasions, see *ibid.,* July 22, 1870; May 5, 1875; May 16, 1877; *Richmond Dispatch,* April 9, July 6, 1866; *Nashville Daily Press and Times,* August 2, 1866; June 23, 1868; *Montgomery Daily Advertiser,* January 1, 1891.

8. *Richmond Dispatch,* October 25, 1875; *Nashville Banner,* October 15, 1887; *Atlanta Constitution,* September 1, 1885. See also the description of the memorial procession for President Garfield, *ibid.,* September 27, 1881.

9. Montgomery *Alabama Enterprise,* July 10, 1886; estimate of the bishop in Samuel J. Barrows, "What the Southern Negro is Doing for Himself," *Atlantic Monthly,* LXVII (June 1891), 805–15; *Atlanta Constitution,* July 25, August 8, 1880.

10. For a sample of black outings, see Nashville *Republican Banner,* July 2, August 20, September 19, 1871; *Atlanta Constitution,* May 8, 1871.

11. *Atlanta Constitution,* February 11, 1882; June 27, 1890; J. H. Chataigne (comp.), *Chataigne's Directory of Richmond for 1891* (Richmond, 1891), pp. 750–51; *Raleigh Directory 1886,* pp. 18–19; James T. Haley (comp.), *Afro-American Encyclopedia or, the Thoughts, Doings and Sayings of the Race* (Nashville, 1896), p. 212; for the role of the Freedmen's Bank, see, for example, Nashville *Republican Banner,* March 9, 1871; for Dorsette Hall, see Bertha Thomas McClain, *Montgomery Then and Now As I Remember* (Montgomery, 1960), p. 12.

12. *Raleigh Directory, 1886, passim; Richmond Dispatch,* September 3, 1880, used the expression "Black Belt"; Haley, *Afro-American Encyclopedia,* pp. 211–12; for Atlanta, see E. R. Carter, *The Black Side: A Partial History of the Business, Religious, and Educational Side of the Negro in Atlanta, Georgia* (Atlanta, 1894), pp. 22–24.

13. *Nashville Banner,* March 5, 1888; Tintagil Club, *Official Guide to the City of Montgomery* (Montgomery, 1920), pp. 27–28; C. J. Allardt (comp.), *Montgomery City Directory for 1891* (Montgomery, 1891), p. 14; Montgomery *Alabama Enterprise,* July 10, 1886; Montgomery *Herald,* February 5, April 2, 1887.

14. *Atlanta Constitution,* August 23, 1889.

15. For Taylor's political views, see *Atlanta Constitution,* December 25, 1889; February 13, July 6, 1890; Scott's claim in advertisement in Smith, *Montgomery Directory, 1880–1881,* p. 207; for Lowery, see Nashville *Tennessee Tribune,* December 19, 1870; Nashville *Republican Banner,* May 21, 1874; for Pledger, see *Atlanta Constitution,* October 27, 1885; for Mitchell, see William J. Simmons, *Men of Mark: Eminent, Progressive and Rising* (Cleveland, 1887), pp. 314–20.

16. *Atlanta Constitution,* June 20, 1885; Atlanta *Weekly Defiance,* quoted *ibid.*

17. Quoted *ibid.,* October 27, 1885. Despite such harassment, the *Defiance* lost none of its bite. Two years later a Burnett editorial said in part:

> Hell is too pleasant a place for that rich white man of the south who has gained all of his wealth by the hard, unpaid for strokes of the negro on a thousand acres of the red hills of Georgia and whose ancestry have seen generations after generations of negroes perish at the burdens placed upon them, and now rolling in the wealth thus acquired, think that a cent of their money is too good for negro education (quoted *ibid.,* April 27, 1887).

18. For Duke's account of the matter, see his letter to the editor, *Montgomery*

Daily Advertiser, August 21, 1887, published under the headline "A Cheeky Letter from the Exile."

19. Richmond *Virginia Star,* November 11, 1882. In presenting his case, the editor used a tactic popular among both blacks and whites who called for better treatment of the Negroes. He reminded whites of the debt owed the former slaves who had faithfully served the unprotected old, young, and women on the homefront during the Civil War.

20. *Richmond Planet,* January 4, May 24, 1890; Richmond *Virginia Star,* August 27, 1881.

21. Montgomery *Herald,* February 5, 1887; *Richmond Planet,* August 9, June 7, 1890. See also *ibid.,* April 12, 1890. Earlier the editor of the Savannah *Colored Tribune,* July 8, 1876, had reminded whites caught up in the Centennial that "the first blood shed for American liberty was that of a negro, Crispus Altucks [*sic*]."

22. Montgomery *Colored Citizen,* April 26, 1884; *Richmond Planet,* August 30, 1890. Davis's purchase further illustrates the segregated housing pattern in the city. His new home was opposite the all-Negro Swayne School. The lot was probably part of the tract of land earlier bought by the American Missionary Association and set aside for sale to prospective black homeowners.

23. Montgomery *Colored Citizen,* April 12, 1884.

24. *Ibid.;* Montgomery *Weekly Advance,* September 11, 1880.

25. Nashville *Colored Tennessean,* October 14, 1865; letter of "Ivanhoe" to the editor, Richmond *Virginia Star,* August 27, 1881; *ibid.,* April 30, 1881; Atlanta *Weekly Defiance,* October 8, 22, 1881. Gilbert Osofsky mentions that prior to 1914 many Southern black women came north on tickets supplied by employment and labor agents. These tickets were sometimes called "Justice's Tickets" (Gilbert Osofsky, *Harlem: The Making of a Ghetto* [New York, 1966], p. 29). In fact, the tickets were "Justis's Tickets."

26. Carter, *Black Side,* p. 121; assessment of the *Star* by William Saunders, *Through the Light Continent* (London, 1879), p. 78; Richmond *Virginia Star,* May 11, 1878; social parasite charge leveled by *Southern Independent* and quoted approvingly in Montgomery *Herald,* February 5, 1887.

27. Nashville *Republican Banner,* December 4, 1874.

28. Noble L. Prentis, *Southern Letters* (Topeka, 1881), p. 163; *Atlanta Constitution,* August 31, 1890.

29. *Richmond Dispatch,* January 1, 1880; for discussion topics, see *ibid.,* April 17, 1875; *Richmond Planet,* February 21, 1885; June 12, 1886; *Atlanta Constitution,* April 24, 1870; September 3, 16, 1875.

30. *Nashville Banner,* September 13, 1884. The Colored Y.M.C.A., however, opened its library to the public (*ibid.,* November 21, 1888).

31. *Atlanta Constitution,* July 2, 1879; March 7, 1880; June 2, July 17, December 9, 1881; March 16, 20, 1884.

32. *Richmond Dispatch,* October 21, 1890; Montgomery *Colored Citizen,* May 3, 1884; *Nashville Banner,* March 12, April 28, 30, October 28, 1887.

33. J. W. A. Sanford to his son, January 5, 1886, John William Augustine Sanford Papers, Alabama Department of Archives and History.

34. August Meier and David Lewis, "History of the Negro Upper Class in Atlanta, Georgia 1890–1958," *Journal of Negro Education,* XXVIII (Spring 1959), 130–39.

35. *Atlanta Constitution,* February 21, 1877; *Raleigh Farmer,* quoted *ibid.,* Janu-

ary 29, 1881; Wendell P. Dabney (ed.), *Maggie L. Walker: Her Life and Deeds* (Cincinnati, 1927), pp. 34–35.

36. Nashville *Republican Banner*, June 25, November 21, 1873; Nashville *Daily American*, June 10, 14, 1879; *Nashville Banner*, July 5, 1887.

37. *Ibid.*, January 1, 1885. Many of those people already named participated in various protest meetings during the 1880s. W. H. Young called to order a large group of blacks assembled at St. John's A.M.E. to condemn the massacre of Negroes at Carrollton, Mississippi. J. H. Keeble served as secretary. Keeble was also a member of the Committee on Resolutions, which included J. H. Dismukes and W. A. Hadley (*ibid.*, March 26, 1886). Three years earlier, at a meeting called to urge the appointment of black teachers, the Committee on Resolutions included among its nine members Young, J. C. Napier, S. R. Walker, T. A. Sykes, and Henry Harding. Another of its members was the Congregational minister W. A. Sinclair, who also served as chairman of the 1886 meeting (*ibid.*, June 9, 1883).

38. Nashville *Daily American*, January 1, 1880; *Nashville Banner*, October 3, 1883; September 11, July 29, 1885.

39. Nashville *Daily American*, December 27, 1878.

40. For Napier, see G. F. Richings, *Evidences of Progress Among Colored People* (10th ed.; Philadelphia, 1903), p. 268; W. N. Hartshorn, *An Era of Progress and Promise 1863–1910: The Religious, Moral and Educational Development of the American Negro Since His Emancipation* (Boston, 1910), p. 415; for Vandervall, see *Richmond Dispatch*, September 18, 1885; for Steele, see *Atlanta Constitution*, May 4, 1884; Carter, *Black Side*, pp. 187–89.

41. *Nashville Banner*, November 4, 1890; *Atlanta Constitution*, July 20, 1881 (see also Eugene M. Mitchell, "Queer Place Names in Old Atlanta," *Atlanta Historical Bulletin*, I [April 1931], 29); for the Willingham Building, see *Atlanta Constitution*, January 7, 1872; August 10, 1879; February 3, April 1, May 3, 1882; September 25, 1889.

42. Raleigh *Tri-Weekly Standard*, March 22, 1866; T. F. Brockwell, "Raleigh in 1870: A Detailed Description of the City's Business District as It Appeared Fifty-Six Years Ago," *Raleigh Times*, June 8, 1926; *Montgomery Daily Advertiser*, September 6, 1865; *Richmond Dispatch*, August 30, 1870.

43. Nashville *Daily American*, June 7, 1876; *Atlanta Constitution*, May 12, 1882; for the catastrophic wake, see *ibid.*, October 10, 1876.

44. *Richmond Dispatch*, October 20, 1866; *Atlanta Constitution*, February 13, November 18, 1881.

45. *Nashville Daily Press and Times*, October 6, 1865.

46. *Ibid.*, August 12, 1865; Montgomery *Colored Citizen*, April 26, 1884; *Richmond Planet*, October 4, 1890. See also letter of James M. Jackson to the editor, Montgomery *Herald*, February 19, 1887; speech of W. B. Mathews, Atlanta principal, reprinted in Hartshorn, *Era of Promise and Progress*, p. 58.

47. *Atlanta Constitution*, April 2, 1881.

48. Nashville *Republican Banner*, May 31, July 15, 22, August 11, 1874; *Nashville Banner*, September 18, 1886; interview of "C.E." in Nashville *Daily American*, August 20, 1885. C.E. is described as a young man not in politics. In a letter to the editor (*ibid.*, August 17, 1885), he had previously written that "decent colored people are inconvenienced by the present system, as are also respectable whites, from the fact that they have no protection against objectionable contact with persons of their own race."

49. Quoted in *Atlanta Constitution*, January 28, 1883. The article included the endorsement of segregation by Frances Willard, founder and president of the W.C.T.U. On March 10, 1887, the West Atlanta W.C.T.U. was organized at Friendship Baptist Church by a group of middle-class blacks which included the wife of the Reverend E. R. Carter (Carter, *Black Side*, p. 43).

50. *Nashville Banner*, February 19, 24–25, October 11, August 24, 1886.

51. *Ibid.*, February 20, March 6, August 11, 1888; appeal of Peter Lowery in Nashville *Daily American*, October 21, 1879.

52. Richard Morse, *The History of the North American YMCA*, quoted in Raube Watten, "History of the YMCA," in "Contributions to Richmond History," Assembled by the Virginia Capital Centennial Commission as Part of the Richmond Bicentennial Celebration April 30–September 25, 1937, p. 8, Valentine Museum, Richmond; Nashville *Daily American*, June 20, 1876.

53. The sample includes Negro leaders from Montgomery, Nashville, Richmond, and Atlanta who could be located in the 1870 and 1880 federal manuscript census schedules. Because the designation of an individual as "mulatto" or "black" reflected the opinion of the census-taker, these findings must be treated with caution.

54. *Atlanta Constitution*, January 7, 1885.

55. *Nashville Banner*, August 20, 1889. For a similar conclusion about the greater importance of wealth and cultural attributes among Negroes in New Orleans, see John W. Blassingame, *Black New Orleans 1860–1880* (Chicago, 1973), pp. 152–56.

56. Prohibition is discussed in Chapter 13; the generation gap, in the Epilogue.

57. *Richmond Dispatch*, August 17, 1870; January 22, June 14, 1875; for other agents, see *ibid.*, January 6, June 21, 1870. For the early efforts of labor agents in Montgomery, see Montgomery *Alabama State Journal*, January 17, 20, 1874.

58. Studies of Northern urban blacks confirm the presence of a significant urban element in the pre-1910 migration to Northern cities. See, for example, Osofsky, *Harlem*, p. 29; W. E. B. Du Bois, *The Philadelphia Negro* (reprinted; New York, 1967), p. 76. Additional evidence for the existence of a two-step migration to the North—with rural blacks moving first into Southern cities and then on to the North—can be found in Zane L. Miller, "Urban Blacks in the South, 1865–1920: An Analysis of Some Quantitative Data on Richmond, Savannah, New Orleans, Louisville, and Birmingham," in *The New Urban History: Quantitative Explorations by American Historians*, ed. Leo F. Schnore (Princeton, 1975), pp. 187–93.

59. Nashville *Daily American*, May 18, 1876; October 16, 1879.

60. *Nashville Union and American*, September 28, October 10, 1869; Nashville *Republican Banner*, May 20–21, 1875.

61. Nashville *Daily American*, June 3, 1879; Young quoted *ibid.*, July 10, 1879; *ibid.*, August 17, 1879. See also letter of J. H. Burrus to the editor, Nashville *Daily American*, December 26, 1879.

62. Montgomery *Weekly Advance*, September 11, 1880.

63. Nashville *Republican Banner*, May 22, August 15, 1875. See also Alrutheus Ambush Taylor, *The Negro in Tennessee* (Washington, D.C., 1941), p. 120. The Board of Commissioners of the convention included among its seven members W. A. Sizemore of Edgefield and three prominent Nashville blacks, Nelson Walker, Henry Harding, and B. A. Holmes.

64. *Atlanta Constitution*, January 28, 1873.

65. Letter to the editor, *ibid.*, January 21, 1875; *ibid.*, March 10, 1876. At the

height of the migration fervor in 1879, the Atlanta politician and businessman Moses H. Bentley introduced the following resolution at the National Colored Emigration Conference held in Nashville: "Resolved: that before taking final steps towards emigration, we ask for and demand our political rights in the south." For the opposition to emigration by Raleigh's James H. Harris, see his testimony in U.S. Senate, 46th Cong., 2nd Sess., *Report and Testimony of the Select Committee of the United States Senate to Investigate the Causes for the Removal of the Negroes from the Southern States to the Northern States* (Washington, D.C., 1880), Part I, 106.

66. Napier and Keeble quoted in *Nashville Banner*, February 23, 1888. Napier had earlier supported emigration because the Negro had been denied "almost every privilege that is calculated to elevate him in his moral, intellectual and political status" (quoted in Nashville *Daily American*, May 9, 1879).

67. For example, Napier's personal political victories during the 1880s, plus the concessions he was able to win for blacks, probably brought about the shift in his position on emigration.

68. *Atlanta Constitution*, November 30, December 2, 8, 1890. Schell had been born a slave in 1857, the son of his master. In 1867 he was apprenticed as a shoemaker and soon after moved to Atlanta. After working at a variety of jobs, he opened a small grocery and shoe shop. By the 1890s he was already one of the city's wealthiest blacks, the owner of both an impressive residence and a dry goods business housed in his three-story brick building (Carter, *Black Side*, pp. 141–44; J. W. Gibson and W. H. Crogman, *Progress of A Race or The Remarkable Advancement of the American Negro* [rev. ed.; Atlanta, 1902], p. 283).

69. Quoted in *Atlanta Constitution*, December 2, 1890.

70. *Southern Appeal*, quoted *ibid.*, November 26, 1890; disclosure of fraud, *ibid.*, December 29, 1890.

11.　FROM RECONSTRUCTION TO REDEMPTION

1. North Carolina, *Private Laws* (1866), p. 5; Tennessee, *Acts* (1865), p. 195. See also, for example, *Nashville Daily Press and Times*, September 30, 1866; *Montgomery Daily Advertiser*, December 5, 1865.

2. Letter of "Proxter" to the editor, *Montgomery Daily Advertiser*, August 27, 1865; *Atlanta Constitution*, June 24, 1868; testimony of B. R. Grattan of Richmond in U.S. Congress, 39th Cong., 1st Sess., *Report of the Joint Committee on Reconstruction* (Washington, D.C., 1866), Part II, 162–63.

3. Testimony of Dr. James P. Hambleton, in *Joint Committee Report on Reconstruction*, Part III, 167; *Montgomery Daily Ledger*, September 4, 1865; *Atlanta Constitution*, June 24, 1868; *Montgomery Daily Advertiser*, January 24, 1866.

4. Sister to Alexander M. McPheeters, Sr., September 16, 1868, Alexander M. McPheeters, Sr., Papers, Duke University Library, Durham, North Carolina; Drury Lacy to his daughter, May 2, 1868, Drury Lacy Papers, Southern Historical Collection, University of North Carolina Library, Chapel Hill; Sallie Munford Talbott to her husband, October 22, 28, 1867, Box 21, Munford-Ellis Papers, Duke University Library.

5. Holden quoted in Raleigh *Daily Standard*, May 12, 1865; *Nashville Daily Press and Times*, April 24, 1865.

6. Testimony of Mailton J. Safford [*sic*] in *Joint Committee Report on Reconstruction*, Part III, 62.

7. August Meier, *Negro Thought in America 1880–1915* (Ann Arbor, 1966), pp. 3–16, but especially pp. 5–6, 11–12. The memorial of the Freedmen's Convention in Raleigh which was submitted to the North Carolina Constitutional Convention in the fall of 1865 is reprinted in Sidney Andrews, *The South Since the War: As Shown by Fourteen Weeks of Travel and Observation in Georgia and the Carolinas* (Boston, 1866), pp. 128–30.

8. William Hepworth Dixon, *The New America* (2 vols.; 6th ed.; London, 1867), II, 329; John Richard Dennett, *The South As It Is 1865–1866*, edited with an introduction by Henry M. Christman (reprinted; New York, 1967), pp. 26–27. Some Negroes continued to have reservations about the franchise even after it was awarded. Caesar Shorter, a Montgomery Conservative and former body servant to the wartime governor, stated in 1871 that the Fifteenth Amendment should have been delayed for five years since blacks did not have "enough sense" to vote. Nor in his opinion were Negroes fit to hold office (testimony of Caesar Shorter, in U.S. Congress, 42nd Cong., 2nd Sess., *Testimony Taken by the Joint Select Committee to Inquire Into the Condition of Affairs in the Late Insurrectionary States* [Washington, D.C., 1872], IX, 1074–75).

9. Resolution quoted in *Nashville Daily Press and Times*, June 28, 1866; letter of Holland Thompson to the editor, Mobile *Nationalist*, March 7, 1867.

10. Reverend Henry S. Fox, "A Vacation Tour of South and West," in *The National Freedman*, I (September 15, 1865), 265.

11. Raleigh, *Amended Charter* (1867), pp. 3–4; Atlanta, Minutes of the Atlanta City Council, November 27, 1868, Office of the City Clerk, Atlanta City Hall; *Atlanta Constitution*, June 16, 1869; Alrutheus Ambush Taylor, *The Negro in Tennessee 1865–1880* (Washington, D.C., 1941), p. 57.

12. Samuel P. Richards, "Diary," March 24, 1867, Atlanta Historical Society; *Scott's Monthly Magazine*, VI (September 1868), 647.

13. Raleigh *Tri-Weekly Standard*, October 3, 1867; William Asbury Christian, *Richmond: Her Past and Present* (Richmond, 1912), p. 291; *Nashville Daily Press and Times*, August 3, 1867; Franklin M. Garrett, *Atlanta and Environs: A Chronicle of Its People and Events* (3 vols.; New York, 1954), I, 739. Atlanta was the only one of Georgia's five largest cities to have more white than black registrants (C. Mildred Thompson, *Reconstruction in Georgia: Economic, Social, Political, 1865–1872* [reprinted; Gloucester, Mass., 1964], p. 187).

14. Alrutheus Ambush Taylor, *The Negro in the Reconstruction of Virginia* (Washington, D.C., 1926), p. 227; John W. Beverly, *History of Alabama* (Montgomery, 1901), pp. 203–206; Raleigh *Tri-Weekly Standard*, November 23, 1867; Richards, "Diary," December 21, 1867.

15. Rapier was elected in 1872 with an almost 3,000-vote majority, but was narrowly defeated for reelection in 1874 (Montgomery *Alabama State Journal*, November 16, 1872; November 14, 1874); Elaine Joan Nowaczyk, "The North Carolina Negro in Politics, 1865–1876" (unpublished M.A. thesis, University of North Carolina, 1957), pp. 199–200; Beverly, *History of Alabama*, pp. 203, 205–206.

16. *Atlanta Constitution*, December 9, 1870; Montgomery, Minutes of the Montgomery City Council, January 1, 1872; August 1, 1870; February 6, 1871, Alabama Department of Archives and History, Montgomery; *Nashville Union*

and Dispatch, September 29, October 2, 12, 1867; *Nashville Daily Press and Times,* October 2, 1868; Raleigh *Daily Standard,* July 14, 1868. For Finch's background, see E. R. Carter, *The Black Side: A Partial History of the Business, Religious, and Educational Side of the Negro in Atlanta, Georgia* (Atlanta, 1894), pp. 74–77, and Clarence A. Bacote, "William Finch, Negro Councilman and Political Activities in Atlanta During Early Reconstruction," *Journal of Negro History,* XL (January 1955), 341–64. The other Atlanta councilman was George Graham, an obscure forty-year-old railroad worker.

17. Nashville, Minutes of the Nashville Board of Aldermen, October 22, 1867, Office of the Metropolitan Clerk, Davidson County Building and Nashville City Hall, Nashville; *Nashville Union and Dispatch,* October 29, 1867.

18. Nashville Board of Aldermen Minutes, May 21, June 17, 1868; *Nashville Union and Dispatch,* October 29, 1867; L. Branson (ed.), *The North Carolina Business Directory 1869* (Raleigh, 1869), p. 152; Raleigh *Daily News,* March 25, 1872; Wake County, Minutes of the Wake County Board of Commissioners, August 19, 1870; August 18, 1871, North Carolina Department of Archives and History, Raleigh; *Montgomery Weekly Advertiser,* May 28, 1867; *Nashville Daily Press and Times,* May 8, 1868.

19. *Richmond Dispatch,* March 16–18, April 1, 11, 30, 1870; Christian, *Richmond,* pp. 314–24; Jack P. Maddex, Jr., *The Virginia Conservatives 1867–1879: A Study in Reconstruction Politics* (Chapel Hill, 1970), pp. 89–90.

20. *Nashville Daily Press and Times,* August 3, 1867; *Nashville Union and Dispatch,* September 29, 1867; Alden quoted *ibid.,* October 11, 1867.

21. Nashville *Republican Banner,* September 27, 1868; for charges of fraud, see *ibid.,* September 26, 1868; *Nashville Union and American,* November 4–5, 1868; Nashville *Republican Banner,* September 26, 1868; *Nashville Daily Press and Times,* September 29, 1868.

22. *Nashville Daily Press and Times,* June 29, 1869; Nashville *Republican Banner,* September 26, 1869. For a defense of Alden's administration, see Gary L. Kornell, "Reconstruction in Nashville, 1867–1869," *Tennessee Historical Quarterly,* XXX (Fall 1971), 277–87.

23. *Atlanta Constitution,* December 3, 1868; December 3, 1869.

24. Atlanta, *Code* (1870), p. 41; *Atlanta Constitution,* December 9, 1870.

25. *Atlanta Constitution,* December 8–9, 1870; Atlanta *Daily New Era,* December 8, 1870.

26. *Atlanta Constitution,* December 9, 1870.

27. *Ibid.,* November 11, December 7, 1871; November 7, December 5, 1872; December 4, 1873.

28. See, for example, *ibid.,* December 5, 1879; December 2, 1880. For the reaction of a prominent black politician, see *ibid.,* March 24, 1884.

29. *Nashville Union and American,* November 2, 1869; North Carolina, *Public Laws* (1876–1877), p. 228; Raleigh, *Amended Charter* (1876), p. 10.

30. Raleigh *Daily News,* May 7, 1872; Raleigh *Daily Sentinel,* April 26, 1873.

31. Raleigh *Daily Sentinel,* May 5, 1874; August 5, 1875.

32. Raleigh, *Amended Charter* (1876), pp. 8–10; Raleigh *Daily Sentinel,* April 22, 1874; April 23, 1875; Bureau of the Census, *Eleventh Census: Population* (Washington, D.C., 1893), I, Part I, 261.

33. Raleigh *Daily Sentinel,* April 22, 1874; April 23, 1875; for subsequent registration, see, for example, *ibid.,* March 25, 27, 1875.

34. *Ibid.,* May 3, 1875; for Republican presidential victories, see *ibid.,* November 12, 1876; Raleigh *News and Observer,* November 6, 1880.

35. Richmond, Minutes of the Richmond City Council, December 30, 1867, Office of the City Clerk, Richmond City Hall. In January 1868 the lines were slightly altered, evidently to reduce the overly high concentration of Negroes in Monroe Ward. The ward gained some whites and in turn gave some of its blacks to neighboring Clay (*ibid.*, January 13, 1868).

36. Bureau of the Census, *Ninth Census: Population* (Washington, D.C., 1872), I, 280.

37. Richmond, *Charter* (1870), p. 3; Richmond Board of Health Census, 1874, reprinted in *Richmond Dispatch*, January 1, 1875. As of 1890, Jackson contained 3,274 eligible black and 998 eligible white voters. Three of the other five wards had less than 3,050 males of voting age (Bureau of the Census, *Census, 1890*, I, Part I, 823).

38. "Thomas A. Kercheval," *Biographical Directory Tennessee General Assembly 1796–1969* (Preliminary No. 21), Lincoln County, p. 28. The fight over redistricting can be followed in the Nashville *Republican Banner*, July 4, 8, 25, August 18, 26–28, 1875.

39. *Montgomery Daily Advertiser*, May 5–6, 1875; Montgomery *Alabama State Journal*, April 20, May 5, 1875; August 6, 1876; Montgomery, Message of the Mayor, *Annual Message of the Mayor of Montgomery and Reports for the Various City Officers and Standing Committees of the City Council for the Fiscal Year Ending April 30, 1877* (Montgomery, 1877), p. 8; Alabama, *Acts* (1876–1877), pp. 254–57.

40. *Montgomery Daily Advertiser*, April 26, May 5, 1875; April 8, May 2, 1877. For Democratic endorsement of reduced city limits, see *ibid.*, December 22, 1875; February 4, 1877. For Republican opposition, see Montgomery *Alabama State Journal*, December 31, 1875. For unsuccessful Republican attempts to enlarge the city limits in order to bring in more Negro voters, see *Montgomery Daily Advertiser*, April 4, December 3, 1873.

41. *Montgomery Daily Advertiser*, December 5, 1871; Hilary A. Herbert, "Grandfather's Talks About His Life Under Two Flags," pp. 277–78, Southern Historical Collection.

42. Montgomery, *City Code* (1875), pp. 31–35.

43. Montgomery *Alabama State Journal*, December 2, 1873; *Montgomery Daily Advertiser*, February 6, 1875. See also *ibid.*, January 27, 1875.

44. Montgomery, *City Code* (1875), pp. 39–40. The Republican *Alabama State Journal*, which had endorsed earlier election bills, strongly condemned the new measure, especially the change in election day. See, for example, January 31, February 2, 28, 1875. Registration dropped from 2,779 in 1873 to 2,131 two years later (*ibid.*, November 21, 1873; *Montgomery Daily Advertiser*, April 26, 1875).

45. Charles Nordhoff, *The Cotton States in the Spring and Summer of 1875* (New York, 1876), p. 92. For Republican charges that Democrats were buying certificates, see Montgomery *Alabama State Journal*, April 7–9, 28, 1875. By manipulating the voting requirements after Mayor Alden was removed from office, Tennessee Redeemers were able to add 2,700 whites to Nashville's voting rolls (*Nashville Union and American*, July 27, 1869; Thomas B. Alexander, "Political Reconstruction in Tennessee 1865–1870," in *Radicalism, Racism and Party Realignment: The Border States during Reconstruction*, ed. Richard O. Curry [Baltimore, 1969], pp. 72–73).

46. This, of course, was nothing new. During the 1867 Constitutional Convention, blacks had been threatened with the loss of their jobs for voting independently

(*Richmond Enquirer,* October 25–26, 1867; letter of B. L. Canedy, October 26, 1867, in *The Freedmen's Record,* III [November 1867], 173; letter of M. L. Kellogg, in *The American Missionary,* XII [February 1868], 25).

47. *Richmond Dispatch,* May 13, 1870.

48. See, for example, *ibid.,* May 23, 25, 28, 1870.

49. *Ibid.,* November 26, 1870.

50. *Ibid.,* May 26, 28, 1870.

51. *Ibid.,* May 31, June 1, 1870.

52. *Ibid.,* May 18, 28, 31, 1870.

53. *Ibid.,* June 6, July 21, 30, November 10, 1870.

54. *Ibid.,* November 10, 26, 1870.

55. *Nashville Union and American,* December 6, 1872; Monroe N. Work (comp.), "Some Negro Members of Reconstruction Conventions and Legislatures and of Congress," *Journal of Negro History,* V (January 1920), 114; Raleigh, Minutes of the Raleigh City Council, May 17, 1881, North Carolina Department of Archives and History; Raleigh, *Annual Reports of the Mayor and Officers of the City of Raleigh for Fiscal Year Ending February 28, 1889* (Raleigh, 1889), p. 6. Richmond committee assignments can be followed in the city directories beginning in 1881. An occasional assignment to Elections, Schools, and Claims and Salaries was the closest blacks came to positions of real power. As during Reconstruction, officeholders in the three cities continued to be chosen primarily from the ranks of skilled laborers and petty tradesmen such as grocers, with an occasional professional like attorney Napier or editor Mitchell.

56. For Napier's and Griswold's attempts to secure black police, see, for example, Nashville *Republican Banner,* February 28, April 25, 1873; *Nashville Banner,* January 13, February 24, 1882; February 24, 1888; for their interest in better streets, see, for example, Nashville, Minutes of the Nashville Common Council, February 27, 1882, Office of the Metropolitan Clerk, Davidson County Building and Nashville City Hall; for the controversy over the location of the Nashville packing plant, see *Nashville Banner,* June 21, 25, 30, October 25, 1881; for the Jackson Ward park issue, see Richmond, Minutes of the Richmond Common Council, August 18, October 3, 1887; June 7, August 6, 1888; June 3, 1889; April 7, 1890, Office of the City Clerk, Richmond City Hall; for the accomplishments of Richmond council members, see Luther Porter Jackson, *Negro Office-Holders in Virginia 1865–1895* (Norfolk, 1945), p. 83; for Dunston's contribution, see Raleigh City Council Minutes, August 6, 1880; Raleigh, *Annual Reports,* 1883–1884, p. 35.

57. In all cases, however, the equipment of the Negroes was inferior to that of the whites. In Raleigh, for example, the all-black Victor Company with its hand engine had equipment valued at $5,000; the all-white Rescue Steam Engine Company's equipment was worth $7,000. The Negro Bucket and Ladder Company's equipment was valued at $500; that of the other two white companies, $3,500 and $1,500. And both black units were housed in the same rundown fire station apart from the whites (Raleigh, *Annual Reports,* 1883–1884, p. 36; *ibid.,* 1890–1891, pp. 52, 54).

58. See, for example, Nashville *Daily American,* November 11, 1875; August 8, 1877; September 25, October 18, 1879; January 3, September 15, 1880; November 4, 1884; *Nashville Banner,* September 13, 1881; January 7, September 15, 1887; July 19, 1889.

59. *Directory of the City of Raleigh for 1887* (Raleigh, 1887), p. 57; Wilmoth Annette Carter, "The Negro Main Street of a Contemporary Urban Com-

munity" (unpublished Ph.D. dissertation, University of Chicago, 1959), p. 78;
Raleigh City Council Minutes, April 9, 1880. As late as 1890, several blacks
were appointed Republican ward judges by the Democratic-controlled Board
of County Commissioners, perhaps in order to remind whites of the links between blacks and the Republican Party (Raleigh *News and Observer*, October 9, 1890).

60. For Cargill, see *Atlanta Constitution*, November 11, 13, 15, 1881; for the new
position of janitor, see *ibid.*, July 2, 1889.

61. Nashville *Daily American*, January 4, 1877; *Richmond Dispatch*, June 14,
1870; *Raleigh Register*, March 27, 1878; for Negro postal workers and Ellison's
contract, see Montgomery *Alabama Enterprise*, February 27, 1886; December
18, 1887.

62. J. H. Chataigne (comp.), *Richmond Directory 1882-1883* (Richmond, 1882),
p. 18; J. H. Chataigne (comp.), *Richmond City Directory 1888* (Richmond,
1888), p. 18.

63. *Atlanta Constitution*, September 23, 1875; June 14, 1882; August 15, 20,
1889; for the controversy involving the appointment of the black clerk, see
ibid., August 6-9, 1889; for the number of black postal employees in 1889, see
ibid., November 19, 1889; for Henry Craig, see Arthur Williams, "The Participation of Negroes in the Government of Alabama 1867-1874" (unpublished
M.A. thesis, Atlanta University, 1946), p. 37. For the changing fortunes
under Democratic and Republican administrations of Montgomery's black
mailmen (called "coon carriers" by the leading Democratic newspaper),
see *Montgomery Daily Advertiser*, September 1-2, 1885; March 1, 1890. The
Republican postmaster in Raleigh refused to put a black man at the general
delivery window because of the close contact with white women (Raleigh
News and Observer, March 9, 1890).

64. For Alexander, see *Savannah Tribune*, September 14, 1889; for Napier, see
Commission Certificates for 1875 and 1877, J. C. Napier Papers, Fisk University Library, Nashville; for Sykes, see *Nashville Banner*, April 20, 1881; for
Rapier, see Ross A. Smith (comp.), *The Montgomery City Directory for 1880-
1881* (Montgomery, 1880), p. 245; Joel Davis (comp.), *Montgomery Directory
1883-1884* (Montgomery, 1883), p. 24; for Stewart and Clarkson, see J. H.
Chataigne (comp.), *Richmond Directory for 1885* (Richmond, 1885), p. 66;
for Lindsay, see Jackson, *Negro Office-Holders*, p. 25; for Boyd and Cox, see
Richmond Dispatch, December 24, 1870; April 17, 1880; for Young, see W. N.
Hartshorn, *An Era of Progress and Promise 1863-1910: The Religious, Moral
and Educational Development of the American Negro Since His Emancipation*
(Boston, 1910), p. 462; for Pledger, see *Atlanta Constitution*, January 1, 1885;
for Wimbish, see *Savannah Tribune*, September 14, 1888. In order for Pledger
to get his position he had to resign as Republican State Chairman (Vincent P.
DeSantis, "Negro Dissatisfaction with Republican Policy in the South 1882-
1884," *Journal of Negro History*, XXXVI [April 1951], 152).

65. For Rucker, see Hartshorn, *Era of Progress and Promise*, p. 429; J. W. Gibson
and W. H. Crogman, *Progress of A Race or The Remarkable Advancement of
the American Negro* (rev. ed.; Atlanta, 1902), pp. 286-88; Clarence A. Bacote,
"Negro Officeholders in Georgia Under President McKinley," *Journal of Negro
History*, XLIV (July 1959), 226; for Oliver, see *Richmond Dispatch*, May 9,
1867; September 27, 1870; for Heard, see *Atlanta Constitution*, January 10,
1890; for Clarkson's dismissal under Cleveland, see *Richmond Dispatch*, July 2,
1885.

66. For McHenry, see Carter, *Black Side,* pp. 178–80; for Casswell, see Raleigh *Daily Sentinel,* August 3, 1868; for Paul, see C. A. Bryce, "Good Old Days When Jackson Ward Was a Political Battleground," *Richmond Times Dispatch,* May 8, 1921; for Wadkins, see *Nashville Banner,* March 25, 1881; for Sumner, see Work, "Some Negro Members of Reconstruction," p. 114.

12. THE SEARCH FOR ALTERNATIVES TO ONE-PARTY ALLEGIANCE

1. *Richmond Dispatch,* July 24, 1873; February 10, 1880; Josiah Crump, N. V. Bacchus, W. H. Carter, and R. A. Paul to William A. Mahone, December 21, 1881, William A. Mahone Papers, Duke University Library, Durham, North Carolina; *Richmond Planet,* April 12, 1890.
2. *Atlanta Constitution,* April 30, 1880; McHenry quoted *ibid.,* March 5, 1882; *ibid.,* March 11, 1889; September 16, 1890.
3. See, for example, Nashville *Republican Banner,* October 5, 1873; April 12, 1874; petition to President Garfield, March 21, 1881, J. C. Napier Papers, Fisk University Library, Nashville; excerpt from Nashville *Tennessee Star* editorial by George T. Robinson, reprinted in *Nashville Banner,* May 21, 1887; vote against the Harrison administration in *Nashville Banner,* June 16, 1890. For similar protests in Raleigh, see Raleigh *News and Observer,* August 23, 27, 1890.
4. Richmond leader quoted in *Richmond Dispatch,* May 24, 1870; Nashville *Republican Banner,* October 23, 1872; letter of J. Munroe Cockrill to the editor, Nashville *Daily American,* August 13, 1876 (italics added); *ibid.,* October 22, 29, 1876. Occasionally such protests bore fruit: see *Nashville Banner,* September 16, 18, 1882.
5. Bentley quoted in *Atlanta Constitution,* November 4, 1876; resolutions reported in Nashville *Daily American,* August 8, 1879.
6. *Richmond Planet,* May 31, 1890.
7. C. A. Bryce, "Good Old Days When Jackson Ward Was a Political Battleground," *Richmond Times Dispatch,* May 8, 1921. Bahen thus resembled other leading Republican grocer-politicians like Nashville's T. J. Slowey and the owner of Atlanta's Willingham Building. For the important political role played by antebellum grocers especially in matters concerning blacks, see Richard C. Wade, *Slavery in the Cities: The South 1820–1860* (New York, 1964), pp. 85–87, 146–60, 253–55. For the demographic character of Bahen's neighborhood, see J. H. Chataigne (comp.), *Chataigne's Directory of Richmond for 1891* (Richmond, 1891), pp. 1002–1003. For biographical information, see Bureau of the Census, Manuscript Census Schedules, Population, 1870, Virginia, Henrico County, City of Richmond, Jefferson Ward, p. 126. (Jackson Ward had not been created yet.)
8. *Richmond Dispatch,* May 27, 1882; *Richmond Planet,* May 31, 1890. Although 28 of the 48 members of the two Council chambers chosen in 1882 were incumbents, only two aldermen out of Jackson's eight-man delegation were reelected.
9. Nashville *Daily American,* July 20, August 22, 27, 1880; August 20, 1885.
10. Young quoted in *Nashville Banner,* May 12, 1888; for especially strong criticism of Young's nomination, see Nashville *Daily American,* July 20, 1888; letter of "XYZ" to the editor, *Nashville Banner,* July 21, 1888.

11. *Nashville Banner*, July 20, 1888; white delegate quoted in Nashville *Daily American*, July 20, 1888.

12. Raleigh *North Carolina Republican*, November 12, 1880, quoted in Frenise A. Logan, *The Negro in North Carolina 1876–1894* (Chapel Hill, 1964), p. 16; Nashville *Republican Banner*, November 7, 1872; Nashville *Daily American*, August 12, 30, 1876; *Richmond Dispatch*, November 4–5, 1890.

13. The Georgia delegation to the 1880 Convention which included one white and one black delegate from Atlanta was the only one in which blacks outnumbered whites. Four years later Georgia sent an all-white delegation (*Atlanta Constitution*, April 24, 1880; August 10, 1884).

14. *Ibid.*, August 4, 1882; *Nashville Banner*, June 17, 1886; August 14, 1890; *Richmond Dispatch*, January 30, 1880.

15. *Atlanta Constitution*, October 17, 1883; August 27, September 16, 1890; *Nashville Banner*, June 7, 1882; *Montgomery Daily Advertiser*, August 3, 1890. The county committees tended to be heavily weighted with Negro members. The Davidson County Republican Executive Committee for 1874–1875, for example, included eight Negroes and six whites (Nashville *Republican Banner*, July 12, 1874).

16. *Nashville Union and Dispatch*, May 16, 1867; *Richmond Dispatch*, September 9, 1880; *Montgomery Weekly Advertiser*, May 21, 1867; for the pattern in selecting officers, see, for example, *Richmond Dispatch*, August 4, 1870; *Nashville Banner*, June 12, October 7, 1886; June 14, 1890.

17. *Richmond Dispatch*, August 4, 20, 1870.

18. *Ibid.*, January 29, September 9, 1880. A similar split took place during the 1874 Congressional campaign. Backing the white incumbent were Lewis Lindsay, C. J. S. Bowe, and R. A. Paul; supporting his white challenger were Landon Boyd, Joseph Cox, and Royall White (*ibid.*, October 8, 1874).

19. Nashville *Daily American*, December 5, 1883; *Atlanta Constitution*, August 23, 1889; March 28, 1888. For other divisions among blacks over patronage, see Nashville *Republican Banner*, July 26, 1868; *Atlanta Constitution*, January 8, April 19, 1876; April 9, 1880; Raleigh *News and Observer*, February 1, 1890.

20. Raleigh *Daily Standard*, April 14, 1868; testimony of P. T. Sayre, in U.S. Congress, 42nd Cong., 2nd Sess., *Testimony Taken by the Joint Select Committee to Inquire Into the Condition of Affairs in the Late Insurrectionary States* (Washington, D.C., 1872), VIII, 357 (hereafter cited as *KKK Hearings*).

21. *Nashville Daily Press and Times*, April 12, 1867; Central Committee quoted *ibid.*, June 7, 1867; *ibid.*, April 8, 1868; *Nashville Banner*, October 1, 1889.

22. *Atlanta Constitution*, April 9, 1880; letter of "A Republican" to the editor, Montgomery *Colored Citizen*, April 12, 1884.

23. Atlanta *Daily New Era*, October 1, 1870, cited in Robert E. Perdue, "The Negro as Reflected in the *Atlanta Constitution, Atlanta Intelligencer* and *Atlanta Daily New Era* from 1868–1880" (unpublished M.A. thesis, Atlanta University, 1963), p. 16; letter of A. A. Carter to the editor, Nashville *Daily American*, September 19, 1875; interview of Kercheval, *ibid.*, October 4, 1887.

24. For Hunnicutt, see Jack P. Maddex, Jr., *The Virginia Conservatives 1867–1879: A Study in Reconstruction Politics* (Chapel Hill, 1970), pp. 50–51; Alrutheus Ambush Taylor, *The Negro in the Reconstruction of Virginia* (Washington, D.C., 1941), pp. 209–12; for Buck, see *Atlanta Constitution*, October 22, 1882; for Manly, see *Richmond Dispatch*, July 2, 1875, and Chapter 7 of this study; for Lawrence, see *Nashville Banner*, August 8, 1889.

25. *Richmond Dispatch,* November 7, 1870. Chandler had run for Congress in 1865 as an opponent of Negro suffrage (*ibid.,* May 24, 1870). He and his running mates for mayor and city sergeant had also been leaders of the Know Nothing movement in antebellum Richmond. Other scalawags including Thomas A. Kercheval also had been involved in the Know Nothing movement and thus provide support for those scholars who find sizable Whig and Know Nothing representation among postbellum native Republicans. See, for example, Warren A. Ellem, "Who Were the Mississippi Scalawags?" *Journal of Southern History,* XXXVIII (May 1972), 217–40.

26. Testimony of James H. Clanton, in *KKK Hearings,* VIII, 239.

27. W. M. Smith to William A. Mahone, November 9, 1883, Mahone Papers. Smith was chairman of the Richmond Coalition Campaign Committee.

28. *Atlanta Constitution,* March 25, April 3, 9–11, May 2, 1884; Carrier quoted *ibid.,* March 20, 1890; letter of Colonel A. L. Harris to the editor, *ibid.,* March 18, 1890.

29. *Nashville Banner,* August 16, 1886; August 18, 25, 1888.

30. The convention fight is reported *ibid.,* September 26–27, October 4–5, 1888.

31. *Ibid.,* October 7, 1890. Symbolic of the differences between the races, blacks and whites sat on opposite sides of the hall.

32. *Ibid.,* April 27, 1889; Grandison quoted in *Atlanta Constitution,* January 3, 1888.

33. Nashville *Daily American,* January 29, 1880; *Nashville Banner,* September 13, 17, November 29, December 1, 1887; letter of "A Colored Voter" to the editor, *ibid.,* August 5, 1890.

34. *Nashville Banner,* August 3, 1888; Atlanta black quoted in *Atlanta Constitution,* November 30, 1887. See also Montgomery *Herald,* April 2, 1887.

35. Excerpt from *Weekly Defiance* reprinted in *Atlanta Constitution,* February 5, 1882; Fifth Ward Negroes' statement in *Atlanta Constitution,* December 1, 1887; letter of "Phoenix" to the editor, Montgomery *Alabama Enterprise,* July 10, 1886.

36. Letter of John McGowan to the editor, Nashville *Republican Banner,* August 19, 1874; letter of "C.E." to the editor, Nashville *Daily American,* August 17, 1885.

37. See, for example, letter of W. F. Anderson to the editor, *Nashville Banner,* October 10, 1883; letter of T. G. Ryman to the editor, *ibid.,* September 25, 1883. A *Nashville Banner* editorial, September 20, 1883, strongly defended the right of "sober, capable and honest" Negroes to hold office. See also Nashville *Daily American,* October 10–11, 1883.

38. Nashville *Daily American,* October 13, 1883; *Nashville Banner,* October 12, 1883.

39. See, for example, *Nashville Banner,* October 12, 1883. Aside from his active campaigning, Anderson had nominated the victorious mayoral candidate (Nashville *Daily American,* September 19, 1883).

40. *Nashville Banner,* October 17, 1883; Colyar quoted *ibid.,* October 13, 1883. Ironically, many of the men saluting Young soon would be calling him an agitator for his efforts to secure representation for blacks.

41. Nashville, Message of the Mayor, *Annual Reports of the Various Officers Connected with the Different Departments of the City of Nashville for the Year Ending September 30, 1884* (Nashville, 1884), p. 5.

42. The controversy over the composition of the new fire company can be followed in *Nashville Banner,* November 8, 1884; January 14–15, September 5, 1885.

(One possible reason for the appointment of Gowdey might have been to remove him from the Council. He was replaced by a white.) For Gowdey's support of free water, see Nashville, Minutes of the Nashville City Council, December 13, 1883, Office of the Metropolitan Clerk, Davidson County Building
and Nashville City Hall, Nashville; for Anderson's reward, see *Nashville Banner*, November 9, 1883; Napier's view expressed in a letter to J. M. Dickinson,
April 14, 1909, Dickinson Family Papers, Box 24, Folder 11, Tennessee State
Library and Archives, Nashville (italics added). See also Napier's assessment
of the reform campaign in Monroe N. Work (comp.), "Some Negro Members
of Reconstruction Conventions and Legislatures and of Congress," *Journal of
Negro History*, V (January 1920), 115.

43. *Nashville Banner*, October 8, 1885; Young quoted *ibid.*, October 6, 1885.
44. Nashville *Daily American*, October 9, 1885; for disclosures of fraud on both
    sides, see *Nashville Banner*, October 9–10, 1885; for bloc voting, see *ibid.*,
    October 8, 1885; for final results, see Nashville *Daily American*, October 9,
    1885.
45. *Nashville Banner*, April 23, 1886. Among those present were J. C. Napier,
    W. H. Young, J. H. Keeble, J. H. Dismukes, W. A. Hadley, and the Reverend
    George W. Bryant.
46. Robinson quoted in Nashville *Daily American*, August 18, 1890. Those present
    at the founding of the club included Alfred Menefee, J. H. Dismukes, and
    Jesse Woods. J. C. Napier and Henry Harding were expected to attend, but
    they did not appear. See letter of Jesse Woods to the editor, *Nashville Banner*,
    August 20, 1887, and letter of Alfred Menefee to the editor, *ibid.*, for a de-
    fense of the club's objectives.
47. Nashville *Daily American*, October 5–6, 1887. Included on the campaign com-
    mittee for the ticket of Bosley and his running mates were J. C. Napier, J. H.
    Keeble, B. J. Hadley, S. R. Walker, Abram B. Bradford, and Alfred Menefee.
    No Negroes served on the Knights of Labor's committee (*ibid.*, October 7,
    1887). See *ibid.*, October 14, 1887, for the election results. Going down to de-
    feat with Bosley were three of his four running mates.
48. See, for example, *Richmond Dispatch*, October 28, 1880; *Atlanta Constitution*,
    February 20, September 24, November 8, 1878; Nashville *Daily American*,
    August 30, November 6–7, 1878.
49. For a description of the campaign and the final results, see *Richmond Dis-
    patch*, May 22–29, 1886 (the reform candidate for city sergeant triumphed
    because of a 2,280–212 margin in Jackson Ward). For interest in equalization
    of wages, see *ibid.*, November 5, 1887; for the armory site, see Richmond,
    Ordinances (1886–1888), p. 128. For discussions leading up to the passage
    of the appropriation, see Richmond, Minutes of the Richmond Common Coun-
    cil, February 2, 1886; December 5, 1887; January 3, February 6, May 7, 1888,
    Office of the City Clerk, Richmond City Hall. For earlier efforts to secure an
    armory, see *ibid.*, January 3, 1881; May 26, 1882.
50. *Richmond Dispatch*, October 22, 27–28, 1880; Harris quoted *ibid.*, April 29,
    1880. See also O. M. Stewart to William A. Mahone, September 21, 1883,
    Mahone Papers, and endorsement of Mahone in Richmond *Virginia Star*, April
    30, 1881.
51. For the lack of support for the Readjusters among Richmond whites, see Henry
    Hudnall to William A. Mahone, November 9, 1883, Mahone Papers; letter of
    William Nott to William A. Mahone, November 7, 1883, *ibid.*; for the con-

tribution of the Readjusters to the education of Richmond blacks, see Chapter 7 of this study.

52. *Atlanta Constitution*, October 8, 1886; December 3, 1890; Atlanta, Minutes of the Atlanta City Council, December 14, 1890, Office of the City Clerk, Atlanta City Hall; Nashville *Daily American*, October 5, 1887; letter of D. P. Lane to the editor, Raleigh *News and Observer*, July 31, 1890; for Richmond, see *Savannah Tribune*, June 1, 1889.

53. Pledger quoted in *Atlanta Constitution*, November 22, 1884; McHenry quoted *ibid.*, December 6, 1884; for Negro support of statewide Democratic candidates, see, for example, activities of the Colored Colquitt Club during the 1880 campaign, *ibid.*, September–October 1880, *passim;* editorial of Atlanta *Weekly Defiance* endorsing Conservatives like Stephens and Gordon, quoted *ibid.*, December 11, 1886.

54. Montgomery *Colored Citizen*, May 3, 1884; Montgomery *Herald*, April 2, 1887; Nashville *Daily American*, August 17, 20, 1885; *Nashville Banner*, August 17, 1886. See also *Richmond Planet*, March 22, 1890.

55. *Montgomery Daily Advertiser*, July 22, 1872. See also letter of Levi Mastin to the editor, *ibid.*, March 21, 1872.

56. *Nashville Banner*, October 10, 1882; Terry quoted in Nashville *Daily American*, September 28, 1877; testimony of Caesar Shorter, in *KKK Hearings*, IX, 1074–76. The *Montgomery Daily Advertiser* delighted in printing letters of Negroes who wished to announce their switch from the Republican to the Democratic Party. See, for example, letter of J. B. Nettles to the editor, April 7, 1875; letter of Jeff Wallace to the editor, April 17, 1875.

57. *Nashville Union and Dispatch*, April 7, 1867; *Richmond Dispatch*, May 25, 1876. Dungee later was driven from his pulpit for his efforts on behalf of the Democrats (*ibid.*, February 20, June 22, 1877). For accounts of Williams's activities, see *Nashville Union and Dispatch*, April 10, 30, October 15, 1867; *Nashville Union and American*, November 5, 1868; August 30, 1870.

58. Montgomery *Weekly Advance*, September 11, 1880.

59. Letter of James A. Scott to Colonel Fred A. Conkling, reprinted in Nashville *Daily American*, October 1, 1880. For a similar comparison between Republicans and Democrats, see the statement of Richmond's Colored Hancock and English Club, *Richmond Dispatch*, August 5, 1880.

60. *Atlanta Constitution*, April 21, December 25, 1889.

61. Taylor quoted *ibid.*, July 6, February 13, 1890; letter of C. H. J. Taylor to the editor, *ibid.*, November 16, 1889. There is no record of Taylor's convention ever having taken place.

62. *Nashville Banner*, November 4, 1884; *Richmond Dispatch*, October 25–26, 1889. The Reverend John Jasper, a longtime foe of Wells and an opponent of political activity by clergymen, refused to sign the 1889 circular. For his reasons, see *Nashville Banner*, October 30, 1889. For further evidence of Negro identification with the Republican Party in Raleigh and Montgomery, see testimony of John O. Kelly in U.S. Senate, 46th Cong., 2nd Sess., *Report and Testimony of the Select Committee of the United States Senate to Investigate the Causes for the Removal of the Negroes from the Southern States to the Northern States* (Washington, D.C., 1880), Part I, 245; J. W. A. Sanford to his son, April 30, 1889, John William Augustine Sanford Papers, Alabama Department of Archives and History, Montgomery.

63. Letter of Samuel Lowery, Moses R. Johnson, T. J. Bell, and D. L. Lapsley to

Senator Charles Sumner informing him of resolutions passed by a local meeting of blacks, quoted in Nashville *Republican Banner*, August 11, 1872; Nashville *Daily American*, July 25, 1885; letter of "Colored Citizen" to the editor,
Nashville Banner, July 27, 1885.

13. RESOLVING THE UNCERTAINTIES:
TOWARD ELIMINATION OF THE BLACK VOTE

1. *Atlanta Constitution*, September 8, 1889; Charles M. Blackford to Robert
   Taylor Scott, August 16, 1889, Robert Taylor Scott Papers, Virginia Historical
   Society, Richmond.
2. *Atlanta Constitution*, October 31, November 21, 1868; December 27, 1878;
   January 14, 1879; August 10, 1885; *Montgomery Weekly Advertiser*, December 31, 1867; *Richmond Dispatch*, August 12, 1870.
3. Nashville *Daily American*, August 24, 1876; Nashville *Republican Banner*,
   July 26, 1872. *Atlanta Constitution*, August 1, 1887, announced that the newspaper would challenge Republican attempts to disfranchise the blacks: "We are
   in favor of negro suffrage, not because the race is prepared for it, but because
   it gives the democratic party of the south additional power." Implicit was the
   suggestion that the newspaper would no longer support Negro suffrage if it
   became harmful to the Democratic Party. For a sample of Negro Democratic
   clubs in one city, see *Montgomery Daily Advertiser*, July 31, August 17, 1868;
   July 31, August 4, 10, 1872; July 11, 16, 1880.
4. Speaker quoted in *Atlanta Daily Sun*, December 5, 1870; Nashville *Republican
   Banner*, September 28, 1868; Stahlman quoted in Nashville *Daily American*,
   October 7, 1877.
5. Testimony of Willard Warner, in U.S. Congress, 42nd Cong., 2nd Sess., *Testimony Taken by the Joint Select Committee to Inquire Into the Condition of
   Affairs in the Late Insurrectionary States* (Washington, D.C., 1872), VIII, 35
   (hereafter cited as *KKK Hearings*); *Montgomery Weekly Advertiser*, October
   15, 1867.
6. Endorsement of Negro weekly published in Atlanta by C. E. Yarboro, *Atlanta
   Constitution*, August 6, 1890. See also *Montgomery Daily Advertiser*, November 12, 1890.
7. Quoted in Montgomery *Weekly Advance*, September 3, 1881. See also *Montgomery Daily Advertiser*, November 23, 1880.
8. Testimony of J. H. Clanton, in *KKK Hearings*, VIII, 228–29; Nashville *Republican Banner*, November 4, 1868; Nashville *Daily American*, November 4,
   1880; *Atlanta Constitution*, November 10, 1876; *Richmond Dispatch*, May 28,
   1870. For other claims of intimidation against Negro voters, see *Atlanta Constitution*, November 8, 1884; *Nashville Banner*, August 14, 1886; testimony of
   P. T. Sayre, in *KKK Hearings*, VIII, 362; *Montgomery Daily Advertiser*, December 7, 1871; August 3–4, 1872; letter of Henry Davis to the editor, *ibid.*, May
   6, 1875. Despite Democratic charges, heckling was the most common form of
   harassment. In 1871 former Senator Willard Warner, a white Republican
   carpetbagger from Montgomery, told a Congressional committee that some
   blacks were working for the Democrats in his city, but "of course the pressure
   is very strong upon the colored people to vote all one way." A Negro Republican, Charles Mahone, added that any black who encouraged support for the

NOTES TO PAGES 309–315

Democrats "would be in a little difficulty." These views were corroborated by Caesar Shorter, Montgomery's leading Negro Democrat. He stated that violence was rarely used against himself or his followers, but threats were frequent and he was often "abused right smartly" (*KKK Hearings*, VIII, 35; *ibid.*, IX, 1072, 1077–79). Similarly, a longtime Richmond resident remembered that Negroes who voted Democratic in the Virginia capital had to cast their ballots "amid hoots and jeers of crowds of their own hostile color" (C. A. Bryce, "Good Old Days When Jackson Ward Was a Political Battleground," *Richmond Times Dispatch*, May 8, 1921).

9. Nashville *Republican Banner*, August 5, 1874; *Richmond Dispatch*, November 9, 1883. See especially *Atlanta Constitution*, October 4, 1876; September 10, 1882; October 31, 1884.

10. *Atlanta Constitution*, October 30, 1883; Nashville *Republican Banner*, August 7, 1874; *Richmond Dispatch*, April 23, 1890.

11. See, for example, Raleigh *Daily Sentinel*, May 27, 1875; *Nashville Banner*, September 28, 1883.

12. *Nashville Banner*, September 27, 1888.

13. *Richmond Dispatch*, December 9, 1870. See also *ibid.*, May 1870 and October 1870, *passim*.

14. *Richmond Dispatch*, May 1, 1880; November 9, 1883 (italics added). See also Raleigh *Daily News*, May 22, 1877; *Raleigh Register*, August 13, 27, 1884.

15. Nashville *Republican Banner*, August 6, 1874; *Nashville Banner*, August 1, 1882; November 15, 1884.

16. Atlanta Democrat quoted in *Atlanta Constitution*, September 17, 1876; *Richmond Dispatch*, October 7, 1870; June 22, 1877; Montgomery *Herald*, April 2, 1887. For earlier examples of white primaries in Atlanta, see *Atlanta Constitution*, October 4, 1872; November 12, 1875. For an invitation to "every white man" in Raleigh's Second Ward to organize a Democratic club, see Raleigh *News and Observer*, October 10, 1890.

17. *Richmond Dispatch*, March 9, 1875; May 25, 27, 1876 (italics added).

18. *Atlanta Constitution*, October 23, December 8, 1881 (see also *ibid.*, November 21, 1875; October 22, 1890). The two Nashville papers were *The World* and *Daily American*. For the discounting of the rumors, see *Nashville Banner*, October 29–31, 1884.

19. *Richmond Dispatch*, November 10, 1879; April 28, 1880; circular quoted *ibid.*, October 26, 1889. See also *ibid.*, April 29, May 4–5, 1880.

20. *Nashville Union and American*, November 10, 1870; September 29, 1872; Nashville *Republican Banner*, November 8, 1872; Nashville *Daily American*, November 4, 1880; for pleas for unity, see, for example, *ibid.*, April 14, July 24, 1878.

21. *Richmond Dispatch*, November 7, 1870; November 1, October 28, 11, 1875.

22. *Atlanta Constitution*, September 11, December 5–6, 1878; October 8, 1882.

23. *Ibid.*, December 4–5, 1879; Nashville *Daily American*, August 8, 1882; *Nashville Banner*, July 12, August 8, 1884. Cargile finished second with 1,058 votes to the winner's 1,863. The candidate who withdrew had amassed 510 votes before dropping out. Burrus lost 8,841–4,519. Gowdey, with 1,496 votes, fell 600 short of victory.

24. For the thesis that the Populist–Bourbon rivalry brought about disfranchisement in the 1890s, see C. Vann Woodward, *The Strange Career of Jim Crow* (3rd rev. ed.; New York, 1974), Chapter iii and *passim*.

25. *Atlanta Constitution*, November 15, 1885. For general discussions of the local

option campaigns, see John Hammond Moore, "The Negro and Prohibition in Atlanta 1885–1887," *South Atlantic Quarterly*, LXIX (Winter 1970), 38–57; Edgar G. Epps, "The Participation of the Negro in the Municipal Politics of the City of Atlanta 1867–1908" (unpublished M.A. thesis, Atlanta University, 1955), pp. 26–32.

26. *Atlanta Constitution*, November 13, December 3, 1885; for the payment of poll taxes and providing of refreshments, see *ibid.*, October 29, 1885. Even the speakers on the platform at the tent meeting were seated according to race.

27. Pledger quoted *ibid.*, November 21, 1885; Parker remark *ibid.*, October 30, 1885.

28. *Ibid.*, November 3, 1885; letter to the editor, *ibid.*, November 24, 1885. Liquor taxes and license fees went toward the support of public schools.

29. *Ibid.*, November 24–26, 1885. For a pre-election assessment of the importance of the black vote, see *ibid.*, October 29, 1885. According to the Atlanta correspondent of the *Richmond Dispatch*, December 1, 1885, the drys won because of black support.

30. The various maneuvers can be followed in *Atlanta Constitution*, October 27– November 5, 1886.

31. Registration figures *ibid.*, November 16, 1887. For a steady barrage of prohibition news, see *ibid.*, from the end of October through election day, November 27, 1887.

32. For statements of prohibition advocates including Bentley, McHenry, Gaines, and Carter, see *ibid.*, November 2, 9, 1887 (Bentley later charged that the prohibitionists had reneged on their promise to him [*ibid.*, March 22, 1890]); for Pledger's views and charges of white manipulation, see *ibid.*, November 8, 1887.

33. *Ibid.*, November 27, December 6, 1887.

34. *Ibid.*, October 17, 19–20, 24, November 27, 1888; judge quoted *ibid.*, March 20, 1890.

35. Excerpt reprinted *ibid.*, August 2, 1888.

36. *Richmond Dispatch*, December 1, 1885; *Atlanta Constitution*, April 27, 1886; Atlanta observer quoted *ibid.*, April 6, 1886. In its rundown of the final vote, the *Richmond Dispatch*, April 27, 1886, suggested that many blacks who worked in tobacco factories voted wet because they feared that if liquor were prohibited, tobacco might be outlawed next. It seems, however, that the strength of the wets among blacks was largely due to the control exercised by white saloonkeepers and grocers in Jackson Ward.

37. Josephus Daniels, *Tar Heel Editor* (Chapel Hill, 1939), pp. 306–307; R. H. Whitaker, *Whitaker's Reminiscences: Incidents and Anecdotes* (Raleigh, 1905), p. 197.

38. For campaign activities, see, for example, Nashville *Daily American*, September 30, 1887; *Nashville Banner*, June 27, September 24, 28, October 1, 1887; for the vote breakdown by wards, see *ibid.*, September 30, 1887.

39. Nashville *Daily American*, October 17, 1887.

40. Quoted in *Chicago Times* and reprinted in Nashville *Daily American*, November 19, 1880. The man was typical of Southern whites who exaggerated the corruption of Reconstruction and the purity of Redemption. See, for example, C. Vann Woodward, *Origins of the New South 1877–1913*, Vol. IX of *A History of the South*, eds. Wendell Holmes Stephenson and E. Merton Coulter (Baton Rouge, 1951), pp. 68–69.

41. Letter of J. Staunton Moore, November 16, 1886, in J. Staunton Moore, *Reminiscences: Letters, Poetry, and Miscellaneous* (Richmond, 1903), pp. 94–95.
42. *Richmond Planet*, May 17, 1890; Bryce, "Good Old Days in Jackson Ward"; *Richmond Dispatch*, November 7, 1888; William Cameron to William A. Mahone, November 2, 1883, William A. Mahone Papers, Duke University Library, Durham, North Carolina.
43. Alexander K. McClure, *The South: Its Industrial, Financial and Political Condition* (Philadelphia, 1886), pp. 79–80, 82.
44. Bryce, "Good Old Days in Jackson Ward."
45. See, for example, Montgomery *Herald*, April 2, 1887; *Nashville Banner*, August 3, 1882.
46. *Richmond Dispatch*, October 16, 21, 1875; October 14, 1883.
47. Hilary A. Herbert, "Grandfather's Talks About His Life Under Two Flags," pp. 278–79, Southern Historical Collection, University of North Carolina Library, Chapel Hill; Montgomery *Colored Citizen*, May 3, 1884; *Richmond Dispatch*, April 13, 24, 26, 1890.
48. *Richmond Dispatch*, November 15–25, December 14–15, 1875; Bryce, "Good Old Days in Jackson Ward." The results of the municipal elections held in 1876 provide further evidence of the fraudulent nature of the 1875 count. The First Precinct gave the Conservatives 280 votes and the Republicans 174 votes, a closer approximation of the anti-Conservative strength (*Richmond Dispatch*, May 27, 1876).
49. Charles Nordhoff, *The Cotton States in the Spring and Summer of 1875* (New York, 1876), p. 103; for Mitchell's complaints, see, for example, Richmond, Minutes of the Richmond Common Council, December 3, 1888, Office of the City Clerk, Richmond City Hall; *Richmond Planet*, June 14, 1890; for the distribution of voting precincts, see *Richmond Dispatch*, November 10, 1876; July 16, 1880; Richmond, *Ordinances* (1892), pp. 19–21. See also Savannah *Colored Tribune*, November 13, 1876; Henry Hudnall to William A. Mahone, October 30, 1883, Mahone Papers.
50. E. Thompson to William A. Mahone, October 15, 1885, Mahone Papers; *Richmond Planet*, March 22, 1890.
51. *Richmond Dispatch*, November 6, 1889. As a result, Mahone carried Jackson by a relatively slim margin of 784 to 669. In all the other wards the Mahone vote was only a few less than the number of registered black voters. For Conservative denial of using separate lines to limit the number of black votes, see *ibid.*, November 8, 1876.
52. It can be assumed that such practices were common throughout the urban South. The cities noted here are singled out because documentation was readily available. For separate voting boxes in the 1887 Augusta municipal election, see *Atlanta Constitution*, December 8, 1887; for the intended use of separate voting lines in the upcoming presidential election in Atlanta, see *ibid.*, November 7, 1876; for the existence of separate white and black precincts in the 1880 federal elections in Norfolk, see *Richmond Dispatch*, October 22, 1880; for separate registration books in Raleigh, see North Carolina, *Private Laws* (1874–1875), pp. 531–32 and in Richmond, see *Richmond Dispatch*, November 13, 1875; Richmond Common Council Minutes, January 6, 1890.
53. See, for example, *Richmond Planet*, May 17, 24, 1890; *Richmond Dispatch*, November 13, 1875; Beverley B. Munford, *Random Recollections* (Richmond, 1905), p. 130; quotation by Bryce, "Good Old Days in Jackson Ward."

54. Letter of William A. Kirkham to the editor, *Richmond Dispatch*, November 13, 1885 (italics added). See rebuttal in letter of Robert A. Martin to the editor, *ibid.*, November 15, 1885. Martin, also of Petersburg, called for a continued attempt to divide the Negro vote and put an end to the color line in politics. He also pointed out that any attempt to disfranchise blacks would provoke retaliation from Northern Republicans such as John Sherman. Martin's position therefore represented not only the dwindling number of white Democrats who sincerely defended Negro suffrage, but also that larger number whose hostility was at least partly checked by fear of Northern intervention.

55. Nashville *Daily American*, August 4–5, 1876; Charter of 1883 in Nashville, *Laws* (1893), pp. 8–12; letter of "X.X." to the editor, Montgomery *Colored Citizen*, May 17, 1884; Montgomery *Alabama Guide*, November 1884; Chattanooga legislation reported in *Nashville Banner*, February 22, 1889; Jackson developments reported *ibid.*, September 18, 1889; *Atlanta Constitution*, January 22, 1890. Despite the gerrymandering in Chattanooga, the Republicans elected their mayor and a majority of the aldermen in the 1889 municipal elections (*Nashville Banner*, October 10, 1889).

56. *Atlanta Constitution*, June 15, November 5, 1884; for early Republican complaints about the poll tax, see *ibid.*, September 28, 1873.

57. *Ibid.*, October 5, 1876; October 20, 1882; November 1, 1885. Savannah election officials were also less demanding about the qualifications of white voters (Savannah *Colored Tribune*, November 13, 1876).

58. For the new registration law, see *Atlanta Constitution*, November 3, 1890; for both the registration figures and the comment about Negro defaulters, see *ibid.*, September 21, 1884.

59. Alrutheus Ambush Taylor, *The Negro in the Reconstruction of Virginia* (Washington, D.C., 1926), pp. 266–67; Richmond *Virginia Star*, May 11, 1878.

60. *Richmond Dispatch*, May 23–24, 1878; November 6, 1879; quotation, August 17, 1880. See also *ibid.*, August 8, 1880.

61. *Ibid.*, November 9, 1883; January 2, 1888.

62. Paul Lewinson, *Race, Class and Party: A History of Negro Suffrage and White Politics in the South* (reprinted; New York, 1965), p. 72; *Nashville Banner*, September 24, 1887; August 5, 1890. In 1879 approximately one-third of the 6,500 assessed poll taxes were paid (Nashville *Daily American*, November 7, 1879).

63. *Nashville Banner*, April 3, 1889; the law is reprinted *ibid.*, April 5, 1889; *Memphis Avalanche* quoted *ibid.*, July 8, 1890.

64. *Nashville Banner*, September 16, October 11, 1889; for a good description of the voting aids, see *ibid.*, October 9–10, 1889. For the first time the Republicans lost the Fourth Ward which had the largest number of blacks in the city and had sent several blacks to the City Council. The Democratic mayoral candidate won 119 votes compared to 85 and 25 for his Republican and Prohibition challengers. There were 222 registered black voters as compared to 191 whites, so clearly a larger percentage of the whites turned out.

65. *Ibid.*, August 1, 8–9, October 13, November 5, 1890; quotation *ibid.*, August 8, 1890.

66. That story is best told in J. Morgan Kousser, *The Shaping of Southern Politics: Suffrage Restriction and the Establishment of the One-Party South* (New Haven, 1974), one of the few studies that appreciates Tennessee's pioneering role.

67. On fusion in Raleigh, see Helen G. Edmonds, *The Negro and Fusion Politics in North Carolina 1894–1901* (Chapel Hill, 1951), pp. 126–27 and *passim*.

EPILOGUE. RACE RELATIONS AND SOCIAL CONTROL

1. For similar speculation on the relationship between antebellum free Negroes and postbellum black leadership, see Ira Berlin, *Slaves Without Masters: The Free Negro in the Antebellum South* (New York, 1974), pp. 384–85. Charleston and New Orleans were two other cities where the presence of vital antebellum free Negro communities favorably influenced postwar developments. See especially John W. Blassingame, *Black New Orleans 1860–1880* (Chicago, 1973).
2. C. Vann Woodward, *The Strange Career of Jim Crow* (3rd rev. ed.; New York, 1974), pp. 65, 7, 3–109 *passim*.
3. George Brown Tindall, *South Carolina Negroes 1877–1900* (Columbia, 1952); Charles E. Wynes, *Race Relations in Virginia 1870–1902* (Charlottesville, 1961); Frenise A. Logan, *The Negro in North Carolina 1876–1894* (Chapel Hill, 1964); Henry C. Dethloff and Robert P. Jones, "Race Relations in Louisiana, 1877–1898," *Louisiana History,* IX (Fall 1968), 301–23; Blassingame, *Black New Orleans;* Dale A. Somers, "Black and White in New Orleans: A Study in Urban Race Relations, 1865–1900," *Journal of Southern History,* XL (February 1974), 19–42; Joel Williamson, *After Slavery: The Negro in South Carolina During Reconstruction 1861–1877* (Chapel Hill, 1965); Vernon Lane Wharton, *The Negro in Mississippi 1865–1890* (Chapel Hill, 1947); Richard C. Wade, *Slavery in the Cities: The South 1820–1860* (New York, 1964); Roger A. Fischer, "Racial Segregation in Ante Bellum New Orleans," *American Historical Review,* LXXIV (February 1969), 926–37; Roger A. Fischer, "The Post-Civil War Segregation Struggle," eds. Hodding Carter *et al., The Past as Prelude: New Orleans 1718–1968* (New Orleans, 1968), pp. 288–304; Roger A. Fischer, *The Segregation Struggle in Louisiana 1862–77* (Urbana, 1974); Berlin, *Slaves Without Masters.*
4. See, for example, William Archibald Dunning, *Reconstruction Political and Economic 1865–1877,* Vol. XXII of *The American Nation: A History,* ed. A. B. Hart (New York, 1907); J. G. de Roulhac Hamilton, *Reconstruction in North Carolina* (reprinted; Gloucester, Mass., 1964); Walter L. Fleming, *Civil War and Reconstruction in Alabama* (reprinted; Gloucester, Mass., 1949).
5. See, for example, John Hope Franklin, *Reconstruction: After the Civil War* (Chicago, 1961); Kenneth M. Stampp, *The Era of Reconstruction 1865–1877* (New York, 1965); Alan Conway, *The Reconstruction of Georgia* (Minneapolis, 1966); Williamson, *After Slavery.*
6. Lawrence J. Friedman, *The White Savage: Racial Fantasies in the Postbellum South* (Englewood Cliffs, N.J., 1970); Forrest G. Wood, *Black Scare: The Racist Response to Emancipation and Reconstruction* (Berkeley and Los Angeles, 1970); and *The Era of Reconstruction 1863–1877* (New York, 1975). The Republicans are not without their defenders among younger scholars. See especially Michael Les Benedict, *A Compromise of Principle: Congressional Republicans and Reconstruction 1863–1869* (New York, 1974).
7. See, for example, Allen W. Trelease, "Republican Reconstruction in North

Carolina: A Roll-Call Analysis of the State House of Representatives, 1868–1870," *Journal of Southern History*, XLII (August 1976), 319–44.

8. Gilbert Thomas Stephenson, *Race Distinctions in American Law* (New York, 1910), p. 214. See also John Snyder, "Prejudice Against the Negro," *Forum*, VIII (October 1889), 222.

9. *Richmond Dispatch*, March 9, 1875. The difference between the younger and older Ellis is also evident in their first names. The father retained the common slave name of Caesar while his son had a "white man's name" which he had perhaps chosen for himself. It should not be assumed that only the young sought to enjoy the privileges granted in the Civil Rights Act of 1875. It does seem, however, that they were far more likely than their elders to challenge the barriers established by white society.

10. *Atlanta Constitution*, May 30, 1890.

11. *Nashville Banner*, December 22, 1888; *Nashville Tribune* editorial, reprinted in Nashville *Fisk Herald*, VIII (July 1890), 15.

12. Nashville *Fisk Herald*, VII (October 1889), 11–12; *ibid.*, VII (March 1889), 12. See also W. H. Crogman, "Negro Education—Its Helps and Hindrances," a speech delivered before the National Teachers' Association, at Madison, Wis., July 16, 1884, reprinted in the author's *Talks for the Times* (Atlanta, 1896), p. 65; speech of the Reverend C. N. Grandison of Clark University, quoted in *Atlanta Constitution*, January 3, 1888. Grandison argued that "you cannot educate men and then deprive them of their God given rights. It is not the ignorant man who is asking for better accommodations at the hotels, in the cars, and in waiting rooms, but the educated negro."

13. Letter of Flavia Canfield to a friend in Topeka, Kansas, reprinted in Nashville *Daily American*, July 20, 1889.

14. Letter of W. A. Sinclair to the editor, *ibid.*, October 4, 1881.

15. August Meier and Elliott Rudwick, "Negro Retaliatory Violence in the Twentieth Century," *New Politics*, V (Winter 1966), 41–51.

16. See Howard N. Rabinowitz, "The Conflict between Blacks and the Police in the Urban South 1865–1900," *The Historian*, XXXIX (November 1976), 70–71.

17. *Atlanta Constitution*, August 18–19, 1868.

18. *Ibid.*, September 27–28, 1881.

19. *Ibid.*, July 14, 1881; Atlanta *Weekly Defiance*, October 29, 1881.

20. *Atlanta Constitution*, August 17, 25–26, 1883. The police commissioners responded by ordering policemen to arrest any persons, white or black, who might follow them while they were taking in a prisoner (*ibid.*, August 31, 1883).

21. *Ibid.*, July 5, August 1, 7, 1888. For Burnett's interest in joining the force, see *ibid.*, April 2, 1885.

22. *Ibid.*, October 22, November 13, 1888. It is unlikely that Burnett's second such intervention was due to coincidence. Either he was trying to prove to the police that he could be of use on the force or else he was already working for them in an undercover capacity.

23. *Ibid.*, March 25, 1895, quoted in Eugene J. Watts, "The Police in Atlanta, 1890–1905," *Journal of Southern History*, XXXIX (May 1973), 176.

A Note on Sources

This note will consider only the most important primary sources used in this study. I have discussed the basic secondary sources in the Preface and Epilogue, and those readers interested in a more detailed, though still selected, list of sources are referred to the footnotes and to my Ph.D. dissertation, "The Search for Social Control: Race Relations in the Urban South, 1865–1890" (2 vols.; University of Chicago, 1973), II, 892–932.

Newspapers published in the five sample cities provided a wealth of information. Unfortunately, to the victors belonged the press, and, especially for the post-Reconstruction period, I was forced to rely mostly on white Democratic papers. When used with care and some healthy skepticism, however, these extremely partisan papers revealed much about black and white attitudes and behavior. These newspapers included for Atlanta, *Constitution* (1868–1890), *Daily Intelligencer* (1865–1866); for Raleigh, *Daily Sentinel* (1868–1875), *Daily News* (1872, 1875, 1877), *Weekly Progress* (1865–1867), *Register* (1884–1886), *News and Observer* (1880, 1885, 1889–1891); for Nashville, *Dispatch* (1865–1867), *Union and Dispatch* (1867–1868), *Union and American* (1868–1875), *Republican Banner* (1871–1875), *Daily American* (1875–1890), *Banner* (1881–1890); for Montgomery, *Daily Ledger* (1865–1866); *Daily Advertiser* (1865–1890); for Richmond, *Dispatch* (1865–1890).

Though less extensive, the white Republican press provided valuable information on the relationship between black and white Republicans. Those papers most frequently consulted were for Atlanta, *Daily New Era* (1866–1870); for Raleigh, *Daily Standard* (1865–1866, 1868–1869), *Tri-Weekly Standard* (1866–1867), *Register* (1877–1878), before it changed sides; for Nashville, *Daily Press and Times* (1865–1869), *Tennessee Tribune* (1870–1871); for Montgomery, *Daily State Sentinel* (1867–1868), *Alabama State Journal* (1868–1876). Scattered issues are all that remain of most of the period's numerous weekly and monthly local black newspapers. The only sustained runs I found were for Richmond's *Virginia Star* (1878–1882) and *Planet* (1885–1886, 1888–1890) and Nashville's student newspaper *Fisk Herald* (1887–1890). Of the other black newspapers, periodic issues were located for Atlanta, *Weekly Defiance* (1881); for Nashville, *Colored Tennessean* (1865–1866); for Montgomery, *Republican Sentinel* (1872, 1878), *Weekly Advance* (1880–1881, Democratic), *Alabama Guide* (1884); *Colored Citizen* (1884); *Herald* (1886–1887); *Alabama Enterprise* (1886). To compensate for the relative scarcity of local white and black Republican newspapers and to broaden my understanding of conditions in other cities, I examined newspapers in nearby towns which had correspondents in one of my five principal cities. These included the white-edited Mobile *Nationalist* (1865–1868) and the black papers *Savannah Tribune* (1886–1889; also when known as the *Colored Tribune*, 1875–1876) and *Huntsville Gazette* (1881–1887).

Especially valuable were the monthly journals and annual reports published by the Northern missionary societies. Letters from teachers and agents in the field were filled with information about the welfare, religious, and educational efforts of the societies. Among the journals were *The American Missionary* (1865–1890), *The American Freedman* (1866–1867), *The Freedmen's Record* (1865–1871), and *The National Freedman* (1865–1866). Further information about the societies and the conditions in the South was gleaned from the American Missionary Association Archives now available on microfilm and housed at the Amistad Research Center, Dillard University, New Orleans, but examined by me at Fisk University in Nashville. Also useful were J. W. Alvord, *Letters from the South Relating to the Condition of Freedmen Addressed to Major General O. O. Howard* (Washington, D.C., 1870) and Henry L. Swint (ed.), *Dear Ones at Home: Letters from Contraband Camps* (Nashville, 1966).

Other pieces of correspondence were disappointing. The papers of the various governors of the five states, a rich vein for the study of statewide race relations, were less helpful because of my concentration on capital cities. There was relatively little correspondence concerning the five cities in these collections, indicating that most information about local conditions was gained by first-hand observation or was transmitted in person. A few manuscript collections were of greater value. Most noteworthy were Jabez Lamar Monroe Curry Letters (Alabama Department of Archives and History and Duke University Library); Dickinson Family Papers (Tennessee State Library and Archives); Hilary A. Herbert Collection (Southern Historical Collection, University of North Carolina Library, Chapel Hill); William A. Mahone Papers (Duke University Library); Munford-Ellis Papers (Duke University Library); William Henry Ruffner Papers (Virginia State Library); John William Augustine Sanford Papers (Alabama Department of Archives and History); Wager Swayne Papers (Alabama Department of Archives and History). The private papers of those blacks who were politically active in the five cities under study during this period were, in general, not pertinent. These include James H. Harris Papers (North Carolina Department of Archives and History); Charles N. Hunter Papers (Duke University Library); J. C. Napier Papers (Fisk University Library).

Published and unpublished diaries and memoirs were more helpful. Among them were Sarah G. Follansbee, "Diary," 1867–1868 (Alabama Department of Archives and History); Josiah Gorgas, "Journal," 1864–1878 (Southern Historical Collection, University of North Carolina Library, Chapel Hill); John Berrien Lindsley, "Diary," 1862–1866 (Tennessee State Library and Archives); Myrta Lockett Avary, *Dixie After the War* . . . (New York, 1906); T. F. Brockwell, "Raleigh in 1870 . . ." *Raleigh Times*, June 8–16, 1926; C. A. Bryce, "Good Old Days When Jackson Ward Was a Political Battleground," *Richmond Times Dispatch*, May 8, 1921; Josephus Daniels, *Tar Heel Editor* (Chapel Hill, 1939). The few accounts by blacks were especially useful in re-creating the institutional framework of the black community. They include Wendell P. Dabney (ed.), *Maggie L. Walker: Her Life and Deeds* (Cincinnati, 1927); Charles N. Hunter, *Review of Negro Life in North Carolina with My Recollections*, Vol. I, No. 1 (Raleigh, no date); Bertha Thomas McClain, *Montgomery Then and Now As I Remember* (Montgomery, 1960); Richard R. Wright, Jr., *87 Years Behind the Black Curtain: An Autobiography* (Philadelphia, 1965).

Travelers from the North and abroad who toured the South throughout the period left accounts of their visits which vary greatly in perceptiveness and reliability but which remain an indispensable source for understanding postbellum race relations. Over thirty were used in this study. The most informative include Sidney Andrews, *The South Since the War* . . . (Boston, 1866); Sir George Campbell, *White and Black* . . . (London, 1879); John Richard Dennett, *The South As It Is 1865–1866* (reprinted; New York, 1967); William Hepworth Dixon, *The New America* (2 vols.; 6th ed.; London, 1867); Edward King, *The Southern States of North America* (London, 1875); David Macrae, *The Americans at Home* (2 vols.; Edinburgh, 1870); Charles Nordhoff, *The Cotton States in the Spring and Summer of 1875* (New York, 1876); Noble L. Prentis, *Southern Letters* (Topeka, 1881); Whitelaw Reid, *After the War* . . . (London, 1866); William and W. F. Robertson, *Our American Tour* . . . (Edinburgh, 1871); William Saunders, *Through the Light Continent* (London, 1879); Robert Somers, *The Southern States Since the War 1870–1871* (New York, 1871); David Thomas, *My American Tour* . . . (Bury, 1868); J. T. Trowbridge, *A Picture of the Desolated States and the Work of Restoration, 1865–1868* (Hartford, 1868); Charles Dudley Warner, *Studies in the South and West with Comments on Canada* (New York, 1889). One of the few accounts by a Negro is former runaway slave William Wells Brown's *My Southern Home* . . . (Boston, 1880).

The major national periodicals during the period contained articles of varying importance on Southern race relations in practically every issue. Of greatest value were Samuel J. Barrows, "What the Southern Negro is Doing for Himself," *Atlantic Monthly*, LXVII (June 1891), 805–15; George Washington Cable, "The Freedmen's Case in Equity," *Century Magazine*, XXX

(January 1885), 409–18; and "The Silent South," *Century Magazine*, XXX (September 1885), 674–91; "Color Prejudice," *Nation*, XLIX (July 11, 1889), 26–27; Alfred H. Colquitt, "Is the Negro Vote Suppressed?" *Forum*, IV (November 1887), 268–78; Henry W. Grady, "In Plain Black and White," *Century Magazine*, XXX (April 1885), 909–17; "The Negro in Southern Politics," *Nation*, XLI (July 23, 1885), 67; John Snyder, "Prejudice Against the Negro," *Forum*, VIII (October 1889), 218–24. Two articles by prominent blacks were Frederick Douglass, "The Color Line," *North American Review*, CXXXII (July 1881), 567–77; and J. C. Price, "Does the Negro Seek Social Equality?" *Forum*, X (January 1891), 559–64.

Important sources for biographical information about blacks and descriptions of black schools, churches, hospitals, and fraternal orders were the compilations published around the turn of the century by blacks and whites to publicize the achievements of Negroes since emancipation. Though marred by numerous factual errors and unabashed plagiarism, these works are extremely valuable if used with caution. As with the two best, E. R. Carter, *The Black Side . . . Negro in Atlanta, Georgia* (Atlanta, 1894) and William J. Simmons, *Men of Mark . . .* (Cleveland, 1887), they often were written by clergymen. Among the many consulted were Charles Octavius Boothe, *The Cyclopedia of the Colored Baptists of Alabama* (Birmingham, 1895); J. W. Gibson and W. H. Crogman, *Progress of A Race or The Remarkable Advancement of the American Negro* (rev. ed.; Atlanta, 1902); W. N. Hartshorn, *An Era of Progress and Promise . . .* (Boston, 1910); G. F. Richings, *Evidences of Progress Among Colored People* (Philadelphia, 1903).

Though published after 1890, the volumes edited by W. E. B. Du Bois in the Atlanta University Publications Series provided detailed information about the economic, social, and religious life of blacks throughout the urban as well as the rural South. Most useful were *Economic Co-operation Among Negro Americans* (Atlanta, 1907); *Efforts for Social Betterment Among Negro Americans* (Atlanta, 1909); *The Negro American Family* (Atlanta, 1908); *The Negro Artisan* (Atlanta, 1902); *The Negro Church* (Atlanta, 1903); *The Negro Common School* (Atlanta, 1901); *The Negro in Business* (Atlanta, 1899). Few records of local black institutions are extant, though two exceptions are *Charter and By-Laws of the Friends Asylum for Colored Orphans* (Richmond, 1883) and *Minutes of Raleigh's Excelsior Lodge No. 21 of Colored Masons, 1875–1886* (North Carolina Department of Archives and History).

Federal documents shed further light on the status of Southern urban blacks. These include J. W. Alvord, *Semi-Annual Reports on Schools and Finances of Freedmen* (Washington, D.C., 1866–1870); U.S. Congress, 39th Cong., 1st Sess., *Report of the Joint Committee on Reconstruction* (Washington, D.C., 1866); U.S. Congress, 42nd Cong., 2nd Sess., *Testimony Taken by the Joint Select Committee to Inquire Into the Condition of Affairs in the Late Insurrectionary States* (Washington, D.C., 1872); U.S. Senate, 46th Cong., 2nd Sess., *Report and Testimony of the Select Committee of the*

United States Senate to Investigate the Causes for the Removal of the Negroes from the Southern States to the Northern States (Washington, D.C., 1880).

The published volumes of the federal censuses for 1860, 1870, 1880, and 1890 helped me to trace the expansion of the urban Negro population, and the occupational data for the nation's largest cities in the 1890 volume facilitated the division of workers in Richmond, Nashville, and Atlanta into the broad employment categories found in Chapter 4. A special census volume, *Report on the Social Statistics of Cities*, Part II (Washington, D.C., 1887) contained useful descriptive material and a brief history of every city studied except Raleigh. Extremely helpful in placing in perspective late-nineteenth-century developments affecting urban blacks was another special volume, *Negro Population 1790–1915* (Washington, D.C., 1918).

Even more useful than the published census data were the Manuscript Population Schedules for 1870 and 1880. (The 1890 schedules were destroyed in a fire, and the 1900 schedules have only recently been opened to scholars on a restricted basis.) For both years enumerators listed an individual's name, age, state of birth, sex, color (white, mulatto, or black), occupation, and literacy. The 1870 census schedules also contained each individual's estimate of his or her real and personal property; the 1880 version clearly identified the relationship of each individual to the head of a household and gave the state of birth of each resident's parents. The schedules thus provided a broad range of biographical material for individual blacks and a general picture of the economic status of a given town's black community prior to 1890. They also enabled me to make a rough estimate of the extent and nature of residential segregation, although even that estimate suffers from the fact that street names and house numbers in the 1870 and, to a lesser degree, in the 1880 schedules were often missing. These returns are located in the National Archives and state archives and are available on microfilm.

State records helped place the experience of urban blacks within a broader perspective. I examined the constitutions, codes, and annual acts of each state in order to trace changes in the legal status of blacks. Legislative journals permitted me to follow the course of relevant legislation and to weigh the contribution of local blacks elected to the state legislatures. Extremely helpful were the reports of state superintendents of education and of such state institutions as penitentiaries, insane asylums, and institutions for the education of the blind, deaf, and dumb.

The rich and largely overlooked sources of local history made my task much easier. There are numerous guidebooks and booster histories for each city which, though usually neglecting the black population, helped convey the flavor and character of the city and its white population. City directories which gave the occupation and address of each alphabetically listed person were especially useful after the 1870s when compilers made a greater effort to include the growing number of blacks. Blacks were identified by a "c," "col.," or asterisk after their name or, as in Raleigh, sometimes confined to a Jim Crow section. The most prominent blacks also were listed with white residents of similar occupations in the part of the directory devoted to businesses. Black churches, schools, clubs, militia, and fire companies were listed separately from their white counterparts. By the 1890s the directories for Montgomery, Richmond, and Atlanta had a section with residents arranged by street address which permitted me to do the residential mapping found in Chapter 5.

Municipal and county records provided a previously untapped resource. Richmond, Nashville, and Atlanta city council minutes from 1865 to 1890 (from 1862 in the case of Nashville) were examined, as were the partial minutes extant for Montgomery and Raleigh. Complete board of education minutes remain for every city but Raleigh. Also useful were the charters and ordinances of each city. By the 1880s all five cities published detailed reports of municipal departments which provided further information on education, housing conditions, welfare services, and crime. Published and unpublished annual messages of the mayors also revealed white attitudes and policies toward blacks. Tax records, deeds, and will books found in city halls and state archives furnished added economic data about leading blacks. Court records in Raleigh and Richmond complemented the extensive treatment of court activity in the newspapers.

Excellent photographic and map collections were consulted in the numerous archives, libraries, and historical societies I visited. The picture files at Richmond's Valentine Museum merit special praise. Published collections of photographs include *Artwork of Nashville* (Chicago, 1894) and *Artwork of Montgomery, Alabama* (Chicago, 1894). The final sources worth noting are the cities themselves. Despite the "progress" of the past hundred years, much of the late nineteenth century still survives, preserving elements of race relations in the urban South the historian must not overlook.

Index

Abbott, Lyman, 154–55
Abernathy, Ralph David, 215
Abyssinian Library (Atlanta), 239–40
Adair, G. W., 233
Adams, John, 62
Adams, John H., 277
Agricultural and mechanical associations, black, 80
Alabama: antimiscegenation law, 45; apprenticing law, 34; black conventions in, 262; chain gangs in, 50; closing of Freedmen's Hospital in, 134; convict leasing in, 139; Insane Hospital in, 137, 146, 148, 374; Institution for the Deaf and Dumb and Blind in, 137, 151; jurors in, 39–40; militia companies in, 228; orphanage in, 135; prisons in, 139, 370; public schools in, 165; Redemption of, 12
Alden, A. E., 17, 265, 267–68, 307
Alexander, N. H., 280
Alvord, J. W., 205
American Baptist Home Mission Society, 163, 202, 377
American Freedmen's and Union Commission, 153–54
American Missionary Association: and black housing, 102, 400; and education, 153–54, 156–57, 161–63, 166, 174, 176, 380; and religion, 202, 207, 217; and welfare services, 129. See also Missionary societies, Northern

Anderson, W. F., 295–96, 411
Andrews, Sidney, 6–7
Angier, Nedom, 34
Annexations, 101, 124, 293, 323
Arthur, Chester, 290
Ash, William H., 251
Ashby, Nathan, 214
Ashcraft, E. S., 292
Athens, Georgia, 23, 230
Atlanta, Georgia, 13, 15, 19; absence of black firemen in, 228, 266, 329; absence of black justices of the peace in, 37, 329; absence of black police in, 41, 266, 329; absence of Radical control in, 259; annexations in, 101; as archetype of the New South, 8; black businesses in, 78, 81, 84–89, 93, 359–60, 403; black elite in, 239–40, 243, 251; black emigration from, 251–53; black expositions in, 80; black jurors in, 41, 59; black office-holding in, 263, 265, 268–69, 329; black press in, 231–33, 236, 353, 399; black professionals in, 37, 90–94, 172, 174–78, 205, 208, 211, 213, 215–19, 221–23, 315–17, 382, 384, 395–97, 420; blacks and the Democratic Party in, 278–79, 300–303, 305–9, 311, 314, 321–24, 327, 414; blacks and the Republican Party in, 279–81, 283–84, 286–91, 294, 410; churches in, 202–9, 211–12, 215–19, 221–24,

427

and survey of black self-help efforts,
372
Duke, J. C., 233
Dungee, J. W., 301, 413
Dunning, W. A., 332
Dunston, Norfleet, 266, 277–78

Easley, Smith, 229, 317
Edwards, Alba M., 354
Elite, black, 240–43, 248–52, 402
Ellison, Stewart, 278–79
Ellyson, Henry K., 267, 275–76
Emancipation Day celebrations, 229–
30, 293
Emigration, black, 249–53, 402–3
Epidemics, 5, 17, 120–22, 131, 149
Ewing, Taylor, 90–91
Excelsior Lodge No. 21 of Colored
Masons (Raleigh), 227
Exclusion, of blacks: from bars, 188;
from boardinghouses, 388; from
brothels, 189; from city council
committees, 277–78; from institutions
for the deaf, dumb, and blind, 128,
136–37, 151; from fire departments,
228, 266, 329; from hospitals, 128,
131, 135, 151; from hotels, 182–84,
188, 388; from houses of refuge,
135; from insane asylums, 128, 132;
from judgeships, 37, 329; from medical dispensaries, 131; from militia
companies, 228; from nominating
conventions, 311; from officeholding,
265, 301; from orphanages, 128, 135;
from parks, 182, 187, 189–90, 389;
from police departments, 41, 266,
329; from poorhouses, 128–30; from
primaries, 311, 314; from railroad
waiting rooms, 188; from restaurants,
182–84, 188, 388, 391; from schools,
162, 164–65, 382; from skating rinks,
184–85; from streetcars, 182, 184,
195; from swimming pools, 190, 389;
from theaters, 182, 184, 386; from
unions, 69–70; from voting, 257,
259–60
Excursions, black, 196–97, 229–30, 346
Expositions, 15, 80, 190–91, 211–12

Fifteenth Amendment, 194, 229, 404
Finch, William: and black education,

166, 265; and conflict with W. J.
Gaines, 221; political career of, 265,
313; and prohibition campaigns, 316
Finley, Peyton, 264
Fire companies, black, 228, 230, 236,
266, 278, 296, 329, 407
First African Baptist Church (Rich-
mond), 199–200, 203, 206–7, 209–
10, 212–13, 217, 392, 396
First Baptist Colored Church
(Raleigh), 200, 203
First Colored Baptist Church (Mont-
gomery), 200, 203, 211, 214–15, 239
First Colored Baptist Church (Nash-
ville), 200, 204–7, 220–21
Fischer, Roger A., 331, 386, 391
Fisk, Clinton B., 21, 23, 33, 66–67, 155
Fisk Jubilee Singers, 30, 206, 240, 242
Fisk University (Nashville), 16, 102–3,
157, 162–63, 174, 202, 211, 240, 242
Fleming, John, 168
Flipper, Henry O., 195
Flipper, J. S., 219, 222
Florida, 182
Follansbee, Sarah, 23
Forrester, Richard, 178, 299
Foster, Aaron, 63
Foster, James A., 215
Fourteenth Amendment, 38, 229, 262
Fourth of July, 24, 228–30, 338
Franklin, John Hope, 377
Fraternal societies, black, 140, 227–28,
236
Freedmen's Aid Society, 102, 157, 163
Freedmen's Bank, 81–83, 88, 211, 230–
31, 302, 358, 396
Freedmen's Bureau, 80; and education,
153–57, 160, 166; freedmen camps
of, 100; and judicial proceedings, 32–
34; and return of freedmen to coun-
tryside, 20–21; and vagrancy laws,
36; and welfare services, 23, 127–32,
140, 143, 367
Freedmen's Union Commission, 117
Friedman, Lawrence J., 332
Friends Asylum for Colored Orphans
(Richmond), 135, 144–45, 147, 243,
374
Friendship Baptist Church (Atlanta),
204, 206, 212, 215–16, 224, 240,
316, 396, 402

Fulton County (Atlanta), 94, 135, 139–
40, 147, 286, 315
Funders, 216
Fusion, 327

Gaines, W. J.: and clashes with congre-
gation, 221–22; as community leader,
229; and opposition to white teach-
ers, 382; and prohibition campaigns,
315–17
Galveston, Texas, 4
Gamble, Tip, 292
Gammon Theological Seminary, 163
Gardner, L., 218
Garfield, James, 272, 283, 285, 337
Garner, A. A., 92
Garrison, William Lloyd, 238, 241
Georgia: Academy for the Blind in,
136, 144, 146, 373; antimiscegenation
law in, 34, 45; convict leasing in,
139, 150; first black lawyer in, 37;
Institution for the Deaf and Dumb
in, 136, 146–47, 369; jurors in, 39;
local option law in, 315; Lunatic
Asylum in, 148; militia companies
in, 228; orphanage in, 135; peonage
in, 50; prisons in, 138–39, 370, 375;
public schools in, 164–65; Republican
Party in, 410
Gerrymandering, 98, 270–75, 314, 406,
418
Gilbert, M. W., 397
Gordon, John B., 300
Gowdey, C. C., 295–96, 314, 323, 412,
415
Grady, Henry W., 8–9, 69, 117, 138,
302
Graham, George, 405
Grand Fountain of the United Order
of True Reformers, 83–84, 140
Grandison, G. N., 293, 420
Grant, U. S., 269, 285, 303
Graves, A. A., 384
Great Britain Board of Trade, 90, 118–
19
Greeley, Horace, 303
Greenback Party, 298–99, 312
Greenville, North Carolina, 43
Grey Eagle Fire Company (Mont-
gomery), 228, 236
Griswold, Thomas, 278

Hadley, B. J., 241–42, 412
Hadley, W. A., 241, 401, 412
Hale, Ann, 113–14, 143
Hale, James, 87, 94, 143, 249
Hale, James Infirmary. See James Hale
Infirmary
Hamilton, Alexander, 87
Hannon, Allen, 201
Harding, Henry: as advocate of hiring
black teachers, 401; background of,
88; business activities of, 88, 116;
and color differences among blacks,
249; and Colored Fairgrounds, 88;
and emigration, 402; and Freedmen's
Bank, 82, 88; and social activities
of, 241–42; and Tammany Club, 412
Hardy, Iza Duffus, 191
Hardy, Lady Duffus, 69
Harris, C. O., 286
Harris, Cornelius, 287, 299
Harris, James H.: as advocate of black
representation on boards of state
institutions, 145; as advocate of
hiring black teachers, 174; as city
councilman, 265, 277; as delegate to
constitutional convention, 264; as
delegate to Republican National Con-
vention, 286; and North Carolina
Institution for the Blind and Deaf
and Dumb, 145; and emigration,
403; as state legislator, 265
Harris, Joel Chandler, 30, 347
Harris, John, 199
Harrison, Benjamin, 283, 290
Hartshorn Memorial College (Rich-
mond), 163, 211
Hayes, I. W., 94
Hayes, Rutherford B., 272
Heard, Jack, 281
Henrico County (Richmond), 40, 299
Herbert, Hilary A., 187, 320
Herndon, Alonzo, 86
Hershaw, L. M., 384
Holden, William, 81, 261, 290
Holmes, B. A., 402
Holmes, James Henry, 200, 217
Hood, J. W., 223
Hooper, Bob, 86
Hopkins, Richard, 96
Howard, Charles Wallace, 22
Howard, David T., 84–85, 117, 239, 37?